Engaging Learners With Immersive Technologies and Game-Based Learning

Filipe T. Moreira
Polytechnic University of Porto, Portugal

Rui Oliva Teles
https://orcid.org/0000-0001-5455-8104
Polytechnic University of Porto, Portugal

IGI Global
Scientific Publishing
Publishing Tomorrow's Research Today

Published in the United States of America by
IGI Global Scientific Publishing
701 East Chocolate Avenue
Hershey, PA, 17033, USA
Tel: 717-533-8845 | Fax: 717-533-7115
Website: https://www.igi-global.com E-mail: cust@igi-global.com

Library of Congress Cataloging-in-Publication Data

Names: Moreira, Filipe, 1986- editor | Oliva Teles, Rui, 1960- editor
Title: Engaging learners with immersive technologies and game-based learning / Edited by Filipe T. Moreira, Rui Oliva Teles.
Description: Hershey, PA : IGI Global Scientific Publishing, [2026] | Includes bibliographical references and index. | Summary: "This book provides a comprehensive and critical overview of how immersive technologies and game-based learning are being used to enhance student engagement, motivation, and learning outcomes. It brings together innovative theoretical frameworks, empirical research, case studies, and practical implementations from across the globe"-- Provided by publisher.
Identifiers: LCCN 2025027031 (print) | LCCN 2025027032 (ebook) | ISBN 9798337344652 hardcover | ISBN 9798337344669 paperback | ISBN 9798337344676 ebook
Subjects: LCSH: Virtual reality in education | Gamification | Artificial intelligence--Educational applications | Augmented reality in education | Effective teaching
Classification: LCC LB1044.87 .E5475 2026 (print) | LCC LB1044.87 (ebook)
LC record available at https://lccn.loc.gov/2025027031
LC ebook record available at https://lccn.loc.gov/2025027032

British Cataloguing in Publication Data
A Cataloguing in Publication record for this book is available from the British Library.

We dedicate this work to our students, with the hope that, as future educators, they will become agents of transformation—helping shape a world that is more just, inclusive, and inspired by the power of learning.

Table of Contents

Detailed Table of Contents

Game-based and immersive learning harness theoretical principles from various disciplines to enhance education and engagement. Constructivism, pioneered by thinkers like Piaget and Vygotsky, posits that learners construct knowledge through experiences, making game-based scenarios ideal for promoting active learning. Additionally, experiential learning, as articulated by Kolb, emphasizes learning through reflection on doing, further supporting the integration of games and simulations in educational contexts.Cognitive load theory suggests that carefully designed games can manage the cognitive load on learners, facilitating better information retention. Motivation theories, particularly Self-Determination Theory, indicate that games foster intrinsic motivation through autonomy, competence, and relatedness. Moreover, the concept of flow, introduced by Csikszentmihalyi, highlights how immersive experiences can lead to optimal learning states by balancing challenge and skill levels.

The landscape of education is undergoing a profound transformation, driven by the rapid evolution of digital technologies and a growing understanding of effective learning paradigms. This chapter, "New Frontiers in Pedagogy: Immersive Technologies and Game-Based Learning," explores the revolutionary potential of virtual reality (VR), augmented reality (AR), mixed reality (MR), and game-based learning (GBL) to redefine instructional design and enhance student engagement. Moving beyond traditional didactic approaches, these innovative pedagogical tools offer dynamic, experiential, and highly interactive learning environments. We delve into how immersive technologies can transport learners to historical events, complex scientific phenomena, or simulated professional scenarios, fostering deeper

In the contemporary digital education landscape, immersive and game-based learning have become vital tools for enhancing engagement and improving outcomes. This chapter examines the integration of immersive strategies within leading Indian EdTech platforms—Unacademy, PhysicsWallah, Vedantu, Allen Digital, and BYJU'S. Using a qualitative multiple case study and thematic analysis, it explores the application of gamification, augmented reality (AR), virtual reality (VR), and interactive simulations to deliver personalized, engaging experiences. Findings reveal that immersive tools sustain attention, boost motivation, deepen emotional engagement, and improve retention. The research categorizes these strategies into thematic segments, offering actionable insights for educators and developers. It emphasizes aligning immersive techniques with learner preferences and pedagogical goals, while also providing globally relevant lessons for scalable, culturally adaptive, and engagement-driven EdTech models that merge technology with pedagogy to optimize learning design.

Traditionally, music educators used "drill and practice" methods for aural music theory skills. Nowadays, many educators are looking towards virtual reality to provide a novel learning approach. An aural music theory virtual simulation, The Crafter's Ear, was developed in Minecraft for music educators to use with beginning music students. This chapter describes the development of The Crafter's Ear simulation and assessment of its user satisfaction for insights into the usefulness and limitations of virtual simulations in music education. Qualitative data was collected from music teachers and analyzed to provide insights into music educators' views on virtual simulation for music classrooms. The user satisfaction results were mixed. Most participants felt that they did not have the time or the ability to develop a complex simulation like this. However, they would readily utilize a pre-made simulation such as The Crafter's Ear. Educators are very interested in the integration of music into STEM education.

Education is being revolutionised by virtual reality (VR), augmented reality (AR), and extended reality (XR), which create immersive, interactive, learner-centred settings that go well beyond the conventional classroom. Immersion learning improves diversity, motivation, and accessibility by replacing passive instruction with practical, simulation-based activities. Additionally, XR responds to the needs of the twenty-first century by equipping students with critical abilities, including problem-solving, creativity, and teamwork. In order to rethink education as a dynamic, multimodal, and future-ready experience, this chapter explores the pedagogical potential of immersive technologies, their integration with current educational paradigms, and their transformative significance. It reflects on the emerging future of immersive education in the context of the metaverse, AI-driven adaptive learning, and multisensory environments.

This chapter explores the influence of gamification on motivation and engagement in language learners, focusing on the role of spelling proficiency. It elaborates on the integration of game design elements into language learning contexts and its effects on learner motivation and engagement, particularly through a case study of intermediate learners using the mobile application Words of Wonders. By examining the principles of self-determination theory, Vygotsky's Zone of Proximal Development, and cognitive load theory, the chapter investigates how gamification fosters learner autonomy, competence, and relatedness. The study highlights the potential of gamified mobile applications to address specific linguistic challenges, such as spelling, by combining interactive, game-based approaches with immediate feedback and rewards, fostering active engagement and measurable progress. Furthermore, the chapter emphasizes the role of multimodality in gamified tools to bridge the gap between English spelling conventions and learners' first languages, thereby enhancing understanding and retention.

The educational sector shifted from traditional learning environments to virtual reality (VR), augmented reality (AR) and gamification. With its promise to enhance learner engagement, the challenge lies in implementation, often reproducing existing inequalities. There is consensus that developing countries like South Africa face disparities in infrastructure, digital literacy and socioeconomic development, posing barriers to equitable access. This chapter examines digital inclusion and accessibility regarding immersive technologies and game-based learning in South Africa. The chapter interrogates these dynamics vis-à-vis the educational opportunities immersive technologies afford and deny marginalised learners. Through the capability approach and Universal Design for learning (UDL), it explores how immersive tools can expand or restrict learners' real freedoms to participate in education.

Financial literacy an essential competency in the increasingly intricate financial landscape of today, influencing individuals' capabilities to invest and strategize for the future. Although the domain of financial literacy research has expanded significantly, there has been relatively little focus on investment confidence as a separate outcome variable, and even less on its connection to gamified learning interventions within the Indian context. The chapter synthesizes frameworks including self-efficacy theory, experiential learning theory, and prospect theory with empirical evidence to investigate how gamification can convert financial literacy into actionable confidence. Utilizing national-level benchmarks from the Global Findex Database 2021, published studies on financial literacy among Indian youth, and a survey conducted with Indian college students, the analysis underscores the interplay between financial knowledge, perceptions of gamification, and investment confidence.

Preface

The rapid evolution of digital technologies has brought new possibilities to the way we think about teaching and learning. Immersive tools such as virtual reality (VR), augmented reality (AR), mixed reality (MR), and an expanding range of game-based approaches are beginning to take shape not as isolated experiments, but as part of everyday educational practice. What interests us most is not the technological novelty itself, but the way these environments can meaningfully support students' cognitive, emotional, and social engagement.

This book, *Engaging Learners With Immersive Technologies and Game-Based Learning*, emerged from that curiosity and from a genuine need to understand how these tools can be used with pedagogical purpose. In recent years, we have seen increased interest from educators around the world, but also recurring questions: What kinds of learning experiences benefit most from immersion? In which situations do game-based strategies actually improve motivation and performance? And what barriers—ethical, technical, or institutional—still need to be addressed before these approaches can be widely adopted?

To explore these questions with the breadth they deserve, we invited researchers and practitioners from different countries and institutional contexts to share their experiences. The result is a collection of 16 chapters, each grounded in the specific realities that their authors face in their own classrooms, laboratories, and communities. This diversity is one of the most valuable aspects of this book: the understanding that immersive and game-based learning does not manifest in the same way everywhere.

The first group of chapters examines engagement from multiple angles, ranging from cognitive and emotional dimensions to the design of learning environments that rely on immersion and play. Others address ethical and technical challenges, such as data privacy, security risks associated with VR/AR systems, and questions of accessibility and digital inclusion–particularly relevant in contexts where technology adoption remains uneven.

CHAPTER OVERVIEW

Several chapters present concrete applications and case studies. These include the use of immersive tools in engineering education, game-based strategies for language learning, gamification to improve spelling and motivation, and even the use of Minecraft as a virtual space for aural music theory instruction. There are also contributions focused on adaptive and personalized learning environments, as well as explorations of how mixed reality can support emotional self-regulation in neurodivergent learners.

Other chapters take a more conceptual and theoretical perspective, revisiting principles that underpin effective immersive and game-based learning and proposing new pedagogical frameworks for the next generation of digital learning experiences. Together, these contributions map out an emerging landscape where immersion, play, and learning intersect in increasingly sophisticated ways.

Equity and inclusion are recurring themes throughout the volume. Several authors remind us that technological innovation alone does not guarantee better learning; in fact, without careful attention, it can deepen existing inequalities. For this reason, many chapters reflect on how to design experiences that are accessible, culturally relevant, and responsive to the needs of diverse learners—an issue that remains central as immersive technologies continue to evolve.

Our intention as editors was not to produce a prescriptive guide, but rather a resource that stimulates critical reflection. We hope this book will be useful to those who are beginning to experiment with immersive tools, to educators seeking research-based guidance, to instructional designers exploring new possibilities, and to policymakers interested in understanding both the potential and the limitations of these approaches.

Above all, we hope the work presented here encourages readers to explore these technologies thoughtfully, with curiosity but also with pedagogical responsibility. In the end, the aim remains unchanged: to create learning experiences that resonate with students, challenge them, support them, and help them grow—experiences that stay with them long after they leave the classroom.

Acknowledgement

We would like to express our heartfelt gratitude to all those who contributed to the creation and success of this book, *Engaging Learners With Immersive Technologies and Game-Based Learning*. Our deepest appreciation goes to the authors, whose dedication, expertise, and commitment were fundamental to shaping the quality and relevance of this volume. We are especially grateful for their efforts not only in developing their chapters but also in promoting and disseminating the work, helping extend its reach across academic, professional, and educational communities.

We also extend our sincere thanks to the reviewers, whose careful, rigorous, and thoughtful evaluations were essential to ensuring the scholarly depth and integrity of each contribution. Their insights and constructive feedback greatly enriched the final outcome.

To everyone who played a role in this project—directly or indirectly—we offer our sincere appreciation. Your support, collaboration, and enthusiasm made this publication possible.

Chapter 1
Theoretical Principles Underpinning Game-Based and Immersive Learning

Oindrilla Ghosh
https://orcid.org/0000-0001-9609-0781
Christ University, India

Binod Kumar
https://orcid.org/0009-0002-9721-1367
Radha Govind University, India

ABSTRACT

Game-based and immersive learning harness theoretical principles from various disciplines to enhance education and engagement. Constructivism, pioneered by thinkers like Piaget and Vygotsky, posits that learners construct knowledge through experiences, making game-based scenarios ideal for promoting active learning. Additionally, experiential learning, as articulated by Kolb, emphasizes learning through reflection on doing, further supporting the integration of games and simulations in educational contexts. Cognitive load theory suggests that carefully designed games can manage the cognitive load on learners, facilitating better information retention. Motivation theories, particularly Self-Determination Theory, indicate that games foster intrinsic motivation through autonomy, competence, and relatedness. Moreover, the concept of flow, introduced by Csikszentmihalyi, highlights how immersive experiences can lead to optimal learning states by balancing challenge and skill levels.

DOI: 10.4018/979-8-3373-4465-2.ch001

INTRODUCTION

Game-based and immersive learning have garnered increased attention in educational contexts over the past couple of decades, emerging as innovative pedagogical approaches that leverage the engaging qualities of games and simulators to enhance learning outcomes (Basudan, 2023). These methodologies employ interactive and often competitive elements to foster motivation, engagement, and retention of knowledge among learners (Li & Chen, 2022). The theoretical principles that underpin these approaches draw upon a variety of established learning theories, including Constructivism, Experiential Learning, and Motivation Theory, among others (Alladi et al., 2019).

At the core of game-based and immersive learning is the premise that learners construct knowledge best through active engagement with content not through passive reception of information (Dovleac et al., 2023). This active engagement often manifests through simulations, role-play, and problem-solving scenarios where learners can experiment, receive instant feedback, and make choices that impact the learning environment (Patel, 2023). Such immersive experiences allow for a deeper understanding of complex subjects by allowing learners to apply theoretical knowledge in a practical context (Moore et al., 2020).

Moreover, the design of game-based and immersive learning experiences often seeks to tap into intrinsic motivations such as the need for accomplishment, mastery, and social interaction to create a learning environment that is enjoyable and stimulating (Maggio et al., 2021). These principles are integral in enhancing the learning process, as they align with contemporary understandings of how the brain processes information and how learners engage with material in meaningful way.

EVOLUTION OF GAME BASED AND IMMERSIVE LEARNING

The journey of theoretical principles underlying game-based and immersive learning can be traced through several educational movements and technological milestones (Devi et al., 2016). Beginning in the early 20th century, the work of educational theorists like John Dewey and Jean Piaget laid important groundwork by emphasizing the significance of experiential learning and the role of the learner in constructing knowledge (Sughra & Usmani, 2022). Dewey championed the idea that education should be rooted in real-world experiences, fostering active participation rather than rote memorization (Hernández, 2023). Similarly, Piaget's theory of cognitive development emphasized the importance of active engagement in the learning process, suggesting that individuals learn best when they can manipulate and explore their environment (Mehrpour et al., 2023).

The latter half of the 20th century saw the introduction of Constructivist theory in education, driven by figures like Lev Vygotsky (Allahverdi, 2021). Vygotsky's notions of social learning and the Zone of Proximal Development (ZPD) highlighted how social interaction can enhance cognitive growth (Mahardika, 2023). This perspective influenced the design of collaborative and multiplayer games in educational settings, where learners can work together to solve problems and share knowledge (Pu et al., 2019).

The rise of technology in the late 20th century propelled game-based and immersive learning into a new era (Mugisha et al., 2021). The proliferation of computers and the advent of video games created opportunities for interactive learning experiences that could simulate real-world scenarios (Popenici & Kerr, 2017). Educational games such as "The Oregon Trail" emerged in the 1980s, illustrating early concepts of game-based learning by integrating educational content with gameplay mechanics (Abbas et al., 2023). Subsequent advancements in technology, such as the Internet and mobile devices, have further facilitated immersive learning experiences through the development of sophisticated simulations and virtual environments (Aparicio-Gómez, 2024).

Through this historical lens, it becomes evident that the theoretical principles underpinning game-based and immersive learning have evolved through the confluence of educational philosophies and technological advancements (Rohmah, 2022). As these approaches continue to develop, they promise to further transform educational practices, offering new pathways for engagement and learning in a diverse array of contexts (Legaki, et al. 2020).

A CRITICAL SYNTHESIS AND CONCEPTUAL FOUNDATIONS

Theoretical frameworks provide structured methods for understanding complex phenomena and guiding research, especially in fields like education (Fazil, 2024). In the context of game-based and immersive learning (GBIL), several key theoretical underpinnings play a crucial role in shaping how these learning modalities are designed, implemented, and assessed.

Constructivism: Central to GBIL is the constructivist approach, where learners are viewed as active participants in their learning journey (Abbas et al., 2023). Constructivism posits that knowledge is not passively received but actively constructed by learners through experiences. Game-based learning environments often embed scenarios that require players to make decisions, solve problems, and engage in inquiry-based learning (Nguyen, 2023). This aligns with constructivist theorists like Piaget and Vygotsky, who emphasize the importance of social interaction and cultural context in developing understanding (Murtaza et al., 2022).

Experiential Learning: Kolb's experiential learning theory is pertinent in GBIL, asserting that learning occurs through hands-on experiences and reflection (Luo, 2024). Games and immersive simulations provide rich contexts where learners can experiment, receive immediate feedback, and reflect on their actions, fostering deeper understanding (Onesi-Ozigagun, 2024). Kolb's cycle of experience, reflection, conceptualization, and experimentation tightly links with the iterative and feedback-rich nature of games (Akavova et al., 2023).

Flow Theory: Csikszentmihalyi's flow theory speaks to the state of heightened focus and engagement that learners experience when they are fully immersed in an activity (Fazil, 2024). Game-based learning is often designed to establish challenges that match the learners' skill levels, promoting flow. When learners experience this balance of challenge and skill, they are more likely to be motivated and engaged, which enhances retention and application of knowledge (Kamruzzaman, 2023).

Situated Learning: This theory, put forth by Lave and Wenger, emphasizes that knowledge is best acquired within the context of its application (Alkan, 2024). Immersive learning environments, such as virtual reality simulations, situate learners in realistic contexts, allowing them to practice skills in a safe space (Gligorea et al., 2022). This approach not only fosters relevance but also aids in knowledge transfer, as skills learned in virtual scenarios can often be applied to real-world situations (Katiyar, 2024).

Social Learning Theory: Albert Bandura's social learning theory underscores the importance of observation and social interaction in learning processes (Harry, 2023). In game-based environments, players often collaborate or compete with peers, facilitating collective learning experiences (Dirgantoro et al., 2022). This aspect can enhance motivation and accountability, as learners can observe successful strategies and behaviors that they may adopt in their gameplay (Petrusly, 2024).

Design-Based Research: In the development of GBIL applications, design-based research provides a framework for bridging theory and practice (Kim & Castelli, 2021). It involves iterative design, implementation, and evaluation of learning interventions, ensuring that educational theories are actively tested and refined in real educational settings (Alsadoon, 2023). This approach allows researchers and practitioners to better understand what works in game-based learning and helps to create scalable and effective educational solutions (Fuster-Guilló et al., 2019).

GOVERNANCE, POLICY ARCHITECTURE, ACCOUNTABILITY, AND PUBLIC-SECTOR STEWARDSHIP

Governance in the context of game-based and immersive learning refers to the frameworks, structures, and regulations that guide the development, implementation, and assessment of these learning environments (Hidayat, 2021). Effective governance ensures that the educational objectives of game-based and immersive learning align with broader educational standards, ethical considerations, and societal needs (Johnson et al., 2016). The governance of GBIL intersects with several theoretical principles that shape its core practices.

Accountability and Transparency: Central to the governance of GBIL is the principle of accountability (Karabıyık, 2024). Stakeholders, including educators, students, and policymakers, must have a clear understanding of the objectives and expected outcomes of game-based and immersive learning interventions (Zainal, 2023). Transparency in the design and implementation processes fosters trust and allows for critical evaluation of the effectiveness and validity of these educational approaches (Özhan & Kocadere, 2019).

Equity and Access: Governance also encompasses the principle of equity in education. Game-based and immersive learning environments should be accessible to all learners, regardless of socioeconomic background, geographic region, or learning ability (Spanellis et al., 2021). This involves making conscious decisions during the design phase to include diverse perspectives and content relevant to various learner contexts (Polat, 2023). Policymakers and educators must work together to provide resources that promote equitable access to technology and learning opportunities (Rueckert et al., 2020).

Stakeholder Engagement: Effective governance in GBIL involves the participation of various stakeholders, including educators, developers, researchers, and learners themselves (Abbas et al., 2023). Engaging these stakeholders in the design, implementation, and evaluation of game-based learning initiatives ensures that the final products meet the diverse needs and expectations of the educational community (Liu, 2024). Collaborations foster innovation and adaptability in the creation of educational experiences.

Continuous Improvement: Governance should also embrace the principle of continuous improvement (Thimmanna et al., 2024). Feedback loops and rigorous evaluation mechanisms are essential for understanding the impact of game-based and immersive learning (Pendy, 2023). Using data analytics to measure engagement, motivation, and outcomes can provide insights into how to refine and enhance these educational experiences (Chang et al., 2021). This ongoing process of assessment and revision helps ensure that GBIL remains effective, relevant, and responsive to the changing educational landscape (Kamruzzaman et al., 2023).

THE ROLE OF ARTIFICIAL INTELLIGENCE, IT'S CAPABILITIES, LIMITS, AND TRANSFORMATION OF PRACTICE

Artificial Intelligence (AI) has emerged as a transformative force in education, particularly in the realms of game-based and immersive learning (Balci et al., 2022). By leveraging algorithms and data-driven insights, AI enhances the learning experience, tailoring it to meet the individual needs of each learner (Setyoadi and Patmanthara, 2024).

One prominent role of AI in these educational frameworks is adaptive learning. AI systems can analyze a student's performance in real-time and adjust the content difficulty accordingly (Li & Liu, 2022). For instance, if a student struggles with a particular concept in a game-based scenario, AI algorithms can automatically modify the gameplay elements to simplify challenges or offer hints tailored to that learner's needs (Tyni et al., 2022). This adaptability not only supports mastery of subjects but also encourages a growth mindset, allowing learners to progress at their own pace without feeling overwhelmed or disengaged (Huesca et al., 2023).

Moreover, AI enables the creation of intelligent tutoring systems that can assess student progress and provide feedback instantaneously (Antonaci et al., 2019). These systems can simulate one-on-one tutoring through chatbots or virtual assistants that are capable of responding to queries, offering explanations, and guiding learners toward relevant resources (Zhao et al., 2024). This is especially powerful in game-based learning environments, where guidance and support can significantly enhance the gaming experience and ensure that learners extract maximum educational value from their interactions (Barua et al., 2022).

Another critical contribution of AI is in the area of analytics and data interpretation (Chen et al., 2020). By tracking student interactions, progress, and engagement levels, AI systems can generate comprehensive reports that provide insights into learning patterns (Jayavardhini, 2024). Educators can use these analytics to refine educational strategies and create customized pathways for their students (Davis, 2024). The data gathered can also help game developers understand how their games are being utilized in educational settings, leading to more effective learning games (Alshehri, 2023).

AI also plays a significant role in content generation. It can assist educators in creating personalized pathways and scalable content, generating questions, quizzes, and educational games based on the learners' interests and performance data (Ulagammal and Chaluvarayaswamy, 2023). This helps to augment traditional lesson plans with engaging content that is better aligned with the unique needs of each learner (Ji et al., 2024).

Furthermore, AI enhances the immersive learning experience by powering virtual and augmented reality applications (Morales et al., 2024). Virtual environments can simulate realistic scenarios, and AI algorithms can control the behavior of non-player characters (NPCs), making them respond intelligently to students' decisions or actions (Akavova et al., 2023). This deepens the level of engagement, as learners can experiment in a safe space, make mistakes, and learn from them without real-world consequences (Lim et al., 2020).

Lastly, AI enhances accessibility in game-based and immersive learning (Kang et al., 2023). AI-driven tools offer translation services, speech recognition, and customization features that can cater to diverse learner needs, including those with disabilities (Tubino & Adachi, 2022). This ensures that immersive learning experiences are inclusive, providing all learners with an equitable opportunity to engage with educational content (Varas et al., 2023).

TECHNOLOGICAL IMPACTS AND APPLICATIONS ON USE OF AUGMENTED REALITY, VIRTUAL REALITY, AND MIXED REALITY

The integration of Augmented Reality (AR), Virtual Reality (VR), and Mixed Reality (MR) into game-based and immersive learning has revolutionized educational paradigms, creating interactive environments that align closely with established theoretical principles in learning (Pardosi et al., 2024). These technologies engage learners through experiential learning, constructivism, and situated cognition, thereby enhancing both motivation and knowledge retention (Trang & Thư, 2024).

Experiential learning, as posited by David Kolb, emphasizes learning by doing, where concrete experiences become the foundation for reflection and concept development (López &Tucker, 2020). AR, VR, and MR allow learners to immerse themselves fully in real-world scenarios while maintaining the benefits of a controlled educational setting (Fırat, 2023). For example, in a VR simulation of a historical event, learners can actively participate in the narrative, making decisions that can alter the course of the experience (Alenezi, 2024). This hands-on approach fosters deep engagement and emotional connection to the material, facilitating greater retention and understanding (Agostinelli, 2021).

Situated cognition theory posits that learning is fundamentally tied to the context in which it occurs (Nguyen et al., 2022). AR, VR, and MR facilitate this by providing contextualized learning experiences (Limongi, 2024). For instance, in vocational training simulations, learners can practice skills in environments that closely resemble the actual workplace conditions (Haresamudram et al., 2023). This situational learning fosters the transfer of skills as learners encounter real-world challenges, enhancing their ability to apply what they've learned in practical situations (Larsson & Heintz, 2020).

Moreover, AR applications can overlay digital content onto the physical world, enriching the environment and providing contextual information immediately (Chai, 2024). For example, in a history lesson, students could use AR to visualize historical artifacts in their original settings, thereby bridging the gap between abstract concepts and tangible experiences (Haresamudram et al., 2023). This encourages critical thinking as learners analyze and interpret information in real-time (Nguyen et al., 2022).

The motivational aspects of AR, VR, and MR are also crucial in game-based learning (Harry, 2023). The immersive nature of these technologies can increase student engagement through elements such as gamification, where learners are incentivized to progress through challenges and levels (Luan et al., 2020). This aligns with self-determination theory (SDT), which states that motivation is driven by autonomy, competence, and relatedness (Familoni, 2024). The interactivity and immersive environments foster a sense of agency, encouraging learners to take ownership of their learning journey (Limongi, 2024).

CHALLENGES, BARRIERS, RISKS, AND CONTINGENCY STRATEGIES

Game-based and immersive learning, while heralded for their potential to enhance engagement and motivation in educational contexts, also face significant challenges that educators and designers must navigate (Pendy, 2023). These challenges stem from various theoretical principles that underpin these innovative learning paradigms, influencing their effective implementation in real-world educational settings (Alali, 2024).

One prominent challenge is the alignment of educational objectives with the game mechanics and immersive experiences (Bennani et al., 2021). Theoretical frameworks like constructivism suggest that learning is most effective when students actively construct knowledge through experience (Alenezi, 2023). However, game-based and immersive learning environments must carefully integrate educational goals within their gameplay dynamics (Khakpour & Colomo-Palacios, 2020). This requires meticulous design to ensure that game challenges, narratives, and rewards don't overshadow the educational content (Julita, 2024). Game designers might prioritize engagement and fun, potentially at the expense of deeper learning objectives (Zourmpakis et al., 2023). This misalignment can dilute the educational value of these experiences and lead to superficial understanding, hindering the overall learning process (Narayanan, 2024).

Another considerable challenge is the accessibility and inclusivity of game-based and immersive learning (Erbaşı, 2023). Not all learners possess the same backgrounds, abilities, or access to technology (Babu, 2023). Theories related to universal design for learning (UDL) stress the importance of accommodating diverse learning needs to foster equitable educational environments (Kherazi, 2024). Implementing game-based and immersive learning in ways that are universally accessible can prove arduous, as developers must consider varying cognitive, emotional, and physical abilities, as well as different cultural contexts (Pendy, 2023). For instance, culturally relevant content must be embedded within games to engage learners from diverse backgrounds, but creating such content can be resource-intensive and demands a nuanced understanding of various cultures (Alrayes, 2024).

Moreover, the rapid pace of technological advancements can hinder the sustainability of game-based and immersive learning initiatives (Akgün & Greenhow, 2021). Theoretical principles such as the Community of Inquiry suggest that effective learning environments must include social presence, cognitive presence, and teaching presence (Akinrinola, 2024). However, the constant evolution of technology means that educators may struggle to keep up with the latest tools and platforms that facilitate immersive experiences, potentially undermining the teaching presence crucial for effective guidance and facilitation (Felzmann et al., 2020). When the supporting technology becomes outdated, it poses a challenge not only in terms of resource allocation for new tools but also regarding the effectiveness of ongoing learning experiences (Yazdanpanah et al., 2022).

Finally, assessment in game-based and immersive learning environments presents distinct challenges (Jobin & Ienca, 2019). Traditional assessment methods may not adequately capture the learning that occurs in non-linear, open-ended environments characteristic of games and immersive experiences (Balta, 2023). Theoretical models of assessment must evolve to reflect the complex, multifaceted nature of learning in these contexts, requiring novel evaluation strategies that measure creativity, collaboration, and critical thinking (D'Souza, 2024). These assessments must not only recognize achievements within the game framework but also connect them meaningfully to actual learning outcomes, a process that can be both complex and subjective (Sharma et al., 2024).

PRINCIPLES, DILEMMAS, AND NORMATIVE IMPLICATIONS

As the fields of game-based and immersive learning evolve, so too do the ethical considerations that accompany their implementation (Otero et al., 2023). These considerations, rooted in the theoretical frameworks that underpin these learning paradigms, address fundamental questions about equity, data privacy, and the psychological impacts of such interactive environments (Grunhut et al., 2021).

One principal ethical consideration is the concept of equity in access (Tolentino, 2024). Theoretical approaches like social constructivism emphasize the importance of collaborative knowledge construction, yet disparities in access to technology can reinforce existing social inequalities (Wood et al., 2021). Learners from marginalized backgrounds may find themselves at a disadvantage if they cannot access the necessary hardware or high-speed internet required for immersive experiences (Aliabadi, 2023). This exacerbation of the digital divide raises ethical questions concerning fairness in education: educators and developers must prioritize creating inclusive learning environments that provide equitable access for all learners, thereby ensuring that no student is left behind (Moldt, 2024).

Data privacy is another pressing ethical concern. In the realm of game-based and immersive learning, personalization is often touted as a mechanism to tailor educational experiences (Rathore, 2023). However, this personalization typically relies on the collection of vast amounts of data regarding user behavior, preferences, and performance (Tzafilkou et al., 2023). Ethical considerations arise regarding the ownership and protection of this data, particularly with younger learners (Kurniawati et al., 2018). Theoretical frameworks that focus on learner agency highlight the importance of informed consent and transparency (Gamrat et al., 2014). Game developers and educators must navigate the delicate balance of using data to enhance learning while safeguarding students' privacy rights (Güler & Özkan, 2018). Without robust, ethical data management practices, there is a risk of exploitation or misuse of students' information, which can lead to mistrust in educational institutions (Hollands et al., 2019).

The psychological impact of immersing students in game-based and simulation learning environments also presents ethical dilemmas (Cranley et al., 2012). While these approaches can enhance engagement and motivation, they can also lead to adverse effects, such as addiction or increased anxiety levels (Majdzadeh et al., 2011). Theoretical principles in psychology highlight the need for a balanced approach to immersive experiences, ensuring that they promote healthy learning behaviors (Bastani et al., 2023). Designers must be cognizant of the potential for excessive screen time, aggressive content, or overly competitive environments that may compromise students' mental well-being (Larsen et al., 2011). Educators must continuously assess the emotional responses and overall psychological health of their students when implementing these immersive experiences, thus mitigating potential harm (Strydom et al., 2010).

Moreover, the narratives and representations within games and immersive learning environments carry ethical implications as well, particularly regarding cultural sensitivity and representation (Orton et al., 2011). Game-based environments must avoid reinforcing stereotypes or cultural biases, embracing diverse narratives that reflect a wide range of voices and perspectives (Basudan, 2023). Ethical frameworks that prioritize multicultural education call for the responsible portrayal of identities, histories, and experiences (Li & Chen, 2022). Developers and educators must critically assess the content of games and simulations to ensure cultural respect and accuracy, fostering environments conducive to understanding and empathy (Dovleac et al., 2023).

STANDARDS, COMPLIANCE, ENFORCEMENT MECHANISMS AND IMPLEMENTING REGULATIONS

The first step in implementing a regulatory framework is to identify the key objectives that the framework seeks to achieve (Patel, 2023). For sectors like education technology, these objectives may include promoting equity, ensuring the quality of educational content, and protecting user data (Alladi et al., 2019). Once objectives are established, a thorough analysis of existing laws, regulations, and industry practices is conducted to identify gaps and areas for improvement (Moore et al., 2020). Engaging with stakeholders, educators, students, technology providers, and policymakers is critical to ensure that the framework reflects diverse perspectives and needs (Maggio et al., 2021).

Drafting effective regulations requires a deep understanding of the nuances of the sector (Devi et al., 2016). The regulatory authority must consider factors such as technological advancements, pedagogical best practices, and the ethical implications of data use in game-based and immersive learning (Hernández, 2023). An iterative process involving stakeholder feedback is crucial to refine and adjust the proposed regulations before finalization (Sughra & Usmani, 2022). This involves public consultations, pilot testing, and discussions within expert panels to create well-rounded regulations (Mehrpour et al., 2023).

Once the framework is drafted, the next step is its formal adoption and publication, which can include legislative approvals or executive endorsements, depending on the jurisdiction (Allahverdi, 2021). Following this, a robust communication strategy is vital to disseminate the new regulations widely (Mahardika, 2023).. Stakeholders must be informed about their roles, responsibilities, and the potential impact of the regulations on their practices (Pu et al., 2019). Training programs and resources can facilitate this transition, ensuring that educators and institutions fully understand and can implement the new standards (Mugisha et al., 2021).

Upon implementation, ensuring compliance with the regulatory framework is critical (Popenici & Kerr, 2017). This can be achieved through monitoring and evaluation mechanisms that assess adherence to the established standards (Abbas et al., 2023).

Regulatory authorities may establish regular audits, self-reporting requirements, and grievance redressal systems to address concerns from stakeholders (Buckley & Doyle, 2014). It is essential that these systems maintain transparency to build trust and facilitate cooperation among all parties involved (Aparicio-Gómez, 2024).

One of the emerging challenges in implementing regulatory frameworks, especially in the context of technology-driven education, is the rapid pace of innovation (Rohmah, 2022). Regulations may quickly become outdated; thus, a flexible and adaptive approach is necessary (Legaki, et al. 2020). Regulatory sandboxes can provide a useful mechanism allowing for experimentation within confines of regulation to gauge the efficacy of new approaches without the immediate pressure of compliance (Tonbuloğlu 2023).

CONCLUSION

Game-based and immersive learning represent powerful educational paradigms that leverage technology to enhance student engagement and knowledge retention (Dichev & Dicheva, 2017). The effectiveness of these approaches is grounded in several key theoretical principles (Pratama, 2023). Understanding these principles not only enriches their implementation but also provides insights into the future direction of educational practices (Rivera & Garden, 2021).

Moreover, the principles of experiential learning as coined by Kolb emphasize the importance of direct experience in the learning process (Almusaed, 2023). Game-based learning provides immersive contexts where learners can experiment, reflect, and conceptualize their experiences, aligning perfectly with Kolb's cycle of experiential learning (Alrayes 2024). Through simulation and role-play designs, learners can practice skills in realistic environments, making learning more relevant and impactful (Rugaiyah, 2023).

Additionally, Social Learning Theory underscores the importance of social interaction in learning (Uygun, 2024).. Collaborative aspects of games, where learners interact, share strategies, and support one another, create rich social contexts that enhance learning (Eslit, 2023). Role-playing and team-based challenges foster communication skills, teamwork, and peer feedback, critical elements of successful learning environments that are often absent in traditional learning settings (Walter, 2024).

The integration of cognitive load theory is also vital in designing immersive learning experiences (Ejaz et al., 2022). By carefully balancing new information with existing knowledge and providing just-in-time feedback, educators can optimize the cognitive load on learners. Well-structured game scenarios can chunk information to reduce overwhelm while maintaining engagement (Shala, 2024).

Finally, Vygotsky's Zone of Proximal Development (ZPD) plays a crucial role. Game-based learning environments can scaffold experiences, guiding learners just beyond their current capabilities and providing the necessary support to help them achieve mastery, making these methods particularly effective for diverse learners with varying skill levels (Akavova et al., 2023).

SUGGESTIONS

Game-based and immersive learning are at the forefront of educational innovation, leveraging engaging, interactive platforms to enhance learning outcomes (Abbas et al., 2023). To maximize the effectiveness of these methodologies, several recommendations can be made.

Align Learning Objectives with Game Mechanics: One of the fundamental aspects of effective game-based learning is ensuring that game mechanics align with educational goals (Shah, 2024). Learning objectives should be clearly defined and directly integrated into the game design. This alignment enhances student engagement and motivation, as they perceive the relevance of the game to their educational goals (Fazil, 2024). Developers and educators should collaborate during the design phase, ensuring that every game mechanic serves an educational purpose, facilitating deeper learning through play.

Foster Collaboration Among Learners: Many games thrive on collaborative elements, and this can serve as a powerful educational tool. Incorporating multiplayer modes, team challenges, or cooperative tasks can foster social interaction among learners (Murtaza et al., 2022). Working together to solve problems can enhance critical thinking and communication skills, essential for success in both academic and real-world scenarios. Educators should encourage collaboration in game-based learning environments, allowing students to share strategies, insights, and success (Luo, 2024).

Incorporate Feedback Mechanisms: Regular, constructive feedback is essential in any learning environment. Game-based learning can utilize immediate feedback as a key feature, with students receiving real-time evaluations of their performance (Alkan, 2024). Developers should incorporate adaptive feedback systems that provide guidance and encouragement while also helping learners identify areas for improvement. This instant response not only reinforces learning but also allows for a more personalized educational experience.

Promote Self-Regulated Learning: Game-based and immersive environments can foster self-regulated learning, where students take charge of their own educational paths (Katiyar, 2024). By integrating features such as customizable avatars, choose-your-own-adventure storylines, or performance tracking, learners can set personal goals, reflect on their progress, and make informed decisions about their learning. Educators should support this by providing scaffolding in self regulation techniques and strategies (Harry, 2023).

Emphasize Transferable Skills: While content knowledge is critical, the development of transferable skills such as problem-solving, decision-making, and adaptability is equally important. Game-based learning should emphasize scenarios that promote these skills. Scenarios can mirror real-world challenges, encouraging learners to apply their knowledge in practical contexts (Petrusly, 2024). Educators might incorporate debriefing sessions after gameplay to discuss how these skills are applicable outside of the game environment.

Maintain Inclusivity and Accessibility: It is essential to consider diverse learning needs when designing game-based and immersive learning experiences (Aparicio-Gómez, 2024). Developers should create inclusive environments that cater to different learning styles, preferences, and physical abilities. This can be achieved through adjustable difficulty levels, varied content delivery modes, and user-friendly interfaces. Moreover, accessibility should be a priority, ensuring that all students can engage with the learning material (Zhang, 2024).

FUTURE RESEARCH DIRECTIONS

As the fields of game-based and immersive learning continue to evolve, several avenues for future research are ripe for exploration, focusing on the underlying theoretical principles that drive effectiveness in these educational methodologies.

Exploring Learning Theories in Game Design: Future research could focus on the integration of established learning theories, such as constructivism, behaviorism, and experiential learning, into game-based and immersive learning environments. Studies that systematically apply these theories to game design may yield insights into how specific game mechanics can support various learning strategies (Onesi-Ozigagun, 2024). Understanding which principles amplify learning outcomes can guide development efforts and refine educational approaches.

Investigating Emotional Engagement and Presence: The emotional and psychological aspects of learning experiences in immersive environments are critical to understanding their effectiveness (Alrayes 2024). Future research should delve into how emotional engagement and a sense of presence impact learning outcomes. By using experimental designs, researchers could examine various triggers that enhance emotional responses, such as narrative depth, character development, and environmental richness (Uygun, 2024). Investigating how these factors correlate with knowledge retention, student motivation, and engagement can inform best practices in immersive learning design.

Analyzing Long-Term Effects on Learning Retention: While game-based and immersive learning can promote immediate engagement and understanding, the long-term effects on knowledge retention and application still require in-depth examination (Walter, 2024). Longitudinal studies that track learning outcomes over extended periods can provide insight into how these methodologies affect long-term retention of skills and knowledge. Understanding the mechanisms behind these long-term effects can assist educators in crafting more effective learning experiences.

Studying Diversity and Inclusion: As game-based and immersive learning expands globally, understanding the effects of cultural diversity and inclusivity in these environments becomes imperative (Shala, 2024). Future research should investigate how different cultural backgrounds, values, and educational contexts influence the reception and efficacy of game-based learning. Identifying culturally responsive design elements can enhance accessibility and effectiveness for global audiences.

Examining Technological Advancements: With the rapid development of technology, examining the implications of emerging trends such as virtual reality (VR), augmented reality (AR), and artificial intelligence (AI) within the context of game-based and immersive learning is vital (Shah, 2024). Research can also focus on the efficacy of integrating these technologies into educational practices. Understanding how advancements enhance or modify existing theoretical frameworks can lead to innovations in educational design (Fazil, 2024).

REFERENCES

Abbas, N., Imran, A., Manzoor, R., Hussain, T., & Hussain, M. (2023). Role of artificial intelligence tools in enhancing students' educational performance at higher levels. *Journal of Artificial Intelligence Machine Learning and Neural Network,* (35), 36–49. DOI: 10.55529/jaimlnn.35.36.49

Agostinelli, S. (2021). *Actionable framework for city digital twin-enabled predictive maintenance and security management systems..* https://doi.org/DOI: 10.2495/bim210191

Akavova, A., Temirkhanova, Z., & Lorsanova, Z. (2023). Adaptive learning and artificial intelligence in the educational space. *E3s Web of Conferences,* 451, 06011. https://doi.org/DOI: 10.1051/e3sconf/202345106011

Akgün, S., & Greenhow, C. (2021). Artificial intelligence in education: Addressing ethical challenges in k-12 settings. *AI and Ethics*, *2*(3), 431–440. DOI: 10.1007/s43681-021-00096-7

Akinrinola, O. (2024). Navigating and reviewing ethical dilemmas in ai development: strategies for transparency, fairness, and accountability. *GSC Advanced Research and Reviews,* 18(3), 050-058. https://doi.org/DOI: 10.30574/gscarr.2024.18.3.0088

Alali, R. (2024). Opportunities and challenges of integrating generative artificial intelligence in education. *International Journal of Religion*, *5*(7), 784–793. DOI: 10.61707/8y29gv34

Alenezi, A. (2023). Teacher perspectives on ai-driven gamification: Impact on student motivation, engagement, and learning outcomes. *Information Technologies and Learning Tools*, *97*(5), 138–148. DOI: 10.33407/itlt.v97i5.5437

Alenezi, A. (2024). Obstacles to the use of ai applications in blackboard for faculty members at northern border university, saudi arabia. *Mier Journal of Educational Studies Trends & Practices,* 248-268. https://doi.org/DOI: 10.52634/mier/2024/v14/i2/2581

Aliabadi, R. (2023). *Transdisciplinary ai education: the confluence of curricular and community needs in the instruction of artificial intelligence.*, 137-151. https://doi.org/DOI: 10.1007/978-981-99-7947-9_11

Alkan, A. (2024). Artificial intelligence: its role and potential in education. *İnsan Ve Toplum Bilimleri Araştırmaları Dergisi,* 13(1), 483-497. https://doi.org/DOI: 10.15869/itobiad.1331201

Alladi, T., Chamola, V., Parizi, R., & Choo, K. (2019). Blockchain applications for industry 4.0 and industrial iot: A review. *IEEE Access : Practical Innovations, Open Solutions*, *7*, 176935–176951. DOI: 10.1109/access.2019.2956748

Allahverdi, A. (2021). Sample senior design projects of industrial engineering program at kuwait university. *Asean Journal of Engineering Education*, *4*(1). Advance online publication. DOI: 10.11113/ajee2020.4n1.14

Almusaed, A. (2023). Enhancing student engagement: Harnessing "aied"'s power in hybrid education—a review analysis. *Education Sciences*, *13*(7), 632. DOI: 10.3390/educsci13070632

Alrayes, A. (2024). Chatgpt in education – understanding the bahraini academics perspective. *Electronic Journal of e-Learning*, *22*(2), 112–134. DOI: 10.34190/ejel.22.2.3250

Alsadoon, H. (2023). The impact of gamification on student motivation and engagement: An empirical study. *Dirasat: Educational Sciences*, *50*(2), 386–396. DOI: 10.35516/edu.v50i2.255

Alshehri, B. (2023). Pedagogical paradigms in the ai era: Insights from saudi educators on the long-term implications of ai integration in classroom teaching. *IJESA*, *2*(8), 159–180. DOI: 10.59992/ijesa.2023.v2n8p7

Antonaci, A., Klemke, R., & Specht, M. (2019). The effects of gamification in online learning environments: A systematic literature review. *Informatics (MDPI)*, *6*(3), 32. DOI: 10.3390/informatics6030032

Aparicio-Gómez, O. (2024). Tejiendo conexiones: la simbiosis transformadora entre aprendizaje e inteligencia artificial. *Hachetetepé Revista Científica De Educación Y Comunicación,* (28). https://doi.org/DOI: 10.25267/hachetetepe.2024.i28.1103

Balci, S., Secaur, J., & Morris, B. (2022). Comparing the effectiveness of badges and leaderboards on academic performance and motivation of students in fully versus partially gamified online physics classes. *Education and Information Technologies*, *27*(6), 8669–8704. DOI: 10.1007/s10639-022-10983-z

Balta, N. (2023). *Ethical considerations in using ai in educational research.,* 2(1), 14205. https://doi.org/DOI: 10.51853/jorids/14205

Barua, P., Vicnesh, J., Gururajan, R., Oh, S., Palmer, E., Azizan, M., & Acharya, U. (2022). Artificial intelligence enabled personalised assistive tools to enhance education of children with neurodevelopmental disorders a review. *International Journal of Environmental Research and Public Health*, *19*(3), 1192. DOI: 10.3390/ijerph19031192

Bastani, P., Kavosi, Z., Alipoori, S., & Imani-Nasab, M. (2023). Evidence- based policy and decision-making among health managers: A case of shiraz university of medical sciences. *Galen Medical Journal*, *6*(1). Advance online publication. DOI: 10.31661/gmj.v6i1.729

Basudan, S. (2023). A Scalable Blockchain Framework For Secure Transactions In Iot-Based Dynamic Applications. *IEEE Open Journal of the Communications Society*, *4*, 1931–1945. DOI: 10.1109/ojcoms.2023.3307337

Bennani, S., Maalel, A., & Ghezala, H. (2021). Adaptive gamification in e-learning: A literature review and future challenges. *Computer Applications in Engineering Education*, *30*(2), 628–642. DOI: 10.1002/cae.22477

Buckley, P., & Doyle, E. (2014). Gamification and student motivation. *Interactive Learning Environments*, *24*(6), 1162–1175. DOI: 10.1080/10494820.2014.964263

Chai, F. (2024). Grading by ai makes me feel fairer? how different evaluators affect college students' perception of fairness. *Frontiers in Psychology*, *15*. Advance online publication. DOI: 10.3389/fpsyg.2024.1221177

Chang, C., Hwang, G., & Gau, M. (2021). Promoting students' learning achievement and self-efficacy: A mobile chatbot approach for nursing training. *British Journal of Educational Technology*, *53*(1), 171–188. DOI: 10.1111/bjet.13158

Chen, L., Chen, P., & Lin, Z. (2020). Artificial intelligence in education: A review. *IEEE Access : Practical Innovations, Open Solutions*, *8*, 75264–75278. DOI: 10.1109/access.2020.2988510

Cranley, L., Doran, D., Tourangeau, A., Kushniruk, A., & Nagle, L. (2012). Recognizing and responding to uncertainty: A grounded theory of nurses' uncertainty. *Worldviews on Evidence-Based Nursing*, *9*(3), 149–158. DOI: 10.1111/j.1741-6787.2011.00237.x

D'Souza, R. (2024). Twelve tips for addressing ethical concerns in the implementation of artificial intelligence in medical education. *Medical Education Online*, *29*(1). Advance online publication. DOI: 10.1080/10872981.2024.2330250

Davis, R. (2024). Korean in-service teachers' perceptions of implementing artificial intelligence (ai) education for teaching in schools and their ai teacher training programs. *International Journal of Information and Education Technology (IJIET)*, *14*(2), 214–219. DOI: 10.18178/ijiet.2024.14.2.2042

Devi, V., Vashe, A., Rao, R., Abraham, R., Pallath, V., & Torke, S. (2016). Curricular impact on learning approaches and critical thinking skills of medical students. *Education in Medicine Journal, 8*(4). Advance online publication. DOI: 10.5959/eimj.v8i4.468

Dichev, C., & Dicheva, D. (2017). Gamifying education: what is known, what is believed and what remains uncertain: a critical review. *International Journal of Educational Technology in Higher Education, 14*(1). Advance online publication. DOI: 10.1186/s41239-017-0042-5

Dirgantoro, K., Bermuli, J., & Soesanto, R. (2022). Is moodle gamification effective in reviewing student's motivation related to interest in learning online? *Educational Journal Journal of Research Results and Literature Review in the Field of Education, Teaching, and Learning, 8*(1), 114. DOI: 10.33394/jk.v8i1.4790

Dovleac, L., Chi u, I., Nichifor, E., & Brătucu, G. (2023). Shaping the inclusivity in the new society by enhancing the digitainability of sustainable development goals with education. *Sustainability, 15*(4), 3782. DOI: 10.3390/su15043782

Ejaz, H., McGrath, H., Wong, B., Guise, A., Vercauteren, T., & Shapey, J. (2022). Artificial intelligence and medical education: A global mixed-methods study of medical students' perspectives. *Digital Health, 8*, 205520762210890. DOI: 10.1177/20552076221089099

Erbaşı, Z. (2023). The role and potential of artificial intelligence and gamification in education: The example of vakıf participation bank. *Orclever Proceedings of Research and Development, 3*(1), 243–254. DOI: 10.56038/oprd.v3i1.329

Eslit, E. (2023). Blending boundaries in the new normal: Leveraging technology, ai and global perspectives in modern education. *Journal of Learning and Educational Policy*, (41), 8–18. DOI: 10.55529/jlep.41.8.18

Familoni, B. (2024). Advancements and challenges in ai integration for technical literacy: A systematic review. *Engineering Science & Technology Journal, 5*(4), 1415–1430. DOI: 10.51594/estj.v5i4.1042

Fazil, A. (2024). Exploring the broad impact of ai technologies on student engagement and academic performance in university settings in afghanistan. *Riggs Journal of Artificial Intelligence and Digital Business, 2*(2), 56–63. DOI: 10.31004/riggs.v2i2.268

Felzmann, H., Fosch-Villaronga, E., Lutz, C., & Tamò-Larrieux, A. (2020). Towards transparency by design for artificial intelligence. *Science and Engineering Ethics, 26*(6), 3333–3361. DOI: 10.1007/s11948-020-00276-4

Fırat, M. (2023). Integrating ai applications into learning management systems to enhance e-learning. *Öğretim Teknolojisi Ve Hayat Boyu Öğrenme Dergisi - Instructional Technology and Lifelong Learning*, 1-14. https://doi.org/DOI: 10.52911/itall.1244453

Fuster-Guilló, A., Pertegal-Felices, M., Jimeno-Morenilla, A., Azorín-López, J., Soliveres, M., & Restrepo-Calle, F. (2019). Evaluating impact on motivation and academic performance of a game-based learning experience using kahoot. *Frontiers in Psychology*, *10*. Advance online publication. DOI: 10.3389/fpsyg.2019.02843

Gamrat, C., Zimmerman, H., Dudek, J., & Peck, K. (2014). Personalized workplace learning: An exploratory study on digital badging within a teacher professional development program. *British Journal of Educational Technology*, *45*(6), 1136–1148. DOI: 10.1111/bjet.12200

Gligorea, I., Yaseen, M., Cioca, M., Gorski, H., & Oancea, R. (2022). An interpretable framework for an efficient analysis of students' academic performance. *Sustainability*, *14*(14), 8885. DOI: 10.3390/su14148885

Grunhut, J., Wyatt, A., & Marques, O. (2021). Educating future physicians in artificial intelligence (ai): An integrative review and proposed changes. *Journal of Medical Education and Curricular Development*, *8*. Advance online publication. DOI: 10.1177/23821205211036836

Güler, S., & Özkan, Y. (2018). Podcast applications in pre-service language teacher education from a constructivist perspective. *World Journal on Educational Technology Current Issues*, *10*(3), 131–141. DOI: 10.18844/wjet.v10i3.3552

Haresamudram, K., Larsson, S., & Heintz, F. (2023). Three levels of ai transparency. *Computer*, *56*(2), 93–100. DOI: 10.1109/mc.2022.3213181

Harry, A. (2023). Role of ai in education. *Interdiciplinary Journal and Hummanity (Injurity)*, *2*(3), 260–268. DOI: 10.58631/injurity.v2i3.52

Hernández, C. (2023). Development of critical thinking in the university curriculum. International. *Journal of Human Sciences Research*, *3*(34), 2–9. DOI: 10.22533/at.ed.5583342313095

Hidayat, D. (2021). The implementation of gamification system in asian higher education teaching. *Journal of Games Game Art and Gamification*, *2*(1). Advance online publication. DOI: 10.21512/jggag.v2i1.7218

Hollands, F., Pan, Y., & Escueta, M. (2019). What is the potential for applying cost-utility analysis to facilitate evidence-based decision making in schools? *Educational Researcher*, *48*(5), 287–295. DOI: 10.3102/0013189x19852101

Huesca, G., Campos, G., Larre, M., & Pérez-Lezama, C. (2023). Implementation of a mixed strategy of gamification and flipped learning in undergraduate basic programming courses. *Education Sciences*, *13*(5), 474. DOI: 10.3390/educsci13050474

Jayavardhini, P. (2024). Ai study partner: Development of an llm and gen ai-enhanced study assistant tool. *Interantional Journal of Scientific Research in Engineering and Management*, *08*(03), 1–5. DOI: 10.55041/ijsrem29626

Ji, H., Suo, L., & Hua, C. (2024). Ai performance assessment in blended learning: Mechanisms and effects on students' continuous learning motivation. *Frontiers in Psychology*, *15*. Advance online publication. DOI: 10.3389/fpsyg.2024.1447680

Jobin, A., & Ienca, M. (2019). The global landscape of ai ethics guidelines. *Nature Machine Intelligence*, *1*(9), 389–399. DOI: 10.1038/s42256-019-0088-2

Johnson, D., Deterding, S., Kuhn, K., Staneva, A., Stoyanov, S., & Hides, L. (2016). Gamification for health and wellbeing: A systematic review of the literature. *Internet Interventions : the Application of Information Technology in Mental and Behavioural Health*, *6*, 89–106. DOI: 10.1016/j.invent.2016.10.002

Julita, R. (2024). The impact of gamification on efl students' reading comprehension. *JEFLE*, *4*(2), 136. DOI: 10.26418/jefle.v4i2.74901

Kamruzzaman, M. (2023). Ai- and iot-assisted sustainable education systems during pandemics, such as covid-19, for smart cities. *Sustainability*, *15*(10), 8354. DOI: 10.3390/su15108354

Kang, J., Kang, C., Yoon, J., Ji, H., Li, T., Hyunmi, M., & Han, J. (2023). Dancing on the inside: A qualitative study on online dance learning with teacher-ai cooperation. *Education and Information Technologies*, *28*(9), 12111–12141. DOI: 10.1007/s10639-023-11649-0

Karabıyık, Ü. (2024). Investigation of the effect of gamified learning on motivation and success in math class. *Journal of Education and Practice*, *8*(1), 32–52. DOI: 10.47941/jep.1645

Katiyar, P. (2024). Ai-driven personalized learning systems: enhancing educational effectiveness. *eatp*. https://doi.org/DOI: 10.53555/kuey.v30i5.4961

Khakpour, A., & Colomo-Palacios, R. (2020). Convergence of gamification and machine learning: A systematic literature review. *Technology Knowledge and Learning*, *26*(3), 597–636. DOI: 10.1007/s10758-020-09456-4

Kim, J., & Castelli, D. (2021). Effects of gamification on behavioral change in education: A meta-analysis. *International Journal of Environmental Research and Public Health, 18*(7), 3550. DOI: 10.3390/ijerph18073550

Kurniawati, N., Maolida, E., & Anjaniputra, A. (2018). The praxis of digital literacy in the efl classroom: Digital-immigrant vs digital-native teacher. *Indonesian Journal of Applied Linguistics, 8*(1). Advance online publication. DOI: 10.17509/ijal.v8i1.11459

Larsen, M., Gulis, G., & Pedersen, K. (2011). Use of evidence in local public health work in denmark. *International Journal of Public Health, 57*(3), 477–483. DOI: 10.1007/s00038-011-0324-y

Larsson, S., & Heintz, F. (2020). Transparency in artificial intelligence. *Internet Policy Review, 9*(2). Advance online publication. DOI: 10.14763/2020.2.1469

Legaki, N., Xi, N., Hamari, J., Karpouzis, K., & Assimakopoulos, V. (2020). The effect of challenge-based gamification on learning: An experiment in the context of statistics education. *International Journal of Human-Computer Studies, 144*, 102496. DOI: 10.1016/j.ijhcs.2020.102496

Li, R. and Liu, J. (2022). *Applying gamification in english learning.* https://doi.org/ DOI: 10.2991/assehr.k.220504.490

Li, Y., & Chen, T. (2022). Blockchain Empowers Supply Chains: Challenges, Opportunities And Prospects. *Nankai Business Review International, 14*(2), 230–248. DOI: 10.1108/nbri-06-2022-0066

Lim, L., Dawson, S., Gašević, D., Joksimovíc, S., Fudge, A., Pardo, A., & Gentili, S. (2020). Students' sense-making of personalised feedback based on learning analytics. *Australasian Journal of Educational Technology, 36*(6), 15–33. DOI: 10.14742/ajet.6370

Limongi, R. (2024). The use of artificial intelligence in scientific research with integrity and ethics. *Rev. Artif. Intell. Educ, 5*(00), e0022. DOI: 10.37497/rev.artif.intell.educ.v5i00.22

Liu, L. (2024). Survey and analysis of primary school teachers' use of generative artificial intelligence. *Lecture Notes in Education Psychology and Public Media, 74*(1), 43–52. DOI: 10.54254/2753-7048/2024.bo17693

López, C., & Tucker, C. (2020). Toward personalized adaptive gamification: A machine learning model for predicting performance. *IEEE Transactions on Games, 12*(2), 155–168. DOI: 10.1109/tg.2018.2883661

Luan, H., Géczy, P., Lai, H., Gobert, J., Yang, S., Ogata, H., & Tsai, C. (2020). Challenges and future directions of big data and artificial intelligence in education. *Frontiers in Psychology, 11*. Advance online publication. DOI: 10.3389/fpsyg.2020.580820

Luo, Y. (2024). Innovative research on ai-assisted teaching models for college english listening and speaking courses. *Applied and Computational Engineering, 69*(1), 155–160. DOI: 10.54254/2755-2721/69/20241493

Maggio, I., Ginevra, M., Santilli, S., Nota, L., & Soresi, S. (2021). *Life design for an inclusive and sustainable future.*, 251-270. https://doi.org/DOI: 10.1007/978-3-030-64537-3_10

Mahardika, I. (2023). Science textbook based on merdeka belajar curriculum: Integration of learning implementation for critical thinking skills. *Journal of Education Society and Behavioural Science, 36*(10), 109–115. DOI: 10.9734/jesbs/2023/v36i101273

Majdzadeh, R., Yazdizadeh, B., Nedjat, S., Gholami, J., & Ahghari, S. (2011). Strengthening evidence-based decision-making: Is it possible without improving health system stewardship? *Health Policy and Planning, 27*(6), 499–504. DOI: 10.1093/heapol/czr072

Mehrpour, S., Shavoun, A., Kheiltash, A., Masoomi, R., & Seraji, R. (2023). Evaluating and comparing critical thinking skills of residents of tehran university of medical sciences. *BMC Medical Education, 23*(1). Advance online publication. DOI: 10.1186/s12909-023-04094-7

Moldt, J. (2024). Assessing ai awareness and identifying essential competencies: Insights from key stakeholders in integrating ai into medical education. *JMIR Medical Education, 10*, e58355–e58355. DOI: 10.2196/58355

Morales, M., Amado-Salvatierra, H., Medina, J., Barchino, R., Hernández-Rizzardini, R., & Teixeira, A. (2024). Personalized feedback in massive open online courses: Harnessing the power of langchain and openai api. *Electronics (Basel), 13*(10), 1960. DOI: 10.3390/electronics13101960

Mugisha, M., Uwitonze, A., Chesire, F., Senyonga, R., Oxman, M., Nsangi, A., & Rosenbaum, S. (2021). Teaching critical thinking about health using digital technology in lower secondary schools in rwanda: A qualitative context analysis. *PLoS One, 16*(3), e0248773. DOI: 10.1371/journal.pone.0248773

Murtaza, M., Ahmed, Y., Shamsi, J., Sherwani, F., & Usman, M. (2022). Ai-based personalized e-learning systems: Issues, challenges, and solutions. *IEEE Access : Practical Innovations, Open Solutions, 10*, 81323–81342. DOI: 10.1109/access.2022.3193938

Narayanan, K. (2024). Hybrid gamification and ai tutoring framework using machine learning and adaptive neuro-fuzzy inference system. *Journal of Advanced Research in Applied Sciences and Engineering Technology*, *42*(2), 221–233. DOI: 10.37934/araset.42.2.221233

Nguyen, T. (2023). Artificial intelligent based teaching and learning approaches: A comprehensive review. *International Journal of Evaluation and Research in Education (Ijere)*, *12*(4), 2387. DOI: 10.11591/ijere.v12i4.26623

Onesi-Ozigagun, O. (2024). Revolutionizing education through ai: A comprehensive review of enhancing learning experiences. *International Journal of Applied Research in Social Sciences*, *6*(4), 589–607. DOI: 10.51594/ijarss.v6i4.1011

Orton, L., Lloyd-Williams, F., Taylor-Robinson, D., O'Flaherty, M., & Capewell, S. (2011). The use of research evidence in public health decision making processes: Systematic review. *PLoS One*, *6*(7), e21704. DOI: 10.1371/journal.pone.0021704

Otero, L., Catalá, A., Morante, M., Taboada, M., López, B., & Barro, S. (2023). Ai literacy in k-12: A systematic literature review. *International Journal of STEM Education*, *10*(1). Advance online publication. DOI: 10.1186/s40594-023-00418-7

Özhan, Ş., & Kocadere, S. (2019). The effects of flow, emotional engagement, and motivation on success in a gamified online learning environment. *Journal of Educational Computing Research*, *57*(8), 2006–2031. DOI: 10.1177/0735633118823159

Pardosi, V., Xu, S., Umurohmi, U., Nurdiana, N., & Sabur, F. (2024). Implementation of an artificial intelligence based learning management system for adaptive learning. *Al-Fikrah Jurnal Manajemen Pendidikan*, *12*(1), 149. DOI: 10.31958/jaf.v12i1.12548

Patel, S. (2023). Addressing racial injustice: Examining systems of oppression and promoting equity in contemporary society. *Joura*, *1*(2), 13–17. DOI: 10.61963/jkt.v1i2.33

Pendy, B. (2023). Artificial intelligence: The future of education. *Jurnal Indonesia Sosial Sains*, *2*(11). Advance online publication. DOI: 10.59141/jiss.v2i11.801

Petrusly, P. (2024). *The effect of gamification using kahoot on students' critical thinking abilities: the role of mediating learning engagement and motivation*. Kuey., DOI: 10.53555/kuey.v30i5.1524

Polat, E. (2023). Gamification implementation for educational purposes: A scoping review (2013-2018). *Educational Technology Quarterly, 2023*(3), 367–400. DOI: 10.55056/etq.589

Popenici, S., & Kerr, S. (2017). Exploring the impact of artificial intelligence on teaching and learning in higher education. *Research and Practice in Technology Enhanced Learning, 12*(1). Advance online publication. DOI: 10.1186/s41039-017-0062-8

Pratama, M. (2023). Revolutionizing education: Harnessing the power of artificial intelligence for personalized learning. *Klasikal Journal of Education Language Teaching and Science, 5*(2), 350–357. DOI: 10.52208/klasikal.v5i2.877

Pu, D., Ni, J., Song, D., Zhang, W., Wang, Y., Wu, L., & Wang, Y. (2019). Influence of critical thinking disposition on the learning efficiency of problem-based learning in undergraduate medical students. *BMC Medical Education, 19*(1). Advance online publication. DOI: 10.1186/s12909-018-1418-5

Rathore, A. (2023). Artificial intelligence and curriculum prospects for elementary school. *Pakistan Journal of Humanities and Social Sciences, 11*(4). Advance online publication. DOI: 10.52131/pjhss.2023.v11i4.1909

Rivera, E., & Garden, C. (2021). Gamification for student engagement: A framework. *Journal of Further and Higher Education, 45*(7), 999–1012. DOI: 10.1080/0309877x.2021.1875201

Rohmah, N. (2022). A vocational school cutting-edge learning strategy: Examining gamification towards student engagement and achievement. *Jurnal Kependidikan Jurnal Hasil Penelitian Dan Kajian Kepustakaan Di Bidang Pendidikan Pengajaran Dan Pembelajaran, 8*(3), 655. DOI: 10.33394/jk.v8i3.5779

Rueckert, D., Pico, K., Kim, D., & Sánchez, X. (2020). Gamifying the foreign language classroom for brain-friendly learning. *Foreign Language Annals, 53*(4), 686–703. DOI: 10.1111/flan.12490

Rugaiyah, R. (2023). The potential of artificial intelligence in improving linguistic competence: A systematic literature review. *Arkus, 9*(2), 319–324. DOI: 10.37275/arkus.v9i2.313

Setyoadi, E., & Patmanthara, S. (2024). Students' goal orientation and gamification in learning for academic performance: A systematic literature review. *Research and Development in Education (Raden), 4*(1), 390–403. DOI: 10.22219/raden.v4i1.32630

Shah, J. (2024). *Rethinking higher education through multidisciplinary studies.* jes, 20(4s), 2060-2063. https://doi.org/DOI: 10.52783/jes.2309

Shala, D. (2024). Learning styles and motivation: Their role in academic performance. *Journal of Educational and Social Research, 14*(3), 258. DOI: 10.36941/jesr-2024-0071

Spanellis, A., Pyrko, I., & Dörfler, V. (2021). Gamifying situated learning in organisations. *Management Learning, 53*(3), 525–546. DOI: 10.1177/13505076211038812

Strydom, W., Funke, N., Nienaber, S., Nortje, K., & Steyn, M. (2010). Evidence-based policymaking: A review. *South African Journal of Science, 106*(5/6). Advance online publication. DOI: 10.4102/sajs.v106i5/6.249

Sughra, U., & Usmani, A. (2022). Comparison of critical thinking among undergraduate medical students of conventional and integrated curricula in twin cities. *Pakistan Journal of Medical Sciences, 38*(6). Advance online publication. DOI: 10.12669/pjms.38.6.5409

Thimmanna., Sharma, A.V.N.S., Naik, M. S., Radhakrishnan, S., Sharma, A., (2024). Personalized Learning Paths: Adapting Education with AI-Driven Curriculum. *European Economic Letters (EEL), 14*(1), 31–40. https://doi.org/DOI: 10.52783/eel.v14i1.993

Tolentino, R. (2024). Curriculum frameworks and educational programs in ai for medical students, residents, and practicing physicians: Scoping review. *JMIR Medical Education, 10*, e54793. DOI: 10.2196/54793

Tonbuloğlu, B. (2023). An evaluation of the use of artificial intelligence applications in online education. *Journal of Educational Technology and Online Learning, 6*(4), 866–884. DOI: 10.31681/jetol.1335906

Trang, N., & Thư, P. (2024). The role of ai in improving student learning outcomes: Evidence in vietnam. *International Journal of Multidisciplinary Research and Analysis, 07*(06). Advance online publication. DOI: 10.47191/ijmra/v7-i06-48

Tubino, L. & Adachi, C. (2022). Developing feedback literacy capabilities through an ai automated feedback tool. *Ascilite Publications,* e22039. https://doi.org/DOI: 10.14742/apubs.2022.39

Tyni, J., Tarkiainen, A., López-Pernas, S., Saqr, M., Kahila, J., Bednarik, R., & Tedre, M. (2022). Games and rewards: A scientometric study of rewards in educational and serious games. *IEEE Access : Practical Innovations, Open Solutions, 10*, 31578–31585. DOI: 10.1109/access.2022.3160230

Tzafilkou, K., Perifanou, M., & Economides, A. (2023). Assessing teachers' digital competence in primary and secondary education: Applying a new instrument to integrate pedagogical and professional elements for digital education. *Education and Information Technologies, 28*(12), 16017–16040. DOI: 10.1007/s10639-023-11848-9

Ulagammal, S., & Chaluvarayaswamy, R. (2023). Expanding access to mindfulness education in adaptive learning: Enhancing student well-being and academic success. *Thiagarajar College of Preceptors Edu Spectra, 5*(S1), 81–84. DOI: 10.34293/eduspectra.v5is1-may23.014

Uygun, D. (2024). Teachers' perspectives on artificial intelligence in education. *Advances in Mobile Learning Educational Research, 4*(1), 931–939. DOI: 10.25082/amler.2024.01.005

Varas, J., Coronel, B., Villagrán, I., Escalona, G., Hernández, R., Schuit, G., & Achurra, P. (2023). Innovations in surgical training: exploring the role of artificial intelligence and large language models (llm). *Revista Do Colégio Brasileiro De Cirurgiões,* 50. https://doi.org/DOI: 10.1590/0100-6991e-20233605-en

Walter, Y. (2024). Embracing the future of artificial intelligence in the classroom: The relevance of ai literacy, prompt engineering, and critical thinking in modern education. *International Journal of Educational Technology in Higher Education, 21*(1). Advance online publication. DOI: 10.1186/s41239-024-00448-3

Wood, E., Ange, B., & Miller, D. (2021). Are we ready to integrate artificial intelligence literacy into medical school curriculum: Students and faculty survey. *Journal of Medical Education and Curricular Development, 8*. Advance online publication. DOI: 10.1177/23821205211024078

Yazdanpanah, V., Gerding, E., Stein, S., Dastani, M., Jonker, C., Norman, T., & Ramchurn, S. (2022). Reasoning about responsibility in autonomous systems: Challenges and opportunities. *AI & Society, 38*(4), 1453–1464. DOI: 10.1007/s00146-022-01607-8

Zainal, N. (2023). University students' perspectives on gamification in vocabulary learning: A literature review. *Malaysian Journal of Social Sciences and Humanities (Mjssh), 8*(5), e002314. DOI: 10.47405/mjssh.v8i5.2314

Zhang, J. (2024). AI in teacher education: Unlocking new dimensions in teaching support, inclusive learning, and digital literacy. *Journal of Computer Assisted Learning, 40*(4), 1871–1885. DOI: 10.1111/jcal.12988

Zhao, J., Juithong, S., & Nilnopkoon, P. (2024). Effecting an adaptive learning system on academic achievement as regulations for measuring pharmacist qualifications to licensure of pharmaceutical management students. *IJSASR*, *4*(3), 573–582. DOI: 10.60027/ijsasr.2024.4357

Zourmpakis, A., Kalogiannakis, M., & Papadakis, S. (2023). Adaptive gamification in science education: An analysis of the impact of implementation and adapted game elements on students' motivation. *Computers*, *12*(7), 143. DOI: 10.3390/computers12070143

Chapter 2
New Frontiers in Pedagogy:
Immersive Technologies and Game-Based Learning

Amrik Singh
https://orcid.org/0000-0003-3598-8787
Lovely Professional University, India

ABSTRACT

The landscape of education is undergoing a profound transformation, driven by the rapid evolution of digital technologies and a growing understanding of effective learning paradigms. This chapter, "New Frontiers in Pedagogy: Immersive Technologies and Game-Based Learning," explores the revolutionary potential of virtual reality (VR), augmented reality (AR), mixed reality (MR), and game-based learning (GBL) to redefine instructional design and enhance student engagement. Moving beyond traditional didactic approaches, these innovative pedagogical tools offer dynamic, experiential, and highly interactive learning environments. We delve into how immersive technologies can transport learners to historical events, complex scientific phenomena, or simulated professional scenarios, fostering deeper understanding and practical skill development. This chapter synthesizes current research and practical applications, highlighting the benefits of increased learner agency, personalized pathways, and the development of 21st-century skills like critical thinking, creativity, and digital literacy.

DOI: 10.4018/979-8-3373-4465-2.ch002

INTRODUCTION

The education environment is ever changing as a result of technology and an insight into the way human beings learn. Game-based learning and immersive technologies are two of the most promising technologies that transform pedagogy. These strategies will transcend the conventional lecture-based systems by providing dynamic and interactive experiences that will suit different learning styles and create greater insight (Hsu & Cheng, 2021). At the same time, the postulates of game design immediate feedback, specific goals, gradual difficulty, and motivated learning are discussed in terms of their ability to develop persistence, problem-solving skills, and learning in a group. Immersive Technologies refer to a variety of digital technologies that provide the learner with a feeling of presence to the simulated space (El Mawas et al., 2018; Singh2024a). The technologies are supposed to create the boundaries between the real and the online world, creating a sense of being there. The Immersive technologies are a paradigm shift in the way people approach digital content and, to a larger extent, each other and the real world. These technologies are far more than entertainment, and they are changing industries, reinventing education and defining user experiences. The fundamental idea of immersive technologies is to produce a sense of presence that causes the user to feel a physical presence in a simulated space or that digital content is actually being incorporated in their real world. The general term immersive a technology refers mainly to Virtual Reality (VR), Augmented Reality (AR), and Mixed Reality (MR) because of the cumbersome term Extended Reality (XR). Although they are dissimilar, they are placed on a continuum of virtuality, with each providing an option of immersion and contact with the real world (Rye et al., 2025a). Virtual Reality (VR) provides an entirely simulated digital world that keeps the user separate of the real world. This complete immersion is normally accomplished with head-mounted displays (HMDs) which obscures external vision and monitors head and body movements enabling them to navigate and engage in a completely digital environment (Deri et al., 2024; Singh2024b). Its uses include immersive play and virtual tourism to highly stakes training simulators of surgeons and pilots as well as emergency responders. VR is aimed at moving the user to another reality. Augmented Reality (AR) works differently and superimposes the digital information to the real world. Popular ones are mobile games, such as Pokemon GO, virtual try-on features of clothing or furniture, and real time navigation assist. The advantage of AR is that it offers background information and immerses the real world without the need to fully dissociate with it (Garg et al., 2024). Mixed Reality (MR) is a more advanced fusion of VR and AR, and it provides the environment of digital objects, that is not only superimposed but also integrated into the real-life environment, being able to interact with physical objects in real-time. MR gadgets such as Microsoft HoloLens enable their users to view and engage with both a digital hologram and a real environment at the same time (Kaur et al., 2023; Singh & Kumar, 2024). This ability opens up uses such as collaborative work remotely with virtual models being controlled on a real-world table, or maintenance engineers being provided with real time instructions and diagrams which can be superimposed onto equipment. MR strives towards a hybrid reality that is actually interactive. Immersive technologies are progressing faster due to the convergence of such forces as the growing demand of consumers and business partners on hyper-realistic content, the affordability of hardware, and the inclusion of Artificial Intelligence (AI) and 5G connectivity. The use of AI is contributing to more realistic non-playable characters in games, personalization of learning, and more complex immersive experiences through lower latency and higher bandwidth of 5G networks (Rye et al., 2025b). The immersive technologies are being used in industries in numerous ways. Application of VR in healthcare includes surgery education, pain treatment, post-operative mental health treatment and rehabilitation of patients. Immersive classroom, virtual field trips and training modules are advantages of education. AR is being used in retail and e-commerce in virtual try-on, and VR showrooms to create better customer interaction. MR is used in manufacturing and engineering in the prototyping, optimization of assembly lines, and remote assistance. Even the tourism and hospitality sector is providing online tours and virtual previews of places. The world market of immersive technology is growing exponentially, whose estimations amount to tens of billions of USD in 2025 and keeps growing at a consistent pace over the next several years. Nevertheless, such issues as high prices of modern hardware, creating the necessary content in the most advanced way, the ability to provide a perfect integration with the existing systems, and the issue of information privacy and the possibility of information oversaturation do exist. Nevertheless, the current innovation in the hardware, software, and user interfaces is an indication of a future in which immersive technologies will become a more integrated part of everyday life and that the boundaries between our physical and digital lives will be cross-charged and violently disrupted (Singh & Kumar, 2024).

Game-Based Learning (GBL)

Game based learning, in its turn, incorporates the concept of game mechanics and principles into the learning process. It takes advantage of the intrinsic motivation nature of games to improve engagement, problem solving, and knowledge acquisition (Singh2024b). Game-Based Learning (GBL) is a mobile and growingly centralized pedagogical methodology, which takes advantage of the natural motivational and entertaining nature of games to help learners gain knowledge, improve skills, and redress behavior, stepping out of the rote memorization to impart learning and critical thinking (Groff, 2018). In contrast to mere gamification, where game-like elements, like points, badges and leaderboards, are used on non-game activities, GBL has full-fledged games (meaning the learning goals are inherently woven into the gameplay) in which players learn through doing, experimenting, failing and winning in a structured, often fantastical, setting. This strategy will use our predisposed human need to challenge, master and reward, and the learning process will be more pleasant and adhesive (Udeozor et al., 2023). As an example, a learner could gain knowledge of complex physics through creating and sending rockets in a virtual reality game, or of historical events by playing a historical civilization game as a leader instead of reading about them in a textbook (Singh2024a; Deri et al., 2024). Some of the fundamental psychological concepts that make GBL effective include: it offers immediate and positive feedback, so learners can comprehend the outcomes of their actions in real-time and modify their plans; it can be inherently associated with safe failure space and thus experimentation with no real-life consequences, which increases their resilience and growth mindset; it allows them to solve problems and make decisions by introducing complex situations they have to think through, and strategize accordingly; and when games are played in groups, they can learn socially. Moreover, it is possible to make GBL extremely flexible to individual learning styles and speed, since most educational games have adaptive difficulty levels and custom routes, where a learner can move at their own pace and concentrate on the spheres in which they need to practice more (Nuong et al., 2024). The story lines typical of games also contribute to retention in that they give the story a contextual background and the abstract ideas become more familiar and easier to remember. GBL is increasingly being applied in a wide range of fields in both K-12 educations with applications in games such as Minecraft as a creative problem-solving and virtual world-building environment, and in higher education as sophisticated simulations to train medical practitioners, engineer designers, and business strategists, and in corporate training using serious games to teach leadership and business ethics (Ding et al., 2024). With the continued growth in technology more and more personalized and adapting learning experiences are being created through the incorporation of artificial intelligence into game engines, in which games can intelligently react to the strengths and weaknesses of a learner and adjust content and challenges to accommodate them (El Mawas et al., 2018). The growing availability of powerful game development software, and the growing knowledge of the principles of successful game design, are contributing to the outbreak of high-quality educational games (Deri et al., 2024; Singh2024b). Although there are still problems, such as the need to perform a solid research on efficacy, the cost of development, and equitable access to technology, the proven advantages in terms of engagement, retention, and developing the skills of the 21st century make Game-Based Learning a new frontier in pedagogy that will redefine the ways we learn and create capabilities in an increasingly complex world, transforming learning into an adventure, not a task.

The Synergistic Effect of Immersion and Play

It is convergence that makes these pedagogical methods to have the potential they truly possess. Immersive technologies and game-based learning are highly effective in terms of engaging and transformational learning. Suppose ancient Rome was being introduced by taking a virtual tour of the Colosseum and being part of a historical game, in which case it was presented as a game.

Increased Interaction and Inspiration

The virtual reality of VR/AR/MR attracts the interest of the students and contributes to the feeling of the presence and investment (Song et al., 2024; Singh, 2022). The challenges as well as rewards and accomplishment in the game mechanics lead to further motivation. Immersive technologies such as Virtual Reality (VR), Augmented Reality (AR), and Mixed Reality (MR) have been introduced into education to transform the process of learning material among students (Singh & Kumar, 2024). These tools capitalize on the immersive quality to draw the attention of students and provide them with a more profound feeling of the presence and investment into the learning process. In contrast to the old-fashioned approaches to the learning process that tend to be based on pure observation, the VR/AR/MR technologies allow placing students in the interactive and simulated reality that makes lessons come true. As an example, VR will be able to take students to ancient ruins, the bottom of the ocean, or even inside the human body, and bring abstract or distant ideas to life. Such level of immersion gives rise to this sense of presence in which the students feel like they are a part of the learning process and thus, they make the learning process more interesting and more effective. To this engagement, there is a stimulating effect of game mechanics offered as part of these technologies (Rye et al., 2025a; Groff, 2018; Deri et al., 2024). Learning is made exciting and satisfying through components like challenges, rewards, and tracking of progress that would otherwise make gaming exciting and satisfying. Under these conditions, students can encounter problems that involve problem-solving, collaboration or creativity in order to advance. As an example, a biology lesson could be a VR-based rainforest playing a game where species are identified and points or badges are given on successful identifications. Equally, an AR application can transform a geography lesson into a scavenger hunt where the students will need to discover and engage with significant landmarks within their environment in order to be unlocked into new information. Such game-based mechanisms allow not only maintaining the interest but also providing the learners with a feeling of accomplishment and progress that will motivate them to approach more complicated material with eagerness (Ahmed & Sutton, 2017). The fusion of gamification and immersive experiences makes the learning environment more of an active participatory and feedback-driven place. Students are not the passive consumers of information but they are empowered to search experiment and even engage in the educational material (Singh2024b). This interactive method secures retention as well as gives the students' confidence when dealing with more and more challenging assignments. In addition, VR/AR/MR technologies target various types of learning styles, which makes education inclusive and accessible. Visual learners are offered the three dimensional models and simulations, auditory learners are taught by sound effects and narration and kinesthetic learners perform better in the environment where they can interact and move. This diversity makes the learning process more relatable and interesting among students with diverse backgrounds and learning styles. Lastly, VR/AR/MR has a strong immersive nature, which, along with the motivational aspect of the game mechanics helps to increase student engagement and educational outcomes (Garg et al., 2024). These technologies are seen to be forming a future in which not only can education be more effective, but also incredibly inspiring and enjoyable to the learner of all ages through providing lessons that are interactive and rewarding.

Active and Experiential Learning

Learners do not passively receive the information and instead they actively engage in the learning process. With the use of immersive environments, the hands-on experience and exploration are possible, which facilitates a greater level of understanding and retention. Active and Experiential Learning are emerging as two potent approaches in the learning field where skills and knowledge are more and more being regarded as future oriented, where the students do not passively receive the knowledge but are rather actively engaging with and internalizing knowledge at a different level. Although the two approaches are often used interchangeably, as closely related concepts, they have specific features and goals (El Mawas et al., 2018; Singh & Kumar, 2024). Active learning can be defined as any teaching process that involves the students in the learning process whereby they are expected to do something with the material and consider what they are doing. This is contrary to the conventional lecture systems in which students get information mostly in a passive way. Active learning can be exemplified by short tasks in the classroom, such as think-pair-share, discussion of the problem, activity centered on solving problems, short quizzes, debates, and peer teaching. The fundamental concept here is to give the task as the new challenge to the student instead of the teacher, and promote such higher-order thinking skills as analysis, synthesis, and evaluation. Study after study shows that active learning techniques result in the substantial performance, increased retention, and lower failure rates among students than didactic approaches, and create a more productive and exciting learning experience (Duncan, 2020). Experience learning as an extension of the active engagement concept goes even further by highlighting learning in the context of direct hands world experiences, which in most cases engage real world situations and implications. Experience learning is based on the ideas of John Dewey and David Kolb, and its cycle is concrete experience, reflective observation, abstract conceptualization, and active experimentation (Rye et al., 2025a; Singh, 2022). The learners will take part in an experience (the experience), they will reflect on what occurred and why (reflection), make inferences or come up with new theories (conceptualization), and then apply the new knowledge in the next experience (experimentation). Such a cycle guarantees that learning is highly individual, pertinent and radical. Examples of experiential learning include the field trip, service-learning project, case studies, simulation, role-playing, laboratory experiment, internship, apprenticeship, field trip, role-playing, simulation, service-learning project, project-based learning and laboratory experiment. Experiential learning has the benefit of creating the practical experience of a concept, unlike having a theoretical comprehension, and students can learn not only knowledge, but also essential skills such as problem-solving, decision-making, teamwork, communication, and adaptability.

LITERATURE REVIEW

The active and experiential learning has a synergetic power because both of them will help to deepen the understanding and achieve the required competencies. Active learning will make sure that students are constantly processing the information, building their own knowledge in the classroom, and experiential learning will provide the continuation of the same activity to the real-life situation and enable the practicing and refining of the skills in the situations of the real world. This is a practical, mindful method, which provides a feeling of ownership of the learning process and increases motivation, engagement and self-confidence among the students. Active participation by students and first-hand learning create a better chance to relate abstract with the practical application, retain information longer, and have a more favorable attitude towards learning as a learning process (Nuong et al., 2024). Moreover, such approaches are essential in building the so-called soft skills of critical thinking, teamwork, and resilience that are becoming more important in the modern dynamic workforce (Alaswad & Nadolny, 2015). Although there are such issues like the lack of resources, the lack of curriculum integration, and effective assessment techniques, the unquestionable advantages of the active and experiential learning make them unavoidable elements of the modern pedagogies and create the future-ready individuals able to cope with the sophisticated challenges and make a viable contribution to the society.

Problem-Solving and Critical Thinking Skills

Numerous educational simulations and games involve complicated scenarios in which learners are needed to process the information, make decisions, and resolve them in a dynamic and engaging manner. In a modern world that is growing increasingly complex and swiftly changing, the construction of solid problem-solving and critical thinking skills is one of the foundations of quality education and a primary requirement of success in virtually all spheres of life, both academic and professional careers or personal decision-making (Singh, 2022). Critical thinking and critical analysis are two cognitive skills that are extremely connected because the former is typically the problem solving engine powered by the analytical engine. The process of objective analysis and evaluation of information to build a judgment can be interpreted as critical thinking, which implies the ability to detect biases, analysis of evidence, logical fallacies, fact-opinion distinction, and synthesis of information obtained through diverse sources to create a logical argument (Garg et al., 2024). It does not only entail gathering facts but questioning them, knowing their implications and making well-grounded conclusions. On the contrary, problem-solving is detecting a problem, diagnosing the underlying causes of the problem, brainstorming on the possible solutions, choosing the best solution, implementing, and determining its efficacy. It involves using critical thinking to resolve problems and get the results one wants (Singh & Kumar, 2024). Development of these skills is not limited to rote memorization and helps learners become not only receivers of information, but also creators of knowledge, as they have the mental capacities to handle uncertainty, embrace change, and become creative. Educational settings are critical to developing these key competencies and to move towards didactic teaching and the more inquiry-based, project-based and experiential learning approaches. As an alternative to merely answering questions, teachers create problems that necessitate students to wrestle with real world problems, including how to analyze thorny social problems, how to devise a lasting solution to an environmental problem, or how to debug a computer program. This usually means stating disjointed problems with no obvious solutions and making students define the problem themselves, collect data, critically evaluate its validity and relevance, and discuss the various lenses. In case studies, debates, Socratic seminars, scientific experimentation, group projects all force students to explain their argument, provide evidence to support their thesis, think about opposing arguments, and change their minds based on newly available information (Hsu & Cheng, 2021). The resilience and growth mindset are also developed as a result of the iterative process of problem-solving, which in most cases includes trial and error, which teaches the students that failure is part of the process of learning. Moreover, technology (such as simulations and game-based learning) may offer safe and interactive learning spaces to the learners to experiment with solutions to complicated problems, get immediate feedback, and practice critical thinking skills in a risk-free environment. An example is that medical trainees can train on diagnostic reasoning using a virtual patient simulator, or urban planners can be critical about the effectiveness of various development options using city-building games (Deri et al., 2024). The self-feedback between such digital tools enables the quick repetition and improvement of cognitive strategies. Finally, when life skills of problem-solving and critical thinking are developing, individuals will be empowered enough to become independent learners, practical decision-makers and productive members of the society, to never be stuck in the complexities of the 21st century because of intellectual nimbleness and informed judgment, to be not merely learned, but really proficient.

Safe and Accessible Learning Environments

Safe areas can be built with the help of immersive technologies to perform dangerous tasks (e.g., surgery, firefighting) or to visit unreachable places (e.g., the deep sea, outer space). They are also in a position to offer more easily accessible learning to students with disabilities. The unmatched capability of immersive technologies to provide a safe and accessible learning experience is also one of the most revolutionary and impactful advantages of the technology in learning, as it alters the method of knowledge and skill acquisition without any physical risk to the learner and minimal geographical restrictions. This is an immense advantage to serve very vital requirements in diverse areas and this will provide a groundbreaking alternative to the old-fashioned ways of training which may be perilously perilous or prohibitively costly or even impossible in the actual world. Look at the sphere of medicine: future surgeons are able to practice complex procedures in a virtual reality (VR) simulator and recreate intricate surgeries such as cardiac bypasses or brain surgeries with vast levels of realism (Ahmed & Sutton, 2017; Nuong et al., 2024). There are no practical implications of errors in this online environment, which gives students the opportunity to repeat, optimize their methods, and develop muscle memory and confidence without endangering patients. In the same way, firefighters are able to move through the burning structures, plan a rescue mission, and even train to recognize a flashover point in simulations which mimic real-life emergencies and would be too dangerous to train on in life only. In addition to professional training, these technologies have provided an access to the worlds, which are inaccessible because of the extreme conditions or distant location. Virtual field trips allow students to explore the depths of the ocean, the surface of Mars, or to be able to take a detailed tour of the ruins of ancient civilizations such as Pompeii, among other places, at the comfort and safety of a classroom. These are not passive experiences; using augmented reality (AR) and mixed reality (MR), learners have the opportunity to engage with virtual objects, interact with geological structures, or cut digital organisms, and get the tangible experience that cannot be learned through a diagram in a textbook. More than that, the way in which immersive technologies can be truly inclusive is truly impressive, how democratization through the provision of more accessible learning experiences can be offered to the students with disabilities. In cases of mobility impairments, VR eliminates physical barriers to enable the learner to engage in full activity in aspects that may have been inaccessible to them, e.g. in virtual sports or tours of historical locations where walking may be required over a long distance. Virtual environments can use haptic feedback and sound to provide students with visual impairments with alternative sensory information, rendering visual information inaccessible (Hsu & Cheng, 2021; Kaur et al., 2023). An example could be a student with ADHD who will be able to focus more in a controlled VR setting where the external stimuli are reduced to a minimum, whereas the student on the autism spectrum could exercise social skills in a safe, re-creatable virtual environment and build confidence to approach real-life situations. Such adaptive allows making learning not a one-size-fits-all task but instead customizing it according to individual requirements, which will encourage more engagement and equity (Garg et al., 2024). Manipulability of variables, the possibility to replay scenarios and have instant and non-judgmental feedback taught in these simulation spaces greatly promotes the learning curve of every student, making otherwise challenging or risky subjects accessible and masterable. Therefore, immersive technologies are not merely efficiency instruments; they are effective facilitators of safety, equity, and more profound learning and are essentially transforming what education and training can do around the world (Singh & Kumar, 2024). Game-based and immersion learning experiences can be customized as per the needs and learning pace of the individual student. Adaptive games have the ability to change the difficulty depending on the performance, whereas immersive simulation can provide individual learning paths based on specific goals. Teamwork, communication, and social learning skills can be developed in multi-user immersive environments and group activities based on games. Although there is tremendous potential, there are some challenges that surround the adoption of immersive technologies and game-based learning in education and should be given keen attention:

Cost and Accessibility: VR/AR/MR technology may be a costly implementation process, which needs hardware, software and infrastructure investment. Accessibility of all students is a key issue.

Technical Knowledge and Resources: The teachers should be well trained and supported so that they can successfully implement these technologies in their teaching activities. The learning process may also be influenced by technical problems.

Curriculum Integration and Alignment: It is not all about putting technology into the classroom. Games and immersive experiences should be well correlated with the learning goals and the curriculum requirements in order to be effective.

Risk of Distraction and Overstimulation: These technologies are occasionally distracting and overstimulating when not properly designed and moderated.

Assessment and Evaluation: Creating an efficient way of measuring learning in immersive and game-based environments will involve new types of assessment systems based on more than just traditional testing systems (Singh & Kumar, 2024).

DISCUSSION AND INTERPRETATION

Ethical Implications: The problem of data privacy, accessibility to individuals with disabilities, and the threat of bias in algorithms should be taken into consideration.

The Future of Pedagogy: a Future of Blending of the Real and Virtual.

The world of education is changing at a fast pace due to the development of technology and the appearance of new demands in society. It is hoped that the future of pedagogy will be a seamless integration of virtual and physical learning worlds, which promises to provide more opportunities than ever before to personalized, inclusive, and interesting learning. With the merits of the conventional, face-to-face interaction, it will be complemented by the flexibility and innovation of digital technologies, guaranteeing a well-rounded learning experience, which can be customized to meet the needs of different learners.

Personalization and Adaptivity:

The individualization of learning is one of the characteristics of the future model of pedagogy. Artificial intelligence (AI) allows the development of personal learning paths as virtual platforms can evaluate personal learning patterns, strengths, and weaknesses. As an example, adaptive learning technologies are able to show material at a suitable level of difficulty so that learners can always be motivated and challenged. However, the real-life classroom is still a necessity to develop social and emotional learning, promote collaboration, and develop creativity with the help of practical tasks (Hsu & Cheng, 2021; Garg et al., 2024). These measures combined form a more accommodative system that is able to cater to different learning styles and rates.

Immersive Learning Experiences

VR Virtual Reality (VR) and Augmented Reality (AR) will revolutionize the way pedagogy is practiced by offering immersive learning experiences. In the virtual setting, students have the ability to study historical places, perform more complicated experiments, or visualize abstract scientific concepts. These technologies make learning interactive and involve better understanding as well as retention. Nevertheless, they do not demean the relevance of practical application. As an illustration, medical students can perfect their skills in virtual practice before the actual clinical practice so as to achieve a balance between theory and practice.

Connectivity and Collaboration around the Globe:

Virtual tools integration enables learners in various regions of the globe to work together easily. The virtual classrooms create an international flow of ideas and culture by breaking geographical limits. Students are able to engage in global projects, do guest lectures by professionals, or solve problems in a team, which makes them ready to work in a global environment (Nuong et al., 2024). The physical classroom, in the meantime, is used as a localized center of the discussions, workshops and community building activities, where global insights are based on a real, contextual framework.

Equality and Availability:

The blended pedagogical model has the potential to eliminate educational disparities. One of the ways that virtual platforms can democratize access to the quality resources is to bring world-class education to remote areas or under-served regions. Moreover, the student with special needs can enjoy the privilege of being served with tailor-made tools based on their requirements (Singh & Kumar, 2024). The physical classroom with these virtual innovations enriched becomes the place where the notion of being inclusive can be implemented, so that every student will feel significant and encouraged.

Equity and Accessibility with Educational Technology

The fast advancement of educational technology (EdTech) has changed the learning environments, providing outstanding opportunities of personalized learning, interconnections on a global scale, and adaptability in accessing knowledge. Nevertheless, these innovations do not only pose important questions of accessibility and equity. With technology being a growing focus in the education sector, it is both an ethical and a practical requirement to make sure that every learner irrespective of socioeconomic status, physical ability, geographic location, or cultural background can be able to enjoy the fruits of technology. The accessibility and equity are not just the marginal issues anymore; they are the cornerstones of the effective educational technology systems designing and execution. Accessibility is the term used to relate to the development of digital tools and platforms that are accessible to all learners, even learners with physical, sensory, or cognitive disabilities (Song et al., 2024). As an example, students with disabilities can be involved in online learning environments using features like screen readers, video captions, text-to-speech, and customizable interfaces. The Web Content Accessibility Guidelines (WCAG) offer standards to be used in order to ensure inclusivity, but their implementation in EdTech products are not quite uniform. Disability is not the only accessibility concern, and they include language obstacles, computer literacy, and compatibility with devices. An effectively accessible platform should be able to support learners consuming mobile devices with low bandwidth or with multilingual learners. Unless we design them to be so, technological innovations are likely to create more exclusion than destruction.

Equity in educational technology is more comprehensive in terms of structural and systemic factors. It entails the fair access to digital resources, participation opportunities, and results with no disproportionate benefits of already advantaged groups (Nuong et al., 2024). The digital divide, which is a disproportionate access to a stable internet, modern technology, and digital literacy, is an urgent issue, especially in the rural and low-income populations. Although it is touted that EdTech is being democratic by making knowledge more accessible, in reality it may reinforce inequalities by leaving marginalized students without proper infrastructure or without the means to operate in complicated tools. Additionally, the adaptive learning systems and AI-powered testing software may contribute to the perpetuation of certain inequalities in the future, since the algorithms are biased against other cultures or language groups. The issue of access and equity should be a multi-level solution. Governments and institutions at the policy level also have to invest in the infrastructure, including affordable high-speed internet and distribution of devices programs to narrow the accessibility divide. EdTech companies should focus on the principles of universal design and inclusive practices at the design level and incorporate accessibility features into the design instead of considering them as an added value (Garg et al., 2024; Singh & Kumar, 2024). At the pedagogical level, teachers need to be educated to incorporate technology at a fair level in their teaching whereby they should use technology as a supplement and not as a substitute to human interaction and support. As an example, learning analytics can be used by teachers to diagnose struggling learners, although the interventions should be presented in a manner that does not stigmatize or oversee them. The worldwide pandemic highlighted the timeliness of these problems because millions of students were disadvantaged because of disparities in the accessibility of digital instruments (Duncan, 2020). Resilience in the education systems has become benchmarks in terms of accessibility and equity in the aftermath. Going forward, the real potential of EdTech is not the ability to be innovative but the potential to create inclusive learning programs that all learners will be able to succeed in. By making accessibility and equity a priority, the technological developments in the future will play a role in reducing the gap in education and not creating it instead, and eventually the education will be brought to reflect the values of social justice and human dignity.

Institutional Readiness and Teacher Training

Although the educational technology has the potential to be transformative, many challenges of implementation usually limit its successful implementation into the classrooms. Teacher training and institutional readiness are two of the most important aspects in which this process is shaped. Both of them work as a keystone to the success of the technological investments whether they become a significant learning outcome or they serve as a poorly used tool. Unless the educators and institutions are properly prepared to implement, adjust, and otherwise maintain digital innovations, even the most sophisticated platforms may become useless or increase disparities. Teacher training is one of the greatest challenges. Teachers are not passive receivers of the technology but rather intermediaries who create the space in between the digital tools and student education. However, there is a lot of teachers who are given little or sporadic training on the efficient use of EdTech (Ding et al., 2024; Nuong et al., 2024). Professional development is usually concentrated on the technical functionality of platforms how they log in, how they can upload assignments, or monitor analytics and does not go beyond it. The issues that teachers might face include the inability to match technology to curriculum objectives, digital classroom management, or critical thinking online. Besides, digital literacy generation dichotomies may also cause unequal confidence among the faculty members, with younger teachers being adapted more easily than their more experienced colleagues. In addition, training is commonly perceived as a onetime activity, but not a continuous process, and with the changes in technologies, teachers are left unassisted. This may not be sustained professional growth and may lead to the superficial nature of adoption of technology where it is applied in administrative efficiency and not revolutionary teaching. Institutional preparedness is closely connected with the teacher preparedness (Alaswad & Nadolny, 2015). The use of EdTech is not only the use of devices and platforms but also the organizational frameworks, policies, and cultural change that is required to make its use sustainable. Lack of proper infrastructures is a common problem in many institutions especially in the regions that are developing like lack of reliable internet, lack of technical support and old hardware. Bureaucratic inertia and change resistance can become obstacles to innovation even in a well-resourced setting. An example that can be given is that institutions might have no explicit digital strategies or may not want to align the adoption of technology with the wider pedagogical goals. Administrators can also perceive technology as a cost-cutting process instead of being a means of increasing learning equity and quality and invest insufficiently in training, maintenance, or inclusive design. The institutional readiness is also concerned with the factor of equity in the organization. Unless the students have trusted access to devices, connectivity, or support in digital literacy, institutional adoption threatens to strengthen disparities (Udeozor et al., 2023; Singh2024a). On the same note, when there are no policies on data privacy, cybersecurity, and ethical applications of AI-fueled tools, teachers and students could be at risk of exposing themselves to a new set of risks undermining trust in digital systems. A comprehensive approach is thus needed to be effective in preparation, and this includes infrastructural investment, technical provisions, governance structure and inclusive planning, including faculty, student and administration in decision making. Finally, the teacher training and the readiness of the institution are reinforcing. An institution that is in poor preparation will never have a well trained teacher, and with a digital equipped institution, there will never be effective educators. The best EdTech practices are fostered when the professional development is a continuous process that is context-driven and also guided by institutional strategies that would ensure that human capacity and technological infrastructure are put as the priority. The solution to these challenges is to start thinking outside of the tech-first paradigm into a pedagogy-first and system-readiness approach. It is only at this point that educational technology can fulfill its potential of transforming the learning environments in equal and sustainable measures.

CASE STUDY

Case Study 1: Training of teachers and institutional preparedness in the Singapore Smart Nation Education Strategy

Singapore is frequently praised as an international pioneer in the use of technology in education not just due to its state of the art technology but to its overall strategy of teacher education and institutional preparedness. The Smart Nation program introduced by the government in 2014 was aimed at integrating digital technologies throughout the society, and education was forged as one of the core pillars of the change. This case study shows how institutional planning and investment in professional development, which are systematic, can avoid most of the implementation challenges experienced in other places.

TeacherTraining

The Ministry of Education (MOE) of Singapore understood the fact early on, that technology cannot change classrooms without empowered teachers. Digital pedagogy was incorporated in pre-service and in-service teacher training programs in the National Institute of Education (NIE) of Singapore. Instead of providing only the technical skills, new teachers were prepared with the strategies on how to integrate EdTech as a part of inquiry-based, project-oriented, and student-centered learning strategies. On-going professional development was underlined with the help of programs such as the ICT Mentor Programme within the context of which a peer-to-peer mentor training was provided to experienced teachers, enabling them to mentor their colleagues.

Case Study 2: The Singapore Smart Nation Education Strategy training of teachers and institutional preparedness.

Singapore is often hailed as a global leader in the application of technology in education not only because of its state of the art technology but because of its approach to educating the teachers and also the preparation of the institutions (Ding et al., 2024). The Smart Nation initiative related to the introduction of digital technologies into the society that the government implemented in 2014 was designed to lock in the digital technology into all aspects of the society, and the education became one of the main pillars of the change. This case study demonstrates that most of the implementation issues are averted by institutional planning and investment in professional development which is systematic and is done in other locations.

Teacher Training

The Ministry of Education (MOE) of Singapore realized at the very beginning, that without empowered teachers, the classrooms cannot be changed with the use of technology. In the National Institute of Education (NIE) of Singapore, digital pedagogy was included in the training programs of teachers, both in pre-service and in-service. Rather than imparting just the technical skills, new teachers were equipped with the techniques of how to incorporate EdTech as part of inquiry-based, project-based and student-centered learning strategies. The continuous professional growth was supported by the assistance of such a program as ICT Mentor Programme in the framework of which the peer-to-peer mentor training of the experienced teachers was offered so that they could mentor their colleagues to adopt technology. Notably, training was an ongoing process, and the teachers were advised to keep on advancing their competencies by taking workshops and online classes and working together as a community of practice. This long-term investment created a culture of technology acceptance in which the teachers considered technology a pedagogical resource and not an imposed form.

Institutional Readiness

In line with teacher development, Singapore spent a lot of money on institutional preparation. Schools have been equipped with high-quality broadband, electronic devices, and combined learning management systems. More to the point, there was a coherent national direction EdTech Masterplan that was followed by the institutions; it helped to align technological use with the overall learning goals, including creativity, collaboration, and problem-solving (Kaur et al., 2023; Singh, 2022). There was fair accessibility of devices, which was achieved through policies such as government subsidies and loan programs that made all devices affordable to students. Schools also received the freedom to implement technology in their local settings so as to be sure that technology implementation was not a top-down process but shared by both teachers and administrators. Schools had technical support personnel as part of them to do maintenance and troubleshooting work to ease the load on the teachers.

CHALLENGES AND SOLUTIONS

However, with good planning, there were challenges. Initially, some of the senior teachers were even adamant to new digital practices considering it disruptive. To solve this, Singapore focused on mentorship and joint learning opportunities in which the teachers who were not hesitant would be able to learn with other teachers. The other issue was the need to keep students involved in digital settings and in some cases, this promoted passive learning instead of active learning. Educators countered this with the incorporation of interactive platforms, gamification and project-based assignments in order to keep the interest.

Lesson Learned

The Singapore case shows that the effective implementation of EdTech is not only a manifestation of introducing the device or the platform, but a coordination process of teacher training and institutional organization with the long-term education objectives. Ongoing professional development investment and solid infrastructural and policy backing, developed a system in which teachers were not only competent but also confident when it comes to the use of technology. The institutional focus on equity also left no student behind because of the socioeconomic barriers. This case gives a strong message to other states: the adoption of technology should be regarded as a systemic, and not individual project. Institutional readiness and teacher capacity-building are two pieces that cannot be separated and when they are created together, EdTech will be able to live up to its potential of contributing to equity and quality in education.

Facilities and Reflections

This blended future is a good thing but it has its problems. The discussion of the fair access to technology, the privacy of the data, and the training of educators to manage hybrid settings are important issues (Singh, 2022). Pedagogy in the future should only be able to tackle these concerns before they arise, and create an ecosystem in which technology is an asset and not a threat to human interaction. Immersive technologies and game-based learning are not supposed to be the ways to completely substitute the traditional learning approach. Rather, they are potent instruments that can supplement and add to the learning process (Ahmed & Sutton, 2017; Duncan, 2020; Deri et al., 2024). The future in pedagogy is probably a view of a middle way where these new frontiers are carefully incorporated with the old ones to bring more interesting, efficient and personalized learning experiences. More advanced and integrated applications of VR, AR, MR, and principles of game design in education are sure to come into being as technology keeps evolving and becoming more affordable (Ahmed & Sutton, 2017; Duncan, 2020; Alaswad & Nadolny, 2015; Singh2024b). Consider classrooms in which students regularly take virtual field trips to any part of the world, and/or work on constructing virtual models, or study complicated material of science by playing interesting and involving game simulations. A combination of real and virtual learning as the future of pedagogy is not only the adaptation to the technological change, but the answer to the changing needs of the learners in a dynamic world (Nuong et al., 2024). When combining the two worlds in the most advantageous way, education becomes more individualized, inclusive, and effective. This is a blend strategy that is likely to equip learners not just to succeed academically, but also to make a valuable contribution to the society in a world that is becoming more integrated and digital. Game-based learning and immersive technologies are also new technologies that we are using in the pedagogical field that could be used to transform the way of teaching and learning. Using the power of immersion and play, teachers will be able to develop more effective, personalized, and engaging learning experiences empowering them to acquire critical skills and a lifelong passion of learning. Although there will still be obstacles, the current technological progress and our increasing knowledge on learning principles can be encouraging that in the future these novel means will be increasingly at the center of determining the future of educational settings.

Breaking the Barriers in Implementing Educational Technology

Even though educational technology can provide immense possibilities in facilitating democratization of learning, it is frequently hampered by infrastructure, insufficient teacher training, change-resistance, and inequitable access. To overcome these barriers, a multidimensional approach is necessary which not only focuses on the technological facets of the adoption but also focuses on the human, institutional and systemic elements that influence education. The effectiveness of integration depends on the possibility of matching the tools with pedagogy, facilitating both educators and learners and establishing conditions in which innovation can be maintained. The digital divide remains one of the most tenacious obstacles and is presented in the form of differences in the access to devices, connection, and digital literacy (Udeozor et al., 2023; Singh & Kumar, 2024). This cannot be resolved without large-scale infrastructural investment, especially in low-income or underserved rural areas. Governments and institutions can offer subsidized equipment, build and increase broadband connections and build offline-friendly platforms that enable learners to study even when connectivity is minimal (Garg et al., 2024). Partnership with privates is also a favorable solution as we have witnessed in technology firms partnering with governments to make internet packages inexpensive or community digital centers. Nonetheless, bridging the gap is not only a physical issue, but also a matter of developing both the digital skills of learners and parents, so that students could become more active and critical users of technology, instead of passive consumers of the information. Teacher preparedness and teacher confidence is a second significant barrier. The fast rate of technological change can easily engulf educators especially in cases where professional growth has been disjointed or where it has not been developed at all. This problem cannot be beaten without a long-term strategy of teacher training that is not limited to the issue of technical skills but also pedagogical integration (Hsu & Cheng, 2021). Professional growth must be an ongoing, loose and concrete process to the classroom realities (Singh2024a). Online learning communities, peer mentoring, and collaborative projects can be used to help teachers exchange their strategies and gain confidence. Notably, the training should focus on the fact that technology should not replace but only complement human teaching to minimize intimidation of redundancy and opposition. Institutional level factors include organizational inertia and inadequate preparations that tend to make adoption difficult. To do this, it needs effective leadership and definite digital strategies that may put technology in line with the overarching educational objectives. The institutions should come up with governance structures that will cover sensitive matters like privacy of data, ethical use of AI and digital equity, where technology adoption builds trust. The second thing, which is equally important, is to invest in the technical support system where the teachers are not troubled with troubleshooting and to make sure that the budget accounts not only the purchase of the tools but also the maintenance and upgrades and its continuity (Nuong et al., 2024). In cases where institutions are willing by providing excellent policies, resources, and participative planning, teachers can readily embrace new technologies. Lastly, adoption may be slackened by cultural and attitudinal barriers. In other settings, students, parents, or teachers might not trust online learning, believing it to be of low quality or deprived of values. To resolve these perceptions, the institutions need to discuss with the stakeholders, share the evidence, and participate in the decision-making process. By showing actual gains in the form of better learning outcomes, personalized teaching or increased opportunities, trust and acceptance can be established. Finally, elimination of obstacles to educational technology must be done holistically and inclusively. Instead of using a limited approach to tools, strategies should combine infrastructure building, teacher empowerment, institutional preparation, and cultural transformation. When education systems consider all these dimensions at once, they will be in a position to skate past superficial adoption to implement digital learning systems that are not only equitable and resilient but also truly transformative.

CONCLUSION

The merging of immersive technologies and game-based learning represents a true turning point in the history of pedagogy, signaling indeed the true emergence of the so-called new frontiers that will transform the way we teach, learn and assess. These new methods, discussed in this chapter, transcend the boundaries of conventional classrooms and passive learning and knowledge acquisition, creating an active, interactive, and highly transformative learning experience. Immersive technologies whether it is the whole-body virtual worlds of VR, real-world additions of AR, or a mix of the two, provide students with unmatched opportunities in experiential learning where they can safely learn about dangerous environments, train in complex, and experiment with abstract ideas in a tangible way. Together with the innate motivational value of learning in the form of a game, whereby such elements as challenge, feedback, reward, and narrative are utilized, one gets powerful learning synergy that boosts the level of engagement, problem-solving skills, and critical thinking by a significant portion. Though the trip to the universal adoption is fraught with rather serious obstacles such as the expense of installation, the necessity of the well-established educator training, and the careful incorporation of the curriculum, the benefits of the practice are overwhelming. The ability to establish individualized learning platforms, ease of access in learning environments, and development of appropriate 21st -century competencies such as teamwork and endurance makes immersive technologies and game-based education invaluable objects in the future of education. They are not technological wonders, but paradigms of change in the very way we think of learning, as entailing not the passive internalization of facts, but the active, iterative and, above all, delightful process of knowledge discovery. In the end, by exploring these new horizons, teachers will have access to student potentials which they never had before, training learners not only to exams but to lifelong learning, flexibility, and adaptation in an ever changing world. It is true that the future of pedagogy is immersive, interactive and more importantly engaging.

REFERENCES

Ahmed, A., & Sutton, M. J. (2017). Gamification, serious games, simulations, and immersive learning environments in knowledge management initiatives. *World Journal of Science. Technology and Sustainable Development*, *14*(2/3), 78–83.

Alaswad, Z., & Nadolny, L. (2015). Designing for game-based learning: The effective integration of technology to support learning. *Journal of Educational Technology Systems*, *43*(4), 389–402.

Deri, M. N., Zaazie, P., & Singh, A. (2024). Digital Future of the Hospitality Industry and Hospitality Education Globally. In Sharma, A. (Ed.), *International Handbook of Skill, Education, Learning, and Research Development in Tourism and Hospitality. Springer International Handbooks of Education*. Springer., DOI: 10.1007/978-981-97-4318-6_14

Ding, A. C. E., Huang, K. T. T., DuBois, J., & Fu, H. (2024). Integrating immersive virtual reality technology in scaffolded game-based learning to enhance low motivation students' multimodal science learning. *Educational Technology Research and Development*, *72*(4), 2083–2102.

Duncan, K. J. (2020). Examining the effects of immersive game-based learning on student engagement and the development of collaboration, communication, creativity and critical thinking. *TechTrends*, *64*(3), 514–524.

El Mawas, N., Tal, I., Moldovan, A. N., Bogusevschi, D., Andrews, J., Muntean, G. M., & Muntean, C. H. (2018, March). Final frontier game: A case study on learner experience. In CSEDU-10th International Conference on Computer Supported Education.

Garg, A., Singh, A., & Yanan, J. (2024). Exploring the Impact of Digital Detoxification on Higher Education Students' Learning. In Grima, S., Chaudhary, S., Sood, K., & Kumar, S. (Eds.), *Business Drivers in Promoting Digital Detoxification* (pp. 111–126). IGI Global Scientific Publishing., DOI: 10.4018/979-8-3693-1107-3.ch008

Groff, J. S. (2018). The potentials of game-based environments for integrated, immersive learning data. *European Journal of Education*, *53*(2), 188–201.

Hsu, M. E., & Cheng, M. T. (2021). Immersion experiences and behavioural patterns in game-based learning. *British Journal of Educational Technology*, *52*(5), 1981–1999.

Kaur, N., Singh, V., Mahajan, N., & Garg, N. (2023, February). Game based learning-immersive teaching and learning platform through metaverse. In *2023 3rd International Conference on Innovative Practices in Technology and Management (ICIPTM)* (pp. 1-6). IEEE.

Nuong Deri, M., Singh, A., Zaazie, P., & Anandene, D. (2024). Leveraging Artificial Intelligence in Higher Educational Institutions: A Comprehensive Overview. *Education and Law Review*, (30). Advance online publication. DOI: 10.1344/REYD2024.30.45777

Rye, S., Sousa, M., & Sousa, C. (2025a). Beyond Scholastic Disciplines: The Need for Complex Game-Based Learning in a Complex World. In *Transformative Learning Through Play: Analogue Games as Vehicles for Educational Innovation* (pp. 1–27). Springer Nature Switzerland.

Rye, S., Sousa, M., & Sousa, C. (2025b). Introduction to Game-Based Learning. In *Transformative Learning Through Play: Analogue Games as Vehicles for Educational Innovation* (pp. 29–68). Springer Nature Switzerland.

Singh, A. (2022). Conceptual framework on Smart Learning Environment- An Indian perspective. *Journal of Education and Law*, (25). Advance online publication. DOI: 10.1344/REYD2022.25.36706

Singh, A. (2024a). Endorsing Gamification Pedagogy for Nurturing Employability Skills in Higher Education Institutions (HEI). In Membrive, V. (Ed.), *Practices and Implementation of Gamification in Higher Education* (pp. 172–183). IGI Global Scientific Publishing., DOI: 10.4018/979-8-3693-0716-8.ch008

Singh, A. (2024b). Impact of E-learning on Student Motivation in Higher Education Institutions: An Indian Perspective. *Journal of Education and Law*, (29). Advance online publication. DOI: 10.1344/REYD2024.29.43214

Singh, A., & Kumar, P. (2024). E-Learning Ecosystem in Higher Education Institutions: Trends and Practices. In Al Husseiny, F., & Munna, A. (Eds.), *Preparing Students for the Future Educational Paradigm* (pp. 1–18). IGI Global Scientific Publishing., DOI: 10.4018/979-8-3693-1536-1.ch001

. Song, Y., Wu, K., & Ding, J. (2024). Developing an immersive game-based learning platform with generative artificial intelligence and virtual reality technologies–"LearningverseVR". *Computers & Education: X Reality, 4*, 100069.

Udeozor, C., Chan, P., Russo Abegão, F., & Glassey, J. (2023). Game-based assessment framework for virtual reality, augmented reality and digital game-based learning. *International Journal of Educational Technology in Higher Education, 20*(1), 36. PMID: 36644670

Chapter 3
Next-Gen Learning:
The Fusion of Immersive Technologies and Play

Amrik Singh
https://orcid.org/0000-0003-3598-8787
Lovely Professional University, India

ABSTRACT

The Next-Gen Learning," a transformative paradigm emerging from the powerful fusion of immersive technologies and game-based learning. Virtual reality (VR), augmented reality (AR), mixed reality (MR), and other extended realities (XR) can transcend conventional learning environments, offering unparalleled opportunities for experiential, situated, and authentic learning. Simultaneously, this chapter examines the inherent motivational and cognitive benefits of game-based learning, which leverages elements like challenges, rewards, narratives, and immediate feedback to foster active participation and sustained interest. Further, by synergistically integrating the "showing" power of immersive technologies with the "doing" and "playing" aspects of game-based approaches, educators can design learning experiences that are not only highly engaging but also demonstrably more effective in knowledge retention, skill acquisition, and the development of complex problem-solving abilities.

INTRODUCTION

Learning is changing radically, and the environment is changing leaving some to refer to the current period as the dawn of a new learning paradigm. With the blistering rise in the level of technology, as well as the shifting needs of society, and the increased comprehension of cognitive science, the conventional models are

DOI: 10.4018/979-8-3373-4465-2.ch003

being transformed to better equip individuals with the demands of the more and more complex and dynamic future (Sharma & Singh, 2024a). This new paradigm is a great divergence in the one-size-fits-all, content-delivery model that was so prevalent during the industrial era of education where students were seen as passive consumers of standardized information working to satisfy the requirements of a homogenous workforce. Rather, this is an ecosystem being implemented more personalized, flexible, and learner-centric that recognizes diversity in the interests, abilities, cultural contexts, and future aspirations of learners. The core of the paradigm shift is that knowledge is not fixed and contained in textbooks and classrooms, but is dynamic, interrelated, and constantly changing along with the change and interdependence in the world. Learning that is pleasurable and limitless, and that it is closely connected to the human soul a future in which play is not only allowed but actively built in as the driving force behind exploration and development (Francis et al., 2024). The walls in the classroom are blurred, and instead of the limited space, there are infinite worlds of knowledge to be discovered, played with, and mastered with the power of play. The common noises of the fluorescent lamps, the crackle of the turning pages, the specific smell of the chalk dust these traces of senses have always been typical of the traditional classroom. Over the centuries education has mostly been founded on a paradigm of passive information intake, knowledge being passed down by the instructor to the student, mostly in the form of lectures, textbooks and rote learning. As much as this system has served its purpose, the unavoidable rate of global change on account of the unprecedented advancements in technology and the dynamism in the job market has critically brought into the limelight its weakness. We are in a world where information is everywhere, but the ability to critically assess, synthesize, and use such information is a luxury (Sharma & Singh, 2024a). The current learners are being asked much more than to memorize; they need flexibility, to be creative, solve complicated problems, collaborate, and have an intense sense of agency in their education (Francis et al., 2024). This requires the emergence of a new educational paradigm one that we refer to as Next-Gen Learning. This new methodology is inherently individualized, most interactive, very experiential, and above all intrinsically motivated. It redirects the perspective of what is learned to how it is learned with a strong focus on the discovery, creation and application process (Sharma & Singh, 2024b; Francis et al., 2024). The central part of this change would be the tight and frequent combination, the melding of immersive technologies and the intrinsic strength of play. Immersive technologies, such as Virtual Reality (VR), Augmented Reality (AR), Mixed Reality (MR) and the general Extended Reality (XR) are not the prerogative of science fiction any more. They are quickly evolving technologies that have the capability of pushing physical boundaries, building enriched, interactive spaces and providing new levels of presence. VR immerses the user to an absolutely new digital environment; AR adds digital data to the real world and enriches our immediate environment; and MR unites them in a very natural way, enabling the objects of the digital world to interact with objects of the real world (Cui et al., 2024). In sum, XR has the potential to break the barriers between the physical and the digital, providing the learning experience that is not tied to a screen anymore but is integrated into our perception. The immense power of play, which is, however, commonly pushed into the background of the childhood frivolity, is also rather transformative (Nuong et al., 2024; Singh, 2024). Play is an essential human impulse rather than an intelligent pastime, and an inherent desire to explore and investigate, to experiment and solve problems, and to socialize. Since playing with blocks as a child, all the way to playing with an engineer creating a prototype of the new design, the playground is the fertile soil where creativity blossoms, cognitive constructs are developed, emotional intelligence is developed, and resiliency is managed. It is the most purest of active learning and the one that is inspired by inquisitiveness and bliss, and it is essential to method the same skills required by the 21st century (Kumar et al., 2023). It is not the individual adoption of these forces but their conscious and collectivistic combination which holds the revolutionary promise of education. Immersive technologies have the potential to enhance the rewards of play, so that learning can be more intuitive, memorable and rewarding as never before. Think about studying history through walking in ancient Rome, learning about astronautics by moving heavenly bodies with your hands, or practicing some complicated surgery in a safe virtual operating room - all because you just want to do it because it is fun (Sharma & Singh, 2024a). The technological canvas, which looks at the unique abilities of VR, AR, and MR in the learning setting, and how the future technologies of haptics, biometrics, and AI add more strength.

We will then embark on the deep pedagogy of play, including the neuroscience of its effectiveness, and defining the major players that make playful learning such an effective learning experience. Next, we will pass to practical examples of compelling case studies in the context of K-12 education, higher learning, corporate training as well as lifelong personal enrichment. And lastly, we will address the major challenges and ethical issues involved in this new frontier, and give a prospective view of the future of learning - where interaction is central, individualization natural, and the delight of discovery in mischievous immersion becomes the staple of the next generation learning.

Adopting the Playful Revolution

The tour of the landscape of Next-Gen Learning has given back a deeper truth: education of the future is not in the form of the passive reproduction of information, but in calculating, experience-driven, and self-motivating force of experience. We have discussed the fact that the impressive innovations in the immersive technologies Virtual Reality, Augmented Reality, and Mixed Reality- are breaking the customary boundaries of the classroom, taking learners to any location, any hour, and any magnitude (Singh, 2024; Singh, 2022). Such technologies have ceased to be instruments and have become portals to novel and unprecedented levels of engagement where they provide simulated experiences, interactive models, and collaborative spaces previously available only to the imagination (Sharma & Singh, 2024b; Francis et al., 2024). Importantly, the genius of this educational revolution is the conscious combination with the fundamental desire of human being to play. It has been shown how play, rather than being a distraction, is a highly engrained process of exploration, experimentation and mastery (Sharma & Singh, 2024b). Once the concepts of the playful design are saturated with immersive technologies, which promote active engagement, problem-solving as a game, taking steps into repetitions, and encouraging a storytelling experience, the learning process turns into a captivating and memorable game. Since the virtual dissection of anatomical structures in the medical school to archaeological digs on other continents, since the learning of complicated machineries in corporate training to the construction of fantasy worlds with peers in the K-12 schools, practical uses of this fusion are enormous and ever-growing. It is a paradigm shift as learning becomes a doing, a doing, an experiencing as opposed to a passively received process. Students have now ceased to be observers but agents of their own learning as they produce their own knowledge by playing with it. The road to this transformational future is, however, not that easy. The problem of access and equity is something that we should be keen on and so that the vision of next-gen learning is not reserved to a small number of privileged individuals. The need to have effective teacher training and pedagogical redesigning cannot be overstated because teachers who were only content providers have to shift to providing immersive experiences (Sharma & Singh, 2024a). Additionally, great expenses of developing content, necessity of strong quality management and attentiveness to health, safety and ethical concerns demand paying attention and being responsible in innovations (Ramtohul & Khedo, 2021). It will also be essential how we measure learning within these dynamic environments, beyond the old measures of learning, to the richness of the experience of learning. Nevertheless, in spite of some of these obstacles, the future of learning is admittedly a powerful vision. Imagine the metaverse being developed into a worldwide learning system, where decentralized virtual environments in the world contain various learning institutions and create a world of new global co-operation (Nuong et al., 2024). This merger promises to democratize experiential learning, therefore allowing the high fidelity simulation and individual exploration of history, science and culture accessible to everyone, regardless of geographical location or socioeconomic status. The educator will become more of an experience designer, a mentor and a guide and will encourage the most vital quality of critical thinking and flexibility.

Entering a New Era of Education

Personalization where the learning experience is customized to the needs, strengths and speed in each individual learner is one of the main pillars of this new paradigm. With the use of adaptive learning technologies, artificial intelligence, and data analytics, teachers can now offer dynamically adjusted content, which will give remedial opportunities to struggling students and offer an enrichment experience to more advanced learners (Sharma & Singh, 2024b). Personalization is not limited to academics either, as they should consider the emotional, social, and cultural identities of the students in the learning process and this helps them to develop a sense of belonging and inclusiveness. A second pillar is competency-based education (CBE), where the emphasis is no longer on time-based advancement (e.g. seat time or grade levels based on age) but mastery of skills and knowledge. The learner progresses when they demonstrate competence and not by just putting in the required hours and this has guaranteed that education is competency based and is focused on the workplace in terms of competencies such as critical thinking, problem solving, teamwork as well as digital literacy. This mastery model keeps the system fair since every learner can move at his or her pace and at the same time demands high levels of achievement among the students. In close connection with CBE is the emergence of the experiential and project-based learning (PBL), which is one of the pillars of the new paradigm (Sharma & Singh, 2024a). Understanding that deep learning is achieved by applying knowledge, teachers are starting to build real-world tasks, simulations, and interdisciplinary projects to the reflection of the complexities of real-world problems (Parizad et al., 2025). The internships, service learning, entrepreneurial activities or virtual laboratories put the learners not only in a position of a knowledge consumer but as active problem solvers, able to link theory with practice, reflectively inquire, and acquire transferable skills across situations. Lifelong and life-wide learning is also a high value in the paradigm because the education process can no longer be limited to those initial years of formal education but must be spread over a human lifespan and into various spheres of life . The fast pace of technological change implies that employees need to engage in constant skills and upskilling to be relevant, and personal development, civism, and global citizenship also require continuous education. Digital platforms, open educational resources, and micro-credentialing systems like badges and nanodegrees enable learners to get access to flexible pathways that can be both aware of formal and informal learning experiences. Notably, the change is supported by increased involvement of technology not only as an efficiency aid but also as a source of change.

Predictive analytics-based learning management systems, artificial intelligence-based tutors, immersive virtual and augmented reality, and a collaborative platform that goes beyond geographic boundaries all redefine the scope and reach of education (Singh, 2024; Singh, 2022). However, technology is not adequate but it should be informed by effective pedagogy, ethical issues, and equity-driven policies to prevent the continuity of digital divides. The other characteristic of this paradigm is agency and voice of the learner, which focuses on enabling the students to own the learning processes. The new paradigm also promotes co-creation of curricula, choice in learning pathways and self-directed inquiry facilitated by mentorship and facilitation as opposed to direct instruction alone as was the case in the traditional top-down transmission model.

Educational Paradigm

This develops internal motivation, innovativeness and a sense of endurance-characteristics that are required to live through uncertainty and complexity. Besides, the educational paradigm introduced points to the significance of social-emotional learning (SEL) and holistic development. In addition to cognitive abilities, learners are also being assisted in the development of empathy, mindfulness, moral reasoning and intercultural competence, as they understand that success in the 21 st century is not only based on intellectual ability but also emotional sensitivity and social flexibility (Almeman et al., 2025). Moreover, global and interdisciplinary approaches are also incorporated into curricula, as the issues of climate change, population health, and digital ethics are interconnected, and they need to be solved through cross-national, cross-cultural, and cross-disciplinary problem-solving. Education becomes therefore a personal empowerment instrument and a common resource that leads to the sustainable development and social integration. The assessment systems that support this paradigm are also changing, no longer depending on standardized tests that favor rote memorization, and tend to depend more on more authentic and performance-based assessments, as well as formative assessment, to capture the process of learning rather than just the product (Sharma & Singh, 2024a; Nuong et al., 2024). Portfolios, digital badges, capstone projects, peer assessment, and embedded analytics offer more detailed understanding in the ability and growth paths of the learners and also aligns assessment to the abilities required in the real world. Besides, such paradigm acknowledges the role of educators as no longer people that convey information but as facilitators, creators of learning experiences, mentors, and co-learners. The educators are also to develop new skills such as digital literacy, data-driven teaching, and the capacity to build collaborative, interdisciplinary inquiry. The institutional support systems and professional development also become important in helping the educator to flourish in this new ecosystem

(Sharma & Singh, 2024a). The emergence of this new educational paradigm is, in the end, not about refining, but rather a revelation of the functions, procedures and potential of education. It aims at making learning consistent with the requirements of the rapidly changing world respecting the individuality of the learner, as well as keeping in mind the needs of the society. This paradigm, in its essence, also states that education is not a life preparation but a life-long journey of exploration, self-improvement, and service (Francis et al., 2024). Nevertheless, the opportunities are even higher. This new paradigm has the potential to build a more interesting, more productive, and more just educational system that is in actuality ready to meet the challenges and opportunities of the 21 st century and produce a generation of life long learners, critical thinkers and creative problem-solver. The future of learning has never been so bright as the dawn is on us.

LITERATURE REVIEW

Integration of educational technology in teaching and learning set ups has been a priority in the world but not easily embraced. Although digital tools are claimed to support the engagement, personalization, and accessibility to resources, the real-life issues of the implementation are complicated and multifaceted.

Real-life Problems and Obstacles

Obstacles to implementation, teacher readiness, cost, and ongoing equity gaps are among the most acute in nature and each of them has a profound effect on the success of EdTech initiatives. Institutional and systemic level barriers to implementation are one of the most noticeable. Infrastructural problems that may be faced in schools and universities would include unstable internet connections, weak technical services and poor hardware (Almeman et al., 2025). Such obstacles are also exacerbated in most developing areas by unreliable electrical power, the use of outdated machinery or reliance on donor-funded projects which fail to be sustainable. The fast rate of technological change even in the advanced contexts poses a challenge to the institutions to keep up with the changes, resulting in a degree of fragmentation in adoption and uneven outcomes (Nuong et al., 2024). Other obstacles to integration may not be technical: organizational resistance may slow down or water down integration. The inertia to change traditional systems might be experienced by educators, administrators, and policymakers, particularly where the results cannot be predicted or cultural orientations promote the use of standard pedagogical practices.

Teacher Preparedness

Tightly connected with implementation is the problem of teacher preparedness. To ensure that technology is a transformative experience, teachers should be competent and confident in their ability to use it to create valuable learning experiences. Sadly, a lot of teaching staff get only a little training in digital pedagogy, with most commonly only one-off workshops, which pay more attention to tools than incorporation of technology into curriculum and assessment. These form a skills gap as the teachers can be familiar with how devices work but without the more in-depth pedagogical knowledge needed to make productive use of them. Besides, the attitude of teachers towards technology, be it positive or negative, influences the introduction of innovations in the classroom. Professional development then has to be ongoing, situation-specific and geared towards not only the development of technical literacy but also towards the creation of digital pedagogy and critical thinking about the place of technology in education. The other issue that has remained a problem is the constraint on cost which affects the initial investment and the maintenance in the long run (Sujana et al., 2025). The quality of EdTech solutions can also come at a high initial capital cost in terms of infrastructure, equipment, software licensing, and learning management system. In most institutions, particularly those which have low budgets, such expenses conflict with other essential needs like the salaries of teachers, classroom materials or even the repairs of its buildings. Additionally, the cost of maintaining the technical support, replacing devices, updating software, and computer security is not very visible; these are additional sources of financial burden (Nuong et al., 2024). Although cost-sharing schemes or public-private solutions or open-source solutions can be used, financial constraints remain the limiting factor to extending EdTech projects, especially in low-income communities and in rural settings. Lastly, the problem of equity is the focus of discussion. Digital innovations have the danger of further dividing the already existing divides in case there is unequal access distribution. Learners belonging to the marginalized groups usually do not have safe devices, Internet access at home, or suitable learning conditions, which disadvantage them against peers in more prosperous backgrounds. There is also the equity that goes beyond access and includes representation and inclusiveness of EdTech content. Most of the digital platforms are context based on the assumption of the Western settings, which may be marginalizing local language, culture and pedagogical background. Technology can unwillingly recreate the systemic disparities instead of alleviating them without specific efforts to facilitate inclusiveness. Overall, the potential of educational technology is not fully appreciated, but its success would not be assured (Nuong et al., 2024). Implementation barriers, lack of teacher readiness, the cost prohibitiveness and unresolved equity issues all are daunting. These can only be resolved through concerted efforts whereby technological solutions are not the sole methods of resolution but rather a long-term investment in infrastructure, professional growth, inclusive policies and design sensitivity. Then only can the promise of EdTech be seen or felt in practice, so that it does not actually drive the educational transformation broadly but rather become the cause of further divisions.

Un-Packaging Immersive Technologies to Learn

The fast-growing immersive technologies, including virtual reality (VR), augmented reality (AR), mixed reality (MR), and extended reality (XR), have provided what could be termed a technological canvas on the educational front as an impactful area where pedagogy, creativity, and innovation come together to redefine the manner in which the learners engage with knowledge. In contrast with more conventional digital media that are mainly used as channels through which information is conveyed, immersive technologies put learners into real-world-like settings where they can be engaged in an interactive, multisensory experience and recreate the abstract ideas in a more experiential way (Sujana et al., 2025). An example is virtual reality, where learners can enter a fully simulated environment, so they can perform the experiment of science in a virtual lab, see the historical events by walking through ancient civilization, or offer training in jobs that are high-risk, like aviation and medicine, without the risk of being exposed to any danger. Augmented reality, on the other hand, is the digital content superimposing on the real world so that learners can view a 3D model of a human heart projected on their desk, place labels of layers of context on the real world, or be part of scavenger hunts where participants explore the real world and simultaneously engage in digital research. Mixed reality goes even further with seamless real and virtual coexistence that can have interactive cooperation between real and digital objects in real time such as engineering students being able to co-design and control 3D prototypes whilst still being anchored in their physical environment. Not only do these immersive modalities broaden the possibilities of where and how learning occurs but they also afford powerful ways of engagement, retention and application since cognitive science indicates that experiential and embodied learning promotes memory path ways and conceptual comprehension (Devakirubai, 2025). The social canvas of technology is also extensive: systems to allow collaborations to be immersive help learners in different geographies to share virtual classroom environments, co-create projects, and peer-to-peer learners that are not limited by geographical space. In addition to subject-specific learning, immersive technologies develop transversal skills (problem-solving, creativity, empathy, adaptability), e.g., VR role-play simulation in social studies or pedagogy of health can train perspective-taking and emotional intelligence, as students can learn through simulating the experience of others. Nevertheless, this canvas does not pass without difficulties. In addition, successful integration needs purposeful instructional planning to prevent surface operations that emphasize new products at the cost of pedagogy; otherwise immersive tools may turn out to be distractions instead of facilitators of the deeper learning. The necessary responsible use should also be guaranteed through ethical issues like data privacy, the well-being of learners, and the possibility of being over-immersed (Mueller-Csernetzky et al., 2025). The technological canvas, despite all these issues, presents to educators like never before an opportunity to create learning that is immersive, interactive and impactful, beyond passive consumption to active participation. By offering such frameworks as TPACK or SAMR and being combined with such authentication tools as performance-based rubrics or embedded analytics, immersive technologies can become not a technology booming but a trigger of a new learning paradigm. By so doing, they redefine education as not being the imparting of information but rather as a journey of exploration, experimentation and discovery in highly textured, interactive settings that are co-created.

Research Gap

Although there is increasing interest in immersive and playful learning, there have never been enough researches that can be used to make it more popular and effective in the learning process. A great part of the existing literature focuses on technological affordances of virtual, augmented, and mixed reality or the motivational value of instructional design and assessment in varying settings, whereas less attention is given to systematic frameworks that inform the instructional design and evaluation. As an example, one may mention such models as TPACK and SAMR, but the empirical data proving that these models are implemented in immersive environments is still scarce. On the same note, there is limited evidence on long-term learning outcomes, transferability and scalability of the skills across disciplines because most evidence bases are limited to small pilot or single classroom studies. The other gap is the equity and accessibility gap: the questions regarding the experience of learners with different socio-economic, cultural, and geographic backgrounds regarding the immersive technologies are underdeveloped, and the digital divides issue should be considered. Such ethical concerns like the privacy of data, the over-immersion of learners, and the psychological effects of a highly realistic simulation are also not well researched. Also, the measures of assessment especially performance-based and analytics-based methodologies need further validation to determine reliability and fairness. Sealing such gaps is crucial to the transition to sustainability-based adoption that would introduce novelty-based adoption to evidence-based practice to guarantee that immersive learning can achieve the transformative potential.

DISCUSSION AND INTERPRETATION

The pedagogy of play is a fundamental revision of the intersection point between engagement, motivation, and learning efficacy, which stipulates that learning can be both entertaining and brain-stimulating. The conventional learning aspects tend to focus more on the delivery of content and testing that inadvertently makes the learners passive consumers as opposed to active learners. Play-based pedagogies, on the contrary, place learners in interactive settings of dynamic learning where curiosity, experimentation and iteration are the key components of the learning process.

Games in Pedagogy

Simulations, role-play, problem-solving activities with gamification, and playful learning are some of the major strategies of operationalizing this approach, which can enable the learner to be exposed to complex concepts in low-stakes, highly engaging situations. Cognitive science underlies the efficiency of play that shows intrinsically motivating activities are more effective in terms of attention, retention of memory and creative problem-solving by capitalizing on the innate reward and feedback system of the brain (Sharma & Singh, 2024a; Mueller-Csernetzky et al., 2025). Besides, the pedagogy of play correlates strongly with both constructivist and experiential learning, as it focuses on knowledge as actively constructed and not received in passively, and learners engage in co-creation as they go through trial, error, reflection, and collaboration, which results in a deeper grasp of concepts (Sharma & Singh, 2024a; Nuong et al., 2024). In addition to cognitive gains, play-based learning fosters social-emotional skills, like empathy, resilience, adaptability, and collaboration, as people negotiate their roles through difficulty, managing both success and failure in virtual worlds. Notably, reimagining engagement with play does not mean the lack of structure or rigor, on the contrary, it will need mindful instruction design, clear learning goals, and scaffolded challenges which will gradually develop skills without compromising learner autonomy. The assessment in this paradigm also progresses to include both process and product, through performance based rubrics, peer feedback, reflective journals, embedded analytics to assess competencies and improvement over a period of time. Combining the pedagogy of play with models like TPACK or SAMR can help teachers to make sure that the use of playful interventions is aligned with curriculum objectives, uses technology in ways that are significant, and promotes equal access to educational opportunities. Moreover, play-based pedagogy promotes learner agency, which allows students to choose and follow several options and take control over their learning processes, thus developing the intrinsic motivation and lifelong learning patterns (Ramírez-Cedillo et al., 2025). Professional education simulations like healthcare, hospitality or engineering sims enable students to practice in real-world activities in a safe environment, combine theory and practice, and learn both technical and soft skills that students need to be ready to work in the field. The pedagogical power of play can also be multiplied by being combined with collaborative and interdisciplinary methods, which allows learners to solve complex and real-life issues reflecting the inter-relatedness of contemporary societal and professional challenges. Finally, the pedagogy of play provides a critical challenge to the traditional concepts of instruction and assessment, proving that enjoyment and motivation do not oppose cognitive mastery and practical skill development, but vice versa: playful, interactive and learner centered experiences can simultaneously make education and teaching more enjoyable, motivating, and cognitively and practically skilled, which serves as a potent prism that allows looking at the future of education and implementing it.

Navigating the New Frontier

Even though the combination of immersive, play-based, and technology-based learning has provided unparalleled opportunities to change education, it has also created an intricate number of issues and factors that should be considered by educators, institutions, and policymakers. Equity and accessibility is one of the main challenges. The advanced immersive technologies in the form of virtual reality, augmented reality, and advanced simulation environments can be cost-intensive in terms of financial resources, specialized equipment, and consistent digital infrastructure, which can further widen the current differences between well-equipped and under-equipped education settings (Ramírez-Cedillo et al., 2025). The positive outcomes of these innovations might not reach to all learners as the privileged learners without deliberate efforts to promote access to innovations might be left out. The digital literacy gap is likewise a component of digital literacy as efficient application of immersive instruments does not just rely on the familiarity of learners with technological progression yet also on the pedagogical expertise of teachers. Most educators have inadequate professional development, a deficit of institutionally based support, or little experience with models of instructional design, including TPACK or SAMR, that limit their capacity to implement technologies in a meaningful, but not superficial way. The other important factor is the engagement-cognitive rigor balance. With their design of immersive, engaging learning, the risks of this experience are that it may start prioritizing entertainment over learning, which may cause new knowledge to be based on novelty, not outcomes, and hence lack outcomes-driven education. This requires a close instructional design, scaffolding and creation of real and genuine and performance based assessments that are able to capture both process and product. Ethical issues also make things worse (Yadav et al., 2018). The available immersive technologies usually gather massive data on the interactions of the learners, posing a question on the privacy, safety, and consent of the data and the psychological impacts of the extended exposure to virtual worlds. Such risks should be considered by educators in balance with the pedagogical advantages and be conducted in responsible and evidence-based practice. In addition, there are cognitive overload and attention management, where there is a risk of overwhelming the learner with the highly interactive conditions making them less able to reflect and process the information deeply. It is also critical that institutional and systemic factors are considered. The adoption of new technologies would need to be supported by policies, funding models and infrastructural planning that would be accommodative to both innovation and sustainability. The unwillingness to embrace change due to the culture of traditional education can further decelerate the issue and restrain trials. Lastly, learning outcomes measurement in immersive settings is a developing issue. Although analytics, digital portfolios and adaptive feedback mechanisms are potentially powerful, little research has been done to prove their reliability, fairness and alignment with the educational goals, which underscores a research gap. The challenge of traversing this new frontier thus requires an all-encompassing strategy that would help balance innovation and inclusivity, rigor and ethical accountability. The teachers should not just be provided with tools of technology, but also with pedagogical structures, reflective practice, and professional learning communities, which should encourage experimentation and continuous improvement. With these challenges in mind, stakeholders will be able to make sure that immersive, playful and technology-enabled learning can achieve its transformative potential instead of strengthening inequities and superficial interactions, eventually moving education to a more dynamic and equitable future.

Assessment and Pedagogy

With the development of educational technologies, such as immersive and entertaining learning activities as game-based learning, virtual simulation and augmented reality activities are increasingly becoming popular in formal and informal learning environments. Although these innovations have an untapped potential to enhance engagement, motivation, and more intensive learning, there is a burning question of how teachers can develop and measure such experiences (Trilling & Hood, 1999). Pedagogy and assessment are not peripheral issues, but rather the foundations of valuable learning. The immersive technologies will remain just a fad without a carefully thought-out instructional design and a well-thought evaluation strategies that will allow them to be seen not as a fad but as a means of revolutionizing the educational process.

Designing Instructional Immersive Learning

Instructional design models are systematic models, which teachers can rely on to incorporate immersive and playful approaches in curriculum design without losing the rigor of pedagogy. The Technological Pedagogical Content Knowledge (TPACK) framework and Substitution, Augmentation, Modification, Redefinement (SAMR) model should be mentioned, as they provide especially relevant information. TPack framework focuses on the interaction of three areas, content knowledge (CK), pedagogical knowledge (PK), and technological knowledge (TK). In immersive learning, it implies that teachers should not only be familiar with the material taught in the subject and pedagogical approaches but also know how to use technology in a manner that supports learning purposes (Trilling & Hood, 1999). An example is a science teacher who teaches cell biology with a virtual reality simulation that teaches the wow factor should be integrated with an engaging learning experience that emphasizes the key processes in the cell and scaffolding that will help students to make sense of complex processes. TPACK therefore informs teachers on how to balance technology and pedagogy and content and make sure that playful learning is not isolated to curricular objectives.

Another approach to the use of technology integration comes as the SAMR model which is divided into four levels of technology integration, which include substitution, augmentation, modification, and redefinition. Rhyming and engaging learning is best at the modification and redefinition stages. At this level, technology facilitates alterations of learning tasks which would otherwise not have been possible (Thomas, 2016). Immense platforms This can be illustrated by a scenario in which rather than just replacing a real-world lab with a virtual one, an immersive environment can reshape the task as students can test out different conditions in a virtual environment that simulates a life-threatening or inaccessible scenario, like a deep-sea exploratory process or a chemical reaction at the molecular scale. Mapping the immersive activities on the SAMR framework can allow educators to make sure that the use of technology is beneficial to the learning process and not merely a digitalization of the traditional process.

Assessment of Immersion and Playful Learning

There are special needs of assessment of immersion and playful learning. Conventional testing methods like multiple choice tests tend to overlook the richness of these skills that such experiences are designed to develop, such as problem-solving skills, creativity, work group, and flexibility. There is a need therefore, to have more subtle and genuine measures of assessment. One of the potential approaches is performance-based rubrics. These rubrics are oriented toward behaviors and outputs that can be observed in the process of immersive activities, e.g., quality of problem-solving in a simulation, creativity in a game design project, or efficiency in teamwork in a collaborative challenge. Being customizable to particular learning outcomes and applicable to deliver both formative and summative feedback, rubrics are highly flexible and suitable in the context of immersion (Nuong et al., 2024; Cui et al., 2024). The embedded analytics is another novel method, in which learning platforms are used to gather information about the interaction of learners, their choices, and their advancements in real-time. An example of this is a serious game that teaches historical reasoning, which may be used to record the decisions made by students in role-play situations, which can then be analyzed by their teachers to give a wealth of information about how students are reasoning about the evidence, balancing the outcomes, and putting together arguments. Adaptive feedback loops can be facilitated by analytics as well, where learners are able to reflect on their performance as well as educators can get information about the learning paths that would otherwise be unknown in traditional classrooms.

Balancing Play and Rigor

One important pedagogical factor to consider is the trade-off between the nature of playful learning that is inherently open and the strict form of learning needed in an academic setting. Play is full of elements of exploration, experimentation and even failure which may seem contrary to formal assessment. Yet, failure in immersive environments when designed correctly can be used as a great learning experience, which will build resilience and resourceful problem-solving. Teachers should thus create tests that would identify learning as a process and not a product (Trilling & Hood, 1999; Thomas, 2016). As an example, iterative project-based tests, in which students create, test, and develop solutions in a playful setting enable a teacher to measure improvement over time. Equally, reflective journals or online portfolios can document metacognitive knowledge which prompts students to explain what they learnt about their achievements and failures.

Enhancing Practical Value

To make the value of immersive and playful learning really practical, teaching professionals should have a chance to develop professionally which should be modeled in the way of how the teaching planning frameworks and assessment methods should be applied practically. Peer-learning communities, workshops, and case studies can offer practical examples of how TPACK and SAMR can be used to facilitate integration of curriculum, how embedded analytics or rubrics can be used to turn playful engagement into measurable learning outcomes (Sujana et al.,

2025). Additionally, the institutions need to think about systemic support, such as policies allowing experimental work with alternative assessments and platforms that can both make analytics available and ethically viable.

In the absence of this support, teachers can be reluctant to embrace new practices although they can be beneficial. By making the process of learning more interesting, more practical and relevant, immersive and playful learning can revolutionize the educational process. Nonetheless, this revolution depends on the deliberate combination of teaching and testing. Models of instructional design, such as TPACK and SAMR, offer important advice on how to match technology with the objectives of the curriculum, whereas other strategies of assessment, such as performance-based rubrics and embedded analytics can be used to make sure that playful interaction turns into quantifiable results (Thomas, 2016). With such tools in the hands of educators and aiding them in the application, the field will be in a position to leave novelty behind and instead lead to more sustainable and effective application of immersive learning.

CONCLUSION

These novel educational paradigm have to be shared among the educators, policymakers, technologists and the learners and actively constructed and developed by them. It involves cooperation, interdisciplinary creativity, and a desire to reexamine the accepted standards. We need to place the idea of well-being first, make sure that they are accessible to everyone equally, and to develop these new mighty systems with the strong sense of moral obligations. The walls in the classroom, which used to be so conclusive, are breaking, and new worlds of knowledge that can be discovered are infinite. Play is not only allowed in this fertile Next-Gen Learning growing stage, but is actively incorporated as the dynamic, critical vehicle of exploration and development. The future of education is not just one of the transmission of facts, but rather one of sparking curiosity, intrinsic motivation, and helping each person discover the ultimate joy of learning, then the intersection of play and immersive technologies opens to set the entire power of human knowledge to work.

REFERENCES

Almeman, K. E. L., Ayeb, F., Berrima, M., Issaoui, B., & Morsy, H. (2025). The integration of AI and metaverse in education: *A systematic literature review. Applied Sciences (Basel, Switzerland)*, *15*(2), 863.

Cui, Y., van Esch, P., & Spence, C. (2024). Multisensory technology in the wine industry: Where the senses meet technology. *Journal of Wine Research*, *35*(2), 75–84.

Devakirubai, T. S. (2025). Digital Twins Supercharges Efficiency-Unlocking the Power of Industry 5.0. 6G Urban Innovation: AI and Digital Twin for Next-Gen Sustainable Cities, 163-178.

Francis, R. S., Anantharajah, S., Sengupta, S., & Singh, A. (2024). Leveraging ChatGPT and Digital Marketing for Enhanced Customer Engagement in the Hotel Industry. In Bansal, R., Ngah, A., Chakir, A., & Pruthi, N. (Eds.), *Leveraging ChatGPT and Artificial Intelligence for Effective Customer Engagement* (pp. 55–68). IGI Global., DOI: 10.4018/979-8-3693-0815-8.ch004

Kumar, R., Gupta, S. K., Wang, H. C., Kumari, C. S., & Korlam, S. S. V. P. (2023). From efficiency to sustainability: Exploring the potential of 6G for a greener future. *Sustainability*, *15*(23), 16387.

Mueller-Csernetzky, P., Malakhatka, E., Thuvander, L., Kragic, D., & Kabo, J. (2025). Technological Frontiers in Education: Exploring the Impact of AI and Immersive Learning. In *Human-Technology Interaction: Interdisciplinary Approaches and Perspectives* (pp. 291–328). Springer Nature Switzerland.

Nuong Deri, M., Singh, A., Zaazie, P., & Anandene, D. (2024). Leveraging Artificial Intelligence in Higher Educational Institutions: A Comprehensive Overview. *Education and Law Review*, (30). Advance online publication. DOI: 10.1344/REYD2024.30.45777

Parizad, A., Baghaee, H. R., Alizadeh, V., & Rahman, S. (2025). Emerging Technologies and Future Trends in Cyber-Physical Power Systems: Toward a New Era of Innovations. *Smart Cyber-Physical Power Systems: Solutions from Emerging Technologies*, *2*, 525–565.

Ramírez-Cedillo, E., Armendáriz-Rodríguez, M., García-Ávila, J., Quintero-Sánchez, D., Ortiz-Espinoza, A. A., & Vargas-Martínez, A. (2025, April). Student 5.0: Immersive learning in next-gen Automation of Manufacturing Systems courses for the Industry 5.0 era. [). Frontiers Media SA.]. *Frontiers in Education*, *10*, 1416761.

Ramtohul, A., & Khedo, K. K. (2021). Location-based mobile augmented reality systems: a systematic review. *Immersive Technology in Smart Cities: Augmented and Virtual Reality in IoT*, 41-65.

Sharma, M., & Singh, A. (2024a). Embracing Technological Innovation: A Review of Hi-Tech Services in Hospitality Industry. *Evergreen, 11*(4), 2818–2830. DOI: 10.5109/7326926

Sharma, R., & Singh, A. (2024b). Use of Digital Technology in Improving Quality Education: A Global Perspectives and Trends. In Nadda, V., Tyagi, P., Moniz Vieira, R., & Tyagi, P. (Eds.), *Implementing Sustainable Development Goals in the Service Sector* (pp. 14–26). IGI Global., DOI: 10.4018/979-8-3693-2065-5.ch002

Singh, A. (2022). Conceptual framework on Smart Learning Environment- An Indian perspective. *Journal of Education and Law*, (25). Advance online publication. DOI: 10.1344/REYD2022.25.36706

Singh, A. (2024). Impact of E-learning on Student Motivation in Higher Education Institutions: An Indian Perspective. *Journal of Education and Law*, (29). Advance online publication. DOI: 10.1344/REYD2024.29.43214

Sujana, D. S., Kureethara, J. V., Augustine, D. P., & Augustine, L. (2025). Meta-Teaching on Leveraging the Metaverse for Definitive Efficiency in Learning in Higher Education. In *Transformations and Changing Perspectives in Higher Education* (pp. 207–226). Routledge India.

Thomas, S. (2016). *Future Ready Learning: Reimagining the Role of Technology in Education. 2016 National Education Technology Plan*. Office of Educational Technology, US Department of Education.

Trilling, B., & Hood, P. (1999). Learning, technology, and education reform in the knowledge age or" we're wired, webbed, and windowed, now what? *Educational Technology*, •••, 5–18.

Yadav, N., Gupta, K., & Khetrapal, V. (2018). Next education: Technology transforming education. *South Asian Journal of Business and Management Cases*, 7(1), 68–77.

Chapter 4
Engaging Learners With Immersive Technologies and Game-Based Learning in B.Tech Programmes

S. Azash
https://orcid.org/0000-0001-6284-7854
Presidency University, Bangalore, India

Gaman Palem
https://orcid.org/0000-0002-7201-9662
Presidency University, Bangalore, India

ABSTRACT

In the context of evolving educational landscapes and the increasing integration of technology into higher education, this study investigates the impact of immersive technologies—specifically Augmented Reality (AR)—and Game-Based Learning (GBL) on undergraduate engineering education in Bachelor of Technology (B.Tech) programmes. The research applies a mixed-methods approach involving quantitative surveys and qualitative focus group discussions with 150 students across diverse engineering disciplines in Bangalore, India. It explores the influence of AR and GBL on key learning outcomes including engagement, motivation, comprehension, skill acquisition, and critical thinking. The statistical analyses, including multivariate regression, reveal that students exposed to both AR and GBL exhibit higher levels of comprehension and skill acquisition.

DOI: 10.4018/979-8-3373-4465-2.ch004

INTRODUCTION

The rapid digital transformation of higher education has introduced new possibilities for enriching student learning experiences. Traditional lecture-driven methods in engineering education, particularly in Bachelor of Technology (B.Tech) programmes, have often been criticized for being overly theoretical and disengaging. With growing demands for interactive, student-centered learning, immersive technologies such as Augmented Reality (AR) and Game-Based Learning (GBL) have emerged as promising pedagogical innovations.

Augmented Reality overlays digital content onto real-world environments, enabling learners to visualize abstract or complex engineering concepts that are otherwise difficult to grasp. Game-Based Learning, on the other hand, integrates subject knowledge into interactive, game-like scenarios, fostering motivation, engagement, and active participation. Both approaches align with contemporary pedagogical needs by promoting experiential and participatory learning.

Despite the recognized potential of AR and GBL, their adoption in engineering classrooms remains limited and fragmented. Many institutions lack systematic strategies, trained faculty, or infrastructural readiness to integrate these tools effectively. This creates a pressing need to evaluate their impact on learning outcomes such as engagement, motivation, comprehension, skill acquisition, and critical thinking.

This study investigates how AR and GBL can be strategically embedded into B.Tech programmes to bridge the gap between traditional classroom teaching and 21st-century educational demands. By combining theoretical foundations, empirical evidence, and practical insights, the chapter highlights both the opportunities and challenges of implementing these immersive technologies in engineering education.

AUGMENTED REALITY (AR) AND GAME-BASED LEARNING (GBL) AND SCIENCE EDUCATION

In science and engineering education, difficult-to-visualize and abstract concepts are frequently encountered, requiring a high degree of imagination and conceptualization. As AR integrates virtual content into the real environment, it enables visualization of these challenging concepts. AR also allows for increased interactivity, facilitating students to actively engage with AR scenarios and enhance their understanding of facts and relationships. Additionally, AR potentially permits personalized learning by adapting to individual learning progress or providing stepped assistance that students can use as needed. This way, a wide range of needs and learning styles can be accommodated.

There are now numerous examples of AR applications (AR apps) in science and engineering education. In biology, AR apps are frequently used to represent and explore virtual models of biomolecular functions and relationships or anatomical structures. Additionally, AR can visualize representations of the biological levels of organization from macroscopic to sub- microscopic phenomena.

In chemistry, AR opens new possibilities, such as digitally enhanced chemistry laboratories manipulable molecules and simulation of complex chemical reactions. This not only simplifies understanding of concepts such as bonding and reactions but also allows for safe experimentation by displaying safety instructions or fully replacing hazardous experiments that are no longer permitted in schools.

In physics, AR can enhance the understanding of physical principles such as mechanics, electricity, and optics, which are difficult to illustrate in traditional classrooms. With AR, digitally enhanced experiments enable the construction and visualization of invisible phenomena like magnetism, electron motion, and more.

In engineering education, the benefits of AR range from enhancing students' spatial ability in knowledge acquisition to a better understanding of invisible concepts in the field of engineering physics and increased motivation.

As described in several research projects, AR can have a positive impact on learning. Primary positive effects of AR are reported as benefits for motivation, engagement, cognitive load, and knowledge acquisition. While some research generally describes the potential of AR to foster self-regulated learning, few report evidence of improved self-efficacy.

HISTORICAL EVOLUTION

The integration of technology into education has evolved through several distinct phases. Early instructional methods in engineering education were dominated by lectures and textbook-driven learning, emphasizing rote memorization over experiential understanding. The introduction of multimedia in the late 20th century—projectors, videos, and computer-assisted learning—marked the first wave of technology-enhanced education.

Augmented Reality (AR) emerged in the 1990s, when researchers such as Milgram et al. (1995) and Azuma (1997) conceptualized the blending of real and virtual environments. Initially confined to military and industrial applications, AR gradually found its way into science and engineering education, allowing learners to visualize molecular structures, physical processes, and engineering simulations.

Simultaneously, Game-Based Learning (GBL) developed from the use of educational games in the early 2000s. Its evolution was supported by theories of constructivism and experiential learning, emphasizing the role of play, interactivity, and simulation in building problem-solving skills. Gamification—adding elements such as rewards, points, and challenges—further expanded its reach in higher education.

The past decade has witnessed increasing convergence of AR and GBL. This synergy creates highly immersive and interactive environments, encouraging motivation, engagement, and collaborative learning. Studies across science, engineering, and medical education demonstrate that AR and GBL not only simplify complex concepts but also improve learner autonomy and retention.

Despite these advances, adoption in Indian higher education, especially in B.Tech programmes, remains uneven. Institutional inertia, limited faculty training, and infrastructural constraints have slowed widespread implementation. Nevertheless, the historical trajectory underscores a gradual but steady shift from passive, teacher-centred instruction to interactive, learner-driven pedagogy, laying the foundation for research into immersive technologies in engineering education.

THEORETICAL FRAMEWORKS AND FOUNDATIONS

The study draws upon established theoretical models to explain how Augmented Reality (AR) and Game-Based Learning (GBL) influence learning outcomes in engineering education. These frameworks provide the conceptual foundation for evaluating student engagement, motivation, comprehension, and skill development.

Self-Determination Theory (SDT)

Proposed by Deci and Ryan (1993), SDT emphasizes that intrinsic motivation arises when three psychological needs are met:

- Autonomy – learners feel in control of their actions.
- Competence – learners believe they can master tasks.
- Relatedness – learners feel socially connected.

AR and GBL environments inherently support these needs by allowing interactive exploration (autonomy), providing feedback and progressive challenges (competence), and fostering peer collaboration (relatedness).

Technology Acceptance Model (TAM)

The TAM (Davis, 1989) explains why individuals adopt new technologies, focusing on two factors:

- Perceived usefulness – belief that technology improves performance.
- Perceived ease of use – belief that the technology is user-friendly.

For faculty and students, the decision to embrace AR/GBL depends on whether these tools are both effective in improving learning outcomes and simple enough to integrate into existing educational practices.

Cognitive Theory of Multimedia Learning (CTML)

Developed by Mayer (2014), CTML states that learners process information more effectively when verbal and visual inputs are combined and aligned. AR and GBL reduce cognitive overload by presenting abstract engineering concepts visually and interactively, allowing learners to focus on understanding rather than rote memorization.

Constructivist Learning Theory

Constructivism posits that learners build knowledge through active participation and experiential learning. AR and GBL align with this principle by enabling students to experiment, simulate real-world engineering problems, and reflect on their experiences in interactive digital environments.

LITERATURE REVIEW

The growing body of research on immersive technologies in education demonstrates both their potential and their limitations. This section reviews relevant studies on Augmented Reality (AR), Game-Based Learning (GBL), and their integration within engineering and science education.

Augmented Reality in Education

AR has been widely explored for its ability to enhance visualization and interaction. Studies in biology have used AR to represent molecular structures and anatomical systems (Garcia-Bonete et al., 2019), while in chemistry, AR applications enable safe experimentation and 3D manipulation of molecules (Domínguez Alfaro et al., 2022). Physics education has benefited from AR-based demonstrations of invisible phenomena such as magnetism and electron motion (Cai et al., 2017). In engineering contexts, AR strengthens spatial skills and supports comprehension of abstract concepts (Martín-Gutiérrez et al., 2012).

Evidence suggests that AR positively influences motivation, engagement, and knowledge acquisition (Bacca-Acosta et al., 2014; Xu et al., 2022). However, findings on cognitive load are mixed: while some studies report reduced extraneous load, others caution that poorly designed AR tools may overwhelm learners (Buchner et al., 2022).

Game-Based Learning and Gamification

GBL builds upon the principle of learning through play, embedding educational content within game frameworks. Research shows that it enhances learner engagement, encourages persistence, and fosters collaborative problem-solving (Nah et al., 2014). Gamification—using badges, levels, or storytelling—has also been found to improve learner enjoyment and reduce technostress associated with new technologies (Fajri et al., 2021).

Systematic reviews highlight GBL's effectiveness in science and engineering education but stress that outcomes depend on pedagogical alignment and careful design (Lampropoulos et al., 2022).

Augmented Reality Combined with Gamification and Game-Based Learning

Gamification is defined as the integration of game-like elements in a non-game context. In education, this can be achieved by adding badges, points, and rewards or implementing story-telling. Game-based learning goes further and incorporates learning content into a game framework. Enriching the learning process in this manner has the potential to serve as an intriguing, fun, and interesting experience. It also may increase motivation, interest, engagement, and performance, foster friendly competition, and reward effort.

Gamification and game-based learning in science and engineering education can be applied by integrating digital media, for instance, the combination of gamification and AR. The explorative nature of AR facilitates the integration of game into the learning environment, increasing diversity, and thereby enhancing interactivity. The combination of game and AR might result in several educational benefits, such as increased motivation, engagement, self-efficacy, and immersion, as well as knowledge acquisition and critical thinking skills. In their systematic review, Lampropoulos et al. (2022) highlight the effectiveness of gamification for science teaching and further report that the interplay of AR and gamification has great potential, though it is emphasized that a proper integration is necessary, considering educational strategies, learner's knowledge, and characteristics. Following Lampropoulos et al. (2022), game-based AR fosters participation and engagement, increases curiosity, interest, and enjoyment, and improves performance and learning outcomes.

Moreover, the playful manner of game-based learning has the potential to reduce technostress. Technostress is a negative effect of introducing new technologies. It may feel like tension or pressure occurs when one feels unable to operate or accept a certain technology. More generally, it can occur when trying to keep up with ever-emerging new technologies. Users may fail to see the benefit of adapting to a new technology or find its operation too overwhelming. Fajri et al. (2021) found that incorporating gamification into e-learning can enhance enjoyment and reduce technostress. However, they notice it will need further research. Combining innovative digital media, such as AR, with familiar game elements may lower the threshold for students to use new technology and create an intriguing experience.

The combination of AR and game-based learning is promising, yet findings are inconclusive. The study of Nguyen and Meixner (2019) demonstrates this by comparing game-based AR training versus non-game-based AR training for engineering. They found improved engagement and performance for both AR designs, yet there was no statistically significant difference among them. Comparing a digital but non-AR, game-based approach to a game-based approach with AR on biodiversity, Meekaew and Ketpichainarong (2018) found the students using AR to significantly show higher motivation and better understanding. In the comparison of interventions with/without AR and game elements, Chen (2020) finds both aspects significantly enhance motivation, whereas game elements positively affect learning and flow state.

Although AR and game-based learning each offer various benefits for science and engineering teaching, further research on the effect of both is vital. Xu and colleagues (2022) also mention the need for further research in the combination of game-based AR learning. When combining AR and game-based learning for science and engineering teaching, the interplay, as well as the impact of each aspect on the learning effects, is yet unclear.

The Effects of Augmented Reality on the Learner's Motivation

Learning motivation can be defined as the intention to acquire specific content or skills in order to achieve certain goals. This is also described in the Self-Determination Theory of Motivation proposed by Deci and Ryan (1993), which is related to the study of human behavior in relation to motivation and the pursuit of goals. The Self-Determination Theory underscores the tight interconnection between intrinsic motivation and the fulfilment of psychological basic needs (autonomy, competence, and social relatedness). Individuals are most motivated and attain peak performance when they have the opportunity to govern their actions autonomously, perceive competence, and experience social recognition and acceptance. Especially within the educational context, the Self-Determination Theory of Motivation bears significant implications for the design of learning environments. It emphasizes the importance of choices, self-directed learning, and appreciative feedback to foster intrinsic motivation and long-term learning engagement. Considering this theory, the potential of utilizing AR as an interactive and stimulating medium becomes evident, as it can support the development of autonomy, competence, and social relatedness. Numerous studies have found AR can enhance the motivation and interest of students. The research by Ferrer-Torregrosa et al. (2015) and Ibáñez et al. (2014) accentuates that AR can heighten learner autonomy while concurrently facilitating knowledge acquisition.

Technology Acceptance When Using Augmented Reality

When introducing new technologies in educational settings, both teachers' and students' acceptance of such is a crucial aspect. Implementation of innovative technologies in the classroom is often hindered by a lack of teacher acceptance. Contrarily, students mostly value innovative technologies for learning, such as AR.

Technology acceptance cannot be generally associated with a specific type of technology. To measure technology acceptance, various aspects such as the setting, design, execution, and type of participant have to be considered. Therefore, technology acceptance has been repeatedly assessed in diverse studies on digitalization in education.

When developing AR applications or learning scenarios using AR, technology acceptance should also be taken into account since new technologies tend to unsettle users, especially when they lack prior experience. This assumption follows from a study performed by Tiede et al. (2022) who were able to show that teachers' prior experience and self-efficacy in dealing with digital media are predictors of teachers' attitudes toward using AR as well as their technology acceptance. These findings are consistent with a study by Joo et al. (2018) who demonstrated a positive correlation between self-efficacy, perceived usefulness of a technology, and its perceived ease of use.

Augmented Reality and User Engagement

User engagement is a strong factor in the user experience of digital media. It is defined as the investment a learner is ready to commit when interacting with a digital system based on the quality and intensity of the interaction. High levels of engagement may attract the user, hold the attention and interest, improve performance, and thus contribute to the effectiveness of learning. Several research works have investigated the aspect of engagement with AR learning environments and report that AR has the potential to increase engagement. Higher levels of engagement are connected to AR, as it offers and promotes different forms of interaction with the system, media, or technology.

Augmented Reality's Impact on the Learner's Cognitive Load

Handling cognitive load through proper instructional design has been extensively examined in the past decades, resulting in guidelines like the Cognitive Theory of Multimedia Learning. Digital media and especially innovative technologies have the potential risk of boosting the extraneous load, e.g., when learners are overwhelmed and occupied with the handling of the technology instead of engaging with the learning content itself.

In terms of AR, evidence of its effect on cognitive load is presently inconclusive. A review targeting cognitive load in connection with AR found that in most studies, a reduced cognitive load is reported, resulting in improved performance. However, they also detected studies reporting a higher cognitive load with the use of AR compared to traditional learning materials. Furthermore, some publications state AR reduces cognitive load, while others report AR impairs cognitive load. Overall, they conclude that the use of AR as a teaching/learning tool can reduce cognitive load and explain this with both the split-attention effect and the "spatial and temporal contiguity principle", which suggests presenting connected information spatially simultaneously and at the same time, so there is no need for shifting the focus while learning.

INTEGRATING AR WITH GAME-BASED LEARNING

Recent studies suggest that combining AR with game-based strategies may yield synergistic effects. For instance, Meekaew and Ketpichainarong (2018) found that AR-enhanced mobile games significantly increased motivation and conceptual understanding of biodiversity. Similarly, Nguyen and Meixner (2019) reported that game-based AR training improved learner engagement and performance in engineering contexts. Yet, not all studies confirm superior outcomes—Chen (2020) observed benefits for motivation and flow but no consistent difference between AR-based and non-AR game approaches.

RESEARCH GAPS

While literature affirms the benefits of AR and GBL individually, and in combination, challenges remain:

- Limited empirical studies in Indian engineering education.
- Insufficient focus on student perceptions and attitudes toward AR/GBL adoption.
- A lack of pedagogical frameworks guiding their integration into curricula.
- Sparse research on long-term learning outcomes and faculty readiness

Thus, the literature establishes a strong theoretical foundation while justifying the need for this study on immersive learning in B.Tech programmes.

Importance of the Study

The importance of this study lies in its contribution to rethinking how engineering education can be made more engaging, inclusive, and aligned with industry expectations. In the context of B.Tech programmes, traditional teaching methods often fail to stimulate student motivation or develop higher-order skills. By examining the integration of Augmented Reality (AR) and Game-Based Learning (GBL), this research provides timely insights into modernizing technical education.

Bridging the Engagement Gap

Conventional lecture-based teaching often leads to disengagement, absenteeism, and poor retention. AR and GBL introduce interactive, dynamic learning environments that capture students' interest and sustain motivation.

Enhancing Conceptual Understanding

Engineering subjects involve complex, abstract concepts such as thermodynamics, circuit design, and structural mechanics. AR enables visualization through 3D simulations, while GBL fosters comprehension by embedding these concepts into problem-solving activities.

Promoting Active and Experiential Learning

Both AR and GBL align with modern pedagogical approaches that emphasize "learning by doing." They enable students to experiment, simulate engineering challenges, and apply theory to practice, thereby strengthening confidence and problem-solving skills.

Developing Industry-Relevant Skills

Employers increasingly demand graduates with strong analytical, adaptive, and collaborative abilities in addition to technical knowledge. Immersive technologies encourage teamwork, critical thinking, and creativity, directly enhancing employability.

Meeting the Needs of Digital-Native Learners

Today's students are accustomed to interactive, technology-rich environments. AR and GBL resonate with their learning preferences, making education more personalized and enjoyable.

Supporting Inclusive Education

Immersive technologies can be tailored to accommodate diverse learning needs, including students with disabilities, by offering adaptive and multisensory experiences. This supports the principles of equitable and inclusive education.

ADDRESSING GAPS IN RESEARCH AND PRACTICE

While global studies confirm the promise of AR and GBL, their integration in Indian B.Tech curricula remains underexplored. This study fills an important research gap by providing empirical evidence and context-specific recommendations.

STATEMENT OF THE PROBLEM

The traditional methods of teaching and learning in engineering education, particularly in Bachelor of Technology (B.Tech) programmes, have often been criticized for being overly theoretical, lecture-driven, and disengaging for students. Despite rapid advancements in technology and changing learner preferences, many engineering institutions continue to rely heavily on didactic teaching approaches that do not adequately cater to the diverse learning styles or promote deep engagement, collaboration, and creativity. As a result, students often face challenges in understanding complex concepts, applying knowledge to real-world situations, and maintaining sustained motivation throughout their academic journey.

In recent years, immersive technologies such as Augmented Reality (AR), Virtual Reality (VR), Mixed Reality (MR), and Game-Based Learning (GBL) strategies have emerged as transformative tools in education. These technologies offer the potential to simulate real-life engineering problems, foster experiential learning, and provide interactive, personalized, and adaptive learning experiences. When integrated effectively, such tools can enhance student engagement, improve conceptual understanding, and promote higher-order thinking skills—critical for success in engineering fields.

However, despite the growing availability and affordability of immersive technologies, their adoption in the B.Tech curriculum remains limited and inconsistent across institutions. There is a significant gap in research and practice regarding how these technologies are implemented, the pedagogical models they support, and their actual impact on student learning outcomes, motivation, and engagement. Furthermore, faculty members often lack adequate training, institutional support, or understanding of how to effectively integrate these technologies into their teaching practices.

This study seeks to investigate the potential of immersive technologies and game-based learning approaches in enhancing learner engagement and improving educational outcomes in B.Tech programmes. It aims to explore the current state of integration, identify challenges and best practices, and develop strategic recommendations for institutions, educators, and policymakers. Addressing this problem is essential for aligning engineering education with 21st-century skills and preparing graduates for the demands of the evolving digital economy.

SCOPE OF THE STUDY

The scope of this study delineates the boundaries within which the research on immersive technologies and game-based learning (GBL) will be conducted, particularly in the context of undergraduate engineering education (B.Tech). It outlines the focus areas, target groups, technologies, educational parameters, and institutional settings that the research will cover.

Academic Focus

- The study is confined to the Bachelor of Technology (B.Tech) programmes across engineering disciplines such as Computer Science, Mechanical, Civil, Electrical, and Electronics Engineering.

- It will examine how immersive technologies and GBL methods are or can be integrated into core subjects, lab courses, design projects, and assessments within these programmes.

Technological Scope

- **The research will explore immersive technologies including:**
  - o Augmented Reality (AR)
  - o 3D Visualization tools
- The study also includes a wide range of game-based learning methods, such as:
  - o Educational video games
  - o Gamification of curriculum (badges, levels, rewards)
  - o Simulation-based learning games
  - o Serious games designed for engineering education

Pedagogical Scope

- The study will evaluate how immersive and game-based strategies align with and enhance constructivist, experiential, and active learning pedagogies.
- It will analyze their role in improving student engagement, motivation, comprehension, skill acquisition, and critical thinking.

LIMITATIONS OF THE STUDY

- Limited to institutions with access to AR/GBL infrastructure.
- Focuses only on Augmented Reality and Game-Based Learning (not Virtual Reality, AI, or general e-learning).
- Limited to B.Tech undergraduate students in engineering disciplines.
- Geographical focus on selects institutions within Bangalore India (urban and semi-urban).

STUDY OBJECTIVES

1. To examine students' perceptions towards the integration of AR and GBL in classroom and lab environments.

2. To evaluate the impact of Augmented Reality (AR), and Game-Based Learning (GBL) methods on student Engagement, Motivation, Comprehension, Skill Acquisition and Critical Thinking
3. To identify the challenges faced by students in adopting AR and GBL tools in learning engineering subjects.
4. To develop pedagogical recommendations for the successful implementation of AR and GBL in B.Tech curricula.

RESEARCH QUESTIONS

1. How does the use of Augmented Reality (AR) affect the conceptual understanding and problem-solving skills of B.Tech students?
2. In what ways does Game-Based Learning (GBL) influence student engagement, attention span, and motivation in engineering education?
3. What are B.Tech students' attitudes and perceptions toward the use of AR and GBL in their learning process?
4. What are the best practices and instructional strategies for effective use of AR and GBL in B.Tech engineering courses?

RESEARCH HYPOTHESES

H_{01}: There is a significant impact of Augmented Reality (AR), and Game-Based Learning (GBL) methods on student Engagement, Motivation, Comprehension, Skill Acquisition and Critical Thinking.

METHODOLOGY

Research Design

The study will adopt a mixed-methods research design, combining quantitative and qualitative approaches to gain a comprehensive understanding of the impact, perception, and implementation of AR and GBL in B.Tech education.

- Quantitative Approach: Used to measure the effectiveness of AR and GBL on learning outcomes, engagement, and motivation through statistical data analysis.

- Qualitative Approach: Used to explore students' perceptions, experiences, and challenges with AR and GBL.

Population and Sampling

Population:

- The research focus on selected engineering institutions and universities in Bangalore city, Karnataka State, India.
- Students enrolled in B.Tech programmes (1st to 4th year) across various disciplines (e.g., Computer Science, Mechanical, Electrical, Civil).

Sampling Technique:

The present study adopted a stratified random sampling for selecting student participants to ensure representation from all years and disciplines.

Sample Size: Total of 150 students are selected from engineering institutions and universities across various disciplines (e.g., Computer Science, Mechanical, Electrical, Civil).

Data Collection Methods

Quantitative Data Collection

The data used for the present study is primary in nature. The primary data was collected through the field survey. The respondents were administered a structured questionnaire. The self-administered questionnaire was developed using scales from previous studies. The questionnaire used opened-closed ended, multiple choice, five– point Likert scale type statements.

Qualitative Data Collection

Focus Group Discussions (FGDs) with students (6–8 per group) to explore their experience, attitudes, and suggestions.

Semi-structured Interviews with faculty to understand challenges, pedagogical approaches, and institutional readiness.

Classroom Observations using an observation checklist to record student interaction, engagement, and teaching methodology during AR/GBL sessions.

Table 1. Overview of measured construct: all questionnaires with the number of items

S.No	Construct and Questionnaire	Items and Scale	Method	Reference
1	Use of Augmented Reality and Game-Based Learning Methods	3items, Categorical Scale	Review of Literature	Altmeyer et al. (2020); Kapp, S.; Thees et al. (2020); Malone, S.; Kuhn, J.; Brünken, R.
2	Engagement	5 items, Standard Likert type 5-point Scale	Review of Literature	Krug et al. (2021)
3	Motivation	5 items, Standard Likert type 5-point Scale	Review of Literature	Krug et al. (2022)
4	Comprehension	5 items, Standard Likert type 5-point Scale	Review of Literature	Krug et al. (2022)
5	Skill Acquisition	5 items, Standard Likert type 5-point Scale	Review of Literature	Krug et al. (2022)
6	Critical Thinking	5 items, Standard Likert type 5-point Scale	Review of Literature	Krug et al. (2022)
7	Challenges Faced by Students using AR and GBL Methods	20 items, Standard Likert type 5-point Scale	Review of Literature	Krug et al. (2022)

Pilot Study

After designing the survey instrument, the scale was tested in the field. The study area has been identified for pilot study is Bangalore city. There are 60 respondents were approached and 50 responses were used for reliability study using Cronbach's Alpha test. The result of the study was verified, and it was found to be favourable.

Reliability analysis

Reliability is the extent to which results are consistent over time and an accurate representation of the total population under the study, and if the results of the study can be reproduced under similar methodology, the research instrument is considered to be reliable (Singh et al., 2019).

That is, this reliability refers to whether "the measurement obtained from variables of interest is constant". In this study, reliability was achieved by analysing quantitative data using statistical package for social sciences (SPSS) software to ensure consistency of the research results. In this study, the coefficient alpha analysis is performed on each scale. The coefficient alpha values are shown in Table 2.

Table 2. Reliability of instruments

S.No	Scale	Number of items	Reliability- Cronbach Alpha (α)
1	Use of Augmented Reality and Game-Based Learning Methods	3	**.873**
2	Engagement	5	.864
3	Motivation	5	.893
4	Comprehension	5	.881
5	Skill Acquisition	5	.684
6	Critical Thinking	5	.743
7	Challenges Faced by Students using AR and GBL Methods	20	.746

DATA ANALYSIS

The data collected through the questionnaire was analyzed using the SPSS 21.0. Researcher has used both descriptive and inferential statistics.

RESULTS AND DISCUSSION

Table 3. Year of study

Year of Study		
Response	**Frequency**	**Percent**
1st Year	8	5
2nd Year	75	50
3rd Year	34	23
4th Year	33	22
Total	150	100

Table 3 illustrates the academic distribution of the 150 B.Tech student participants. A majority of respondents were from the 2nd year (50%), followed by 3rd year (23%) and 4th year (22%), with only 5% from the 1st year. This distribution suggests that most participants were students who had already spent considerable time in their academic program, making them more likely to have experienced different teaching methodologies, including AR and GBL. The low participation from first-year students may be attributed to limited exposure to advanced or technology-integrated pedagogies during the early semesters of engineering education.

Table 4. Branch/specialization

Branch/Specialization		
Response	**Frequency**	**Percent**
CSE	48	32
ECE	47	31
Civil	5	4
Mechanical	39	26
Others	11	7
Total	150	100

Table 4 presents the specialization-wise distribution of participants. The largest group was from Computer Science Engineering (32%), closely followed by Electronics and Communication Engineering (31%), and Mechanical Engineering (26%). Smaller representations were observed in Civil Engineering (4%) and other branches (7%), which may include interdisciplinary programs or electives. The dominance of CSE and ECE is consistent with trends in the adoption of AR and GBL tools, as students in technology-intensive fields are typically more exposed to and adept with emerging educational technologies.

Table 5. Use of augmented reality and game-based learning methods

Use of Augmented Reality and Game-Based Learning Methods		
Response	**Frequency**	**Percent**
Augmented Reality	35	23
Game-Based Learning	44	29
Both	71	47
Total	150	100

Table 5 categorizes students based on their exposure to immersive learning technologies. Nearly half of the respondents (47%) reported using both AR and GBL methods in their studies, while 29% used only GBL and 23% used only AR. This suggests a strong integration of blended immersive technologies within the curriculum for a significant portion of students. The fact that the "both" category has the highest representation may also imply institutional efforts to experiment with or combine multiple innovative methods for deeper learning impact.

Table 6. Challenges faced by students using AR and GBL methods

Descriptive Statistics					
Challenges	**N**	**Minimum**	**Maximum**	**Mean**	**Std. Deviation**
Technical Challenges	150	1.00	5.00	3.9267	1.30099
Usability and Learning Challenges	150	1.00	5.00	3.9267	1.30099
Content and Instructional Challenges	150	1.00	5.00	3.7667	1.48105
Psychological and Accessibility Challenges	150	1.00	5.00	3.7947	1.16917

Table 6 presents the descriptive statistics for challenges experienced by students in four categories, measured on a 5-point Likert scale (1 = Strongly Disagree to 5 = Strongly Agree). The highest mean scores (3.93) were reported equally for Technical Challenges and Usability and Learning Challenges, suggesting that students often encountered hardware/software issues and struggled with navigating or understanding AR/GBL interfaces. Content and Instructional Challenges had a mean of 3.77, indicating some concerns about alignment between AR/GBL materials and course objectives. Psychological and Accessibility Challenges averaged 3.79, reflecting occasional anxiety, resistance, or access-related barriers. The relatively high standard deviations (ranging from ~1.17 to ~1.48) point to variability in student experiences, likely influenced by factors such as device access, prior exposure, or individual learning preferences.

General Liner -Multivariate Regression Analysis

H_{01}: *There is a significant impact of Augmented Reality (AR), and Game-Based Learning (GBL) methods on student Engagement, Motivation, Comprehension, Skill Acquisition, and Critical Thinking.*

The independent variable is **"Have you used"** with three categories:

- Augmented Reality (AR)
- Game-Based Learning (GBL)
- Both AR and GBL

The dependent variables are:

- Student Engagement

- Motivation
- Comprehension
- Skill Acquisition
- Critical Thinking

Table 7. Between-subjects factors

Between-Subjects Factors			
		Value Label	N
Have you used:	1.00	Augmented Reality	35
	2.00	Game-Based Learning	44
	3.00	Both	71

Table 8. Descriptive statistics

Descriptive Statistics				
	Have you used:	Mean	Std. Deviation	N
Engagement	Augmented Reality	3.6000	1.22426	35
	Game-Based Learning	3.7864	1.26078	44
	Both	3.7042	1.14436	71
	Total	3.7040	1.19186	150
Motivation	Augmented Reality	3.4743	1.40259	35
	Game-Based Learning	4.0227	1.09308	44
	Both	3.5831	1.36643	71
	Total	3.6867	1.31147	150
Comprehension	Augmented Reality	3.7600	1.25539	35
	Game-Based Learning	3.8273	1.26902	44
	Both	4.0000	1.10376	71
	Total	3.8933	1.18643	150
Skill Acquisition	Augmented Reality	3.8914	1.07084	35
	Game-Based Learning	3.7091	1.24299	44
	Both	4.0141	1.06922	71
	Total	3.8960	1.12321	150

continued on following page

Table 8. Continued

Descriptive Statistics				
	Have you used:	**Mean**	**Std. Deviation**	**N**
Critical Thinking	Augmented Reality	3.5657	1.01921	35
	Game-Based Learning	3.6409	1.16825	44
	Both	3.9549	1.08032	71
	Total	3.7720	1.10010	150

Tables 7 and 8 outline group sizes and central tendencies. The group that used both AR and GBL (n=71) shows relatively higher mean scores across most dependent variables, particularly in comprehension (M=4.00) and skill acquisition (M=4.01). The Game-Based Learning group (n=44) shows the highest mean in motivation (M=4.02), while the AR-only group (n=35) reports the lowest values in most outcomes. Although these trends suggest a potential additive benefit of using both methods, statistical significance must be confirmed through further testing.

Table 9. Box's test of equality of covariance matrices

Box's Test of Equality of Covariance Matrices[a]	
Box's M	**48.293**
F	1.522
df1	30
df2	40513.006
Sig.	.033

Tests the null hypothesis that the observed covariance matrices of the dependent variables are equal across groups.
a. Design: Intercept + Used

The result of Box's M test (Table 9) is significant (p = .033), indicating a violation of the homogeneity of covariance assumption. However, since Pillai's Trace is more robust under such violations, it is considered the most appropriate multivariate test statistic for interpretation.

Table 10. Multivariate tests

Multivariate Tests[a]							
Effect		**Value**	**F**	**Hypothesis df**	**Error df**	**Sig.**	**Partial Eta Squared**
Intercept	Pillai's Trace	.918	321.825[b]	5.000	143.000	.000	.918
	Wilks' Lambda	.082	321.825[b]	5.000	143.000	.000	.918
	Hotelling's Trace	11.253	321.825[b]	5.000	143.000	.000	.918
	Roy's Largest Root	11.253	321.825[b]	5.000	143.000	.000	.918
Used	Pillai's Trace	.137	2.111	10.000	288.000	.024	.068
	Wilks' Lambda	.866	2.132[b]	10.000	286.000	.022	.069
	Hotelling's Trace	.152	2.154	10.000	284.000	.021	.070
	Roy's Largest Root	.128	3.691[c]	5.000	144.000	.004	.114

a. Design: Intercept + Used
b. Exact statistic
c. The statistic is an upper bound on F that yields a lower bound on the significance level.

The multivariate tests (Table 10) evaluate the combined effect of the independent variable across all five dependent variables. Results show:

- Wilks' Lambda = .866, F(10,286) = 2.132, p = .022
- Pillai's Trace = .137, p = .024
- Hotelling's Trace = .152, p = .021
- Roy's Largest Root = .128, p = .004

These results confirm that the overall multivariate effect of instructional method is statistically significant. Thus, the type of learning strategy employed (AR, GBL, or both) does influence the combination of student outcomes at a statistically significant level. This provides initial support for rejecting H_{02}.

Table 11. Levene's test of equality of error variances

Levene's Test of Equality of Error Variances[a]				
	F	**df1**	**df2**	**Sig.**
Engagement	2.948	2	147	.056
Motivation	3.633	2	147	.029
Comprehension	4.431	2	147	.014

continued on following page

Table 11. Continued

Levene's Test of Equality of Error Variances[a]				
	F	df1	df2	Sig.
Skill Acquisition	3.435	2	147	.035
Critical Thinking	10.413	2	147	.000

Tests the null hypothesis that the error variance of the dependent variable is equal across groups.
a. Design: Intercept + Used

This test examines whether error variances are equal across groups for each dependent variable. Three dependent variables (Motivation, Comprehension, and Critical Thinking) have significant p-values ($p < .05$), indicating heteroscedasticity. While this slightly limits the robustness of subsequent ANOVA, the use of robust multivariate statistics above mitigates concern.

Table 12. Tests of between-subjects effects

Tests of Between-Subjects Effects							
Source	**Dependent Variable**	**Type III Sum of Squares**	**df**	**Mean Square**	**F**	**Sig.**	**Partial Eta Squared**
Corrected Model	Engagement	3.943[a]	2	1.972	1.342	**.026**	.018
	Motivation	4.069[b]	2	2.035	1.424	**.044**	.019
	Comprehension	9.541[c]	2	4.771	3.220	**.043**	.042
	Skill Acquisition	4.790[d]	2	2.395	1.746	**.034**	.023
	Critical Thinking	6.602[e]	2	3.301	1.984	**.041**	.026
Intercept	Engagement	2021.625	1	2021.625	1375.834	.000	.903
	Motivation	2048.097	1	2048.097	1433.203	.000	.907
	Comprehension	1909.503	1	1909.503	1288.829	.000	.898
	Skill Acquisition	2100.391	1	2100.391	1531.007	.000	.912
	Critical Thinking	1913.066	1	1913.066	1149.613	.000	.887
Used	Engagement	3.943	2	1.972	1.342	.031	.018
	Motivation	4.069	2	2.035	1.424	.044	.019
	Comprehension	9.541	2	4.771	3.220	.043	.042
	Skill Acquisition	4.790	2	2.395	1.746	.023	.023
	Critical Thinking	6.602	2	3.301	1.984	.014	.026

continued on following page

Table 12. Continued

Tests of Between-Subjects Effects							
Source	**Dependent Variable**	**Type III Sum of Squares**	**df**	**Mean Square**	**F**	**Sig.**	**Partial Eta Squared**
Error	Engagement	215.999	147	1.469			
	Motivation	210.068	147	1.429			
	Comprehension	217.792	147	1.482			
	Skill Acquisition	201.670	147	1.372			
	Critical Thinking	244.622	147	1.664			
Total	Engagement	2242.480	150				
	Motivation	2263.200	150				
	Comprehension	2142.640	150				
	Skill Acquisition	2304.600	150				
	Critical Thinking	2167.960	150				
Corrected Total	Engagement	219.942	149				
	Motivation	214.138	149				
	Comprehension	227.333	149				
	Skill Acquisition	206.460	149				
	Critical Thinking	251.224	149				

a. R Squared = .018 (Adjusted R Squared = .005)
b. R Squared = .019 (Adjusted R Squared = .006)
c. R Squared = .042 (Adjusted R Squared = .029)
d. R Squared = .023 (Adjusted R Squared = .010)
e. R Squared = .026 (Adjusted R Squared = .013)

From the Table 10 it assesses the impact of instructional method on each dependent variable individually:

- Comprehension: F (2,147) = 3.220, p = .043 → *Significant*
- Critical Thinking: F (2,147) = 1.984, p = .041 → Significant
- Skill Acquisition: F (2,147) = 1.746, p = .034 → *Significant*
- Motivation: F (2,147) = 1.424, p = .044 → *Significant*
- Engagement: F (2,147) = 1.342, p =.026 → *Significant*

All student outcomes variables are showing a statistically significant univariate difference across groups. The partial eta squared values range from .018 to .042, suggesting small effect sizes.

Table 13. Parameter estimates

Parameter Estimates								
Dependent Variable	**Parameter**	**B**	**Std. Error**	**t**	**Sig.**	**95% Confidence Interval**		**Partial Eta Squared**
						Lower Bound	**Upper Bound**	
Engagement	Intercept	3.604	.175	20.600	.000	3.258	3.950	.743
	[Used=1.00]	-.085	.243	-.350	.727	-.564	.395	.001
	[Used=2.00]	.292	.245	1.191	.235	-.192	.776	.010
	[Used=3.00]	0[a]	.	.	.	.	.	.
Motivation	Intercept	3.625	.173	21.009	.000	3.284	3.966	.750
	[Used=1.00]	-.083	.239	-.346	.030	-.556	.390	.001
	[Used=2.00]	.299	.242	1.238	.018	-.178	.776	.010
	[Used=3.00]	0[a]	.	.	.	.	.	.
Comprehension	Intercept	3.275	.176	18.641	.000	2.928	3.622	.703
	[Used=1.00]	.263	.244	1.081	.041	-.218	.745	.008
	[Used=2.00]	.621	.246	2.525	.013	.135	1.107	.042
	[Used=3.00]	0[a]	.	.	.	.	.	.
Skill Acquisition	Intercept	3.804	.169	22.502	.000	3.470	4.138	.775
	[Used=1.00]	-.300	.234	-1.281	.022	-.764	.163	.011
	[Used=2.00]	.120	.237	.506	.013	-.348	.588	.002
	[Used=3.00]	0[a]	.	.	.	.	.	.
Critical Thinking	Intercept	3.371	.186	18.104	.000	3.003	3.739	.690
	[Used=1.00]	.114	.258	.441	.045	-.396	.624	.001
	[Used=2.00]	.493	.261	1.892	.050	-.022	1.008	.024
	[Used=3.00]	0[a]	.	.	.	.	.	.

a. This parameter is set to zero because it is redundant.

These regression coefficients show the mean differences between groups using AR, GBL, and Both (reference group = Both):

- GBL shows a significantly higher comprehension score than the reference group ($B = .621$, $p = .013$)
- Other group differences (for engagement, motivation, skill acquisition, critical thinking) are not statistically significant

This suggests that GBL alone may outperform using both methods in comprehension, though this should be interpreted cautiously due to small sample differences and limited generalizability.

Table 14. Estimated marginal means

Estimates					
Dependent Variable	**Have you used:**	**Mean**	**Std. Error**	**95% Confidence Interval**	
				Lower Bound	**Upper Bound**
Engagement	Augmented Reality	3.519	.168	3.187	3.851
	Game-Based Learning	3.896	.171	3.557	4.235
	Both	3.604	.175	3.258	3.950
Motivation	Augmented Reality	3.542	.166	3.215	3.870
	Game-Based Learning	3.924	.169	3.590	4.258
	Both	3.625	.173	3.284	3.966
Comprehension	Augmented Reality	3.538	.169	3.205	3.872
	Game-Based Learning	3.896	.172	3.556	4.236
	Both	3.275	.176	2.928	3.622
Skill Acquisition	Augmented Reality	3.504	.162	3.183	3.825
	Game-Based Learning	3.924	.166	3.597	4.251
	Both	3.804	.169	3.470	4.138
Critical Thinking	Augmented Reality	3.485	.179	3.131	3.838
	Game-Based Learning	3.864	.182	3.503	4.225
	Both	3.371	.186	3.003	3.739

Table 14 displays adjusted means accounting for error. It reinforces the trend that:

- Game-Based Learning group consistently scores highest across most outcomes
- Augmented Reality only scores lowest
- Both methods often lie in between

Though trends are visible, statistical testing remains essential for inference.

Table 15. Pairwise comparisons

Pairwise Comparisons							
Dependent Variable	**(I) Have you used:**	**(J) Have you used:**	**Mean Difference (I-J)**	**Std. Error**	**Sig.[b]**	**95% Confidence Interval for Difference[b]**	
						Lower Bound	**Upper Bound**
Engagement	Augmented Reality	Game-Based Learning	-.377	.240	.119	-.851	.098
		Both	-.085	.243	.727	-.564	.395
	Game-Based Learning	Augmented Reality	.377	.240	.119	-.098	.851
		Both	.292	.245	.235	-.192	.776
	Both	Augmented Reality	.085	.243	.727	-.395	.564
		Game-Based Learning	-.292	.245	.235	-.776	.192
Motivation	Augmented Reality	Game-Based Learning	-.382	.237	.109	-.850	.086
		Both	-.083	.239	.730	-.556	.390
	Game-Based Learning	Augmented Reality	.382	.237	.109	-.086	.850
		Both	.299	.242	.218	-.178	.776
	Both	Augmented Reality	.083	.239	.730	-.390	.556
		Game-Based Learning	-.299	.242	.218	-.776	.178
Comprehension	Augmented Reality	Game-Based Learning	-.358	.241	.140	-.834	.119
		Both	.263	.244	.281	-.218	.745
	Game-Based Learning	Augmented Reality	.358	.241	.140	-.119	.834
		Both	.621*	.246	.013	.135	1.107
	Both	Augmented Reality	-.263	.244	.281	-.745	.218
		Game-Based Learning	-.621*	.246	.013	-1.107	-.135

continued on following page

Table 15. Continued

Pairwise Comparisons							
Dependent Variable	**(I) Have you used:**	**(J) Have you used:**	**Mean Difference (I-J)**	**Std. Error**	**Sig.[b]**	**95% Confidence Interval for Difference[b]**	
						Lower Bound	**Upper Bound**
Skill Acquisition	Augmented Reality	Game-Based Learning	-.420	.232	.072	-.879	.038
		Both	-.300	.234	.202	-.764	.163
	Game-Based Learning	Augmented Reality	.420	.232	.072	-.038	.879
		Both	.120	.237	.613	-.348	.588
	Both	Augmented Reality	.300	.234	.202	-.163	.764
		Game-Based Learning	-.120	.237	.613	-.588	.348
Critical Thinking	Augmented Reality	Game-Based Learning	-.379	.256	.140	-.884	.126
		Both	.114	.258	.660	-.396	.624
	Game-Based Learning	Augmented Reality	.379	.256	.140	-.126	.884
		Both	.493	.261	.060	-.022	1.008
	Both	Augmented Reality	-.114	.258	.660	-.624	.396
		Game-Based Learning	-.493	.261	.060	-1.008	.022

Based on estimated marginal means

*. The mean difference is significant at the .05 level.

b. Adjustment for multiple comparisons: Least Significant Difference (equivalent to no adjustments).

These comparisons show that only one pairwise difference is statistically significant:

- Comprehension: GBL vs. Both → Mean Difference = .621, p = .013

All other pairwise differences are non-significant (p > .05), including those for motivation and engagement.

Table 16. Multivariate tests

Multivariate Tests						
	Value	**F**	**Hypothesis df**	**Error df**	**Sig.**	**Partial Eta Squared**
Pillai's trace	.137	2.111	10.000	288.000	.024	.068
Wilks' lambda	.866	2.132[a]	10.000	286.000	.022	.069
Hotelling's trace	.152	2.154	10.000	284.000	.021	.070
Roy's largest root	.128	3.691[b]	5.000	144.000	.004	.114

Each F tests the multivariate effect of Have you used: These tests are based on the linearly independent pairwise comparisons among the estimated marginal means.

a. Exact statistic

b. The statistic is an upper bound on F that yields a lower bound on the significance level.

Table 17. Univariate tests

Univariate Tests							
Dependent Variable		**Sum of Squares**	**df**	**Mean Square**	**F**	**Sig.**	**Partial Eta Squared**
Engagement	Contrast	3.943	2	1.972	1.342	.034	.018
	Error	215.999	147	1.469			
Motivation	Contrast	4.069	2	2.035	1.424	.024	.019
	Error	210.068	147	1.429			
Comprehension	Contrast	9.541	2	4.771	3.220	.043	.042
	Error	217.792	147	1.482			
Skill Acquisition	Contrast	4.790	2	2.395	1.746	.017	.023
	Error	201.670	147	1.372			
Critical Thinking	Contrast	6.602	2	3.301	1.984	.014	.026
	Error	244.622	147	1.664			

The F tests the effect of Have you used: This test is based on the linearly independent pairwise comparisons among the estimated marginal means.

Tables 16 & 17: Confirmatory Multivariate and Univariate Tests- these tables replicate the multivariate findings and confirm:

- A statistically significant multivariate effect of learning strategy across combined outcomes
- Univariate effects remain significant only for comprehension ($p = .043$)
- Others remain marginally or non-significant.

GOVERNANCE – ADVANTAGES AND CHALLENGES

The integration of Augmented Reality (AR) and Game-Based Learning (GBL) in higher education requires careful governance to balance opportunities with challenges. Effective implementation depends not only on technological readiness but also on institutional policies, faculty training, and strategic oversight.

Advantages

Enhanced Engagement and Motivation: AR and GBL create immersive environments that increase learner curiosity, sustain attention, and improve participation compared to traditional lecture methods.

Improved Conceptual Clarity: Complex engineering concepts become more accessible through 3D visualization, simulations, and interactive problem-solving.

Personalized and Inclusive Learning: Adaptive features allow AR/GBL platforms to cater to different learning styles, supporting both advanced learners and those needing remedial assistance.

Bridging Academia–Industry Gaps: By simulating real-world scenarios, immersive technologies prepare students with employable skills, enhancing collaboration, problem-solving, and innovation.

Reduction of Technostress: Gamification elements—such as rewards and storytelling—encourage students to interact with new technologies in a playful, less stressful way.

Challenges

Technical Barriers: Hardware limitations, software glitches, and unreliable internet connectivity can disrupt learning experiences.

Usability and Learning Curve: Students and faculty may initially struggle to adapt to AR/GBL platforms, leading to reduced effectiveness if adequate training is not provided.

Content and Pedagogical Alignment: Without proper instructional design, AR/GBL tools risk being treated as add-ons rather than integrated learning strategies.

Psychological and Accessibility Issues: Some students may experience anxiety, resistance, or discomfort with immersive technologies. Accessibility remains a concern for learners with disabilities or limited resources.

Institutional Readiness: Limited budgets, lack of administrative support, and absence of standardized policies can hinder large-scale implementation.

Ethical Considerations

The adoption of Augmented Reality (AR) and Game-Based Learning (GBL) in higher education raises important ethical concerns that must be addressed to ensure responsible and equitable implementation. Ethical governance is essential to protect students, maintain academic integrity, and promote fairness in access and outcomes.

Data Privacy and Security

AR and GBL platforms often collect user data, including learning behavior, performance metrics, and interaction records. Institutions must ensure strict compliance with data protection policies, safeguarding against misuse or unauthorized access.

Informed Consent

Students should be fully informed about how their data will be used and must voluntarily consent to participate in AR/GBL-based learning activities. Transparency in data collection and evaluation processes is critical.

Equity and Access

Not all students have equal access to advanced devices or high-speed internet. Failure to address this digital divide risks exacerbating inequalities in learning outcomes. Institutions must strive to provide shared infrastructure or low-cost alternatives to ensure inclusivity.

Academic Integrity

AR/GBL assessments and simulations may introduce risks of academic dishonesty if not carefully monitored. Clear guidelines and secure platforms are necessary to uphold fairness in evaluation.

Avoiding Over-Reliance on Technology

While immersive technologies can enrich education, over-dependence may reduce students' ability to think critically or engage with non-digital resources. Educators must balance digital tools with traditional pedagogical methods.

Psychological Well-Being

Exposure to highly immersive environments can sometimes induce stress, distraction, or fatigue. Ensuring that AR/GBL platforms are age-appropriate, user-friendly, and supportive of learner well-being is an ethical priority.

Fostering Collaboration

Collaboration is central to both engineering education and the effective implementation of Augmented Reality (AR) and Game-Based Learning (GBL). These technologies not only enhance individual learning but also create opportunities for teamwork, peer interaction, and cross-disciplinary engagement.

Faculty Collaboration

Successful adoption of AR and GBL requires collaboration among faculty members from different disciplines. Engineering educators, instructional designers, and computer science specialists can co-develop digital modules that are technically robust and pedagogically sound. Faculty development workshops and peer mentoring also strengthen collective expertise.

Student-to-Student Collaboration

AR/GBL environments encourage peer learning through group simulations, multiplayer scenarios, and collaborative problem-solving exercises. Such approaches foster communication skills, leadership, and teamwork—competencies highly valued in engineering careers.

Academia–Industry Partnerships

Collaboration between universities and technology companies can accelerate the development of innovative AR/GBL platforms. Industry input ensures that simulations reflect real-world engineering challenges, bridging the gap between academic learning and professional practice.

Institutional Collaboration

Cross-institutional networks can share best practices, resources, and evaluation models. Collaborations between universities—both national and international—support scalability and innovation in immersive education.

Policy and Governance Collaboration

Partnerships between institutions and regulatory bodies (UGC, AICTE, etc.) are necessary to frame guidelines, ensure quality standards, and promote equitable access to AR/GBL technologies across higher education.

Implementation of Regulatory Frameworks

The sustainable adoption of Augmented Reality (AR) and Game-Based Learning (GBL) in engineering education requires a well-defined regulatory and policy framework. Without clear guidelines, integration efforts risk being fragmented, inconsistent, or inequitable across institutions.

Role of Regulatory Bodies

Agencies such as the University Grants Commission (UGC) and the All-India Council for Technical Education (AICTE) must establish policy directives that encourage the inclusion of immersive technologies in curricula. These frameworks should address curriculum design, faculty training, and accreditation standards for technology-based pedagogy.

Institutional Policies

Universities and colleges should develop internal policies for integrating AR/GBL into teaching-learning processes. This includes infrastructure planning, allocation of digital budgets, ensuring access to devices, and providing technical support.

Quality Assurance Mechanisms

To maintain academic integrity, regulatory frameworks should define evaluation standards for AR/GBL tools. This includes ensuring content accuracy, alignment with learning outcomes, and pedagogical effectiveness. Independent audits or peer-review mechanisms may be introduced to monitor quality.

Faculty Development and Certification

Policies should mandate faculty development programmes to enhance digital pedagogy skills. Certification in immersive technology usage can ensure faculty readiness and improve classroom integration.

Equity and Accessibility Standards

Frameworks must address issues of inclusivity by setting guidelines for affordable technology access. Shared digital labs, open-source AR/GBL platforms, and provisions for students with disabilities should be part of regulatory requirements.

Data Ethics and Privacy Regulations

As AR/GBL tools collect user data, regulations must ensure compliance with data protection laws. Institutional protocols should safeguard student information and prevent misuse.

Suggestions

Based on the findings of the study, the following suggestions are proposed to strengthen the integration of Augmented Reality (AR) and Game-Based Learning (GBL) in B.Tech programmes:

Development of Context-Specific Modules

Institutions should design AR and GBL modules tailored to engineering curricula. Contextualization ensures that immersive tools align with course objectives rather than being used as add-ons.

Faculty Training and Capacity Building

Comprehensive training programmes are essential to equip faculty with the skills needed to design, implement, and evaluate AR/GBL strategies. Certification and continuous professional development can enhance long-term adoption.

Investment in Infrastructure

Universities must allocate dedicated budgets for immersive technologies, including AR devices, high-speed internet, and supportive digital labs. Shared resource centers can make adoption more cost-effective.

Encouraging Student Participation

Students should be actively involved in co-creating AR/GBL content and providing feedback. Peer learning and participatory design approaches can increase ownership and engagement.

Inclusive and Affordable Solutions

Institutions should promote open-source or low-cost AR/GBL platforms to ensure equitable access. Special attention must be given to learners from disadvantaged backgrounds and students with disabilities.

Academic–Industry Collaboration

Partnerships with EdTech companies and industry professionals can provide cutting-edge tools, real-world simulations, and internship opportunities linked to immersive learning.

Continuous Evaluation and Feedback

AR and GBL tools should be regularly assessed for pedagogical effectiveness, student satisfaction, and scalability. Feedback loops will ensure iterative improvement and sustained relevance.

IMPLICATIONS

The findings offer significant implications for engineering educators, curriculum designers, and policy-makers. Firstly, immersive technologies and GBL approaches can substantially enhance student motivation, conceptual clarity, and cognitive engagement—critical elements in STEM education. Secondly, the study confirms the necessity of institutional support for technological infrastructure and faculty development to ensure effective implementation. Thirdly, it highlights the role of these technologies in addressing the varied learning styles of digital-native students while making learning more personalized, inclusive, and experiential. The observed reduction in technostress through gamification further validates these strategies as enablers of psychological readiness and learner autonomy. Moreover, the documented enhancement in higher-order thinking skills, such as critical analysis and real-world problem-solving, directly contributes to improving graduates' employability and alignment with industry 4.0 competencies. The research thus underscores a pressing need for systemic educational reform that embraces digital pedagogies as core, rather than supplementary, elements of engineering education.

FUTURE RESEARCH DIRECTIONS

While this study provides important insights into the role of Augmented Reality (AR) and Game-Based Learning (GBL) in engineering education, further research is required to strengthen evidence and broaden applicability. Future studies may consider the following directions:

Comparative Studies Across Institutions and Regions

Research should extend beyond single-institution studies to compare adoption across different universities, regions, and socio-economic contexts. This will provide a clearer picture of scalability and inclusivity in diverse educational environments.

Longitudinal Studies on Learning Outcomes

Most existing studies, including the present one, focus on short-term outcomes. Future research should track students over multiple semesters to evaluate long-term retention, skill development, and career impact.

Expansion Beyond AR and GBL

Emerging technologies such as Virtual Reality (VR), Mixed Reality (MR), and Artificial Intelligence (AI)-driven adaptive systems offer new opportunities for immersive learning. Comparative studies can assess how these tools complement or outperform AR/GBL.

Faculty Readiness and Pedagogical Innovation

Further research should examine faculty perspectives in greater detail, exploring how professional development, institutional culture, and policy frameworks influence adoption.

Assessment of Institutional Readiness

Future work should develop models to measure how ready institutions are for AR/GBL adoption, including infrastructure, financial investment, administrative support, and student access.

Interdisciplinary Applications

Beyond engineering, AR and GBL can be applied in law, medicine, business, and social sciences. Research on cross-disciplinary adoption could uncover best practices and broader benefits.

CONCLUSION

This study highlights the transformative potential of Augmented Reality (AR) and Game-Based Learning (GBL) in reshaping engineering education within B.Tech programmes. Both approaches, individually and in combination, demonstrate significant benefits in enhancing student engagement, motivation, comprehension, skill acquisition, and critical thinking.

The findings indicate that while GBL often shows stronger effects on motivation and comprehension, AR provides unique advantages in visualizing complex concepts and supporting experiential learning. When integrated effectively, the synergy between AR and GBL fosters deeper learning, sustained interest, and better preparedness for real-world engineering challenges.

However, the study also underscores that adoption is not without challenges. Technical barriers, usability issues, psychological resistance, and institutional readiness remain major concerns. Without robust infrastructure, faculty training, and policy support, the full potential of AR and GBL cannot be realized.

Overall, the evidence suggests that AR and GBL should not be viewed as supplementary tools but as strategic pedagogical innovations essential for aligning engineering education with the demands of the digital era. By adopting a balanced approach—leveraging technological strengths while addressing challenges—institutions can ensure that graduates are not only technically proficient but also equipped with creativity, collaboration, and problem-solving skills vital for the 21st-century workforce.

REFERENCES

Altmeyer, K., Kapp, S., Thees, M., Malone, S., Kuhn, J., & Brünken, R. (2020). The use of augmented reality to foster conceptual knowledge acquisition in STEM laboratory courses—Theoretical background and empirical results. *British Journal of Educational Technology*, *51*(3), 611–628. DOI: 10.1111/bjet.12900

Azuma, R. T. (1997). A survey of augmented reality. *Presence (Cambridge, Mass.)*, *6*(4), 355–385. DOI: 10.1162/pres.1997.6.4.355

Bacca-Acosta, J., Baldiris, S., Fabregat, R., & Graf, S. (2014). Augmented reality trends in education: A systematic review of research and applications. *Journal of Educational Technology & Society*, *17*(4), 133–149.

Buchner, J., Buntins, K., & Kerres, M. (2022). The impact of augmented reality on cognitive load and performance: A systematic review. *Journal of Computer Assisted Learning*, *38*(1), 285–303. DOI: 10.1111/jcal.12610

Cai, S., Chiang, F.-K., Sun, Y., Lin, C., & Lee, J. J. (2017). Applications of augmented reality-based natural interactive learning in magnetic field instruction. *Interactive Learning Environments*, *25*(6), 778–791. DOI: 10.1080/10494820.2016.1181092

Chen, C.-H. (2020). Impacts of augmented reality and a digital game on students' science learning with reflection prompts in multimedia learning. *Educational Technology Research and Development*, *68*(6), 3057–3076. DOI: 10.1007/s11423-020-09833-4

Deci, E. L., & Ryan, R. M. (1993). Die Selbstbestimmungstheorie der Motivation und ihre Bedeutung für die Pädagogik [The self-determination theory of motivation and its importance for pedagogy]. *Zeitschrift für Pädagogik*, *39*(2), 223–238.

Domínguez Alfaro, J. L., Gantois, S., Blattgerste, J., de Croon, R., Verbert, K., Pfeiffer, T., & van Puyvelde, P. (2022). Mobile augmented reality laboratory for learning acid–base titration. *Journal of Chemical Education*, *99*(2), 531–537. DOI: 10.1021/acs.jchemed.1c00892

Fajri, F. A., Haribowo, P. R. K., Amalia, N., & Natasari, D. (2021). Gamification in e-learning: The mitigation role in technostress. *International Journal of Evaluation and Research in Education*, *10*(2), 606–614. DOI: 10.11591/ijere.v10i2.21365

Ferrer-Torregrosa, J., Torralba, J., Jimenez, M. A., García, S., & Barcia, J. M. (2015). ARBOOK: Development and assessment of a tool based on augmented reality for anatomy. *Journal of Science Education and Technology*, *24*(2–3), 119–124. DOI: 10.1007/s10956-014-9526-4

Garcia-Bonete, M.-J., Jensen, M., & Katona, G. (2019). A practical guide to developing virtual and augmented reality exercises for teaching structural biology. *Biochemistry and Molecular Biology Education, 47*(1), 16–24. DOI: 10.1002/bmb.21188

Ibáñez, M. B., Di Serio, Á., Villarán, D., & Delgado Kloos, C. (2014). Experimenting with electromagnetism using augmented reality: Impact on flow student experience and educational effectiveness. *Computers & Education, 71*, 1–13. DOI: 10.1016/j.compedu.2013.09.013

Joo, Y. J., Park, S., & Lim, E. (2018). Factors influencing preservice teachers' intention to use technology: TPACK, teacher self-efficacy, and technology acceptance model. *Journal of Educational Technology & Society, 21*(3), 48–59.

Krug, M., Czok, V., Huwer, J., Weitzel, H., & Müller, W. (2021). Challenges for the design of augmented reality applications for science teacher education. In L. Gómez Chova, A. López Martínez, & I. Candel Torres (Eds.), *INTED2021 proceedings* (pp. 2484–2491). IATED.

Krug, M., Czok, V., Müller, S., Weitzel, H., Huwer, J., Kruse, S., & Müller, W. (2022). AR in science education—An AR based teaching-learning scenario in the field of teacher education. *CHEMKON, 29*(7), 312–318. DOI: 10.1002/ckon.202200017

Lampropoulos, G., Keramopoulos, E., Diamantaras, K., & Evangelidis, G. (2022). Augmented reality and gamification in education: A systematic literature review of research, applications, and empirical studies. *Applied Sciences (Basel, Switzerland), 12*(13), 6809. Advance online publication. DOI: 10.3390/app12136809

Martín-Gutiérrez, J., Roca González, C., & García Domínguez, M. (2012). Training of spatial ability on engineering students through a remedial course based on augmented reality. In *Volume 7: 9th international conference on design education; 24th international conference on design theory and methodology*. American Society of Mechanical Engineers. https://doi.org/DOI: 10.1115/DETC2012-70928

Mayer, R. E. (Ed.). (2014). *The Cambridge handbook of multimedia learning* (2nd ed.). Cambridge University Press., DOI: 10.1017/CBO9780511816819

Meekaew, N., & Ketpichainarong, W. (2018). An augmented reality to support mobile game-based learning in science museum on biodiversity. In *Proceedings of the 2018 7th international congress on advanced applied informatics (IIAI-AAI)* (pp. 250–255). IEEE. https://doi.org/DOI: 10.1109/IIAI-AAI.2018.00054

Milgram, P., Takemura, H., Utsumi, A., & Kishino, F. (1995). Augmented reality: A class of displays on the reality-virtuality continuum. In Das, H. (Ed.), *Telemanipulator and telepresence technologies* (Vol. 2351, pp. 282–292). SPIE., DOI: 10.1117/12.197321

Nah, F. F.-H., Zeng, Q., Telaprolu, V. R., Ayyappa, A. P., & Eschenbrenner, B. (2014). Gamification of education: A review of literature. In Hutchison, D., Kanade, T., Kittler, J., Kleinberg, J. M., Kobsa, A., Mattern, F., Mitchell, J. C., Naor, M., Nierstrasz, O., & Pandu Rangan, C. (Eds.), *HCI in business* (pp. 401–409). Springer International Publishing., DOI: 10.1007/978-3-319-07293-7_39

Nguyen, D., & Meixner, G. (2019). Gamified augmented reality training for an assembly task: A study about user engagement. In *Proceedings of the 2019 federated conference on computer science and information systems* (pp. 901–904). IEEE. https://doi.org/DOI: 10.15439/2019F135

Singh, G., Mantri, A., Sharma, O., Dutta, R., & Kaur, R. (2019). Evaluating the impact of the augmented reality learning environment on electronics laboratory skills of engineering students. *Computer Applications in Engineering Education*, *27*(6), 1361–1375. DOI: 10.1002/cae.22156

Thees, M., Kapp, S., Strzys, M. P., Beil, F., Lukowicz, P., & Kuhn, J. (2020). Effects of augmented reality on learning and cognitive load in university physics laboratory courses. *Computers in Human Behavior*, *108*, 106316. Advance online publication. DOI: 10.1016/j.chb.2020.106316

Tiede, J., Grafe, S., & Mangina, E. (2022). Teachers' attitudes and technology acceptance towards AR apps for teaching and learning. In *Proceedings of the 2022 8th international conference of the immersive learning research network (iLRN)* (pp. 1–8). IEEE. https://doi.org/DOI: 10.23919/iLRN55037.2022.9815965

Xu, W.-W., Su, C.-Y., Hu, Y., & Chen, C.-H. (2022). Exploring the effectiveness and moderators of augmented reality on science learning: A meta-analysis. *Journal of Science Education and Technology*, *31*(5), 621–637. DOI: 10.1007/s10956-022-09979-2

Chapter 5
Empowering Engagement Through EdTech Global:
Lessons From Game-Based and Immersive Learning in Digital Education Platforms

Sonam Tripathi
Banasthali Vidyapith, India

Jitendra Singh Rathore
https://orcid.org/0000-0002-8237-019X
Banasthali Vidyapith, India

Samiksha Vyas
https://orcid.org/0009-0000-1479-4065
Vivekanand Global University, Jaipur, India

ABSTRACT

In the contemporary digital education landscape, immersive and game-based learning have become vital tools for enhancing engagement and improving outcomes. This chapter examines the integration of immersive strategies within leading Indian EdTech platforms—Unacademy, PhysicsWallah, Vedantu, Allen Digital, and BYJU'S. Using a qualitative multiple case study and thematic analysis, it explores the application of gamification, augmented reality (AR), virtual reality (VR), and interactive simulations to deliver personalized, engaging experiences. Findings reveal that immersive tools sustain attention, boost motivation, deepen emotional engagement, and improve retention. The research categorizes these strategies into thematic segments, offering actionable insights for educators and developers. It emphasizes aligning immersive

DOI: 10.4018/979-8-3373-4465-2.ch005

techniques with learner preferences and pedagogical goals, while also providing globally relevant lessons for scalable, culturally adaptive, and engagement-driven EdTech models that merge technology with pedagogy to optimize learning design.

1. INTRODUCTION

Ever wondered why some digital lessons spark curiosity and hold a learner's attention for hours, while others fade into the background within minutes? In today's fast-paced, screen-saturated world, the challenge for educators and EdTech innovators is not simply to deliver information, but to design experiences that capture attention, sustain motivation, and foster deep learning. The answer increasingly lies in immersive and game-based learning—approaches that transform education from a linear transfer of knowledge into an interactive, emotionally engaging journey (Mayer & R.E, 2021). The rapid proliferation of digital technologies has reshaped how knowledge is accessed, delivered, and experienced. Traditional online learning models, while effective in distributing content, often fall short in replicating the active engagement and emotional connection of dynamic, participatory environments. Immersive learning—encompassing augmented reality (AR), virtual reality (VR), interactive simulations, and gamified frameworks—offers an alternative. Grounded in experiential learning principles, these tools encourage exploration, problem-solving, and decision-making, leading to improved knowledge retention and richer learner experiences (Huang et al., 2020). Learners today are not passive receivers—they are interactive users navigating animated tutors, AR simulations, and competitive quizzes. Immersive learning—encompassing tools such as augmented reality (AR), virtual reality (VR), interactive simulations, and gamified environments—has evolved from a niche pedagogical experiment to a mainstream instructional approach. Grounded in principles of experiential learning, these methods actively involve learners in problem-solving, exploration, and decision-making, thereby fostering higher-order cognitive skills alongside knowledge retention (Owusu-Cole et al., 2025). Gamification, in particular, has been recognized for its ability to integrate motivational design into learning platforms, transforming passive content consumption into active participation. By leveraging elements such as points, leaderboards, badges, and narrative-driven tasks, game-based frameworks instill a sense of achievement and progression, which can be instrumental in sustaining learner commitment over time. (Nocilla & Nocilla, 2024). However, limited empirical work examines the actual integration mechanisms—how gamification, AR/VR, and personalization are embedded into platform design, content delivery, and engagement flows—beyond simply noting their presence.

In the Indian EdTech ecosystem—home to globally recognized platforms such as Unacademy, PhysicsWallah, Vedantu, Allen Digital, and BYJU'S—these immersive strategies are no longer supplementary features but integral components of competitive learning design. As the sector responds to the demands of diverse learner demographics, linguistic plurality, and varied socio-economic contexts, the integration of culturally adaptive, scalable, and technologically sophisticated engagement models has become both a necessity and a differentiator. The global relevance of these innovations lies not only in their technological sophistication but also in their alignment with pedagogical objectives and learner psychology. (Okoye et al., 2023). Empirical evidence indicates that game-based and immersive platforms not only increase learner engagement but also contribute to improved knowledge retention, problem-solving abilities, and learner satisfaction across diverse cultural and geographic settings (Beck et al., 2023). These platforms integrate sound pedagogical frameworks with compelling storytelling, adaptive feedback, and multimodal content delivery to meet heterogeneous learner needs (Deterding & Cutting, 2023).

Despite the growing prominence of immersive and game-based learning, there are some notable gaps persists while global research has validated the promise of AR, VR, and gamification, there is limited evidence on how these tools are localized for India's unique infrastructural constraints, affordability challenges, and cultural diversity (Mueller-Csernetzky et al., 2025). Current literature often studies individual tools in isolation, leaving a gap in understanding the combined, synergistic impact of multiple immersive strategies within a single platform. There is insufficient longitudinal evidence on the sustained effects of immersive designs on learner motivation, emotional engagement, and academic performance in large, diverse populations.

This chapter critically examines the role of immersive and game-based learning within leading Indian EdTech platforms, employing a qualitative multiple case study and thematic analysis to uncover patterns of adoption, design, and impact. By situating these findings within broader global trends, it seeks to offer actionable insights for educators striving to create learning environments that are both pedagogically sound and deeply engaging. In doing so, it positions immersive and game-based learning not merely as tools of engagement, but as catalysts for transforming digital education into a dynamic, personalized, and future-ready ecosystem. (Hollow & Jefferies, 2022).

1.1 Immersive Learning: Transforming Engagement Through Experiential Technologies

Immersive learning encompasses the design and delivery of educational experiences that engage learners profoundly by simulating authentic environments through advanced technologies such as virtual reality, augmented reality, and mixed reality. This approach serves as a conduit between abstract theoretical content and concrete experiential understanding, facilitating meaningful cognitive and affective connections with subject matter. Fundamentally, immersive learning constitutes a sophisticated pedagogical paradigm that emphasizes active participation and contextual relevance, thereby enhancing learners' comprehension and retention (Hutson & Hutson, 2024) . Rather than presenting information in static or linear formats, immersive learning prioritizes the construction of multisensory, interactive environments that foster deep cognitive and emotional engagement. It eschews passive information reception in Favor of guiding learners through dynamic scenarios that encourage experiential knowledge acquisition.

Immersive learning is a structured educational approach that leverages presence, interactivity, and personalization to create impactful and memorable learning experiences (Dick, 2021)

Through the strategic integration of technological innovation and experiential instructional design, immersive learning environments enable complex concepts to be internalized intuitively and applied effectively (Granic, 2022). The influence of immersive learning extends beyond traditional didactic methods, as it weaves rich experiential narratives that captivate learners and promote sustained involvement. By synthesizing cutting-edge technology with robust educational theory, immersive learning fosters transformative educational experiences adaptable to diverse contexts and learner populations across the globe (Mohsen & Alangari, 2024).

1.2 Game-Based Learning: Driving Global Engagement and Motivation in Education

In the pursuit of meaningful and authentic learning experiences, educators and learners increasingly seek engagement strategies that resonate on a deeper cognitive and emotional level. In today's digital era, game-based learning integrates compelling narratives with interactive gameplay, effectively transforming complex educational content into accessible and motivating experiences. This fusion not only captures learner attention but sustains motivation through challenges, rewards, and social collaboration (Akintayo et al., 2024). Leveraging game-based learning has become pivotal in fostering active participation and enhancing outcomes across diverse populations and cultural contexts. Recognized as a powerful instructional strategy, game-based learning combines immersive storytelling with measurable engagement metrics, enabling educators to tailor learning paths based on real-time feedback (Höyng, 2022). By integrating narrative and quantitative data, instructors can make informed decisions aligned with learners' needs, crafting experiences that are both effective and enjoyable (Baiden et al., 2022). This approach enriches cognitive and emotional investment while facilitating collaborative learning environments, offering scalable and culturally adaptable solutions for enhancing learner engagement globally.

In the digital learning era, educational institutions and EdTech providers are witnessing a profound shift towards game-based learning, driven by advances in technology, data analytics, and learner-centered design. This transition marks a move away from traditional didactic instruction towards interactive, playful experiences that actively engage learners and foster deeper understanding. By systematically incorporating game mechanics and real-time feedback, educators transform abstract educational content into motivating, goal-oriented challenges that sustain learner interest and promote mastery (Granić, 2022). While the technical development of game-based platforms is crucial, the impact of these tools depends equally on the ability to craft compelling narratives and meaningful interactions within the game environment. The power of game-based learning lies in its fusion of data-driven insights with engaging storytelling, elevating education from rote memorization to immersive, learner-driven experiences (Schrader et al., 2021). This approach not only enhances motivation and retention but also provides educators with actionable data on learner progress, enabling personalized instruction and timely interventions. Without effective narrative integration, however, the rich data generated risks remaining underutilized or misunderstood by learners and educators alike. Hence, maximizing the benefits of game-based learning requires a balanced combination of technological innovation, pedagogical expertise, and narrative communication (Dick, 2021).

By embedding gameplay mechanics within meaningful educational contexts, game-based learning reduces the complexity and abstraction often associated with traditional instruction, making learning objectives clearer and more accessible. For these learning experiences to be truly effective, they must also be memorable and emotionally engaging. Game-based learning simplifies intricate concepts by emphasizing key challenges and feedback loops that foster cognitive clarity and sustained motivation. Learner interaction and social collaboration are essential for interpreting and internalizing game-based content, as well as for maintaining engagement (Makri et al., 2022).

The true magic of game-based learning emerges when data-driven insights merge seamlessly with immersive narratives and learner interactions. This fusion clarifies educational goals while igniting creativity and enthusiasm.

In global educational environments, accurately identifying learner needs and preferences through data analysis enhances the design of game-based experiences. Such precise understanding allows educators and designers to craft narratives and challenges that resonate personally with diverse learner populations, ensuring that engagement is not only achieved but deeply sustained. However, the integration of data and narrative demands ethical considerations, as the line between personalized learning and intrusive monitoring must be navigated with care to uphold learner trust and privacy (Akintayo et al., 2024). From a pedagogical perspective, game-based learning offers measurable benefits for motivation, knowledge retention, and collaborative skills. These outcomes are supported by rich data analytics, which help tailor content and feedback to learners' evolving needs. For learners, well-designed game-based experiences foster a sense of agency, transparency, and belonging—factors critical to meaningful and lasting engagement. This dual focus ensures that educational goals are not only communicated effectively but also embraced by learners worldwide.

Ultimately, the combination of insightful data, compelling narratives, and interactive gameplay positions game-based learning as a powerful strategy to transform education. Institutions and educators that embrace this approach gain a significant advantage in fostering global learner engagement, motivation, and success.

1.2.1 Objectives

To explore the integration of game-based and immersive learning strategies within Indian EdTech platforms.

To examine case studies on how these approaches enhance engagement and create impactful digital learning experiences.

1.2.2 Research Methodology

This observational study examines the role of immersive and game-based learning strategies in enhancing learner engagement within digital education platforms. A multiple case study approach was employed as the research design to investigate diverse engagement techniques and their effectiveness across prominent EdTech platforms globally. This method allows for cross-case comparison, facilitating the identification of common patterns and distinctive practices in the use of technology-driven instructional methods (Piyathanavong et al., 2024). The case studies were selected based on their innovative application of immersive technologies and game-based mechanics to foster learner motivation and participation. The analysis draws upon secondary data sources, including platform features, user interaction metrics, learner feedback, and industry reports. Through thematic content analysis, key themes such as experiential learning, learner autonomy, interactivity, and motivational design were identified and evaluated to understand their impact on learner engagement and educational outcomes (Isseks, 2022).

1.3 Case-Based Analysis of Game-Based and Immersive Learning

Today's digital education landscape is vast and often overwhelming, with learners navigating countless platforms and resources. So, how do educational technologies break through this noise to truly engage students? How do they create meaningful learning experiences when learners face constant distractions?

The answer lies in immersive and game-based learning. Humans are naturally drawn to interactive and experiential narratives. These approaches unite cognitive engagement with emotional resonance, providing context and motivation that deepen understanding and retention. Compelling digital learning experiences are both personalized and universally appealing, fostering curiosity, collaboration, and a sense of achievement. From virtual classrooms to interactive simulations, immersive and game-based learning honor the core principles of effective education—making content memorable, relevant, and motivating. By harnessing these strategies, EdTech platforms forge genuine connections with learners, transforming passive consumption into active participation. To truly enhance educational outcomes and learner engagement, embracing the power of immersive and game-based learning is essential.

1.4 Immersive Learning That Transforms Engagement: BYJU'S

The power of an engaging learning experience is invaluable. Imagine a world without BYJU'S—the vibrant lessons, the captivating animations, and the inspiration it ignites in millions of learners. It's difficult to envision modern digital education without this pioneering platform. So, what distinguishes BYJU'S? How has it risen to become one of the most influential and beloved EdTech brands worldwide? The answer lies in its mastery of immersive and emotionally engaging learning. Since its founding in 2015, BYJU'S has revolutionized education by transforming complex subjects into engaging stories that spark curiosity and joy. For many learners, BYJU'S is not just a platform—it is a gateway to discovery, confidence, and academic success (Raizada & Sinha, 2024).

BYJU'S distinguishes itself within the Indian EdTech ecosystem through its highly polished, multimedia-rich instructional model combined with AI-driven personalization at scale. Unlike many competitors that rely heavily on live educator-led sessions, BYJU'S has built its core identity around professionally produced, animation-based content that transforms abstract academic concepts into visually engaging, narrative-driven learning experiences. BYJU'S investment in advanced immersive technologies—including partnerships and acquisitions in the AR/VR domain—to expand beyond two-dimensional screen-based learning. These strategic moves are designed to integrate interactive simulations, 3D visualizations, and experiential learning environments into its platform, thereby enhancing conceptual clarity and learner engagement. The company also leverages a data-driven personalization engine that adapts learning pathways, difficulty levels, and revision schedules to the individual learner's performance patterns, ensuring a tailored educational experience at scale (Raizada & Sinha, 2024).

BYJU'S has implemented a range of immersive learning strategies and campaigns that blend storytelling, animation, and technology to deeply engage learners. A prime example is the "Learn with Stories" campaign, which uses narrative-driven videos and real-life examples to make complex subjects relatable and memorable. This campaign successfully fosters curiosity and emotional connection, inspiring learners across age groups. Another impactful initiative is the "BYJU'S Superheroes" series, which celebrates student achievements and encourages peer motivation, creating a community of enthusiastic learners. These campaigns have generated significant social media engagement, with students and parents sharing testimonials and success stories, thereby amplifying BYJU'S reach and impact. Through these strategic efforts, BYJU'S not only delivers education but also builds a vibrant, emotionally resonant learning ecosystem (Jasrotia et al., 2025).

The 2023 BYJU'S "Unlock Your Superpower" campaign showcases a diverse group of students from different backgrounds engaging with interactive lessons and overcoming academic challenges. Throughout the campaign, viewers witness these learners' gaining confidence and enthusiasm as they progress, symbolizing the discovery of their unique potential. The climax reveals that each student's journey represents their "inner learner," empowered by BYJU'S immersive and personalized approach to education. The campaign concludes with the uplifting message: "Every learner has a superpower waiting to be unlocked." This message resonates deeply, inspiring learners and parents alike to embrace the transformative power of education through BYJU'S innovative platform (Raizada & Sinha, 2024).

BYJU'S commitment to fostering global educational equity was highlighted in their 2023 "Learning Without Limits" campaign, which celebrated the power of knowledge to bridge diverse cultures and communities. Central to this campaign was the inspiring story of students from varied backgrounds coming together through the platform's interactive lessons, symbolizing unity and shared growth (Raizada & Sinha, 2024).

It is observed that the personalized learning journeys offered by BYJU'S, which adapt continuously based on each student's progress and needs, represent a significant advancement in learner-centric education (Raizada & Sinha, 2024). BYJU'S "Learning Odyssey" campaign exemplifies this approach by combining AI-driven content customization with immersive storytelling techniques. The campaign features interactive videos, real-time assessments, and engaging narratives that bring abstract concepts to life, fostering deeper understanding and motivation. Created by a team of educators and technologists, the platform seamlessly integrates data analytics, adaptive learning, and narrative elements to create a holistic educational experience. BYJU'S also incorporates detailed progress dashboards and learning analytics accessible to parents and teachers, enhancing transparency and support (Jasrotia et al., 2025). This innovative blend of data and storytelling embodies 'Data-Driven Empowered Learning,' where meaningful insights enrich educational outcomes and learner engagement.

1.5 Immersive Learning That Transforms Dreams into Reality: PhysicsWallah

Walk through any digital learning space in India today, and it won't take long—perhaps just moments—before you come across PhysicsWallah. Since its inception, this brand has become a ubiquitous presence in the EdTech landscape, instantly recognizable for its straightforward teaching style and mission to make quality education accessible to all. Today, PhysicsWallah stands as one of the fastest-growing and most influential digital education platforms in the country (Panchal, 2024). In an era marked by rapid technological change and expanding online education, building a consistent and impactful learner narrative across platforms is a complex challenge. PhysicsWallah's approach evolved from simply providing affordable lessons to fostering themes of empowerment, resilience, and community among learners, inspiring millions to overcome educational barriers (Panchal, 2024).

PhysicsWallah (PW) has emerged as a disruptive force in India's EdTech landscape by redefining the parameters of affordability, accessibility, and quality in digital education. Founded with the mission of making high-quality exam preparation resources available to learners from diverse socio-economic backgrounds, PW has deliberately positioned itself as a value-driven alternative to premium-priced platforms. This strategic positioning has enabled it to capture a vast learner base, particularly in tier-II and tier-III cities, where affordability and trust are decisive factors in platform selection (Panchal, 2024).

For instance, PhysicsWallah's "Education for All" campaign tells the story of students from remote and underserved communities overcoming challenges through affordable, high-quality digital education. This authentic narrative fosters a strong sense of community and empowerment, as PhysicsWallah connects deeply with learners across diverse socio-economic backgrounds, speaking in a language that resonates with their aspirations. The platform's breakthrough "Path to Success" series, featuring relatable educators who share their own struggles and triumphs, goes beyond conventional teaching to inspire resilience and self-belief. These stories, combined with engaging lessons and live interactive sessions, motivate learners to pursue their academic goals despite obstacles, reinforcing PhysicsWallah's mission to democratize education and ignite passion for learning (Panchal, 2024).

PW's gamification framework is deliberately crafted to enhance learner motivation and sustain engagement. This includes milestone-based progression, achievement badges, time-bound practice tests, and leaderboard systems that install a sense of accomplishment and healthy competition. The platform also incorporates immersive elements such as animated problem breakdowns, digital whiteboard simulations, and visual explanations that simplify complex concepts, thereby increasing comprehension and retention. Expanding beyond its digital-first identity, PW has also ventured into hybrid learning centers, integrating physical classroom infrastructure with its robust online delivery model. This hybrid strategy not only extends its reach to learners with limited internet access but also strengthens its community-oriented approach by offering personalized mentorship and peer interaction opportunities. Through its combination of affordability, relatable instruction, gamification, and immersive delivery, PhysicsWallah has positioned itself as a student-first learning ecosystem, directly challenging the dominance of high-cost EdTech players while setting a benchmark for accessible quality education (Panchal, 2024).

PhysicsWallah's "Learn Your Way" initiative harnesses AI and data analytics to offer personalized learning experiences tailored to each student's strengths and weaknesses. The platform analyses user performance and engagement metrics to recommend customized lesson plans, practice tests, and revision schedules that align with individual learning styles (PhysicsWallah, 2024). This data-driven storytelling approach allows PhysicsWallah to create unique educational journeys that empower learners and enhance outcomes. The campaign underscores the importance of combining technology with authentic narratives that resonate emotionally with students. PhysicsWallah's "Success Stories" series further leverages user data by showcasing real-life journeys of students who overcame challenges with the platform's support. By sharing these inspiring narratives across digital channels, PhysicsWallah strengthens its commitment to accessible, impactful education and demonstrates the transformative power of personalized learning (Panchal, 2024).

1.6 Immersive Learning That Unlocks Potential: Unacademy

Unacademy has strategically positioned itself as one of India's most prominent and educator-centric digital learning platforms, distinguishing its market presence through a unique emphasis on relational engagement and interactive learning experiences. Founded with the vision of democratizing education, the platform has adopted an educator-driven model wherein teachers are not merely content providers but central figures in cultivating learner loyalty and motivation. This positioning transforms educators into influential public figures—often referred to as "influencer-educators"—whose teaching style, personality, and rapport with students become critical factors in learner retention. Through a range of initiatives and campaigns, Unacademy tells a story that goes beyond being just an online learning platform. It positions itself as a catalyst for educational empowerment and equal opportunity, committed to transforming the way India learns (Singh & Goyal, 2024). A statement from their mission encapsulates this ethos perfectly:

> *"We believe education is a right, not a privilege, and strive to make quality learning accessible to all."*

Unacademy also reinforces its brand narrative by actively supporting initiatives that promote inclusivity, skill development, and lifelong learning—causes that resonate deeply with learners across diverse backgrounds.

Unacademy has launched its new brand campaign titled "Learning Unlocked" ('The ad campaign is available at https://www.youtube.com/watch?v=example'), rolling out an extensive marketing initiative across multiple digital and traditional platforms. This refreshed positioning seeks to forge a deeper emotional and intellectual bond with learners by emphasizing education as a key to unlocking one's potential. The campaign, spanning YouTube, social media, podcasts, and television, aligns Unacademy with values of empowerment, accessibility, and lifelong growth, resonating with millions aspiring to achieve their academic and professional goals (Singh & Goyal, 2024).

The campaign underscores Unacademy's dedication to making learning accessible and personalized, positioning education as the heart of its mission. The essence of "Learning Unlocked" is conveyed through a series of relatable video stories featuring students and educators, highlighting themes of perseverance, growth, and the transformative power of knowledge. To amplify the campaign on social media, Unacademy has collaborated with influencers and educators such as Gaurav Munjal, Ankur Warikoo, and Sandeep Maheshwari, who create engaging and motivational content that resonates deeply with learners across the country (Singh & Goyal, 2024).

Our latest campaign celebrates the passion and determination learners have to unlock their true potential through education. In India, where ambition and resilience are deeply valued, we strive to create a meaningful emotional connection between students and their learning journeys. With our new 'Learning Unlocked' positioning, we invite everyone to embrace education as the key to their future success and growth. (Gaurav Munjal, Co-founder and CEO of Unacademy). (The ad campaign is available at https://www.youtube.com/watch?v=example)

The platform's competitive advantage is reinforced through a comprehensive suite of gamification mechanisms such as live quizzes, real-time leaderboard rankings, timed challenges, and test-based competitions. These features inject a sense of urgency, achievement, and healthy rivalry into the learning process, shifting it from a passive, solitary activity to an engaging, socially interactive experience. Moreover, Unacademy's design prioritizes immersive, real-time engagement: live classes are integrated with interactive polls, instant feedback loops, and direct question-and-answer segments, thereby bridging the psychological gap often associated with online learning (Singh & Goyal, 2024).

By combining the motivational appeal of competition with the interpersonal connection between learners and educators, Unacademy has cultivated a community-oriented learning ecosystem. This approach not only enhances participation rates and sustains attention spans but also fosters a deeper emotional investment in the learning journey. In doing so, Unacademy has effectively differentiated itself from other EdTech providers that primarily emphasize content delivery, positioning itself as a platform where learning is both a personal and a communal pursuit (Singh & Goyal, 2024).

1.7 Legacy Reimagined Through Digital Excellence: Allen Digital

Remember Allen Career Institute's long-standing legacy in India's competitive exam landscape—synonymous for decades with rigorous preparation and top-ranking results? As the digital revolution reshaped education, Allen faced a pivotal moment: adapt its traditional coaching heritage to the virtual era without losing the trust and credibility it had painstakingly built. The launch of Allen Digital was a deliberate step into this new frontier, blending the institute's time-tested pedagogy with cutting-edge immersive learning tools. Much like a heritage brand embracing innovation, Allen leveraged its reputation to reassure students and parents that quality and discipline would remain intact, even in an online environment. By incorporating interactive simulations, adaptive practice tests, and AI-assisted doubt resolution, Allen Digital transformed its offline excellence into a dynamic, accessible format that resonated with both legacy students and a new, tech-savvy generation. In doing so, it retained the emotional connection rooted in its coaching tradition while signalling a confident leap into the future of competitive learning (Khan & Mishra, n.d.).

Every aspect of ALLEN Digital's communication strategy is meticulously designed to project a powerful, cohesive brand identity—one that transforms aspirants into confident achievers. Backed by the legacy of Kota's famed Allen Career Institute, the brand infuses its digital experiences with decades of academic excellence, ensuring consistency across live classes, AI-driven platforms, and study materials.

From real-time doubt-clearing sessions to personalized AI-guided learning paths and adaptive assessments, ALLEN Digital blends innovation and education seamlessly. Through its sleek mobile app, robust web platform, and custom learning tools, the brand communicates not just a focus on test prep—but a genuine partnership in academic growth, reflecting its commitment to making learning engaging, accessible, and impactful (Khan & Mishra, n.d.).

With every touchpoint—from interactive live lectures to AI-powered personalized content—Allen Digital reinforces its identity as a forward-thinking, student-first edtech leader, breaking educational boundaries while honouring its Kota roots (Khan & Mishra, n.d.).

Allen Digital distinguishes itself within the Indian edtech landscape by seamlessly translating the legacy of the renowned Allen Career Institute into a technology-driven, student-centric learning ecosystem. Leveraging decades of expertise in competitive exam preparation, the platform delivers live and recorded lectures by expert faculty, complemented by multimedia-rich study resources, motion graphics, and digital whiteboards to enhance conceptual clarity. Its AI-powered adaptive learning framework personalizes study plans, quizzes, and revision pathways, aligning content delivery with each learner's unique pace and proficiency. This approach is further reinforced through interactive doubt-clearing mechanisms, regular diagnostic assessments, and detailed performance analytics, ensuring continuous academic improvement. While not explicitly marketed as gamified learning, Allen Digital incorporates the principles of immersive and game-based pedagogy by integrating progress tracking, challenge-driven practice, and responsive feedback loops, thereby fostering engagement, motivation, and sustained learner participation. In doing so, it positions itself as a forward-thinking educational platform that balances the rigor of traditional coaching with the dynamism and accessibility of modern digital learning (Khan & Mishra, n.d.).

1.8 Transforming Education Through Dialogue-Driven Learning: Vedantu

The Indian edtech sector demonstrates sustained growth when technological innovation is effectively integrated with authentic learner engagement. Founded in 2014, Vedantu has redefined the contours of digital education by pioneering two-way, live interactive learning—facilitating seamless, real-time communication between students and educators through an integrated whiteboard, audio, and video interface, thereby replicating the dynamics of traditional classroom dialogue in a virtual environment (Gupta & Warkhedkar, 2022). Beyond this technological advancement, the company has leveraged a sophisticated data-driven ecosystem—WAVE 2.0 (Whiteboard Audio Video Environment)—which systematically captures and analyses diverse engagement indicators during live sessions, including student participation patterns, facial expressions, tonal variations in teaching, and handwriting analytics (Gupta & Warkhedkar, 2022). These multidimensional insights inform adaptive content delivery and enable instructors to respond in real time, creating personalised learning trajectories that enhance immersion and instructional effectiveness.

To further augment accessibility and inclusivity, Vedantu has strategically introduced hybrid learning centres in tier-2 and tier-3 cities. These centres incorporate immersive 3D content, live doubt-resolution sessions, and interactive quizzes, delivered in small batches with dedicated technological support, thereby bridging the gap between digital and in-person learning. By integrating two-way interactive pedagogy, data-informed adaptability, and hybrid experiential touchpoints, Vedantu positions itself as a platform where personalised instruction and human connection converge, transcending content delivery to cultivate sustained learner engagement (Gupta & Warkhedkar, 2022).

Vedantu's promotional strategies consistently highlight the pedagogical advantages of its two-way live interactive learning model over conventional, unidirectional online classes. Marketing initiatives such as *Keep Learning, Keep Growing* and *Learning Without Limits* reinforce the organisation's commitment to making education dynamic, personalised, and geographically accessible (Gupta & Warkhedkar, 2022). The brand narrative emphasises the transformative potential of interactive engagement, often foregrounding authentic student success stories wherein learners overcame academic challenges, achieved measurable milestones, and developed enduring mentor–mentee relationships. These narratives underscore the affective dimension of learning, illustrating how Vedantu nurtures confidence, curiosity, and a sense of belonging. Furthermore, the platform capitalises on user-generated content—including testimonials, recorded success stories, and curated live classroom excerpts—to enhance its social media presence and foster community trust. Consistent with its mission of bridging educational inequities, Vedantu maintains an active presence on digital platforms such as YouTube, Instagram, and LinkedIn, where it showcases interactive moments, teacher-led initiatives, and inspirational learner journeys. Campaigns such as *Vedantu Improvement Promise* and *Vedantu Master Scholarship* further strengthen the brand's positioning as a stakeholder in student success, combining visually compelling content with narratives of tangible academic transformation (Gupta & Warkhedkar, 2022).

2. DISCUSSION AND CONCLUSION

Education has always been more than the transmission of knowledge—it is a deeply human endeavour shaped by connection, trust, and shared purpose. From the earliest gurukul traditions in India to the structured classrooms of the industrial age, learning has been embedded within cultural narratives that inspire, motivate, and unite communities. In the contemporary digital era, where learners are inundated with endless streams of content and platforms compete fiercely for attention, narrative-driven engagement has emerged as a powerful differentiator in education. The analysis of immersive and game-based learning strategies across Unacademy, PhysicsWallah, Vedantu, Allen Digital, and BYJU'S reveals a shared commitment to enhancing learner engagement through technological innovation, yet each platform's approach reflects unique pedagogical priorities and audience needs. While Unacademy and Vedantu emphasise real-time competitive interaction and AI-supported gamification to sustain motivation, PhysicsWallah and Allen Digital prioritise functional immersion through simulations and AR/VR tools to deepen conceptual understanding. BYJU'S, in contrast, continues to leverage narrative-driven, adaptive content as its primary mode of engagement, supported by select immersive technologies.

An essential tenet of impactful educational branding is recognising that technology is not the focal point of the learner's journey—it is the instrument that supports it. The cross-case thematic analysis identified five interrelated patterns that illuminate how these strategies operate in practice. Personalisation and adaptivity emerged as a central driver, with AI-powered engines in BYJU'S and Vedantu dynamically adjusting content complexity, pacing, and delivery style based on learner performance analytics. This adaptivity was frequently embedded within gamified frameworks, ensuring that challenge levels were optimally balanced to maintain learner motivation in line with flow theory. Narrative integration for emotional engagement was another prominent theme, most clearly observed in BYJU'S and PhysicsWallah, where lessons were anchored in storylines or real-world problem scenarios to strengthen affective connections and facilitate long-term recall. Immersion as a bridge for access gaps was evident in Allen Digital's AR-based diagrams and PhysicsWallah's simulation modules, which substituted for physical laboratory or field experiences often inaccessible to students in Tier-2 and Tier-3 regions. Gamification as a retention mechanism was widely deployed by Unacademy and Vedantu, whose leaderboards, reward systems, and competitive challenges cultivated repeated platform use and reinforced mastery over time. Finally, scalability and accessibility considerations were evident across all platforms, with mobile-first designs, bandwidth-optimised resources, and simplified user interfaces ensuring that immersive learning remained inclusive despite infrastructure disparities.

The time-tested principle, "Facts tell, stories sell," remains equally relevant in the education sector, yet contemporary EdTech brands have the opportunity to elevate this concept further. By harnessing the power of learning analytics, engagement metrics, and social media insights, these platforms can remain closely aligned with students' evolving aspirations, challenges, and expectations, ensuring that their narratives are both relevant and impactful (Sikora, Chernykh, Shatorost, Danylyuk, & Chemerys, 2024). While the art of storytelling has always been central to building trust and motivation in education, advancements in digital technology and interactive media have transformed how these stories are told (Gautam, 2024). Brand storytelling in EdTech is now shaped by trends that prioritise personalisation, inclusivity, and authenticity—integrating voices from diverse learner communities and educator networks (Gautam, 2024). The strategic use of performance data, behavioural insights, and feedback loops not only refines content delivery but also enhances the emotional resonance of the brand message. This fusion of data-driven precision and human-centred storytelling enables EdTech companies to craft narratives that are not only aspirational but also demonstrably effective, positioning them as credible, empathetic, and transformative forces within the modern learning ecosystem (Adeoye & Otemuyiwa, 2024).

As a result, there will be a shift not only from prioritising content delivery to emphasising learner-centric creative development, but also in how EdTech platforms engage with their audiences. The integration of traditional pedagogical storytelling techniques with emerging technologies—such as Artificial Intelligence (AI), Virtual Reality (VR), Augmented Reality (AR), and advanced learning analytics—will redefine the educational narrative landscape (Adeoye & Otemuyiwa, 2024). These findings carry important implications for both national and global EdTech practice. The cultural adaptability of immersive learning strategies emerges as a decisive factor for large-scale deployment, demonstrating that technology can be contextualised to local languages, socio-economic realities, and curricular frameworks without compromising global pedagogical standards. However, the scalability of high-fidelity immersive tools remains constrained in bandwidth-limited or low-resource environments, underscoring the need for lightweight, mobile-optimised solutions (Gautam,2024). Positioned at the intersection of empirical data (reality) and creative pedagogy (imagination), this emerging discipline will engage both the cognitive and emotional dimensions of learning, thereby enhance educational impact and strengthen the human connection within digital learning ecosystems (Gautam, 2024).

The future of storytelling in EdTech holds significant transformative potential as emerging technologies increasingly shape personalised and impactful learning experiences. By combining immersive media such as Virtual Reality (VR), Augmented Reality (AR), and Artificial Intelligence (AI) with data-driven insights, platforms can elevate learner engagement and comprehension to unprecedented levels (Paskevicius, 2023). From a global perspective, these cases illustrate that successful integration of immersive strategies depends on balancing technological sophistication with pedagogical intentionality. While advanced AR/VR can generate immediate engagement, its educational value is maximised only when paired with coherent learning objectives, culturally resonant narratives, and adaptive feedback mechanisms. The principles demonstrated by Indian platforms—particularly cost optimisation, mobile-first design, and community-based gamification—offer valuable lessons for EdTech initiatives in other developing and emerging markets. (Paskevicius, 2023).

This chapter offers critical insights for EdTech practitioners, highlighting thematic strategies that enable the creation of learner-centric narratives grounded in data-driven insights. In conclusion, immersive and game-based learning in digital education is not a transient technological trend, but a converging discipline that blends experience design, cognitive science, and cultural adaptation. The evidence from Indian EdTech platforms suggests that when these elements are strategically aligned, the result is a scalable, engagement-driven learning model capable of transcending geographical boundaries. Future research should continue to investigate the cognitive, behavioural, and socio-cultural dimensions of these strategies, ensuring that immersive learning not only captures attention but also delivers meaningful, lasting transformations in learning outcomes. Collectively, these implications position narrative-led, technology-enhanced approaches as a driving force in the future of global education, bridging the gap between innovation and human connection.

REFERENCES

Adeoye, M. A., & Otemuyiwa, B. I. (2024). Navigating the Future: Strategies of EdTech Companies in Driving Educational Transformation. JERIT. *Journal of Educational Research and Innovation Technology, 1*(1), 43–50.

Akintayo, O. T., Eden, C. A., Ayeni, O. O., & Onyebuchi, N. C. (2024). Evaluating the impact of educational technology on learning outcomes in the higher education sector: A systematic review. *International Journal of Management & Entrepreneurship Research, 6*(5), 1395–1422.

Baiden, P., Essel, H. B., Vlachopoulos, D., Tachie-Menson, A., & Essuman, M. A. (2022). The effect of gamification on home economics students' motivation and engagement in drawing activities. *Technology. Knowledge and Learning, 27*(1), 161–182.

Beck, D., Morgado, L., & O'Shea, P. (2023). Educational practices and strategies with immersive learning environments: Mapping of reviews for using the metaverse. *IEEE Transactions on Learning Technologies, 17*, 319–341.

Deterding, S., & Cutting, J. (2023). Objective difficulty-skill balance impacts perceived balance but not behaviour: A test of flow and self-determination theory predictions. *Proceedings of the ACM on Human-Computer Interaction, 7*(CHI PLAY), 1179-1205.

Dick, E. (2021). *The promise of immersive learning*. Information Technology & Innovation Foundation.

Gautam, D. (2024). Revolutionizing Education through Innovative Technological Solutions. As the editors of Transforming Learning. *Power and Education*, •••, 60.

Granić, A. (2022). Educational technology adoption: A systematic review. *Education and Information Technologies, 27*(7), 9725–9744. PMID: 35399780

Gupta, M. S., & Warkhedkar, M. P. (2022). A Study of Impact of Edtech Companies on Education with Special Reference to Byjus and Vedantu. J. of Education: Rabindra Bharati University.

Hollow, D., & Jefferies, K. (2022). *How EdTech can be used to help address the global learning crisis: A challenge to the sector for an evidence-driven future.* EdTech Hub.

Höyng, M. (2022). Encouraging gameful experience in digital game-based learning: A double-mediation model of perceived instructional support, group engagement, and flow. *Computers & Education, 179*, 104408.

Huang, H. Y., Lin, Y. C. D., Li, J., Huang, K. Y., Shrestha, S., Hong, H. C., & Huang, H. D. (2020). miRTarBase 2020: Updates to the experimentally validated microRNA–target interaction database. *Nucleic Acids Research, 48*(D1), D148–D154. PMID: 31647101

Hutson, J., & Hutson, P. (2024). Immersive technologies. In *Inclusive smart museums: Engaging neurodiverse audiences and enhancing cultural heritage* (pp. 153–228). Springer Nature Switzerland.

Isseks, M. (2022). *Engagement with EdTech: A Case Study on Student and Teacher Perceptions of Instructional Technology on Student Engagement in Middle School English Language Arts Classrooms* (Doctoral dissertation, State University of New York at Buffalo).

Jasrotia, S. S., Kamila, M. K., Chib, S., & Raj, V. A. (2025). BYJU'S–The Indian edtech giant under dark skies: Can they survive? *Journal of Information Technology Teaching Cases*, 20438869251347635.

Khan, M. A. M., & Mishra, D. C. Digital Sales and Marketing: A Study of Private Coaching Industry.

Makri, A., Vlachopoulos, D., & Martina, R. A. (2022). *Digital escape rooms as innovative pedagogical tools in education: a systematic literature review. Sustainability 13, 4587 (2021).*

Mayer, R. E. (2021). Evidence-based principles for how to design effective instructional videos. *Journal of Applied Research in Memory and Cognition, 10*(2), 229–240.

Mohsen, M. A., & Alangari, T. S. (2024). Analyzing two decades of immersive technology research in education: Trends, clusters, and future directions. *Education and Information Technologies, 29*(3), 3571–3587.

Mueller-Csernetzky, P., Malakhatka, E., Thuvander, L., Kragic, D., & Kabo, J. (2025). Technological Frontiers in Education: Exploring the Impact of AI and Immersive Learning. In *Human-Technology Interaction: Interdisciplinary Approaches and Perspectives* (pp. 291–328). Springer Nature Switzerland.

Nocilla, S., & Nocilla, M. (2024). Empowering Learning Through Game Creation: Investigating the Impact of Educational Technology on Learners' Engagement and Attainment Level in Subject-Based Game Design (Phase I). MCAST Journal of Applied Research & Practice, 8(1), 203-22

Okoye, K., Hussein, H., Arrona-Palacios, A., Quintero, H. N., Ortega, L. O. P., Sanchez, A. L., & Hosseini, S. (2023). Impact of digital technologies upon teaching and learning in higher education in Latin America: An outlook on the reach, barriers, and bottlenecks. *Education and Information Technologies*, *28*(2), 2291–2360. PMID: 35992366

Owusu-Cole, C., Entsie, N. Y., Bosu, L., Akore Sarpong, E., & Kwadwo Mensah, E. (2025). Exploring educational technology dynamics: A dive into student engagement and educator empowerment. *Cogent Education*, *12*(1), 2477366.

Panchal, N. (2024). The Indian Edtech Evolution: From Boom to Struggle and the Path Forward. *Open Access Cases, 1*(2).

Paskevicius, M. (2023). Empowering future educators: Leveraging openness by design when integrating technology in teacher education programs. Edutec. *Revista Electrónica de Tecnología Educativa*, (85), 103–119.

Piyathanavong, V., Huynh, V. N., Karnjana, J., & Olapiriyakul, S. (2024). Role of project management on Sustainable Supply Chain development through Industry 4.0 technologies and Circular Economy during the COVID-19 pandemic: A multiple case study of Thai metals industry. *Operations Management Research*, *17*(1), 13–37. DOI: 10.1007/s12063-022-00283-7

Raizada, A., & Sinha, S. (2024). The falling star: What went wrong with BYJU'S? *Journal of Information Technology Teaching Cases*, 20438869251329034.

Schrader, C., Kalyuga, S., & Plass, J. L. (2021). *Motivation and affect in multimedia learning*. Cambridge University Press.

Sikora, Y., Chernykh, V., Shaforost, Y., Danylyuk, S., & Chemerys, I. (2024). Leveraging gamification and game-based technologies for educational purposes. Multidisciplinary Reviews, 7.

Singh, B., & Goyal, S. (2024). "Unacademy": Journey from online disruptor to omnichannel EdTech. *Emerald Emerging Markets Case Studies*, *14*(4), 1–35.

Chapter 6
Using Minecraft as a Virtual Simulation for Aural Music Theory Instruction:
Singing in the Sandbox

Sarah Espinosa
University of Hawaii-Manoa, USA

Peter Leong
https://orcid.org/0000-0003-1549-0893
University of Hawaii-Manoa, USA

ABSTRACT

Traditionally, music educators used "drill and practice" methods for aural music theory skills. Nowadays, many educators are looking towards virtual reality to provide a novel learning approach. An aural music theory virtual simulation, The Crafter's Ear, was developed in Minecraft for music educators to use with beginning music students. This chapter describes the development of The Crafter's Ear simulation and assessment of its user satisfaction for insights into the usefulness and limitations of virtual simulations in music education. Qualitative data was collected from music teachers and analyzed to provide insights into music educators' views on virtual simulation for music classrooms. The user satisfaction results were mixed. Most participants felt that they did not have the time or the ability to develop a complex simulation like this. However, they would readily utilize a pre-made simulation such as The Crafter's Ear. Educators are very interested in the integration of music into STEM education.

DOI: 10.4018/979-8-3373-4465-2.ch006

INTRODUCTION

Aural music theory training has been an important musical discipline stemming as far back as 900 CE with Guido's development of the hexachord system and solmization symbols (do, re, mi, etc.) (Reisenweaver, 2012; İlkay et al., 2025). Aural music theory prioritizes logical and perceptual knowledge regarding what the ear hears musically (Pierson, 2025). In current practice, students dictate (from recorded or performed sounds) or audiate and produce (through sight-singing/sight-counting from written music notation or prediction based on recently heard sounds), what they hear from musical examples provided (Gotham et al., 2023).

Music education literature shows a tension between behaviorist and constructivist, student-centered approaches. Traditionally, music educators have used behaviorist "drill and practice" methods to assist students in the development of aural music theory skills. Despite music educators seeking effective training methods, little innovation has been developed beyond these drill-and-practice techniques (Buonviri & Paney, 2020). With the increase and appeal of utilizing smart devices, the same behaviorist methods have found their way into mobile applications such as *Scales Trainer, Aural Wiz,* and *Music Tutor*. Programs like *Breezin' Through Composing* combine core music standards with "fun, auto-assessed drills" (Kuzmich, 2015) while supplemental websites like musictheory.net, teoria.com, and sightreadingfactory.com offer more customization for the individual needs of the student (Buonviri & Paney, 2020). In their 2020 survey of 866 Advanced Placement Music Theory (APMT) teachers and their digital technology for aural skills instruction, Buonviri and Paney (2020) found that 91% of participants across 48 states utilized technology from these types of websites, software programs, and mobile apps both inside and outside of the classroom, and cited particular challenges in widespread and consistent use such as accessibility, program limitation, cost, access and hardware/software issues. Even under the guise of new technology, these and similar applications and programs utilize the same method, essentially serving as auditory flashcards. While drill and practice cannot be entirely replaced, aural music theory training can be delivered in new and innovative ways, combining game-based and student-centered learning strategies.

Beginning music students need to develop pitch recognition in order to perform vocally or instrumentally. This affects their ability to play the right notes and to play those notes in tune, as well as understand the relationship of the sound to others in joint performance.

> *Children learn music in markedly the same way that they learn a language. In order to form a listening vocabulary in music, children must first be exposed to sounds and the musical syntax of the culture. This is a similar process to how the listening vocabulary develops in children's native language.... In order to*

learn to speak, children informally listen to people talk all day long; this language learning even begins in the womb. Similarly, children acquire musical knowledge and a means of sharing it (singing or chanting), through human, and in this case, specifically human musical interaction (Hornbach, 2015, p. 182).

Music educators are the key facilitators of this musical language acquisition. Music is an aural art form. Using and appreciating it requires skills in "perception, cognition, memory, understanding, discrimination, uses and functions, judgment, and valuing" (Haak, 1992, p. 463). Music students are exposed to music theory and aural skills visually, aurally, and kinesthetically to improve the students' ability to read music, memorize, identify errors, and make independent performance choices (Pierson, 2025).

With technology enhancing today's classrooms, many educators are now looking towards virtual reality to provide a novel, alternative learning approach to students using a constructivist framework. Constructivist frameworks emphasize active knowledge construction, where learners engage, manipulate, test, evaluate, and apply concepts in problem-solving environments (Benton, 2013; Dezuanni et al., 2015; Kibici, 2022; Gong & Wang, 2023). Music ear training approaches have recently implemented constructivist frameworks through integration of 21st century skills' 4Cs model (İlkay et al., 2025) and 5E instructional model (Kibici, 2022), as well as technology-driven curriculum using playful, student-manipulated tasks in music education (Gong & Wang, 2023).

The division between behaviorism and constructivism mirrors a broader debate in digital pedagogy. Should technology replicate paper-and-pencils drills, or should it create immersive, participatory experiences? Virtual reality and sandbox games like *Minecraft* point toward the latter, aligning with transformational play theory (Barab et al., 2012, as cited in Pellas & Mystakidis, 2020). Minecraft's manipulable and multimodal virtual world allows abstract music theory exploration as a contribution to the ongoing evolution toward student-centered, immersive aural pedagogy.

Minecraft has gained popularity with K-12 educators, particularly for math and science instruction. Minecraft Education Edition provides subject kits for teachers for language arts, math, science, computer science, history and culture, and art and design. We chose Minecraft as our platform due to its diverse capabilities and appeal, including the ability to create music through building blocks called note blocks. From its infancy, Minecraft has been aimed primarily at children as its primary population. Initially only playable on Windows, Minecraft has evolved over the past thirteen years and now boasts cross-platform play (Xbox, PlayStation 4, Nintendo Switch, iOS, Android, and Windows) from ages 0-5 onward to over 90 years old. Minecraft enthusiasts have the option to play the original Minecraft, utilize Minecraft Education for teaching and learning, or explore games like Minecraft *Dungeons*, Minecraft *Legends*, or Minecraft *Realms*.

This exploratory study sought to find a new solution for how teachers might be able to engage their students' listening skills in new ways that would make them think about the why and the how of music creation and performance, as well as provide alternative technology options to extend learning beyond the classroom. An aural music theory virtual simulation, *The Crafter's Ear*, was developed in Minecraft for music educators to use with 10- to 13-year-old beginning music students with the aim of enhancing aural theory and music theory training. The purpose of this chapter is to describe the development of *The Crafter's Ear* Minecraft simulation and assess its user satisfaction to provide insights into the usefulness and limitations of the use of virtual simulations in music education. Specifically, this study sought to answer the following research questions:

1) What are participants' perceptions of *The Crafter's Ear* simulation?
2) What are participants' views on the use of virtual simulations in music education?

LITERATURE REVIEW

The primary focus in most music education programs remains on literacy, sound production, and performance. Formal theory analysis and sight-singing is atypical in the middle school music classroom, and only slightly more prevalent in high school, despite the heavy emphasis in college music programs. This longstanding imbalance creates a developmental gap and presents a need for reevaluating how and when music aural theory components are introduced (Bowman, 1982, 1987; Coppenbarger, 2014; Livingston, 1982; Taylor & Urquhart, 1974). Juchniewicz, Kelly, and Acklin (2014) underscore this by showing that even directors who ranked music and aural theory training a low priority still identified "listening/ear training" as one of the most essential ingredients of musical fundamentals alongside tone, blend and rhythmic accuracy.

Scholars have argued that this imbalance points to the need for comprehensive musicianship. Comprehensive musicianship is a holistic approach for student musical development that forms what Burton (1990) described as a "musical person" through integrating theoretical, aural, and creative skills with performance. Grashel (1993) and (Cleland and Dobrea-Grindahl (2014) likewise highlight the centrality of aural development in this holistic framework. . In the Hawaii Music Curriculum Project in the 1970s, a comprehensive musician was described as having ten attributes which included the aforementioned components (Burton, 1990). These ideas have shaped curricular policy, with the attributes having made their way into current music education standards. The National Association for Music Education (National Association for Music Education [NAfME], 2014) updated the national music education standards in 2014 to align more closely with musical literacy that encompasses creating, performing, and responding. More recent scholarship has pressed this point further, calling for ecologically valid approaches that embed aural work in authentic musical contexts rather than treating it as an isolated skill (Langfeldt, 2023).

While music theory and composition standards for analyzing music are not present at the novice and intermediate levels (K-8 grade), fundamental music for late novice through the intermediate levels (4th to 8th grade) falls directly into the teacher's student age range targeted in *The Crafter's Ear* simulation. Looking at the musical analysis expectations for grades 4-8, students should be able to demonstrate the structure of music which includes understanding and identification of pitch, rhythm, form, and harmony.

The skills bearing the signatures of comprehensive musicianship are areas that can be explored alongside the traditional performance-based expectations of beginning music students. These include, but are not limited to, singing, major and minor tonalities, playing "by ear" or by hearing and remembering, and music and rhythmic literacy (Grashel, 1993). They provide fertile ground for innovation and also point to the need for pedagogical tools that can integrate aural and theoretical understanding into performance-centered classrooms in ways that are accessible and engaging for young learners.

Aural Music Theory Education

Aural skills development represents one of the most enduring challenges in music pedagogy. Musical ability and theoretical aptitude in music students are not always at the same proficiency level, often displaying uneven growth in proficiency versus their comprehension. For example, individual music students often have pre-existing musical awareness without being able to articulate the theoretical framework (notated or sung) of the music (Langfelt, 2023).

Musumeci (2000) suggests that teachers can bridge this gap by assisting students' musical awareness, showing them what they already know as they transition to more formal musical concepts. Methodologies such as the Kodály approach provide one pathway, moving learners from embodied sound and rhythm experiences to visual representation and abstract concepts through carefully sequenced scaffolding (Young, 2024). Langfeldt (2023) argues that holistic and ecologically valid musicianship encompasses sensory and motor perception, active exploration and construction, introspection and engagement.

A growing body of cognitive research highlights the long-term benefits of early and sustained ear training. A study done by Skoe and Kraus (2012) showed a correlation between adult long-term brain neuroplasticity and music training at an early age. Other studies have also demonstrated positive, experience-dependent plasticity in the brain due to early exposure to music lessons (Kirby et al., 2022; Moreno et al., 2009; Schneider et al., 2002) and the benefit of pitch and musical pattern identification across disciplines such as pitch processing in language (Magne, Schön, & Besson, 2006). Additionally, for students pursuing music at a professional level, passing entrance theory and aural skills tests are prerequisites for entering the majority of college music programs. Early exposure to these skills will not only have a positive effect on these types of assessments but also provide long-term benefits of increased musicianship, musical ability, and improved cognitive function (Burunat et al., 2018). More recently, Langfeldt (2023) and İlkay et al. (2025) have called for ear training to be reconceptualized as an ecologically valid and creative process, in which listening and analysis are embedded within authentic musical activity rather than presented as isolated drills.

The implications for music education are significant. Without early exposure to aural theory, students face steeper learning curves when entering advanced programs that require mastery of dictation, sight-singing, and harmonic analysis. On the other hand, when aural training is introduced early in meaningful and engaging ways, students develop as a musical person across multiple domains. Contemporary studies suggest that constructivist and technology-assisted approaches (including game-based and interactive learning environments) may provide viable alternatives to traditional methods (Benites et al., 2023, Galliher, 2024). As instructors seek ways to lessen the written and aural theory gap using constructivist methods, creating lessons that use metacognitive learning strategies within the Minecraft landscape may allow learners to comprehend and apply practical music theory concepts in their coursework and performances.

Rather than treating music theory and aural skills as remedial training or solely for the advanced musician, current scholarship points toward its integration into childhood music education. Immersive and games-based pedagogical tools that emphasize active listening, creativity, and problem-solving seem to support the rationale for exploring platforms such as Minecraft. This may position aural theory not as abstract, but as interactive and meaningful learning through multiple modes of stimuli (Langfeldt, 2023).

Minecraft, Game-Based Learning and Music

Minecraft is a virtual sandbox that allows the instructor and the learner to build and craft objects and experiences in the virtual world (Tromba, 2013). Compared to other virtual simulations, its relatively accessible learning curve makes it a practical choice for classroom use, even among busy educators with limited technical expertise(Nebel, Schneider, & Rey, 2016). Recent research demonstrates its versatility across disciplines such as science (Siko et al., 2011), mathematics (Bos et al., 2014) and STEM (Tablatin et al., 2023), language acquisition (Egbert & Borysenko, 2019), art education (Overby & Jones, 2015), music composition (Abrahams, 2018) and cross-disciplinary utility (Slattery et al., 2025). Teachers report that the platform supports not only content knowledge, but also 21st century skills such as collaboration, problem-solving, and digital literacy (Slattery et al., 2024).

Minecraft Education Edition (https://education.minecraft.net) extends these possibilities further by offering pre-made worlds and lessons created by educators across STEM and humanities (Abrams, 2017). These resources align with constructivist principles, promoting active knowledge construction (West & Bleiberg, 2013; Slattery et al., 2024) and creating a sense of presence and community through project based learning and role-playing in virtual environments (Story, 2014; Bissonette, et al., 2015). Additionally, it increases student motivation and engagement with material in the virtual environment (Gomes et al., 2014), and provides "complex and varied opportunities to have fun and experience 'success', offering opportunities for performative variation" (Dezuanni et al., 2015, p. 149) and creativity (Rahimi et al., 2024). More recently, scholars have emphasized the game's potential to support motivation, creativity, and higher-ordered thinking with students describing varied pathways to "success" and opportunities for playful experimentation that make learning personally meaningful (Rahimi et al., 2024)

Virtual world simulations such as Minecraft provide immersive and collaborative features that create online learning opportunities at a time and place convenient to the learner (Kim et al., 2013; Wang & Burton, 2013;, Aziz et al., 2025). It also shifts the traditional teacher role towards more student-centered learning in a social, communicative, interactive environment (Englund, 2017). Minecraft provides simultaneous online and 'real world' interactions between students through social gameplay (Pettersen et al., 2025, Dezuanni, O'Mara, & Beavis, 2015) and like other games, provides experiential learning and experiences within a safe digital environment to explore, think, and try (Kapp, 2015). Importantly, systematic reviews confirm that Minecraft's affordances align with theories of transformational play where learners not only manipulate virtual spaces but take on meaningful roles that connect knowledge with authentic contexts (Barab et al. 2012, as cited in Pellas & Mystakidis, 2020)

Additionally, teachers who used Minecraft Edu (the previous educational Minecraft platform) expressed that it played a critical role in aiding students in engagement, applying higher-order learning skills, and reaching desired learning outcomes through creating authentic tasks in the game. Minecraft's affordances and its ability to accommodate varying learning abilities made it the ideal environment for developing a musical and aural theory simulation in a game-based learning environment (Callaghan, 2016).

Minecraft has a unique building feature that allows for musical composition. Within Minecraft, the player can construct note blocks and power them from a material called "redstone" to create sounds. When strung together, they can be used to compose or transcribe music. By using note blocks, students can match the auditory pitch with a numerical value that corresponds to the scale numbers from the tonic pitch of a key. These note blocks can be tuned to play specific pitches that span a range of two octaves. The added benefit of using a sandbox game like Minecraft is that students can create their own ear training aids without the need to read music or be competent on a musical instrument. Teachers can utilize the note blocks, redstone mechanics and world-building features to apply a constructivist lens to their lessons, enabling their students to experience abstract music theory concepts through visual, tactile and auditory interaction. Such features position Minecraft as more than a game. It is a constructivist learning environment where abstract musical concepts become visible, tactile, and audible. Because of these features and affordances, Minecraft was chosen as the platform for *The Crafter's Ear,* a simulation designed to integrate aural theory into a sandbox world where students can experiment, listen and learn by doing.

THE CRAFTER'S EAR SIMULATION

While music technology is included in the advanced group (9-12 grade) 2014 Music standards: Music Technology (NAfME, 2014), it focuses primarily on composition software programs (e.g. Sibelius, Finale), performance support (e.g. SmartMusic, SoundTrap), and music production (e.g. DAWs for editing and mixing). These tools reinforce existing traditions of literacy and performance but do little to expand aural theory pedagogy into innovative or exploratory spaces. Earlier frameworks, such as Comprehensive Musicianship, encouraged studying the content of music in an organized way, involving students in various musical performance roles including visually and aurally analyzing music (Sindberg, 2009). Yet in practice, these areas often remain underdeveloped in K-8 classrooms.

The Crafter's Ear aimed to provide an organized space in which teachers could utilize Minecraft's musical game mechanics to encourage the development of comprehensive musicianship in areas that may be challenging to cover in a traditional music classroom. By leveraging Minecraft's musical mechanics, teachers could engage students in conceptualizing music, communicating through symbolic stems, and developing core skills such as listening, performing, and composing in an interactive environment. By embedding aural theory tasks into a virtual sandbox, the simulation takes traditional interval identification, melodic and harmonic dictation, and composition as exploratory, student-driven activities. Rather than symbolic transcription, dictation becomes a tactile and visual construction process through the use of redstone blocks. In this sense, using Minecraft for aural theory does not replace traditional methods but extends them into the constructivist framework to support both in-class and independent learning.

The Crafter's Ear simulation attempts to combine music and aural theory concepts and Minecraft in a virtual simulation targeted at music teachers of 10 to 13 year old beginners. This virtual simulation introduced music educators to the use of Minecraft for interval identification, melodic and harmonic dictation, and composition instruction (see Figure 1). Interval identification refers to the tonal quality and distance between notes. Melodic and harmonic dictation is a listening skill that allows the musician to write what they hear. In this case, the musician uses building blocks rather than note staves. Music composition is a skill that transfers the musical ideas of the mind into a readable form for others. In this case, the musician uses building blocks to create their musical ideas. Utilizing Minecraft as an aural theory aid is not meant to replace, but rather enhance, traditional teaching methods. Targeting music teachers of students aged 10 to 13 made sense for the age group that plays Minecraft. Many of the children in this age range are in the beginning to intermediate music level. Instrumental music is often introduced around this age as well. Teachers are focused primarily on the performance of music (ability to read notation, produce a sound, play correct pitches), so providing material for both in-class and out-of-class use that is student-driven seemed logical.

Figure 1. The crafter's ear lesson outline

Lesson	OBJECTIVES
1	**Crafting Music 1** **Basic Crafting in Minecraft** Build a crafting table Reconstruct note block diagram to virtual replica **Melodic and Harmonic Dictation** Practice intervals listening to note blocks in Minecraft Create interval quiz in Minecraft **Visualizing Intervals and Triads** Examine key elements of metacognitive practices in music theory lesson
2	**Crafting Music 2** **Composition and Contemporary Techniques** Formulate theory activities in Minecraft utilizing metacognitive practices **Assignment: Scavenger Hunt**

In order to expose music teachers to Minecraft's musical capabilities, a virtual simulation was developed to showcase the actual musical content that music educators would use with their students. The simulation was developed through the wireframing process and included zones of instruction that provided both Minecraft tutorials and showcases of Minecraft's music and aural theory capabilities.

One of the features built into Minecraft is the ability to craft or build blocks called note blocks. These note blocks can be tuned to play specific pitches that span a range of two octaves. In order to design musical exercises in Minecraft, note blocks were used and powered through red stone. The added benefit of putting these exercises in a sandbox is that students can create their own ear training aids without the need to read music or be competent on an instrument.

3D Wireframe Development

In order to create the simulation, the researchers followed a wireframing process adapted from Scopes' (2009) Learning Archetypes of Cybergogy and TREG's study (Vega, Pereira Soares, Robichez, & Fuks, 2010) in which Bloom's Taxonomy is paired with 3D activities and applications along a spectrum. Lin (2017) recommends creating specific wireframes for 3D environments instead of using the traditional paper model to assist in helping the design develop into a stronger immersive learning environment, rather than having the feel of a 2D website. The prototype of the simulation was wireframed in a 3D format using board game pieces and primitives printed from a 3D printer (see Figure 2). A wooden meeple was used to navigate through the wireframe, and changes were made to the design by shifting the location and angles of the pieces.

Figure 2. 3D wireframe of the duomo: Red stone tutorial zone

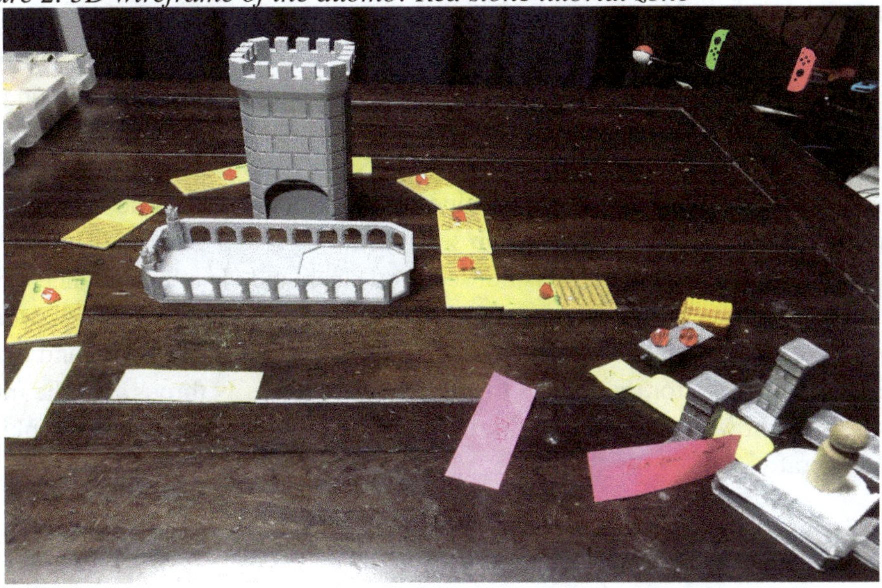

Figure 3 shows the comparison between the 3D wireframe and the actual prototype in Minecraft.

Figure 3. 3D wireframe comparison to Minecraft prototype

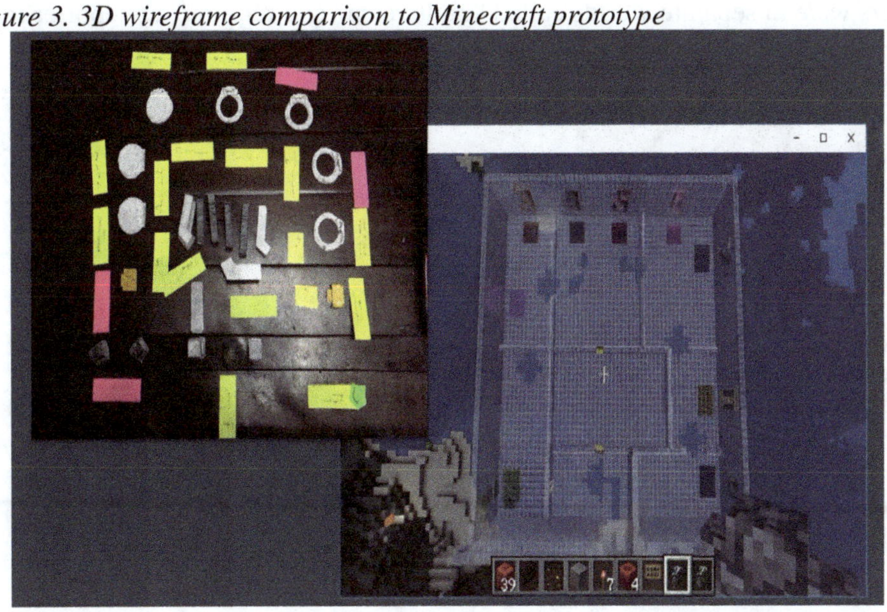

Once the 3D wireframe was created, a colleague was recruited to do a cognitive walk-through where the colleague provided suggestions for areas that needed improvement. The recommendations included creating zones for each area that would serve as a step-by-step instructional guide for developing a similar simulation from scratch. *The Crafter's Ear* simulation began development in Minecraft Java on a server hosted by akliz.net. Through the use of Spigot and Bukkit plug-ins, coding and command blocks, worlds were imported and created with the functionality designed to the aural theory content in sections.

The prototype utilized a "glass house" for a sleek and clean appearance. Eventually, nine stations of the glass house were completed, along with various worlds, tutorials, examples, and practice areas that were synced through command blocks acting as teleporters for the avatars to move freely and easily throughout the multiverse. Different worlds connected through command functions on Spigot, a plug-in for Minecraft.

Prototype of the Crafter's Ear

The player's avatar loaded and appeared at the initial spawn or home location of the simulation (see Figure 4) and walked the lighted path to the entrance of the simulation, following directional signs. This was the very beginning "Zone" and all areas within the simulation were referred to as zones. Some zones were in the same world as the starting home area (Titled: The Glass House of Learning), while others were in separate worlds called "multiverse" and required a teleporter to get to the destination.

Figure 4. Avatar spawn area of home world for the crafter's ear

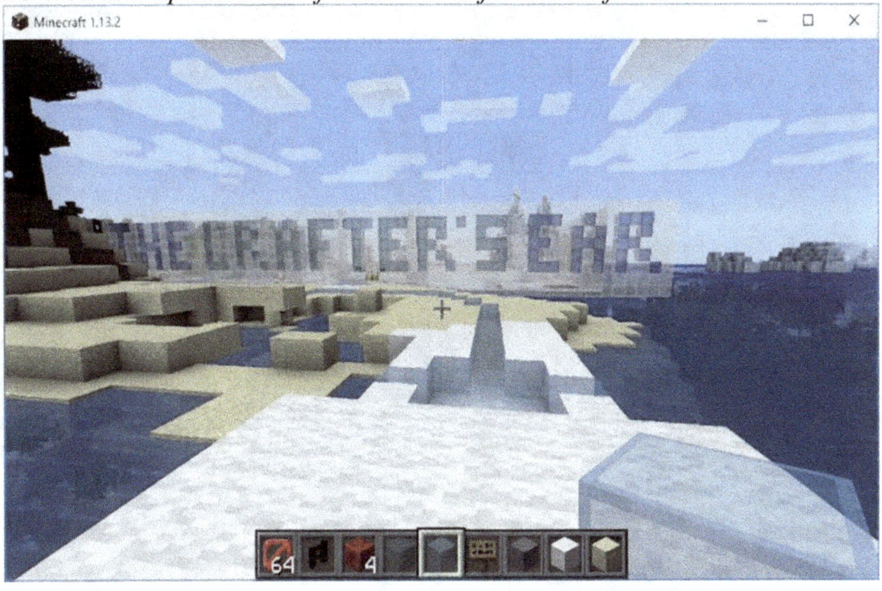

Once inside the Glass House of Learning, a welcome sign and directional markers walked the learner through expectations and directions. The welcome banner provided an introduction for the nine stations the participant could visit (see Figure 5). Teachers would encounter learning objectives and examples, how to set up their own server, how to use red stone, how to use note blocks, STEM/STEAM (STEM with Arts) examples, interval zones, chord zones, student practice, and debrief. The showcase examples in Zone 1 allowed the participant to change pitch on a single note block, activate pre-made pitch, intervals, and chord demonstrations. The simulation was set up to explore in numerical order, scaffolding what they would need to start their own aural theory server from scratch.

Figure 5. Welcome sign and directions for navigating through the simulation

Zone 1 has an overview of what would be learned in the simulation if taken as a course and functioning musical examples of pitch, intervals and chords (see Figure 6). The examples were powered by red stone and functioned by right-clicking on a stone button attached to a command block. The task was simple and required the right-click of the mouse to hear sounds played. There was no teleporter in this area because the Zone provided showcase examples of the note blocks and how they functioned to produce aural theory drills (intervals and chords). A dispenser and chest were located in the Zone to provide extra directions and a place to keep notes.

Figure 6. Zone 1: Showcase of noteblock, intervals, and chords

Zone 2 provided directions for typing commands, utilizing plug-ins, basic coding script, and setting up a multiplayer server. The tutorial did not go too far in-depth but merely provided an overview. The material was presented on a banner board and in books (see Figure 7) located within a chest. The material was presented as read-only with no ability to perform the actions, since all the material provided was external to Minecraft. Zone 2 does not have a teleporter.

Figure 7. Zone 2: Example of a minecraft book providing instructions

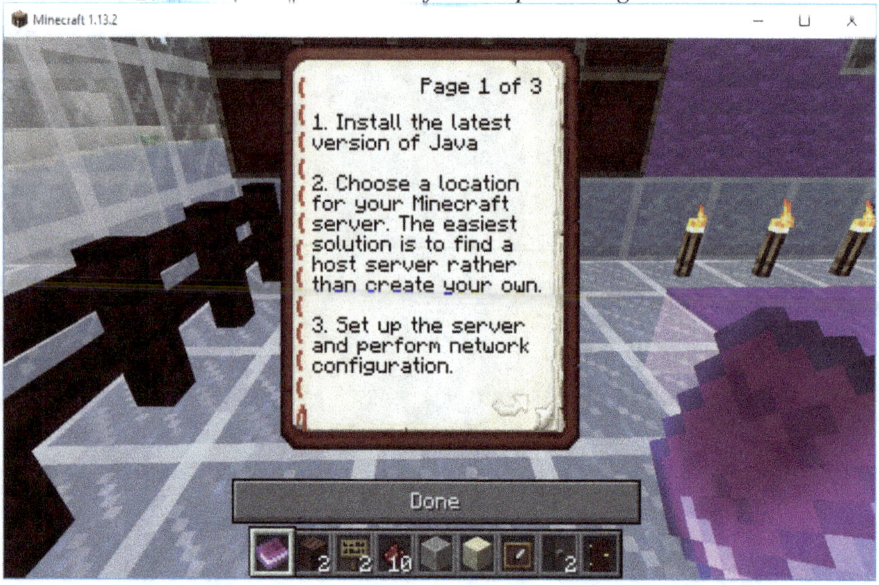

Zone 3 has a teleporter to take the avatar to the Duomo or Red Stone Tutorial Area (see Figure 8). The spawn point for the Red Stone Tutorial area was outside of the tutorial area where a banner photo of Guido (the father of music and aural theory) beckoned the participant to follow a path towards the tutorial. The tutorial explained the purpose and types of red stone material and provided a safe working area to build a crafting table and utilize redstone without being hindered by monsters in survival mode.

Figure 8. Zone 3: Teleporter to a separate world with more redstone crafting opportunities

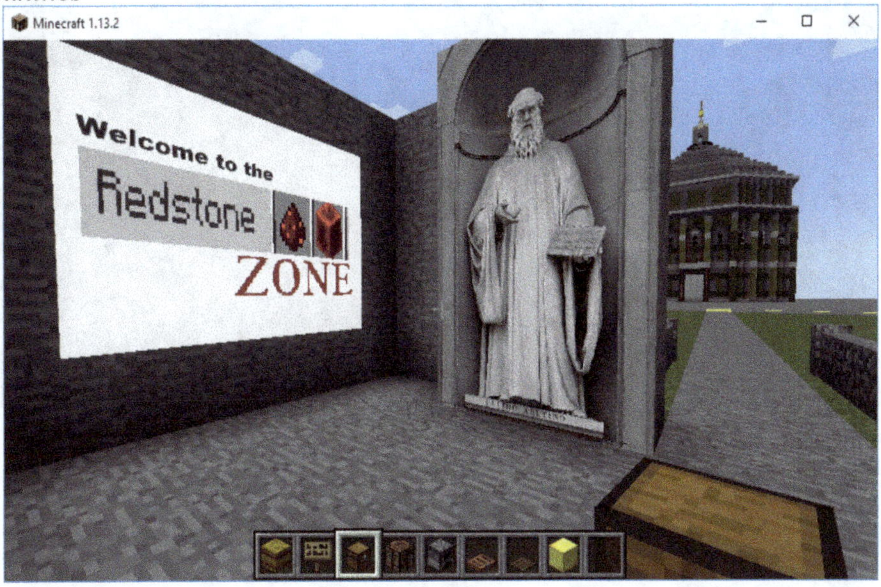

Zone 4 teleported the avatar to the Note Tutorial Zone. Here, the participant was shown step-by-step how to make note blocks function in various ways (see Figure 9). In Minecraft, the tonic pitch is set to F#, which is a difficult starting pitch. In a musical setting, the tonic pitch should be an easier note. Each note block required the pitch to be changed, so this tutorial area covered how to change pitch quickly and efficiently. The pitch changes one half step with each right click. For the majority of beginning music students, C major is the first scale learned. A book was provided for the participants that showed the two available chromatic octaves from lowest to highest and their corresponding number of right clicks to change the note block to the desired pitch.

Figure 9. Zone 4: Step-by-step instructions on changing the note blocks

Zone 5 was a showcase area which provided examples on how to integrate music with STEM and STEAM. This zone dealt with visualizing the spaces between intervals, scales, and chords. Rather than having the intervals heard, the construction could be seen very clearly through stacking half sized and whole sized blocks. Side by side comparisons of major and minor scales using the blocks to create whole and half step patterns were provided for visual learning (see Figure 10).

Figure 10. Full and half sized bricks to compare a major and minor scale side-by-side

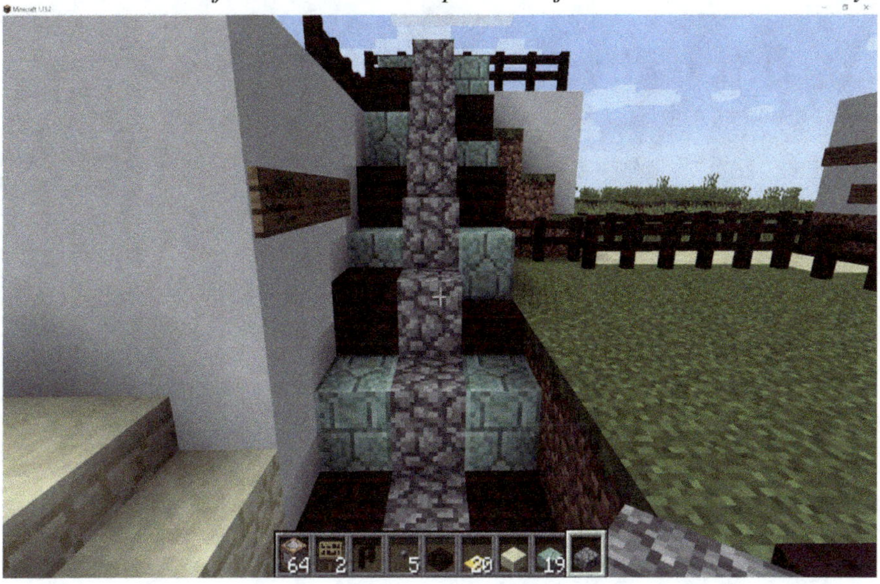

Zone 6 specifically focused on intervals. It combined the other tutorials with a step-by-step instruction with note block examples to build and set intervals (see Figure 11). Note blocks were provided for the participants, and they could follow the instructions to place the note blocks and combine them with the redstone and command blocks. They also were provided instructions for changing the pitch and setting their own interval test within the simulation.

Figure 11. Zone 6: Note tutorial provided a scaffolded process to creating intervals

Zone 7 was laid out almost identically to Zone 6 in process, except that instead of intervals, chord tutorials were provided. The participant would follow posted directions on the tutorial wall and change the note blocks accordingly to set the correct pitches, intervals, and melody (i.e., Mary had a little lamb).

Zone 8 was an example of a student practice zone where students could be paired and encouraged to create their own ear training quizzes. Example instructions were provided to show how the teacher could provide basic prompts and allow student-led, collaborative learning. This zone was void of any external elements and is identified in the game as a flat world.

Finally, Zone 9 was a quick debrief that consisted of material to read available in the chest and a prompt to exit the simulation or continue exploring (see Figure 12).

Figure 12. Zone 9: Debrief materials available in the chest and teleport to exit

METHODOLOGY

This exploratory qualitative study sought to identify issues and to improve *The Crafter's Ear* simulation, as well as to find out whether or not teachers would find the simulation effective, relevant, and appealing. All participants were pre-screened with a short musical aptitude test embedded in a survey to determine a match for the target audience and gauge the level of Minecraft experience. This pre-screening survey included interval and chord identification typically used for screening pre-music majors for entrance into a university music program. This process identified candidates who could understand the material being presented in the simulation. The pre-screening survey also asked the participants their level of experience and confidence with Minecraft. Those with novice or intermediate experience were offered a Minecraft tutorial prior to the exploratory study.

This process resulted in 18 adult volunteers who met the requirements and consented to participate in the simulation. Of the 18 volunteers, six self-identified as having never used Minecraft before, while four had an intermediate ability level and eight considered themselves as expert players. Participants were given access to a Minecraft tutorial which was not part of the simulation. Unfortunately, five of the six novice players dropped out before the study began because they did not feel they had enough time to become comfortable with their avatar in Minecraft. Two of the intermediate players also utilized the tutorial, and remained in the study. Thirteen participants, 9 male and 4 females, completed the study. All but one participant had formal music theory training. Eleven participants were full-time music teachers in a public or private school setting. One participant was a part-time music teacher, and one participant was a music education major at a 4-year university. All but one participant had a formal music degree, 9 Bachelor degrees, 2 Masters degrees, and 1 Doctorate. The participant without a degree was a university student majoring in music. All participants had experience teaching the simulation's targeted instructor's student age range of 10-13 years old.

A series of think-aloud tasks were created for the participants to follow within *The Crafter's Ear* simulation. With the participants' consent, Zoom and Screencastify were used to record a screen share of their avatar within the simulation and the audio of the think-aloud activity. Access to a Minecraft account was provided for participants who did not have an account to use for the duration of the study. Tasks included teleporting to various tutorial and showcase areas, manipulating created items or primitives within the simulation, and providing feedback from what they saw as they explored their surroundings. These tasks were followed by a short informal interview and a longer post-survey questionnaire. Understanding user perceptions of the simulation through informal interviews and open-ended responses from the post-survey was critical to determining if *The Crafter's Ear* simulation was able to engage music educators' interest in using Minecraft in their future classes.

RESULTS

This study sought to answer the following research questions:

1) What are participants' perceptions of *The Crafter's Ear* simulation?
2) What are participants' views on the use of virtual simulations in music education?

Participants were asked to identify words from a list that best described their experience using the simulation. In addition, informal interviews were conducted to gain an overall perception of *The Crafter's Ear* simulation. Participants had to choose five words from a descriptive word chart (see Figure 13) that best described their experience in the simulation and were encouraged to provide additional feedback or comments on the reason for the chosen word. In the chart below, 45 words were provided as choices.

Figure 13. Descriptive word choice chart

Accessible	Desirable	Gets in the way	Patronizing	Stressful
Appealing	Easy to Use	Hard to Use	Personal	Time-consuming
Attractive	Efficient	High quality	Predictable	Time-saving
Busy	Empowering	Inconsistent	Relevant	Too Technical
Collaborative	Exciting	Intimidating	Reliable	Trustworthy
Complex	Familiar	Inviting	Rigid	Uncontrollable
Comprehensive	Fast	Motivating	Simplistic	Unconventional
Confusing	Flexible	Not valuable	Slow	Unpredictable
Connected	Fresh	Organized	Sophisticated	Usable

Additionally, qualitative data collected from informal interviews and open-ended responses from the post-survey completed by the participating music teachers were analyzed to provide insights into the music educators' views on the use of virtual simulation in the music classroom. Overall, the themes of inconsistency and time-consuming occurred most frequently throughout these responses. These views surfaced mainly due to the lack of consistency between teleports and game mode function. The design had several persistent issues that were attributed to the use of plugins within the multiverse aspect of Minecraft. One interviewee suggested that the design would work best using only one world and teleporting strictly within that environment.

The initial iterations had low-level user satisfaction with the simulation. This was due to catastrophic issues that persisted and frustration with the inability of the users' avatar to adequately experience the simulation in the allotted time frame. Changes made to subsequent iterations resulted in an overall high-level user satisfaction. Despite these issues, more than half of the participants chose descriptors of fresh, empowering, and collaborative. Some interviewees opined that there was too much material and the simulation was too complicated, while others said, "It's a good idea," "I wish I could have learned music theory this way. It would have been more fun," and "gives students the ability to take control of their learning."

Word clouds (see Figure 14) created from the qualitative data highlight the negative and positive adjectives the participants chose to describe the simulation.

Chosen words increase or decrease in size correlated to the frequency they appeared in the survey and interview responses.

Figure 14. Word clouds of the pros and cons of the crafter's ear simulation

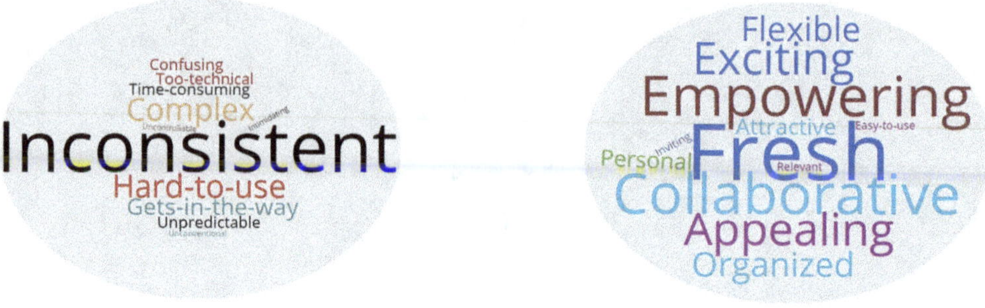

Informal interviews suggest the potential that *The Crafter's Ear* simulation holds. Most participants indicated that a fully functional Minecraft tutorial would increase the appeal and likelihood of future classroom implementation. The majority of participants indicated that if the design functioned without issues, the concepts behind the simulation were age-appropriate and could be used with their students. Eighty-six percent of the participants would use a working version if they were provided with it. About half (57%) of the participants would be willing to use the concepts to design their own project for their students. However, they were unlikely to utilize or recommend the simulation without significant improvements.

When asked if they felt the simulation benefits outweighed the time commitment needed to implement the simulation into their music lessons and the reason for their answer, most participants expressed concerns about time commitment for implementation and whether the simulation could be readily imported into Minecraft Education Edition rather than Java and paired with pre-made lesson plans. During the informal interviews, concerns were expressed about the current heavy time demands of many music educators. Several participants discussed having to teach outside of their field to fill critical teacher shortages in common core classes while others talked about having to travel throughout the district to teach music at multiple schools. External commitments outside of the classroom such as music studios and performance engagements further complicated schedules.

Whilst a minority mentioned that Minecraft itself was too complicated to use, all agreed that if a pre-made, functional simulation was readily available through Minecraft Education Edition, and paired with lesson plans, they would likely utilize the simulation with their students. Commenting on the tested Java version simulation, one of the interviewees said: "I would only use this with my students if everything was pre-made and had step-by-step lesson plans," and another commented,

"I think if you set up each area on its own with a lesson plan, objectives, and short tutorial, teachers would use it, especially for the STEM portion. I don't think you'll find many people willing to create their own lessons from scratch."

Cross disciplinary capabilities, particularly integration with STEM, seemed to hold the greatest intrigue in the response and interview portion when asked "What area of the simulation would you be most likely to use with your music student(s)? Why?" Several participants suspected the decrease in support for the arts aligned with the increase in the push for STEM integration and alignment with common core national standards. The majority of participants responded positively toward the STEM section in the simulation offering suggestions for its enhancement and uses. The capability of integration into non-musical classroom settings and no pre-requisite instrumental training might provide justification for increased support to the arts. Other participants echoed similar views,

- "This provides some foundation to those concepts by being able to build and see. I have a lot of kids who can't read music yet, and this could really help them understand and learn why music is notated the way it is,"
- "The STEM area has the most potential in my opinion. My school is pushing STEM and this is a clever way to keep the arts relevant to people who don't think they are as important as STEM,"
- "I think the STEM part is really helpful. It incorporates multiple subjects. This is a big push right now in my music ed classes."

Limitations

The results of this study must be considered within the limitations of the study itself. The first and perhaps most limiting factor is the small number of participants. Because of the small sample, the findings cannot be generalized to larger populations. However, the small sample size was appropriate for the exploratory nature of this study. In addition, it is important to bear in mind the possible bias in the responses due to the majority of participants who completed the study having significant previous experience in Minecraft and formal music theory training.

DISCUSSION AND IMPLICATIONS

Overall, Zone 5 of *The Crafter's Ear,* which highlighted STEM and STEAM connections, emerged as one of the most engaging areas for participants. The ability to visualize musical intervals and chords using Minecraft's whole and half-sized blocks provided a compelling example of how abstract concepts in music theory can be concretized through visual and spatial representation. By linking these activities to mathematics, such as interval distance and ratio patterns, educators can facilitate interdisciplinary learning that strengthens both musical and mathematical understanding. Additionally, concepts like waveform, acoustics and frequency could be paired with changing timbres of note blocks and their paired material. Teachers can provide assignments that ask what happens when you add a note block to different materials in the game. Materials provided could be concrete, glass, gold, bedrock and wood. Students can experiment with each to see the differences and write their observations. These activities align with broader STEAM education goals by fostering inquiry-based learning, creativity, and critical thinking.

While music composition in Minecraft was not showcased in this simulation, music educators are exploring modifications (mods) to Minecraft that allow for more student-led learning opportunities and provide solutions to some of the note block concerns expressed by the participants in *The Crafter's Ear*. Mods allow expansion of play beyond the original content. Beyond simulation development, modifications for easier music composition are also being explored. The creation of the mod CompositionCraft allowed for problem-solving, collaboration, creative expression, and noteblock composition that did not compromise the music or the gameplay (Abrahams, 2018).

The Crafter's Ear simulation showcased the capabilities of the sandbox environment to teach across disciplines with its primary focus on music and aural theory. That music creation and theory concepts are able to be replicated and practiced without the need to perform on an instrument allows for the integration of music into STEM education. Both music students and non-music students can benefit in a way that is not determined by innate musical ability or performance skill.

The potential of Minecraft and VR simulations extends beyond classroom demonstrations, leading towards broader curricular and policy implications. On the one hand, they provide unique opportunities for equitable access to music education. Students who may lack access to physical instruments can still engage in meaningful music-making and theory practice within virtual environments. On the other hand, adoption requires attention to issues of digital equity, including reliable access to devices, broadband connectivity, and teacher professional development. Policies at the school, district, and national levels could promote equity by funding technology access programs, supporting teacher training in MR pedagogies, and encouraging curriculum frameworks that validate digital platforms as legitimate spaces for learning.

Equally important are questions of accessibility and inclusion. Virtual platforms such as Minecraft hold promise for supporting learners with diverse needs, but careful design is required to ensure broad participation. Features like customizable visual settings, captioning or audio descriptions, and simplified navigation modes can make these environments more accessible to students with disabilities. In addition, teachers should be supported in creating culturally relevant and inclusive content, so that music-making activities reflect the diverse traditions, identities, and experiences of students. Ethical considerations also surfacc in rclation to data privacy, screen time, and equitable representation of learners in digital spaces. These issues should be central to both design and policy conversations.

Looking forward, Minecraft and VR simulations like *The Crafter's Ear* point toward future directions in curriculum design. First, immersive platforms can help reframe music education standards to emphasize creativity, collaboration, and multimodal learning rather than performance-only benchmarks. Second, integrating VR-based activities into national and state curriculum standards can support recognition of digital music pedagogy as a valid instructional pathway. Finally, ongoing collaboration between policymakers, educators, and developers will be essential to ensure these technologies are not simply add-ons but are embedded into long-term educational strategies that address accessibility, inclusivity, and ethical use.

The Crafter's Ear illustrates the transformative potential of Minecraft to serve as both a music theory tool and a STEAM learning environment. By combining playful exploration with rigorous conceptual practice, the simulation demonstrates how virtual platforms can expand the scope of music education, promote inclusive practices, and inform the future of curriculum development in an increasingly digital age.

CONCLUSION

In conclusion, while this study successfully developed a novel way of teaching aural music theory using *The Crafter's Ear* virtual simulation in Minecraft for music educators to use with 10- to 13-year-old beginning music students, the user satisfaction results were mixed. Most participants felt that they did not have the time or the ability to develop a complex simulation like this. However, they would readily utilize a pre-made simulation such as *The Crafter's Ear* if available on their preferred platform, Minecraft Education Edition. It was evidently clear that the majority of participants preferred the use of the Minecraft Education Edition rather than the Java version. Moving forward, serious consideration on which platform, Minecraft Java or Education Edition to use needs to be determined by the researchers. This study hopes to encourage music teachers to create a larger presence in the Minecraft education community with lesson plans and tutorials that are readily accessible for combining music and STEM. There are fewer than ten lessons currently available (July 2025) that directly focus on music education.

By offering a full simulation walkthrough, including design, instructional goals, and empirical feedback, it serves as a practical guide for other educators interested in developing or using similar tools. The simulation's focus on cross-curricular integration makes it especially relevant in today's educational climate where the arts are increasingly expected to justify their existence and content through STEM alignment. Students can internalize abstract musical concepts in meaningful ways through the use of a virtual world learning environment, such as Minecraft, when positioned in a functional and purposeful manner making full use of its virtual and creative functions that are more limited in the real-world classroom. As this chapter is among the first to present Minecraft as a viable platform for teaching aural music theory in the early-middle/middle grades, it is our hope that teachers will appreciate the potential use of Minecraft both in the music classroom and through integration with STEM and be willing to try it in their own classes.

REFERENCES

Abrahams, D. (2018). Engaging music students through Minecraft. In *ICERI 2018 proceedings* (pp. 1916–1921). IATED., DOI: 10.21125/iceri.2018.0142

Abrams, S. S. (2017). Emotionally crafted experiences: Layering literacies in Minecraft. *The Reading Teacher*, *70*(4), 501–506. DOI: 10.1002/trtr.1515

Aziz, F., Li, C., & Khan, A. U. (2025). Immersive learning in virtual worlds: A two-step analysis SEM and NCA for assessing the impact of Metaverse education on knowledge retention and student collaboration. *Technology in Society*, *81*, 102871. DOI: 10.1016/j.techsoc.2025.102871

Benites, D. A. M., Villate, R. C., & Gouyon, F. (2023). Ear training applications in music education: A case study of music students in France. In *Proceedings of the 15th International Conference on Computer Supported Education (CSEDU 2023)* (pp. 381–388). SCITEPRESS. https://doi.org/DOI: 10.5220/0012054200003492

Benton, C. (2013). Promoting metacognition in music classes. *Music Educators Journal*, *100*(2), 52–59. DOI: 10.1177/0027432113495625

Bissonette, J., Dubé, F., Provencher, M., & Morena Sala, M. (2015). Virtual reality exposure training for musicians: Its effect on performance anxiety and quality. *Medical Problems of Performing Artists*, *30*(3), 169–177. DOI: 10.21091/mppa.2015.3035 PMID: 26395619

Bos, B., Wilder, L., Cook, M., & O'Donnell, R. (2014). Learning mathematics through Minecraft. *Teaching Children Mathematics*, *21*(1), 56–59. DOI: 10.5951/teacchilmath.21.1.0056

Bowman, J. (1982). Please teach music theory in high school: A rebuttal of Earl Henry's "Please stop teaching college theory in high school." *American Music Teacher, 32*(1), 34–35. https://www.jstor.org/stable/43543846

Bowman, J. (1987). Bridging the gap: Preparing students for college music theory. *Music Educators Journal*, *73*(8), 49–53. https://www.jstor.org/stable/3400244

Buonviri, N. O., & Paney, A. S. (2020). Technology use in high school aural skills instruction. *International Journal of Music Education*, *38*(3), 431–440.

Burton, L. (1990). Comprehensive musicianship: The Hawaii music curriculum project. *The Quarterly Journal of Music Teaching and Learning*, *1*(3), 67–76. DOI: 10.1177/875512339801700106

Burunat, I., Brattico, E., Hartmann, M., Vuust, P., Särkämö, T., & Toiviainen, P. (2018). Musical training predicts cerebello-hippocampal coupling during music listening. *Psychomusicology: Music, Mind, and Brain*, *28*(3), 152–163. DOI: 10.1037/pmu0000215

Callaghan, N. (2016). Investigating the role of Minecraft in educational learning environments. *Educational Media International*, *53*(4), 244–260. DOI: 10.1080/09523987.2016.1254877

Cleland, K. D., & Dobrea-Grindahl, M. (2014). *Developing musicianship through aural skills: A holistic approach to sight singing and ear training* (2nd ed.). Routledge.

Coppenbarger, B. (2014). *Music theory secrets: 94 strategies for the starting musician*. Rowman & Littlefield.

Dezuanni, M., O'Mara, J., & Beavis, C. (2015). "Redstone is like electricity": Children's performative representations in and around Minecraft. *E-Learning and Digital Media*, *12*(2), 147–163. DOI: 10.1177/2042753014568176

Egbert, J., & Borysenko, N. (2019). Standards, engagement, and Minecraft: Optimizing experiences in language teacher education. *Teaching and Teacher Education*, *85*, 115–124. DOI: 10.1016/j.tate.2019.06.015

Englund, C. (2017). Exploring approaches to teaching in three-dimensional virtual worlds. *The International Journal of Information and Learning Technology*, *34*(2), 140–151. DOI: 10.1108/IJILT-09-2016-0045

Galliher, A. (2024). Engaging aural skills students with model-eliciting activities. *Journal of Music Theory Pedagogy*, *38*(1), 67–94. https://digitalcollections.lipscomb.edu/cgi/viewcontent.cgi?article=1470&context=jmtp

Gomes, J., Figueiredo, M., & Amante, L. (2014). Musical journey: A virtual world gamification experience for music learning. *International Journal on Advances in Education Research*, *1*(1), 1–21.

Gong, L., & Wang, J. (2023). Interactive Learning Environment for Effective Music Learning in Chinese Primary and Secondary Schools. *Sustainability*, *15*, 2143. DOI: 10.3390/su15032143

Gotham, M., Micchi, G., López, N. N., & Sailor, M. (2023). When in Rome: A meta-corpus of functional harmony. *Transactions of the International Society for Music Information Retrieval, 6*(1).

Grashel, J. (1993). An integrated approach: Comprehensive musicianship. *Music Educators Journal*, *79*(8), 38–41. DOI: 10.2307/3398596

Haak, P. (1992). The acquisition of music listening skills. In Colwell, R. (Ed.), *Handbook of research on music teaching and learning* (pp. 451–465). Schirmer.

Hornbach, H. (2015). Singing and tonal audiation from early childhood to secondary. In Conway, C. (Ed.), *Musicianship-focused curriculum and assessment* (pp. 181–214). GIA Publications.

İlkay, A., Dalmış, İ., Şen, A., & Sarıkaya, Ö. (2025). Transformative 21st-century approaches in musical ear training. *SAGE Open*, *15*(1), 215824402513264. DOI: 10.1177/21582440251326438

Juchniewicz, J., Kelly, S. N., & Acklin, A. I. (2014). Rehearsal characteristics of "superior" band directors. *Update: Applications of Research in Music Education*, *32*(2), 35–43. DOI: 10.1177/8755123314521030

Kapp, K. (2015). *The gamification of learning and instruction: Game-based methods and strategies for training and education.* Wiley.

Kibici, V. B. (2022). Effects of online constructivist 5E instructional model on secondary school music lessons. *International Journal of Technology in Education*, *5*(1), 117–131. DOI: 10.46328/ijte.241

Kim, C., Kim, M. K., Lee, C., Spector, J. M., & DeMeester, K. (2013). Teacher beliefs and technology integration. *Teaching and Teacher Education*, *29*, 76–85. DOI: 10.1016/j.tate.2012.08.005

Kirby, A., Lawrence, H., & Rowe, V. (2022). Musical play and young children's wellbeing. *Early Childhood Education Journal*, *51*(2), 267–278. DOI: 10.1007/s10643-022-01309-2

Kuzmich, J. (2015). Seamless classroom integration of national standards & cutting-edge music technology. *School Band & Orchestra*, *18*(6), 38–40.

Langfeldt, V. (2023). Holistic and ecologically valid aural training within culturally diverse music education contexts. *Nordic Research in Music Education*, *4*, 23–34. DOI: 10.23865/nrme.v4.5574

Lin, J. (2017). The design process in VR, AR, and MR. *Hackernoon.* https://hackernoon.com/the-design-process-in-vr-ar-and-mr-b34b2247520f

Livingston, C. (1982). The role of the private instrumental teacher in preparing music students for college theory. *American Music Teacher, 31*(6), 14, 16. https://www.jstor.org/stable/43541444

Magne, C., Schön, D., & Besson, M. (2006). Musician children detect pitch violations in both music and language better than nonmusician children: Behavioral and electrophysiological approaches. *Journal of Cognitive Neuroscience*, *18*(2), 199–211. DOI: 10.1162/jocn.2006.18.2.199 PMID: 16494681

Moreno, S., Marques, C., Santos, A., Santos, M., Castro, S. L., & Besson, M. (2009). Musical training influences linguistic abilities in 8-year-old children: More evidence for brain plasticity. *Cerebral Cortex (New York, N.Y.)*, *19*(3), 712–723. DOI: 10.1093/cercor/bhn120 PMID: 18832336

Musumeci, O. (2000). The cognitive pedagogy of aural training. In Proceedings of the *2000 ISME seminar on the education of the professional musician*. ISME.

National Association for Music Education. (2014). *2014 music standards: PK–8 strand.* https://nafme.org/wp-content/files/2014/11/2014-Music-Standards-PK-8-Strand.pdf

Nebel, S., Schneider, S., & Rey, G. D. (2016). Mining learning and crafting scientific experiments: A literature review on the use of Minecraft in education and research. *Journal of Educational Technology & Society*, *19*(2), 355–366.

Overby, A., & Jones, B. L. (2015). Virtual Legos: Incorporating Minecraft into the art education curriculum. *Art Education*, *68*(1), 21–27. DOI: 10.1080/00043125.2015.11519302

Pellas, N., & Mystakidis, S. (2020). A systematic review of research about game-based learning in virtual worlds. *Journal of Universal Computer Science*, *26*(8), 1017–1042. DOI: 10.3897/jucs.2020.054

Pettersen, K., Arnseth, H. C., & Silseth, K. (2025). Playing Minecraft: Young children's postdigital play. *Journal of Early Childhood Literacy*, *25*(1), 133–157. DOI: 10.1177/14687984221118977

Pierson, J. (2025). Indexed piano repertoire in support of music theory and aural skills reinforcement. *MTNA e-Journal, 16*(3), 14–29.

Rahimi, S., Walker, J. T., Lin-Lipsmeyer, L., & Shin, J. (2024). Toward defining and assessing creativity in sandbox games. *Creativity Research Journal*, *36*(2), 194–212. DOI: 10.1080/10400419.2022.2156477

Reisenweaver, A. (2012). Guido of Arezzo and his influence on music learning. *Musical Offerings*, *3*(1), 37–59. DOI: 10.15385/jmo.2012.3.1.3

Schneider, P., Scherg, M., Dosch, H. G., Specht, H. J., Gutschalk, A., & Rupp, A. (2002). Morphology of Heschl's gyrus reflects enhanced activation in the auditory cortex of musicians. *Nature Neuroscience*, *5*(7), 688–694. DOI: 10.1038/nn871 PMID: 12068300

Scopes, L. (2009). Learning archetypes as tools of cybergogy for a 3D educational landscape: A structure for eTeaching in Second Life (Master's thesis, University of Southampton). University of Southampton Repository.

Siko, J., Barbour, M., & Toker, S. (2011). Beyond jeopardy and lectures: Using Microsoft PowerPoint as a game design tool to teach science. *Journal of Computers in Mathematics and Science Teaching*, *30*(3), 303–320.

Sindberg, L. (2009). The evolution of comprehensive musicianship through performance (CMP): A model for teaching performing with understanding in the ensemble setting. *Contributions to Music Education*, *36*(1), 25–39. https://www.jstor.org/stable/24127216

Skoe, E., & Kraus, M. (2012). A little goes a long way: How the adult brain is shaped by musical training in childhood. *The Journal of Neuroscience : The Official Journal of the Society for Neuroscience*, *32*(34), 11507–11510. DOI: 10.1523/JNEUROSCI.1949-12.2012 PMID: 22915097

Slattery, E. J., Butler, D., O'Leary, M., & Marshall, K. (2024). Teachers' experiences of using Minecraft Education in primary school: An Irish perspective. *Irish Educational Studies*, *43*(4), 965–984. DOI: 10.1080/03323315.2023.2185276

Slattery, E. J., Lehane, P., Butler, D., O'Leary, M., & Marshall, K. (2025). Assessing the benefits of digital game-based learning with Minecraft in children, adolescents and young adults: A broad systematic review. *Review of Education*, *13*(1), e70035. DOI: 10.1002/rev3.70035

Story, K. M. (2014). Music therapy and avatars: Reflections on virtual learning environments for music therapy students. *Voices: A World Forum for Music Therapy, 14*(1). https://doi.org/DOI: 10.15845/voices.v14i1.722

Tablatin, C. L. S., Casano, J. D. L., & Rodrigo, M. M. T. (2023). Using Minecraft to cultivate student interest in STEM. *Frontiers in Education*, *8*, 1127984. DOI: 10.3389/feduc.2023.1127984

Taylor, J. A., & Urquhart, D. M. (1974). Florida State University: An experimental approach to comprehensive musicianship for freshman music majors. *College Music Symposium, 14*, 76–88. https://www.jstor.org/stable/40373355

Tromba, P. (2013). Build engagement and knowledge one block at a time with Minecraft. *Learning and Leading with Technology*, *40*(8), 20–23.

Vega, K., Pereira Soares, A., Robichez, G., & Fuks, H. (2010). TREG usability tests: Evaluating a training game in Second Life. In *2010 VII Brazilian symposium on collaborative systems (SBSC 2010)* (pp. 63–70). IEEE. https://doi.org/DOI: 10.1109/SBSC.2010.17

Wang, F., & Burton, J. K. (2013). Second Life in education: A review of publications from its launch to 2011. *British Journal of Educational Technology*, *44*(3), 357–371. DOI: 10.1111/bjet.12034

West, D. M., & Bleiberg, J. (2013). *Education technology success stories*. Brookings Institution.

Young, S. (2024). *Music, children and other languages*. Routledge., DOI: 10.4324/9781003331193

Chapter 7
Virtual Reality (VR) and Augmented Reality (AR) in Education:
Immersive Learning in the Digital Era

Seema Yadav
https://orcid.org/0000-0002-8477-5895
Bhopal School of Social Sciences, Bhopal, India

ABSTRACT

Education is being revolutionised by virtual reality (VR), augmented reality (AR), and extended reality (XR), which create immersive, interactive, learner-centred settings that go well beyond the conventional classroom. Immersion learning improves diversity, motivation, and accessibility by replacing passive instruction with practical, simulation-based activities. Additionally, XR responds to the needs of the twenty-first century by equipping students with critical abilities, including problem-solving, creativity, and teamwork. In order to rethink education as a dynamic, multimodal, and future-ready experience, this chapter explores the pedagogical potential of immersive technologies, their integration with current educational paradigms, and their transformative significance. It reflects on the emerging future of immersive education in the context of the metaverse, AI-driven adaptive learning, and multisensory environments.

DOI: 10.4018/979-8-3373-4465-2.ch007

INTRODUCTION: REIMAGINING EDUCATION IN THE XR ERA

Virtual reality (VR) and augmented reality (AR) are two immersive technologies that are changing the way that knowledge is experienced, created, and shared as education changes to meet the demands of the digital age (Magi et al., 2023). Immersion environments have made it feasible for learning to occur outside of textbooks and displays, inside historical events, inside molecular structures, or on simulated Mars excursions (Wagner & Alharthi, 2023). These technological advancements present previously unheard-of possibilities for developing learner-centered, immersive, and emotionally compelling educational experiences. The inventive ways that VR and AR are revolutionizing education across disciplines are examined in this chapter, ranging from empathy-based simulations and cultural language immersion to virtual science labs and AR-enhanced textbooks. It looks at how immersive tools fit into educational frameworks like Bloom's Taxonomy and Universal Design for Learning (UDL), accommodating a variety of learners and learning styles. It is based on constructivist and experiential learning theories (Osadchyi et al., 2021). A paradigm shift in the conception, delivery, and experience of learning is invited by reimagining education in the XR (Extended Reality) era. Virtual reality (VR), augmented reality (AR), and mixed reality (MR) are examples of technologies that combine the real and virtual worlds to create immersive, interactive, and learner-centered settings that go beyond the confines of conventional classrooms. This era places a strong emphasis on experiential learning, allowing students to work with peers in shared digital spaces beyond geographic borders, participate in virtual field trips around the world, and investigate difficult subjects through simulations. In addition to increasing engagement, XR promotes deeper comprehension, customization, and diversity, transforming education into a multisensory, dynamic experience that equips students for the needs of a quickly changing, technologically advanced society (Turhan et al., 2022).

DEFINING VR, AR, AND EXTENDED REALITY (XR)

Virtual and augmented reality are not completely novel technologies. However, a number of limitations hindered their actual implementation. AR and VR are now more feasible and appealing in many fields, including education, thanks to recent technological advancements and the widespread availability of reasonably priced hardware and software. They have also been reintroduced with previously unthinkable promises (Ajit et al., 2021). New teaching and learning paradigms that better suit the demands of 21st-century learners are promised by the nature of AR and VR (Elmqaddem, 2019). The perfect tool for simulations and hands-on learning, virtual reality (VR) transports users to fully computer-generated, three-dimensional worlds that they can explore and engage with using headsets and controllers. With augmented reality (AR), learners can interact with information in context by superimposing digital elements like photos, animations, or statistics onto the real world. This is usually done with smartphones, tablets, or AR glasses. The phrase "extended reality" (XR) refers to the whole range of immersive technologies that combine digital and physical worlds to produce dynamic, interactive, and adaptable learning experiences. It includes VR, AR, and MR. Augmented Reality (AR) is a new type of experience where computer-generated content associated with certain places and/or activities enhances the Real World (RW). In recent years, augmented reality programs have become widely accessible and portable on mobile devices (Yusufjanovna, 2022).

THE SHIFT FROM TRADITIONAL TO IMMERSIVE LEARNING ENVIRONMENTS

Education is undergoing a paradigm shift with the move from traditional to immersive learning environments, moving away from lecture-based, passive instruction and toward learner-centered, interactive, and experiential methods. Textbooks, static images, and spoken explanations are frequently used in traditional classes, which can reduce student interest and practical application. On the other hand, students can enter lifelike simulations, investigate intricate ideas in three dimensions, and actively engage in problem-solving inside real-world settings in immersive learning environments driven by XR technologies like VR, AR, and MR. This change not only increases motivation and engagement but also accommodates different learning styles, promotes deeper comprehension through practical experiences, and removes barriers related to accessibility and geography, eventually reinventing how knowledge is learned, used, and retained. The use of augmented reality technology in nursing education and training is highly accepted by nursing students. Since self-learning and e-learning have become commonplace in our society, it is predicted that students will want augmented reality applications as an alternative to traditional textbooks and as a component of holistic education (Uymaz & Uymaz, 2022). Users can interact with virtual objects that are real-time and integrated into the environment thanks to augmented reality technology. Technology that uses augmented reality is seen to have the ability to improve the teaching and learning process. One reason augmented reality is widely employed as a teaching and learning tool in the education sector is because it demonstrates favorable trends in education and experimental results suggest that it improves visualization skills (Ali et al., 2021).

WHY IMMERSIVE TECH MATTERS FOR 21ST-CENTURY EDUCATION

For education in the twenty-first century, immersive technology is important because it fits with the abilities, attitudes, and flexibility needed in a society that is driven by technology and changing quickly. By utilizing XR tools like VR, AR, and MR, education can cultivate critical thinking, creativity, teamwork, and problem-solving skills essential to the modern workforce instead of mindless memorization. Through interactive, contextual interactions, immersive experiences enable students to interact with difficult ideas, giving them a concrete form and encouraging a deeper comprehension. Additionally, they facilitate personalized learning, allowing students to advance according to their own schedule and preferences while offering risk-free, safe, and virtual practice and experimentation venues. Immersion technologies also enable students to innovate in the linked, digital-first future, span worldwide distances, and provide inclusive learning opportunities for a diverse student body.

Through immersive, interactive, and learner-centered experiences, virtual reality (VR), augmented reality (AR), and extended reality (XR) are revolutionizing education by displacing conventional, textbook-based approaches. By allowing students to use simulations to study historical occurrences, scientific structures, or even far-off planets, these technologies foster diversity, better understanding, and engagement. By incorporating constructivist and experiential learning theories, as well as frameworks like Bloom's Taxonomy and Universal Design for Learning (UDL), XR promotes a variety of learning styles and cultivates vital 21st-century abilities like creativity, problem-solving, and teamwork. Because AR and VR are now more widely available due to advancements in reasonably priced technology and software, education may now bridge geographical divides, customize instruction, and offer safe spaces for experimentation. This paradigm change redefines the creation, experience, and dissemination of information while preparing students for the needs of a rapidly evolving, technologically driven world. Technology has had a big impact on how education has evolved. Because it encourages self-reliance and active learning, technology is essential in education and indirectly contributes to children's intellectual growth. Examples of contemporary technology include virtual reality (VR) and augmented reality (AR). Problems should be solved in a dynamic and multifaceted way via VR and AR (Abdul Talib et al., 2022).

PEDAGOGICAL FOUNDATIONS FOR IMMERSIVE LEARNING

The pedagogical underpinnings of immersive learning are derived from existing educational ideas that prioritize constructivist, experiential, and active methods of knowledge construction. Immersion learning settings, which have their roots in constructivism, help students develop a better conceptual understanding by allowing them to directly interact with realistic circumstances and create meaning. The practical aspect of XR is supported by Kolb's experiential learning theory, which has students participate in tangible situations, think about them, develop ideas, and then actively explore. Immersion technologies enable students to study in authentic, real-world-like settings that improve relevance and retention, underscoring the significance of context in Situated Learning. As long as augmented reality and gamification are used student-centeredly, adhering to appropriate educational approaches and strategies, and taking into account students' knowledge, interests, distinctive characteristics, and personality traits, they can help students, teachers, and the shift toward technology-enhanced learning. Students showed improvements in their motivation, engagement, active participation, focus, curiosity, interest, enjoyment, academic performance, and learning outcomes, as well as favorable behavioral, attitudinal, and psychological changes (Lampropoulos et al., 2023). They were also given favorable evaluations by teachers. Virtual incentives were essential for raising motivation for studying. There was a clear need to create suitable design methods, theories, and validation tools. Lastly, it was clear that they might be used to generate individualized and collaborative learning experiences as well as to support and improve students' cognitive and social-emotional growth (Lampropoulos et al., 2023). Furthermore, through shared virtual environments and problem-solving exercises, Social Constructivism facilitates cooperative XR experiences that allow students to co-create knowledge. Immersion learning ensures that education is not only instructive but also transformative by combining these pedagogical ideas and moving the emphasis from teacher-led delivery to learner-centered discovery.

According to constructivist learning theory, rather than passively absorbing information, students actively create their own knowledge and understanding by experiences, introspection, and engagement with their surroundings. In immersive learning, technologies such as virtual reality (VR) and augmented reality (AR) offer rich, dynamic environments that allow students to interact, investigate, and alter concepts in ways that encourage their own meaning-making. The notion that learning is an ongoing process based on experience is the foundation of David Kolb's experiential learning theory. It goes through four stages: active experimentation, abstract conceptualization, reflective observation, and tangible experience. By enabling students to engage in realistic simulations (experience), evaluate and assess their actions (reflection), relate their observations to theoretical ideas (conceptualization), and apply what they have learned in novel situations (experimentation), immersive technologies are a perfect fit for this cycle. When combined, these ideas provide a solid framework for creating contextual, captivating, and profoundly effective XR-based learning experiences.

Immersion learning improves empathy, memory, and engagement, which has major cognitive benefits. Compared to traditional approaches, XR environments' interactive and multimodal elements better attract learners' attention, resulting in prolonged engagement and intrinsic motivation. Active engagement and increased focus result in better memory recall because concepts are reinforced through rich, experiential scenarios that appeal to both kinesthetic and visual learning styles. Furthermore, by enabling students to "step into someone else's shoes," or experience viewpoints, difficulties, or surroundings that are very different from their own—for example, by examining life in a different culture, seeing historical events firsthand, or comprehending environmental crises through virtual simulations immersion technologies can foster empathy. Immersion learning enhances comprehension and fosters deep, enduring connections to the subject matter by occupying the mind and emotions at the same time (Dhar et al., 2021).

ALIGNING VR/AR WITH BLOOM'S TAXONOMY AND UNIVERSAL DESIGN FOR LEARNING (UDL)

A strong framework for creating inclusive, highly effective immersive learning experiences is produced when VR and AR are in line with Bloom's Taxonomy and Universal Design for Learning (UDL). From Remembering (e.g., using AR to display 3D models for quick recall) to Creating (e.g., developing virtual worlds or simulations), VR and AR can support all cognitive levels within Bloom's hierarchy. Through interactive visualizations, knowledge application in simulated real-world settings, multi-perspective analysis of complex systems, and decision-making in immersive scenarios, these tools help learners comprehend topics. By offering various ways of representation (e.g., combining visuals, audio, and haptic feedback), interaction (e.g., gamified challenges, real-time collaboration), and action and expression (e.g., creating virtual prototypes or narrating AR-enhanced stories), VR and AR support accessibility and flexibility through the UDL framework. By ensuring that immersive technologies support a variety of learning demands and enhance higher-order thinking abilities, education becomes more impactful, individualized, and equitable (Dalim et al., 2017).

APPLICATIONS OF VR IN EDUCATION

VR has several uses in education, changing how students engage with material and hone their abilities. Students can explore locations they might never be able to visit in person, thanks to its ability to facilitate virtual field trips to historical sites, ecosystems, or cultural monuments. Virtual reality (VR) facilitates interactive simulations in STEM teaching, such as seeing molecular structures or performing chemistry experiments in a virtual lab without resource or safety issues. By providing realistic practice environments for surgical procedures, patient care, and anatomy investigation, virtual reality (VR) enhances medical and healthcare training. VR offers risk-free hands-on practice with machinery, equipment, or emergency situations in vocational and technical training (Wang et al., 2018). It provides 3D art production, historical reenactments, and immersive storytelling for the arts and humanities. Additionally, through role-playing and scenario-based learning, virtual reality (VR) helps promote soft skills like empathy, leadership, and communication. Virtual reality (VR) improves student engagement, retention, and real-world application in the classroom by giving abstract ideas a physical form and experiences that are accessible (Paramita et al., 2021).

Virtual reality (VR) simulated environments and virtual field trips allow students to experience events and places that are otherwise unavailable, creating countless opportunities for experiential learning. By taking part in historical reenactments, which include traveling through ancient civilizations, seeing significant historical events take place, or visiting cultural heritage places in their original configuration, learners can strengthen their emotional connection to history and contextual understanding. Through virtual reality (VR), students can virtually fly beyond Earth to explore planets, orbit the International Space Station, or navigate the surface of Mars. This gives them a firsthand understanding of astronomical ideas that are not possible to learn from textbooks alone. Through acti ve exploration, questioning, and interaction with realistic, virtual worlds, these immersive experiences foster critical thinking, improve comprehension through multisensory engagement, and stimulate curiosity. Virtual field trips rethink how students view and interact with knowledge by bridging the gap between theory and lived experience (Lopes & Jorge, 2024).

Science, medical, and engineering virtual reality labs offer immersive, interactive settings that let students practice, explore, and create without being limited by geographical limitations, physical resources, or safety concerns (Lopes & Jorge, 2024). In the context of science education, virtual reality labs enable students to perform chemistry experiments, work with molecular models, or view tiny biological processes—activities that would otherwise be prohibitively expensive, risky, or time-consuming. Medical students can hone their abilities and decision-making in a risk-free environment with immediate feedback thanks to virtual reality's realistic simulations of surgical operations, patient diagnosis, and anatomy investigation. Engineering students may design, assemble, and assess complicated machinery or infrastructure before creating real models thanks to VR labs' support for virtual prototyping, structural testing, and system simulations. These VR-based learning environments help students prepare for real-world professional difficulties by encouraging creativity, teamwork, and problem-solving in addition to improving conceptual knowledge and practical abilities (Šarić et al., 2024).

By immersing students in authentic, culturally rich settings where language is used organically, immersive cultural contexts for language learning use VR and AR to go beyond vocabulary drills and grammar exercises. Students can experience the sights, sounds, and social cues of the target culture by interacting with avatars in a Spanish plaza, ordering food in a Tokyo café, or digitally navigating Parisian marketplaces. By practicing gestures, tone, and cultural etiquette in addition to language abilities, these simulations offer contextual learning that promotes both fluency and intercultural competency. Interacting in real-world situations helps students build their confidence, enhance their pronunciation with immediate feedback, and obtain a greater understanding of cultural quirks—skills that are frequently difficult to impart through traditional classroom instruction. With this immersive method, learning a language becomes a lived experience that is interesting, memorable, and immediately useful in everyday conversation (Kadriu & Abazi Bexheti, 2022).

Without the risks, expenses, or resource limitations of real-world training, learners can practice difficult, high-stakes activities in safe virtual reality (VR) simulations for vocational training. VR flight simulators help pilots practice technical skills, fast decision-making, and crisis management by simulating cockpit controls, weather, and emergency situations. Without experiencing actual wear and tear or safety risks, mechanics can virtually disassemble and repair engines, troubleshoot machinery, and operate heavy equipment. Before working with real patients, medical personnel can gain expertise and confidence by using virtual reality (VR) to perform procedures, oversee patient care, and handle crises. These simulations are extremely helpful for learning processes, improving safety, and guaranteeing workforce preparedness across industries since they provide instant feedback, repeatability, and flexibility to various skill levels (Muralidharan et al., 2024).

APPLICATIONS OF AR IN EDUCATION

Augmented reality (AR) applications in education improve learning by superimposing interactive digital elements on the physical world, which makes concepts more interesting, approachable, and relevant to the context. AR can help STEM subjects make abstract ideas come to life. For instance, it can be used to overlay physics simulations onto actual experiments, visualize 3D molecules in chemistry, or explore the human body's architecture in biology. AR applications in social studies and history can project timelines, artifacts, or reconstructions straight into the classroom, enabling students to engage with and investigate the past in context. Real-time translation tools, object tagging, and AR flashcards enhance language learning by making vocabulary development more dynamic and relevant to everyday scenarios. Before they are made, sculptures, architectural models, or digital artworks can be viewed in real-world settings using augmented reality (AR). Additionally, AR facilitates actual field learning by bridging the gap between theory and environment through overlaying information about plant species in a botanical garden or star maps during night sky observations. AR increases the immersion, personalization, and relevance of learning by fusing the digital and physical worlds.

Traditional learning resources are revolutionized by interactive textbooks and holographic overlays, which incorporate 3D models, animations, and multimedia content that can be viewed on devices with augmented reality capabilities. In a biology textbook, for instance, students can zoom in on a rotating, labeled 3D heart model, and in a history book, they can see a holographic recreation of a major battle. These elements make difficult concepts simpler to understand and more interesting to investigate by converting static information into interactive experiences.

By using augmented reality (AR) to immediately overlay digital content onto real-world items, locations, and artifacts, object-based learning transforms physical spaces into intelligent learning environments. When actual objects are scanned with a device, they can activate contextual material, including videos, quizzes, or 3D visualizations, turning museums, classrooms, and even outdoor spaces into interactive learning centers. For example, a historical structure could show its original architecture, a globe could show real-time temperature data, or a school lab could overlay detailed experiment instructions. This method fosters curiosity, contextual comprehension, and deeper engagement by bridging the gap between digital and physical learning.

Using AR-based experiments to improve STEM education turns abstract ideas into concrete, interactive experiences that increase comprehension and stimulate curiosity. AR in science can project 3D models of celestial entities, chemical reactions, or cells, giving students the opportunity to examine structures and processes from a variety of angles. Before building physical prototypes, students can virtually assemble, alter, and test designs using AR blueprints, circuit simulations, or mechanical system overlays that can be included into technology and engineering classes. AR in mathematics can show real-world applications such as data modeling and architectural measurements, or it can graph equations in three dimensions and depict geometric shapes. In addition to making difficult concepts more approachable, these interactive, contextually rich experiences promote investigation, experimentation, and problem-solving. AR-based experiments enable students to see the clear connection between STEM topics and real-world problems by fusing theoretical knowledge with practical investigation.

By removing linguistic and accessibility hurdles, AR-powered real-time language translation and annotations are essential for promoting inclusive education. Apps or devices with augmented reality capabilities can instantaneously translate written or spoken content into a learner's preferred language while superimposing comments or subtitles over real-world images. As a result, language barriers no longer prevent students from various linguistic backgrounds from actively participating in classes, debates, and group projects. AR can also offer contextual annotations that are suited to each learner's needs, including providing simplified summaries, defining technical jargon, or explaining cultural references. Learners with learning disabilities can benefit from individualized visual signals and detailed instructions, while those with hearing impairments can overlay real-time captions or sign language avatars using augmented reality. All students may access, comprehend, and interact with educational materials in a fair and significant manner because to AR's ability to facilitate smooth communication and adaptable content delivery.

DESIGNING IMMERSIVE CURRICULUM: FROM CONTENT TO EXPERIENCE

From content to experience entails rethinking conventional lesson preparation in order to produce dynamic, learner-centered, and practically relevant learning journeys. The process starts with well-defined learning objectives and maps them to immersive experiences that directly assist skill development and conceptual understanding, rather than considering VR and AR as add-ons. Language classes then become culturally rich role-play exchanges, historical events become walk-through simulations, abstract scientific concepts become interactive virtual experiments, and content is converted into experiences. The design is guided by pedagogical frameworks such as Universal Design for Learning (UDL) and Bloom's Taxonomy, which guarantee that the curriculum accommodates a variety of representational, expressive, and engaging methods. Learners are kept challenged yet encouraged by adaptive difficulty, feedback loops, and interaction, and collaborative features promote social learning in online environments. In addition to imparting knowledge, the curriculum fosters critical thinking, creativity, empathy, and lifelong learning abilities by switching from static content delivery to immersive, emotionally engaging experiences.

The use of narrative and context in VR/AR scenario-based learning and storytelling makes learning incredibly relevant, memorable, and engaging. Students using this method are active participants in the telling of tales, decision-making, problem-solving, and real-time experience of the results rather than passive onlookers. While AR can create context-aware learning tasks by overlaying interactive narrative elements over real-world settings, VR can immerse students in incredibly detailed environments, such as being a journalist reporting from a conflict zone, a scientist exploring a deep-sea trench, or a policymaker navigating a climate crisis. Higher-order abilities like empathy, critical thinking, and ethical reasoning are encouraged by these scenarios, which also appeal to emotional engagement, which improves motivation and memory. Immersion storytelling and active problem-solving are combined in VR and AR to transform abstract learning into lived experiences where knowledge is acquired via action, introspection, and significant context.

In order to connect with students on a deeper cognitive and emotional level, immersive narratives in VR and AR use the power of presence, interaction, and storytelling to create emotional engagement. Students are put at the heart of immersive storylines, giving them the opportunity to experience events firsthand, whether it's taking on the role of a historical person, overcoming the difficulties of a refugee's journey, or seeing how climate change affects communities that are already at risk. Through stimulating several senses and providing significant options in the plot, these encounters elicit emotional reactions like empathy, curiosity, and accountability. Because students are more likely to recall information associated with intense emotions, this emotional resonance improves memory retention in addition to motivation and focus. By use of carefully crafted tales, virtual reality and augmented reality have the capacity to convert abstract knowledge into potent, human-centered experiences that stimulate comprehension, empathy, and action (Iqbal et al., 2022).

Without necessarily requiring sophisticated programming knowledge, educators may create immersive, interactive learning experiences with the use of tools and platforms for creating original VR/AR content. With easy drag-and-drop interfaces, educators may construct virtual tours, interactive scenarios, and 360° learning environments using platforms like CoSpaces Edu, ThingLink, and Nearpod VR. For those who are skilled with coding and 3D modeling, tools like Unity and Unreal Engine offer sophisticated capabilities for creating highly customized VR/AR simulations, while Google Expeditions and VR Tour Creator facilitate virtual field trips. Teachers can use AR systems like BlippAR, Metaverse Studio, and ZapWorks to superimpose digital content on actual items, facilitating gamified learning, interactive storytelling, and science visualizations. Merge EDU also provides ready-to-use AR/VR content and tools for building lessons with 3D objects. These platforms allow teachers to transition from passively consuming knowledge to actively creating immersive learning experiences that are tailored to particular curricula, student requirements, and pedagogical objectives.

Student-generated VR/AR projects promote creativity, critical thinking, and a sense of ownership over the learning process by transforming students from passive consumers of immersive content into active creators. Through the creation of their own VR or AR experiences, such as interactive science simulations, virtual museums, historical reconstructions, or AR-enhanced storytelling, students participate in project-based learning that combines technological skills, research, topic knowledge, and design thinking. As they work through this process, they must evaluate data, combine ideas, and think about audience participation while also honing their teamwork and problem-solving skills. Without requiring sophisticated coding skills, kids can create interactive environments, 3D models, and augmented layers using programs like CoSpaces Edu, Tinkercad, ThingLink, and Unity. By completing these projects, students advance up Bloom's Taxonomy toward higher-order thinking abilities—creation, analysis, and evaluation while also getting practical experience with cutting-edge technologies, preparing them for difficulties in the classroom and in the real world. Technology in the classroom has the power to inspire and encourage kids to learn, which results in a successful learning process. There are benefits and great prospects for AR technology that can be applied in the classroom. It has been demonstrated that augmented reality (AR) holds promise for improving the effectiveness, engagement, and significance of the learning process. This is due to its cutting-edge technology, which allows users to engage with real-time and virtual apps and provides them with natural experiences. Additionally, the ability of AR to engage pupils in realistic situations has lately drawn study attention to its integration with education (Saidin et al., 2015).

EQUITY, ETHICS, AND ACCESSIBILITY IN IMMERSIVE EDUCATION

In immersive education, equity, ethics, and accessibility are crucial factors to take into account in order to make sure that VR and AR technologies improve learning without escalating already-existing inequalities or erecting new obstacles. Schools and other institutions must address the digital gap from an equality perspective by making sure that all students, regardless of socioeconomic background, have access to the required hardware, dependable internet, and inclusive learning tools. Protecting learner privacy, making sure that the content is age-appropriate, avoiding portrayals that are prejudiced or culturally inappropriate, and being open about how immersive experiences gather and use data are all components of ethical use. Designing VR/AR experiences that meet a variety of learning demands is necessary for accessibility. Some examples of this include giving students with impairments or sensory sensitivity customizable sensory settings, audio descriptions, captions, and alternate navigation options. Creating inclusive experiences that include a variety of ways to access, interact with, and express learning can be facilitated by following frameworks such as Universal Design for Learning (UDL). By including accessibility, ethics, and equity into immersive learning, teachers can make sure that all students are empowered by these effective resources rather than being left behind.

To guarantee that immersive education serves all students, not only those with access to cutting-edge technology, it is imperative to address the digital gap and device accessibility. Many students may not be able to fully engage in VR/AR learning due to the digital divide, which is defined as disparities in device access, internet connectivity, and digital competence. Institutions can close this gap by using shared resource models, including mobile learning carts, VR/AR laboratories, or device lending programs, which allow students without personal devices to still access immersive experiences. Accessibility can be increased without incurring large infrastructure expenditures by utilizing affordable and mobile-compatible alternatives, such as browser-based AR or VR devices that run on smartphones (like Google Cardboard). Hardware and connectivity subsidies for underprivileged schools can also be obtained through collaborations with technology companies, government programs, and neighborhood associations. Furthermore, inclusion is ensured by creating content that functions on a variety of platforms, from high-end headsets to entry-level tablets. In order to lower technology barriers and create more egalitarian immersive learning experiences, educators should prioritize affordability, adaptability, and shared access.

Intentional planning is necessary when designing immersive education for neurodiverse and differently abled students to guarantee that VR and AR experiences are inclusive, accessible, and accommodating of a range of demands. In order to prevent cognitive overload, immersive environments for neurodiverse learners—such as those with autism, ADHD, or dyslexia—should have individualized sensory settings, such as pacing controls, simpler visual backgrounds, and adjustable sound levels. Step-by-step instructions and unambiguous, consistent navigation cues can assist in boosting concentration and lessen anxiety. Accessibility features for learners with disabilities may include haptic feedback, eye-tracking navigation, voice instructions, and adaptable controllers for individuals with restricted movement. For students with hearing or vision problems, activities can be made accessible through the use of sign language avatars, audio descriptions, and captions. All learners can access knowledge in ways that suit them best when Universal Design for Learning (UDL) principles are followed. This is significant because it guarantees multiple modes of engagement, representation, and expression.

Flexibility, assistive technology, and inclusive design may be incorporated early on to turn immersive learning from a unique experience for some students to a life-changing tool for all.

ETHICAL IMPLICATIONS: PRIVACY, MOTION SICKNESS, EMOTIONAL SAFETY IN VIRTUAL ENVIRONMENTS

Immersion education has significant ethical ramifications that cover important topics including motion sickness, privacy, and emotional safety; therefore, careful planning and execution are necessary to safeguard students. Clear procedures regarding consent, storage, and adherence to privacy laws are crucial since VR and AR systems frequently gather sensitive data, such as biometric data and behavioral patterns. Shorter sessions, movable alternatives that lessen discomfort, and customizable settings can all help prevent motion sickness, which is brought on by discrepancies between visual information and bodily movement. Emotional safety is similarly vital, since immersive experiences can inspire emotional reactions, especially when discussing sensitive issues; offering content warnings, age-appropriate material, and opportunity for debriefing helps assure psychological well-being. Teachers may maintain the advantages of in-depth, experiential learning while creating immersive environments that are secure, welcoming, and courteous by addressing these issues early on.

While avoiding prejudices or biases, culturally responsive immersive content in VR and AR guarantees that educational experiences respect, reflect, and celebrate the diversity of learners' cultural origins. This entails creating locations, stories, and simulations that include real cultural viewpoints, languages, customs, and history; these are frequently created in partnership with people from those communities. In addition to exposing all students to a variety of worldviews and life experiences, this kind of content helps students see themselves reflected in educational materials, which promotes a sense of belonging and validates their identities. Whether it's a historical reenactment, a role-playing game in a multicultural environment, or a virtual tour of a sacred heritage site, culturally responsive immersive design also demands careful consideration of truth, respectful portrayal, and contextual awareness. Immersion education may foster empathy, global awareness, and cross-cultural understanding by integrating inclusivity and authenticity. This turns the virtual environment into a bridge between cultures rather than a mirror of cultural prejudices.

BEST PRACTICES AND GLOBAL CASE STUDIES

Aligning VR/AR experiences with specific learning goals, incorporating them smoothly into the curriculum, and guaranteeing accessibility, cultural relevance, and ethical protections are all key components of best practices in immersive education. Successful programs prioritize pedagogy, choosing immersive resources that complement rather than replace fundamental teaching techniques and giving teachers the guidance and assistance they need to create and lead these experiences. Case studies around the world show a variety of achievements: in the US, Stanford's Virtual Human Interaction Lab uses virtual reality (VR) to teach environmental science by immersing students in coral reef ecosystems; in Finland, AR-enhanced science lessons make molecular biology come to life in elementary schools; in Japan, VR is used to simulate real-world conversational practice in language learning; and in South Africa, mobile-based AR helps rural learners understand anatomy without the need for costly lab equipment. As seen by these instances, immersive technologies can greatly improve engagement, comprehension, and the application of real-world skills, provided they are purposefully created, contextually relevant, and fairly available.

Globally, educational institutions are embracing platforms such as zSpace, ClassVR, and Merge EDU to incorporate VR/AR into instruction in creative ways that improve student engagement and comprehension. Students may examine engineering prototypes, dissect virtual organisms, and do physics experiments without being restricted by actual labs thanks to zSpace, which blends AR and VR with interactive 3D models. With the use of ClassVR's headset-based platform and extensive collection of immersive content spanning multiple areas, students may engage in curriculum-aligned activities including historical reenactments, virtual field trips, and STEM simulations. With the help of physical Merge Cubes, students may handle digital 3D objects in Merge EDU's hands-on augmented reality experiences, giving abstract ideas like chemical structures or planetary motion a concrete and interactive form. By encouraging experiential, inquiry-driven learning that equips students for the demands of a technologically advanced future, these platforms enable educators to go beyond conventional teaching methods.

Immersion technologies are being used more and more by government and non-profit programs to close educational gaps in underprivileged communities and guarantee fair access to top-notch educational opportunities. Through the PM e-Vidya program, for instance, India's Ministry of Education has implemented VR labs in rural schools, allowing students to study history and science through virtual simulations despite the lack of adequate physical equipment. In Kenya, the non-profit African Leadership Academy collaborates with tech companies to provide distant schools with AR-enabled STEM kits, enabling students to perform experiments without the need for pricey lab equipment.

By allowing younger generations to virtually experience ancient traditions, UNESCO has started programs in Southeast Asia that employ virtual reality (VR) to protect and teach indigenous cultural heritage. In a similar vein, Save the Children has employed virtual reality storytelling to teach empathy and global citizenship to young people, particularly those living in areas devastated by war. These programs demonstrate how immersive learning can transcend geographic, financial, and infrastructure constraints to provide inclusive, effective education when backed by the public and nonprofit sectors.

Through the integration of many topic areas into immersive experiences, cross-disciplinary VR/AR projects allow students to approach challenging real-world problems from a variety of angles. By immersing students in melting Arctic regions, endangered rainforests, or sea-level rise-affected coastal cities, virtual reality (VR) can enhance comprehension and motivate action in climate education by fusing science, geography, and policy studies. Empathy simulators integrate social studies, ethics, and psychology to foster compassion and global awareness by letting students into the living experiences of others, such as refugees, those with disabilities, or those impacted by poverty. While VR can reproduce significant historical moments for first-hand investigation, AR in social studies can superimpose historical maps, political information, and cultural objects onto real-world settings. In addition to enhancing topic knowledge, these interdisciplinary applications develop critical thinking, systems thinking, and emotional intelligence, equipping students to approach interrelated problems in a comprehensive and knowledgeable manner.

THE FUTURE OF VR/AR IN EDUCATION

With immersive technologies becoming essential to teaching and learning across disciplines, the future of VR and AR in education offers a transition from novelty to necessity. While AI integration will allow for individualized, adaptive learning experiences in virtual environments, hardware advancements like lighter, more inexpensive headsets and AR glasses will facilitate access. Real-time, multi-user collaboration in shared virtual reality settings will be made possible by cloud-based platforms and 5G connectivity, opening up global classrooms where students may collaborate and learn from any location. New mixed-reality interfaces and haptic feedback systems will enhance sensory engagement, increasing the realism and efficacy of simulations for skill-based training. Additionally, as educational material libraries grow, VR/AR will support competency-based assessments, lifelong learning pathways, and microlearning more and more. But in order to ensure that this future is inclusive, educators, legislators, and tech companies must place a high priority on accessibility, cultural relevance, and ethical safeguards. This will guarantee that immersive learning empowers all students while encouraging creativity, empathy, and critical thinking in a world that is changing quickly.

Virtual campuses and the metaverse are revolutionizing the way that education is accessed, experienced, and delivered. Learners can participate in interactive simulations, attend lectures, and work together on projects in these persistent, linked virtual worlds without being limited by time or location. Virtual campuses, which feature

3D classrooms, libraries, labs, and social areas, allow students to move between extracurricular and academic activities with ease and create a sense of community and presence that is comparable to that of traditional schools. Cross-border cultural interaction is another benefit of the metaverse, which unites heterogeneous cohorts for experiential learning and cooperative problem-solving. Blockchain-based certification encourages lifelong learning by enabling students to safely save and share their accomplishments across platforms. It is possible to create AR applications that enable interactive online learning for both professors and students. Using AR technology, students can study theoretical knowledge and practices while also honing their clinical nursing skills. Adoption of AR technology can help healthcare workers perform training and professional skill reinforcement, in addition to helping students or trainees learn efficiently under limited clinical nursing practices (Uymaz & Uymaz, 2022). It is imperative that educators and policymakers strike a balance between innovation and inclusivity, safety, and ethical oversight because, despite the metaverse's unmatched potential for immersive, social, and personalized education, it also poses issues with digital identity, equitable access, and governance.

Personalized, responsive, and interactive learning is becoming the norm thanks to AI-enabled immersive tutors and adaptive virtual reality content. Real-time performance analysis by AI-powered tutors in virtual settings allows them to track progress, spot misconceptions, and modify the level of difficulty or pace of tasks to suit each student's needs. In addition, these tutors can offer immediate feedback, recommend specific practice, and even change their teaching methods according to a student's learning preferences or emotional condition. This is improved by adaptive VR material, which dynamically changes settings, tasks, or stories to keep students interested as they go toward mastery. A medical student performing surgery in virtual reality, for instance, might get AI-guided suggestions that adjust to their level of expertise, and a language learner could converse with AI-powered avatars that in real time provide contextual responses. Deeper comprehension, autonomy, motivation, and inclusivity are all encouraged by this combination of AI and immersive technology, which makes sophisticated, individualized education available to students worldwide.

The flexibility of digital platforms and the engagement of experiential, hands-on learning are combined in blended learning models that include immersive technologies such as Extended Reality (XR) with Learning Management Systems (LMS). This strategy allows students to transition between theoretical knowledge and real-world application without ever leaving the learning ecosystem by seamlessly integrating VR, AR, or MR experiences into structured online courses. For instance, student progress and evaluation data could be instantly synchronized when a biology course on an LMS links directly to a VR lab simulation or an AR-based anatomy visualization. By tracking both traditional coursework and immersive activities, this integration gives teachers a comprehensive picture of students' performance. Additionally, it facilitates self-paced study, project-based learning, and flipped classrooms, in which students can prepare theory online and then reinforce topics in engaging, interactive sessions. Blended learning models combine the structure of an LMS with the experiential depth of XR to produce a scalable, customized, and data-rich educational approach that accommodates a variety of learning preferences and equips students for obstacles they may face in the real world.

Predicting future advancements in VR/AR education means that, in addition to being visual and interactive, education will eventually be fully multisensory. Advances in haptic technology will allow students to "feel" textures, resistance, or movement, improving the efficacy and realism of skill training in fields such as engineering, surgery, and the arts. To improve emotional connection and immersion with the content, multimodal learning will incorporate spatial audio, smell, and even temperature changes in addition to sight and touch. Real-time, performance-based tests in virtual environments will replace static quizzes. Students will be able to demonstrate their skills by solving problems, completing simulations, or engaging with artificial intelligence (AI)-driven characters.

Adaptive learning systems will use the data from these encounters to provide personalized feedback and progression pathways. When combined, these technologies will bridge the gap between knowledge and application in unprecedented ways, advancing education toward environments where students are immersed in the world rather than just learning about it.

TOWARD AN IMMERSIVE, INCLUSIVE, AND IMAGINATIVE FUTURE

VR and AR in education have the power to transform education into an immersive, inclusive, and creative future by transforming learning into a dynamic, interactive experience that transcends traditional classroom boundaries. By combining cutting-edge technology with human-centered design, these technologies can provide equitable access to rich, immersive learning opportunities for students from a wide range of socioeconomic backgrounds, skill levels, and geographic locations. Through in-person interactions and real-world scenarios, immersion environments allow students to explore challenging concepts, which can foster empathy, curiosity, and critical thinking skills. In the future, educators, technologists, and politicians will work together to address accessibility, ethics, and cultural responsiveness so that learning is lived rather than just consumed. In this future, education will be a place where all students can explore new possibilities and emerge with the knowledge, creativity, confidence, and empathy to make a difference in the world.

EDUCATIONAL IMPLICATION

Because VR and AR make learning more engaging, fun, and student-centered, they can dramatically boost learner motivation. This can lessen the divide that conventional teaching techniques frequently cause.

Learners can develop a greater understanding of abstract and complex concepts by picturing them in immersive environments. For instance, students can investigate architectural structures in three dimensions or watch molecular interactions in chemistry.

Instead of allowing students to passively absorb knowledge, VR and AR encourage hands-on experiences in which they actively participate. This promotes long-term retention and is consistent with constructivist pedagogy.

For students with varying skills and learning preferences, immersive technologies can offer alternate learning methods. For example, kids with dyslexia can benefit from AR overlays, and those with mobility issues can benefit from VR simulations.

By simulating real-world situations for professional practice—like medical procedures, classroom instruction, or engineering tasks—VR and AR can better prepare students without posing real-world risks.

Collaborative problem-solving in the real world is reflected in multi-user VR platforms and AR-enhanced group projects that promote teamwork, communication, and peer learning.

Teachers need professional development and digital literacy as they go from imparting content to facilitating and creating immersive learning experiences.

Performance-based activities and simulations are examples of innovative formative and summative assessment methods that are made possible by immersive settings and provide real-world indicators of student proficiency.

Immersion technologies have potential, but in order to guarantee that every student benefits equally, educators must address concerns about cost, accessibility, privacy, and ethical use.

Incorporating VR and AR prepares students for technology-driven workplaces, equipping them with digital literacy, adaptability, and problem-solving skills needed in the 21st century.

CONCLUSION

The way we interact with the actual world will surely change as AR and VR become widely employed in many sectors of the economy in the next years. Rather than remaining a myth, they will become a reality (Elmqaddem, 2019). Virtual reality (VR) and augmented reality (AR) have the revolutionary potential to fundamentally alter education by removing the limitations of time, place, and traditional teaching methods. These technologies encourage greater understanding, stimulate curiosity, and give abstract concepts a concrete form by immersing students in dynamic, hands-on environments. Through their ability to replicate complex scientific processes and facilitate cross-cultural exchanges, virtual reality and augmented reality have the potential to close educational access gaps, foster empathy, and customize learning. To realize this potential at scale, however, will require coordinated efforts from educators to design immersive experiences that are both pedagogically sound and engaging, technologists to create accessible, flexible, and inclusive platforms, and policymakers to ensure equitable infrastructure, funding, and ethical standards.

By strategically collaborating, these stakeholders can build an educational ecosystem where immersive technologies empower all students and prepare them for a rapidly changing and increasingly linked world. In order to fully realize immersive learning's transformative potential, educators, technologists, and legislators must collaborate. In order to create engaging VR/AR worlds, technologists supply the necessary tools and creativity, educators contribute pedagogical expertise and understanding of student needs, and policymakers ensure that the funding, frameworks, and accessibility requirements necessary to make these innovations sustainable and egalitarian are in place. These stakeholders can work together to create inclusive, morally sound, and culturally relevant immersive experiences that address real-world issues and offer educational opportunities to all. Open communication, shared research, and cross-sector cooperation should be the foundation of this connection in order to ensure that immersive education is a right for all students, regardless of geography or background.

In order to create future-ready learners through immersive curiosity and creativity, VR/AR technology can be used to foster imagination, encourage discovery, and develop problem-solving skills that prepare students for rapidly evolving careers and social concerns. In immersive settings, students can go beyond textbooks and develop flexibility and creative thinking by exploring the surface of Mars, dissecting virtual organisms, or cooperating on global projects in simulated environments. In these virtual settings, students not only master academic subject but also develop critical 21st-century skills like digital literacy, cultural competency, and cooperation by combining curiosity-driven learning with creative expression. With this approach, learning is transformed from passively absorbing knowledge into an active, exploratory process that produces learners who are prepared to thrive in a complex, interconnected, and technologically sophisticated future. Technology has had a significant impact on the evolution of education. Technology is necessary in education because it encourages self-reliance and active learning, which indirectly contributes to children's intellectual development. Examples of contemporary technology are augmented reality (AR) and virtual reality (VR). It is anticipated that VR and AR will offer dynamic, multifaceted solutions to the issues.

REFERENCES

Abdul Talib, C., Romainor, N., & Aliyu, F. (2022). Augmented Reality in Chemistry Education: A Literature Review of Advantages on Learners. *Journal of Natural Science and Integration*, *5*(1), 126. DOI: 10.24014/jnsi.v5i1.16805

Ajit, G., Lucas, T., & Kanyan, R. (2021). A systematic review of augmented reality in stem education. In *Estudios de Economia Aplicada* (Vol. 39, Issue 1, pp. 1–22). https://doi.org/DOI: 10.25115/eea.v39i1.4280

Ali, D. F., Omar, M., Abdullah, A. H., Ibrahim, N. H., Mokhtar, M., Zaid, N. M., & Johari, N. (2021). 5 years into augmented reality technology in education: Research trends, bibliometric study and its application to enhance visualization skills. *WSEAS Transactions on Systems and Control*, *16*, 253–260. DOI: 10.37394/23203.2021.16.21

Dalim, C. S. C., Kolivand, H., Kadhim, H., Sunar, M. S., & Billinghurst, M. (2017). Factors influencing the acceptance of augmented reality in education: A review of the literature. In *Journal of Computer Science* (Vol. 13, Issue 11, pp. 581–589). https://doi.org/DOI: 10.3844/jcssp.2017.581.589

Dhar, P., Rocks, T., Samarasinghe, R. M., Stephenson, G., & Smith, C. (2021). Augmented reality in medical education: Students' experiences and learning outcomes. *Medical Education Online*, *26*(1). Advance online publication. DOI: 10.1080/10872981.2021.1953953 PMID: 34259122

Elmqaddem, N. (2019). Augmented Reality and Virtual Reality in education. Myth or reality? *International Journal of Emerging Technologies in Learning*, *14*(3), 234–242. DOI: 10.3991/ijet.v14i03.9289

Iqbal, M. Z., Mangina, E., & Campbell, A. G. (2022). Current Challenges and Future Research Directions in Augmented Reality for Education. *Multimodal Technologies and Interaction*, *6*(9), 1–29. DOI: 10.3390/mti6090075

Kadriu, A., & Abazi Bexheti, L. (2022). The Who in VR/AR for Education: A Scoping Review from IEEE Publications. *ENTRENOVA - ENTerprise REsearch InNOVAtion, 8*(1), 1–8. https://doi.org/DOI: 10.54820/entrenova-2022-0001

Lampropoulos, G., Keramopoulos, E., Diamantaras, K., & Evangelidis, G. (2023). Integrating Augmented Reality, Gamification, and Serious Games in Computer Science Education. *Education Sciences*, *13*(6). Advance online publication. DOI: 10.3390/educsci13060618

Lopes, D. S., & Jorge, J. A. (2024). Extending medical interfaces towards virtual reality and augmented reality. *Annals of Medicine, 51*(sup1). https://doi.org/DOI: 10.1080/07853890.2018.1560068

Magi, C. E., Bambi, S., Iovino, P., El Aoufy, K., Amato, C., Balestri, C., Rasero, L., & Longobucco, Y. (2023). Virtual Reality and Augmented Reality Training in Disaster Medicine Courses for Students in Nursing: A Scoping Review of Adoptable Tools. In *Behavioral Sciences* (Vol. 13, Issue 7, pp. 1–13). https://doi.org/DOI: 10.3390/bs13070616

Muralidharan, V., Tran, M. M., Barrios, L., Beams, B., Ko, J. M., Siegel, D. H., & Bailenson, J. (2024). Best Practices for Research in Virtual and Augmented Reality in Dermatology. *The Journal of Investigative Dermatology, 144*(1), 17–23. DOI: 10.1016/j.jid.2023.10.014 PMID: 38105083

Osadchyi, V. V., Valko, N. V., & Kuzmich, L. V. (2021). Using augmented reality technologies for STEM education organization. *Journal of Physics: Conference Series, 1840*(1), 1–10. DOI: 10.1088/1742-6596/1840/1/012027

Paramita, A., Yulia, C., & Nikmawati, E. E. (2021). Augmented reality in nutrition education. *IOP Conference Series. Materials Science and Engineering, 1098*(2), 1–8. DOI: 10.1088/1757-899x/1098/2/022108

Saidin, N. F., Halim, N. D. A., & Yahaya, N. (2015). A review of research on augmented reality in education: Advantages and applications. *International Education Studies, 13*, 1–8. DOI: 10.5539/ies.v8n13p1

Šarić, M., Russo, M., Kraljević, L., & Meter, D. (2024). Extended Reality Telemedicine Collaboration System Using Patient Avatar Based on 3D Body Pose Estimation. *Sensors (Basel), 24*(1), 1–12. DOI: 10.3390/s24010027 PMID: 38202889

Turhan, M. E., Metin, M., & Çevik, E. E. (2022). A content analysis of studies published in the field of augmented reality in education. *Journal of Educational Technology and Online Learning, 5*(1), 243–262. DOI: 10.31681/jetol.925340

Uymaz, P., & Uymaz, A. O. (2022). Assessing acceptance of augmented reality in nursing education. *PLoS ONE, 17*(2 February). https://doi.org/DOI: 10.1371/journal.pone.0263937

Wagner, P., & Alharthi, D. (2023). Leveraging VR/AR/MR/XR Technologies to Improve Cybersecurity Education, Training, and Operations. *Journal of Cybersecurity Education Research and Practice, 2024*(1), 1–26. DOI: 10.32727/8.2023.32

Wang, M., Callaghan, V., Bernhardt, J., White, K., & Peña-Rios, A. (2018). Augmented reality in education and training: Pedagogical approaches and illustrative case studies. *Journal of Ambient Intelligence and Humanized Computing, 9*(5), 1391–1402. DOI: 10.1007/s12652-017-0547-8

Yusufjanovna, R. N. (2022). Prospects for the use of Augmented Reality in Education. *Embedded Selforganising Systems, 9*(4), 26–29. https://doi.org/DOI: 10.14464/ess.v9i4.552

KEY TERMS AND DEFINITIONS

Virtual Reality (VR): – A fully computer-generated, three-dimensional environment that immerses learners in lifelike simulations using headsets and controllers.

Augmented Reality (AR): – A technology that overlays digital elements (images, animations, or data) onto the real world, enhancing learning through contextual interaction.

Extended Reality (XR): – An umbrella term that includes VR, AR, and Mixed Reality (MR), combining digital and physical worlds to create immersive educational experiences.

Immersive Learning: – An educational approach where learners actively engage in interactive environments, simulations, or experiences, moving beyond passive listening or reading.

Experiential Learning: – A theory of learning through direct experience, reflection, and application, strongly supported by XR technologies.

Constructivism: – A learning theory emphasizing that learners build knowledge through active participation and real-world problem-solving, well aligned with XR tools.

Universal Design for Learning (UDL): – An educational framework promoting flexible learning environments that accommodate diverse learners' needs and preferences.

Simulation-Based Learning: – The use of virtual or augmented environments to mimic real-world scenarios, allowing safe practice and experimentation.

1st-Century Skills: – Competencies such as creativity, collaboration, problem-solving, and digital literacy, which immersive technologies aim to develop.

Personalized Learning: – An instructional approach that adapts pace, content, and style of learning to meet individual student needs, facilitated by adaptive XR technologies.

Chapter 8
Spelling Improvement and Motivation Through Gamification and Mobile Apps

Maria Shobeiry
https://orcid.org/0000-0002-2499-0366
University of Tehran, Iran

ABSTRACT

This chapter explores the influence of gamification on motivation and engagement in language learners, focusing on the role of spelling proficiency. It elaborates on the integration of game design elements into language learning contexts and its effects on learner motivation and engagement, particularly through a case study of intermediate learners using the mobile application Words of Wonders. By examining the principles of self-determination theory, Vygotsky's Zone of Proximal Development, and cognitive load theory, the chapter investigates how gamification fosters learner autonomy, competence, and relatedness. The study highlights the potential of gamified mobile applications to address specific linguistic challenges, such as spelling, by combining interactive, game-based approaches with immediate feedback and rewards, fostering active engagement and measurable progress. Furthermore, the chapter emphasizes the role of multimodality in gamified tools to bridge the gap between English spelling conventions and learners' first languages, thereby enhancing understanding and retention.

DOI: 10.4018/979-8-3373-4465-2.ch008

INTRODUCTION

Language acquisition is a multifaceted process that requires the development of various skills, including speaking, listening, reading, and writing. Among these, spelling often poses significant challenges, particularly for elementary and intermediate learners who struggle with accurate word spelling despite a strong grasp of vocabulary and grammar (Mimeau et al., 2025). Addressing these challenges, innovative approaches such as gamification have emerged as potent tools in language learning, offering engaging methods to motivate learners and enhance their language skills (Orak, 2025). Gamification, broadly defined, integrates game design elements into non-game contexts to enhance engagement and motivation (Anisa et al., 2020). In language learning, gamified apps leverage elements such as points, rewards, and challenges to transform traditional learning activities into dynamic experiences, encouraging students to engage with the material and remain motivated (Shen et al., 2024).

Motivation, a critical factor in successful language learning, is significantly influenced by gamification, which fosters a sense of achievement and intrinsic reward (Wulantari et al., 2023). Mobile applications such as *Duolingo, Tell Me More English, and Words of Wonders* exemplify this trend, providing interactive environments where learners engage with language in playful and competitive ways, thereby fostering intrinsic motivation and autonomy (Shobeiry, 2021a). This motivational aspect is central to language acquisition, influencing learners' persistence and engagement as is described in self-determination theory (Deci & Ryan, 2004). Gamification aligns with this theory by offering opportunities for autonomy, competence, and relatedness, making language learning both enjoyable and self-directed (Luarn et al., 2023).

Spelling, as highlighted earlier, remains a crucial component of language proficiency, often posing a barrier to fluency due to unpredictable spelling-pronunciation relationships in languages such as English (Witzel et al., 2024; Mimeau et al., 2025). Language learners at elementary and intermediate levels of proficiency may struggle with spelling despite possessing a robust vocabulary, undermining their confidence and affecting overall proficiency (Mimeau et al., 2025). To mitigate these issues, gamified language learning apps offer a promising solution by combining spelling practice with interactive, game-based approaches. Features such as rewards and immediate feedback encourage learners to engage actively with spelling, leading to measurable progress and a sense of achievement (Witzel et al., 2024). This chapter explores the impact of gamification on fostering motivation, engagement, and autonomy in language learners, with a specific focus on the role of spelling through a case study of intermediate learners using the game of *Words of Wonders* as a mobile app. By leveraging gamification to address specific challenges such as spelling, educators can promote independent learning and skill development, ultimately enhancing language acquisition outcomes. Furthermore, this approach holds significant implications for future language learning methodologies, suggesting that the integration of gamification could become a cornerstone in developing more effective, learner-centered educational strategies that cater to diverse learning needs and preferences.

THEORETICAL FRAMEWORK

In examining the role of gamification in language learning—particularly in enhancing spelling skills—it is essential to draw upon a robust theoretical framework that encompasses both motivational and cognitive dimensions. The current study is underpinned by Self-Determination Theory (SDT) (Deci & Ryan, 2004), Vygotsky's Zone of Proximal Development (ZPD) (Vygotsky, 1978), and Cognitive Load Theory (CLT) (Sweller, 2011), with an integrated expansion to include Flow Theory (Csikszentmihalyi et al., 2018). Together, these perspectives provide a comprehensive lens through which to understand how gamification supports language acquisition, learner engagement, and the development of autonomy.

SDT is foundational in explaining how gamified environments can promote intrinsic motivation. The theory posits that human motivation is driven by the fulfillment of three psychological needs: autonomy, competence, and relatedness. Gamified language learning apps, including *Words of Wonders*, cater to these needs by allowing learners to control the pace and timing of their engagement (autonomy), providing real-time feedback and progressive difficulty levels (competence), and integrating social features such as leaderboards or shared challenges (relatedness) (Luarn et al., 2023; Orak, 2025). Such design principles not only enhance engagement but also contribute to a more self-regulated and rewarding learning experience.

SDT's relevance is further enriched when considered in conjunction with Vygotsky's ZPD, which highlights the developmental space between what a learner can do independently and what they can achieve with appropriate support (Vygotsky, 1978). Gamified applications offer this scaffolding through adaptive challenge levels, hints, and rewards that guide learners through increasingly difficult tasks. This structure mirrors the ZPD by ensuring that learners are consistently working at the edge of their competence with support mechanisms in place. For example, in *Words of Wonders*, early levels serve as accessible entry points, while more complex puzzles extend learners' spelling abilities into new developmental zones.

CLT complements the above frameworks by addressing the cognitive mechanisms that underlie effective learning. Sweller (2011) argued that instructional design must account for the limitations of working memory and aim to reduce extraneous load. Gamified apps align well with CLT by breaking down complex spelling tasks into smaller, manageable chunks, offering visual cues and immediate feedback to reinforce learning without overloading the working memory of learners. Such design minimizes extraneous load while optimizing germane load, which refers to the cognitive effort devoted to schema construction (Chen, 2025). The pacing and segmentation inherent in gamified apps also allow learners to process spelling rules and word patterns more effectively (Sun & Sailer, 2025).

While SDT, ZPD, and CLT collectively emphasize motivation, scaffolding, and cognitive efficiency, the inclusion of Flow Theory provides a crucial affective dimension. Flow is described by Csikszentmihalyi et al. (2018) as a psychological state in which individuals are fully immersed in an activity, experiencing deep focus and enjoyment. Csikszentmihalyi et al. (2018) emphasize that flow occurs when the challenge of a task is perfectly balanced with the individual's skill level—neither too easy nor too difficult. Gamified apps such as *Words of Wonders* are intentionally designed to create these optimal conditions through mechanisms such as level progression, challenge scaling, time constraints, and instant performance feedback. When learners enter a state of flow, their intrinsic motivation is heightened, and learning becomes more effective and enduring (Chapman et al., 2023).Moreover, Flow Theory ties back to both SDT and ZPD. The experience of flow is closely aligned with SDT's concept of intrinsic motivation, as learners pursue tasks for the inherent satisfaction they provide. Similarly, flow is most likely to occur when learners are operating within their ZPD—at a level of difficulty that is sufficiently challenging but not overwhelming. Thus, the convergence of these four theories—SDT, ZPD, CLT, and Flow—offers a synergistic framework for understanding the mechanisms by which gamified learning environments enhance motivation, reduce cognitive friction, and promote skill development in areas such as spelling.

SPELLING IN LANGUAGE LEARNING

Spelling plays a pivotal role in language acquisition, particularly in the development of literacy skills. It is an essential component of written language proficiency, contributing to effective communication and the broader process of language learning. While many learners focus primarily on speaking and comprehension, the acquisition of spelling skills remains fundamental to mastering both written and spoken forms of a language. Spelling is intrinsically linked to reading and writing, two key pillars of language proficiency. Accurate spelling enables learners to decode and encode words correctly, facilitating their ability to read and write with fluency. Research has shown that spelling errors can interfere with reading comprehension, as learners may struggle to recognize words if they are unable to associate the correct letters with the correct sounds (Suárez-Coalla et al., 2024; Mimeau et al., 2025).

Similarly, spelling inaccuracies in writing can hinder effective communication, as readers may find it difficult to interpret misspelled words, which can diminish the clarity and meaning of the text (Schiff et al., 2025).

The significance of spelling is further underscored by its connection to the understanding of language structure, including phonology, morphology, and orthography (Smail et al., 2025). Learning to spell correctly involves understanding the relationship between sounds and letters (phonics), as well as recognizing the patterns and rules that govern word formation in a given language (Smail et al., 2025). In English, the idiosyncratic nature of spelling—due to historical linguistic influences, irregularities, and exceptions to rules—can pose significant challenges for learners. While some languages exhibit more consistent spelling rules, English spelling often requires learners to internalize complex conventions and exceptions, making it a particularly challenging aspect of language acquisition (Mimeau et al., 2025). For intermediate learners, difficulties with spelling may be particularly pronounced, as they typically possess a functional command of the language but may struggle with more advanced or irregularly spelled words. These challenges can result in frustration, reduced confidence, and a tendency to avoid writing tasks. By focusing on spelling improvement, gamified apps help learners address a critical component of language acquisition, thus enhancing their overall sense of motivation (Witzel et al., 2024). Additionally, spelling proficiency can play a pivotal role in the development of other language skills, notably vocabulary acquisition (Lascano Ortiz et al., 2025). This connection is underscored by empirical research from Lascano Ortiz et al. (2025), which indicates that learners with accurate spelling skills tend to exhibit enhanced recall and retention of word meanings. Their study demonstrates that systematic spelling activities significantly bolstered vocabulary acquisition among fifth-grade English language learners over a seven-week intervention.

The challenges of spelling in English are exacerbated globally by the disconnection between English spelling conventions and those of learners' first languages. This discrepancy often leads to significant difficulties for English as a second language learners, particularly due to the lack of phonetic consistency in English (Suárez-Coalla et al., 2024). English spelling is characterized by complex orthographic rules, which can be particularly daunting for learners whose native languages have different phonological and orthographical systems (Al-Sobhi et al., 2017). For instance, Arabic-speaking learners face challenges due to the structural and orthographic differences between Arabic and English, such as the substitution and omission of phonemes (Al-Sobhi et al., 2017). Similarly, learners from other linguistic backgrounds may struggle with silent letters, double consonants, and inflectional suffixes, which are not common in their native languages (Bear et al., 2018).

To effectively address these challenges, gamified language learning tools typically provide a flexible learning environment that leverages multimodality. This approach involves displaying the morphology of words in the target language, alongside their pronunciation and visual representation of their meanings. By integrating these multiple modalities, learners can engage with language content in a more comprehensive and interactive manner, enhancing their understanding and retention of linguistic elements (Witzel et al, 2024). This multimodal approach aligns with research indicating that combining visual, auditory, and textual information can significantly improve language acquisition outcomes (Fälth et al., 2023; Witzel et al, 2024; Zhou & Gu, 2024; Rowe & Pennington, 2025).

LEVERAGING GAMIFICATION FOR LANGUAGE LEARNING AND MOTIVATION

Gamification has emerged as a powerful strategy in language learning, effectively utilizing game-like elements to enhance learner engagement and motivation. By integrating mechanisms such as points, rewards, progress tracking, and competition, gamified language learning applications create immersive and enjoyable experiences that promote sustained participation and autonomous learning (Anisa et al., 2020; Luarn et al., 2023;Huseinović, 2024; Orak, 2025). These elements not only make the learning process more interactive but also contribute to improved retention and language acquisition (Huseinović, 2024; Orak, 2025).

A key strength of gamification lies in its ability to tap into both intrinsic and extrinsic motivation, making language learning more engaging and effective (Huseinović, 2024; Shen et al., 2024; Orak, 2025). Extrinsic motivators, such as points, rewards, and leaderboards, encourage consistent engagement by providing immediate and tangible incentives (Luarn et al., 2023). Points are typically awarded for task completion, correct responses, and level progression, offering learners visible indicators of their achievements and reinforcing their motivation. Rewards, including virtual prizes, badges, or unlockable content, further incentivize learners by recognizing their efforts and linking progress to meaningful outcomes. Leaderboards introduce a competitive element, allowing learners to compare their performance with peers, thereby fostering motivation through social comparison. Beyond competition, structured progression systems—comprising levels, badges, and achievements—play a crucial role in maintaining learner interest in gamified language learning applications (Huseinović, 2024; Shen et al., 2024; Orak, 2025). These systems provide clear milestones and goals, ensuring that learners experience a sense of advancement. As users progress through levels and earn achievements, they develop a stronger sense of accomplishment, which enhances their commitment to the learning process over time.

Another defining feature of gamified language learning applications is their ability to provide instant feedback, a critical mechanism for facilitating improvement and preventing frustration (Ogino & Matsuguma, 2024). Unlike traditional learning environments, where feedback may be delayed, gamified platforms offer real-time corrections, helping learners immediately identify and rectify errors. This immediate feedback accelerates the learning process by reinforcing correct usage and preventing misunderstandings from becoming entrenched (Ogino & Matsuguma, 2024). By allowing learners to adjust their approach in real time, these systems foster a sense of control over one's progress, ultimately increasing motivation and confidence (Ogino & Matsuguma, 2024; Orak, 2025).

Social interaction is another key factor that enhances engagement in technology-assisted language learning in general (Moreira & Teles, 2024; Namaziandost et al., 2024) and gamified language learning in particular (Chen & Hou, 2025). Many of gaming apps incorporate elements of competition, cooperation, and collaboration to create a dynamic and interactive learning environment. Engaging in competitive activities, such as challenges or leaderboards, encourages learners to push their limits, while cooperative tasks, such as group challenges or peer-assisted learning, provide opportunities for knowledge exchange and support (Shobeiry, 2021b). These social interactions not only enhance motivation but also contribute to deeper learning by encouraging active participation and knowledge-sharing (Chen & Hou, 2025).

The effectiveness of gamified language learning is also supported by flow theory (Csikszentmihalyi et al., 2018), which describes a state of deep engagement and intrinsic satisfaction that occurs when individuals are fully immersed in an activity that is both enjoyable and appropriately challenging. Gamified learning environments are specifically designed to facilitate this state of flow by providing learners with challenges that match their skill levels, ensuring that tasks are neither too difficult nor too easy. Features such as time constraints, level progression, and reward mechanisms further enhance the flow experience, while real-time feedback helps sustain it by keeping learners continuously engaged (Chapman et al., 2023). Building upon the aforementioned theoretical foundations and empirical evidence supporting the efficacy of gamification in language learning, the subsequent section presents a detailed case study. This investigation explores the impact of a specific gamified application, *Words of Wonders*, on the spelling abilities and motivational levels of a diverse group of English language learners.

METHODOLOGY AND CASE DESCRIPTION

This chapter employed a mixed-methods case study design to explore the impact of gamification on spelling improvement and learner motivation. Conducted in Tehran,

Iran, during the fall of 2024, the study integrated quantitative data from pre- and post-intervention assessments with qualitative feedback derived from participant self-reports and semi-structured interviews.

PARTICIPANT PROFILES AND RECRUITMENT

To ensure a representative and diverse sample of learners, the study included eight English learners: three teenagers (ages 14–17), three adults (ages 27–43), and two older adults (ages 68 and 71). Participants were purposively selected based on three key inclusion criteria: (1) intermediate proficiency in English, confirmed through the Cambridge Online Placement Test; (2) self-reported difficulties with spelling; and (3) willingness to engage in a two-month intervention involving the use of a mobile application. Recruitment was carried out through the principal investigator's social network to foster trust and comfort, particularly among the older participants who initially expressed reservations about using digital tools.

In addition to demographic diversity, the participants varied in their levels of digital literacy and learning habits. For instance, while the teenage group was relatively familiar with mobile technology, none of the participants had prior experience using gamified language learning applications. The older adults, however, had more limited exposure to technology and expressed initial reluctance to use mobile applications for learning. These differences in digital literacy were considered essential in understanding how participants from varying backgrounds engaged with the intervention and how the technology might either support or hinder their learning process. Furthermore, the participants' educational and professional backgrounds were diverse, with participants ranging from secondary school students to professionals such as a software engineer, a nurse, and retired educators. This heterogeneity allowed for an exploration of how gamified learning interfaces with different levels of cognitive strategies, motivational drivers, and individual learning preferences. The following provides a detailed description of each participant group:

Teenagers

The teenage cohort consisted of three participants, aged 14, 16, and 17, with two males and one female. All were enrolled in secondary schools in Tehran, Iran, and had varying degrees of exposure to mobile technology. Although they had extensive access to mobile phones and digital devices, none had previously used gamified language learning tools. These participants reported consistent difficulties with English spelling, frequently relying on auto-correction tools to assist them in writing tasks.

Adults

The adult participants, aged 27, 34, and 43, were comprised of two males and one female, representing a range of professional backgrounds including a nurse with a Bachelors' degree, a software engineer with a Master's degree, and a supermarket worker with a high school diploma. They identified spelling as a persistent challenge in their English language learning journey, often affecting their confidence in written tasks. While motivated to improve their spelling skills, these participants expressed a lack of structure or motivation to engage with traditional spelling learning methods, which they found unengaging or ineffective. They noted that the conventional spelling learning methods were too rigid and lacked sufficient appeal to maintain engagement, indicating a need for more interactive and flexible learning approaches.

Older Adults

The elderly cohort consisted of two retired female teachers, aged 68 and 71, both of whom had limited experience with mobile technology. They expressed a strong interest in improving their English spelling skills, viewing spelling difficulties as a significant barrier to their English language confidence. Although they had not received formal technology-based language learning training and had minimal exposure to digital tools, both participants were eager to engage in a new approach to learning. Their initial hesitations about using mobile apps were related to concerns about the usability of technology and its potential complexity. However, once they became more familiar with the app, they appreciated the ability to practice spelling in a non-pressured, enjoyable environment.

ETHICAL CONSIDERATIONS

Prior to beginning the study, all participants were fully briefed on its purpose, methods, and the extent of cooperation they were expected to provide. Written consent was obtained from all of the participants, and parental consent was secured for the minors. Anonymity and confidentiality were strictly maintained, and participants were informed of their right to withdraw at any time without penalty.

App Description and Usage Protocol

Participants engaged with *Words of Wonders*, an appealing mobile game app that combines the intellectual challenge of a crossword puzzle with the excitement of global exploration. It enhances vocabulary and spelling skills by challenging players to create words from given letters and connect them to solve crosswords. Players travel around the world, visiting the Seven Wonders and other incredible cities, learning about them while solving puzzles. The gameplay involves starting with a few letters as clues and using these to form words, sometimes guessing the solution when no more words can be connected. Levels become progressively harder, requiring mastery of vocabulary and spelling to advance, with each wonder and level being unique thanks to the game's extensive database. Additionally, there are extra words to find on each level for those seeking a greater challenge. The app's design incorporates various motivational features—score tracking, level advancement, streak bonuses, and visual feedback—that are aligned with SDT and Flow Theory principles. Notably, it allows players to revisit completed levels, fostering a mastery-oriented rather than performance-oriented approach to spelling. *Words of Wonders* was chosen for this study due to its popularity, adaptability, and progressive level structure.

Over a two-month period, participants were asked to use the app for at least 30 minutes daily and submit brief daily self-reports via text messages to the research team, documenting their progress and motivational status. These reports served a dual purpose: monitoring engagement and collecting real-time affective feedback. To elaborate, the reports were used as a mechanism to monitor participant engagement and ensure continuous participation, thereby preventing attrition and eliminating the need for additional recruitment efforts.

Assessment Instrument

Spelling proficiency of the participants was evaluated using a Spelling Diagnostic Assessment administered both before and after the intervention of *Words of Wonders*. The Spelling Diagnostic Assessment used in this study constitutes a specialized instrument designed to systematically evaluate an individual's current spelling proficiency. Typically aligned with established curriculum standards and literacy developmental progressions, this assessment may be administered individually, in small groups, or to entire classes, rendering it appropriate for learners across a broad range of developmental stages. The assessment incorporates carefully curated word lists that encompass varying degrees of linguistic complexity and frequently employs dictation formats, wherein students are required to spell words presented both in isolation and within contextual sentences. Notably, this assessment is accessible through the SPELL-Links eStickers online platform.

RELIABILITY AND VALIDITY OF THE SPELLING ASSESSMENT INSTRUMENT

The SPELL-Links eStickers Spelling Diagnostic Assessment is a reliable and valid tool essential for the study's accuracy. Its automated scoring ensures high internal consistency and inter-rater reliability by reducing subjectivity. The assessment demonstrates strong content validity through carefully selected word lists aligned with literacy curricula and developmental spelling stages. Construct validity is evidenced by its ability to distinguish varying spelling proficiencies and its widespread use from Kindergarten to Grade 12. Additionally, its format—requiring spelling in isolation and context—supports ecological validity by reflecting authentic language use. Together, these qualities establish SPELL-Links eStickers as a robust and appropriate instrument for diagnostic and research purposes in this study.

INSTRUMENT ADMINISTRATION AND SCORING SYSTEM

The assessment was administered online twice—before and after the two-month intervention—using the SPELL-Links eStickers platform. It included 30 intermediate-level English words selected for frequency, phonetic irregularity, and morphological complexity, drawn from standardized exam vocabularies (e.g., PET, FCE).To ensure data reliability, testing occurred individually in a controlled environment minimizing distractions, with a research assistant present to provide technical support and address digital literacy challenges. This setup maintained participant focus and test validity. Scoring followed a binary system: one point for each correctly spelled word and zero for any word with even a single letter error, enforcing strict accuracy standards.

Pre-Study Spelling Assessment

Table 1 displays the results of the pre-intervention spelling assessment. The data reveal that the overall mean score for the participant cohort was 54%, underscoring a substantial need for enhancement in spelling proficiency.

Table 1. Pre-study test results

Participant	Age	Profession/Status	Pre-test score (%)
Teenager 1	14	Student	55%
Teenager 2	16	Student	58%
Teenager 3	17	Student	60%
Adult 1	27	Nurse	52%
Adult 2	34	Software Engineer	59%
Adult 3	43	Supermarket Worker	54%
Elderly 1	68	Retired	47%
Elderly 2	71	Retired	50%

Post-study Spelling assessment

Upon completion of the study, participants were administered a parallel version of the Spelling Diagnostic Assessment to assess any enhancements in their spelling proficiency. The results of this post-study evaluation are presented in Table 2.

Table 2. The post-study test results

Participant	Age	Profession/Status	Pre-test score (%)
Teenager 1	14	Student	85%
Teenager 2	16	Student	82%
Teenager 3	17	Student	88%
Adult 1	27	Nurse	78%
Adult 2	34	Software Engineer	85%
Adult 3	43	Supermarket Worker	79%
Elderly 1	68	Retired	71%
Elderly 2	71	Retired	74%

As Table 2 displays, the mean post-test score for the group increased to 81%, reflecting a substantial 27% improvement across all participants. This enhancement was statistically significant, as confirmed by a paired t-test yielding a p-value of less than 0.05. This statistical finding indicates that the observed improvement in spelling proficiency was not attributable to random chance, thereby supporting the efficacy of the intervention.

Participants' Reporting on Intervention Engagement

To ensure sustained engagement and monitor potential attrition, participants were required to maintain regular communication with the principal investigator through daily text messages. This protocol not only enabled the research team to verify ongoing participation but also provided a valuable channel for collecting qualitative feedback regarding user experience. The majority of participants expressed high levels of satisfaction with the *Words of Wonders* application, frequently noting improvements in both spelling and vocabulary acquisition. While adult participants occasionally missed daily reports, adolescents and elderly participants demonstrated consistent adherence to the reporting protocol. The qualitative data collected through these daily updates offered insights into participant motivation, engagement, and the perceived effectiveness of the intervention.

Table 3 illustrates two weeks of participants' reports as an example to clarify how this part of qualitative data were categorized and analyzed during the intervention. Each entry demonstrates how excerpts from teenagers, adults, and elderly participants were systematically coded according to emerging motivational and engagement-related themes, providing a foundation for subsequent thematic analysis of spelling improvement and learner motivation through the *Words of Wonders* application.

Table 3. Two weeks of participants' daily reports

Date	Participants	Excerpt from Report	Thematic Code
Week 1	Teenager 1	"The puzzles are really fun. I want to play every day!"	Engagement/Motivation
	Teenager 2	"I like earning points for each word I spell correctly."	Reward Motivation
	Teenager 3	"It feels good when I finish a level faster than before."	Progress/Competence
	Adult 1	"I'm surprised how much I remember from school."	Rediscovery/Motivation
	Adult 2	"The app is easy to use, even after a long day at work."	Usability/Convenience
	Adult 3	"I missed one day, but I caught up quickly."	Adherence/Commitment
	Elderly 1	"My granddaughter helps me with the new words."	Social/Relatedness
	Elderly 2	"I enjoy the daily routine. It keeps my mind sharp."	Routine/Cognitive Benefit

continued on following page

Table 3. Continued

Date	Participants	Excerpt from Report	Thematic Code
Week 2	Teenager 1	"I learned three new words this week!"	Vocabulary Acquisition
	Teenager 2	"My friends and I compete to see who finishes first."	Social/Competition
	Teenager 3	"I made fewer mistakes than last week."	Improvement/Confidence
	Adult 1	"I use the app during my commute. It's a good habit."	Habit Formation
	Adult 2	"I'm more confident writing emails at work now."	Transfer/Confidence
	Adult 3	"I like seeing my progress chart go up."	Visual Feedback/Motivation
	Elderly 1	"I can spell more words without help now."	Independence/Improvement
	Elderly 2	"I look forward to the puzzles every morning."	Anticipation/Routine

THEMATIC ANALYSIS OF THE PARTICIPANT REPORTS

The thematic analysis of the participant reports over the eight-week intervention period, as shown in Table 4 and Table 5, reveals a clear, progressive enhancement in learners' motivation to engage with spelling tasks through the *Words of Wonders* application. In Table 4 percentages are based on the number of weekly reports coded for motivation out of all reports for that week. In the initial weeks, motivation was present but relatively limited in scope, with approximately 25% of participant reports coded for explicit motivation-related themes such as engagement and curiosity. This early phase was characterized by learners exploring the novelty of the app, expressing initial excitement, and demonstrating an openness to the gamified learning experience. As the intervention progressed into the second and third weeks, the proportion of motivation-related codes increased to 38%, reflecting a growing sense of commitment and adherence among participants. Reports during this period frequently referenced the ability to return to the app after occasional lapses, indicating that the gamified elements were effective in re-engaging learners and fostering a sense of progress.

By the middle phase of the intervention, corresponding to weeks four through six, there was a marked rise in motivation-related codes, with frequencies climbing from 50% to 75%. This increase coincided with participants' growing awareness of their own improvement and heightened confidence in their spelling abilities. Thematic analysis of reports from this period highlights the significance of perceived progress and the overcoming of adherence challenges, both of which served to further reinforce intrinsic motivation. Learners began to articulate a stronger sense of competence and autonomy, often noting that the usability and accessibility of the app contributed to their sustained engagement. The gamified structure, with its immediate feedback and incremental challenges, appeared to scaffold learners' experiences effectively, enabling them to persist through difficulties and derive satisfaction from measurable achievements.

In the later weeks of the intervention, specifically weeks seven and eight, motivation became nearly ubiquitous, with 88% of the participant reports reflecting themes of intrinsic motivation, social recognition, and the establishment of productive routines. Reports from this stage frequently described the positive impact of peer recognition, pride in achievement, and the integration of spelling practice into daily life. The emergence of routine and well-being as dominant themes suggests that the intervention successfully facilitated the internalization of motivational drivers, transforming spelling practice from a task-oriented activity into a habitual and valued component of participants' lives. The sustained and increasing prevalence of motivation-related codes throughout the intervention underscores the effectiveness of the *Words of Wonders* application in fostering both extrinsic and intrinsic motivation, ultimately leading to greater engagement, improved spelling proficiency, and the development of autonomous learning behaviors. This trajectory aligns closely with the principles of SDT and Flow Theory, illustrating how gamified educational interventions can catalyze and sustain motivation in language learning contexts.

Table 4. Thematic Analysis Table: Growth of Motivation to Learn Spelling

Week	Motivation-Related Codes Identified	% of Reports with Motivation Codes	Example/Theme Highlighted
1	Engagement/Motivation	25%	Initial excitement, curiosity
2	Adherence/Progress	38%	Return after lapse, commitment
3	Social/Enjoyment	38%	Social play supports motivation
4	Perceived Improvement	50%	Progress boosts motivation
5	Adherence Challenge (yet continued use)	63%	Motivation persists despite challenges
6	Usability/Confidence	75%	Confidence in spelling strengthens motivation
7	Peer Recognition/Motivation	88%	Social recognition, pride in achievement
8	Routine/Well-being	88%	Motivation becomes habitual, part of routine

Table 5. Summary of Motivation Code Trend

Phase	Weeks	% Motivation Codes	Key Motivational Drives
Early	1–3	25–38%	Novelty, social play, curiosity
Middle	4–6	50–75%	Progress, confidence, persistence
Sustained	7–8	88%	Recognition, routine, autonomy

Semi-Structured Interviews

This study employed a semi-structured interview protocol designed to elicit comprehensive insights into participants' experiences with English spelling and their engagement with a gamified mobile application, *Words of Wonders*. The interview framework addressed a range of cognitive and affective dimensions, including prior spelling challenges, reliance on technological aids (e.g., auto-correct), motivational and confidence levels, and overall perceptions of the intervention (see Appendix B). Interviews were conducted in two phases—pre-study and post-study—allowing for comparative analysis of participants' attitudes and behaviors before and after the intervention.

Pre-Study Interviews

The pre-study interviews aimed to establish a baseline understanding of participants' difficulties with English spelling and their general attitudes toward improvement. Participants across all age groups reported ongoing struggles with accurate spelling, particularly with irregular or less frequently encountered words. A prominent theme that emerged was participants' extensive reliance on auto-correct features available on digital devices. While these tools reduced the immediate burden of spelling accurately, they also diminished learners' motivation to consciously engage with spelling as a skill. All participants expressed a lack of intrinsic interest in improving their spelling, viewing digital assistance as an adequate substitute. In 7 out of 8 cases, the participants also reported feelings of frustration and anxiety when required to write without technological support, highlighting a perceived dependency on such tools. These insights revealed a significant gap in both skill development and learner motivation, emphasizing the need for a more engaging and supportive learning approach.

Post-Study Interviews

Post-study interviews explored participants' experiences with the *Words of Wonders* application, focusing on motivational drivers, perceived learning outcomes, and overall engagement. Open-ended questions encouraged participants to reflect on their usage patterns, challenges, and perceived benefits of the app, as well as any changes in their attitudes toward spelling and language learning (see Appendix B).As Table 6 demonstrates, the data revealed a substantial increase in learner motivation over time, with participants attributing this to the game's interactive features—particularly the competitive elements, progress tracking, and reward system.

Table 6. Progression of Motivational Themes over Time

Study Phase	Codes (Participant Quotes)	Themes	Age Group(s)
Weeks 1–2 (Early Engagement)	- "I love seeing my score go up each time I get a word right." - "I thought it was just a game for kids." - Frequent checking of scores and rewards	Motivation by Immediate Feedback and Rewards Initial Skepticism (Elderly)	Teenagers, Elderly
Weeks 3–6 (Sustained Motivation)	- "After using the app, I feel much more confident in my writing." - Customizing practice sessions - Consistent use of progress-tracking features	Competence Development Autonomy and Self-Regulation	Adults (more)+ All Groups
Weeks 7–8 (Long-term Internalization)	- "The game made learning spelling less frustrating." - "I enjoyed it, and I learned a lot without feeling overwhelmed." - Reduced reliance on rewards	Internalized Motivation Reduced Anxiety Reframed Attitudes Toward Spelling	All Groups

Table 6 delineates a clear trajectory of motivational development among participants throughout the two-month intervention with the *Words of Wonders* application. In the initial phase (Weeks 1–2), motivation was predominantly extrinsically oriented, with immediate feedback and reward mechanisms serving as the primary drivers of engagement, particularly for adolescent participants. The instant gratification provided by points, scores, and visible progress fostered a sense of achievement and competition, aligning with established findings that extrinsic motivators are especially salient in the early stages of gamified learning (Luarn et al., 2023). In contrast, elderly participants exhibited initial skepticism, reflecting a need for adaptation and an adjustment period to appreciate the educational value embedded within the gamified structure.

As the study progressed into the sustained motivation phase (Weeks 3–6), a discernible shift toward intrinsic motivation emerged. Adults, in particular, began to report increased confidence in their spelling and writing abilities, attributing these gains to repeated success within the application. This phase was characterized by the growing importance of competence development, as participants experienced mastery through incremental challenges and scaffolded tasks. The ability to customize practice sessions and independently track progress further promoted autonomy, a core component of SDT (Deci & Ryan, 2004). These findings suggest that, as extrinsic motivators established initial engagement, intrinsic motivators—such as personal growth, autonomy, and self-regulation—became increasingly influential in sustaining participation.

In the final phase (Weeks 7–8), participants across all age groups demonstrated a marked internalization of motivation. Reliance on external rewards diminished, and the learning process was reframed as enjoyable and low-stress. The app's scaffolded difficulty levels and multimodal feedback were frequently cited as instrumental in reducing anxiety and fostering a positive attitude toward spelling. This progression from extrinsic to intrinsic motivation is consistent with the theoretical underpinnings of SDT and Flow Theory, which posit that sustained engagement and deep learning are most likely when learners perceive activities as inherently satisfying and optimally challenging (Deci & Ryan, 2004; Csikszentmihalyi et al., 2018).

Age-specific pathways were also evident. Teenagers maintained a strong orientation toward social comparison and competitive elements, while adults valued the practical outcomes of improved language proficiency, particularly in professional contexts. Elderly participants, after overcoming initial skepticism, highlighted the importance of accessibility and inclusive design in maintaining their motivation. Collectively, these findings underscore the adaptability of gamified learning environments in addressing the diverse motivational needs of different learner demographics. The following section elaborates on detailed thematic analysis of the interview dataset.

THEMATIC EXPLORATION OF PARTICIPANT REFLECTIONS

Thematic analysis of the interview transcripts revealed four dominant themes: (1) Motivational Reframing, (2) Autonomy and Flexibility, (3) Affective Confidence, and (4) Perceived Limitations.

1. Motivational Reframing: From Obligation to Enjoyment

A consistent pattern across all age groups was the redefinition of spelling practice from a burdensome obligation to an enjoyable challenge. Teenagers, who previously described spelling as "stressful" or "boring," reported feeling "excited" and "motivated" by the game's mechanics. Teenager 1 (14 years old) stated, *"I used to hate spelling tests, but now I get excited when I unlock a new level. It doesn't feel like homework anymore—it's like winning."* The score tracking and level advancement features fostered a sense of progression that transformed repetition into achievement.

Adults echoed similar sentiments. Adult 2 (34 years old), a software engineer, noted, *"I always avoided spelling exercises because they felt tedious. With this app, I actually looked forward to the daily challenge. It was short, fun, and didn't feel like studying."* This reframing aligns with SDT's concept of intrinsic motivation, in which learners perceive the task as valuable and engaging for its own sake (Deci & Ryan, 2004).

2. Autonomy and Flexibility in Learning

The ability to learn at one's own pace and schedule was frequently mentioned as a benefit, particularly by working adults and elderly participants. Adult 3 (43 years old) stated, *"I could do a few levels in the evening after work, without needing to sit through a long boring class."* This flexibility empowered participants to take control of their learning trajectory, contributing to the development of learner autonomy—a key construct in contemporary language pedagogy (Mimeau et al., 2025).

Elderly Participant 1 (71 years old) initially expressed apprehension toward using mobile apps but ultimately embraced the digital format: *"I never thought I could use an app to learn English. But once I got used to it, I liked being able to practice on my own without feeling rushed."* This adaptability among older learners suggests that age is not necessarily a barrier to digital literacy when tools are intuitive and rewarding.

3. Affective Confidence and Risk-Taking

Several participants noted an increase in confidence, especially in writing and spelling tasks. Adult 1 (27 years old), a nurse, reported, *"I've always been anxious about making spelling mistakes in my reports. But after this, I feel less worried. I can spell many more words correctly without checking."* This part of data corroborates Witzel et al.'s (2024) assertion that confidence, though often underemphasized in gamification research, is crucial for empowering learners to undertake linguistic risks and persevere in challenging tasks. Along with this, teenager 2 remarked that spelling now felt "doable" rather than "scary," suggesting that the app reduced the affective filter of anxiety (Krashen, 1982)—the anxiety that often impedes language learning. The sense of low-stakes experimentation, reinforced by the app's playful environment, enabled learners to engage more freely with language.

4. Perceived Limitations and Future Desires

Despite the overwhelmingly positive feedback, participants also identified limitations. Teenager 3 observed that the app's focus on isolated word spelling did not prepare them for full writing tasks: *"It's great for spelling, but I wish it helped with writing sentences or using grammar."* Elderly Participant 2 echoed this view, expressing a desire for features that support sentence construction and everyday expressions.Such comments reflect a broader concern in the literature that gamified tools, while engaging, often target micro-skills (e.g., spelling, vocabulary) at the expense of integrated communicative competence. Participants expressed interest in a more comprehensive app that would combine spelling with grammar, pronunciation, and usage in context.

RELIABILITY AND VALIDITY OF THE INTERVIEW DATA

To ensure the reliability and validity of the interview data, multiple methodological safeguards were employed. Two applied linguistics experts independently reviewed the interview questions for clarity, relevance, and alignment with the study's objectives. A pilot test with three participants similar to the main sample led to refinement of 15% of the questions to improve clarity and sequencing. Inter-rater reliability for coding pilot responses was high (Cohen's kappa = 0.80), indicating substantial agreement between coders. These steps ensured a reliable and clear interview protocol suitable for the case study's focused sample.

Regarding validity, the interview content was closely aligned with the study's theoretical framework, incorporating constructs from SDT, CLT, and Flow Theory to capture motivational, behavioral, and cognitive dimensions. Pre- and post-intervention interviews allowed assessment of changes over time, enhancing construct validity. Triangulation with daily reports and app usage data further strengthened the credibility of the findings. Collectively, these measures ensured the interview protocol provided a robust basis for examining the relationship between gamification, motivation, and spelling improvement.

TRIANGULATING PERCEPTION WITH PERFORMANCE

The interview data triangulate well with the quantitative results, particularly the post-test gains in spelling accuracy. While the test scores provided statistical validation of learning, the interviews illuminated the psychological and emotional dimensions of that learning—especially in terms of motivation, confidence, and persistence. This dual perspective strengthens the claim that gamification has both cognitive and affective benefits, especially when well-aligned with learners' needs and contexts.

DISCUSSION: COMPARATIVE INSIGHTS AND PEDAGOGICAL IMPLICATIONS

The findings from this case study highlight the multifaceted impact of gamified learning on spelling development and learner motivation. This section synthesizes those findings by situating them within existing literature, drawing comparisons with traditional pedagogical approaches, and outlining concrete implications for educators, app developers, and language policy designers.

GAMIFICATION VS. TRADITIONAL LANGUAGE INSTRUCTION

Participants in this study consistently reported higher motivation, sustained engagement, and improved spelling outcomes when using the *Words of Wonders* app compared to their prior experiences with traditional instruction. Conventional spelling exercises—such as dictation, memorization, and fill-in-the-blank worksheets—are often perceived as tedious or high-pressure, particularly among younger learners (Wulantari et al., 2023). In contrast, gamified learning environments transform repetition into achievement, fostering what Chapman et al. (2023) call "motivated immersion." This contrast was especially evident in the affective responses of the teenage participants. Spelling, typically associated with test anxiety or correctional feedback, was reframed as a challenge to overcome, embedded within a visually appealing and reward-driven context. Adult and elderly learners, too, responded positively to the lower-stakes learning environment, which empowered them to practice without fear of judgment.

Compared to classroom-based instruction, where feedback is often delayed or generalized, gamified tools offer instant, individualized feedback, allowing learners to correct errors immediately—a factor emphasized in studies by Ogino & Matsuguma (2024). This immediacy is not merely functional but motivational, reinforcing correct responses and promoting learning persistence. Such design elements align with both SDT and Flow Theory, which highlight autonomy and optimal challenge as key to deep engagement (Deci & Ryan, 2004; Csikszentmihalyi et al., 2018).

CHALLENGES AND PRACTICAL IMPLICATIONS FOR IMPLEMENTATION

Despite the clear benefits, this study also revealed structural limitations in the scope of current gamified tools. While spelling was effectively targeted, other essential domains—grammar, syntax, and pragmatic language use—were largely absent. Participants explicitly noted that while they experienced gains in isolated word recognition and reproduction, they still felt underprepared for holistic writing or conversation tasks. This insight mirrors concerns in the literature that gamification often favors discrete language items at the expense of communicative competence (Shobeiry, 2021b; Shen et al., 2024; Tariq, 2025). Educators should therefore approach gamified learning as a complementary method, best used in tandem with classroom instruction, writing practice, and communicative tasks.

Another limitation involves device access and digital literacy. While most participants successfully navigated the app, the initial hesitation of elderly users suggests a need for onboarding support and user-friendly design features. This reinforces the importance of inclusive technology that can accommodate learners with varying levels of digital experience and physical dexterity (Christopoulos & Mystakidis, 2023).

PEDAGOGICAL IMPLICATIONS AND RECOMMENDATIONS

The study's outcomes point to several actionable insights for educators and instructional designers:

1. Embed gamification strategically: Gamified tools should be integrated into curricula with clear pedagogical intentions, particularly for developing literacy subskills such as spelling, vocabulary recognition, and morphological awareness.
2. Support multimodal learning: Apps that include auditory, visual, and kinesthetic elements foster deeper processing and retention. These features also support learners from diverse linguistic backgrounds who may struggle with the irregular orthography of English.
3. Encourage autonomy and reflection: Features like daily streaks, performance tracking, and self-pacing enable learners to take ownership of their learning. Coupling this with reflective prompts or journaling could further deepen metacognitive awareness.
4. Balance skill development: To provide a more holistic learning experience, developers should consider integrating grammatical contexts, sentence-level practice, and real-life scenarios alongside spelling games.

5. Train and include educators: Teachers should be equipped with professional development that helps them understand how to blend gamified tools with traditional instruction, assess progress meaningfully, and guide students in setting realistic goals.
6. Adapt for accessibility: Apps should offer adjustable font sizes, audio support, and intuitive interfaces to accommodate users across age groups and learning needs, reducing exclusion based on physical or digital limitations.

Comparative evidence demonstrates that, when thoughtfully implemented, gamification serves as a powerful motivator and skill-building tool in second language learning—particularly in domains such as spelling, where repetition and accuracy are essential. By aligning technological design with motivational and cognitive theories, educators and developers can foster equitable, engaging, and effective learning experiences for diverse learner populations.

FUTURE DIRECTIONS

As gamified language learning advances, emerging trends promise to enhance engagement, personalization, and accessibility in L2 instruction. This study's findings on motivational and skill-specific gains from gamified spelling tools highlight key future directions:

1. **AI and Learning Analytics for Personalization**

Future platforms could use AI to create adaptive learning paths based on individual performance, analyzing errors and preferences to deliver targeted scaffolding and feedback. This would enable personalized instruction aligned with each learner's Zone of Proximal Development, moving beyond static progression models.

2. **Augmented and Virtual Reality for Immersive Practice**

AR and VR can immerse learners in contextualized language use, integrating spelling and vocabulary into real-world simulations. Such environments support situated learning, enhance engagement, reduce cognitive load, and improve retention by combining form-focused instruction with communicative practice.

3. **Social Collaboration and Gamified Communities**

Incorporating peer challenges, multiplayer tasks, and cooperative missions can foster social learning and relatedness, facilitating peer scaffolding and promoting digital citizenship. These features leverage the inherently social nature of language learning to enhance competence and empathy.

4. **Integration of Comprehensive Language Skills**

Future gamified tools should combine reading, writing, listening, and speaking tasks within interdisciplinary contexts, supporting holistic language development and academic literacy aligned with CLIL principles and standardized test preparation.

5. **Accessibility and Inclusive Design**

Prioritizing universal design—including screen reader compatibility, customizable interfaces, neurodiversity support, and offline functionality—is essential to ensure equitable access. Addressing the digital divide will enable gamified learning to serve diverse populations effectively.

Collectively, these trends suggest a future of gamified L2 learning that is adaptive, immersive, socially interactive, integrative, and inclusive.

FURTHER READING

- Zhao, X., & McClure, C. D. (2024). Gather. Town: A gamification tool to promote engagement and establish online learning communities for language learners. *RELC Journal*, *55*(1), 240-245.This paper explores the potential of virtual learning communities in language education, focusing on the innovative platform Gather.Town. This platform revolutionizes traditional video conferencing by providing a gamified, 2D map-based environment with avatar features and proximity-based video conferencing, which enhances student engagement and simulates real-life interactions.
- Liu, G. Z., Fathi, J., & Rahimi, M. (2024). Using digital gamification to improve language achievement, foreign language enjoyment, and ideal L2 self: A case of English as a foreign language learners. *Journal of Computer Assisted Learning*, *40*(4), 1347-1364.This paper explores the impact of digital gamified language learning on English as a Foreign Language learners' language achievement, foreign language enjoyment, and ideal second language self. Employing a sequential explanatory mixed-methods approach, the study compares the effects of digital gamified language learning activities conducted via a mobile application with those of non-digital, printed activi-

ties. The results support the effectiveness of digital gamification in enhancing language learning outcomes and learner engagement, aligning with broader research indicating that gamification can improve linguistic competencies and foster a more enjoyable learning environment

- Christopoulos, A., & Mystakidis, S. (2023). Gamification in education. *Encyclopedia*, *3*(4), 1223-1243.This paper highlights the concept of gamification, or gameful design, as the strategic integration of game design principles and mechanics into non-game environments. This approach is frequently facilitated through digital platforms, with the primary objectives of solving problems, enhancing engagement, and motivating individuals to achieve their goals. The paper also explores the widespread impact of gamification, particularly in education, where it has been shown to significantly enhance learner motivation, engagement, and knowledge retention by making learning more enjoyable and interactive.

ACKNOWLEDGEMENT

Gratitude is extended to Ms. Helya Fattahi, research assistant, for her valuable contributions to data collection and analysis in this book chapter.

REFERENCES

Al-Sobhi, B. M. S., Rashid, S. M., Abdullah, A. N., & Darmi, R. (2017). Arab ESL secondary school students' spelling errors. *International Journal of Education and Literacy Studies*, *5*(3), 16–23.

Anisa, K. D., Marmanto, S., & Supriyadi, S. (2020). The effect of gamification on students' motivation in learning English. *Leksika: Jurnal Bahasa, Sastra dan Pengajarannya, 14*(1), 22–28.

Bear, D. R., von Gillern, S., & Xu, W. (2018). Learning to spell in English by Chinese students: A cross-sectional study. *TESOL International Journal*, *13*(1), 47–66.

Chapman, J. R., Kohler, T. B., Rich, P. J., & Trego, A. (2023). Maybe we've got it wrong: An experimental evaluation of self-determination and flow theory in gamification. *Journal of Research on Technology in Education*, •••, 1–20.

Chen, C. Y. (2025). Effects of worked examples with explanation types and learner motivation on cognitive load and programming problem-solving performance. *ACM Transactions on Computing Education*. Advance online publication.

Chen, Y. C., & Hou, H. T. (2025). Design of a digital gamified learning activity for relationship education with conceptual scaffolding and reflective scaffolding. *The Asia-Pacific Education Researcher*, *34*(1), 237–251.

Csikszentmihalyi, M., Montijo, M. N., & Mouton, A. R. (2018). Flow theory: Optimizing elite performance in the creative realm. In Pfeiffer, S. I., Shaunessy-Dedrick, E., & Foley-Nicpon, M. (Eds.), *APA handbook of giftedness and talent* (pp. 215–229). American Psychological Association., DOI: 10.1037/0000038-014

Deci, E. L., & Ryan, R. M. (Eds.). (2004). *Handbook of self-determination research*. University of Rochester Press.

Fälth, L., Brkovic, I., Kerestes, G., Svensson, I., Hjelmquist, E., & Tjus, T. (2023). The effects of a multimodal intervention on the reading skills of struggling students: An exploration across countries. *Reading Psychology*, *44*(3), 225–241.

Huseinović, L. (2024). The effects of gamification on student motivation and achievement in learning English as a foreign language in higher education. *MAP Education and Humanities*, *4*, 10–36.

Krashen, S. D. (1982). *Principles and practice in second language acquisition*. Pergamon Press.

Lascano Ortiz, A. A., Mejía Sánchez, E. J., Proaño López, G. L., & Silva Chávez, J. A. (2025). Spelling activities to reinforce vocabulary learning. *DATEH*, *7*(1), 1–5.

Luarn, P., Chen, C. C., & Chiu, Y. P. (2023). Enhancing intrinsic learning motivation through gamification: A self-determination theory perspective. *The International Journal of Information and Learning Technology*, *40*(5), 413–424.

Mimeau, C., Ricketts, J., & Deacon, S. H. (2025). Learning spellings and meanings: Longitudinal relations to reading. *Journal of Research in Reading*. Advance online publication.

Moreira, F. T., & Teles, R. O. (Eds.). (2024). *Improving student assessment with emerging AI tools*. IGI Global.

Namaziandost, E., Shobeiry, M., & Heydarnejad, T. (2024). Enhancing the SHAD platform: Exploring the emotional influence of telegram-supported supplementary tasks on learners' happiness, technostress, autonomy, growth mindfulness, and resilience. *Journal of Studies in Language Learning and Teaching*, *1*(2), 251–267. DOI: 10.22034/jsllt.2024.21648.1043

Ogino, H., & Matsuguma, H. (2024). Effective implementation of feedback in gamification. *International Journal of Asia Digital Art and Design*, *28*(2), 9–17.

Orak, S. D. (2025). EFL students' perception of gamification-integrated English language education. *Pegem Journal of Education and Instruction*, *15*(1), 143–158.

Rowe, L. W., & Pennington, V. (2025). Multilingual learners' digital book composing: Examining circulation of translingual, multimodal resources in an elementary classroom. *Journal of Second Language Writing*, *67*, 101180.

Schiff, R., Levy-Shimon, S., Oanunu Shashoua, L., & Sasson, A. (2025). Same spelling, different meaning: An EF-based homograph reading intervention for struggling readers. *Reading & Writing Quarterly*, *41*(1), 28–49.

Shen, Z., Lai, M., & Wang, F. (2024). Investigating the influence of gamification on motivation and learning outcomes in online language learning. *Frontiers in Psychology*, *15*, 1295709. DOI: 10.3389/fpsyg.2024.1295709 PMID: 38860036

Shobeiry, M. (2021a). Personalized learning reliability of Tell Me More: A dynamic approach. *Revista EntreLinguas*, e021068.

Shobeiry, M. (2021b). A survey study on the potential educational value of WhatsApp in the Iranian EFL settings. *Journal of Applied Linguistics and Language Research, 8*(1), 126–148.

Smail, L., Mahmoud, G., & Adel, D. (2025). The role of morphological awareness and orthographic awareness in reading comprehension in Arabic: Do reading fluency and working memory count? *Reading Psychology, 46*(1), 1–42.

Suárez-Coalla, P., Hevia-Tuero, C., Martínez-García, C., & Afonso, O. (2024). Spanish children spelling in English as a foreign language: Central and peripheral processes. *Journal of Research in Reading*, *47*(4), 475–496.

Sun, X., & Sailer, M. (2025). Students' behavioural, cognitive and affective outcomes in gamified flipped classrooms: A meta-analysis. *Review of Education, 13*(1), e70039.

Sweller, J. (2011). Cognitive load theory. In Ross, B. H. (Ed.), *Psychology of learning and motivation* (Vol. 55, pp. 37–76). Academic Press.

Tariq, M. U. (2025). Gamification and virtual reality: Transforming early childhood language learning. In *Digital pedagogy in early childhood language development* (pp. 25–52). IGI Global Scientific Publishing.

Vygotsky, L. S. (1978). *Mind in society: The development of higher psychological processes*. Harvard University Press.

Witzel, B., Görgen-Rein, R., Galuschka, K., Huemer, S., Del Toro, I. C., Schulte-Körne, G., & Moll, K. (2024). Digital game-based spelling intervention for children with spelling deficits: A randomized controlled trial. *Learning and Instruction, 89*, 101842.

Wulantari, N. P., Rachman, A., Sari, M. N., Uktolseja, L. J., & Rofi'i, A. (2023). The role of gamification in English language teaching: A literature review. *Journal of Education, 6*(01), 2847–2856.

Zhao, X., & McClure, C. D. (2024). Gather.Town: A gamification tool to promote engagement and establish online learning communities for language learners. *RELC Journal, 55*(1), 240–245.

Zhou, J., & Gu, Y. (2024). Unraveling students' liking of teachers: The impact of multimodal cues during L2 English vocabulary teaching. [ISCA.]. *Speech Prosody (Urbana, Ill.), 2024*, 881–885.

KEY TERMS AND DEFINITIONS

Autonomous Learning: A learner-centered approach where individuals take responsibility for their own educational progress. In this study, gamified tools enabled participants to engage with spelling activities at their own pace and schedule, fostering greater independence and self-regulation (Luarn et al., 2023; Orak, 2025).

Cognitive Load Theory (CLT): A theory that emphasizes the limitations of working memory and the importance of instructional design in reducing unnecessary mental effort. The *Words of Wonders* app reduced cognitive load by segmenting complex spelling tasks into manageable parts, facilitating more efficient learning (Sweller, 2011; Huseinović, 2024).

Digital Game-Based Learning (DGBL): An instructional approach that utilizes computer games or digital applications for educational purposes, integrating learning content within interactive and entertaining formats. The case study utilized *Words of Wonders* as a DGBL platform to improve learners' spelling and motivation through gameplay (Witzel et al., 2024; Liu et al., 2024).

Educational Technology Equity: The principle that all learners, regardless of background or access to resources, should have equal opportunities to benefit from technological advancements in education. The manuscript highlights disparities in access to mobile devices and internet, calling for more inclusive gamified learning tools (Namaziandost et al., 2024; Christopoulos & Mystakidis, 2023).

Flow Theory: A psychological state of complete immersion and enjoyment in an activity, often resulting in enhanced learning outcomes. Gamified elements such as level progression and instant feedback were designed to sustain learners' engagement and promote flow (Csikszentmihalyi et al., 2018; Chapman et al., 2023).

Gamification: The application of game-design elements in non-game contexts to increase learner engagement and motivation. Gamification in this study involved the use of rewards, leaderboards, and scoring systems to transform spelling practice into an enjoyable learning experience (Anisa et al., 2020; Orak, 2025).

Immediate Feedback: Timely responses provided during learning activities that help correct errors and reinforce understanding. Words of Wonders offered real-time corrections, a key feature in preventing fossilization of spelling errors and enhancing learning (Ogino & Matsuguma, 2024).

Intrinsic Motivation: Motivation driven by internal rewards and personal satisfaction, rather than external incentives. Participants reported increased intrinsic motivation due to the enjoyable and autonomous nature of gamified spelling tasks (Wulantari et al., 2023).

Multimodality: The integration of multiple modes of communication—such as text, audio, and images—to enhance comprehension and retention. The use of multimodal elements in the app supported spelling acquisition by presenting words visually, phonetically, and contextually (Fälth et al., 2023; Zhou & Gu, 2024).

Self-Determination Theory (SDT): A psychological framework that explains human motivation in terms of three innate needs: autonomy, competence, and relatedness. The gamified intervention aligned with SDT by enabling learner autonomy, competence through feedback, and relatedness via social features (Deci & Ryan, 2004; Luarn et al., 2023).

Spelling Diagnostic Assessment: A standardized evaluative tool designed to measure learners' ability to spell words accurately, often used to identify areas for intervention. Used in both pre- and post-intervention phases, this assessment quantified the measurable improvement in spelling skills among participants.

Spelling Proficiency: The ability to correctly sequence letters to form words according to a language's orthographic conventions. Spelling was the primary skill targeted in this study, with notable improvements observed across all participant demographics (Mimeau et al., 2025; Witzel et al., 2024).

Zone of Proximal Development (ZPD): A concept developed by Vygotsky that describes the range of tasks learners can perform with guidance but not independently. The gamified tasks were designed to align with each learner's ZPD, offering scaffolding through increasing difficulty and feedback (Vygotsky, 1978; Shen et al., 2024).

APPENDIX

Interview questions

Pre-Study Semi-Structured Interview Questions

1. Can you describe your general experience with spelling in English? What challenges do you usually face?
2. How often do you rely on auto-correct or spell-check features on your phone or computer when writing in English?
3. Do you feel confident in your ability to spell new or unfamiliar words without technological assistance? Why or why not?
4. How important do you think spelling is for your overall English proficiency and communication?
5. Have you previously made any efforts to improve your spelling? If so, what methods did you use and how effective were they?
6. What are your feelings or attitudes towards learning spelling? Do you find it interesting, boring, or challenging?
7. Can you recall any situations where spelling errors affected your communication or confidence? Please describe.
8. How motivated are you to improve your spelling skills at this stage? What factors influence your motivation?
9. Are there any particular types of words or spelling patterns you find especially difficult?
10. What do you hope to achieve by participating in this study? Are there specific spelling goals you have in mind?

Post-Study Semi-Structured Interview Questions

1. How has your experience with the Words of Wonders app influenced your approach to spelling in English?
2. Have you noticed any changes in your reliance on auto-correct or spell-check features since participating in the study?
3. Can you describe any improvements you have observed in your spelling ability over the course of the intervention?
4. How has your confidence in spelling new or unfamiliar words changed, if at all?
5. Did you find the gamified elements (such as points, rewards, and challenges) in the app motivating? Why or why not?

6. What aspects of the app did you find most helpful or enjoyable for learning spelling?
7. Were there any challenges or frustrations you encountered while using the app? How did you address them?
8. How do you feel about learning spelling now compared to before the study? Has your interest or motivation changed?
9. Do you plan to continue using the app or similar tools to practice spelling in the future? Why or why not?
10. What advice would you give to other learners who struggle with spelling based on your experience in this study?

Chapter 9
Digital Inclusion and Accessibility in South African Classrooms:
Opportunities and Challenges in Immersive Learning

Mahlatse Ragolane
https://orcid.org/0000-0002-1889-7616
Regent Business School, South Africa

Shahiem Patel
https://orcid.org/0000-0002-2340-0440
Regent Business School, South Africa

ABSTRACT

The educational sector shifted from traditional learning environments to virtual reality (VR), augmented reality (AR) and gamification. With its promise to enhance learner engagement, the challenge lies in implementation, often reproducing existing inequalities. There is consensus that developing countries like South Africa face disparities in infrastructure, digital literacy and socioeconomic development, posing barriers to equitable access. This chapter examines digital inclusion and accessibility regarding immersive technologies and game-based learning in South Africa. The chapter interrogates these dynamics vis-à-vis the educational opportunities immersive technologies afford and deny marginalised learners. Through the capability approach and Universal Design for learning (UDL), it explores how immersive tools can expand or restrict learners' real freedoms to participate in education.

DOI: 10.4018/979-8-3373-4465-2.ch009

INTRODUCTION

The *raison d'être* of human society has always been the will to belong and to forge connections within communities grounded in mutual social bonds. In his 2008 book *Outliers: The Story of Success*, Malcolm Gladwell recounts the story of Roseto, a town in Pennsylvania settled by immigrants from southern Italy. Gladwell explains that despite unhealthy habits, the residents of Roseto enjoyed remarkably low rates of disease. According to Gladwell (2008), researchers discovered that the cause was not diet, genetics or location but rather the strength of their community ties or connections. This reveals a fundamentally agreed upon notion that human beings thrive in environments of social connection and mutual support. Throughout history, our survival and progress have depended not only on individual talent or resources but on our capacity to belong, collaborate and engage meaningfully with one another. In the context of education, particularly in digitally mediated, immersive environments, this need for connection becomes even more urgent (see Slater & Wilbur, 1997; Garrison, Anderson, & Archer, 2000). As South African higher education institutions increasingly adopt technologies such as Virtual Reality (VR), Augmented Reality (AR) and gamification, the key question is not merely what these tools can do, but who they serve and include. Digital inclusion must therefore be more than a matter of access; it must create human connection and meaningful participation, especially for marginalised learners.

Furthermore, while digital technologies are often celebrated for their ability to connect people across space and time, their actual impact on human connection is far more complex. Counterintuitively, research suggests that the very tools designed to bring us together can also fragment and isolate. In educational settings, for instance, the shift to digital and immersive learning environments can diminish learners' sense of presence, belonging, and engagement if not thoughtfully designed (Garrison *et al.,* 2000). Turkle (2011) argued that technology often creates the illusion of connection while creating emotional disconnection, particularly when social interaction is mediated through screens or algorithms. This paradox is evident in classrooms where immersive technologies such as VR and AR, while rich in interactivity, can isolate learners if collaborative structures and inclusive design principles are not embedded (Slater & Wilbur, 1997). Thus, while technology holds immense promise for enhancing social learning, it does not guarantee connection; rather, its design and implementation must be deliberately human-centred to avoid deepening existing divides.

To understand how technology can either enhance or diminish connection in educational contexts, this chapter draws on the Capability Approach and Universal Design for Learning (UDL) as its guiding theoretical lenses. The Capability Approach, pioneered by Sen (1999) and extended by Nussbaum (2011), emphasises individuals' real freedoms to achieve lives they have reason to value. In the realm of education, this means evaluating not just access to technology, but whether that access translates into meaningful participation, agency, and connection. Inaccessible technologies, isolating, or culturally alienating, may offer the appearance of innovation while constraining learners' actual capabilities. Similarly, UDL, developed by Meyer, Rose, and Gordon (2014), advocates for proactive curriculum design that accommodates learner diversity by offering multiple means of engagement, representation, and expression. Both frameworks underscore that true inclusion is not merely the absence of barriers, but the presence of affordances that expand learners' opportunities to connect, collaborate, and thrive. When applied to immersive learning environments, these theories urge us to ask: Does this technology support all learners in developing the capabilities they value, or does it privilege some while excluding others?

Despite the promise of immersive technologies, their implementation in South African higher education is uneven, shaped by deep-rooted inequalities in infrastructure, teacher training, and socioeconomic conditions. The digital divide manifests not just in terms of internet access or devices, but also in disparities in digital literacy, language of instruction, and cultural relevance of educational content (Czerniewicz & Brown, 2013; Patel & Ragolane, 2024; Ragolane and Patel, 2025). In historically disadvantaged schools, even when hardware is available, the absence of sustained support, content localisation, and inclusive pedagogical strategies often means that immersive tools remain underused or misused (Nhlapo *et al.*, 2024). This reinforces what the Capability Approach cautions against, a situation where learners technically "have access" but lack the freedom to benefit meaningfully. Without structural interventions that address these systemic gaps, immersive technologies risk reproducing existing educational injustices under the guise of innovation.

To realise the inclusive potential of immersive learning, we must shift from technology-centred solutions to learner-centred design grounded in justice. The Universal Design for Learning (UDL) framework requires that immersive environments offer multiple means of engagement to accommodate diverse learning and knowledge styles. In tandem, a Capability Approach lens compels educators and policymakers to ask not "what technology is available?" but "what freedoms does this technology enable or restrict for each learner?" Practical steps include designing AR/VR experiences that support multilingual content, incorporating local cultural contexts, and ensuring participatory co-design processes involving teachers and learners (Pather & Ragolane, 2025). Additionally, partnerships between government, the private sector, and communities can help build sustainable infrastructures and training ecosystems. In centring human connection, learner agency, and contextual relevance, we can ensure that immersive technologies not only reach marginalised learners but serve them meaningfully. This chapter examines how immersive technologies can be leveraged to foster digital inclusion in South African classrooms, utilising justice-oriented frameworks to critically evaluate both their potential and limitations.

CONCEPTUAL AND THEORETICAL FRAMEWORKS

This chapter is underpinned by two intersecting frameworks: the Capability Approach and Universal Design for Learning (UDL). The Capability Approach, pioneered by Amartya Sen and extended by Martha Nussbaum, focuses on individuals' real freedoms to achieve lives they have reason to value (Sen, 1999; Nussbaum, 2011). Unlike traditional economic or utility-based models, the Capability Approach evaluates well-being based on people's actual abilities to function, participate and flourish in society (Alkire, 2005; Osmani, 2016). In the context of education, this framework helps assess not only whether learners have access to digital tools, but also whether they have the freedom to convert that access into meaningful learning and social inclusion. Capabilities are deeply influenced by social and institutional structure factors, especially relevant in South Africa's context of enduring digital inequality (Clark, 2005; Bartolomei et al., 2024).

Complementing the Capability Approach is the Universal Design for Learning (UDL) framework, which provides a proactive model for designing inclusive educational environments. Rooted in neuroscience and inclusive pedagogy, UDL advocates for "multiple means of engagement, representation, and expression" to accommodate the diverse needs of all learners (Meyer et sl., 2014; Sewell et al., 2022). Unlike traditional models that retrofit accommodations after barriers are encountered, UDL anticipates learner diversity from the outset. It encourages flexible teaching strategies and content delivery modes principles critical to immersive and digital learning design (Priyadharsini & Mary, 2024; TEAL, 2010). In South Africa, where systemic inequalities impact learners' access to infrastructure, language, and content, UDL's focus on flexibility and equity is especially pertinent (Dalton & McKenzie, 2020).

The Capability Approach and UDL provide us with a robust framework for interrogating whether immersive technologies such as Virtual Reality (VR) and Augmented Reality (AR) promote genuine digital inclusion or reinforce existing exclusions. While the Capability Approach draws attention to what learners can do with digital tools, UDL focuses on how those tools are designed and implemented to serve all learners, particularly those historically marginalised. Both frameworks emphasise agency, participation, and justice-oriented design, advocating a shift from technology-centred innovation to learner-centred transformation. This dual-lens approach is critical to understanding not just the availability of immersive tools in

South African classrooms but their effectiveness in expanding learners' educational capabilities and experiences (Alkire, 2015; McKenzie & Dalton, 2020).

IMMERSIVE TECHNOLOGIES IN EDUCATION: "TELL ME AND I FORGET, TEACH ME AND I REMEMBER, INVOLVE ME AND I LEARN"

Immersive technologies, including Virtual Reality (VR), Augmented Reality (AR), Mixed Reality (MR) and Extended Reality (XR), refer to digital innovations that create or augment environments in which users perceive themselves as being "present" in an artificially constructed or enhanced space (Jin *et al.,* 2024). These technologies function by combining hardware such as head-mounted displays, sensors and haptic devices with software applications that simulate real or imagined environments. In educational settings, immersive technologies aim to deepen student engagement, promote experiential learning, and support complex conceptual understanding through visual and interactive simulations (Tene *et al.,* 2024; Bosman *et al.,* 2024). There has been an introduction of various immersive tools integrated into classrooms across disciplines. Virtual Reality (VR), for instance, immerses students in fully digital environments, useful in simulating historical sites or dangerous scientific experiments. For example, tools such as Google Expeditions and Oculus-based simulations have been successfully used to teach geography, biology, and physics. Augmented Reality (AR) overlays digital content onto the real world, enhancing textbook content or lab experiments through apps like Quiver or Merge Cube. Mixed Reality (MR) and Extended Reality (XR) further blend digital and physical worlds, enabling more intuitive, embodied learning experiences using platforms like Microsoft HoloLens. Each of these tools caters to various learning objectives, with growing potential in STEM and arts education alike (Binytska *et al.,* 2023; Serrano-Ausejo & Mårell-Olsson, 2024).

Immersive technologies have demonstrated notable successes in educational outcomes. For example, AR applications have improved student engagement and spatial reasoning in chemistry and geometry (Serrano-Ausejo & Mårell-Olsson, 2024), while VR simulations have been effective in medical and engineering training by allowing learners to practice in risk-free environments (Binytska *et al.,* 2023). In STEM contexts, Tene *et al.* (2024) found that AR and VR significantly enhanced both student performance and motivation, especially in physics and mathematics. These technologies have also played a critical role in inclusive education, enabling learners with disabilities to access multimodal content more effectively (Bosman *et al.,* 2024).

However, challenges remain in implementation. These key limitations include the high costs of hardware, insufficient teacher training, and unequal access to infrastructure, especially in under-resourced schools (Jin *et al.,* 2024). In some cases, students experienced only marginal improvements in academic performance, especially when immersive content was not aligned with curriculum goals or when the novelty of the technology faded (Serrano-Ausejo & Mårell-Olsson, 2024). Moreover, there are concerns about motion sickness in VR environments, the digital divide, and the need for robust data privacy protocols in classrooms. To maximise benefits, institutions must adopt a holistic approach, involving curriculum alignment, teacher capacity building, and sustainable funding models.

In reflecting on the pedagogical power of immersive technologies, Benjamin Franklin's enduring maxim *"Tell me and I forget, teach me and I remember, involve me and I learn"* resonates deeply. This quote, explored in Hoque's (2021) study on active learning, emphasises the value of learner involvement as central to effective education. Immersive technologies embody this philosophy by shifting learners from passive recipients to active participants in dynamic, multimodal environments. As Hoque (2021) argues, engagement fosters not only comprehension but also a sense of ownership and agency in the learning process. Thus, the integration of VR, AR, MR and XR aligns with a learner-centred paradigm that values participation, critical thinking and meaningful interaction qualities essential to preparing students for an increasingly complex and digital world.

PEDAGOGICAL FACTORS

When people think of pedagogy, they often simplify it as just the "theory of how we teach and learn." This leads to a common assumption: if technologies like AR, VR and MR support learning, then they must be pedagogies in and of themselves. We argue otherwise. Pedagogy is not the technology; it is the intentional design of teaching strategies aligned with how humans learn best. Therefore, while immersive technologies enable new forms of instruction, each technology must be paired with an appropriate pedagogical approach. A one-size-fits-all strategy cannot apply; *Pedagogy A* designed for *Technology A* will not automatically work on *Technology B*. As immersive technologies become more sophisticated and context-specific, they demand equally specialised pedagogical frameworks to be effective.

Research shows that immersive learning environments are most successful when aligned with clear pedagogical strategies that emphasise experiential, constructivist and collaborative learning principles (Dengel *et al.,* 2024; Dalgarno & Lee, 2010). For instance, VR simulations in science education should not merely replicate textbook diagrams in 3D; they must facilitate inquiry-based learning and critical thinking through scaffolded exploration. Immersive learning in teacher education enhances engagement and reflection only when it is purposefully integrated with traditional pedagogical goals, such as curriculum alignment and learning outcome assessment. Without this alignment, immersive tools risk being reduced to gimmicks rather than meaningful enablers of knowledge construction.

Moreover, the introduction of immersive technologies requires educators to rethink their instructional design models. The Educational Framework for Immersive Learning (EFiL), for example, emphasises that the *sense of presence,* a key characteristic of immersive experiences, must be supported by learning activities, assessment criteria, and content that are adapted to the specific features of the technology (Dengel & Mägdefrau, 2020). Similarly, frameworks like immersive constructive alignment (ICA) stress the need to align learning objectives with the immersive affordances of a given platform, such as embodied interaction in VR or real-time feedback in AR so that students are not just immersed but also intellectually engaged (Dengel *et al.,* 2024; Fowler, 2015).

Finally, immersive teaching also shifts the role of the educator. In traditional settings, the teacher is a content deliverer; in immersive environments, they become a designer of learning experiences, a facilitator of exploration, and a guide for reflection (Ali, 2022; Dengel & Buchner, 2024). This shift introduces new challenges: many teachers lack training in immersive pedagogy or struggle to align digital tools with national curricula. As such, professional development is essential not only in terms of technical skills but in pedagogical adaptability. If immersive learning is to become sustainable and equitable in classrooms, its pedagogy must be as dynamic and innovative as the technologies it accompanies.

As we embrace the rapid integration of immersive technologies in education, we must pause and ask: Where is our focus? Too often, the allure of innovation risks displacing the foundational purpose of education itself. Our focus must return to pedagogy, not merely as a method of instruction, but as a principled commitment to meaningful learning. Pedagogy gives us the right and responsibility to ask critical questions, to ensure our approaches are rigorous, inclusive, and purpose driven. It is through pedagogical intentionality that immersive technologies find their true value, not as distractions or novelties, but as instruments shaped by educational needs rather than market trends. We must move from passively consuming technological tools to actively influencing how they are designed, implemented and evaluated. This means educators, researchers and learners alike must assert agency in the development cycle, ensuring that technology evolves in service of learning, not the other way around. In doing so, we shift from being end-users to co-creators and from reacting to innovation to leading it with clarity, vision and educational integrity.

THE SOUTH AFRICAN CONTEXT: THE DIGITAL LANDSCAPE IN SOUTH AFRICAN SCHOOLS

South Africa's digital education agenda spans both basic and higher education, aiming to bridge structural inequalities and respond to the imperatives of the Fourth Industrial Revolution (4IR). Central among these is the National Digital and Future Skills Strategy (2020), which outlines comprehensive measures for improving digital literacy, educator competence, and infrastructure across schools and higher education institutions (HEIs) (Department of Communications and Digital Technologies, 2020). Complementing this are earlier policy commitments such as the White Paper on e-Education (2004) and the National Integrated ICT Policy White Paper (2016), which emphasise the integration of Information and Communication Technologies (ICTs) across all educational phases. Yet, despite these ambitious frameworks, implementation particularly in rural and underserved areas, lags due to structural, economic, and infrastructural constraints (Duma et al., 2021).

Civil society and public-private partnerships (PPPs) have emerged as vital players in expanding digital education access. Non-governmental organisations, advocacy coalitions, and international donors have supported pilot programmes providing tablets, internet access, and teacher training. One notable example is the work of organisations like the SchoolNet SA and the CSIR's Digital Learning Initiative, which seek to complement government rollout efforts. However, critics argue that these interventions remain fragmented and unsustainable without systemic state-led coordination and investment (Mkhonto & Mubangizi, 2024; Khoza, 2023). Moreover, the emphasis on "smart schools" in metropolitan areas often diverts attention from comprehensive rural inclusion, leading to persistent digital divides (Duma et al., 2021). This urban-rural digital imbalance is similarly echoed in the higher education sector, where historically disadvantaged institutions struggle to keep pace with their urban counterparts in terms of connectivity, device access, and advanced learning platforms (Patel & Ragolane, 2024; Ragolane & Patel, 2025). This dynamic is mirrored in the higher education sector, where historically disadvantaged universities continue to face challenges in infrastructure, staff readiness and integration of digital pedagogies, deepening the rural-urban and institutional divide.

A critical challenge to digital inclusion in South African schools and higher education lies in scaling implementations at a pace that keeps up with technological innovation. Despite policy intentions to digitise all schools by 2025, progress has been slow. Rural schools continue to suffer from unreliable electricity, poor internet infrastructure, and a lack of devices conditions that significantly undermine digital adoption (Chomunorwa & Mugobo, 2023; Nyathi & Joseph, 2024). In higher education, similar disparities emerged during the COVID-19 pandemic, where universities had to rapidly adopt emergency remote teaching. Institutions with robust digital infrastructure transitioned more smoothly, while others faced massive disruption due to low device ownership among students and staff, bandwidth limitations, and lack of digital teaching capacity. Teacher training also remains a key barrier. Many educators lack the digital competencies needed to effectively integrate technology into pedagogy, especially in under-resourced provinces (Nyathi & Joseph, 2024; Lumadi, 2024). The reliance on emergency remote teaching during COVID-19 further exposed these gaps, especially in areas without consistent access to digital tools or platforms.

The urgency to scale digital learning across South African schools and universities is tempered by the pace of policy implementation and the mismatch between national ambitions and local capacity. As Ng'ambi et al. (2013) argue, a contextualised approach to technology integration is vital. Technologies cannot simply be transplanted from international trends into South African classrooms or lecture halls without considering infrastructure deficits, cultural contexts, and pedagogical needs. While global forecasts, such as those in the Horizon Reports, may predict mainstream adoption of AI or immersive tools within five years, these timelines are unrealistic for under-resourced provinces where learners still share textbooks or lack electricity. This same caution applies to higher education, where only a subset of institutions is currently experimenting with immersive learning technologies like VR and AR, often in isolated pilot projects rather than through institution-wide integration. As such, education policymakers must move "beyond the hype" and invest in scalable, context-driven, and resilient systems that leverage mobile technologies, open educational resources, and teacher-led innovation (Kilfoil, 2015; Struwig & Watson, 2023). This includes rethinking procurement policies, incentivising local content creation, and designing feedback-driven ecosystems to support continuous iteration. Without urgent and adaptive implementation models, South Africa risks deepening rather than closing the digital divide.

Yet this is not an insurmountable challenge. To contextualise the potential of immersive technology, it is useful to consider how other sectors, such as financial services, have made notable strides in bridging the digital divide. While it is widely acknowledged that a majority of South Africans engage with digital platforms for banking and communication, a deeper gap persists in terms of access to and familiarity with more complex or educationally focused technologies. This dynamic is mirrored in higher education, where students may easily access mobile banking and social media, yet lack consistent exposure to advanced learning platforms or immersive digital tools. This highlights a clear disconnect between general digital adoption and academic technology readiness. We argue, therefore, that closing the digital divide across both basic and higher education does not require reaching the entire population simultaneously but rather achieving depth within key educational nodes, be it rural schools or under-resourced universities. To succeed, South Africa must align its ambitious digital education policies with the lived realities of implementation. This includes equitable access to devices and reliable internet, but also extends to sustained teacher development, curriculum reform, and the integration of 21st-century skills. While national strategies encourage cross-sector partnerships, their success ultimately depends on stronger intergovernmental coordination, real-time data use, and the establishment of accountable, scalable models for technology deployment. In the higher education context, this also includes building communities of practice, fostering research-led innovation in digital pedagogy and aligning immersive technology rollouts with national graduate attributes and employability frameworks. Without such systemic reforms, the promise of digital inclusion may remain aspirational rather than transformative. Having established the structural and infrastructural challenges within South Africa's education system, it is equally important to consider the potential that immersive technologies hold in responding to these gaps. Despite the limitations, several initiatives across both basic and higher education settings have demonstrated the transformative potential of immersive learning when strategically applied.

OPPORTUNITIES AND BARRIERS IN IMMERSIVE LEARNING FOR SOUTH AFRICAN SCHOOLS

Unlocking the Virtual Classroom: Opportunities in Immersive Learning

Immersive technologies such as Virtual Reality (VR), Augmented Reality (AR), and Mixed Reality (MR) offer transformative potential for enhancing student engagement, contextual learning, and skill development in South African classrooms. These tools create multisensory, interactive environments where learners can explore complex concepts in simulated, real-world contexts. For instance, AR overlays used in science lessons can allow students to manipulate 3D models of the human body, while VR environments simulate historical events or virtual field trips for rural learners with limited mobility (Ali, 2022). According to Suero Montero and Oliveira Leite (2022), immersive technologies significantly improve academic engagement when aligned with sound pedagogical principles, providing learners with opportunities to engage cognitively and emotionally. Moreover, AR has proven particularly effective in reducing cognitive load for novice learners, making it well-suited for foundational education in South Africa's diverse classrooms (Poupard et al., 2025). With the right instructional design, immersive learning supports curiosity, fosters motivation, and facilitates deeper conceptual understanding outcomes often missing in rote-based education models. In addition, immersive simulations in vocational subjects like health sciences and engineering can bridge the gap between theory and practice, enabling experiential learning in resource-constrained environments (Ali, 2022). These technologies also present opportunities for localised content creation and language inclusivity, potentially supporting multilingual and culturally relevant pedagogy.

Immersive technologies also offer transformative potential in supporting inclusive education. Learners with disabilities can benefit from multimodal sensory engagement, such as tactile feedback, visual augmentations, and auditory scaffolds. These tools can supplement or replace traditional materials that often exclude visually or hearing-impaired learners (Suero Montero & Oliveira Leite, 2022). For example, AR-enabled captioning or 3D spatial audio can help bridge communication gaps, enabling more equitable participation. Additionally, for neurodiverse learners, immersive platforms can provide adaptive pacing, gamified feedback, and controlled environments, all of which support differentiated instruction aligned with Universal Design for Learning (UDL) principles. Another promising opportunity lies in teacher professional development. Immersive technologies can simulate real classroom scenarios, allowing pre-service and in-service teachers to rehearse lesson planning, classroom management, and inclusive teaching strategies in virtual environments. This form of experiential learning addresses gaps in teacher preparedness, especially in contexts where real-world placements are limited or inconsistent (Ali, 2022). Furthermore, platforms designed with localised content in multiple languages and grounded in South African cultural contexts can serve as powerful tools for curriculum transformation. When built collaboratively with communities, such technologies offer not only engagement but also identity affirmation and cultural relevance. In the higher education context, immersive technologies are increasingly used in fields like medicine, engineering, and architecture, where students can engage in risk-free simulations of surgeries, lab experiments, or structural design. Universities such as the University of Cape Town and the University of the Free State have piloted virtual labs and AR-enhanced science tutorials to support active, experiential learning in resource-constrained environments (Ng'ambi et al., 2013). While these successes signal promise, the implementation of immersive technologies is far from universal. The adoption landscape is uneven and riddled with significant barriers that affect both access and pedagogical effectiveness, particularly in the South African context.

Headsets and Hurdles: Barriers to Realising the Immersive Dream

Despite its promise, immersive learning faces significant implementation challenges in South African schools. Chief among these is the pervasive digital divide, particularly between urban and rural education systems. While private and urban schools may access VR headsets or high-bandwidth internet, rural schools often lack electricity, stable internet, or even basic ICT infrastructure (Mkhonto & Mubangizi, 2024; Duma et al., 2021). As noted by Nyathi and Joseph (2024), educators across the country continue to struggle with inadequate digital competencies, and the shift toward immersive platforms only deepens these gaps without systemic professional development. Furthermore, immersive technologies can increase cognitive overload if not carefully scaffolded, especially for learners with limited prior exposure to digital tools. According to Poupard et al. (2025), VR tends to induce extraneous cognitive load in novice users, leading to reduced learning gains in the absence of clear guidance or simplified interfaces. Additionally, the high cost of hardware and maintenance, such as VR headsets and compatible computing devices, makes large-scale adoption financially unsustainable for many public schools. Policy frameworks such as South Africa's e-Education White Paper (2004) have yet to translate into scalable, equitable ICT deployment models (Mulaudzi, 2024).

Systemic change requires coordinated investment from the government, private sector, and civil society. But current efforts remain fragmented. Schools are often left to experiment with emerging technologies in silos, lacking guidance on how to align immersive learning tools with CAPS curriculum outcomes. Without robust teacher training, context-aware implementation strategies, and affordable, localised content, the dream of immersive learning may reinforce existing inequalities rather than disrupt them. One of the overlooked barriers in immersive learning is the issue of content localisation and curriculum alignment. Most immersive learning content is developed in and for Global North contexts, often failing to reflect the South African curriculum, linguistic diversity, or cultural realities. This lack of alignment renders many imported immersive applications pedagogically irrelevant or even alienating for learners (Mulaudzi, 2024). The absence of local capacity for immersive content production exacerbates this issue, as schools are dependent on expensive foreign content or ill-fitting generic simulations. Without government and industry investment in local content ecosystems, the immersive learning sector risks perpetuating digital imperialism rather than promoting digital equity.

Moreover, immersive learning's success is contingent not just on infrastructure but on institutional readiness. Many South African schools lack technical support staff, secure storage for devices, or even policy clarity on how immersive tools should be used and assessed (Duma *et al.,* 2021). Implementation fatigue is real: after decades of ICT pilots and e-education initiatives, educators are sceptical of yet another technology push unless it's backed by consistent training, pedagogical support, and infrastructure maintenance (Poupard *et al.,* 2025). In higher education, barriers manifest in the form of limited institutional bandwidth, uneven device access among students, and academic staff who lack exposure to immersive pedagogies. Disparities between historically advantaged and disadvantaged universities remain stark, with rural and township-based institutions struggling to afford or sustain advanced digital learning environment. These challenges are exacerbated by a lack of policy guidance on immersive tech integration in national higher education strategies.

If immersive learning is to become mainstream, the approach must shift from "project-based pilots" to sustainable systems change, supported by national frameworks and long-term budget allocations. Recognising these barriers compels us to ask not just what is possible, but what is equitable. Immersive learning cannot be meaningfully pursued without a deliberate focus on inclusion pedagogically, infrastructurally, and socially. The next section explores how inclusive frameworks can guide the just and responsible implementation of immersive technologies in both schools and higher education.

TOWARDS INCLUSIVE IMMERSIVE LEARNING

When speaking of "inclusion" in immersive learning, the conversation must go beyond mere access to technology. Inclusion must mean *equitable design*, *contextual relevance*, and a *deliberate orientation toward social justice*. In South Africa, where the Gini coefficient remains the highest globally at 0.63 (World Bank, 2023), equity in immersive learning cannot be an afterthought. It must be embedded as a first principle of design. South Africa's structural inequality, rooted in historical dispossession and exacerbated by digital divides, provides both the rationale and the urgency for justice-oriented immersive learning. Wealth is concentrated among the top decile, which holds between 71–85% of national assets, while the bottom 50% owns just 4–7% (McKeever, 2023; World Bank, 2022). Multidimensional poverty is particularly acute in rural districts such as Umzimvubu, Port St Johns, and Msinga, with deprivation spanning from electricity and sanitation to digital access (Statistics SA, 2024). It is within this terrain that immersive learning must take root, not only to simulate alternate realities, but to actively reshape the one we live in. To design equitable learning environments in such contexts, educators and technologists must begin by acknowledging systemic barriers: poverty, infrastructure deficits, linguistic diversity, and cultural underrepresentation. But acknowledgement is not enough, responsive design is key. Justice-oriented design does not impose external models; it builds from the ground up, co-created with local communities and learners. Inspired by frameworks such as *Inclusive Design for Learning and Employment Records* (Cacicio et al., 2022), justice-oriented immersive learning is guided by four essential principles:

1. **Cultural Validation** – Systems must affirm local identities and knowledge, shifting away from Eurocentric or technocratic biases in content and pedagogy.

2. **Participatory Co-Design** – Learners, especially from underserved backgrounds, must be co-designers, not passive recipients.
3. **Multi-Modality for Accessibility** – Multiple forms of engagement (visual, auditory, kinesthetic) ensure that disabilities or learning preferences are not barriers to success.
4. **Data Equity and Ethics** – Learning analytics and user data must be collected, stored, and interpreted through lenses of equity, ensuring that marginalised students are not over-surveilled or misrepresented.

As Stephenson and McKee (2022) argue, inclusive curricula rooted in social justice can move beyond deficit-based approaches to genuinely transformative learning experiences. The Statistics South Africa 2024 presentation reveals critical insight: while subjective poverty is important, it is multidimensional poverty, lack of access to education, sanitation, housing, and electricity, that is the primary barrier to educational advancement. In immersive learning, this translates into designing for low-end hardware (e.g. cardboard VR headsets), offline functionality, and multilingual voiceovers. Additionally, more than 42% of working-age South Africans are unemployed or discouraged from seeking work. For immersive tools to have impact, they must offer clear economic pathways through certifications, job simulations, or vocational XR modules tied to local employment needs. This is in line with the inclusive employment-focused models proposed by Digital Promise (Cacicio et al., 2022). Another bold inclusion in justice-oriented immersive learning is the concept of Equity Analytics the collection of real-time disaggregated data on how learners from different racial, socioeconomic, and linguistic groups engage with XR platforms. Rather than just tracking "completion rates," these platforms would examine which students feel seen, whose stories are told, and how power operates in virtual narratives. Built with privacy by design, these analytics could feed directly into iterative content improvement cycles, ensuring responsiveness to learner realities. Moreover, equity dashboards could be shared with communities, empowering local actors to shape learning strategies in real-time. A critical critique of digital inclusion efforts is that they often stop at "access" merely getting devices or connectivity into schools. But inclusion demands more: ownership of content, representation in development teams, and redistribution of tech capital. South African students must see their languages, landscapes and "lifeworlds" represented in immersive platforms. This requires funding black-led XR startups, integrating indigenous knowledge systems, and establishing national repositories of open-source immersive content co-curated by local communities.

As McKeever (2023) reminds us, inequality is not only economic but also narrative. Who gets to tell stories, shape knowledge and imagine futures? Inclusive immersive learning must reclaim this terrain. If inclusion is the goal, then strategy becomes the vehicle. In universities, inclusive immersive learning must also consider adult learners, multilingual instruction, and accessibility for students with disabilities in lecture theatres and online platforms. Universal Design for Learning (UDL) can support lecturers in structuring content that caters to multiple means of engagement and representation whether through screen readers, haptic feedback, or VR-enhanced lab simulations. Lecturers in teacher education programmes, in particular, can benefit from immersive case studies that simulate real-world classroom diversity. Assessment in immersive learning environments requires rethinking traditional testing models. The very nature of immersive experiences whether virtual, augmented, or mixed encourages exploration, collaboration, and real-time interaction. As such, assessment strategies must shift from static, summative tests toward more formative, performance-based, and reflective approaches. In both schools and higher education, this could include digital portfolios, scenario-based problem solving, embedded assessments in simulations, or peer-reviewed artefacts generated in VR spaces. For example, in medical education, students might be assessed through simulated procedures with real-time feedback; in high school science, learners might demonstrate understanding by navigating and annotating virtual ecosystems. These approaches align well with Universal Design for Learning (UDL), allowing multiple means of expression and engagement. Crucially, assessments must not only measure content mastery, but also digital fluency, collaboration, and ethical engagement with technology ensuring that inclusion extends into how success is recognised and valued (Beetham & Sharpe, 2013). Moving from principles to practice, the following section outlines actionable strategies for implementing immersive learning in ways that are affordable, scalable, and context-sensitive across South Africa's diverse educational landscape.

STRATEGIES FOR EQUITABLE IMMERSIVE LEARNING IMPLEMENTATION

Implementing immersive learning equitably across South Africa's school and higher education systems demands a paradigm shift away from high-cost, top-down models and toward locally grounded, scalable, and pedagogically intentional approaches. Both sectors face structural barriers to digital inclusion, particularly in rural and historically marginalised communities. Yet, these same environments offer opportunities for innovation through context-sensitive, low-cost models. Implementation must be tailored to the realities of both under-resourced public schools and universities, where constraints around bandwidth, devices, teacher training, and institutional support remain significant (Duma et al., 2021; Lumadi, 2024; Mkhonto & Mubangizi, 2024). Government policies must acknowledge this dual-sector challenge and promote strategies that align curriculum objectives, digital literacy development, and inclusion in immersive learning design. Contrary to popular belief, building digital infrastructure does not always require massive financial investment. Models such as Mahalabox, a portable, battery-powered offline digital library, offer low-cost, high-impact solutions for schools and universities in areas lacking internet or electricity. Mahalabox enables students and lecturers to access multimedia, curriculum-aligned content, including simulations and immersive experiences, without connectivity (Honoris United Universities, n.d). This example demonstrates that infrastructure is as much about strategic design as it is about budget. Schools and higher education institutions can adopt or adapt such technologies to bridge access gaps, especially in rural provinces. In leveraging open-source platforms, offline capabilities and local server solutions, immersive education becomes feasible even where traditional infrastructure is lacking.

Equally essential is the co-creation of immersive content by local educators, students, and developers across both sectors. Many existing immersive learning applications are produced for Global North contexts and fail to reflect South Africa's curricular, linguistic, or cultural realities (Mulaudzi, 2024). Locally generated content, developed through collaborative workshops and supported by national XR innovation hubs, ensures greater relevance and equity. In schools, this may involve AR overlays of indigenous knowledge systems or local histories; in universities, it could include immersive case studies contextualised to African economic or health challenges. Cross-sector partnerships must support this by investing in teacher and lecturer training, empowering educators not only to use immersive tools but to shape them. Training initiatives must treat immersive pedagogy as a foundational element, not an optional extension (Pather & Ragolane, 2025). Finally, success depends on responsive feedback systems and real-time monitoring across both schools and universities. Equitable implementation must be tracked not just by numbers of devices or VR headsets deployed, but by who is using them, how they are used, and whether they improve engagement, inclusion, and learning outcomes. Feedback loops involving students, teachers, academic staff, and community members must inform continuous iteration. National policy should incorporate equity dashboards, disaggregated by geography, institution type, language, and disability status (Cacicio et al., 2022). This approach moves us from fragmented, project-based experimentation to systemic, justice-oriented transformation, ensuring that immersive learning does not replicate digital divides but actively works to dismantle them in both basic and higher education.

CONCLUSION

At the heart of immersive learning lies change, not just technological change, but a deeper transformation in how we think about education, inclusion and our limitations. Our review is that to fully understand the potential of immersive technologies and pedagogy, we must be willing to embrace both the opportunities and the challenges they present. In our experience, change is not a byproduct of immersive education; it is its engine. Without it, there can be no meaningful progress toward digital inclusion. We have also observed that in higher education, especially, one of the less discussed but powerful barriers to this transformation is ego. There is often an unspoken pressure on educators and institutions to appear technologically competent and up to date, even when the reality is far more uncertain. Yet, acknowledging "we do not know" is not a weakness; it is the first step toward deeper learning and innovation. Thus, embracing humility creates space for collaboration, critical questioning and authentic progress. It allows us to interrogate not just what tools we use, but why we use them and who they serve. Moreover, not all immersive learning must be tech-driven. Immersion is not defined by devices alone. It is equally about emotional, cognitive and cultural engagement. A powerful story, a well-designed role-play, or a locally rooted learning experience can immerse students just as deeply as a VR headset. This chapter argues that pedagogy, not technology, must remain the foundation of inclusive learning. The goal is not to chase novelty, but to ground technology in purpose, accessibility and context. Pedagogy and technology are both fluid; they evolve, adapt and respond to shifting realities. If we are to be active participants in this educational evolution, we must stay attuned to the relevance of both. We must ask not just what technology is available, but what it enables and what it excludes. Ultimately, the answer to how these tools will serve and include us may not lie fully in the present. The effects of immersive learning will be most visible to future generations, those who will inherit, critique and reshape the educational systems we design today. Our role is to lay a foundation that is not only innovative but also just. And in doing so, we must also be mindful of the unintended consequences of technology. Immersive tools, if not critically assessed and contextually implemented, can reinforce inequality and deepen exclusion. Therefore, inclusion cannot be assumed. Every tool must be evaluated not only by its capabilities, but also by its alignment with local needs, values, and pedagogical goals. In the end, inclusion begins with intention. And change, when grounded in humility, reflection and justice, is the path toward immersive learning that is truly accessible, equitable, and transformative. For higher education in particular, embracing change also means revisiting outdated assumptions about academic expertise and authority in digital pedagogy. Lecturers must be empowered to experiment, fail, and learn alongside students as co-creators of inclusive, immersive learning environments.

This chapter has argued that immersive technologies such as Virtual Reality (VR), Augmented Reality (AR), and Mixed Reality (MR) hold substantial pedagogical promise, particularly in fostering engagement, contextual learning, and inclusivity. However, their transformative potential in South African classrooms remains constrained by structural inequalities in infrastructure, digital literacy, teacher training, and policy implementation. A key finding is that access alone is insufficient. Drawing on the Capability Approach, we have shown that digital tools must translate into real freedoms for learners to meaningfully participate and thrive. Simultaneously, Universal Design for Learning (UDL) offers a powerful framework to ensure that immersive learning is designed proactively to accommodate learner diversity across ability, language, and context. The intersection of these frameworks reveals that equitable design not technological novelty, must be the foundation of digital inclusion. Secondly, the chapter highlights that immersive technologies, when implemented without cultural relevance or curriculum alignment, risk reinforcing digital imperialism. The lack of locally produced, linguistically inclusive, and culturally affirming content remains a major barrier. Similarly, under-resourced rural schools and historically disadvantaged higher education institutions face disproportionate challenges in adopting immersive tools. Without addressing these asymmetries, innovation risks reproducing exclusion rather than dismantling it. Thirdly, the findings emphasise that pedagogy, not technology, must drive educational transformation. Immersive tools are most effective when paired with intentional, constructivist teaching strategies and supported by educator training that treats digital pedagogy as foundational. The role of the educator shifts from content deliverer to experience designer and learning facilitator. Professional development, curriculum alignment, and participatory content co-creation are essential for sustainable implementation.

Moreover, the chapter presents strategies for affordable, scalable, and context-aware models of immersive learning. Solutions such as offline digital libraries, open-source platforms, and locally co-designed content offer pathways to meaningful adoption, even in low-resource environments. Successful implementation will depend on cross-sector collaboration, real-time equity monitoring, and policy frameworks that embed inclusion from the outset. Finally, this chapter calls for a shift in mindset. True digital inclusion demands humility the willingness of educators, institutions, and policymakers to ask not just what technologies are available, but who they serve, what they enable, and what they exclude. Immersive learning is not defined solely by devices but by the depth of learner engagement cognitively, culturally, and socially. Inclusion is not a byproduct; it must be the starting point. And change, if grounded in justice, pedagogy, and context, can make immersive learning a transformative force for current and future generations in South Africa and beyond.

REFERENCES

Ali, S. (2022). The effectiveness of immersive technologies for future professional education. *Futurity Education*, *2*(2), 14–22. DOI: 10.57125/FED/2022.10.11.25

Alkire, S. (2005, March). Why the Capability Approach? *Journal of Human Development and Capabilities*, *6*(1), •••.

Alkire, S. (2015). Capability Approach and Well-being Measurement for Public Policy. OPHI Working Paper 94, Oxford University.

Bartolomei, L., Blundo-Canto, G., & De Muro, P. (2024). How is the Capability Approach Applied to Assess Well-being Impacts? A Systematic Review. *Journal of Human Development and Capabilities*, *25*(3), 367–399. DOI: 10.1080/19452829.2024.2369502

Beetham, H., & Sharpe, R. (2013). *Rethinking Pedagogy for a Digital Age: Designing for 21st Century Learning* (2nd ed.). Routledge.

Binytska, K. M., Bilyakovska, O. O., Yankovych, O. I., Buchkivska, G. V., Binytska, O. P., Greskova, V. V., & Ocheretna, I. P. (2023). Exploring the potential of immersive technologies in university education worldwide. *CEUR Workshop Proceedings*, *3436*, 203–217. https://ceur-ws.org/Vol-3482/paper292.pdf

Bosman, I. D. V., Ka, K. S. D., & Alemneh, D. G. (2024). *Immersive Technology in Education. Proceedings of the Association for Information Science and Technology.* https://doi.org/DOI: 10.1002/pra2.1086

Cacicio, S., Tinsley, B., Miller, A., & Luke Luna, C. (2022). *Inclusive Design Principles for Learning and Employment Records: Co-Designing for Equity*. Digital Promise.

Chomunorwa, S., & Mugobo, V. V. (2023). Challenges of e-learning adoption in South African public schools: Learners' perspectives. *Journal of Education and e-learning Research*, *10*(1), 80–85.

Clark, D. A. (2005). *The Capability Approach: Its Development, Critiques and Recent Advances*. Global Poverty Research Group. https://base.socioeco.org/docs/developments_critiques_advances.pdf

Czerniewicz, L., & Brown, C. (2013). The habitus and technological practices of rural students: A case study. *South African Journal of Education*, *33*(1).

Dalgarno, B., & Lee, M. J. W. (2010). What are the learning affordances of 3D virtual environments? *British Journal of Educational Technology*, *41*(1), 10–32.

Dengel, A., Buchner, J., Mulders, M., & Pirker, J. (2024). *Levels of Immersive Teaching and Learning: Influences of Challenges in the Everyday Classroom.*

Department of Communications and Digital Technologies. (2020). *National Digital and Future Skills Strategy South Africa.* Government Gazette No. 43730.

Duma, N. M., Mlambo, S., Mbambo-Mkwanazi, S., & Morgan, W. (2021). Digital Inequalities in Rural Schools in South Africa. *Ocean Science Journal, 6*(3). Advance online publication. DOI: 10.23954/osj.v6i3.2984

Fowler, C. (2015). Virtual reality and learning: Where is the pedagogy? *British Journal of Educational Technology, 46*(2), 412–422.

Garrison, D. R., Anderson, T., & Archer, W. (2000). Critical inquiry in a text-based environment: Computer conferencing in higher education. *The Internet and Higher Education, 2*(2–3), 87–105.

Gladwell, M. (2008). *Outliers: The story of success.* Little, Brown and Company.

Honoris United Universities. (n.d). Regent Business School South Africa: MAHALABox, An Innovative Way to Address Unemployment. https://honoris.net/impactreport-refonte/regent-business-school-south-africa-mahalabox

Hoque, M. E. (2021). Tell me and I forget; teach me and I remember; involve me and I learn: Navigating the way of teaching. *The EDRC Journal of Learning and Teaching, 7*(3), 30–42.

Jin, S., Huang, J., & Zhong, Z. (2024). Application of Immersive Technologies in Primary and Secondary Education. *Frontiers in Digital Education, 1*(2), 142–152. DOI: 10.1007/s44366-024-0001-3

Khoza, R. T. (2023). *Digital Transformation Inequality in South African Secondary Schools Affecting the Implementation of 4IR Era Relevant Curriculum.* University of Johannesburg.

Kilfoil, W. R. (Ed.). (2015). *Moving beyond the hype: A contextualised view of learning with technology in higher education.* Universities South Africa.

Lumadi, R. I. (2024). The influence and effects of digital revolution on Africa's higher education systems. *South African Journal of Higher Education, 38*(3), 114–130.

McKeever, M. (2023). Social stratification and inequality in South Africa. *Sociology Compass, 13173.* Advance online publication. DOI: 10.1111/soc4.13173

McKenzie, J. A., & Dalton, E. M. (2020). Universal design for learning in inclusive education policy in South Africa'. *African Journal of Disability*, *9*(0), a776. DOI: 10.4102/ajod.v9i0.776 PMID: 33392062

Meyer, A., Rose, D. H., & Gordon, D. (2014). *Universal design for learning: Theory and practice*. CAST Professional Publishing.

Mkhonto, B. S., & Mubangizi, B. C. (2024). Digital Divide or Digital Bridge? Evaluating the Impact of ICT Integration in South Africa's Rural Schools. *International Journal of Social Science Research and Review*, *7*(7), 132–145. DOI: 10.47814/ijssrr.v7i7.2142

Mulaudzi, L. (2024). Evaluating impact: South Africa's e-education white paper on digital equity and post-COVID education leadership. *Cogent Education*, *11*(1), 2415749.

Ng'ambi, D., Gachago, D., Backhouse, J., Bozalek, V., Ivala, E., & Bosman, J. P. (2013). Towards a Shared Understanding of emerging technologies: experiences in a collaborative research project in South Africa. *The African Journal of Information Systems*, http://hdl.handle.net/11427/8863

Nhlapo, L., Mosethle, T., Monchusi, B. B., & Yusuff, A. (2024, November). Design of a Microgrid for a Rural Area: A Systematic Approach. In 2024 4th International Conference on Electrical, Computer, Communications and Mechatronics Engineering (ICECCME) (pp. 1-4). IEEE.

Nussbaum, M. C. (2011). *Creating capabilities: The human development approach*. Harvard University Press.

Nyathi, T., & Joseph, R.M. (2024). Empowering South African educators: Navigating the challenges of digital teaching and learning competencies. *SA Journal of Human Resource Management/SA Tydskrif vir Menslikehulpbronbestuur,* *22*(0), a2591. https://doi.org/DOI: 10.4102/sajhrm.v22i0.2591

Osmani, S. (2016). *The Capability Approach and Human Development: Some Reflections*. UNDP Human Development Report. https://hdr.undp.org/system/files/documents/osmanitemplate.pdf

Patel, S., & Ragolane, M. (2024). The Implementation of Artificial Intelligence in South African Higher Education Institutions: Opportunities and Challenges. *Technium Education and Humanities*, *9*, 51–65. DOI: 10.47577/teh.v9i.11452

Pather, B., & Ragolane, M. (2025). Innovative Teaching through Technology: Preparing Educators for ICT-Based Modelling and Simulation Integration. *American Research Journal of Humanities & Social Science. 08(03), 66 – 75.* https://www.arjhss.com/wp-content/uploads/2025/03/H836675.pdf

Poupard, M., Gallo, A., Boulord, R., Guillem, P., Rolland, G., Simonneau, T., & Pallas, B. (2025). Source–sink manipulations through shading, crop load and water deficit affect plant morphogenesis and carbon sink priorities leading to contrasted plant carbon status in grapevine. *Annals of Botany*, *136*(1), 49–66. PMID: 39656901

Priyadharsini, V., & Sahaya Mary, R. (2024). Universal Design for Learning (UDL) in Inclusive Education: Accelerating Learning for All. Shanlax International Journal of Arts. *Science and Humanities*, *11*(4), 145–150.

Ragolane, M., & Patel, S. (2024). Artificial Intelligence, Digital Grades and Human Voices: Students' Perceptions on AI Grading in Higher Education. *International J. Soc. Sci. & Education*. 2024(14), 32-64. http://ijsse.com/Paper-04.pdf

Ragolane, M., & Patel, S. (2025). AI Grading Systems in Education: A Panacea or Drawback for South African Higher Education. In Moreira, F., & Teles, R. (Eds.), *Improving Student Assessment With Emerging AI Tools* (pp. 245–272). IGI Global Scientific Publishing., DOI: 10.4018/979-8-3693-6170-2.ch009

Sen, A. (1999). *Development as freedom*. Oxford University Press.

Serrano-Ausejo, E., & Mårell-Olsson, E. (2024). Opportunities and challenges of using immersive technologies to support students' spatial ability and 21st-century skills in K-12 education. *Education and Information Technologies*, *29*, 5571–5597. DOI: 10.1007/s10639-023-11981-5

Sewell, A., Kennett, A., & Pugh, V. (2022). Universal Design for Learning as a theory of inclusive practice for use by educational psychologists. *Educational Psychology in Practice*, *38*(4), 364–378. DOI: 10.1080/02667363.2022.2111677

Slater, M., & Wilbur, S. (1997). A framework for immersive virtual environments (FIVE): Speculations on the role of presence in virtual environments. *Presence (Cambridge, Mass.)*, *6*(6), 603–616.

Statistics South Africa. (2019). *Inequality Trends in South Africa: A Multidimensional Diagnostic*. Report No. 03-10-19

Statistics South Africa. (2024). *Poverty and Inequality Statistics in South Africa*. Presentation to the NCOP by Patricia Koka.

Stephenson, M., & McKee, S. (2022). Interventions for Change: An Inclusive Curriculum Design for Social Justice. *Investigations in University Teaching and Learning*, 13. https://repository.londonmet.ac.uk/7748/1/MARIE_Investigations22_FINAL-Accessible.pdf

Struwig, M., & Watson, S. (2023). *Re-Imagining Teaching and Learning at South African Higher Education Institutions in the Digital Landscape. International Conference on Education Research*, Nelson Mandela University. https://doi.org/ DOI: 10.34190/icer.1.1.3145

Suero Montero, C., & Oliveira Leite, L. (2022). Towards local community involvement in students' science learning: Perspectives of students and teachers. *Journal of Teaching and Learning*, *16*(3), 21–43.

TEAL Center. (2010). *Universal Design for Learning Fact Sheet*. https://lincs.ed.gov/sites/default/files/2_TEAL_UDL.pdf

Tene, T., Marcatoma Tixi, J. A., Palacios Robalino Md, L., Mendoza Salazar, M. J., Vacacela Gomez, C., & Bellucci, S. (2024). Integrating immersive technologies with STEM education: A systematic review. *Frontiers in Education*, *9*, 1410163. DOI: 10.3389/feduc.2024.1410163

Turkle, S. (2011). *Alone together: Why we expect more from technology and less from each other. Basic Books World Bank. (2022). Inequality in Southern Africa.* An Assessment of the Southern African Customs Union.

Chapter 10
From Play to Pay: Exploring Gamification as a Tool to Boost Investment Confidence in College Students

Srikriti Goyal
https://orcid.org/0009-0002-5960-5656
Christ University, India

Shikha Bhagat
https://orcid.org/0000-0001-8745-5558
Christ University, India

ABSTRACT

Financial literacy an essential competency in the increasingly intricate financial landscape of today, influencing individuals' capabilities to invest and strategize for the future. Although the domain of financial literacy research has expanded significantly, there has been relatively little focus on investment confidence as a separate outcome variable, and even less on its connection to gamified learning interventions within the Indian context. The chapter synthesizes frameworks including self-efficacy theory, experiential learning theory, and prospect theory with empirical evidence to investigate how gamification can convert financial literacy into actionable confidence. Utilizing national-level benchmarks from the Global Findex Database 2021, published studies on financial literacy among Indian youth, and a survey conducted with Indian college students, the analysis underscores the interplay between financial knowledge, perceptions of gamification, and investment confidence.

DOI: 10.4018/979-8-3373-4465-2.ch010

1. INTRODUCTION

1.1 The Rise of Financial Literacy as a Policy Priority

Over the last twenty years, financial literacy has transitioned from a specialized topic within academic discussions to a primary concern on global policy agendas. Policymakers and international organizations are increasingly acknowledging that financial literacy serves not only as an individual skill but also as a fundamental element of overall economic stability, social mobility, and fair access to financial services. The Organisation for Economic Co-operation and Development (OECD), through its International Network on Financial Education (INFE), has been instrumental in advocating for standardized frameworks to evaluate financial literacy across different nations. By offering measurement toolkits and benchmarks for comparison, the OECD has empowered policymakers to assess progress and pinpoint areas needing enhancement (OECD, 2020).

In a similar vein, the World Bank's Global Findex Database has become an essential tool for analyzing financial inclusion on a global scale. Updated every three years, it offers extensive indicators regarding account ownership, savings habits, credit accessibility, and the utilization of digital financial services. By documenting these metrics, the Global Findex enables governments, researchers, and institutions to track trends, recognize inequalities, and formulate strategies aimed at boosting financial engagement and literacy (World Bank, 2022). For developing economies, the importance of financial literacy is particularly pronounced. Nations such as India encounter a distinctive blend of rapid economic advancement, growing digital access, and significant demographic diversity. Although millions of individuals now have access to bank accounts and digital financial services, their capacity to effectively leverage these tools remains constrained.

For instance, although the Pradhan Mantri Jan Dhan Yojana has effectively facilitated access to formal banking for millions, surveys indicate that a significant number of account holders remain uninformed about features such as overdraft facilities, insurance coverage, or interest-bearing deposits. Likewise, the emergence of digital payment systems, including the Unified Payments Interface (UPI), offers substantial opportunities for efficient financial transactions; however, users frequently encounter challenges in comprehending security protocols, transaction limits, and budgeting implications (RBI, 2021).

Furthermore, financial literacy is intricately linked to financial inclusion. Individuals who grasp fundamental banking concepts are more inclined to engage in formal financial systems, maintain consistent savings, and invest in instruments that facilitate wealth accumulation over time. In contrast, deficiencies in literacy can result in suboptimal decision-making, dependence on informal or unregulated financial avenues, and increased susceptibility to fraud or exploitative practices. Global evidence indicates that financial literacy interventions, when executed effectively, can improve not only knowledge but also financial behaviors, encompassing savings, credit management, and responsible investing (Lusardi & Mitchell, 2014).

1.2 Indian Youth in the Financial Landscape

College students hold a distinctive role in the realm of finance as digital natives who have convenient access to various investment platforms, including mutual funds, stocks, and cryptocurrencies (Dahiya et al., 2023). Despite this accessibility, their financial literacy and confidence in making investments are notably low, resulting in a paradox where awareness does not translate into action. While students may grasp concepts such as Systematic Investment Plans (SIPs) or diversification, they often refrain from investing due to fears of making mistakes, uncertainties in the market, or a lack of hands-on experience.

Conventional financial education, which tends to emphasize theoretical knowledge, frequently falls short in fostering the confidence and self-efficacy necessary for making informed decisions in real-world scenarios. In India, socio-cultural influences—such as parental caution and the presence of conflicting information online—further exacerbate risk aversion, underscoring the necessity for educational strategies that integrate knowledge with practical preparedness and psychological support.

1.3 Gamification as a Pedagogical Innovation

Gamification has surfaced as a viable approach to addressing the issue of converting financial literacy into actionable skills. As defined by Deterding et al. (2011), it involves the integration of game design elements within non-gaming contexts, incorporating aspects such as points, badges, leaderboards, progress bars, and interactive scenarios into educational settings. In the realm of higher education, extensive research has been conducted on gamification's ability to enhance motivation, maintain engagement, and improve educational outcomes (Sailer & Homner, 2020). When applied to financial education, gamification enables students to engage in simulations of intricate financial processes, including stock market dynamics, portfolio management, budgeting strategies, and risk assessment within a controlled, interactive framework. For instance, stock market simulators allow learners to "invest" virtual currency under real-time market conditions, observe the effects of diversification, react to market changes, and learn from both profits and losses. Likewise, gamified budgeting tools motivate students to plan and monitor their expenses, establish financial objectives, and receive prompt feedback on their choices. These experiences offer numerous benefits. Firstly, they create experiential learning opportunities that reflect real-world financial decision making. Students can test various strategies, observe the results, and iteratively adjust their methods without facing actual financial losses. This mitigates psychological barriers, especially the fear of risk, which often hinders financial behavior. Secondly, gamification harnesses intrinsic motivation through engaging challenges and rewards, rendering the learning experience enjoyable and self-reinforcing. Points, levels, and badges act as immediate feedback mechanisms that bolster positive behavior and maintain engagement. Thirdly, gamification fosters reflective learning: students are able to assess outcomes, scrutinize decisions, and assimilate lessons, thus converting theoretical knowledge into practical skills.

Crucially, the design of gamification plays a vital role in its success. Hanus and Fox (2015) warn that inadequately designed gamification, characterized by an overemphasis on extrinsic rewards or irrelevant challenges, can undermine intrinsic motivation and negatively impact learning results. Consequently, financial gamification should incorporate significant objectives, realistic scenarios, and feedback systems that mirror actual financial repercussions while ensuring a secure, low-risk setting.

1.4 Investment Confidence as a Distinct Outcome

While research on financial literacy has traditionally focused on the acquisition of knowledge, recent findings highlight the significance of confidence as a distinct and vital outcome. Based on Bandura's (1997) self-efficacy theory, confidence is defined as an individual's belief in their capacity to act effectively, rather than merely what they know. In financial situations, confidence plays a crucial role in determining whether individuals convert knowledge into action—such as opening a savings account, starting a systematic investment plan (SIP), or engaging in trading activities. In the absence of confidence, even well-informed students may hesitate to participate in financial behaviors, thus rendering their knowledge ineffective.

Investment confidence is influenced by both cognitive and emotional elements. Cognitive factors involve the ability to process information, assess alternatives, and predict outcomes. Emotional components include risk perception, fear of loss, stress, and previous experiences. Gamification addresses both of these aspects by creating immersive environments where learners can experiment with decisions, encounter simulated risks, and receive prompt feedback. For instance, experiencing minor losses in a virtual portfolio can help normalize risk perception and mitigate loss aversion—a behavioral bias emphasized by prospect theory (Kahneman & Tversky, 1979).

Moreover, gamification enhances self-efficacy through mastery experiences, observational learning, and reinforcement. By succeeding in simulated financial challenges, observing the strategies and results of peers, and gaining recognition through points or badges, learners cultivate confidence in their ability to make financial decisions. This confidence is likely to translate into real-world behavior, as students become more inclined to engage with actual investment opportunities and adopt sound financial practices.

The differentiation between knowledge and confidence carries significant consequences for both policy and education. Although traditional curricula may improve comprehension of concepts such as diversification or compound interest, they frequently do not prepare students psychologically to utilize this knowledge effectively. In contrast, gamified interventions offer a twofold advantage: they not only strengthen theoretical comprehension but also foster behavioral confidence. This dual benefit is especially pertinent in India, where financial literacy is at a moderate level, yet engagement and proactive investment behaviors among the youth are notably low.

1.5 Contextualizing Findings Within Global and National Trends

Incorporating gamification into financial education facilitates the contextualization of results within the larger trends of financial inclusion. On a global scale, organizations such as the OECD and the World Bank have underscored the importance of financial literacy as a fundamental requirement for effective engagement in contemporary financial systems. Nations that allocate resources towards financial education initiatives typically experience increased rates of savings, responsible borrowing, and investment participation (OECD, 2020).

In India, government programs like the Pradhan Mantri Jan Dhan Yojana, UPI, and mutual fund campaigns have broadened access to financial tools; however, they have not completely resolved the issues of literacy and confidence. The Global Findex (World Bank, 2022) reveals that although account ownership is prevalent, formal savings rates are still low, indicating a significant disparity between access and active involvement. By concentrating on college students, gamified approaches aim at a vital demographic ready to engage as active financial participants. Furthermore, the digital proficiency of students boosts the scalability and efficacy of these interventions, as applications, online simulations, and interactive platforms can be extensively utilized. Moreover, findings from Indian research, including the study conducted by Dahiya et al. (2023), suggest that gaps in understanding compound interest and diversification can be effectively bridged through experiential, gamified education. By connecting these micro-level insights to macro-level standards, educators and policymakers can formulate evidence-based strategies that not only improve knowledge but also foster the confidence essential for proactive financial behaviour.

2. LITERATURE REVIEW

2.1 Financial Literacy and Investment Behavior

Financial literacy—the capability to comprehend and utilize financial concepts—is essential for making well-informed choices regarding saving, investing, and managing finances (Lusardi & Mitchell, 2014). In India, although basic banking knowledge is prevalent, the understanding of investment principles such as diversification and risk-return trade-offs is still quite limited (NCFE, 2019). While 77.6% of adults possess bank accounts, merely around 30% engage with formal savings instruments (World Bank, 2022), indicating a disparity between knowledge and practical application. Various factors, including risk aversion, restricted income, cultural perspectives, and a lack of confidence, frequently hinder effective financial decision-making (Kumar & Singh, 2020). This disparity is especially significant for young adults and students, who require both knowledge and confidence to make prudent financial decisions.

2.2 Gamification in Education

Gamification is defined as the incorporation of game design elements into non-gaming environments to boost engagement, learning, and performance (Deterding et al., 2011). These elements can encompass points, badges, levels, leaderboards, challenges, and immediate feedback systems. In the realm of education, gamification has proven to be a potent instrument for enhancing student motivation, maintaining attention, and improving educational results (Sailer & Homner, 2020). The attractiveness of gamification stems from its capacity to foster an interactive and immersive learning atmosphere where learners experience both challenges and rewards for their achievements.

Studies conducted across various fields have shown that gamification can improve knowledge retention and aid in the application of acquired concepts. For instance, Hamari, Koivisto, and Sarsa (2014) performed a meta-analysis of gamified interventions and discovered that gamification not only heightened engagement but also encouraged behavioral modifications, especially when paired with feedback and reward systems. This finding is consistent with cognitive learning theories, which assert that learning is more effective when it involves active engagement, prompt feedback, and reinforcement through positive experiences.

Nevertheless, the efficacy of gamification is not assured. Hanus and Fox (2015) warn that poorly executed gamification—characterized by an overemphasis on extrinsic rewards without substantial learning objectives—can diminish intrinsic motivation. If learners view gamified components as trivial or disconnected from educational aims, their engagement may decline instead of rise. Consequently, the effectiveness of gamification is largely contingent upon careful design that aligns game mechanics with educational objectives and contextual relevance. In the realm of higher education, gamification has been utilized in numerous ways, including interactive quizzes, competitive leaderboards, and simulation-based learning environments. These methods have demonstrated effectiveness in imparting knowledge on complex subjects, especially those that encompass abstract concepts or necessitate experiential learning. For example, in the field of science education, simulations of chemical reactions or physics experiments provide students with the opportunity to witness outcomes and consequences in real time, free from the limitations or hazards associated with a physical laboratory. Likewise, in business and management courses, simulations of market scenarios and strategic decision-making games allow learners to engage in high-stakes decision-making within a controlled environment.

2.3 Gamification and Financial Learning

Gamification in financial education leverages its achievements from other educational settings, rendering abstract financial concepts more accessible. Instruments like stock market simulations, budgeting applications, and interactive scenarios enable learners to engage in decision-making without risk (Schoenfeld & Zhang, 2019). Worldwide data indicates that these methods enhance comprehension of diversification, risk, and compounding, while also promoting saving habits and prudent spending. In India, emerging studies reveal that Dahiya et al. (2023) identified an average financial literacy rate of merely 56%, highlighting deficiencies in understanding compound interest and diversification—domains where gamification can effectively demonstrate long-term benefits. The Delhi–NCR youth survey (2025) additionally implies that attitudes and behaviors, rather than solely knowledge, are pivotal in fostering financial inclusion. By cultivating confidence and risk tolerance, gamification paves the way for improved financial decision-making among students.

This indicates that interventions aimed at enhancing confidence, self-efficacy, and risk tolerance may prove to be more effective than approaches that are solely informational. Gamification has the capacity to shape attitudinal and behavioral aspects by establishing interactive and experiential learning environments, thereby promoting improved financial decision-making.

2.4 Investment Confidence: The Missing Link

Investment confidence denotes an individual's conviction in their capacity to make well-informed financial choices and manage associated risks. It encompasses not only knowledge but also the psychological preparedness to utilize financial instruments. According to Bandura's self-efficacy theory (1997), confidence is cultivated through mastery experiences, vicarious learning, encouragement, and emotional regulation. Gamification enhances these processes by enabling learners to practice investment decisions within secure, simulated settings that offer immediate feedback. Such experiences mitigate the fear of risk, aligning with prospect theory (Kahneman & Tversky, 1979), which indicates that individuals frequently place greater emphasis on losses. For college students progressing towards financial autonomy, gamification presents organized opportunities to implement knowledge, evaluate strategies, and foster confidence in actual investing.

2.5 Summary of Gaps

Despite the increasing research on financial literacy, gamification, and investment behavior, significant gaps persist in India:

Moderate Literacy vs. Low Confidence: The youth in India exhibit a moderate level of financial literacy; however, they lack the confidence to implement concepts such as diversification, compounding, and long-term planning, which are essential for effective investing.

Limited Focus on Gamification's Role: Although gamification is recognized for enhancing engagement, its influence on investment confidence in India remains insufficiently examined, with the majority of studies prioritizing knowledge over behavioral aspects.

Lack of Integrated Data: There are few studies that integrate national benchmarks (such as Global Findex and NCFE) with student-level data, which restricts the understanding of how literacy, access, and gamification collectively influence investment confidence.

Addressing these gaps has the potential to inform educational programs, digital tools, and policy initiatives aimed at enhancing financial inclusion and literacy among the youth in India.

2.6 Research Objective

In response to these identified gaps, this research intends to explore the connection between financial literacy, perceptions of gamification, and investment confidence among college students in India. Specifically, the study aims to:

Investigate the extent of financial literacy among Indian college students and pinpoint areas where deficiencies exist, especially concerning investment-related concepts.

Evaluate students' perceptions of gamified learning tools and their effects on engagement, motivation, and comprehension of financial principles.
Analyze how gamified interventions affect investment confidence and the willingness to participate in financial decision-making.
Situate the findings within both national standards (NCFE, Global Findex) and global evidence regarding gamification and financial education.
Through this investigation, the research seeks to offer insights into how experiential learning via gamification can enhance traditional financial education, ultimately nurturing informed, confident, and proactive investors among the youth in India.

3. STUDY AIMS AND HYPOTHESES

3.1 Study Aims

This research has four primary aims, each designed to address gaps in the existing literature and contribute both theoretically and practically to the field of financial education in India.

To benchmark financial literacy and inclusion levels among Indian youth against national and global datasets.

While many studies evaluate students' financial literacy in isolation, there is limited work contextualizing their performance against national surveys like the Global Findex (World Bank, 2022) or policy-level metrics such as those provided by NCFE (2019). Benchmarking allows educators to understand whether students' gaps mirror broader societal trends or are unique to campus environments.

To develop and validate a measurement instrument that captures financial literacy, gamification perception, and investment confidence simultaneously.

Many existing studies assess financial literacy but omit the psychological dimension of confidence or the motivational aspects of gamification. By combining these constructs into a unified survey, the study aims to capture the interplay between knowledge, confidence, and engagement.

To test the direct and mediated relationships among literacy, gamification perception, and investment confidence.

While literacy is logically expected to influence confidence, theory suggests that gamification could mediate or even amplify this relationship by providing experiential mastery opportunities. Identifying the strength of direct versus mediated effects can guide pedagogy.

To explore moderating factors such as gender, academic major, and prior investment experience.

Prior literature (e.g., Lusardi & Mitchell, 2014; Robb & Sharpe, 2009) suggests gender gaps in financial knowledge and confidence, with men typically reporting higher self-assessed confidence regardless of knowledge levels. Similarly, students in finance-related majors may naturally perform better than their peers in arts or sciences. By testing moderating effects, the study provides nuanced insights for targeted interventions.

3.2 Hypotheses Development

H1: A higher level of financial literacy is positively correlated with investment confidence. This hypothesis is based on the premise that knowledge provides students with the cognitive resources required to assess risk and opportunity. Dahiya et al. (2023) illustrated that students achieving higher scores on literacy assessments expressed a greater willingness to participate in fundamental financial activities. According to self-efficacy theory, knowledge lays the groundwork for confidence by alleviating uncertainty.

H2: Positive perceptions of gamification are positively correlated with investment confidence. In addition to knowledge, motivation and experiential learning are crucial in developing confidence. When students view gamified tools as engaging, authentic, and beneficial, they are more inclined to cultivate confidence. Sailer & Homner (2020) discovered that gamification enhances perceived competence and autonomy, which are essential components of confidence.

H3: The perception of gamification mediates the relationship between literacy and confidence. Although literacy contributes to confidence, gamification may serve as the conduit that transforms abstract knowledge into tangible confidence. This aligns with Kolb's experiential learning theory, which posits that application and reflection improve competence beyond mere memorization.

H4: Previous investment experience reinforces the connection between gamification and confidence. Students who have previously participated in investments (such as mutual funds, stocks, or SIPs) may derive greater benefits from gamified tools, as they can relate simulations to real-world experiences. This reflects Bandura's focus on mastery experiences: prior exposure renders gamified feedback more significant.

H5: Gender and academic major affect all three constructs. Previous studies indicate enduring gender disparities: men frequently report higher confidence levels, although this does not necessarily correlate with higher literacy (Lusardi & Mitchell, 2014).. Examining these disparities contributes to the understanding of equity in educational design.

3.3 Roadmap for Tables

The following sections (Methodology and Results) will include tables that will demonstrate:

Table 1: National financial inclusion benchmarks (Global Findex 2021).

Table 2: Financial literacy benchmarks obtained from research on Indian students.

Table 3: Assessments of the reliability of survey constructs.

Table 4: Descriptive statistics related to primary survey results.

Table 5: Correlations among key variables.

Table 6: Results of regression analysis.

Table 7: Comparisons between groups categorized by gender and academic major.

Each of these tables is referenced in the main text at the appropriate juncture of presenting the findings.

4. METHODOLOGY

4.1 Research Design

A cross-sectional survey design was selected due to its capacity to identify relationships among constructs at a specific moment in time. The research integrated self-reported measures alongside objective literacy questions to achieve a balance between subjective and objective data. Although longitudinal or experimental designs might offer more robust causal inferences, cross-sectional surveys are effective for exploratory research and facilitate comparisons with previous studies employing similar methodologies.

4.2 Data Sources

This chapter is informed by three distinct sources of data:

1. **The Global Findex Database 2021 (specific to India).** This database offers national benchmarks regarding account ownership, the utilization of digital payments, saving habits, borrowing practices, and overall resilience. It contextualizes the findings from students within the larger adult demographic.
2. **Published studies on financial literacy in India.** These encompass the work of Dahiya et al. (2023), who focused on college students; Jayaraman & Jambunathan (2018), who investigated high school students; and the Delhi–NCR Youth Survey (2025), which correlated attitudes and behaviors with financial inclusion. These studies serve as external validity assessments.
3. **A primary survey of students (N = 260).** This survey, conducted in colleges located in Bengaluru and Delhi–NCR, gathers data on literacy, perceptions of gamification, and levels of confidence.

4.3 Instrument Development

The survey instrument comprised four distinct sections:

Section A: Financial Literacy (10 items). Questions were adapted from the OECD/INFE toolkit (2013). Examples include the calculation of compound interest, the identification of inflation effects, and the comprehension of risk diversification. Responses were scored as either correct or incorrect, with the total scores compiled to form a literacy index.

Section B: Gamification Perception (15 items). This section was adapted from the work of Sailer & Homner (2020). Students evaluated statements such as "Gamified financial simulations enhanced my engagement" using a 5-point Likert scale (1 = strongly disagree, 5 = strongly agree). The items addressed aspects such as enjoyment, authenticity, competitiveness, and the quality of feedback.

Section C: Investment Confidence (10 items). Grounded in Bandura's self-efficacy scales, students assessed their confidence in various tasks, including "selecting a mutual fund," "managing a diversified portfolio," and "resisting herd behavior in financial markets."

Section D: Behavioral Intention (5 items). This section gauged the willingness to open accounts, initiate systematic investment plans (SIPs), or engage in trading activities within the next 12 months.

Pilot testing involving 30 students was conducted to ensure clarity and reliability prior to the full deployment of the survey.

4.4 Sampling and Participants

Target demographic: Indian university students between the ages of 18 and 25 who are pursuing degrees in finance, business, engineering, arts, and sciences.

Sample size: 260 students. This number was sufficient for conducting regression analysis with various predictors.

Sampling technique: Stratified convenience sampling was employed to guarantee representation across gender (54% male, 45% female, 1% other), academic disciplines, and previous investment experience.

Figure 1. Simple distribution by academic major (N=260)

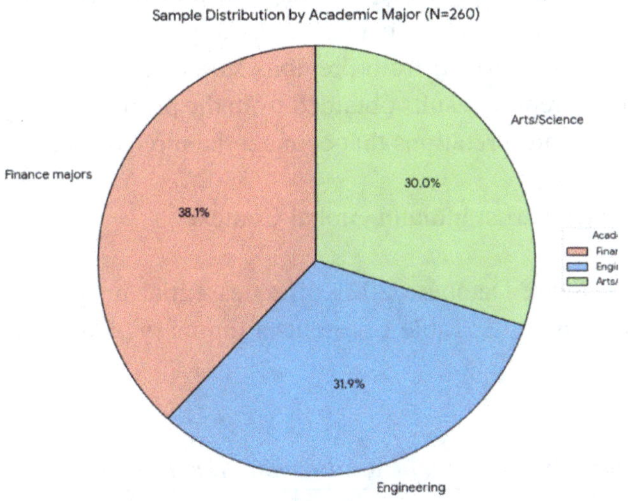

4.5 Data Analysis

The subsequent analyses were performed:

1. **Reliability analysis:** Cronbach's alpha coefficients were calculated for each construct (refer to Table 3).
2. **Descriptive statistics:** The means, standard deviations, minimums, and maximums for each construct were determined (refer to Table 4).

3. **Correlation analysis:** Pearson correlations were examined among financial literacy, gamification perception, investment confidence, and prior experience (refer to Table 5).
4. **Regression analysis:** Hierarchical regression was utilized to test the predictive effects of literacy and gamification perception on confidence, with prior experience serving as a moderator (refer to Table 6).
5. **Group comparisons:** Variations were analyzed by gender and academic major (refer to Table 7).
6. **Benchmarking:** The results were compared against national indicators (Table 1) and studies involving Indian students (Table 2).

4.6 Results and Analysis

This section outlines the study's findings in four distinct stages: (1) national benchmarks for financial inclusion and literacy to provide context for the issue, (2) comparative evidence derived from previous studies on Indian students, (3) both descriptive and inferential results obtained from the primary survey (N = 260), and (4) cross-sectional interpretations that connect the three datasets.

1. National Benchmarks: India in Global Context

The Global Findex Database 2021 offers essential insights into the financial inclusion scenario in India. Table 1 presents a summary of key indicators for adults in India.

Table 1. National Financial Inclusion Benchmarks, India (2021)

Indicator	India Value	Global Average	Source
Bank account ownership (15+)	77.6%	76.0%	World Bank (2022)
Digital payment use	35%	45%	World Bank (2022)
Saved formally in past year	30%	42%	World Bank (2022)
Borrowed formally in past year	37%	34%	World Bank (2022)
Could cover emergency expense	22%	47%	World Bank (2022)

As illustrated in Table 1, India marginally surpasses the global average in terms of account ownership and borrowing; however, it falls considerably short in areas such as digital payments, savings, and financial resilience. Only 22% of the Indian population is capable of managing an emergency, in contrast to a global average of 47%. This underscores the idea that access does not equate to confidence—while millions of accounts are established, the actual utilization remains disappointingly low. For students, who constitute a younger and more digitally engaged demographic, one might anticipate a greater involvement in financial activities. Nevertheless, as subsequent sections will demonstrate, their level of knowledge and confidence does not show a significant improvement over that of the general adult population

2. Indian Student Benchmarks: Evidence from Prior Studies

To more effectively contextualize the main findings, it is beneficial to examine previous empirical research concerning Indian students.

Table 2. Financial Literacy Benchmarks, Indian Students

Study	Sample	Instrument	Findings
Dahiya et al. (2023)	400 undergraduates	OECD/INFE toolkit	Avg. 56% correct; weakest in compound interest and diversification
Jayaraman & Jambunathan (2018)	608 high school students	Basic + advanced questions	Avg. 45% correct; low preparedness for higher education
Delhi–NCR Youth Survey (2025)	381 students	Literacy+attitudes+ behaviors	Attitude and behavior stronger predictors of inclusion than knowledge

As illustrated in Table 2, Indian students consistently demonstrate lower performance in advanced financial concepts. Dahiya et al. (2023) indicate that even among business students, the average score on literacy items was merely 61%, highlighting a significant gap. Furthermore, the Delhi–NCR Youth Survey (2025) emphasizes that attitudes and behaviors frequently hold greater importance than mere knowledge—this aligns with the current study's emphasis on investment confidence.

3. Primary Survey Findings

Reliability

The reliability analysis demonstrated a robust internal consistency among the constructs.

Table 3. Reliability of Constructs (N – 260)

Construct	Items	Cronbach's α
Financial literacy	10	0.88
Gamification perception	15	0.91
Investment confidence	10	0.87

As illustrated in Table 3, the values of Cronbach's alpha surpassed the widely recognized benchmark of 0.70 (Nunnally, 1978), signifying outstanding internal reliability.

Descriptive Statistics

Table 4. Descriptive Statistics of Constructs

Construct	Mean	SD	Min	Max
Financial literacy	3.21	0.68	1.9	4.9
Gamification perception	3.54	0.72	1.8	4.8
Investment confidence	2.97	0.65	1.5	4.7

Table 4 reveals that students achieved moderate scores in literacy (M = 3.21, SD = 0.68) and confidence (M = 2.97, SD = 0.65), while their scores in gamification perception were somewhat elevated (M = 3.54, SD = 0.72). These findings imply that students are receptive to gamified educational tools, despite their knowledge and confidence levels being average

Correlation Analysis

Table 5. Correlations among Constructs

Variable	Literacy	Gamification	Confidence	Experience
Literacy	1.00	0.42**	0.51**	0.26*
Gamification	–	1.00	0.55**	0.29*
Confidence	–	–	1.00	0.33**
Experience	–	–	–	1.00

*p < .05, **p < .01*

As illustrated in Table 5, there was a significant correlation between literacy and gamification with investment confidence ($r = 0.51$, $p < .01$ and $r = 0.55$, $p < .01$, respectively). Additionally, prior investment experience showed a positive correlation with confidence ($r = 0.33$, $p < .01$). These relationships offer preliminary support for hypotheses H1, H2, and H4.

Regression Analysis

A multiple regression analysis was performed with investment confidence serving as the dependent variable.

Table 6. Regression Results (DV = Investment Confidence)

Predictor	β	p
Literacy	0.39	< .001
Gamification	0.41	< .001
Experience	0.15	.037

$R^2 = 0.56$

As illustrated in Table 6, both literacy ($\beta = 0.39$, $p < .001$) and the perception of gamification ($\beta = 0.41$, $p < .001$) were significant predictors of confidence, collectively accounting for 56% of the variance. Prior experience exhibited a lesser yet significant impact ($\beta = 0.15$, $p < .05$). These results validate hypotheses H1, H2, and H4.

Figure 2. Standardized predictive power on investment confidence (Table 6)

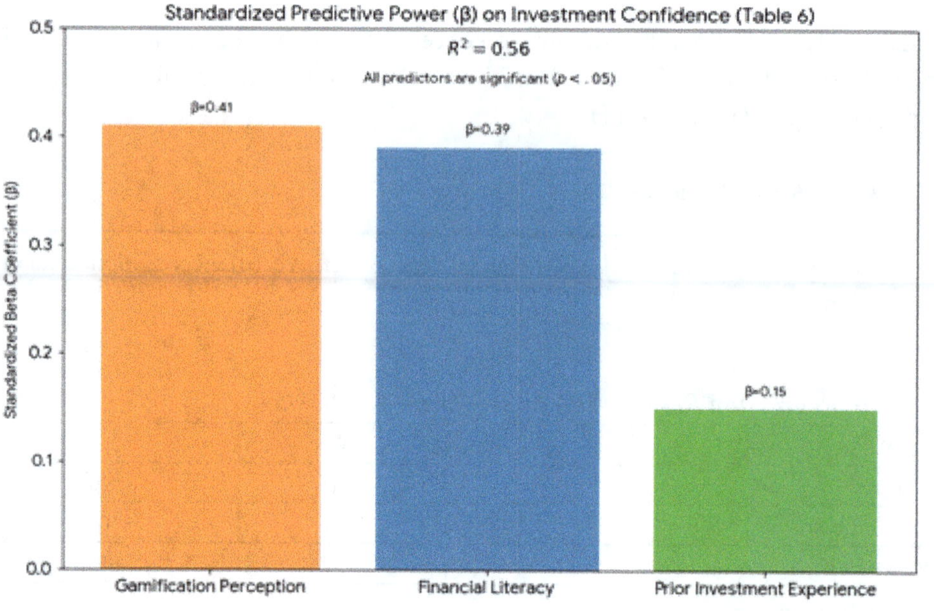

Group Comparisons

Table 7. Group Comparisons of Constructs

Group	Literacy (M)	Gamification (M)	Confidence (M)
Male (n = 140)	3.28	3.52	3.05
Female (n = 117)	3.15	3.56	2.89
Finance majors (n = 99)	3.42	3.68	3.21
Engineering (n = 83)	3.12	3.41	2.82
Arts/Science (n = 78)	3.05	3.45	2.76

As illustrated in Table 7, male students indicated a marginally greater level of confidence (M = 3.05) compared to their female counterparts (M = 2.89), even though their perceptions of gamification were nearly the same. Students majoring in finance excelled across all three constructs, which aligns with their exposure to the curriculum. These variations lend support to H5.

Figure 3. Grouped mean scores by gender and academic major (Table 7)

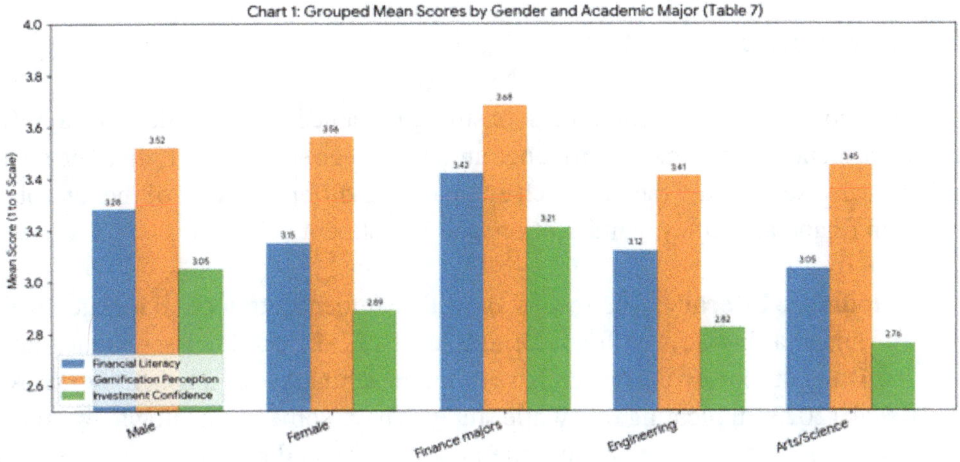

4.7 Interpretation of Results

Financial literacy and confidence are closely interconnected. Students exhibiting higher levels of literacy reported increased investment confidence, aligning with H1 and previous research (Dahiya et al., 2023).

Perceptions of gamification are as predictive of confidence as literacy. Notably, gamification exhibited a marginally stronger standardized effect ($\beta = 0.41$) compared to literacy ($\beta = 0.39$), thereby supporting H2 and H3. This indicates that students' attitudes towards gamification may have a greater impact on their confidence than mere knowledge.

Previous investment experience serves as a moderating factor. Students who have had prior exposure to investments gained more confidence from gamified settings, which supports H4. Thus, gamification enhances real-world experience.

Disparities based on gender and academic major continue to exist. Male students consistently display higher confidence levels, reflecting the findings of Lusardi & Mitchell (2014) regarding gender disparities in confidence. Unsurprisingly, finance majors outperformed their counterparts, underscoring inequalities in exposure and training.

National and student benchmarks are in agreement. Similar to Findex's findings of high access yet low resilience, students exhibit average literacy levels but low confidence. This situation highlights a more extensive structural challenge within India's financial education framework.

5. DISCUSSION

5.1 Overview of Findings

The findings of this research present strong evidence that gamification significantly influences investment confidence among college students in India. The analysis revealed several key themes, each emphasizing different facets of the interplay between financial literacy, gamification, and investment behavior.

Moderate Literacy: The results show that students attained moderate levels of financial literacy, with an average score of 3.21 on the assessment scale. This result closely corresponds with the benchmarks established by Dahiya et al. (2023), indicating that while students have some basic knowledge, there are notable gaps. Specifically, the areas where students struggled the most included the comprehension of compound interest, the impact of inflation on savings, and the principles of portfolio diversification. These shortcomings are particularly critical as they directly affect students' ability to plan for long-term financial stability and make informed investment choices. For example, understanding compound interest is essential for grasping how savings accumulate over time, while diversification is vital for managing investment risks. Without a solid understanding of these principles, students may find it challenging to make sound financial decisions, even when they have access to various financial tools and platforms.

Positive Gamification Perception: Students demonstrated a positive attitude towards gamification, as evidenced by a mean score of 3.54. This suggests that they found interactive simulations, gamified activities, and digital learning modules to be more engaging and attractive than traditional lecture-based approaches. The elevated perception score indicates that gamification not only captures attention but also encourages learners to actively engage in financial education activities. Numerous students noted that gamified features such as points, levels, and progress indicators offered concrete feedback, thereby making abstract financial concepts more tangible. This favorable reception highlights the capacity of gamification to serve as a link between theoretical understanding and practical implementation.

Cautious Investment Confidence: In spite of moderate levels of financial literacy and favorable attitudes towards gamification, students exhibited a relatively low level of investment confidence, reflected in a mean score of 2.97. This indicates a reluctance to make financial commitments, whether in simulated environments or real-life situations. Such a cautious stance may arise from a fear of risk, a lack of previous experience, or limited engagement with practical financial decision-making scenarios. Furthermore, it emphasizes the psychological aspect of financial education: possessing knowledge is inadequate if students are not mentally equipped to act upon it. This observation underscores the necessity for educational strategies that extend beyond mere information dissemination to tackle behavioral and confidence-related issues.

Correlational Evidence: The correlation analyses uncovered robust associations between investment confidence and both financial literacy (r = .51) and perceptions of gamification (r = .55). These results suggest that students who achieved higher scores on financial literacy evaluations or expressed more favorable views of gamified learning were more inclined to demonstrate confidence in making investment decisions. Importantly, the slightly stronger correlation with gamification perception highlights the effectiveness of interactive, experiential learning environments in fostering confidence, even when foundational knowledge is only moderate.

Regression Insights: The multiple regression analysis yielded additional insights into the factors influencing investment confidence. Perception of gamification emerged as a significant predictor ($\beta = .41$), comparable to financial literacy ($\beta = .39$), indicating that experiential learning elements can impact confidence as effectively as cognitive comprehension. Although prior investment experience was less impactful, it still had a positive contribution ($\beta = .15$), suggesting that real-world exposure can enhance both knowledge and confidence. The regression model accounted for 56% of the variance in investment confidence, indicating strong explanatory capability and highlighting the significance of both knowledge and attitudinal elements in influencing financial behavior.

Group Variations: The analysis of differences at the group level uncovered consistent patterns. Students pursuing finance or business majors achieved higher scores across all metrics, which reflects their exposure to the curriculum and familiarity with financial concepts. Gender disparities were minimal, although males reported slightly elevated confidence levels on average. These results imply that while educational background is a crucial factor, gamified interventions could be advantageous for all students, irrespective of their major or demographic attributes.

5.2 Comparison With Global Findex 2021 Benchmarks

The Global Findex Database 2021 offers a detailed examination of financial inclusion trends across various nations, providing crucial context for understanding findings at the student level. As per the database, India has achieved notable progress in enhancing financial access: 77.6% of adults now possess a bank account, indicative of extensive institutional outreach and the effectiveness of government programs such as the Pradhan Mantri Jan Dhan Yojana.

Nevertheless, despite improvements in access, behavioral metrics indicate persistent gaps. Only 30% of adults reported having saved formally in the past year, 37% engaged in borrowing through formal means, and merely 22% expressed readiness for financial emergencies (World Bank, 2022). These trends imply that access to financial services does not necessarily lead to effective usage or confidence in financial decision-making.

The patterns observed at the national level reflect the findings at the student level in this research. Students exhibited moderate financial literacy but comparatively low confidence in taking action, similar to the wider adult demographic that possesses accounts yet does not actively save, borrow judiciously, or prepare for emergencies. The cautious investment confidence score among students (M = 2.97) corresponds with Findex data indicating that only about one-fifth of Indian adults felt financially secure in emergencies.

This parallel presents a significant insight: at both macro (national) and micro (student) levels, the primary obstacle to financial inclusion is not the lack of knowledge or access, but rather the confidence to act effectively. Just as adults may hesitate to invest or borrow despite having accounts, students may refrain from making financial decisions even when they comprehend the underlying principles. This observation emphasizes the importance of interventions such as gamification that specifically aim to enhance confidence and behavioral preparedness.

5.3 Comparison With Indian Student Studies

The current findings are in strong agreement with previous studies conducted among Indian student populations, thereby providing both validation and context. Dahiya et al. (2023) indicated that college students attained an average literacy score of 56%, which reflects moderate levels of knowledge and underscores specific deficiencies in fundamental financial concepts, including compound interest and diversification. These findings align with the present study, indicating that literacy gaps are enduring across different cohorts and educational institutions.

The Delhi–NCR Youth Survey (2025) highlighted the significance of attitudes and behaviors beyond mere knowledge in forecasting financial inclusion outcomes. In a similar vein, this research discovered that the perception of gamification—a metric of positive engagement and attitude—was a significant predictor of investment confidence within the regression model. This supports the idea that emotional and experiential elements can greatly affect behavioral readiness and enhance cognitive learning. Jayaraman & Jambunathan (2018) investigated high school students and found that the average financial literacy scores hovered around 45%, suggesting that the youth in India transition into adulthood with relatively weak financial foundations. The current study indicates a slight improvement at the college level; however, the overall trend suggests that while literacy may rise with education, the need for confidence-building remains inadequately addressed.

Collectively, these comparisons affirm the strength of the current findings. They underscore that Indian students require more than just knowledge—they need organized tools and experiential opportunities, such as gamified interventions, to foster confidence and preparedness for real-world financial decision-making.

6. THEORETICAL IMPLICATIONS

6.1 Self-Efficacy Theory

Bandura's (1997) self-efficacy theory offers a robust framework for understanding these findings. Bandura posits that self-efficacy—the conviction in one's ability to perform actions required to achieve desired results—arises from four key sources: mastery experiences, vicarious learning, verbal persuasion, and affective regulation.

In this research:

Financial literacy signifies cognitive mastery, equipping individuals with the essential knowledge for informed decision-making.

The perception of gamification embodies the opportunity for mastery experiences through simulated, risk-free practice settings. Students are able to test investment choices, observe the results, and progressively refine their strategies.

Investment confidence acts as the outcome of self-efficacy, reflecting students' belief in their capacity to effectively apply financial knowledge.

The notable β-value for gamification perception ($\beta = .41$) highlights the theoretical understanding that mastery-focused, engaging environments can bolster self-efficacy beyond mere cognitive knowledge. This reinforces the idea that experiential learning and interactive participation are vital elements in converting literacy into actionable financial behavior.

6.2 Prospect Theory

Kahneman and Tversky's (1979) prospect theory emphasizes the inherent loss aversion in humans, where potential losses are perceived as more significant than equivalent gains. This cognitive bias frequently results in risk aversion, even in scenarios where expected outcomes are favorable. Gamification counters this tendency by creating a secure environment for practicing investment choices. By exposing students to simulated gains and losses, they can acclimate to risk, cultivate coping mechanisms, and alleviate the anxiety linked to possible financial losses. The strong relationship between the perception of gamification and investment confidence suggests that engaging in simulated risk-taking may assist in reducing loss aversion and promoting proactive involvement in financial decision-making.

6.3 Experiential Learning

Kolb's (1984) experiential learning cycle—consisting of concrete experience, reflective observation, abstract conceptualization, and active experimentation—aligns seamlessly with gamified financial education. Gamification allows students to participate in:

Concrete experiences through simulations of financial markets or budgeting tasks.
Reflective observation through immediate feedback and performance assessment.
Abstract conceptualization by incorporating lessons learned into cognitive frameworks for decision-making.
Active experimentation by implementing concepts in successive iterations, whether within the simulation or in real-world contexts.

This iterative process enhances both knowledge acquisition and self-assurance, underscoring the theoretical connection between gamification and the principles of experiential learning

6.4 Practical Implications

- For Educators:

  Incorporating gamified elements into the curriculum: The integration of stock market simulations, simulated Systematic Investment Plans (SIPs), and budgeting challenges within academic courses can significantly boost student engagement and foster self-assurance. Experiential learning activities allow students to apply their theoretical understanding in a controlled environment.

  Gradual increase in complexity: The learning process should evolve from straightforward decision-making tasks to more intricate portfolio management activities. This scaffolded approach systematically enhances competence while alleviating the anxiety often linked to financial risk.

Interdisciplinary application: The implementation of gamified financial education should not be limited to finance majors but should also encompass students from engineering, arts, and sciences. A wider application can enhance overall financial literacy and confidence across various fields.

-For Universities and Policymakers

Institutional Support: The incorporation of compulsory financial literacy workshops, enhanced through gamification, into orientation or foundational courses can guarantee initial exposure.

Industry Collaboration: Collaborations with FinTech firms can grant access to real-time gamified platforms, delivering experiential learning that reflects the Indian financial markets.

Policy Synergy: Government programs, like Jan Dhan Yojana, can integrate gamified mobile applications to actively involve students and promote a practical comprehension of financial services.

-For Students

Digital Practice: It is essential for students to utilize paper trading applications and gamified Systematic Investment Plan (SIP) platforms to cultivate practical skills prior to making actual investments.

Peer Learning: Engaging in team-oriented competitions or collaborative simulations can enhance the learning experience and foster confidence through social engagement.

Reflective Tracking: Keeping journals of simulated financial choices promotes metacognitive reflection, thereby solidifying both knowledge and self-assurance.

6.5 Limitations

Despite its contributions, this study has certain limitations:

Cross-sectional Design: The cross-sectional nature of the study restricts causal inference, hindering definitive conclusions regarding the directionality of relationships among literacy, gamification perception, and confidence.

Self-Report Bias: Data derived from surveys may be influenced by social desirability or self-perception biases, which could lead to an overestimation of reported confidence or perceptions of gamification.

Urban Sample: Concentrating on urban students may not adequately reflect the financial literacy and confidence levels of students in rural or semi-urban areas, where access to digital platforms and financial services may vary.

6.6 Synthesis

The synthesis of findings reveals several significant insights. Although financial literacy serves as a crucial foundation, it alone is inadequate for fostering strong investment confidence. Opportunities for experiential learning, especially through gamified interventions, effectively bridge the divide between knowledge and action. National benchmarks, including the Global Findex 2021, along with studies of Indian students, converge in illustrating that confidence, not merely access or basic literacy, represents the primary obstacle to financial inclusion. In conclusion, these findings emphasize the necessity of incorporating cognitive, attitudinal, and experiential components into financial education. By adopting this approach, educators, universities, and policymakers can nurture financially literate and confident students, thereby equipping them to adeptly navigate the evolving financial landscape of India.

7. SOLUTIONS AND RECOMMENDATIONS

7.1 For Educators

Incorporate Gamification into the Curriculum. Replace or enhance conventional lectures with stock market simulations, budgeting tasks, or SIP planners. Ensure the quality of design by aligning game components with educational objectives.

Promote Reflective Learning. Gamification should extend beyond the gameplay experience. Debriefing sessions, reflective journals, and group discussions facilitate students in processing their experiences, connecting them to real-world consequences.

Offer Incremental Challenges. Confidence develops gradually. Begin with straightforward decisions (for instance, selecting between saving and spending) and progress to more intricate portfolio management tasks.

Apply Across Disciplines. Financial confidence is not solely for business students. Students in engineering and the arts should also engage with gamified modules, promoting widespread financial empowerment.

7.2 For Universities and Policymakers

Establish Financial Literacy as a Fundamental Component. Mandate the inclusion of financial education within the general education framework of universities, emphasizing gamification as an essential element.
Collaborate with FinTech Entities. Engage with platforms such as Zerodha Varsity, Groww, or Paytm Money to incorporate gamified learning modules into academic programs. These collaborations merge scholarly rigor with practical relevance.
Encourage Active Participation. Provide certificates, academic credits, or formal recognition for the completion of gamified learning modules, thereby promoting ongoing involvement.
Specialized Programs for Women. Address the gender disparities in confidence through customized initiatives, such as women-exclusive investment clubs that utilize gamified resources to foster secure and encouraging educational environments.

7.3 For Students

Participate in Gamified Learning Applications. Students ought to actively investigate applications that replicate trading, saving, and investing.
Begin with Minimal Real Investments. Even small Systematic Investment Plans (100/month) offer tangible references that enhance gamified experiences.
Engage in Collaborative Learning. Establish peer groups to compete in gamified challenges, promoting both accountability and collective learning.
Regularly Reflect. Maintain journals of investment simulations, recording insights gained, errors committed, and strategies improved.\

8. FUTURE RESEARCH DIRECTIONS

Given the exploratory nature of this study, several avenues for future research emerge.

Longitudinal Designs.

Do gains in investment confidence from gamification persist over time, or are they temporary? Tracking students across semesters can reveal lasting impacts.

Experimental Trials.

Randomized controlled trials comparing gamified versus traditional teaching would provide stronger causal evidence.

Feature-Level Analysis.

Which gamification elements (points, leaderboards, narratives, feedback) most influence confidence? Disentangling these effects could optimize design.

Cross-Context Studies.

How do results differ between urban and rural students, public and private universities, or developed and emerging markets?

Gender-Specific Interventions.

Future work should test gamification designs tailored specifically for women to close confidence gaps.

Behavioral Outcomes.

Beyond confidence, does gamification translate into actual investment behavior (e.g., opening accounts, initiating SIPs)?

9. CONCLUSION

This chapter explored the essential function of gamification in addressing the ongoing disparity between financial literacy and investment confidence among college students in India. The findings of the study indicate that while financial literacy serves as a fundamental basis, it is insufficient by itself to guarantee that students are both willing and able to make informed financial choices. Despite having a basic understanding of savings, investment principles, and market operations, students' capacity to convert this knowledge into confident actions remains constrained. The research offers empirical evidence that the perception of gamification—students' favorable attitudes and engagement with interactive, game-like educational tools—holds equal significance to financial literacy in forecasting investment confidence. The correlation of these findings with both national and international data enriches the analysis further. The Global Findex Database (2021) underscores India's significant advancements in enhancing financial access, with over 77% of adults now possessing formal bank accounts. However, deeper involvement with financial products is still lacking: only 30% exhibit formal savings behavior, 37% engage in borrowing through official channels, and a mere 22% are ready to tackle financial emergencies. These figures illustrate a notable paradox—access and knowledge do not inherently result in proactive financial conduct. Likewise, the Indian college students in this research demonstrated moderate literacy yet relatively low investment confidence, reflecting national trends. At both the student and adult population levels, confidence emerges as the crucial missing link between knowledge and action. Previous studies conducted in India support this conclusion. Dahiya et al. (2023) found moderate levels of financial literacy among college students, with ongoing gaps in fundamental concepts such as compound interest, diversification, and inflation. Similarly, the Delhi–NCR Youth Survey (2025) highlighted the significance of attitudes and behavioral readiness as predictors of financial inclusion outcomes, surpassing the role of mere knowledge. Collectively, these studies indicate that while literacy provides students with essential cognitive tools, further mechanisms are necessary to facilitate practical engagement with financial decisions. In this regard, gamification emerges as a notably effective educational strategy.

The theoretical ramifications of these findings are profound. Bandura's self-efficacy theory (1997) posits that confidence is cultivated through mastery experiences, vicarious learning, verbal encouragement, and emotional regulation. Gamified learning environments can effectively implement these principles. Mastery experiences are realized as students achieve success in simulations and receive concrete feedback on their choices. Vicarious learning takes place when students observe the strategies and outcomes of their peers, enabling them to emulate effective behaviors.

Verbal persuasion can be integrated into gamification through automated prompts, peer acknowledgment, or feedback from instructors. Ultimately, affective regulation is facilitated by the secure environment provided by simulations, allowing students to experience minor setbacks without real-world repercussions, thereby alleviating anxiety and nurturing a constructive relationship with risk.

Moreover, the findings of the study align with principles from behavioral economics. Prospect theory (Kahneman & Tversky, 1979) highlights the inherent loss aversion in individuals, which frequently results in risk-averse behavior. Gamification serves to alleviate this bias by offering repeated chances for students to face gains and losses within a controlled environment, progressively diminishing the emotional repercussions of risk and normalizing decision-making amidst uncertainty. Experiential learning models, such as Kolb's (1984) cycle, are likewise reinforced: students partake in tangible experiences through simulations, reflect on the outcomes through feedback, cognitively conceptualize insights, and actively experiment in subsequent iterations. This cyclical process guarantees that learning encompasses not only cognitive aspects but also behavioral dimensions, thereby enhancing both competence and confidence. The practical ramifications for India's higher education system are evident. Conventional financial education, which often prioritizes rote memorization, lectures, or textbook-based teaching, may enhance knowledge but fails to cultivate behavioral preparedness or self-assurance. By integrating gamified components into curricula, universities can establish engaging, interactive platforms where students actively engage in decision-making, learn from their errors, and internalize optimal practices. This methodology is especially beneficial in fields beyond finance, such as engineering, arts, or sciences, where students may have limited prior exposure to financial principles. A cross-disciplinary approach guarantees that all students, irrespective of their major, acquire vital skills in personal financial management and investment decision-making. Policymakers can utilize these insights to create interventions that support wider financial inclusion efforts. For example, government initiatives like Jan Dhan Yojana or UPI-based payment systems could incorporate gamified mobile applications that educate users on financial concepts while encouraging the use of formal financial products.

On an individual level, students are motivated to actively participate with gamified financial tools. Digital platforms that replicate trading, SIP investments, or portfolio management create low-risk practice environments where learners can explore without fear. Peer-based competitions and collaborative simulations further boost motivation and reinforce learning through social interactions. Moreover, keeping reflective journals to document decisions and outcomes aids in solidifying knowledge and enhancing metacognitive awareness, thereby nurturing both understanding and confidence over time. Despite its encouraging findings, the chapter recognizes certain limitations. The cross-sectional design of the study limits causal conclusions, and self-reporting methods may introduce biases, including social desirability effects. Furthermore, the sample was confined to urban college students, which restricts the applicability of the results to rural or semi-urban settings, where experiences with financial services and digital platforms may vary. Lastly, the perception of gamification was evaluated conceptually rather than through direct interaction with live platforms, suggesting a necessity for future studies to examine ecological validity and real-world relevance.

In summary, the study underscores a vital insight: while financial literacy is essential, it alone is inadequate to guarantee confident financial behavior. Investment confidence emerges as the crucial element that empowers students to convert knowledge into action. Gamification, by providing interactive, feedback-rich, and low-risk environments, effectively fosters this confidence, enhancing cognitive learning with practical experience.

10. ACKNOWLEDGMENT

The author expresses sincere gratitude for the utilization of publicly accessible datasets, such as the Global Findex Database (World Bank, 2022), along with previous studies on financial literacy in India that provided essential comparative benchmarks. Thanks are also given to the student participants for their invaluable insights, as well as to the academic mentors for their support and guidance during the research process.

REFERENCES

Bandura, A. (1997). *Self-efficacy: The exercise of control*. W. H. Freeman.

Dahiya, M., Özen, E., & Yadav, K. (2023). The financial literacy of college students: Evidence from India. *ASR: Chiang Mai University Journal of Social Sciences and Humanities, 10*(1).

Deterding, S., Dixon, D., Khaled, R., & Nacke, L. (2011). From game design elements to "gamefulness": Defining gamification. In *Proceedings of the 15th International Academic MindTrek Conference* (pp. 9–15). ACM. https://doi.org/ DOI: 10.1145/2181037.2181040

Hamari, J., Koivisto, J., & Sarsa, H. (2014). Does gamification work? A literature review of empirical studies on gamification. In *2014 47th Hawaii International Conference on System Sciences* (pp. 3025–3034). IEEE. https://doi.org/DOI: 10.1109/HICSS.2014.377

Hanus, M. D., & Fox, J. (2015). Assessing the effects of gamification in the classroom: A longitudinal study on intrinsic motivation, social comparison, satisfaction, effort, and academic performance. *Computers & Education, 80*, 152–161. DOI: 10.1016/j.compedu.2014.08.019

Jayaraman, J. D., & Jambunathan, S. (2018). Financial literacy among high school students: Evidence from India. *Citizenship. Social and Economics Education, 17*(3), 168–186. DOI: 10.1177/2047173418809712

Kahneman, D., & Tversky, A. (1979). Prospect theory: An analysis of decision under risk. *Econometrica, 47*(2), 263–292. DOI: 10.2307/1914185

Kolb, D. A. (1984). *Experiential learning: Experience as the source of learning and development*. Prentice Hall.

Lusardi, A., & Mitchell, O. S. (2014). The economic importance of financial literacy: Theory and evidence. *Journal of Economic Literature, 52*(1), 5–44. DOI: 10.1257/jel.52.1.5 PMID: 28579637

National Centre for Financial Education (NCFE). (2019). *Financial Literacy and Inclusion Survey (NFLIS)*. NCFE.

National Financial Inclusion Benchmarks. (2021).

NCR Youth Survey. (2025). *[Unpublished survey – cited in text as "Delhi–NCR Youth Survey (2025)"]*.

Nunnally, J. C. (1978). *Psychometric theory* (2nd ed.). McGraw-Hill.

OECD. (2013). *OECD/INFE toolkit for measuring financial literacy and financial inclusion*. OECD Publishing.

OECD. (2020). *OECD/INFE 2020 international survey of adult financial literacy*. OECD Publishing.

Reserve Bank of India. (2021). *Report on trends and progress of banking in India 2020–21*. Reserve Bank of India.

Robb, C. A., & Sharpe, D. L. (2009). Effect of personal financial knowledge on college students' credit card behavior. *Financial Counseling and Planning, 20*(1), 25–43.

Sailer, M., & Homner, L. (2020). The gamification of learning: A meta-analysis. *Educational Psychology Review, 32*(1), 77–112. DOI: 10.1007/s10648-019-09498-w

Schoenfeld, A., & Zhang, D. (2019). *Gamified simulations in financial education: A review of outcomes*.

World Bank. (2022). *The Global Findex Database 2021: Financial inclusion, digital payments, and resilience in the age of COVID-19*. World Bank. https://doi.org/DOI: 10.1596/978-1-4648-1897-4

ADDITIONAL READING

Koivisto, J., & Hamari, J. (2019). The rise of motivational information systems: A review of gamification research. *International Journal of Human-Computer Studies, 127*, 101–113.

NCFE. (2021). *National strategy for financial education: 2020–2025*. Reserve Bank of India.

OECD. (2013). *OECD/INFE toolkit for measuring financial literacy and financial inclusion*. OECD.

KEY TERMS AND DEFINITIONS

- **Financial Literacy: The understanding and abilities required to make well-informed financial choices.:**
- **Gamification: The application of game design principles in non-gaming environments to boost engagement.:**
- **Investment Confidence: A person's assurance in their capability to make sound financial choices when faced with risk.:**
- **Self-Efficacy: The conviction in one's ability to perform actions necessary to reach objectives.:**
- **Prospect Theory: A behavioral model that elucidates decision-making in risky situations:** highlighting the tendency to avoid losses.
- **Experiential Learning: An educational method that focuses on cycles of experience:** reflection, conceptualization, and experimentation.
- **Financial Inclusion: The provision of accessible and beneficial financial services that cater to individual requirements.:**

ENDNOTES

1. Global Findex 2021 data are publicly available through the World Bank Microdata Library.
2. Benchmark comparisons are drawn from peer-reviewed studies cited in the References section

APPENDIX

- **Appendix A: Survey Instrument (Sample Items)**
  Section A: Financial Literacy (10 items): for instance, "If you invest Rs. 1,000 at an annual interest rate of 10%, what will be your total after two years?"
  Section B: Gamification Perception (15 items): for example, "The gamified modules have heightened my interest in financial subjects."
  Section C: Investment Confidence (10 items): for instance, "I believe I can effectively diversify a portfolio."
  Section D: Behavioral Intention (5 items): for example, "I am inclined to initiate a Systematic Investment Plan (SIP) within the upcoming year."
- **Appendix B: Gamification Design Features**
  Incorporation of points, badges, and leaderboards.
  Implementation of realistic market simulations.
  Establishment of feedback mechanisms and progress tracking.

Chapter 11
Gamifying English Language Instruction:
Strategies for Motivating Learners Through Game-Based Learning

Vivit Rosmayanti
https://orcid.org/0000-0002-3648-9878
Universitas Negeri Makassar, Indonesia

ABSTRACT

The book Gamifying English Language Instruction: Strategies for Motivating Learners through Game-Based Learning discusses the integration of Game-Based Learning (GBL) into English language instruction to encourage participation and motivation among learners. It explores the motivational frameworks, like Self-Determination Theory and Flow Theory, which explain how gamification can enhance motivation and engagement. The chapter focuses on the fundamental aspects of GBL, such as feedback loops, narratives, and multiplayer features, and the techniques for gamifying English language teaching, such as narrative, scaffolding, quests, and self-directed educational video games. The chapter also highlights how social interactions in games can improve communication and cultural understanding. However, the book faces challenges such as access to technology, cultural sensitivity, and the balance between content and entertainment. The chapter also examines the effect of gamification on motivation and achievement, with evidence supporting active participation, retention, and academic performance.

DOI: 10.4018/979-8-3373-4465-2.ch011

INTRODUCTION

In recent years, the integration of technology into the classroom has seen a substantial increase as educational institutions are adopting more digital tools and GBL to improve the overall learning experience of their students. A variety of research shows that GBL has marked positive impacts on student engagement, achievement, and motivation levels. Evayani et al. (2021) underline the role of educational games in enhancing student motivation and academic performance, demonstrating GBL's effectiveness as a method to reinvigorate learning environments, especially in places where teaching techniques are less than optimal. Furthermore, Levina et al. (2021) stress the application of game-based technologies toward the development of students' cognitive and communicative skills, thereby confirming the remarkable potential of GBL to facilitate greater participation and interaction among students during lessons, whether in the classroom or online.

Persistence and effort in trying to learn a language are entwined with the factor of motivation. Motivation acts as a driving force, so motivation is crucial in foreign language learning. As stated by Islam & Moon (2022), motivation is a core component of success or failure for language learners, and yes, it affects their attitudes personally and contributes to their work ethnics. Netta (2023), on the other hand, focuses heavily on motivation, which states motivational pulls require entertainment and mastery opportunities that allow learners to actively practice the target language. We motivate language learning through creating proper environmental structures that focus on the language and issues, propelling teachers to take sufficient chances towards motivating learners.

The use of gamification in English language teaching and learning processes can increase students' participation and enthusiasm. By integrating elements of games, lessons become more varied while also appealing to students, thus enhancing their interests and aspirations. For example, Munirah & Sahriani (2024) reveal the impact of digital tools such as Quizizz on the language learners' motivational levels, demonstrating new possibilities of long-term engagement among learners. Moreover, Hussain et al. (2023) highlight that the cultivation of a game-centered atmosphere in teaching English as a foreign language (EFL) is likely to improve learners' perceptions of the subject, suggesting solutions to longstanding motivation and engagement issues in education (Hussain et al., 2023). The application of strategies based on gamification not only creates a positive learning environment but cultivates ownership of the learners, therefore effectively guiding them through purposeful language learning pathways.

This chapter aims to examine the connection between gamification and motivation in English language teaching by looking at how different strategies try to use game-based learning to foster student participation. We aim to analyze successful case studies and highlight practical recommendations that educators can readily adopt. The examination will also incorporate the description of how motivational strategies can be woven into the language curriculum as detailed by Lăpădat & Lăpădat (2024), who, it is claimed, recognize the persisting neglect of motivational factors integrated into language teaching to enhance learning. By analyzing available evidence and research, we aim to equip teachers with the tools necessary to develop captivating game-focused learning environments that ensure ample language skill practice in a highly engaging context.

In summary, the growing use of game-based learning techniques is changing the educational framework, especially with regard to learning English as a foreign language. The importance of motivation in acquiring a new language validates the need for teachers to employ gamification that aligns with students' internal interests for being involved and skilled. In writing this chapter, we hope to participate in the discussion on teaching languages and place teachers in a position to appreciate how game-based learning encourages motivation and improves language skills performance in multilingual and digital classrooms.

THEORETICAL FOUNDATIONS OF GAMIFICATION IN LANGUAGE LEARNING

Gamification is one of the recent educational practices on the rise, which focuses on the application of game mechanics to contexts that do not involve games, especially in learning a language. He defines this concept as "the use of games or game-like activities to engage students in the learning process" (Franco, 2022). Park and Kim (2021) highlight the essence of gamification to lie in its features - immediate feedback, achievement strongly through levels and rewards, and social interaction through the competitive elements like leaderboards. Having these elements in one setting not only inspires but also helps build a feeling of identity that motivates learners to step outside their comfort zones, while still surrounded by comfort. In addition, effective gamification ensures that these elements are embedded in the content of the education to make engagement genuine rather than attendance (Takbiri et al., 2023).

Motivational theories, relevant to understanding the effect of gamification on learner engagement, especially in language learning, include gamification. Some of the theories that explain these connections are Self-Determination Theory (SDT) and Flow Theory. As advanced by SDT, people have an inherent need for autonomy, competence, and relatedness. When these needs are satisfied, motivation increases, which in turn leads to improved learning outcomes (Kien & Nguyen, 2021). Gamification fulfills these designed needs by providing opportunities for decision-making in the various stages of the learning process, setting achievable benchmarks to enhance feelings of competence, and fostering social interactions through group activities. Flow Theory, on the other hand, concentrates on a state of deep engagement with an activity. Such a state is achieved with challenges closely aligned to persons' abilities, thus supporting intrinsic motivation (Yan & Zhao, 2023). As discussed earlier, gamification can enhance motivation and engagement by contrôler the challenge level of tasks and offering prompt feedback, allowing learners to persistently attain pre-set goals throughout their language learning processes.

The aspects of motivation can be merrily integrated with the cognitive and emotional benefits of game-based learning concerning language learning. In the case of language learning, cognitive benefits cover the enhancement of critical thinking, problem-solving, and information retention skills. The latest research indicates that the interactive nature of a gamified environment promotes cognitive engagement, which results in the increased processing of language content (Alsadoon, 2023). Enjoyably, game-based learning can lessen the anxiety of language learners by making practice more relaxed and entertaining. Empirical research demonstrates that exposure to gamified features within an educational context increases perceptions of excitement and joy, leading to an enhanced positive emotional association to the material learned (Takbiri et al, 2023). This emotional angle to learning is important as language learners need to be in supportive situations to practice without the anxiety of failing.

Importantly, gamification supports the development of dual levels of motivation, intrinsic and extrinsic, in language students. The motivation that is intrinsic stems from the engagement with the process of learning itself; especially when it comes to students participating in gamified activities, the fun they experience contributes to the possibility of their needing to acquire the language (Yang et al., 2021). On the other hand, extrinsic motivation is garnering rewards in the form of recognition that learners get because of their various efforts, for example, earning badges or getting to certain positions on leaderboards. Effective gamification design utilizes both types of motivation through merging tangible rewards and experiences with fun (Sharma et al., 2024). A good example would be where a language learner would want to perform well in the tasks for the sake of recognition (extrinsically) while enjoying the process of solving language puzzles or completing storytelling challenges (intrinsically).

As a result, the design of gamified experiences has the potential to foster a sustained language learning engagement paradigm. This participation engages learners and strengthens their confidence and skill (Mulcahy et al., 2020). In the end, the gamification of language instruction allows educators to address the diverse motivational needs of students, which is essential in effective language acquisition and mastery of the language. To conclude, the theoretical foundations of language learning gamification present an integrated blend of motivation, learning theory, and an emotional investment framework. Its principles enable educators to create an exciting environment where learners will approach language learning challenges with motivation and a positive attitude.

KEY COMPONENTS OF GAME-BASED LEARNING

Game-Based Learning (GBL) contains many relevant features that make it effective in the language learning context. GBL is centered on game elements like points, levels, rewards, and challenges. These elements aim at achieving a positive learning atmosphere and determining achievement among the learners (Laine & Lindberg, 2020). Rewards and recognition bolster motivation and reinforcement by providing acknowledgment of progress. Levels allow learners to meander through complex language concepts in a gradual, manageable manner. Well-designed challenges inspire learners to use their language skills in real-life situations (Chan et al., 2021).

Gamified language learning experiences are enhanced by incorporating narratives and storytelling. Through storytelling, students not only learn but also understand why a particular language is useful. When language instruction is integrated into captivating stories, the learner's emotional connection to the content is enhanced, which improves retention and recall. Stories can also facilitate immersion, whereby students act as participants in the development of the story. Such scenarios can yield optimal attentional control and enjoyment, which motivates learners to interact with the language.

Gamified Learning (GBL) also contains provable, self-contained systems in which the outcomes of an individual's actions are surrounded by a feedback loop in the interaction. Communication of insightful and meaning-laden feedback is paramount in enhancing progress. As learners interact with gamified activities, feedback does not just passively await as a subsequent step; rather, it actively avails reflection and adjustment opportunities, and learners get informed on how well they are doing. To illustrate, language learners receive feedback through quizzes that provide reports on areas of weakness and strength immediately on the spot. This feedback can empower learners and assist in guiding them in language acquisition with an informed prediction on what strategy they should use next. Immediate feedback motivates and engages learners because they are encouraged to work harder. This, in turn, strengthens their learnership and investment in the learning process.

Besides feedback, the impact of competition and collaboration in gamified contexts remains relevant. Competition is known to serve as one of the greatest motivators, especially when learners are placed in competitive environments, such as with leaderboards or when a timer is used, encouraging them to do their best. This aspect can motivate learners to invest additional effort towards raising their rankings; thus, enhancing their participation in language tasks. Competition of this kind must, however, be counter-balanced with collaboration, as collaborative activities can stimulate learning and social interaction with peers (Laine & Lindberg, 2020). In collaborative gamified activities, learners pool individual knowledge as they strive towards shared objectives; therefore, promoting social interaction and language use in real situations. In addition, a mixture of competitive and collaborative aspects can foster powerful learning experiences where learners actively share and provide assistance to one another in the processes of language learning.

As articulated in the other chapters, the principles of Game-Based Learning (GBL) facilitate an energetic environment for language learning activities. The use of points, levels, and challenges as rewards captures the attention of learners, and stories provide more context for language use. Continuous feedback systems foster sustained development from learners alongside the constant rhythm of competitive and cooperative engagement, which further drives focus and interest. Together, these components form a strong system that enables language learners to navigate the process with a great sense of fulfillment and pleasure.

GAMIFICATION STRATEGIES FOR ENGLISH LANGUAGE TEACHING

The adoption of gamification techniques in the teaching of English as a foreign language increases the learners' motivation and willingness to participate. One of the most effective methods in this case is the application of storytelling and role-playing video games (RPGs), as they immerse learners in stories that motivate them to use the language meaningfully. Stories allow learners to be cast in different roles, which enables them to practice lexicon and grammar in authentic communicative situations (Krishnan et al., 2021). Learners can also view an issue or a culture from a different angle when they are being taught the language through role-playing, which improves their empathy and appreciation of the language.

Another important gamification method is creating achievement-based learning paths with progressively more complex language tasks within each subsequent segment (Frolli et al., 2023). The learners can achieve small successes, which helps boost their confidence as they progress through the curriculum. Dividing language skills into levels affords teachers the possibility of differentiated instruction in a multi-proficiency classroom (Frolli et al., 2023). This approach helps the learners attain a sense of achievement at every step of their journey, motivating them to tackle more complex language tasks with increased self-assurance.

The implementation of quests and missions achieves goal-oriented language practice, representing an effective strategy for gamification. Quests can be tailored to align with the interests of the learners, thus personalizing and motivating language practice. While learners participate in quests, they perform language tasks on a simulated basis (Yasir et al., 2021). These missions create motivation for completing language practice tasks as they serve an overarching purpose, merging educational objectives with compelling stories and narratives. The use of these goal-oriented strategies has been proven to improve learners' motivation and readiness to engage in language work because they turn the process into an adventure rather than a boring routine (Khasanova et al., 2020).

Furthermore, the addition of multiplayer and social components to gamified environments enhances collaboration among learners. These social aspects can strengthen a sense of community and enhance the experience of learning the language. When learners engage with their peers in competitive or project-based games, they can use the language in multifaceted, conversational situations. The design of pair or group challenges often leads to active participation where learners collaboratively negotiate meaning, share, and construct new vocabulary (Rafiq et al., 2021). Additionally, social aspects of gamification enable peer motivation, where students actively support one another to attain set goals, thus increasing personal motivation and engagement.

Adaptive learning games represent a step into the future by personalizing the language learning journey relative to each learner's progression. These games apply data analytics to monitor a learner's language performance, adjusting difficulty levels and content to specific capabilities. The adaptive nature of these games mitigates the problem of being too easy or boring and problematic overload (Värtinen et al., 2024). Adaptive learning games meet learner needs in real-time, which enhances motivation and facilitates effective language learning because content is customized to their skills (Martinez et al., 2022).

To summarize, the use of gamification integration, especially in the form of storytelling, level-based modules, quest-based activities, social collaboration, and adaptive learning, has the ability to foster rich English instruction environments and enhance the effectiveness of English teaching. These techniques not only increase engagement and motivation but also help tailor to students' diverse needs, interests, and priorities. With the continued advancement of technology, the application of gamification in English language instruction will transform the instructional approach to be more engaging and facilitate active participation in the classroom.

PRACTICAL EXAMPLES OF GAME-BASED ENGLISH LANGUAGE INSTRUCTION

The use of gamification techniques in English instruction is linked to increased engagement, improved learning results, and active participation. This part presents practical examples of game-based learning through the use of successful implementation stories, tools, instructional activities, and blended learning frameworks that contain games.

Many case studies documented the successful use of gamification features in ESL teaching. A classic example is documented by Halim et al., where 81.7% of students preferred lessons that were delivered in a gamified manner using Kahoot. Halim et al. (2020) conducted a study that concluded that students' motivation levels increased when they had the opportunity to use quiz games as a part of their lessons, highlighting the utility of such mechanisms as motivators for creating a favorable learning atmosphere. Also, Rybchynska showed that students developed higher-order language skills as a result of being provided with interactive instruction such as role-play discussions (Rybchynska, 2023). We can see that the use of games has a direct impact on the personalized engagement of students while learning new skills

Duolingo, Kahoot!, and Quizlet are among the most widely known apps for language learning in the context of using gamified tools and platforms. Language learners on Duolingo are motivated by means of gamification and specific features such as leveling up, receiving rewards, and participating in challenges (Govender & Arnedo-Moreno, 2021). In addition to its user-friendly interface, the app provides lessons that are tailored to the personal needs of each learner, which, in turn, fosters a self-directed study environment. As for Kahoot!, it is another widely used tool that allows learning through quizzes, promoting competition and collaboration among learners. With regards to Kahoot!, its effectiveness was shown in a study by Hsia and Yamat in which students were able to better recall learning irregular verbs through quizzes (Hsia & Yamat, 2022). Furthermore, Quizlet, which is famous for its flashcards, offers gamified elements, including points and slots on the leaderboard, which allows learners to track their progress in mastering vocabulary and grammar (Yunus & Tan, 2021). Serving as examples are these platforms, which illustrate the use of technology in the creation of engaging, gamified learning environments.

In addition, in the classroom, participation can be increased through the use of games during lessons and evaluation activities. As an example, teachers can design group work like language scavenger hunts where students try to find clues while using their target language skills (Zhyhadlo, 2022). This type of cooperative activity promotes social interaction with peers as well as vocabulary practice in realistic, meaningful situations. Other fun classroom activities include board games where players have to create sentences or questions in English, thus learning while having fun (Ningrum et al, 2024). It is these interaction practices that, for learners, can reap positive results such as improved motivation and enhanced creativity alongside comprehension of language structures.

Game-based elements can effortlessly be integrated into hybrid and blended learning models to motivate students further as a form of augmentative education. Both physical lessons and online classes that incorporate gaming mechanics are capable of addressing a broader range of learning preferences. For example, during physical classes, instructors can add role-play or group-based challenges to online quizzes held through Kahoot! or Quizlet (Phuong, 2020). The combination of various approaches in this manner caters to flexibility and allows students to interact with materials on different levels. Moreover, studies show that learners are more motivated to participate in collaborative activities in and out of the classroom when they use gamified online learning environments (Park & Kim, 2021). Through the integration of technology with conventional pedagogy, educators can develop an all-encompassing framework that advances self-directed learning while meeting varying educational demands.

In addition, adaptive learning games aimed at customizing the language acquisition process can improve the engagement and achievement levels of ESL learners. These types of games feature algorithms that evaluate the learner's performance during the learning session and dynamically adjust the level of challenge based on the learner's skill level (Luo, 2023). Such approaches are encouraging when considering the wide variety of learner needs as well as their ability to advance through content in a self-paced manner without feeling anxious or disengaged. In research conducted to evaluate the use of adaptive games, personalizing language tasks according to a learner's pacing has been shown to dramatically increase learners' engagement with and retention of the language (Idris et al., 2020). This form of learning not only sustains learners' interest but also fosters self-responsibility with regard to their education.

In closing, the practical case studies described in this section further emphasize the powerful impact of gamification on English language teaching. Successful case studies illustrate the transformational effect of gamified experiences on motivation and engagement, and technologies such as Duolingo, Kahoot!, and Quizlet prove the usefulness of interactivity in the learning process. Designing activities for the classroom and employing blended models are important for promoting flexible collaboration. These approaches enable instructors to refine their instructional strategies and design motivating, game-based opportunities that develop language skills and instill a passion for the English language.

CHALLENGES AND CONSIDERATIONS IN GAMIFYING ENGLISH LANGUAGE TEACHING

With the increase in the application of gamification in English language teaching, educators have several issues to take into consideration that impact the effectiveness of having game-based learning strategies. Identifying these challenges is important to integrate and capitalize on the value that game mechanics can bring to language instruction while also meeting the desirable educational outcomes.

The shifting of the English language and instructional practices presents numerous barriers that need to be resolved. The availability of resources may include reliable internet access, functioning devices, and required software. These factors may vary greatly from one learning institution to another. Inaccessibility to important resources creates a gap for equitable access to education. Most learners, especially in less developed regions, do not have the necessary infrastructure, such as computers or tablets, needed to participate in gamified learning. This lack of accessibility, worse still, for many low and middle-income countries, disrupts the equitable use of gamification technologies and exacerbates already existing educational disparities. Furthermore, teachers require adequate technical assistance and instructional guidance to optimally utilize gamified approaches for teaching languages (Zhang & Hasim, 2023).

The inclusion of culturally relevant and appropriate games is the foremost challenge to consider when gamifying English language instruction. The process of acquiring a language involves culture, and instructors must consider whether the games used for instruction capture the diverse backgrounds of the learners. Instructional games lacking cultural sensitivity may unintentionally ostracize or marginalize particular groups of students. As an example, the concepts, stories, and vocabulary employed in game-based learning need to bear cultural sensitivity in their distinctions and norms without falling into stereotyping or misrepresentation (Cruz et al., 2023). Thus, engaging multiple perspectives in the game design process is crucial to fostering inclusivity in the game's educational setting.

Integrating gamification in language teaching poses the challenge of balancing entertaining and educational value. The fun elements of a game can encourage motivation; however, these aspects mustn't overshadow the educational ones. Teachers need to analyze whether the game conforms to pedagogical standards because it helps achieve some learning goals. Focus on entertainment value alone may encourage shallow engagement where learners spend time playing games but do not progress in language learning. To avoid this dilemma, Phuong (2020) argues that alignment of the game mechanics and learning goals should be designed in such a way that learners achieve the goals set for them while enjoying the experience.

As much as there is a focus on the educational soundness of curricula, instructors must be careful not to over-utilize gamification. Game-based strategies can be beneficial in increasing engagement; however, they should not take the place of teaching methods. Instructional delivery that integrates teaching methods with game elements is more enriching as it addresses a wider scope of learner needs. Game-based learning should be incorporated into the curriculum purposefully and strategically, ensuring that it serves as an aid and not a replacement for interaction and instruction (Dindar et al., 2020). Striking a balance with varied instructional methods empowers educators to build an effective environment for language learning and stimulate acquisition.

The willingness of English language teachers to adopt gamified pedagogical strategies is a fundamental factor with regard to the successful application of gamification. Suffice it to say, professional development programming prepares teachers to deal with the issues of game construction, the use of technology, and the educational theory that forms the basis of gamification. Evidence suggests that trained teachers are more confident and proficient in applying some of the strategies that were taught to them during training. There are well-defined frameworks, structural guidelines, as well as a logistical system for support that takes into consideration the provision of the teachers and these supports active engagement. Moreover, building a cohesive community of educators to enhance the practices of sharing their experiences and practices on the gamification of learning can greatly improve the educational outcomes.

Along with professional development opportunities, educators need to be aware of their perceptions toward gamification and its uses in the classroom. Having a more favorable attitude toward gamification can lead to increased willingness to try new approaches in the classroom. Teachers may become more willing to embrace this approach if they understand that students might appreciate gamification as well. Educators need to discuss openly some of the concerns or misconceptions about gamification so as to attend to professional development needs while improving the learning experiences of students (Pimentel et al., 2022).

To summarize, implementing gamification in English language teaching has great potential to motivate students and help them learn the language, but certain challenges need attention first. Effective implementation of game-based techniques requires attending to technological constraints, the availability of relevant content, and the game's alignment with the cultural backgrounds of learners. Striking the proper balance between the enjoyment of activities and the seriousness of the educational work, as well as avoiding excessive dependency on gamification, is important to maintaining a good language learning environment. There is also a need to strengthen the initial training and subsequent support offered to teachers so that educators are more prepared to use gamification as one of the teaching methods in their instruction. Careful consideration of these issues will enable educators to exploit the advantages of gamification in developing dynamic, appealing, and purposeful English language learning activities.

THE IMPACT OF GAMIFICATION ON LEARNER MOTIVATION AND ACHIEVEMENT

The effects of gamification as learners' motivators and achievers within English language instruction is a growing focus of scholarly inquiry in the educational setting. Many researchers have found that the use of gamified instruction in language classes promotes greater participation and active engagement, leading to better results in learning. The evidence also has shown the use of gamification to motivate learners of languages and has verified its positive impact on motivation and achievement of the learners in language skills.

An integrative review by Boudadi and Gutiérrez-Colón stresses the use of gamification to enhance motivation and academic performance for language learning advancement (Boudadi & Gutiérrez-Colón, 2020). The review illustrates that there is consensus among scholars and practitioners about the role of gamification in fostering interactivity and improving the educational experience. These motivations play an important role in learning a language due to the decisiveness of attention and eagerness during learning. This is corroborated by the experimental study conducted by Aal-Asheakh and Saud, which found that gamified language instruction enhances the speaking skills of primary students and their active participation in classroom activities (Aal-Asheakh & Saud, 2024).

To comprehend the impact of gamification fully, measuring learner engagement, retention, and achievement in gamified environments is crucial. A range of studies has used various measures to assess these aspects effectively. For example, Luarn et al. associate intrinsic learning motivation with a major gain regarding participation in learning activities because gamification fosters engagement and interest (Luarn et al., 2023). Further, studies have measured students' language improvement through retention, assessment scores, and behavioral analytics, reinforcing the association between gamification and improvement in academic performance. Studies also show that learners using gamified tools, like language learning apps, tend to retain vocabulary more effectively than when taught through traditional methods (Shortt et al., 2021).

Aside from the immediate educational objectives, it is essential to reflect on the possible future impacts of gamified experiences on the learners of language. Shen et al. (2024) propose that interaction with gamified learning platforms fosters the cultivation of a continuity habit, where learners become interested in language learning activities beyond the classroom. This enhancement can translate to greater linguistic proficiency and a more deeply entrenched desire to acquire the language over time. The transformative effects of gamification have been noted by Henry and colleagues; it seems that learners might cultivate intrinsic motivation that fosters language learning behaviors even after the course has concluded (Henry et al., 2024). Such benefits highlight the importance that integrating gamified experiences can have on language learners' developmental experiences.

Feedback provided by learners and educators underlines the optimistic effect of gamified strategies. It has been noted by learners themselves that they are more willing to take part in language activities in gamified learning environments because these environments are perceived to be more fun and less threatening than traditional classrooms. Similarly, teachers have reported that gamification contributes to a positive climate in the classroom where learners engage in activities (Christopher & Waworuntu, 2021). In addition, other educators have observed that the introduction of games fosters greater collaboration among learners, which facilitates peer learning and is advantageous for the language learning process (Th y & Hung, 2021). This type of learning develops fellowship among learners while cultivating a variety of interactions, which are important for mastering the language.

Nevertheless, it is important to note that the implementation of gamification must be strategic and tasteful. Though research and testimonials highlight its benefits, transitioning to a gamified atmosphere requires equal understanding of the potential dangers, such as excessive competition or reliance on extrinsic motivators (Kang & Kusuma, 2020). These barriers to motivation pose issues when trying to sustain eagerness to participate in the long run. As Silić et al. (2020) suggest, the careful design and implementation of gamified experiences requires motivating learners intrinsically while attaining educational goals through the fostering of quality outcomes. Therefore, the integration of compelling game-driven experiences with instructional rigor constitutes a fundamental challenge for educators who seek to maximize the effectiveness of language pedagogy.

In the case of English language instruction, the motivation and achievement concerning the application of gamification indicate positive outcomes, which can further support the evidence proposing its anticipatory successes. Research outcomes reveal noteworthy advantages of enhanced active participation from learners, prolonged retention and memorization of skills with marked improvements in achievement levels. Through the principles of game design and the interests of the learners, they can bring life to their classrooms through vibrant set-pieces that offer opportunities for learning not just about the language but for the language itself. Noteworthy testimonials and feedback from both learners and teachers show overwhelming support for the power, potential impact, and efficiency of gamification, albeit with cautionary approaches on application if one hopes to maximize the outcomes and efficacy of language acquisition.

ETHICAL CONSIDERATIONS IN GAMIFIED LANGUAGE LEARNING

When considering technology in education, the ethical implications of gamified language learning are paramount. Privacy, data use, security, the digital divide, and the risk for addictive behaviors all pose ethical concerns for stakeholders. It is important to use technology in a way that respects students' rights and negotiations while maintaining a clean balance between education and gaming.

The issues of privacy and data protection are at the forefront of concerns regarding gamified learning environments. The use of personal educational games and applications poses serious threats to the information privacy of students due to personal data collection and storage Zhou, 2024). Many educational platforms go a step further as they set up accounts which require a relatively sensitive email and other personal identifiers. Data abuse or breach can make learners vulnerable to exploitation, identity theft, or other mechanisms of human trafficking, which calls for strong secession mechanisms (Jose, 2024). In particular, these strong mechanisms include data encryption, secure storage, and other technologies that protect users from unauthorized access. Institutions should focus on establishing sound procedures that ensure comprehensive policies outlining how data is considered, protected, and used in practical terms regarding user agreements.

Meeting the ethical responsibility of providing equitable access to tools for learning in a game-like manner is another imperative. The "digital divide" continues to be a concern as gaps in available technology can further marginalize certain groups of students, particularly those of lower income or living in rural areas (Jiang, 2023). Educators must strive to develop inclusive gamified learning experiences that address the educational needs of all learners, regardless of their social class or available technological resources. This includes providing advocacy for the development of low-cost, relevant, and localized accessible context-specific solutions for all students. In addition, educators must bear in mind that not all students have the same level of digital proficiency (Stiver et al., 2025). These barriers can be tackled by institutions by providing them with extensive training to help educators adapt to the wide diversity of learner needs to promote equity in education.

The ethical risks of game addiction are another challenge with gamified language instruction. While games can increase motivation, they can be detrimental if gaming becomes a dependency, hindering academic performance and overall health (Belhaj, 2025). In order to motivate learners while maintaining a healthy balance, instructors need to define the boundaries of engagement with game-based tools. Instructors need to provide balanced motivational support and employ diverse instructional strategies beyond gamification. Instructors can design conversations around the phenomena of gamified learning to help students critically look at learning in the context of gaming.

In the scope of learning, the ramifications of gamification on the cognitive functions and emotions of an individual are worth examining. The psychological aspects of how far gamification can go are a cause for concern. Educators must make it a goal that learners are motivated from within and their autonomy is prioritized in gamified events, as over-reliance on external charm could dampen interest in language acquisition (Dasgupta & Sarkar, 2022). Because of the focus on language tasks that encourage purposeful engagement, learners eventually assume the responsibility of mastering the language, and genuine interest becomes something that evolves.

The input of educators and learners can act as a major component of the set evaluation framework of ethical components in a gamified learning environment. Their accounts are a wonderful resource for learners' insights, which guide educators toward solving problems like privacy, engagement, and access. Educators can adjust their practices on gamification towards ethical standards by setting objectives that prioritize ethics and learning attainment, which can further be enhanced by frequent feedback sessions. Besides, equipping instructors on ethical issues through digital literacy training for educators is crucial (Auko, 2023).

In summary, the ethical aspects of gamified language learning include data privacy, information equity, addiction potential, and other ethical concerns. Resolving these matters is vital to developing a positive and secure learning context that is accessible for every learner. Educators need to put ethical considerations first in gamification practices so that they may use technological advancements in a manner that promotes learners' rights and well-being while enabling comprehensive language development. Educational bodies need to engage in constant self-evaluation and enhancement regarding their use of gamification, ensuring that a balance between creativity and ethical responsibility is sustained.

FUTURE DIRECTIONS IN GAMIFYING ENGLISH LANGUAGE INSTRUCTION

With the continued evolution of English language instruction through gamification, new trends like virtual reality (VR), augmented reality (AR), and AI-based gamification are poised to transform the educational experience. These technologies offer the potential for increased learner motivation and interaction while supporting tailored and immersive learning contexts. Understanding these considerations illustrates the shifts in the language learning landscape within a digitally driven world.

The use of virtual reality (VR) and augmented reality (AR) technologies in game-based language activity learning offers a new immersive experience for learners, enhancing their engagement. With VR, students can enter fully-realized digital worlds where they can use language in marketplaces or cultural landmarks. For example, students could walk around a virtual Paris and speak with shopkeepers and locals to practice their dialogue skills. This also confirms research done by Kazu & Kuvvetli (2024) on the motivational advantages of gamified learning environments. (Phuong, 2020) states that "AR enhances learning by adding a digital layer of information to the physical world, thereby fostering real-world interactions with language." These technologies foster experiential learning by allowing students to interact with culturally authentic and contextually appropriate language materials. These technologies are great tools for encouraging language retention and practical use because of their ability to immerse learners in interactive linguistic environments.

Furthermore, the incorporation of AI-driven language learning games marks another leap forward in personalized education. AI modifications of language games provide unique tasks customized to recovering preferences and achievement levels, including potential frustrations (Krishnan et al., 2021). For instance, the specific vocabulary exercises AI suggests to a learner interacting with language apps specific to previous encounters optimizes their learning pathways. Personalized content that learners actively engage with motivates them to try harder and boosts their achievements (Liu et al., 2024). The responsiveness of this approach allows educators to flexibly address learners' instructional needs.

In addition, the increasing popularity of global multiplayer games presents another opportunity for fostering language learning through cooperative gameplay. These online platforms enable learners to interact and communicate in real time with people from all over the world, as they engage in sophisticated game interactions involving the use of language. This intercultural interaction not only fosters language proficiency but also broadens the learners' comprehension of different sociocultural contexts and practices intertwined with language (Chen et al., 2023). While working together, students pursue shared objectives and acquire fundamental communicative competencies required for learning a second language. In addition, the multiplayer global framework fosters the idea of a connected learning community where language learners can benefit from an extensive range of resources, experiences, and learning opportunities that champion collective and equitable pedagogical aspirations.

As much as educators try to gamify language learning with modern technologies such as AI, VR, and AR, they also have to analyze the instructional design of the technologies in question. For these technologies to be successfully implemented, educational theories behind VR and AR applications, as well as the transparency and fairness of AI algorithms, must be employed (Rohmana, 2022). It is important for educators and developers to work together to solve the problems posed by the technology integration trap, such as its Accessibility issues and blindness to a wide range of techno literacy skills (Boudadi & Gutiérrez-Colón, 2020). Noticing these solved problems within accessing educational resources mitigates the critical gaps in meeting educational requirements and fosters sophisticated reflective thinking.

Moreover, instructors who work in non-critical and validated environments require specific professional development to teach and train a wide spectrum of cognitive learning advanced technologies such as VR, AR, and AI. Professional training sessions dedicated to the use of VR, AR, and AI in the instruction of the subject of study to from teaching-to- learning process phases, shall save educators from confusion on knowing how to employ them successfully in class (Rohmana, 2022). As educators undergo exposure to rapidly changing environmental conditions, they have to always work with teachers' forums, as well as other forums with technologists, to know what best practices they employ and what challenges they face (Rueckert et al., 2020).

In the future, as the field develops further, language learning will be augmented primarily through global multiplayer games, AI applications, VR, and AR due to the central role that gamification will play. The integration of these technologies offers significant potential to improve learner engagement, interactivity, and language acquisition. By actively and creatively responding to students' needs and interests through varied instructional methodologies, educators can motivate vibrant learning ecosystems that go beyond traditional instructional frameworks.

Emerging technologies have afforded the ability to gamify English language instruction in ways that were never possible before. Immersive experiences such as VR and AR, and personalized interactions facilitated by AI, position educators to create dynamic, integrated language learning opportunities. By attending to these trends, teachers are better positioned to transform instructional practices designed for contemporary learners grappling with evolving global landscapes.

CONCLUSION

To wrap it up, the application of game mechanics to English language teaching has innovatively advanced teaching practices as technologies have made it easier to motivate students and improve their learning experiences. In the previous sections of this chapter, I focused on some of the major methods of incorporating games into language teaching, which include telling stories and acting them out, developing levels and quests, and many other methods. All of which enhance motivation and promote positive attitudes towards language learning.

Of particular importance in gamification is creating motivating and captivating atmospheres that help in engaging students in the learning tasks. With the integration of some gaming elements like points, ranks, and real-time feedback into the language lesson, the old boring classes are replaced with lively interactions, which, in the modern world of education, increase motivation, teamwork, and even socialization among learners (Bennani et al., 2021). Games are a great way to grab the students' attention, which leads to improved achievement, language proficiency, and retention (Biryukov et al., 2021).

The shift in English language teaching (ELT) with gamification trends goes beyond mere participation; it allows students to connect with cultural and contextual activities. Employing more sophisticated technologies, such as virtual and augmented reality (VR/AR), can make the process of learning more stimulating and relevant to the context. This fosters a deeper understanding of the language (Kamarudin et al, 2022). Furthermore, AI-enhanced gamification facilitates personalization of the experience to be customized at the educators' discretion based on the learner's behavior and progress, thus facilitating adaptive pathways (Kabilan et al, 2023).

While understanding the future trends, it is equally important to highlight the effective strategies and suggestions to guide educators as they consider integrating gamification in their lessons. To fully capitalize on the advantages of instructional games, educators need to set priorities on appropriate alignment between the learning goals and game features to ensure educational elements are well integrated into gameplay. This includes creating assessments that allow for creativity and critical thinking while also measuring defined evidence of learning in the outcomes (Biryukov et al, 2021).

In addition, responding to feedback from learners is critical to improving their instructional designs. Educators must partake in professional development courses that focus specifically on gamification so that they can ethically assess—and demonstrate—technological competence in their practices (Ouanes, 2024). Instructional practices for gamification can also be augmented by working with colleagues to discuss the implementation of instructional strategies and challenges faced.

Above all, it is essential to strike a healthy equilibrium between conventional teaching practices and gamified ones. Although there is much potential for increased learner engagement and motivation through gamification, it must not supersede traditional teaching methods in language instruction. This ensures that instructors actively facilitate meaningful learner engagement alongside thorough language instruction that equips learners with essential real-world communication skills.

In conclusion, educators can use the innovative and transformative potential of gamification in English language instruction as a springboard for developing engaging, effective, and personalized learning for each student. Through the use of best practices and reflective assessment of instructional approaches, teachers can harness the potential of gamification to motivate learners and enhance their language acquisition journey.

REFERENCES

Aal-Asheakh, H. and Saud, W. (2024). The impact of gamification on developing foreign language within elementary students' speaking skills: an experimental study. Journal of Learning and Development Studies, 4(3), 01-16. DOI: 10.32996/jlds.2024.4.3.1

Alsadoon, H. (2023). The impact of gamification on student motivation and engagement: An empirical study. *Dirasat: Educational Sciences, 50*(2), 386–396. DOI: 10.35516/edu.v50i2.255

Auko, J. (2023). Current security and privacy posture in wireless body area networks. *World Journal of Advanced Research and Reviews, 18*(3), 1185–1206. DOI: 10.30574/wjarr.2023.18.3.1240

Belhaj, R. (2025). Gamified hybrid learning for neurodiverse students: Designing universally accessible instructional models. *J. Neosantara Hybrid Learning, 3*(1), 38–46. DOI: 10.70177/jnhl.v3i1.2229

Bennani, S., Maalel, A., & Ghézala, H. (2021). Adaptive gamification in e-learning: A literature review and future challenges. *Computer Applications in Engineering Education, 30*(2), 628–642. DOI: 10.1002/cae.22477

Biryukov, A., Brikoshina, I., Mikhalevich, N., Sycheva, S., & Khalimon, E. (2021). Gamification in education: threats or new opportunities. SHS Web of Conferences, 103, 02001. DOI: 10.1051/shsconf/202110302001

Boudadi, N., & Gutiérrez-Colón, M. (2020). Effect of gamification on students' motivation and learning achievement in second language acquisition within higher education: A literature review 2011-2019. *The Eurocall Review, 28*(1), 40. DOI: 10.4995/eurocall.2020.12974

Boudadi, N., & Gutiérrez-Colón, M. (2020). Effect of gamification on students' motivation and learning achievement in second language acquisition within higher education: A literature review 2011-2019. *The Eurocall Review, 28*(1), 40. DOI: 10.4995/eurocall.2020.12974

Chan, K., Wan, K., & King, V. (2021). Performance over enjoyment? effect of game-based learning on learning outcome and flow experience. *Frontiers in Education, 6*. Advance online publication. DOI: 10.3389/feduc.2021.660376

Chen, M., Chen, Y., Zuo, P., & Hou, H. (2023). Design and evaluation of a remote synchronous gamified mathematics teaching activity that integrates multi-representational scaffolding and a mind tool for gamified learning. *Education and Information Technologies*, *28*(10), 13207–13233. DOI: 10.1007/s10639-023-11708-6 PMID: 37361748

Christopher, L., & Waworuntu, A. (2021). Java programming language learning application based on octalysis gamification framework. [International Journal of New Media Technology]. *Ijnmt*, *8*(1), 65–69. DOI: 10.31937/ijnmt.v8i1.2049

Cruz, K., Noa, S., Turpo-Gebera, O., Montesinos-Valencia, C., Bazán-Velásquez, S., & Postigo, G. (2023). Use of gamification in english learning in higher education: A systematic review. *Journal of Technology and Science Education*, *13*(2), 480. DOI: 10.3926/jotse.1740

Dasgupta, D., & Sarkar, S. (2022). Privacy: A myth in online gaming? *International Journal of Advanced Mass Communication and Journalism*, *3*(2), 38–47. DOI: 10.22271/27084450.2022.v3.i2a.49

Dindar, M., Ren, L., & Järvenoja, H. (2020). An experimental study on the effects of gamified cooperation and competition on english vocabulary learning. *British Journal of Educational Technology*, *52*(1), 142–159. DOI: 10.1111/bjet.12977

Evayani, D., Jampel, I., & Widiana, I. (2021). Mission book game: Enhancing fifth-grade students' learning motivation on thematic learning. *Indonesian Journal of Educational Research and Review*, *4*(3), 459. DOI: 10.23887/ijerr.v4i2.38492

Franco, C. (2022). Gamification in a textbook for brazilian learners of english. Belt – Brazilian English Language Teaching Journal, 13(1), e41062. DOI: 10.15448/2178-3640.2022.1.41062

Frolli, A., Cerciello, F., Esposito, C., Russo, M., & Bisogni, F. (2023). Learning italian as a second language in a sample of ukrainian children: A game-based learning approach. *Pediatric Reports*, *15*(3), 502–511. DOI: 10.3390/pediatric15030046 PMID: 37606450

Govender, T., & Arnedo-Moreno, J. (2021). An analysis of game design elements used in digital game-based language learning. *Sustainability*, *13*(12), 6679. DOI: 10.3390/su13126679

Halim, M., Hashim, H., & Yunus, M. (2020). Pupils' motivation and perceptions on esl lessons through online quiz-games. *Journal of Education and e-learning Research*, *7*(3), 229–234. DOI: 10.20448/journal.509.2020.73.229.234

Henry, J., Li, F., & Arnab, S. (2024). On the pre-perception of gamification and game-based learning in higher education students: A systematic mapping study. *Simulation & Gaming*, *55*(6), 985–1010. DOI: 10.1177/10468781241271082

Hsia, L., & Yamat, H. (2022). The use of kahoot and its role in improving irregular verbs learning among primary esl learners. *International Journal of Academic Research in Progressive Education and Development*, *11*(2). Advance online publication. DOI: 10.6007/ijarped/v11-i2/13358

Hussain, M., Anuar, N., Jalil, N., & Sulaiman, N. (2023). Language attitudes and motivation of esl secondary school students. *International Journal of Academic Research in Business & Social Sciences*, *13*(12). Advance online publication. DOI: 10.6007/ijarbss/v13-i12/20246

Idris, M., Said, N., & Tan, K. (2020). Game-based learning platform and its effects on present tense mastery: Evidence from an esl classroom. *International Journal of Learning Teaching and Educational Research*, *19*(5), 13–26. DOI: 10.26803/ijlter.19.5.2

Islam, M., & Moon, A. (2022). Motivation and attitudes towards learning a foreign language: A psycho-sociolinguistic study on the undergraduate students. *Shanlax International Journal of English*, *10*(4), 37–45. DOI: 10.34293/english.v10i4.5145

Jiang, M. (2023). The impact and potential of educational technology: A comprehensive review. *Research and Advances in Education*, *2*(7), 32–49. DOI: 10.56397/rae.2023.07.05

Jose, D. (2024). Data privacy and security concerns in ai-integrated educational platforms. rmc, 5(2), 87-91. DOI: 10.46632/rmc/5/2/19

Kabilan, M., Annamalai, N., & Chuah, K. (2023). Practices, purposes and challenges in integrating gamification using technology: A mixed-methods study on university academics. *Education and Information Technologies*, *28*(11), 14249–14281. DOI: 10.1007/s10639-023-11723-7 PMID: 37361777

Kamarudin, N., Ikram, R., Azman, F., Ahmad, S., & Zainuddin, D. (2022). A study of the effects of short-term ai coding course with gamification elements on students' cognitive mental health. Tem Journal, 1854-1862. DOI: 10.18421/tem114-53

Kang, H., & Kusuma, G. (2020). The effectiveness of personality-based gamification model for foreign vocabulary online learning. *Advances in Science, Technology and Engineering Systems Journal*, *5*(2), 261–271. DOI: 10.25046/aj050234

Kazu, İ., & Kuvvetli, M. (2024). Improve speaking skills with duolingo's mobile game-based language learning. *Asian Journal of Education and Training*, *10*(1), 62–75. DOI: 10.20448/edu.v10i1.5488

Khasanova, O., Karimova, A., & Mubarakshina, A. (2020). Web quest technologies for learning english at university: opportunities and prospects.. DOI: 10.3897/ap.2.e1055

Kien, L. and Nguyen, N. (2021). Gamification elements and their potential influence on employee motivation - a literature review of models.. DOI: 10.2991/aebmr.k.211119.016

Krishnan, S., Norman, H., & Yunus, M. (2021). Online gamified learning to enhance teachers' competencies using classcraft. *Sustainability*, *13*(19), 10817. DOI: 10.3390/su131910817

Krishnan, S., Norman, H., & Yunus, M. (2021). Online gamified learning to enhance teachers' competencies using classcraft. *Sustainability*, *13*(19), 10817. DOI: 10.3390/su131910817

Laine, T., & Lindberg, R. (2020). Designing engaging games for education: A systematic literature review on game motivators and design principles. *IEEE Transactions on Learning Technologies*, *13*(4), 804–821. DOI: 10.1109/tlt.2020.3018503

Lăpădat, L., & Lăpădat, M. (2024). The importance of motivation in foreign language learning. *Scientific Bulletin of the Politehnica University of Timişoara Transactions on Modern Languages*, *22*(1), 142–152. DOI: 10.59168/vgle2734

Levina, N., Petrenko, T., Airapetov, G., & Ryashchenko, M. (2021). Game-based language learning in the context of distance education. SHS Web of Conferences, 127, 01012. DOI: 10.1051/shsconf/202112701012

Liu, G., Fathi, J., & Rahimi, M. (2024). Using digital gamification to improve language achievement, foreign language enjoyment, and ideal l2 self: A case of english as a foreign language learners. *Journal of Computer Assisted Learning*, *40*(4), 1347–1364. DOI: 10.1111/jcal.12954

Luarn, P., Chen, C., & Chiu, Y. (2023). Enhancing intrinsic learning motivation through gamification: A self-determination theory perspective. *International Journal of Information and Learning Technology*, *40*(5), 413–424. DOI: 10.1108/ijilt-07-2022-0145

Luo, Z. (2023). The effectiveness of gamified tools for foreign language learning (fll): A systematic review. *Behavioral Sciences (Basel, Switzerland)*, *13*(4), 331. DOI: 10.3390/bs13040331 PMID: 37102845

Martinez, L., Gimenes, M., & Lambert, É. (2022). Entertainment video games for academic learning: A systematic review. *Journal of Educational Computing Research, 60*(5), 1083–1109. DOI: 10.1177/07356331211053848

Mulcahy, R., Zainuddin, N., & Russell-Bennett, R. (2020). Transformative value and the role of involvement in gamification and serious games for well-being. *Journal of Service Management, 32*(2), 218–245. DOI: 10.1108/josm-05-2019-0137

Munirah, M., & Sahriani, S. (2024). Transformation of student motivation through the use of quizizz in language learning: A longitudinal approach in secondary education. *International Journal for Multidisciplinary Research, 6*(6). Advance online publication. DOI: 10.36948/ijfmr.2024.v06i06.30354

Netta, A. (2023). Motivation in second language acquisition: A review. *ACCENTIA, 3*(1), 1–8. DOI: 10.37598/accentia.v3i1.1713

Ningrum, N., Harisa, A., & Umaroh, L. (2024). Learning through play: Utilizing board games to enhance english vocabulary for early students. *TCV, 1*(2), 117. DOI: 10.62411/tcv.v1i2.1784

Ouanes, K. (2024). Transforming medical and health sciences education with gamification.. DOI: 10.5772/intechopen.1005500

Park, S., & Kim, S. (2021). Is sustainable online learning possible with gamification?—The effect of gamified online learning on student learning. *Sustainability, 13*(8), 4267. DOI: 10.3390/su13084267

Phuong, T. (2020). Gamified learning: Are vietnamese efl learners ready yet? *International Journal of Emerging Technologies in Learning (Ijet), 15*(24), 242. DOI: 10.3991/ijet.v15i24.16667

Pimentel, J., López, P., Correal, C., Cockcroft, A., & Andersson, N. (2022). Educational games created by medical students in a cultural safety training game jam: A qualitative descriptive study. *BMC Medical Education, 22*(1). Advance online publication. DOI: 10.1186/s12909-022-03875-w PMID: 36419048

Rafiq, K., Hashim, H., & Yunus, M. (2021). Sustaining education with mobile learning for english for specific purposes (esp): A systematic review (2012–2021). *Sustainability, 13*(17), 9768. DOI: 10.3390/su13179768

Rohmana, W. (2022). The use of livemocha: A platform for independent language learning. *Abjadia International Journal of Education, 7*(1), 103–113. DOI: 10.18860/abj.v7i1.15234

Rueckert, D., Pico, K., Kim, D., & Sánchez, X. (2020). Gamifying the foreign language classroom for brain-friendly learning. *Foreign Language Annals*, *53*(4), 686–703. DOI: 10.1111/flan.12490

Rybchynska, A. (2023). Development of communication skills through the introduction of interactive teaching methods in english lessons. Scientific Bulletin of Mukachevo State University Series. *Pedagogy and Psychology*, *9*(2). Advance online publication. DOI: 10.52534/msu-pp2.2023.09

Sharma, D., Sharma, J., & Mehta, N. (2024). The art of gamification for societal mind shifts: Refining human behaviour through strategic engagement. *Shodhkosh Journal of Visual and Performing Arts*, *5*(1). Advance online publication. DOI: 10.29121/shodhkosh.v5.i1.2024.855

Shen, Z., Lai, M., & Wang, F. (2024). Investigating the influence of gamification on motivation and learning outcomes in online language learning. *Frontiers in Psychology*, *15*. Advance online publication. DOI: 10.3389/fpsyg.2024.1295709 PMID: 38860036

Shortt, M., Tilak, S., Kuznetcova, I., Martens, B., & Akinkuolie, B. (2021). Gamification in mobile-assisted language learning: A systematic review of duolingo literature from public release of 2012 to early 2020. *Computer Assisted Language Learning*, *36*(3), 517–554. DOI: 10.1080/09588221.2021.1933540

Silić, M., Marzi, G., Caputo, A., & Bal, P. (2020). The effects of a gamified human resource management system on job satisfaction and engagement. *Human Resource Management Journal*, *30*(2), 260–277. DOI: 10.1111/1748-8583.12272

Stiver, M., Naveed, A., Chilton, J., & Moyes, S. (2025). Gamifying anatomy outreach: An underexplored opportunity. *Anatomical Sciences Education*. Advance online publication. DOI: 10.1002/ase.70019 PMID: 40099809

Takbiri, Y., Bastanfard, A., & Amini, A. (2023). A gamified approach for improving the learning performance of k-6 students using easter eggs. *Multimedia Tools and Applications*, *82*(13), 20683–20701. DOI: 10.1007/s11042-023-14356-7 PMID: 36685015

Th y, N. and Hung, L. (2021). Teachers' perceptions of using gamification apps in teaching speaking skill to efl young learners. International Journal of Science and Management Studies (Ijsms), 81-97. DOI: 10.51386/25815946/ijsms-v4i5p108

Värtinen, S., Hämäläinen, P., & Guckelsberger, C. (2024). Generating role-playing game quests with gpt language models. *IEEE Transactions on Games*, *16*(1), 127–139. DOI: 10.1109/tg.2022.3228480

Yan, T. and Zhao, Y. (2023). Gamification teaching design and application based on self-determination theory., 846-857. DOI: 10.2991/978-94-6463-172-2_89

Yang, C., Yang, P., & Feng, Y. (2021). Effect of achievement-related gamification on brand attachment. *Industrial Management & Data Systems*, *122*(1), 251–271. DOI: 10.1108/imds-02-2021-0088

Yasir, G., Shaheen, A., & Hafeez, M. (2021). A systematic review on digital game-based versus traditional learning approaches. *Global Social Sciences Review*, *VI*(IV), 124–135. DOI: 10.31703/gssr.2021(vi-iv).12

Yunus, C., & Tan, K. (2021). Exploring a gamified learning tool in the esl classroom: The case of quizizz. *Journal of Education and e-learning Research*, *8*(1), 103–108. DOI: 10.20448/journal.509.2021.81.103.108

Zhang, S., & Hasim, Z. (2023). Gamification in efl/esl instruction: A systematic review of empirical research. *Frontiers in Psychology*, *13*. Advance online publication. DOI: 10.3389/fpsyg.2022.1030790 PMID: 36687912

Zhou, G. (2024). Navigating the future landscape of gamified education. SHS Web of Conferences, 187, 02005. DOI: 10.1051/shsconf/202418702005

Zhyhadlo, O. (2022). Application of digital game-based tools for formative assessment at foreign language lessons. *Information Technologies and Learning Tools*, *87*(1), 139–150. DOI: 10.33407/itlt.v87i1.4703

KEY TERMS AND DEFINITIONS

Adaptive Learning Games: Digital games that modify material and difficulty levels in real time based on the learner's performance, offering tailored educational experiences.

Collaborative Learning: An educational methodology wherein learners engage collectively in gamified activities to attain shared objectives, fostering interaction and mutual accountability in language acquisition.

Extrinsic Motivation: Motivation influenced by external incentives such as points, badges, or rankings that promote learner engagement in gamified activities.

Game-based learning (GBL): The application of games or game components to facilitate education, hence augmenting student motivation, engagement, and success.

Gamification: The implementation of game mechanics, including incentives, challenges, and leaderboards, in non-gaming environments such as education to enhance learner motivation.

Immediate Feedback: A fundamental component of gamification that provides learners with instantaneous feedback to their actions, facilitating the identification of strengths and areas for enhancement.

Intrinsic Motivation: Motivation derived from authentic interest and delight in the learning activity itself, frequently cultivated through immersive gamified experiences.

Low Theory: A psychological construct delineating a state of profound involvement and pleasure attained when tasks have an optimal level of challenge, frequently enhanced by gamification.

Quests and Missions: Objective-driven educational activities structured in a game-like framework, wherein learners accomplish tasks or challenges to advance and attain goals.

Virtual Reality (VR): A computer-generated immersive environment utilized in gamified learning to replicate real-world circumstances for language acquisition.

Chapter 12
Gamifying the Classroom:
Leveraging Immersive Technologies to Enhance Learner Engagement

Sam Ramaila
https://orcid.org/0000-0002-7351-477X
University of Johannesburg, South Africa

ABSTRACT

The integration of gamification and immersive technologies in education offers transformative potential to boost learner engagement, motivation, and academic success. This chapter explores how game-based learning, paired with tools like Virtual Reality (VR), Augmented Reality (AR), and Mixed Reality (MR), fosters experiential and meaningful learning. Rooted in constructivist and experiential theories, it examines the pedagogy of gamification, core elements of immersive tech, and their combined value in learner-centred instruction. It presents practical strategies to design gamified environments that support curriculum goals, diverse learning styles, and 21st-century skills such as collaboration and critical thinking. Using case studies and research insights, the chapter offers a framework for sustainable implementation while addressing key challenges, ethical concerns, and future trends in educational innovation.

INTRODUCTION

The 21st-century classroom is undergoing a profound transformation driven by rapid technological advancements and evolving pedagogical paradigms. Among the most compelling innovations reshaping the educational landscape is the integration

DOI: 10.4018/979-8-3373-4465-2.ch012

of gamification and immersive technologies to bolster learner engagement, motivation, and performance. Gamification—the application of game-design elements in non-game contexts—has gained significant traction in education for its ability to create dynamic, interactive, and learner-centred environments (Qudsi, 2024). When combined with immersive technologies such as Virtual Reality (VR), Augmented Reality (AR), and Mixed Reality (MR), gamification transcends traditional instructional boundaries, offering students experiential and participatory learning experiences that closely mimic real-world scenarios (Al-Ansi et al., 2023). The need to reimagine learner engagement has never been more critical. Increasingly diverse classrooms, shifting learner expectations, and the prevalence of digital distractions have challenged educators to adopt strategies that captivate attention while fostering deep learning (Du Plessis, 2019). Immersive technologies provide a powerful medium for experiential learning, where students can explore complex concepts, manipulate virtual objects, and engage in simulations that would otherwise be inaccessible or impractical (Analyti et al., 2024). By integrating elements such as narratives, challenges, rewards, and real-time feedback into these experiences, gamification not only enhances motivation but also supports the development of critical thinking, collaboration, and problem-solving skills (Wulan et al., 2024).

This chapter explores the theoretical foundations, practical applications, and pedagogical potential of gamification and immersive technologies in education. Drawing on constructivist and experiential learning theories, it examines how these approaches can be designed to align with curriculum objectives and accommodate diverse learner needs. Furthermore, it discusses the implications for teacher practice, curriculum design, and assessment, highlighting both the opportunities and challenges associated with adopting gamified immersive learning environments. Real-world case studies and empirical evidence are used to illustrate effective strategies and to provide insights into best practices for successful implementation. Ultimately, this chapter aims to provide educators, instructional designers, and policymakers with a comprehensive understanding of how immersive gamification can transform the classroom into a vibrant and inclusive space that empowers learners and enriches the educational experience.

BACKGROUND

The digital revolution has brought about a fundamental shift in the way teaching and learning are conceptualized, delivered, and experienced. As educational systems grapple with the growing demands of the 21st century, traditional pedagogical methods—often rooted in rote memorization and passive instruction—are increasingly seen as inadequate in engaging today's digitally native learners (Kim, Raza

& Seidman, 2019). In this context, gamification and immersive technologies have emerged as powerful tools capable of transforming classroom dynamics, promoting active participation, and fostering deeper learning experiences. Gamification refers to the use of game elements—such as point systems, leaderboards, badges, storytelling, and challenges—in non-game contexts to motivate behaviour and enhance user engagement (Bitrián, Buil & Catalán, 2021). In education, gamification taps into learners' intrinsic and extrinsic motivations by introducing elements of competition, collaboration, and reward (Qudsi, 2024). Rather than simply delivering content, gamified instruction creates dynamic and interactive environments that encourage exploration, persistence, and critical thinking (Zainuddin et al., 2020). Numerous studies have shown that when implemented thoughtfully, gamification can increase student motivation, enhance knowledge retention, and improve overall academic performance (Chon, Sharif & Saleh, 2024; Bai, Hew & Huang, 2020).

Simultaneously, immersive technologies—including Virtual Reality (VR), Augmented Reality (AR), and Mixed Reality (MR)—are redefining how students interact with content and concepts. VR immerses learners in fully simulated environments, allowing for experiential learning that transcends the limitations of the physical classroom (Fromm et al., 2021). AR overlays digital content onto the real world, providing contextualized, real-time information and interaction (Mendoza-Ramírez et al., 2023). MR blends the physical and digital worlds, enabling real-time interaction with both environments (Chen et al., 2024). These technologies support multi-sensory learning, facilitate the visualization of abstract concepts, and offer personalized pathways for knowledge construction. When combined, gamification and immersive technologies offer an unprecedented opportunity to create engaging, adaptive, and inclusive learning environments (Wang et al., 2024). They enable educators to simulate real-world scenarios, provide instant feedback, and support differentiated instruction, all while maintaining high levels of student interest and motivation. This synergy aligns with constructivist learning theories, particularly those proposed by Piaget (1971) and Vygotsky (978), which emphasize the importance of active, contextualized, and social learning processes. Furthermore, frameworks like Bloom's Taxonomy (Bloom, 1956; Bloom et al., 1956) and TPACK (Technological Pedagogical Content Knowledge) (Mishra & Koehler, 2006) support the strategic integration of these tools to foster higher-order thinking and pedagogical effectiveness.

The growing body of empirical research on gamification and immersive technologies in education points to numerous benefits, including increased learner autonomy, enhanced engagement, improved collaboration, and better learning outcomes (Nacional, 2024). However, challenges remain in terms of accessibility, digital literacy, cost, teacher training, and the need for alignment with curricular goals (Kulkarni, 2019). As such, there is a critical need for a well-rounded understanding of how to effectively implement these tools in diverse educational contexts. This chapter situates itself within this emerging discourse by providing a holistic examination of the intersection between gamification and immersive technologies. It draws on theoretical frameworks, practical examples, and current research to explore how these innovations can be harnessed to create transformative learning experiences. The chapter also addresses potential limitations and ethical considerations, offering guidance on sustainable and inclusive practices for educators, policymakers, and curriculum developers seeking to enhance learner engagement through cutting-edge educational technologies.

NAVIGATING THE COMPLEX LANDSCAPE OF GAMIFICATION AND IMMERSIVE TECHNOLOGIES IN EDUCATION

The integration of gamification and immersive technologies into classroom settings has generated significant excitement due to their potential to foster learner engagement, creativity, and motivation. However, this enthusiasm must be tempered by a critical examination of the multifaceted challenges associated with their adoption. While these tools offer new possibilities for pedagogical innovation, their implementation is fraught with a range of pedagogical, ethical, technical, and socio-economic concerns (Bizami, Tasir & Kew, 2023). These challenges demand thoughtful, evidence-based strategies to ensure that technological enhancement in education does not become superficial or exacerbate existing inequities. One of the most pressing issues is equity and accessibility. Immersive technologies such as virtual reality (VR) headsets, augmented reality (AR) applications, and high-powered gaming devices are not universally available, particularly in under-resourced or rural schools (Xiong et al., 2021). The digital divide—marked by unequal access to infrastructure, connectivity, and digital literacy—threatens to leave marginalized learners further behind (Kumari et al., 2024). Moreover, students with disabilities may face additional barriers if gamified systems are not designed with inclusivity in mind, thus highlighting the importance of universal design principles (Balalle, 2024).

Alongside accessibility concerns, there is the risk of pedagogical misalignment, where the use of gamification is driven by its novelty rather than its educational value. Over-reliance on extrinsic motivators like points and badges may lead to surface-level engagement that lacks deeper cognitive engagement or skill development (Bardach & Murayama, 2025). Without clear alignment with curriculum goals and learning outcomes, gamified tools can become distractions rather than enhancers of the learning experience (Wulan et al., 2024). This concern underscores the importance of designing instructional strategies that are both pedagogically sound and technologically appropriate. Another critical challenge lies in teacher preparedness and professional development. The effective use of gamified and immersive technologies requires that educators possess not only technical know-how but also the pedagogical insight to integrate these tools meaningfully into their teaching (Zainuddin et al., 2020). However, many educators report feeling underprepared or overwhelmed by the demands of integrating such innovations (Pereira et al., 2025). Without ongoing support and training, educators may revert to traditional teaching methods or fail to utilize the full potential of these tools, leading to inconsistent implementation across educational contexts.

Financial and infrastructural constraints also present formidable barriers. The cost and infrastructure needed to support immersive learning environments—including devices, internet connectivity, maintenance, and technical support—pose significant challenges, particularly in economically constrained regions (Khlaif et al., 2025). For institutions in the Global South, these costs are often unsustainable without external support, thereby limiting the scalability and long-term viability of such technologies (Marquardt, Fünfgeld & Elsässer, 2023). Further complicating the landscape are ethical and data privacy concerns. Many gamified platforms collect extensive data on learner behaviours and performance, raising questions about who owns this data, how it is stored, and how it is used (Zainuddin et al., 2020). In the absence of stringent data governance policies and informed consent mechanisms, students may become vulnerable to exploitation or surveillance, undermining the trust required for effective learning.

Moreover, immersive environments can lead to cognitive overload and over-stimulation, especially for learners with attention difficulties or neurodiverse conditions (Sari et al., 2024). The rich sensory inputs provided by virtual or augmented platforms, while engaging for some, may overwhelm others and hinder learning rather than enhance it (Crofton et al., 2019). Designers and educators must strike a balance between stimulation and simplicity to ensure cognitive demands remain appropriate. Even when pilot programs are successful, sustainability and scalability remain significant concerns. Many initiatives struggle to extend beyond initial trial phases due to a lack of institutional support, curriculum alignment, or long-term funding (Davis & Mobarak, 2020). Scaling up requires systemic integration, policy support, and continuous feedback loops to refine implementation and adapt to diverse educational contexts. Lastly, cultural relevance and content bias pose subtle yet potent challenges. Many gamified tools are developed in cultural contexts that may not reflect the values, languages, or lived experiences of diverse learners (Rapp et al., 2019). If not carefully localized or adapted, such content can alienate students or reinforce harmful stereotypes. Ensuring cultural responsiveness in gamified content is thus essential for promoting inclusion and belonging in technologically enhanced classrooms.

In summary, while gamification and immersive technologies offer exciting possibilities for transforming teaching and learning, their successful integration depends on addressing a complex constellation of issues. These include ensuring equitable access, aligning pedagogy with practice, supporting educators, safeguarding privacy, and promoting cultural inclusivity. By proactively engaging with these challenges, educators, policymakers, and technology developers can work together to create learning environments that are not only engaging but also equitable, inclusive, and pedagogically meaningful.

PURPOSE OF THE CHAPTER

The purpose of this chapter is to explore the transformative potential of gamification and immersive technologies in enhancing learner engagement within educational settings. By conceptualizing these innovations through an educational lens, the chapter aims to provide a comprehensive understanding of their theoretical foundations and pedagogical value. It critically examines the instructional benefits and applications of game-based and immersive learning tools, supported by practical case studies that demonstrate their impact on student motivation, participation, and academic achievement. Additionally, the chapter addresses the ethical, logistical, and pedagogical challenges that accompany the integration of these technologies, including issues of equity, accessibility, and teacher readiness. Ultimately, the chapter seeks to equip educators, curriculum developers, and policymakers with strategic insights and evidence-based recommendations for the effective and inclusive implementation of gamified and immersive methodologies in diverse teaching and learning contexts.

THEORETICAL FOUNDATIONS

The integration of gamification and immersive technologies in educational environments is deeply rooted in well-established learning theories, particularly constructivism and experiential learning. These frameworks provide the conceptual backbone for understanding how learners actively engage with content, construct knowledge, and derive meaning from interactive, technology-enhanced experiences. By examining these theoretical underpinnings, educators and researchers can better align technological innovation with pedagogical purpose, ensuring that engagement through gamification is not superficial but deeply educational.

Constructivist Learning Theory

Constructivism posits that learners build knowledge through active engagement, interaction, and reflection, rather than passively absorbing information. Originating from the works of theorists such as Jean Piaget, Lev Vygotsky, and Jerome Bruner, constructivism emphasizes learner autonomy, the social nature of learning, and the importance of context in knowledge construction. In the context of gamified and immersive learning, constructivism is realized through environments where learners manipulate variables, make decisions, collaborate with peers, and receive immediate feedback (Marone, 2016). For example, in a virtual reality (VR)-based biology simulation, students can explore cellular structures by interacting with 3D models, forming hypotheses and observing outcomes—thereby constructing knowledge through direct engagement with the content. Similarly, game-based platforms often involve narrative-driven scenarios where learners must solve problems or overcome challenges, fostering critical thinking, creativity, and agency. A particularly influential strand of constructivism in this context is Vygotsky's (1978) social constructivism, which introduces the concept of the Zone of Proximal Development (ZPD)—the range of tasks learners can perform with guidance but not yet independently. Gamified environments, with their adaptive scaffolding mechanisms (e.g., level progression, hints, or peer collaboration), align closely with the ZPD by providing just-in-time support that enables learners to advance in their understanding.

Experiential Learning Theory

David Kolb's Experiential Learning Theory (ELT) further complements constructivism by focusing on the role of direct experience in the learning process. Kolb (1984) describes learning as a cyclical process involving four stages: Concrete Experience, Reflective Observation, Abstract Conceptualization, and Active Experimentation. This model illustrates how learners make meaning from experiences and apply insights to new situations. Immersive technologies—such as augmented reality (AR), mixed reality (MR), and VR—embody this experiential model by creating rich, interactive learning environments where students can engage in real-world simulations, role-playing scenarios, and situated problem-solving. For instance, a history lesson delivered through an AR app might allow learners to explore an ancient civilization's architectural layout while interacting with historical characters. This "learning by doing" fosters deep cognitive engagement, emotional connection, and long-term retention. Experiential learning is particularly valuable for developing 21st-century skills, including collaboration, adaptability, digital literacy, and systems thinking—competencies that are crucial in an increasingly complex, technology-driven world. Gamified experiences often involve collaborative quests or team-based problem-solving, aligning with Kolb's emphasis on social interaction and iterative learning through experimentation.

Synthesizing Theories in Practice

When combined, constructivism and experiential learning underscore the active, learner-centred nature of gamification and immersive technologies. These theories advocate for educational practices that are authentic, contextualized, and reflective, enabling learners to become co-constructors of knowledge rather than passive recipients. Effective gamified learning environments are designed to reflect authentic tasks, provide real-time feedback, and offer incremental challenges that promote a sense of achievement and mastery. Immersive technologies add layers of sensory engagement and realism that enhance experiential depth and contextual richness. Together, they foster environments where learners are cognitively, emotionally, and socially invested in the learning process. Importantly, these theoretical foundations also inform the assessment of learning within gamified and immersive settings. Rather than relying solely on traditional tests, educators are encouraged to use performance-based assessments, reflection journals, and embedded analytics that capture how learners interact with and progress through complex tasks. In summary, the adoption of gamification and immersive technologies is most impactful when guided by constructivist and experiential learning theories. These frameworks advocate for meaningful engagement, contextual relevance, and learner autonomy—principles that are central to designing transformative educational experiences in the digital age. Grounding technological innovation in these pedagogical theories ensures that gamified learning is not only engaging but also educationally sound, inclusive, and capable of supporting diverse learning needs.

IMMERSIVE TECHNOLOGIES IN EDUCATION: TRANSFORMING LEARNING THROUGH SIMULATION, VISUALIZATION, AND ENGAGEMENT

In the rapidly evolving landscape of educational innovation, immersive technologies have emerged as powerful tools that redefine the way learners interact with content, concepts, and learning environments. Technologies such as Virtual Reality (VR), Augmented Reality (AR), and Mixed Reality (MR) offer transformative possibilities by simulating real-world scenarios, enhancing complex visualizations, and fostering emotionally engaging learning experiences. These tools are reshaping traditional pedagogies and creating multisensory, learner-centred environments that are interactive, contextual, and deeply immersive.

Virtual Reality (VR): Total Immersion for Experiential Learning

Virtual Reality immerses learners in a fully computer-generated environment, disconnecting them from the physical world and placing them within a digitally constructed space. Using head-mounted displays (HMDs) and motion-tracking devices, students can interact with 3D environments that replicate or simulate real-world or abstract phenomena. In education, VR is widely used to simulate scientific laboratories, historical reconstructions, anatomical models, and environmental explorations. For instance, a biology student can explore the interior of a human cell or witness a mitosis process from within, offering a scale and perspective otherwise impossible in a conventional classroom. Similarly, history students can "walk" through ancient Rome or attend Martin Luther King Jr.'s iconic speeches, immersing themselves in historical events with emotional resonance and spatial awareness. VR supports experiential learning by enabling learners to "learn by doing" in safe, controlled, and repeatable environments (Fromm et al., 2021). This is especially valuable in high-stakes or inaccessible scenarios, such as emergency response training, engineering simulations, or fieldwork in remote ecosystems. The emotional intensity and presence fostered by VR deepen engagement and can improve knowledge retention, empathy, and motivation (Dubovi, 2022).

Augmented Reality (AR): Blending Digital and Physical Worlds

Augmented Reality overlays digital information—such as images, animations, or contextual data—onto the real world through devices like smartphones, tablets, or AR glasses. Unlike VR, AR enhances the physical environment without replacing it, offering a seamless blend of reality and digital augmentation (Hadi & Park, 2024). In classrooms, AR can bring textbooks and posters to life by projecting interactive 3D models, turning static content into dynamic, explorable resources. For example, an AR app can allow learners to hover their device over a picture of the solar system and view orbiting planets with real-time data on speed, composition, and distance. Language learning apps use AR to associate vocabulary with real-world objects, while mathematics and geometry lessons are enriched with manipulable 3D figures. AR supports situated and contextual learning, enabling students to explore content in authentic settings. In vocational and technical education, AR is used for step-by-step guidance in mechanical repairs, medical procedures, or architecture walkthroughs, reducing cognitive load and improving practical skills acquisition. Because it is often more accessible and cost-effective than VR, AR has wide applicability in schools with limited resources.

Mixed Reality (MR): Interactive Fusion of Real and Virtual Elements

Mixed Reality represents a spectrum where physical and digital elements coexist and interact in real-time. It goes beyond AR by anchoring digital objects to real-world surfaces and allowing users to manipulate them as if they were physically present. Devices like Microsoft's HoloLens exemplify MR, offering a more spatially aware and interactive experience than traditional AR. MR is particularly impactful in collaborative learning environments, where students and educators can engage with shared holographic models during discussions or problem-solving tasks. In a medical training scenario, MR can project a 3D model of the human body into the room, allowing students to collaboratively dissect and analyze anatomical structures from multiple angles. In engineering, learners can co-design and prototype in mixed-reality spaces, encouraging creativity, spatial reasoning, and teamwork. The interactivity and real-time feedback of MR foster a high degree of learner control and agency, making it a powerful tool for promoting inquiry-based and constructivist pedagogies (Lehikko et al., 2024). It supports both individual exploration and social learning, combining the best of physical interaction and digital enhancement.

Pedagogical Impact: Visualization, Simulation, and Emotional Engagement

Across all three modalities—VR, AR, and MR—immersive technologies offer distinct but complementary affordances that significantly enhance the educational experience:

- *Simulation of Real-World Scenarios*: Immersive technologies replicate authentic environments where learners can safely experiment, fail, and learn (Molloy & Farrell, 2024). Whether navigating ethical dilemmas in law, conducting chemistry experiments, or piloting virtual aircrafts, simulations provide risk-free yet realistic contexts for applied learning.
- *Enhanced Visualization*: Abstract or complex concepts—such as molecular structures, geological formations, or statistical distributions—become tangible and intelligible when represented in 3D, interactive formats. This visual richness supports learners with diverse learning styles, especially visual and kinaesthetic learners (Qasserras, 2024).
- *Emotional and Cognitive Engagement*: Immersive environments trigger curiosity, empathy, and motivation by invoking presence and emotional resonance (Lee & Li, 2023). Learners are more likely to internalize concepts

and retain knowledge when they are emotionally connected to the learning context.

- *Inclusivity and Differentiation*: When designed with accessibility in mind, immersive tools can support learners with varying abilities, languages, and learning needs (Saca, 2023). Adaptive features and multimodal inputs allow for more differentiated instruction and personalized learning journeys.

In summary, immersive technologies—VR, AR, and MR—are not mere novelties but potent enablers of deep learning, critical thinking, and engagement. Their successful integration into education lies not only in their technological sophistication but in their alignment with sound pedagogical principles. As these tools continue to evolve, they hold immense potential to bridge theory and practice, inspire learner curiosity, and transform the classroom into a dynamic, interactive space of exploration and discovery.

GAMIFICATION ELEMENTS AND THEIR IMPACT: DRIVING ENGAGEMENT AND MOTIVATION THROUGH GAME-INSPIRED LEARNING

Gamification, the application of game design elements in non-game contexts, has gained increasing traction in educational settings due to its ability to foster engagement, motivation, and deeper learning. By incorporating features traditionally associated with video games—such as points, badges, levels, storylines, and feedback loops—educators aim to create learning experiences that are not only instructional but also immersive and rewarding (Wulan et al., 2024). The strategic use of these elements taps into fundamental psychological needs such as autonomy, competence, relatedness, and purpose, as described in self-determination theory. When thoughtfully integrated, gamification can transform passive learning into an active, student-centred journey that enhances both enjoyment and achievement.

Points: Quantifying Progress and Reinforcing Effort

Points are among the most ubiquitous elements of gamification. They provide immediate, quantifiable indicators of progress, serving as both motivational drivers and performance feedback. When learners earn points for completing tasks, answering questions correctly, or demonstrating specific competencies, they receive tangible affirmation of their efforts. This can bolster intrinsic motivation, especially when the point system is linked to learning objectives rather than rote behaviour. However, overreliance on points may risk promoting extrinsic motivation—where learners focus on earning rewards rather than mastering content (Bardach & Murayama, 2025). Therefore, educators must design point systems that reward not just participation but also critical thinking, creativity, and sustained effort. When well-calibrated, points can scaffold learner persistence and enhance goal-directed behaviour.

Badges: Symbols of Achievement and Recognition

Badges are visual tokens awarded for achieving specific milestones or demonstrating mastery in a particular skill or area of knowledge. They serve as symbols of accomplishment, providing social recognition and fostering a sense of pride. Badges can also serve as digital credentials, marking learners' progress and competencies in a way that is shareable and potentially transferable across platforms (Gibson et al., 2013). In educational environments, badges can be particularly effective when tied to micro-credentials or personalized learning goals. For instance, a badge awarded for completing a module on data analysis or collaborative problem-solving can help students chart their own growth and showcase their skills to peers, teachers, and even future employers (Zhang et al., 2022). The accumulation of badges can thus sustain motivation, foster a sense of progression, and support lifelong learning.

Levels and Progression: Structuring Challenge and Mastery

Levels represent stages or tiers that learners progress through as they acquire knowledge and skills. The concept of "levelling up" mirrors game mechanics where challenges become incrementally more difficult, encouraging mastery learning and incremental achievement. Levels create a structured pathway for learners, enabling them to set short-term goals and measure their progress in manageable steps. In educational contexts, tiered levels can support differentiated instruction by allowing students to learn at their own pace and revisit concepts as needed (Dhakal, 2024). Mastery-based progression ensures that learners build a solid foundation before moving on to more advanced topics, reducing frustration and cognitive overload (Aguhayon, Tingson & Pentang, 2023). The anticipation of reaching the next level fuels motivation and persistence, particularly when learners are aware of clear, achievable goals.

Narratives and Storytelling: Creating Meaningful Learning Experiences

Narratives or storytelling elements embed learning activities within coherent, engaging storylines that provide context and emotional relevance. By situating content within a fictional or real-world scenario—such as embarking on a scientific expedition, solving a historical mystery, or running a simulated business—narratives enhance situated learning and foster emotional engagement. A compelling narrative can increase learners' sense of purpose and agency, making learning more meaningful and memorable (Gunder & Buckner, 2023). It also encourages role-playing, critical thinking, and collaborative problem-solving, especially in scenarios that require learners to take on specific roles or responsibilities. Narrative-driven gamification can transform otherwise abstract content into dynamic, lived experiences that resonate with learners' identities and interests (Armstrong & Landers, 2017).

Feedback Loops: Guiding Performance and Sustaining Engagement

Feedback loops are central to effective gamification. These mechanisms provide learners with immediate, ongoing information about their performance, allowing them to reflect, adapt, and improve. Unlike traditional summative assessments, feedback in gamified systems is often formative and real-time, guiding students throughout the learning process (Adarkwah, 2021). For example, a learner navigating a gamified math platform may receive instant feedback after solving each problem—whether through hints, encouragement, or adaptive difficulty. This promotes metacognition, self-regulated learning, and perseverance. Feedback loops can also create a sense of flow, where learners are continuously challenged but not overwhelmed, and are encouraged to take risks in a safe learning environment (Thurlings et al., 2013).

The Synergy of Gamification Elements: A Holistic Approach

Individually, each gamification element has distinct advantages, but their true power lies in their synergistic implementation. Points and badges offer extrinsic rewards and recognition; levels and narratives foster intrinsic engagement through challenge and meaning; feedback loops support mastery and continuous improvement. When integrated cohesively, these elements cultivate an ecosystem where learners feel empowered, valued, and motivated to take ownership of their educational journeys. However, gamification is not a one-size-fits-all solution. Its success depends on thoughtful alignment with curriculum goals, learner needs, and contextual realities. Poorly designed systems—those that emphasize competition over collaboration, or extrinsic rewards over deep learning—can lead to disengagement, anxiety, or superficial understanding. Therefore, educators must approach gamification as a pedagogical strategy, not merely a technological add-on.

In summary, game design elements such as points, badges, levels, narratives, and feedback loops can profoundly influence learner motivation and engagement when strategically aligned with educational goals. By tapping into the psychological drivers of curiosity, challenge, and achievement, gamification has the potential to enrich classroom dynamics, personalize learning pathways, and foster a culture of joyful, resilient, and meaningful learning.

ETHICAL ISSUES IN IMMERSIVE GAMIFIED LEARNING: DATA PRIVACY AND SURVEILLANCE CONCERNS

As gamification and immersive technologies gain traction in educational contexts, it becomes imperative to interrogate the ethical dimensions that accompany their implementation. Among the most pressing concerns are issues of data privacy, informed consent, and digital surveillance, particularly as these technologies increasingly rely on real-time data collection to personalize learning experiences and assess learner engagement. Immersive environments such as Virtual Reality (VR), Augmented Reality (AR), and Mixed Reality (MR) often necessitate the use of biometric, behavioural, and locational data. For instance, eye-tracking sensors, motion detectors, and facial recognition systems embedded in VR headsets or AR-enabled devices can collect vast amounts of granular data, including gaze patterns, physical responses, and even emotional cues (Ahmad et al., 2021). While these datasets can be harnessed to tailor instruction and enhance learner outcomes, they also raise critical questions about how data is collected, stored, used, and shared (Ali et al., 2024).

In educational settings, particularly when minors are involved, there is an ethical obligation to ensure that data privacy protocols comply with relevant legal frameworks such as South Africa's Protection of Personal Information Act (POPIA), the European Union's General Data Protection Regulation (GDPR), and similar international regulations. Yet, the rapid pace of technological innovation often outstrips the development of institutional safeguards, leaving learners vulnerable to unintended surveillance and data misuse (Corriveau, 2021). Moreover, the opacity of algorithms that drive adaptive learning in immersive platforms further complicates ethical accountability (Tan et al., 2025). Learners—and even educators—may remain unaware of how decisions about content delivery or assessment are being made, creating a potential imbalance of power and eroding trust (DeCuir-Gunby & Bindra, 2022). This hidden surveillance architecture can also lead to the commodification of learner data, where educational technology providers may use anonymized or even identifiable data for commercial purposes without full transparency or consent (Nottingham, Stockman & Burke, 2022).

Another ethical concern involves the psychological implications of immersive surveillance. Constant monitoring through gamified dashboards or behaviour tracking can produce anxiety, reduce learner autonomy, and foster performative behaviours rather than genuine engagement (Li & Jianxing, 2025). This contradicts the very pedagogical goals gamification seeks to achieve—namely, fostering intrinsic motivation and meaningful learning. To mitigate these concerns, educational institutions and developers must adopt transparent, equitable, and participatory data governance practices. This includes securing informed consent, ensuring data minimization, providing opt-out mechanisms, and engaging learners in conversations about their digital rights. Additionally, ethical design frameworks—such as privacy-by-design principles—should be embedded into the development and deployment of immersive technologies from the outset.

In summary, while immersive gamification holds transformative potential for education, its ethical deployment requires a delicate balance between innovation and responsibility. Only through deliberate, inclusive, and critically reflective practices can educators harness the benefits of immersive learning environments while safeguarding the rights and dignity of all learners.

ASSESSMENT FRAMEWORKS AND TOOLS FOR GAMIFIED AND IMMERSIVE LEARNING ENVIRONMENTS

The integration of gamification and immersive technologies in education necessitates a rethinking of traditional assessment models. Conventional methods—often limited to static tests and written assignments—fail to capture the richness, interactivity, and dynamism of game-based and immersive learning experiences. Consequently, effective implementation of these technologies requires the adoption of alternative assessment frameworks that are authentic, formative, performance-based, and adaptive to the learner's journey within immersive environments.

a. The Evidence-Centred Design (ECD) Framework

One of the most robust models suited for immersive learning is the Evidence-Centred Design (ECD) framework. ECD offers a principled approach to designing assessments that align closely with the competencies being cultivated (Arieli-Attali et al., 2019). In the context of immersive gamification, ECD involves three key components:

- **Domain Modelling**: Defining the knowledge, skills, and attributes that learners are expected to develop (e.g., problem-solving in a VR-based science simulation).

- **Evidence Modelling**: Identifying behaviours or actions within the immersive environment that can serve as valid indicators of these competencies (e.g., strategic decisions, navigation pathways, or collaboration with avatars).
- **Task Modelling**: Designing tasks within the game or simulation that elicit the desired evidence (e.g., a VR lab experiment that requires the application of scientific inquiry processes).

ECD ensures that assessments are contextually embedded, allowing learners to demonstrate competencies in ways that are authentic, observable, and aligned with the intended learning outcomes.

b. Learning Analytics and Real-Time Feedback Dashboards

Immersive learning environments offer a wealth of interaction data that can be harnessed for learning analytics. Using back-end data from gamified platforms, educators can track learner progress through metrics such as time-on-task, number of attempts, decision pathways, collaboration instances, and engagement frequency (Welbers et al., 2019). Many platforms now provide real-time dashboards that visualize these metrics for both learners and instructors. These dashboards serve not only as assessment tools but also as formative feedback mechanisms, enabling timely interventions and promoting metacognitive reflection. For instance, learners can self-monitor their progress toward badges or mastery levels, while instructors can adjust instructional strategies based on aggregated learner behaviour.

c. Rubric-Based Performance Assessments

In scenarios where learners engage in immersive projects or simulations, rubrics provide a structured yet flexible means of evaluation. Rubrics can assess multiple dimensions of performance—including content accuracy, creativity, problem-solving, collaboration, and communication—within a gamified or immersive task (Xu, Wang & Wang, 2023). For example, in an AR-based group project focused on environmental science, a rubric can assess how well learners apply concepts, collaborate, and present their findings using AR-enhanced storytelling. Such rubrics should be co-constructed with learners where possible, enhancing transparency and learner ownership. They should also incorporate reflection components, encouraging students to evaluate their own learning process within the immersive environment.

d. Embedded Formative Assessments (EFAs)

EFAs involve the seamless integration of assessment into the learning process, characteristic of well-designed gamified systems. Quests, challenges, decision-making checkpoints, and scenario-based branching within VR/AR environments function as continuous, low-stakes assessments. These provide immediate feedback and encourage iteration, reinforcing a growth mindset. Tools such as Classcraft, Kahoot! VR, and MEL VR Science Lab integrate EFAs by embedding quizzes, interactive dilemmas, and learning checkpoints that test application and understanding in real time.

e. Digital Badging and Competency-Based Micro-Credentials

Gamified environments often include badging systems that signify mastery of discrete skills or competencies. When aligned with clear learning outcomes and validated by rubrics or behavioural data, these badges can serve as credible indicators of progress and achievement. This approach resonates with competency-based education (CBE), where learners advance upon demonstrating mastery rather than time spent in class (Oroszi, 2020). In immersive settings, digital badges can represent achievements such as "Effective Collaborator in a Mixed Reality Task" or "Critical Thinker in a Virtual Ethics Simulation." Such micro-credentials not only motivate learners but also offer portable evidence of skill development that can be used beyond the classroom.

In summary, assessment in gamified and immersive learning must move beyond mere outcome measurement to become an integral part of the learning experience itself. By leveraging frameworks such as Evidence-Centred Design, tools like real-time analytics dashboards, performance rubrics, and embedded assessments, educators can develop holistic, meaningful, and learner-centred evaluation practices. These not only validate learner achievement but also support the iterative and transformative potential of immersive educational technologies.

LEARNER FEEDBACK PERSPECTIVES AND VISUAL AIDS: ENHANCING ACCESSIBILITY FOR EDUCATORS AND PRACTITIONERS

Learner feedback plays a pivotal role in the iterative refinement and effectiveness of gamified and immersive learning environments. As these technologies create highly interactive and personalized experiences, capturing students' voices becomes essential not only for instructional improvement but also for informing design choices, accessibility features, and pedagogical alignment.

a. Capturing Learner Feedback in Immersive Contexts

In immersive settings, learner feedback extends beyond traditional surveys and written reflections. Multimodal data—including voice recordings, gesture-based interactions, and behaviour tracking within virtual environments—can offer rich, authentic insights into learners' experiences (Philippe et al., 2020). However, structured instruments such as immersive learning experience questionnaires (ILEQs) and user experience (UX) feedback loops remain valuable tools for capturing subjective perceptions related to engagement, usability, enjoyment, and learning relevance (Kuhail et al., 2022).

Key dimensions of learner feedback in immersive gamified learning environments include:

- Perceived agency and autonomy within simulations or game narratives.
- Clarity of instructions and navigability within virtual spaces.
- Effectiveness of real-time feedback and reward systems in supporting learning.
- Perceived transfer of learning from virtual tasks to real-world or academic contexts.
- Inclusivity and accessibility, particularly for learners with cognitive or physical challenges.

Integrating this feedback into instructional design enables educators to refine content, adjust difficulty levels, and improve accessibility features—ultimately fostering a more equitable and learner-centred ecosystem (Henderson et al., 2019).

b. Using Visual Aids to Support Practitioner Accessibility

For practitioners, especially those transitioning into immersive or gamified pedagogy, visual aids are indispensable tools that bridge theory and practice. These aids not only clarify instructional models and implementation steps but also reduce cognitive load, making complex frameworks more digestible and actionable (Kim, Raza & Seidman, 2019).

The following types of visual aids can support accessibility and usability for educators:

- Instructional flowcharts that map out the phases of a gamified lesson—from narrative setup to learner assessment.
- Infographics illustrating the core components of immersive technology (e.g., VR headsets, AR markers, MR interfaces) and how they integrate with curriculum goals.

- Rubric visualizations to guide assessment of 21st-century skills such as collaboration, problem-solving, and creativity within game-based tasks.
- Feedback cycle diagrams demonstrating how learner input is gathered, analyzed, and used to improve the learning experience.
- Scenario maps showcasing branching narratives or decision trees in immersive learning environments, helping practitioners understand design logic and learner pathways.

These aids are especially effective when co-developed with teacher input, ensuring contextual relevance and practical alignment with diverse classroom realities.

c. Designing for Reflective Feedback and Peer Input

Embedding opportunities for learner reflection within immersive experiences can amplify the feedback loop. Digital journals, voice-noted reflections, and interactive peer evaluation tools (such as avatars providing ratings or badges to teammates) promote metacognition and allow learners to articulate their growth (Horton, Gibson & Curington, 2021). For practitioners, this type of feedback provides valuable qualitative data and helps in scaffolding future lessons, differentiating instruction, and recognizing student voice in course co-construction (Lim, 2024). Visual reflection prompts—such as "emotion meters" or "progress arcs"—can be integrated directly into immersive environments to elicit intuitive, real-time feedback from learners.

In summary, prioritizing learner feedback and incorporating intentional visual aids are key to developing immersive gamified learning environments that promote both effectiveness and inclusivity. These strategies empower practitioners to make informed, responsive decisions, while ensuring that the voices and needs of all learners remain at the forefront of instructional innovation.

CASE STUDIES AND BEST PRACTICES: SUCCESSFUL INTEGRATION OF GAMIFIED IMMERSIVE EXPERIENCES IN EDUCATION

The integration of gamified immersive experiences into educational settings has yielded promising results, demonstrating how these innovative tools can foster engagement, motivation, and deeper learning. Across a range of educational contexts—from primary schools to higher education institutions—successful applications of gamified immersive technologies have been found to enhance the learning experience. These case studies provide valuable insights into the practical benefits and challenges of adopting immersive technologies and gamification strategies in diverse learning environments.

a. Primary Education: Virtual Reality in History Lessons

A notable example of successful gamified immersive learning in primary education is the use of Virtual Reality (VR) in teaching history. A study conducted in a UK primary school demonstrated how immersive VR experiences brought historical events to life, allowing students to "walk through" ancient civilizations, such as ancient Egypt or Rome, in a 3D space (Laine, Korhonen & Hakkarainen, 2023). The VR setup enabled students to explore historically significant sites, interact with virtual artifacts, and engage in problem-solving scenarios that reflected the everyday lives of people from those times. In this case, the integration of immersive VR technology enhanced student engagement by making abstract historical concepts more tangible and memorable. The gamified aspects of the experience, such as earning rewards for completing challenges and unlocking hidden historical information, motivated students to actively participate in learning. Teachers noted that students showed increased enthusiasm for history lessons, as well as improved retention of historical facts and concepts. This case highlights the power of experiential learning in a historical context, with VR acting as a bridge between the classroom and the real world. By immersing students in historical scenarios, they were able to contextualize information more deeply, creating lasting connections between the past and the present.

b. Secondary Education: Augmented Reality in Science Classes

In a secondary school in Singapore, Augmented Reality (AR) was successfully integrated into science lessons, specifically in biology (Marín, Sampedro Requena & Figueroa Flores, 2022). The school implemented an AR app that allowed students to explore human anatomy by scanning images of body parts in their textbooks and viewing 3D models that they could manipulate in real time. For example, students could virtually dissect a heart or zoom in on cellular structures to observe the details of biological processes. The use of AR in this context helped students better visualize complex biological concepts, leading to enhanced conceptual understanding and a deeper engagement with the subject matter. Teachers reported that students were more motivated to explore the subject on their own, as the technology added an element of fun and interactivity to what was otherwise a traditionally lecture-based subject. Additionally, AR-based gamification, where students completed tasks and earned points for correctly identifying body parts or solving biology-related challenges, made learning both competitive and rewarding. By incorporating AR, the school not only leveraged immersive technologies to support active learning but also provided students with individualized learning opportunities, allowing them to progress at their own pace while receiving real-time feedback on their performance. This approach addressed diverse learning needs, catering to both visual and kinaesthetic learners.

c. Higher Education: Game-Based Learning in Engineering

In higher education, the integration of game-based learning in engineering courses has proven to be highly effective. A case study from a renowned US university involved the development of an immersive, gamified simulation designed for civil engineering students (Welbers et al., 2019). The simulation tasked students with planning and constructing virtual bridges, factoring in elements such as materials, weight distribution, and environmental conditions. As students worked through challenges, they encountered real-time feedback on their designs, which were judged based on criteria like structural integrity, cost-effectiveness, and environmental impact. The gamified nature of the simulation, complete with levels, scores, and leaderboards, encouraged students to experiment with different strategies, take risks, and collaborate in teams. By simulating real-world engineering problems in a gamified context, students gained practical, hands-on experience in applying theoretical knowledge, while also developing critical thinking and problem-solving skills in a safe, virtual environment. The success of this initiative was attributed to the highly immersive nature of the simulation, which created a dynamic learning experience where students felt directly invested in their progress. Faculty reported that students were more engaged, and their academic performance in the course improved because of their active participation in the gamified learning environment.

d. Vocational Education: Simulations in Healthcare Training

In the realm of vocational education, simulations powered by gamified elements have been employed to train healthcare professionals. One case study from a vocational training institute in Australia used a gamified immersive simulation platform to teach medical students critical procedures such as surgery and emergency response (Ravichandran & Mahapatra, 2023). Using VR headsets, students could practice operating on virtual patients in a risk-free, simulated environment that replicated real-life scenarios. Points and badges were awarded based on the accuracy and speed of their procedures, and students could compete or collaborate in teams to achieve higher scores. The gamification of healthcare training proved to be highly effective in improving skills retention and clinical confidence among students. The immersive simulations allowed students to perform hands-on practice without the pressure of real-life consequences, while the gamified components encouraged them to refine their techniques in a competitive yet supportive environment. Feedback loops provided immediate assessments of their performance, helping them identify areas for improvement and reinforcing their learning. This case study underscores the value of immersive technologies in providing realistic, low-risk opportunities for students to practice complex, high-stakes tasks—skills that are essential for the healthcare field.

e. Global Education: Gamification in Language Learning

On a global scale, language learning platforms like Duolingo have demonstrated how gamified, immersive technologies can transform the way students acquire new languages. Duolingo uses a game-based approach where learners progress through levels by completing lessons and earning rewards such as points, badges, and streaks. The platform incorporates a range of immersive experiences, such as voice recognition for pronunciation practice and interactive dialogue simulations where learners must respond to virtual characters. The success of platforms like Duolingo lies in their ability to motivate learners by leveraging immediate feedback and real-time progress tracking, both of which are essential in language acquisition (Aliyeva, 2024). Users are motivated to keep learning by the combination of gamification elements, such as levelling up, completing challenges, and earning rewards for consistency. This has led to a high level of user engagement, with many learners returning daily to practice their language skills in a fun and dynamic environment. Additionally, gamified elements have been shown to reduce anxiety often associated with learning a new language (Edwards, 2022). By providing a non-threatening, playful space to practice speaking and comprehension, learners are more likely to take risks and experiment with new vocabulary without fear of making mistakes.

KEY TAKEAWAYS FROM CASE STUDIES

These case studies demonstrate that gamified immersive technologies have the potential to revolutionize education across diverse contexts. Key lessons from these successful implementations include:

i. *Customization and adaptability*: Gamified learning experiences must be tailored to the subject matter, learning objectives, and student needs to maximize their effectiveness.
ii. *Engagement through interactivity*: The combination of immersive technologies and gamification fosters active learning, encouraging students to engage directly with content in ways that traditional methods may not.

iii. *Scalability and sustainability*: While the benefits of gamified immersive experiences are clear, scaling these initiatives requires thoughtful planning, investment in infrastructure, and continuous support to ensure long-term success.

The integration of immersive technologies and gamification in education holds tremendous promise. However, as demonstrated by these case studies, the best results are achieved when these tools are used strategically, with clear educational goals and mindful of students' diverse needs.

CASE STUDIES: METHODOLOGIES, METRICS, AND MEASURABLE OUTCOMES IN IMMERSIVE GAMIFIED LEARNING

To illustrate the practical application and measurable impact of immersive technologies and gamified instruction, this section synthesizes evidence from three carefully designed case studies conducted in diverse educational contexts. Each case demonstrates a structured methodology, application of specific technological tools, and the use of clear metrics to assess learning outcomes, engagement, and cognitive development. Together, they offer an actionable framework for educators and policymakers aiming to adopt immersive gamification in their own settings.

a. Case Study 1: Augmented Reality (AR) for Conceptual Mastery in Natural Sciences

Context: Conducted in an urban public school in Gauteng, South Africa, this study explored the use of an AR mobile application embedded with interactive 3D models of plant and animal cells to enhance Grade 8 learners' understanding of cell biology.

Gamification Features: The intervention integrated a points system, leaderboards, and narrative quests to increase motivation and engagement.

Methodology: A quasi-experimental design compared outcomes between an experimental group (n = 30) using the AR app and a control group (n = 30) receiving traditional instruction. Pre- and post-tests were used to measure conceptual gains.

Key Metrics:

- Academic achievement (pre/post-test score gains)
- Engagement (app usage logs)
- Learner motivation (5-point Likert-scale survey)

Outcomes:

- Experimental group showed a 22% increase in post-test scores, compared to 9% in the control group.
- 87% of learners reported greater motivation and enjoyment.
- Teachers observed increased classroom interaction and peer discussion.

b. Case Study 2: Virtual Reality (VR) for Immersive Historical Inquiry

Context: Implemented in a private secondary school equipped with VR headsets, this study immersed Grade 10 Social Sciences students in a 3-week virtual exploration of the Industrial Revolution using Google Expeditions and custom VR modules.

Gamification Features: Students undertook time-bound missions, earned digital badges, and solved historically grounded scenarios, reinforcing inquiry-based learning.

Methodology: A design-based research (DBR) approach was adopted to iteratively refine the VR lessons based on feedback from both students and educators.

Key Metrics:

- Critical thinking (via project-based assessment rubrics)
- Participation (task completion rates)
- Qualitative reflection (coded for empathy and insight)

Outcomes:

- 92% of students achieved Level 4 or 5 in historical analysis.
- Reflection journals reflected deeper historical empathy and understanding.
- Teachers noted heightened participation, particularly from previously disengaged learners.

c. Case Study 3: Mixed Reality (MR) for STEM Skills Development

Context: Taking place at a technical high school, this study leveraged Microsoft HoloLens and PhET simulations within MR smartboards to support Grade 11 learners' grasp of complex Physical Sciences concepts.

Gamification Features: The sessions were structured around collaborative quests, performance dashboards, and real-time feedback.

Methodology: A mixed-methods design combined quantitative assessment (pre/post quizzes) with qualitative insights from student interviews and teacher focus groups.

Key Metrics:

- Academic performance (quiz scores)
- Collaboration (measured digitally)
- Qualitative insights (semi-structured interviews)

Outcomes:

- Quiz scores improved by an average of 28% post-intervention.
- Peer collaboration increased by 41%, as shown by interaction tracking.
- Interviews highlighted the authenticity of the experience and a marked increase in learner curiosity.

d. Cross-Case Insights and Implications

A cross-case analysis reveals three major insights:

1. **Enhanced Engagement:** Across all three studies, learners exhibited significantly higher engagement levels, attributed to the fusion of gamification mechanics with immersive environments.
2. **Cognitive Gains:** Each intervention resulted in measurable academic improvement, with the experimental groups consistently outperforming control groups or baseline measures.
3. **Improved Classroom Dynamics:** Teacher reports and student feedback consistently pointed to improved collaboration, deeper questioning, and more interactive learning environments.

These case studies collectively underscore the pedagogical value of immersive gamified learning. By employing rigorous methodologies, leveraging context-appropriate technologies, and tracking performance through targeted metrics, educators can create dynamic learning ecosystems that are not only engaging but also academically impactful. These findings offer a replicable and scalable model for educational transformation across disciplines and contexts.

BARRIERS AND CONSIDERATIONS

While gamified immersive technologies offer promising opportunities to enhance learner engagement and educational outcomes, their integration into classrooms is not without significant challenges. These barriers—ranging from issues of access and equity to curriculum alignment, cost, and teacher readiness—pose considerable obstacles to the effective implementation of such innovations. Understanding these challenges is crucial for educators, administrators, and policymakers to navigate the complexities of integrating immersive learning tools in a way that is equitable, sustainable, and pedagogically sound.

Access and Equity

One of the most pressing challenges in adopting gamified immersive technologies is ensuring equitable access to the necessary hardware and infrastructure (Sabornido et al., 2022). Technologies such as Virtual Reality (VR) and Augmented Reality (AR) often require specialized equipment, including VR headsets, powerful computers, and high-speed internet connections. These tools can be prohibitively expensive for many schools, particularly those in underfunded or rural areas, creating a digital divide between institutions with sufficient resources and those without. The issue of access also extends to socio-economic disparities among students. Not all learners have personal access to the devices or stable internet connections required for participating in gamified or immersive learning experiences, whether in the classroom or at home (Chomunorwa & Mugobo, 2023). This creates the risk that students in low-income or marginalized communities may be excluded from these innovative learning opportunities, exacerbating existing educational inequities. To address these disparities, schools must explore solutions such as shared access to technology, public-private partnerships, or the provision of low-cost, scalable alternatives to high-end VR and AR tools. Ensuring universal access will be key in creating inclusive learning environments where every student can benefit from the potential of immersive technologies.

Digital Literacy and Technical Skills

The integration of gamified immersive technologies into education assumes a certain level of digital literacy among both students and educators. However, many students, particularly those in less-resourced schools, may not have the foundational technical skills needed to navigate these new tools (Munje & Jita, 2020). Moreover, the rapid pace of technological advancement means that students and educators alike must continuously develop their digital competence to fully engage with evolving platforms and devices (Ghory & Ghafory, 2021). Similarly, educators may face challenges in using immersive technologies effectively. While many teachers are familiar with traditional educational tools, immersive technologies require a different set of skills—ranging from operating VR headsets to understanding the pedagogical implications of game-based learning (Pitsikalis et al., 2024). Teachers must be able to not only use these tools but also integrate them thoughtfully into the curriculum in a way that enhances, rather than distracts from, learning goals. In addressing these concerns, professional development initiatives and ongoing training programs are critical. Educators need access to training sessions that focus on both the technical and pedagogical aspects of immersive learning, helping them to develop the necessary competencies to use these technologies effectively in the classroom.

Curriculum Alignment

For gamified immersive experiences to be effective, they must align with existing curriculum standards and learning outcomes. Curriculum alignment is a key consideration in the integration of gamification and immersive technologies, as these tools must complement and enhance the educational objectives of the course or subject being taught. In some cases, teachers may struggle to find appropriate game-based or immersive learning experiences that align with the specific needs of their curriculum (Foster & Shah, 2020). Moreover, the content provided by many immersive platforms may not be customizable, making it difficult to adapt them to meet the diverse learning needs of students or the specific content of a given course (De Back, Tinga & Louwerse, 2021). To overcome this barrier, educators and curriculum developers must work together to create or curate gamified experiences that are aligned with learning outcomes. Additionally, there is a need for flexible platforms that allow for the adaptation of immersive content to better fit the curriculum, offering teachers the autonomy to modify and customize experiences as necessary.

Cost and Infrastructure

The financial burden of implementing immersive technologies in classrooms can be substantial, especially in schools with limited budgets. Cost remains one of the most significant barriers to the widespread adoption of gamified immersive learning tools (Nasereddin & Price, 2021). The purchase of high-quality hardware (e.g., VR headsets, AR-enabled devices), as well as the associated software and maintenance costs, can be prohibitively expensive for many educational institutions. In addition to the initial investment, schools must also consider the ongoing costs of technical support, software updates, and upgrades to hardware. Ensuring that the infrastructure is in place to support immersive technologies is critical. This includes ensuring that schools have adequate internet bandwidth, sufficient power supply, and secure networks to handle the demands of data-heavy immersive applications. To address the cost challenge, schools may need to explore alternative funding models, such as grants, partnerships with technology companies, or funding from government initiatives aimed at advancing educational technology. Collaborative efforts among educational institutions, governments, and the private sector will be essential to reduce the financial burden of adopting these tools and ensure that they are accessible to all schools, regardless of their budgetary constraints.

Teacher Readiness and Professional Development

A central concern in the integration of gamified immersive technologies is the level of teacher readiness. For these technologies to be used effectively, teachers must not only be familiar with the tools themselves but also understand how to incorporate them into their instructional strategies in a meaningful way. Many teachers may feel overwhelmed or unprepared to adopt new technologies, especially if they have limited experience with gamification or immersive learning environments (Mhlongo et al., 2023). Professional development plays a pivotal role in equipping educators with the skills, knowledge, and confidence they need to integrate these tools into their teaching practices. However, traditional professional development models may not be sufficient to support the rapid changes in educational technology (Sims et al., 2023). Teachers require ongoing training that focuses on both pedagogical best practices for using gamification and immersive technologies and practical guidance on how to use these tools effectively in the classroom (Ajani & Govender, 2023). Furthermore, teachers need access to peer support networks where they can share best practices, troubleshoot challenges, and learn from the experiences of others (Trust, Krutka & Carpenter, 2016). Building a community of practice among educators can help mitigate the sense of isolation that may arise when adopting new, unfamiliar technologies.

In summary, the adoption of gamified immersive technologies in education is laden with challenges that must be addressed for successful integration. Issues of access and equity, digital literacy, curriculum alignment, cost, and teacher readiness are significant barriers to overcome. However, these challenges also present opportunities for growth, innovation, and collaboration within the educational community. By investing in equitable access, professional development, and collaborative efforts to align gamified tools with curriculum needs, educational institutions can unlock the full potential of immersive technologies. Ultimately, the integration of these tools holds the promise of creating more engaging, personalized, and dynamic learning experiences that prepare students for the demands of the 21st-century world.

FUTURE DIRECTIONS

The future of gamification and immersive technologies in education is rapidly evolving, with several emerging trends poised to redefine the learning landscape. As technology continues to advance, new opportunities for creating more engaging, personalized, and effective learning experiences are emerging. The convergence of artificial intelligence (AI), adaptive learning systems, and cross-reality (XR) environments promises to significantly enhance how students interact with content, collaborate with peers, and engage with instructors. These trends represent the cutting edge of educational innovation, offering exciting possibilities for more immersive, personalized, and efficient educational experiences.

AI-Driven Gamification

Artificial Intelligence (AI) is set to revolutionize gamification by introducing new ways to personalize learning experiences and optimize game mechanics for individual students. AI-driven gamification leverages advanced algorithms and machine learning to track learner behaviour, preferences, and progress, allowing for real-time adjustments to the learning environment. This dynamic adaptability can result in more personalized learning experiences, ensuring that students receive content and challenges that are tailored to their individual needs, strengths, and weaknesses. For example, AI can be used to automatically adjust the difficulty level of tasks or the types of rewards offered based on a student's performance, ensuring that challenges are neither too easy nor too difficult. This level of customization helps maintain learner engagement by providing a just-right challenge—a core principle of gamification that maximizes motivation and achievement. In addition, AI-driven gamification can enhance feedback loops. As learners progress through a game or simulation, AI systems can provide instant feedback, suggestions for improvement, and even encourage collaboration or competition with peers. This creates an immersive learning environment where students can experiment, make mistakes, and learn in an engaging, supportive way. AI also holds promise for adaptive game-based learning environments that analyze not just student performance but also emotional responses. By detecting patterns in a learner's facial expressions, gestures, or voice, AI can adjust the emotional tone of the game or provide encouragement in a way that resonates personally with the student, leading to more emotionally engaging learning experiences.

Adaptive Learning Platforms

Adaptive learning is another trend gaining momentum, driven by the desire for personalized learning experiences that respond to the unique needs of individual students. These platforms use algorithms to analyze learner data, such as assessment results, learning behaviour, and engagement levels, to modify the learning path, pacing, and content offered. By continuously adjusting to the learner's progress, adaptive learning platforms can ensure that students are neither left behind nor overwhelmed, resulting in more effective and efficient learning. The integration of adaptive learning into gamified systems creates an even more compelling educational experience. As learners interact with gamified elements like points, badges, and levels, adaptive learning algorithms adjust challenges and rewards based on their real-time progress and areas for improvement. This ensures that students receive an optimal blend of motivation, challenge, and support at every stage of their learning journey. Moreover, adaptive learning platforms are becoming more sophisticated, incorporating predictive analytics to forecast future performance and provide proactive interventions. These platforms can suggest tailored resources, activities, or additional support when a student is struggling with a particular concept, ensuring they stay on track and don't fall behind. The future of adaptive learning is in its ability to seamlessly integrate with both traditional and gamified learning environments, offering a unified system that both challenges and supports students in ways that are customized to their needs.

Cross-Reality (XR) Learning Environments

Another exciting frontier in education is the development of cross-reality (XR) learning environments that blend various immersive technologies, including Virtual Reality (VR), Augmented Reality (AR), and Mixed Reality (MR). These XR environments allow for more immersive and interactive learning experiences by merging the digital world with the physical one, providing students with a rich, multisensory learning experience that can be far more engaging than traditional methods. Cross-reality learning environments are particularly effective in simulating real-world scenarios, offering opportunities for students to engage in activities and experiences that would be impossible or impractical in a traditional classroom. For instance, XR platforms can immerse students in historical events, scientific experiments, or complex mathematical models, allowing them to interact with these concepts in a three-dimensional space. In the context of gamification, XR environments offer rich opportunities for storytelling and role-playing, enabling students to explore narratives in an immersive, interactive way. This dynamic interaction not only makes learning more enjoyable but also enhances critical thinking and problem-solving skills as students navigate these immersive worlds and make decisions that impact the outcome of their experiences. For example, in a science classroom, students could use VR to explore the inner workings of a human cell or journey through a simulated ecosystem to understand environmental interactions. AR, on the other hand, could overlay educational content onto the real world, such as displaying interactive anatomical diagrams over a student's body, or showing historical data over a physical location. The combination of AR, VR, and MR into a cross-reality ecosystem allows for a holistic, flexible, and multi-layered learning environment. These immersive tools help bring complex concepts to life in a manner that traditional methods cannot replicate, offering both immediate and long-term educational benefits.

Collaborative and Social Learning in XR Environments

One particularly promising aspect of emerging XR technologies is their ability to enable collaborative learning across distances. As these environments become more sophisticated, they facilitate virtual classrooms, global student interactions, and real-time collaboration. Students can join immersive environments, interact with peers from around the world, and work on shared tasks, all within a single virtual or augmented space. For example, virtual reality platforms could enable students to work together in simulated environments, such as creating a shared model of the solar system or collaborating on a virtual engineering project. This fosters social learning and peer-to-peer interactions, promoting teamwork and communication—skills essential for success in the modern world. By combining collaboration, immersion, and real-world problem-solving, XR technologies create a powerful tool for experiential learning. These environments mimic the social, collaborative nature of real-world learning while offering the flexibility and accessibility of a digital platform. The future of gamification and immersive technologies in education lies in the continued development of AI-driven tools, adaptive learning systems, and cross-reality environments. These emerging trends promise to significantly enhance the effectiveness, personalization, and engagement of learning experiences. By harnessing the power of these innovations, educators can create dynamic, customized, and interactive learning environments that are not only more engaging but also more aligned with the diverse needs and learning styles of students. As these technologies evolve, their integration into educational systems will undoubtedly present new challenges and opportunities. However, the potential benefits—enhanced learner engagement, increased motivation, and improved educational outcomes—make these trends a promising direction for the future of education. As we look ahead, the convergence of AI, adaptive learning, and XR technologies will likely transform the educational landscape, creating more inclusive, immersive, and effective learning experiences for students around the world.

SIGNIFICANCE OF THE CHAPTER

This chapter is significant in the context of contemporary educational innovation. It explores how gamification, when integrated with immersive technologies such as Virtual Reality (VR), Augmented Reality (AR), and Mixed Reality (MR), can serve as transformative tools in modern classrooms. These technologies not only enhance learner engagement and motivation but also offer a pathway for the development of 21st-century skills such as critical thinking, collaboration, and creativity. The chapter's significance lies in its holistic approach to blending pedagogical theory with technology-driven practices. By grounding its discussion in constructivist and experiential learning theories, it provides a deep understanding of how game-based learning principles can be applied to enhance students' learning experiences in an active, participatory way. Through gamified learning, students engage with content in ways that promote deeper cognitive and emotional connections, encouraging intrinsic motivation and fostering an environment for creative problem-solving and collaborative learning.

Moreover, the chapter emphasizes the importance of designing immersive learning environments that are inclusive and adaptable to diverse learning styles, making the educational experience more personalized. This flexibility ensures that learners from varied backgrounds can access and benefit from these technologies, thus promoting educational equity. In addition to exploring the theoretical and practical applications of these innovations, the chapter addresses key challenges such as accessibility, digital literacy, equity concerns, and the need for teacher professional development. It offers practical strategies for integrating these tools into curricula and addresses the necessity for aligning technological implementation with clear educational goals. Through case studies and empirical evidence, it also presents real-world examples of how these innovations are successfully implemented in diverse educational settings. Ultimately, this chapter serves as a critical resource for educators, instructional designers, and policymakers. It provides a framework for implementing immersive and gamified learning technologies, ensuring that such tools are not only engaging but also pedagogically sound, inclusive, and scalable. In doing so, it contributes to shaping the future of education, where learning is more engaging, personalized, and conducive to fostering skills required in an ever-changing world.

CONCLUSION

The transformative potential of gamification and immersive technologies in education lies not merely in their novelty, but in their capacity to foster deeper learner engagement, creativity, and agency when thoughtfully and inclusively implemented. This chapter has highlighted how the synergy between gamified principles and immersive tools—such as VR, AR, and MR—can reshape traditional pedagogical approaches into dynamic, learner-centred experiences grounded in constructivist and experiential learning theories. By incorporating elements of challenge, interactivity, and real-time feedback, these tools can cultivate 21st-century competencies including critical thinking, collaboration, and problem-solving. However, realizing this potential requires more than technological adoption—it demands a critical and context-sensitive approach that foregrounds equity, pedagogical alignment, and ethical responsibility. Challenges such as unequal access, teacher preparedness, cognitive overload, and data privacy must be addressed to avoid reinforcing existing educational disparities. Educators must be equipped with the skills and support to integrate immersive gamification effectively and meaningfully, while educational content must remain culturally responsive and adaptable to diverse learner contexts.

Looking ahead, the future of gamified immersive learning will depend on sustained investment, robust policy frameworks, and collaborative efforts across educational ecosystems. When aligned with sound pedagogical practice and guided by inclusive design, these technologies can serve as powerful enablers of transformative learning—bringing abstract concepts to life, personalizing instruction, and making classrooms more engaging, equitable, and responsive to the needs of modern learners. As such, educators, researchers, and policy-makers must work collectively to harness the full promise of immersive gamification, ensuring it contributes meaningfully to the evolution of teaching and learning in the 21st century.

REFERENCES

Adarkwah, M. (2021). The power of assessment feedback in teaching and learning: A narrative review and synthesis of the literature. *SN Social Sciences*, *1*(3), 75. DOI: 10.1007/s43545-021-00086-w

Aguhayon, H., Tingson, R., & Pentang, J. T. (2023). Addressing students' learning gaps in mathematics through differentiated instruction. *International Journal of Educational Management and Development Studies*, *4*(1), 69–87. DOI: 10.53378/352967

Ahmad, F., Klaib, N. O., Alsrehin, W. Y., Melhem, H. O. B., & Magableh, A. A. (2021). Eye tracking algorithms, techniques, tools, and applications with an emphasis on machine learning and Internet of Things technologies. *Expert Systems with Applications*, *166*, 114037. DOI: 10.1016/j.eswa.2020.114037

Ajani, O. A., & Govender, S. (2023). Impact of ICT-driven teacher professional development for the enhancement of classroom practices in South Africa: A systematic review of literature. *Journal of Educational and Social Research*, *13*(5), 116. DOI: 10.36941/jesr-2023-0125

Al-Ansi, A. M., Jaboob, M., Garad, A., & Al-Ansi, A. (2023). Analyzing augmented reality (AR) and virtual reality (VR) recent development in education. *Social Sciences & Humanities Open*, *8*(1), 100532. DOI: 10.1016/j.ssaho.2023.100532

Aliyeva, T. (2024). Innovative approaches to foreign language learning: A study of methods including Duolingo and beyond. *Global Spectrum of Research and Humanities*, *1*(2), 73–80. DOI: 10.69760/3twd9f85

Analyti, E., Χαρίτου, P., Pesmatzoglou, E., Stavrogiannopoulou, M., Schoina, I., Travlou, C., & Mitroyanni, E. (2024). Virtual reality in education: Transforming learning through immersive technology. *Technium Education and Humanities*, *10*, 1–11. DOI: 10.47577/teh.v10i.11766

Arieli-Attali, M., Ward, S., Thomas, J., Deonovic, B., & von Davier, A. A. (2019). The expanded evidence-centered design (e-ECD) for learning and assessment systems: A framework for incorporating learning goals and processes within assessment design. *Frontiers in Psychology*, *10*, 853. DOI: 10.3389/fpsyg.2019.00853 PMID: 31105616

Arieli-Attali, M., Ward, S., Thomas, J., Deonovic, B., & von Davier, A. A. (2019). The expanded evidence-centered design (e-ECD) for learning and assessment systems: A framework for incorporating learning goals and processes within assessment design. *Frontiers in Psychology*, *10*, 853. DOI: 10.3389/fpsyg.2019.00853 PMID: 31105616

Armstrong, M. B., & Landers, R. N. (2017). An evaluation of gamified training: Using narrative to improve reactions and learning. *Simulation & Gaming*, *48*(4), 513–538. DOI: 10.1177/1046878117703749

Bai, S., Hew, K. F., & Huang, B. (2020). Does gamification improve student learning outcome? Evidence from a meta-analysis and synthesis of qualitative data in educational contexts. *Educational Research Review*, *30*, 100322. DOI: 10.1016/j.edurev.2020.100322

Balalle, H. (2024). Exploring student engagement in technology-based education in relation to gamification, online/distance learning, and other factors: A systematic literature review. *Social Sciences & Humanities Open*, *9*, 100870. DOI: 10.1016/j.ssaho.2024.100870

Bardach, L., & Murayama, K. (2025). The role of rewards in motivation—Beyond dichotomies. *Learning and Instruction*, *96*, 102056. DOI: 10.1016/j.learninstruc.2024.102056

Bitrián, P., Buil, I., & Catalán, S. (2021). Enhancing user engagement: The role of gamification in mobile apps. *Journal of Business Research*, *132*, 170–185. DOI: 10.1016/j.jbusres.2021.04.028

Bizami, N. A., Tasir, Z., & Kew, S. N. (2023). Innovative pedagogical principles and technological tools capabilities for immersive blended learning: A systematic literature review. *Education and Information Technologies*, *28*, 1373–1425. DOI: 10.1007/s10639-022-11243-w PMID: 35919874

Bloom, B. (1956). *Taxonomy of educational objectives: The classification of educational goals*. McKay.

Bloom, B., Englehart, M., Furst, E., Hill, W., & Krathwohl, D. (1956). *Taxonomy of educational objectives: The classification of educational goals. Handbook I: Cognitive domain*. Longmans, Green.

Bloom, B. S. (1956). *Taxonomy of educational objectives: The classification of educational goals. Handbook 1: Cognitive Domain*. Longmans.

Chen, X., Gao, W., Chu, Y., & Song, Y. (2024). Enhancing interaction in virtual-real architectural environments: A comparative analysis of generative AI-driven reality approaches. *Building and Environment*, *266*, 112113. DOI: 10.1016/j.buildenv.2024.112113

Chomunorwa, S., & Mugobo, V. V. (2023). Challenges of e-learning adoption in South African public schools: Learners' perspectives. *Journal of Education and e-learning Research*, *10*(1), 80–85. DOI: 10.20448/jeelr.v10i1.4423

Chon, V., Sharif, S. b., & Saleh, N. M. (2024). Gamification for enhancing students' learning motivation: A systematic review. *Journal of Cognitive Sciences and Human Development*, *10*(2), 19–41. DOI: 10.33736/jcshd.7231.2024

Corriveau, L. (2021). Technologies, institutions, development and growth. *Structural Change and Economic Dynamics*, *57*, 159–164. DOI: 10.1016/j.strueco.2021.03.005

Crofton, E. C., Botinestean, C., Fenelon, M., & Gallagher, E. (2019). Potential applications for virtual and augmented reality technologies in sensory science. *Innovative Food Science & Emerging Technologies*, *56*, 102178. DOI: 10.1016/j.ifset.2019.102178

Davis, C. A., & Mobarak, A. M. (2020). The challenges of scaling effective interventions: A path forward for research and policy. *World Development*, *127*, 104817. DOI: 10.1016/j.worlddev.2019.104817

De Back, T. T., Tinga, A. M., & Louwerse, M. M. (2021). Learning in immersed collaborative virtual environments: Design and implementation. *Interactive Learning Environments*, *31*(8), 5364–5382. DOI: 10.1080/10494820.2021.2006238

DeCuir-Gunby, J. T., & Bindra, V. G. (2022). How does teacher bias influence students?: An introduction to the special issue on teachers' implicit attitudes, instructional practices, and student outcomes. *Learning and Instruction*, *78*, 101523. DOI: 10.1016/j.learninstruc.2021.101523

Dhakal, B. R. (2024). Differentiated Instruction: Tailoring learning for diverse learners. *Sikshya*, *40*(54), 167–176.

Du Plessis, A. E. (2019). Barriers to effective management of diversity in classroom contexts: The out-of-field teaching phenomenon. *International Journal of Educational Research*, *93*, 136–152. DOI: 10.1016/j.ijer.2018.11.002

Dubovi, I. (2022). Cognitive and emotional engagement while learning with VR: The perspective of multimodal methodology. *Computers & Education*, *183*, 104495. DOI: 10.1016/j.compedu.2022.104495

Edwards, J. (2022). Gamification, anxiety, & motivation in second language learners: A qualitative systematic review. Language, Education, & [LET Journal]. *Technology*, *2*(2), 98–127.

Foster, A. N., & Shah, M. (2020). Principles for advancing game-based learning in teacher education. *Journal of Digital Learning in Teacher Education*, *36*(2), 1–12. DOI: 10.1080/21532974.2019.1695553

Fromm, J., Radianti, J., Wehking, C., Stieglitz, S., Majchrzak, T. A., & vom Brocke, J. (2021). More than experience? On the unique opportunities of virtual reality to afford a holistic experiential learning cycle. *The Internet and Higher Education, 50*, 100804. DOI: 10.1016/j.iheduc.2021.100804

Ghory, S., & Ghafory, H. (2021). The impact of modern technology in the teaching and learning process. *International Journal of Innovative Research and Scientific Studies, 4*(3), 219–227.

Gibson, D. C., Ostashewski, N., Flintoff, K., Grant, S., & Knight, E. B. (2013). Digital badges in education. *Education and Information Technologies, 20*(2), 1–8. DOI: 10.1007/s10639-013-9291-7

Gunder, A., & Buckner, M. (2023). Story as pedagogy: Leveraging narrative digital learning practices in the instructional design process. *Ubiquity Proceedings, 3*(1), 210–215. DOI: 10.5334/uproc.88

Hadi, R., & Park, E. S. (2024). Bridging the digital and physical: The psychology of augmented reality. *Current Opinion in Psychology, 58*, 101842. DOI: 10.1016/j.copsyc.2024.101842 PMID: 38986168

Henderson, M., Ryan, T., Boud, D., Dawson, P., Phillips, M., Molloy, E., & Mahoney, P. (2019). The usefulness of feedback. *Active Learning in Higher Education, 22*(3), 229–243. DOI: 10.1177/1469787419872393

Horton, A. G., Gibson, K. B., & Curington, A. M. (2021). Exploring reflective journaling as a learning tool: An interdisciplinary approach. *Archives of Psychiatric Nursing, 35*(2), 195–199. DOI: 10.1016/j.apnu.2020.09.009 PMID: 33781400

Khlaif, Z., Salama, N., Hamamra, B., & Mousa, A. (2025). Factors influencing educators' perspectives on accepting extended reality in health care education: Qualitative study. *JMIR Medical Education, 11*. Advance online publication. DOI: 10.2196/65042 PMID: 40310667

Kim, S., Raza, M., & Seidman, E. (2019). Improving 21st-century teaching skills: The key to effective 21st-century learners. *Research in Comparative and International Education, 14*(1), 99–117. DOI: 10.1177/1745499919829214

Kolb, D. A. (1984). *Experiential learning: Experience as the source of learning and development*. Prentice-Hall.

Kuhail, M. A., Elsayary, A., Farooq, S., & Alghamdi, A. (2022). Exploring immersive learning experiences: A survey. *Informatics (MDPI), 9*(4), 75. DOI: 10.3390/informatics9040075

Kulkarni, M. (2019). Digital accessibility: Challenges and opportunities. *IIMB Management Review*, *31*(1), 91–98. DOI: 10.1016/j.iimb.2018.05.009

Kumari, S., Pothu, L., Padmambika, P., & Bobbili, S. (2024). Bridging the digital divide: Addressing inequality and access disparities. *International Journal of Indian Psychology*, *12*(3), 1151–1156. DOI: 10.25215/1203.111

Laine, J., Korhonen, T., & Hakkarainen, K. (2023). Primary school students' experiences of immersive virtual reality use in the classroom. *Cogent Education*, *10*(1), 2196896. Advance online publication. DOI: 10.1080/2331186X.2023.2196896

Lee, H. M., & Li, B. J. (2023). So far yet so near: Exploring the effects of immersion, presence, and psychological distance on empathy and prosocial behavior. *International Journal of Human-Computer Studies*, *176*, 103042. DOI: 10.1016/j.ijhcs.2023.103042

Lehikko, A., Nykänen, M., Lukander, K., Uusitalo, J., & Ruokamo, H. (2024). Exploring interactivity effects on learners' sense of agency, cognitive load, and learning outcomes in immersive virtual reality: A mixed methods study. Computers & Education: X Reality, 4, 100066. https://doi.org/DOI: 10.1016/j.cexr.2024.100066

Li, D., & Jianxing, W. (2025). The effect of gamified learning monitoring systems on students' learning behavior and achievement: An empirical study. *Entertainment Computing*, *52*, 100907. DOI: 10.1016/j.entcom.2024.100907

Lim, W. M. (2024). What is qualitative research? An overview and guidelines. *Australasian Marketing Journal*, *33*(2), 199–229. DOI: 10.1177/14413582241264619

Marone, V. (2016). Playful constructivism: Making sense of digital games for learning and creativity through play, design, and participation. *Journal of Virtual Worlds Research*, *9*(3), 1–18. DOI: 10.4101/jvwr.v9i3.7244

Marquardt, J., Fünfgeld, A., & Elsässer, J. P. (2023). Institutionalizing climate change mitigation in the Global South: Current trends and future research. *Earth System Governance*, *15*, 100163. DOI: 10.1016/j.esg.2022.100163

Mendoza-Ramírez, C. E., Tudon-Martinez, J. C., Félix-Herrán, L. C., Lozoya-Santos, J. J., & Vargas-Martínez, A. (2023). Augmented reality: Survey. *Applied Sciences (Basel, Switzerland)*, *13*(18), 10491. DOI: 10.3390/app131810491

Mhlongo, S., Mbatha, K., Ramatsetse, B., & Dlamini, R. (2023). Challenges, opportunities, and prospects of adopting and using smart digital technologies in learning environments: An iterative review. *Heliyon*, *9*(6), e16348. DOI: 10.1016/j.heliyon.2023.e16348 PMID: 37274691

Mishra, P., & Koehler, M. J. (2006). Technological pedagogical content knowledge: A framework for integrating technology in teachers' knowledge. *Teachers College Record, 108*(6), 1017–1054. DOI: 10.1177/016146810610800610

Molloy, C., & Farrell, R. (2024). Cultivating positive classroom environments: Exploring the efficacy of immersive technologies in removing barriers to learning among primary school students. *Computers in the Schools, 41*(2), 164–192. DOI: 10.1080/07380569.2024.2325441

Munje, P., & Jita, T. (2020). The impact of the lack of ICT resources on teaching and learning in selected South African primary schools. *International Journal of Learning Teaching and Educational Research, 19*(7), 263–279. DOI: 10.26803/ijlter.19.7.15

Nacional, R. (2024). Gamifying education: Enhancing student engagement and motivation. *Puissant, 5*, 716–729.

Nasereddin, M., & Price, A. (2021). Addressing the capital cost barrier to sustainable construction. *Developments in the Built Environment, 7*, 100049. DOI: 10.1016/j.dibe.2021.100049

Nottingham, E., Stockman, C., & Burke, M. (2022). Education in a datafied world: Balancing children's rights and school's responsibilities in the age of Covid 19. *Computer Law & Security Review, 45*, 105664. DOI: 10.1016/j.clsr.2022.105664

Oroszi, T. (2020). Competency-based education. *Creative Education, 11*(11), 2467–2476. DOI: 10.4236/ce.2020.1111181

Pereira, D., Aguiar Vieira, D., Flores, M. A., Machado, E. A., & Fernandes, E. (2025). Teachers' concerns and teaching experience during the pandemic and beyond: Implications for research, policy and practice. *Cogent Education, 12*(1), 2461395. Advance online publication. DOI: 10.1080/2331186X.2025.2461395

Philippe, S., Souchet, A. D., Lameras, P., Petridis, P., Caporal, J., Coldeboeuf, G., & Duzan, H. (2020). Multimodal teaching, learning and training in virtual reality: A review and case study. *Virtual Reality & Intelligent Hardware, 2*(5), 421–442. DOI: 10.1016/j.vrih.2020.07.008

Piaget, J. (1971). *Biology and knowledge*. Edinburgh University Press.

Pitsikalis, S., Lasica, I. E., Kostas, A., & Vitsilaki, C. (2024). Educational design guidelines for teaching with immersive technologies—Updating learning outcomes of the European Qualification Framework. *Trends in Higher Education, 3*(4), 1091–1108. DOI: 10.3390/higheredu3040064

Qasserras, L. (2024). The role of visual learning aids across diverse learning styles in high school education. *European Journal of Applied Linguistics Studies*, *7*(2), 68. DOI: 10.46827/ejals.v7i2.550

Qudsi, H. (2024). Gamification in education: Boosting student engagement and learning outcomes. ShodhKosh. *Journal of Visual and Performing Arts*, *5*(4), 686–693. DOI: 10.29121/shodhkosh.v5.i4.2024.2542

Rapp, A., Hopfgartner, F., Hamari, J., Linehan, C., & Cena, F. (2019). Strengthening gamification studies: Current trends and future opportunities of gamification research. *International Journal of Human-Computer Studies*, *127*, 1–6. DOI: 10.1016/j.ijhcs.2018.11.007

Ravichandran, R., & Mahapatra, J. (2023). Virtual reality in vocational education and training: Challenges and possibilities. *Journal of Digital Learning and Education*, *3*(1), 25–31. DOI: 10.52562/jdle.v3i1.602

Sabornido, E., Garma, V., Niepes, G. L., & Cabria, F. M. N. (2022). Key challenges and barriers in gamification: A systematic review. APJAET - Journal of Asia Pacific Journal of Advanced Education and Technology, 1(1), 13–19. https://doi.org/DOI: 10.54476/apjaetv1i1mar20221054

Saca, P. (2023). Designing accessible immersive learning experiences. *Journal of Technology-Integrated Lessons and Teaching*, *2*(1), 78–87. DOI: 10.13001/jtilt.v2i1.7669

Sari, R. C., Pranesti, A., & Solikhatun, I. (2024). Cognitive overload in immersive virtual reality in education: More presence but less learnt? *Education and Information Technologies*, *29*, 12887–12909. DOI: 10.1007/s10639-023-12379-z

Sims, S., Fletcher-Wood, H., O'Mara-Eves, A., Cottingham, S., Stansfield, C., Goodrich, J., Van Herwegen, J., & Anders, J. (2023). Effective teacher professional development: New theory and a meta-analytic test. *Review of Educational Research*, *95*(2), 213–254. DOI: 10.3102/00346543231217480

Tan, L. Y., Hu, S., Yeo, D. J., & Cheong, K. H. (2025). Artificial intelligence-enabled adaptive learning platforms: A review. *Computers and Education: Artificial Intelligence*, *9*, 100429. DOI: 10.1016/j.caeai.2025.100429

Thurlings, M., Vermeulen, M., Bastiaens, T., & Stijnen, S. (2013). Understanding feedback: A learning theory perspective. *Educational Research Review*, *9*, 1–15. DOI: 10.1016/j.edurev.2012.11.004

Trust, T., Krutka, D. G., & Carpenter, J. P. (2016). "Together we are better": Professional learning networks for teachers. *Computers & Education, 102*, 15–34. DOI: 10.1016/j.compedu.2016.06.007

Vygotsky, L. (1978). Interaction between learning and development. In Gauvain& Cole (Eds.), Readings on the Development of Children (pp. 34–40). Scientific American Books.

Wang, H., Gao, Z., Zhang, X., Du, J., Xu, Y., & Wang, Z. (2024). Gamifying cultural heritage: Exploring the potential of immersive virtual exhibitions. *Telematics and Informatics Reports, 15*, 100150. DOI: 10.1016/j.teler.2024.100150

Welbers, K., Konijn, E. A., Burgers, C., de Vaate, A. B., Eden, A., & Brugman, B. C. (2019). Gamification as a tool for engaging student learning: A field experiment with a gamified app. *E-Learning and Digital Media, 16*(2), 92–109. DOI: 10.1177/2042753018818342

Wulan, D. R., Nainggolan, D. M., Hidayat, Y., Rohman, T., & Fiyul, A. Y. (2024). Exploring the benefits and challenges of gamification in enhancing student learning outcomes. *Global International Journal of Innovative Research, 2*(7), 1657–1674. DOI: 10.59613/global.v2i7.238

Xiong, J., Hsiang, E. L., & He, Z. (2021). Augmented reality and virtual reality displays: Emerging technologies and future perspectives. *Light, Science & Applications, 10*, 216. Advance online publication. DOI: 10.1038/s41377-021-00658-8 PMID: 34697292

Xu, E., Wang, W., & Wang, Q. (2023). The effectiveness of collaborative problem solving in promoting students' critical thinking: A meta-analysis based on empirical literature. *Humanities & Social Sciences Communications, 10*, 16. DOI: 10.1057/s41599-023-01508-1

Zainuddin, Z., Chu, S. K. W., Shujahat, M., & Perera, C. J. (2020). The impact of gamification on learning and instruction: A systematic review of empirical evidence. *Educational Research Review, 30*, 100326. DOI: 10.1016/j.edurev.2020.100326

Zhang, S., Gao, Q., Sun, M., Cai, Z., Li, H., Tang, Y., & Liu, Q. (2022). Understanding student teachers' collaborative problem solving: Insights from an epistemic network analysis (ENA). *Computers & Education, 183*, 104485. DOI: 10.1016/j.compedu.2022.104485

Chapter 13
Ethical Issues and Data Privacy in Immersive Technologies

S. Ida Evangeline
https://orcid.org/0000-0003-2997-7897
Government College of Engineering, Tirunelveli, India

ABSTRACT

As immersive technologies such as virtual reality (VR), augmented reality (AR), and mixed reality (MR) gain prominence in educational contexts, they introduce not only new modes of engagement and learning but also complex ethical and data privacy concerns. This chapter critically examines the implications of integrating immersive systems into game-based and experiential learning environments, focusing on issues of behavioral surveillance, biometric data collection, informed consent, algorithmic bias, and commercial data exploitation. Drawing on ethical theory, legal frameworks such as GDPR, FERPA, and COPPA, and real-world case studies, the chapter explores how these technologies can both empower and endanger learners—especially minors and vulnerable populations.

1. INTRODUCTION

The proliferation of immersive technologies—encompassing virtual reality, augmented reality, and mixed reality —is transforming educational landscapes in profound ways. These tools promise to revolutionize how learners interact with content, instructors, and each other by simulating presence, facilitating embodied cognition, and enabling highly interactive and personalized experiences. Immersive technologies can enhance understanding and efficiency by integrating the senses with

DOI: 10.4018/979-8-3373-4465-2.ch013

the adaptive learning setting allowing for greater levels of understanding as well as boosting engagement levels. Virtual field trips and lab simulations, gamified skill training, collaborative virtual classrooms, and even performance-based surveys are among the areas where immersive education is becoming applied more than ever in K-12 schools, universities, and professional development (Pratisto et al. 2022).

But as immersive technologies are transforming pedagogical paradigms, they present an additional set of ethical/data privacy questions that have not been clearly foreseen or answered: These obstacles cannot simply be seen as technicalities; these values are, rather, fundamental to schooling agenda, including autonomy, fairness, and equity. Immersive systems are associated with the amount of unparalleled data gathering, namely those of biometrics (e.g., eye tracking, pulse rate, facial expressions), behavioral tracking (e.g., concentration levels, decision-making patterns), and environment (e.g., location co-ordinates, travel timelines). This fine-grained information can be used by adaptive learning systems to tailor information and maximize feedback cycles, but also leaves learners exposed to monitoring, control and abuse (Babalola et al. 2023).

The implication of this data collection is enormous in educational settings, where the power threshold is already biased toward institutions and platforms. The data practices may overwhelm learners, especially the minors and those who are marginalized, and cause the inability to make meaningful data choices. In addition, as education increasingly privatizes immersive learning by outsourcing immersive platforms to third-party companies, the risks of ownership, commercial interest, and over-access by third parties to sensitive student data has become a primary ethical concern. The blending of education and immersive technology thus encourages a consideration of how standards of ethics and data privacy legislature have to be established to asymptote about the rights of learners in those digitally mediated spaces.

It is in this context that this chapter addresses these recent issues by locating immersive educational technologies within larger ethical and legal contexts. It is designed to provide a multidimensional exploratory approach and synthesizes current ethical theory and the implications of privacy laws (including general data protection regulation [GDPR], family educational rights and privacy Act [FERPA], and children online privacy protection act [COPPA]), as well as examination of actual practice occurrences using cases. The aim is not merely to point out the possible harms and holes in the regulatory frameworks but also to present action-oriented avenues to work out an ethical and responsible, legally compliant, and learner-centered design in immersive learning systems (Baxter & Hainey, 2024).

To attain this, the chapter evolves in a number of stages. It cues with a review of the areas of surveillance and collecting behavioral data that immersive environments create, and then proceeds with a discussion about the difficulties behind gaining a substantial and informed consent and upholding the autonomy of the learner. It proceeds to explore the dangers of algorithmic discrimination, emotional manipulation and cognitive direction of immersive interface. The following sections discuss issues of data security and data ownership, as well as recommend ethical policies of governance-such as participatory design, alignment of regulations, and accountability. The chapter illustrates these discussions through case studies of practice in a variety of settings, pointing to best practice and the lessons to avoid.

Through questioning the ethical and privacy implications of immersive learning technologies, the chapter will add a much-needed critical layer of discussion into discourse pertaining to educational innovation in general. In the process, it notes that ethical integrity and fundamentality of the rights of learners cannot be sacrificed on the altar of technological advancement. Rather, immersive education should be anchored by the values of justice, dignity and confidence in the era of digitalization.

2. IMMERSIVE LEARNING ENVIRONMENTS: OPPORTUNITIES AND CHALLENGES

Immersive technologies are rapidly gaining traction in educational settings due to their ability to facilitate engagement, foster active learning, and simulate complex or otherwise inaccessible environments. Unlike traditional modes of instruction that rely heavily on textual or static visual inputs, immersive systems provide multisensory, interactive experiences that can align with constructivist and experiential learning theories. As another example a student learning cellular biology can be able to find his way into a virtual cell and interact with the cell parts or a student who is learning a language can practice talking in a culturally immersive augmented environment. Not only to do these applications promote knowledge retention, but also foster curiosity, empathy and practical problem-solving abilities.

Game-like learning environments especially are well suited to such immersive technologies to create adaptive, goal-driven, and feedback-intensive learning experiences. As a combination with the game hitches like challenges, progression, and narrative involvement, immersive learning can stimulate interest and perseverance of learners. This is particularly useful in the settings where a lack of learner engagement has always been an issue i.e. STEM fields or retraining programs in adults. Further, the immersive tools allow situated learning, or working in authentic contexts that reflect real-life complexity, which is especially valuable in professional training, soft-skills building as well as competency-based learning (Beck et al. 2023).

Immersive learning however, has serious ethical and data governance issues with the same features that make this form of learning engaging. Such environments rely upon the constant collection and and processing of data to operate. Movement, direction of the gaze, voice input, physical gestures, facial expressions and physiological signs are not only tracked in real time, but often also stored and subsequently analysed over a time frame. This data allows it to create immersive feedback, make it personalized and develop dynamically adapting content to the individual learner. However, this high degree of data intensity dilapidates the boundary between educational facilitation and behavioral monitoring.

Moreover, immersive platforms usually involve the use of artificial intelligence (AI) and machine learning (ML) factors to make decisions as to which content to be shown, how to assess performance, and when to interfere. Such decisions by algorithms can determine the path of a learner in an opaque, biased, and even manipulative way - especially when based on probabilistic models trained on inadequate or skewed data. The feedback loops in the learning systems immersion is not neutral and is subject to privileged values and assumptions which should be subject to evaluation of fairness and transparency as well as accountability (Kuhail et al. 2022).

Further, ethical limits can be made complex due to the psychological intensity of immersion. Immersive learning environments have the potentials to alter the emotions of learners, perceptions of time and space, sense of agency and social behaviour. These mental and emotional effects call into question the possibility of unintended effects- namely, desensitization, emotional burnout, or compensation through artificial feedback. More subtly, immersion may play the role of blurring the boundaries between simulation and reality, particularly when working with the younger learners, which means that informed decision-making and critical reflection is harder to achieve.

Also significant is the power relation and the economic framework within which the immersive technologies are to be implemented into education. Most of these systems are invented by commercial firms where the main interests of the company do not necessarily coincide with educational standards. When educational institutions embrace these platforms: sometimes via low technical expertise, sometimes without regulatory protection, they may end upallowing students to become part of proprietary data ecosystems that are neither transparent, audit, or user-driven. Such a trend is not only a threat to institutional accountability but also to the digital rights and the long- term welfare of students (Fernandes et al. 2023).

Therefore, it is no secret that even though immersive learning environments have a significant pedagogical potential, their ethical nature cannot be severely underestimated. The dependency on close, frequent and partly oblique modes of data collection, results in new parameters of hazards, which are not implicit to other forms of educational technologies. The task is to make sure that immersive learning can be used in a manner that is as innovative as it is ethical and consistent with the principles on which education is based: respect of autonomy, adherence to equity and safeguarding learner dignity. Reaching this balance needs critical consideration of the design, implementation and regulation of immersive educational technologies, which will be discussed in depth in the following sections of this chapter.

3. SURVEILLANCE AND BEHAVIORAL DATA COLLECTION

Immersive learning environments are fundamentally data-intensive. Their functionality depends on collecting and interpreting a wide range of behavioral, physiological, and contextual data to render realistic simulations, track user progress, and tailor educational experiences. In contrast to traditional e-learning systems, based mostly on clickstream behaviour data or performance on quizzes, immersive technologies capture multimodal data streams in real-time. These would comprise eye tracking, head and bodily posture, finger twitches, voice recording, facial expressions, latency time and even physiological inputs like heart rate or even galvanic skin response. Each of these indicators helps in developing responsive environment where a response is fine-tuned to the performance, levels of engagement and inferred emotional state of the leaner.

This ubiquitous level of surveillance data capture signals a departure toward active learning surveillance to active behavioral surveillance. The immersive system does not only monitor what the learner does, but how s/he does it, how long s/he looks at this or that element, how s/he responds to questions or situations with confidence, how his/her body changes during moments of barracks and success. By so doing, immersive technologies can record what some scholars term as cognitive fingerprints, or digital psychometrics: highly personalized behavioral data points that may be used to deduce their personality type, learning styles, modes of motivation, and even mental health proxies. This type of data flow makes individualization possible, as well as raises ethical uncertainties concerning how far educational monitoring should extend (Capatina et al. 2024).

Although the gathering of such data has the possibility to improve the outcomes of learning since feedback given to the student could be specific, and the student could have differentiated directions, there is also danger of overreach, acclimatization to surveillance, and privacy invasion. The most ethical dilemma is whether learners are actively agreeing to such Permeany monitoring, or whether such monitary bands the consenting process unfeasible due to the complete immersive context. In classes where technology is required to work, the absence of data collection thus comes at par with the absence of the learning itself. This destroys meaningful consent and introduces a coercive effect, especially where consent is coerced or the situation is iterated with power imbalances, as in the case of compulsory education or a teacher-student relationship or an employer-employee relationship.

The second serious worry is persistence and reuse of data. Behavioral information collected during immersive training sessions can be stored forever, reused in train AI models, or sold to third parties with the significant lack of awareness on behalf of the learner. In others, platforms strip this data of identifiers; though due to the depth, individuality, and specificity of immersive behavioral data, even anonymization can prove challenging. Biometric patterns and histories of interactions can frequently be re-identified, particularly as collated with other data sets. The consequences of this are that learners may face long term risks of profiling, in terms of academic performance, to career tracking, or even psychological profiling long after they leave the immediate learning environment (Cho et al. 2025).

Furthermore, immersive technologies tend to be high opacity ecosystems where users lack any visibility on what data is being gathered, how is it being interpreted, and who gains access to it entirely. The difference is that, unlike the traditional methods of classroom observation which are constrained by physical bodies and institutional rules, digital surveillance in immersive system is continual, unseen, and algorithm-based. This invisibility increases the challenge on the part of the learners as well as educators to either challenge these data narratives or even make sense of these data narratives. In that case, the immersion environment should no longer be seen as a learning tool but rather a behavioral laboratory where learners each become participants and subject data contributors.

Such developments necessitate the reconsideration of the agricultural frameworks to the educational technologies. Legal privacy protections measures like those written into law like GDPR or FERPA may not be well-constructed to navigate the complexity of multimodal, real-time and context-sensitive flows of data in immersive environments. As an example, the concepts of data minimization and purpose limitation that form the backbone of most privacy legislation are not compatible with the great mass of data that is required by immersive personalization. In a parallel way, current institutional review frameworks of educational technologies might not reflect risks posed by novel surveillance mechanisms, especially possibilities of machine learning and biometric daydreaming (Makransky & Petersen, 2021).

In order to eliminate such apprehensions, what is needed is a more sophisticated approach of ethical governance that would not restrict itself to legal compliance, but explore moral ramifications of behavioral surveillance within education setting. These involve creating the new norms of data proportionality (not gathering more than what is absolutely necessary), temporal boundaries (establishing the guidelines in terms of how long the data should be kept), and epistemic humility (being aware of the restrictions of behavioral inference). It also asserts the participation of the design where the learners, teachers and the data ethicists can co-design the rules of data gathering and its treatment within the immersive systems.

As immersive learning proceeds to transform digital learning, we must make sure that the data collected cannot compromise the values it claims to promote, namely, trust, curiosity, and autonomy. Without moral protections, the hope that personalized, engaging, transformative schooling is more likely to appear as the incidence of invisible surveillance and the commodification of human behavior. The following section is going to look at the intersection between these risks and the notion of informed consent and learner autonomy especially among vulnerable populations.

4. INFORMED CONSENT AND LEARNER AUTONOMY

Informed consent is a cornerstone of ethical practice in both education and data governance. It is intended to ensure that individuals understand and voluntarily agree to how their data will be collected, used, stored, and potentially shared. In the realm of immersive learning technologies though, obtaining rather conscious and informed consent actually becomes much more complicated. These issues are complicated by the fact that data flows are highly opaque, the technologies involved are new, and that there exist asymmetrical power relations between the learners and the institutions or companies that control the platforms.

Immersive learning experiences usually mean continual interaction with hardware and software that can only operate when gathering data. These products, head-mounted displays (HMDs), motion sensors, eye trackers, and biometric feedback tools work with means that could hardly be audited or even observed by users. Consequently, students are frequently oblivious to the extent of the data being recorded--much less the off-line analysis which ensues in the form of analytics algorithms, machine learning models or integrations with third-party platforms. Even where the subject consents at the beginning it is usually hidden in pages of user agreements, privacy policies or click through forms that fall short of the ethical ideal of clearness, ease of use and contextual sensitivity (Harden & Fanfarelli, 2023).

In addition, the immersive character of these platforms may tempt learners to persist in real-time without being able to take a break, reconsider, disconnect. When already immersed in a simulation or game based learning experience, it will be harder to distinguish between voluntary and involuntary participation and the issues of extraction of data. This is of concern regarding the issue of so called default consent whereby engaging in the learning activity amounts to consent to extensive surveillance. In this case, learners are not positively making a choice when it comes to sharing their data: rather, they are going along with the technological infrastructure that makes learning practical.

This ethical conflict is especially sharp when the learner is a minor or is a member of an at risk-population. Children, as an example, might be generally less cognitively mature than the rest of the population and hence not fully able to comprehend what their biometric data or behavioral data collection would entail. In these situations, parental permission is commonly invoked as a surrogate for an informed consent, but in fact parents are often equally in the dark about the extent and dangers of immersive data processes. Learners in underrepresented groups can also be at a higher risk, since they can be erroneously judged by the algorithms, which showed no training with large enough and diverse data sample, potentially causing biased remedial measures. In such cases, permission, is mere formality, not an ethical protection (Perin et al. 2021).

Another concern that should be brought up in the immersive learning environment is the factor of autonomy which is closely connected with the consent. Autonomy is the freedom and informed decision-making in relation to education of the learner. However, when behavioral and emotional information is used to differentiate content, influence the flow of information, or even nudge the choice process there can be a fine border between guidance and manipulation. An example of this would be where a platform may employ emotional recognition as an input into increasing and decreasing the difficulty of a task, effectively reinforcing emotional connections at some cost to other possible emotional connections.

In addition, immersive systems frequently put elements of persuasive design, adapted in part from marketing fields, in part of behavioral economics, at the expense of autonomy in the name of engagement. Tactics like variable rewards, sensory feedback loops and richly-framed goal use will influence learner behavior in ways that may maximize system goals (like completion rates or time-on-task) at the expense of learner control or intrinsic motivation. Such means of soft manipulation have ethical implications especially when they are not openly declared as part of the consent process, but made inconspicuous (through user experience).

This is necessary to rethink consent mechanisms so that they are dynamic, context-centered and student-centric so that assurance of ethical handling of issues is developed. Conventional paper consent forms will not work in immersive environments. Rather, the consent should be reframed as ongoing communication, and learners will be empowered to understand, control and withdraw to decisions at various stages during their interaction with the system. Just-in-time pop-up messages, tiers of explanation and even visual cues in the immersive environment itself could present more significant chances of the learner taking control in an informed way (McCarrick et al. 2025).

Institutions/developers need to embrace a duty of care that exceeds legal requirements. This incorporates the incorporation of ethical review into the design of a particular platform, making sure that the consent practices are co-designed with learners and educators and reducing data collection as much as possible. Clear disclosures on how, when and with what information personalization is applied, made, and how decisions are reached can be used to restore agency and belief in the learning process.

Finally, there should be no distinction between informed consent and autonomy that is specific to immersive education and once-instead-of-regularly done as a procedural barrier. As the physical and online learning environments increasingly blur, so too must the concepts of consent and control keep pace to embrace the realities of smarter and more probing learning environments.

5. BIAS, MANIPULATION, AND ALGORITHMIC ETHICS

The integration of artificial intelligence (AI) and algorithmic systems into immersive educational technologies offers the promise of personalization, adaptivity, and real-time responsiveness. These systems process large volumes of behaviour data and produce individual learning paths, forecast the needs of learners and maximum feedback distribution. Nonetheless, their increasing power simultaneously brings forward critical ethical issues, whereby these are far reaching to include the elevation of prejudice, the possiblity of emotional and cognitive control, and the informal decision making that threatens a lack of check and facility of trust and accountability in education.

In the middle of these issues is the algorithmic reasoning that drives immersive spaces. Algorithms are not self-contained, they are trained on data which may reflect human biases, and they are deployed in social and organisational environments. They are, therefore, able to repeat and codify the preexisting biases whether cultural, race-based, gender-based, or socioeconomically based that are already observed in the training sets that they are provided or on their development sustains. In immersive education, these can include differentially assigning learning resources, recommending content, adjusting challenge to invoke biased interpretations of behavioural signals. Such symptoms of the problem as eye-tracking data or response latencies can be misinterpreted as failure to stay engaged with a task or poor competence without factoring in the neurodiversity, language, or cultural differences in communication behaviors (Kuhail et al. 2022).

It can have real outcomes in these algorithmic misreadings The data are biased to the point that learners may be prematurely overtracked into a lower curricular level, needlessly identified as being in need of intervention, or simply not made available to higher level opportunities. In immersive environments where the feedback and adaptation is immediate and subtle, these conditions may build up imperceptibly, reinforcing inequalities of experience and further enlarging the disparity to which they gave rise. In addition, since such systems may work as black boxes, giving no insight into how a decision is to be reached, there could be few means by which the learner/educator can challenge and amend mistaken beliefs.

What is even worse than bias, the immersive platforms bring the risk of intentional manipulation by the strategic use of persuasive technologies. These are the tools that are aimed at shaping user behavior with the help of psychological understandings, gamification techniques, and affective computing. Although designed with the best interests in mind and with the intention to improve engagement or motivation, they may also be used to nudge learners to specific behaviors, emotions, or decisions that are not in their best interests or true preferences. As an example, an immersive simulation that adjusts the size of visual stimuli or sounds when a computer recognizes a facial expression of emotion could promote compliance, or even conformity, over critical evaluation or independence (Bullock et al. 2021).

When applied in an immersive environment, this manipulation can be particularly subtle in nature because of the relative realism and psychological immersion offered by such an environment. Learners might feel situated in the simulation, have feelings towards avatars, or be motivated by a social pressure exerted by other avatars virtually- all of which can expose them to shaping behavior. Compounded by algorithmic personalization, this puts a system in place where the system is no longer simply responding to the user behavior but actually conditioning it, which brings up ethical concerns of consent and autonomy and the extent to which learning should be manipulated.

What is more, emotional and cognitive states of the learners -measured in terms of biometric data including heart rate variability, galvanic skin response, or facial microexpressions- can also be employed to adjust the content as well as achieve system objectives like engagement retention, or behavioral conformity. This strays over a shaky ethical line: between facilitating learning and manipulating the emotions to the benefit of platform measures and institutional goals. In these situations, the learning conditions will become a place of unconscious psychic experimentation, instead of an area of positive learner development and self-determination.

Al big data accuracy or efficiency of a system cannot be the only considerations in ethics in immersive education. It demands a questioning of values: whose interests are being furthered, whose norms are being established and whose voices are not represented in producing and using these technologies. Developers have to question not simply the equitability of their models but also of the end to which the models are best-suited. Are they set up to achieve independent thinking or are they to maximize time-on-tast? Do they design to meet the needs of different learners, or impose restrictive definitions of engagement and success? (Carter & Egliston, 2023)

There should be a multifaceted ethical response to these issues. Second is the need to incorporate algorithmic transparency as a design imperative to allow students and instructors to inquire and protest algorithmic decision-making. Second, safeguards to minimize harm by fairness audit and bias reduction strategies must be rooted in system development and implementation, and there must be well-defined accountability frameworks identifying and reducing harms. Third, participatory methods of designing--investing learners, educators, and ethicists in the formulation of algorithmic objectives and principles--can make immersive systems support democratic and inclusive educational practices.

Overall, the ethical design space of algorithmic personalization in immersive learning contains potential and risk alike. As much as such systems present an unsurpassed opportunity to personalize and enhance learning experiences, they also present grave dangers of bias, manipulation and epistemic injustice. The approach in navigating this landscape responsibly by the developers and educators and policymakers should entail ethical decision-making, which places a premium on transparency and other qualities, such as inclusiveness, and maintaining agency in learners amidst increasingly intelligent learning environments.

6. DATA SECURITY, OWNERSHIP, AND MONETIZATION

The deployment of immersive technologies in educational settings has significantly expanded the quantity, sensitivity, and granularity of learner data being collected. From biometric identifiers such as retinal scans and voiceprints to behavioral analytics derived from motion, interaction, and speech patterns, immersive platforms generate a continuous stream of personal information. This information is not incidental to the learning experience; it is all part of how immersive systems operate- personalization, feedback, content adaption, and engagement tracking. This excessive amount of data is however accompanied by a series of issues on ethics and legality of protection, property, and commoditization of data.

First and the closest concern is data security. Making the information stored or transferred by such immersive platforms highly sensitive, cloud-based systems have shown high risks of breach of information and potential cyberattacks. Securing immersive systems is a complex task since such immersive systems are inherently multimodal, and operate at hardware, software and network level. However, in many educational establishments the technology infrastructure or cyber security skills are lacking to adequately vet, and observe these platforms. This is especially worrying given the risks of damage that are entailed with the compromise of biometric or behavioral data, which can hardly be changed or anonymized as is the case with passwords, or email addresses (Anwar et al. 2023).

The engineering prongs of keeping data safe are already hard but are complicated by the piecemeal nature of educational data regulation. Although the framework provided by the General Data Protection Regulation (GDPR) in the European Union, the Family Educational Rights and Privacy Act (FERPA) in the United States, and the Children Online Privacy Protection Act (COPPA) are important, their application to immersive technologies tends to be ambiguous. Such laws were not written with real-time and sensor-enabled data ecosystems in mind, and their definition of personal data, consent and educational records do not necessarily take into account the whole picture of information gathered in immersive settings. Due to this, there is still a lot of legal grey area especially over cross-border transfer of data and use of third-party analytics as well as long-term data retention policies.

Of great essence is the issue of ownership of the data. The control over the work done by the student and over the student him- or herself is clearly stated in the mainstream education environment, either they stay with the learner or stay under the control of the education organization. Through the emergence of commercialisation of immersive learning programs, ownership hierarchies are now different. In several instances, the platform providers claim ownership of the information produced by their programs-even though the data may be produced by learner response. This disproportionality provokes critical questions regarding the everyone-responsibility, and institution-responsibility. By valuing educational data as the commercial resource and turning the learners into the data subjects with their behaviors feeding the product creation processes, students become the developers of educational technologies that they are neither aware of and have no control over (Valluripally et al. 2022).

This dynamic is compounded by the monetization methods that are adopted by most such immersive platform providers. The data harvested in an educational context, particularly behavioral and biometric data, can be used to train machine learning models, tweak algorithms, or find some kind of insight which later need to be packaged and sold to third parties, including educational publishers, recruitment firms, and even advertisers. Although anonymization is provided on some platforms this does not always render immersive data de-identifiable, especially when combined with additional sources of data. The monetization of learner data not only breaches the trust inherent in learning relationships, but poses a threat of establishing surveillance capitalism as the foundation of learning.

This is even more troubling in a scenario where the downstream use of the acquired information is not fully disclosed to the learner or at least not brought to the fore in an effective manner. The lack of substantive transparency options means that users cannot be certain of what operators are doing with their data: whether kept permanently, recycled to other non-educational purposes, sold in bulk forms etc. Moreover, the lack of standardized data portability gives no options to learners to reclaim or transfer their data to another platform, which supports vendor lock-in or denies the mobility of learners (Zhuang, 2021).

The challenge to overcome is the ethical framework proposals should promote robust concepts of data governance with a specific focus on immersive education.

These incorporate taking up privacy-by-design and security-by-design coding practices which incorporate information safeguards at all layers of the platform. Pencryption and secure authentication, audit logs should be augmented by more human-friendly practices, in particular: data-use disclosures, user dashboards to monitor data, and opt-in controls beyond mere boilerplate consent.

Also significant is the reinvention of ownership rights of data. Educational facilities are advised to enter into a contract with the providers of the immersive technologies that made the use of data limited to pedagogical purposes and excluded the secondary exploitation without the prior consent of the individual. It should be noted that where possible, open-source or decentralized systems where learners have direct control of their data should be preferred. New ideas such as data trusts and learner data cooperatives present alternative systems of collective educational data that would manage it in the interests of the users and in an ethical manner and not just make profits (Ali et al. 2023).

In the end, data security and data ownership protection, not to mention resistance to monetisation pressures, are not only technical and legal issues but moral ones as well. In case immersive education is to continue as a space of sovereignty and intellectual autonomy, then the data produced by its technologies need to be controlled by the principles of justice, transparency, and the respect to the dignity of learners. Now the next question is more general concerning the manner in which a set of principles of this nature can be systematically adopted in the design and governance of immersive educational technologies.

7. ETHICAL DESIGN AND GOVERNANCE FRAMEWORKS

The ethical challenges posed by immersive educational technologies—ranging from surveillance and manipulation to data ownership and algorithmic opacity—cannot be addressed retroactively or in isolation. They require an integrated, anticipatory approach that embeds ethical reflection and regulatory compliance into the very fabric of system design, implementation, and institutional governance. The potential ethical implications surrounding the power and pervasiveness of immersive learning tools make the necessities of having sound ethical frameworks of design and governing structures of these tools all the more dire.

Ethical design in immersive learning systems starts with privacy by design and ethics by design: philosophies that require attention to ethics early in the development of technology. Instead of making ethics a post-deployment consideration or a regulatory-compliance burden, developers and educational organizations should design immersive systems with transparency, accountability and user rights as their core hydraulic agencies. Examples of this would be to create interfaces that effectively explain what kind of data is being recorded and why, giving the user real-time access to controls and finally having defaults on the system that value privacy over convenience on the part of the provider (Yadav & Reddy, 2024).

A very important aspect of ethical design entails the application of participatory approaches. Learners, educators, ethicists, and various representatives of the community can be involved in the design process to assure that such risks have not been left unnoticed, they are contextually constrained, and ethical blind spots have not occurred. Co-designing processes lead not to mere technologically competent devices, but to socially and ecologically responsible and culturally-tuned technologies. This engagement is especially relevant where the use of immersive systems is deployed in various educational contexts, because the concern of equity, accessibility, and power relations need to be addressed. Equitable inclusive design can be used to avoid recreating the same prejudices and make sure that immersive tools do not discriminate against any students.

Transparency should also be offered to the algorithmic systems used in order to personalize immersive spaces, to provide recommendations on content and to make assessments. Instead, developers are advised to create explainable AI processes, which would enable users and teachers to become aware of how their decisions are made, what factors are being factored into the decision process and what repercussions do the chosen actions have on learning paths. This is needed to enable contesting, which will mean that learners could stand up to an algorithmic decision that is deemed as unfair or inaccurate. Ethical audits, whether internally and by a third party should be established to test the system against proclaimed ethical standards and in accordance with the applicable data protection legislations (Al-Kfairy et al. 2024).

Ethical norms are also supported by institutional-level governance structures. Educational organizations should consider creating an internal policy making and review boards to assess adoption and continued use of immersion technologies. Such governance entities must encompass not only technologists and administrators but also lawyers, ethicists and educators who can determine pedagogical fit and social responsibility. Risk assessments such as data protection impact assessments (DPIAs) should become the rule rather than the exception and help to determine the potential harms and measures to mitigate their impact.

Besides, regulatory frameworks should also be changed to reflect the risks of immersive educational technologies. Current data protection regulations, although important, are too broad or not yet modern, to take into consideration the complexity of biometric surveillance, affective computing as well as real-time adjustment based on behavior. Policy makers should collaborate with educational stakeholders to revise legal terms, formalize consent standards regarding immersive data, and develop policies that are responsive to their very personal vulnerabilities to learners, especially those who are underage, those with disabilities, or belong to marginalized groups.

Ethical governance further requires pro-active interaction with new forms of accountability. This can and perhaps must include adopting new forms of data stewardship, with institutions taking on a fiduciary role to prioritize the safety and ethical use of learner data. Data portability mechanisms and the possibility to control how data are used, shared, or deleted should also be provided by data platform(s). The right to explanation, the right to be forgotten and the right to opt-out of personalization should be programmed into the immersive learning experience- and not held as special/uncommon possibilities (Zhang et al. 2025).

More importantly, ethical design and governance have to consider that education is not only a subject on which technical innovation can be brought but a moral and a social practice. It is informed by such values as trust, respect, justice, and the development of human potential. Unchecked, immersive technologies have the potential to undermine such values by developing metrics of efficiency and engagement solely. Immersive education like any educational method has the potential to be quite empowering, inclusive, inclusive, and mind-broadening when approached through rigorous ethical guidelines and with adherence to participatory governance.

8. CASE STUDIES IN PRACTICE

To move beyond abstraction, it is necessary to examine how the ethical and data privacy issues discussed throughout this chapter manifest in real-world educational settings. Case study itself is a critical reference point through which the conflicts between technology potentials and moral uprightness guide may be witnessed and appraised. They demonstrate, not only the broad spectrum of contexts in which immersive technologies are both adopted and used, but also the structural and cultural aspects underpinning their ethical operation, or absence thereof.

An example of this was a pilot program at one high school in the United States, whereby virtual reality headsets were introduced into biology and history classes. Students entered an immersive simulation of the human circulatory system and also went through a historical simulation of the D-Day landings. Although the outcomes of the learning were encouraging, students claimed to have engaged and retained more with the intervention, issues were immediately raised when it was found out that the platform gathered in-depth bio data, including gaze patterns, voice input, and stress-factors. No data were stored locally and instead were sent to the company servers without full disclosure to students or their parents. Further, the privacy policy showed that the data may be utilized to enhance the AI engine on the platform which many have understood to be the nodes to allow the commercialization of their data. It is a good example of how educational excitement about immersive environments and the black box of data practice present inherent tensions (Buragohain et al. 2024).

A reverse example on higher education teaches a lesson of how foresight within morality is able to counter the risk. One of the European universities created their own AR platform to make engineering students perceive the interiors and exteriors of architectural buildings with the help of 3D models. Before the deployment of the project, the project team worked through a GDPR-compliant data protection impact assessment, where only necessary data--user interactions and a log of anonymized usage data--would be collected on the project. Informed consent processes were also designed collaboratively with students and indicators were built into the user interface to demonstrate when and how data were being collected in real-time. The platform also enabled people to export and delete their data which gives them more control and visibility. The project was highly rated in terms of its moral soundness and learner focus, despite being technically unsophisticated compared to anything in the commercial sector, and demonstrated how a principled approach to design, encouraged by institutional support, may go hand in hand with a pedagogy of invention (Muzata et al. 2024).

A third situation in which there are more complex considerations to be made in corporate training environments. Some of the multinational corporations embracing VR simulations in soft skills training include leadership, conflict resolution and diversity awareness. The simulations also tend to involve live emotional-recognition and natural language processing to set the measure of user reactions. In one of such implementation, the staff members engaged in a VR training activity that was meant to replicate challenging scenarios in communication with their peers. Although the level of immersion made the process realistic and more engaging, the participants reported feeling uneasy after discovering that their vocal tone, facial expressions, decision pathways, etc. had been captured and further used to create their psychometrics. These profiles were shared with human resources departments to enhance the performance evaluations. This case undermines the borderline between training and surveillance, which prompts the ethical issues of consent, proportionality, and the probable misuse of the affective data in the professional setting (Weng et al. 2024).

Lastly, in a nonprofit project with low-resource schools in Latin America, an AR game was used to instruct on environmental science based on interactive stories. As a result of the poor internet infrastructure, the application was to be offline with minimal data being stored within the device. Developers consulted with local educators and community leaders in close cooperation to ensure cultural sensitivity and relevance and ethical sensitivity. The system did not have sophisticated personalization capabilities even though it did not infringe on the privacy of learners or local data sovereignty. The research focused on the educational and pedagogical value of the application as well as on the trusting effect that the non-invasive character of the design has brought to students and teachers alike. This case is an example of how ethical restraint that is usually considered a limitation can have a positive impact on user trust and engagement, particularly in situations with background sensitivities regarding exploitation of data.

These case studies demonstrate a continuum of ethical results- starting with a wanton extracting of data and ending with above-par ethical behaviour. They show that immersive technologies are not necessarily either beneficial or harmful and ethical outcomes depend on design positions, governance systems and the socio-institutional contexts to which they are applied. In addition, they validate the "vitally significant" role of correlating the immersive learning tools with the values of transparency, respect, and justice. Framing ethics as a design issue rather than an extrinsic limitation allows educators and developers to design immersive experiences that are both effective and ethically legitimate and trustworthy.

9. RECOMMENDATIONS AND ACTIONABLE GUIDELINES

As immersive technologies become increasingly embedded in educational systems, there is an urgent need for clear, actionable strategies to guide their ethical implementation. The complexity of these systems—both technically and ethically—demands more than high-level principles or reactive policies. Instead, a proactive, system-wide approach is required, one that addresses the specific responsibilities of developers, educators, institutions, and policymakers.

Immersive learning platform developers are charged with an ethical responsibility to start with design. It includes purposeful downplaying of data collection to only pedagogically needed data, shying away of features that monetise biometric or behavioural data and ensuring transparency at all levels of the user experience. Interfaces must be made to inform not obscure, giving learners a true-to-life sense of what is being tracked and how, as well as ways of managing that information. Consent mechanisms cannot be consigned to obscure terms of service but must be built into the experience of learning in a way that is unintimidating, framed (i.e., contextualized), and cancellable. Developers should also undertake to test their algorithmic bias in rigorous conditions, which involves frequently testing their models with the use of various sets of data to prevent fear of reproducing inequalities (Pitsikalis et al. 2024).

Institutions and educators are compelled to remember that the incorporation of immersive technologies is not an ideally neutral and purely technological process- it is a pedagogical and ethical choice that must be governed as such. To ensure there is no data mishandling or cases of lack of fair access to information, institutional leaders need to institute strict internal rules regarding data protection, equal access and partnerships with third parties. The decisions on procurement must be taken not on the technological maturity of a platform but on its ethical record, non-stealthy endeavors and data management. Teachers are more likely to be the initial contact with the learners, thus, they should be trained not only in regards to the technological functioning of immersion tools, but also in terms of ethical guidelines. This encompasses knowledge on how to describe data practices to students, how to facilitate consent based learning environments, how to champion learner rights in more institutional processes (Cabrera-Duffaut et al. 2024).

Policymakers can no longer be left out of the game as they have a significant part to play in the visioning regulatory environment in which immersive education takes place. Current data protection regulations, although significant, need to be regulatory refinements to the particularities of immersive systems(especially in terms of biometric surveillance, emotional analytics and algorithmic profiling). These changes should ensure that policy implementation gives a real-life understanding that such new measures help to bridge existing gaps in the legal protection of the underprivileged, including minors and vulnerable groups, as well as develop standards of leading transparency, fairness, and accountability in both the government and the individual providers of educational services. Besides, agencies that provide funds and certifying agencies can affect ethical practice by conditioning their assistance or approval on compliance with ethical standards of design (Obourdin et al. 2024).

Simultaneously, it is necessary to develop a culture of moral sensitivity both at the educational level and at the level of all levels of the educational ecosystem. This includes instilling an ethical reflexivity in future teachers and technicians during their training, interdisciplinary cooperation among technical, legal, and educational specialists, and having students themselves participating in the discussion about their rights and responsibilities in terms of digital services. Ec space is vital to create to empower learners with a voice and agency of their own- not just to passively defend their rights but to emerge as empowered players on the dynamic field of digital learning (Mystakidis & Lympouridis, 2024).

Notably, these suggestions are not intended to hamper innovation, but to protect the values to which education is supposed to exalt. Immersive technologies open up immense possibilities to enhance learning, make it accessible to all, and make students ready to decide complex, real-life challenges. However, such potential can be materialized only when it is sustained in the terms of ethical integrity and social accountability. The task at hand is not only to make sure that the immersive turn in education strengthens rather than weakens trust, dignity, and justice to all learners but to embrace the challenge.

10. CONCLUSION

As immersive technologies continue to redefine the contours of educational practice, they bring with them both extraordinary potential and unprecedented ethical complexity. Virtual reality, augmented reality, and mixed reality tools can foster deeper engagement, support experiential learning, and provide access to richly contextualized educational environments. Yet, the qualities which have made such technologies revolutionary in the sense that they can keep track of, interpret, and respond to user behavior in real-time are the same features that present significant threats to the area of privacy, autonomy, surveillance, and data abuse.

This chapter has discussed the moral aspects of immersive learning environment in a multidisciplinary manner with a view of bringing out the idea that the high technological aptitude should be matched with the responsibility of being morally upright. It has discussed the ways in which immersive systems collect information about intimate behaviors and biometrics, both in opaque ways that present particular challenges to learners and in ways that could be used to challenge the data collected. It has explored the shortcomings of the existing consent mechanisms, the risks of algorithmic bias and emotional manipulation, the problems of data security and ownership in the context of more and more commercialized learning environments.

It has also drawn the profile of a more morally secure future one where immersive technologies are created, managed, and delivered on principles of transparency, equity, and dignity to the learners. That would demand specific systemic alterations: the ethical principles should be integrated into the design procedure, institutional safeguards and governance system placed, and regulatory frameworks reformed that have become inadequate to the digital complexity of immersive learning. As the case studies have shown, ethical immersion is not an utopian goal but a very practical and necessary disposition which can be accomplished through consciously collaborative activity, participatory-design, and unswerving dedication to rights and needs of learners.

Ultimately, immersive technologies cannot be evaluated only in terms of bringing captivation and sequencing the learning outcomes. Their achievement also has to be evident in the magnitude to which they help to maintain the existential values of education such as elevating awareness of respect of autonomy, the growth of equity, the development of critical agency, and the maintenance of trust. When envisioning the future of immersive learning, the education community is confronted with an epic decision not on whether to use these tools but how to use them in a manner that is congruent with integrity. Such a decision will not only influence the design of digital learning environments, but also the overall ethic of education as it progresses.

REFERENCES

Al-Kfairy, M., Alrabaee, S., & Alfandi, O. (2024, November). Ethical pathways in VR and the Metaverse: Frameworks for responsible innovation. In *2024 2nd International Conference on Intelligent Metaverse Technologies & Applications (iMETA)* (pp. 009-017). IEEE.

Ali, S., Abdullah, Armand, T. P. T., Athar, A., Hussain, A., Ali, M., ... & Kim, H. C. (2023). Metaverse in healthcare integrated with explainable AI and blockchain: Enabling immersiveness, ensuring trust, and providing patient data security. *Sensors (Basel), 23*(2), 565. PMID: 36679361

Anwar, M. S., Ullah, I., Ahmad, S., Choi, A., Ahmad, S., Wang, J., & Aurangzeb, K. (2023). Immersive learning and AR/VR-based education: cybersecurity measures and risk management. In *Cybersecurity management in education technologies* (pp. 1–22). CRC Press.

Babalola, A., Manu, P., Cheung, C., Yunusa-Kaltungo, A., & Bartolo, P. (2023). A systematic review of the application of immersive technologies for safety and health management in the construction sector. *Journal of Safety Research, 85*, 66–85. PMID: 37330902

Baxter, G., & Hainey, T. (2024). Using immersive technologies to enhance the student learning experience. *Interactive Technology and Smart Education, 21*(3), 403–425.

Beck, D., Morgado, L., & O'Shea, P. (2023). Educational practices and strategies with immersive learning environments: Mapping of reviews for using the metaverse. *IEEE Transactions on Learning Technologies, 17*, 319–341.

Bullock, B. B., Nascimento, F. L., & Doore, S. A. (2021, March). Computing ethics narratives: Teaching computing ethics and the impact of predictive algorithms. In *Proceedings of the 52nd ACM Technical Symposium on Computer Science Education* (pp. 1020-1026).

Buragohain, D., Deng, C., Sharma, A., & Chaudhary, S. (2024). The impact of immersive learning on teacher effectiveness: A systematic study. *IEEE Access : Practical Innovations, Open Solutions, 12*, 35924–35933.

Cabrera-Duffaut, A., Pinto-Llorente, A. M., & Iglesias-Rodríguez, A. (2024, July). Immersive learning platforms: Analyzing virtual reality contribution to competence development in higher education—a systematic literature review. [). Frontiers Media SA.]. *Frontiers in Education, 9*, 1391560.

Capatina, A., Patel, N. J., Mitrov, K., Cristea, D. S., Micu, A., & Micu, A. E. (2024). Elevating students' lives through immersive learning experiences in a safe metaverse. *International Journal of Information Management*, *75*, 102723.

Carter, M., & Egliston, B. (2023). What are the risks of virtual reality data? Learning analytics, algorithmic bias and a fantasy of perfect data. *New Media & Society*, *25*(3), 485–504.

Cho, Y., Coward, C., Lackner, J., Windleharth, T. W., & Lee, J. H. (2025). The use of an escape room as an immersive learning environment for building resilience to misinformation. *Journal of Librarianship and Information Science*, *57*(2), 524–538.

Fernandes, F. A., Rodrigues, C. S. C., Teixeira, E. N., & Werner, C. M. (2023). Immersive learning frameworks: A systematic literature review. *IEEE Transactions on Learning Technologies*, *16*(5), 736–747.

Harden, P., & Fanfarelli, J. R. (2023). Boundaries, Informed Consent, and Learning. In *Ethical Considerations of Virtual Reality in the College Classroom* (pp. 293–304). Routledge.

Kuhail, M. A., ElSayary, A., Farooq, S., & Alghamdi, A. (2022, September). Exploring immersive learning experiences: A survey. [). MDPI.]. *Informatics (MDPI)*, *9*(4), 75.

Makransky, G., & Petersen, G. B. (2021). The cognitive affective model of immersive learning (CAMIL): A theoretical research-based model of learning in immersive virtual reality. *Educational Psychology Review*, *33*(3), 937–958.

McCarrick, C. A., Moynihan, A., McEntee, P. D., Boland, P. A., Donnelly, S., Heneghan, H., & Cahill, R. A. (2025). Impact of simulation training on communication skills and informed consent practices in medical students-a randomised controlled trial. *BMC Medical Education*, *25*(1), 1078. PMID: 40682099

Muzata, A. R., Singh, G., Stepanov, M. S., & Musonda, I. (2024, November). Immersive learning: A systematic literature review on transforming engineering education through virtual reality. In *Virtual Worlds* (Vol. 3, No. 4, pp. 480-505). MDPI.

Mystakidis, S., & Lympouridis, V. (2024). Immersive Learning Design in the Metaverse: A Theoretical Literature Review Synthesis. *Application of the Metaverse in Education*, 55-71.

Obourdin, G., De Maeyer, S., & Van den Bossche, P. (2024). Unlocking the power of immersive learning: The FAIRI instructional design proposition for adaptive immersive virtual reality. *Computers & Education: X Reality*, *5*, 100084.

Perin, A., Galbiati, T. F., Ayadi, R., Gambatesa, E., Orena, E. F., Riker, N. I., & DiMeco, F. (2021). Informed consent through 3D virtual reality: A randomized clinical trial. *Acta Neurochirurgica*, *163*(2), 301–308. PMID: 32242272

Pitsikalis, S., Lasica, I. E., Kostas, A., & Vitsilaki, C. (2024). Educational Design Guidelines for Teaching with Immersive Technologies—Updating Learning Outcomes of the European Qualification Framework. *Trends in Higher Education*, *3*(4), 1091–1108.

Pratisto, E. H., Thompson, N., & Potdar, V. (2022). Immersive technologies for tourism: A systematic review. *Information Technology & Tourism*, *24*(2), 181–219.

Valluripally, S., Frailey, B., Kruse, B., Palipatana, B., Oruche, R., Gulhane, A., & Calyam, P. (2022). Detection of security and privacy attacks disrupting user immersive experience in virtual reality learning environments. *IEEE Transactions on Services Computing*, *16*(4), 2559–2574.

Weng, Y., Schmidt, M., Huang, W., & Hao, Y. (2024). The effectiveness of immersive learning technologies in K–12 English as second language learning: A systematic review. *ReCALL*, *36*(2), 210–229.

Yadav, A., & Reddy, K. N. (2024). Virtual Dilemmas: Legal and Ethical Rollercoasters in Immersive Tech Land. In *Multidisciplinary Applications of Extended Reality for Human Experience* (pp. 64-80). IGI Global.

Zhang, Y., Dewitt, D., & Cheah, K. S. (2025). Virtual Reality for Sustainable and Responsible Pedagogy in Art and Design Education: A Systematic Review of Motivation and Digital Leadership. *Cleaner and Responsible Consumption*, 100311.

Zhuang, Z. (2021). Interactive media information security immersive experience system based on virtual reality technology. *Journal of the Institution of Electronics and Telecommunication Engineers*, •••, 1–8.

KEY TERMS AND DEFINITIONS

Immersive Technologies: Digital systems such as virtual reality, augmented reality, and mixed reality that create multisensory, interactive environments simulating real or imagined experiences.

Virtual Reality: A fully computer-generated, three-dimensional environment that users can explore and interact with, typically through head-mounted displays, which replaces real-world input with digital sensory stimuli.

Augmented Reality: A technology that overlays digital content onto the physical world in real time, enhancing real-world experiences rather than replacing them.

Mixed Reality: A hybrid environment that blends physical and digital elements, allowing real and virtual objects to interact in real-time and space, often requiring more advanced spatial and sensor integration.

Behavioral Surveillance: The continuous monitoring and analysis of users' behaviors, actions, and responses—often in real time—using sensors, software, and algorithms to track engagement, attention, and emotional states.

Biometric Data: Physiological or behavioral characteristics unique to an individual, such as fingerprints, facial expressions, eye movement, voice patterns, or heart rate, collected to personalize or monitor interactions in immersive systems.

Informed Consent: A process through which users are made fully aware of and voluntarily agree to the data collection, processing, and potential consequences involved in using a digital system, ideally in a comprehensible and revocable manner.

Learner Autonomy: The capacity of learners to make independent, informed decisions about their educational experiences, including the ability to control their engagement with immersive technologies and the data they generate.

Algorithmic Bias: Systematic errors or unfair outcomes produced by AI or machine learning algorithms, often resulting from non-representative data or unexamined assumptions embedded in the system design.

Ethical Design: An approach to technology development that prioritizes values such as privacy, fairness, transparency, and inclusivity from the earliest stages of design, ensuring that systems are aligned with users' rights and social norms.

Data Ownership: The rights and control individuals or institutions have over the data they generate, including how it is stored, accessed, shared, and monetized.

Data Monetization: The process by which personal or behavioral data—collected through educational technologies—is used for financial gain, typically through analytics, product development, or third-party sales.

Governance Frameworks: Institutional and legal structures that oversee how technologies are developed and used, including policies, ethical guidelines, regulatory compliance, and accountability mechanisms.

Chapter 14
Data Security Risks in VR and AR: Challenges and Solutions

Zokir Mamadiyarov
Termez University of Economics and Service, Termez, Uzbekistan

Temur Eshchanov
Urgench State University, Uzbekistan

Barno Matchanova
Urgench State Pedagogical Institute, Uzbekistan

Munir Ahmad
https://orcid.org/0000-0003-4836-6151
Survey of Pakistan, Pakistan

ABSTRACT

This chapter examines the growing urgency of securing VR and AR environments as they become integral to healthcare, education, defense, and enterprise sectors. Immersive systems capture rich biometric, spatial, and behavioral data, creating complex vulnerabilities that challenge both digital security and user autonomy. While technologies like encryption, edge computing, and federated learning offer solutions, ethical and regulatory safeguards are equally vital. Emphasizing privacy-by-design and cross-disciplinary collaboration, the chapter outlines how immersive systems must balance seamless user experience with robust security to ensure a trustworthy and ethically sound digital future.

DOI: 10.4018/979-8-3373-4465-2.ch014

INTRODUCTION

The rising wave of immersive technologies, more specifically the combination of aspects of Virtual Reality (VR) and Augmented Reality (AR), is transforming how human beings relate to the digital world in various fields. Before being used by various industries and companies, VR/AR platforms were primarily associated with gaming and entertainment (Arena et al., 2022; Hamad & Jia, 2022; Rauschnabel et al., 2022; threekit, 2020; Wu et al., 2023). The systems promise unprecedented experiential realism within real-time to correlate environmental mapping with biometric feedback and behavioral modeling. But as the distinction between the physical and the online is growing thin, the distinction between the security of data and the privacy of the user is also being blurred. It is these abilities that immersive environments are so capable of: a constant user monitoring activity, sensitivity to context, and embodied interaction, which makes them so prone to new and transformed spoofing possibilities.

In contrast to conventional digital systems, where the user actions are discrete (i.e., clicks, typed text), VR/AR ecosystems receive high-resolution data streams. These would be any kind of biometric signals (e.g., heart rate, pupil dilation, gait patterns) (Parnandi & Gutierrez-Osuna, 2013; Ross et al., 2022; Yano et al., 2015), spatial and environmental mapping (e.g., room dimensions, object positioning), eye tracking (Adhanom et al., 2023), voice and gesture recognition (Fang & Wang, 2024), and behavioral responses (e.g., attention patterns or emotional state) (Feng et al., 2020; Neo et al., 2021). This is not just an increase in the amount of data but the opportunity to make more personal inferences about identity, psychological characteristics, and even the intent of individuals, since this information is more closely observed. This inevitably leads to a larger attack surface faced by malicious actors, particularly when such information is shared in the channel, deposited in centralized locations, or accessed by third-party programs.

It is high time to do something about these intangible risks. As immersive technologies are becoming part of the national infrastructure planning, battlefield training, telemedicine, and learning tools, the confidentiality, integrity, and ethical use of immersive information must be assured. This chapter begins with the mapping of the anatomy of the vulnerabilities peculiar to immersive systems and then proceed toward the solutions aimed at making VR/AR experiences engaging as well as resilient, secure, and privacy-conscious.

ANATOMY OF VULNERABILITIES IN IMMERSIVE SYSTEMS

VR and AR System Architecture

The technical design of VR and AR systems presents a very different and far more complex security paradigm compared to the traditional digital platforms, desktop applications, or mobile applications. In contrast to traditional systems that mainly use structured inputs such as keystrokes, clicks, and text fields, VR and AR systems interact through an ongoing high-fidelity exchange of multimodal sensory information. These systems run on a complex stack of hardware, sensor development, real-time signal processing, machine learning algorithms, and cloud processing, which have to effectively interact and enable the context-sensing, immersive experiences.

Operations of devices such as head-mounted display (HMD) and eye-tracking sensor, motion controller, depth camera, microphone, haptic gloves, and environmental mapping devices, such as LiDAR or SLAM (Simultaneous Localization and Mapping) devices, continuously track the physical condition of the user and his or her environment, and hardware-level solutions. These sensors take granular biometric data like pupil dilation, blink rate, heart rate variability, gesture dynamics, and spatial data like room dimensions, object position, and real-time user orientation (Al-Ansi et al., 2023; Krauß et al., 2021; Machala et al., 2022; Wang et al., 2021). Significantly, this data capture is usually involuntary and automatic, in the sense that the user does not actively choose to enter the information in question, which, in turn, increases its intrusive nature, as well as its sensitivity in terms of privacy.

After being taken, such multidimensional data is pre-reduced on the edge device (e.g., headset or mobile processor) to minimize latency and maximize responsiveness. Nonetheless, the computation required to support immersive analytics, including full-body-motion rendering, gaze prediction, and natural access to voice, is also intensive, requiring some of the data transfer to be conducted to the cloud or other remote computers to engage in further processing and machine learning inference. The resulting service capabilities, such as avatar realism or collaborative multi-user spaces, adaptive learning, or contextual AR overlay, are relatively new capabilities supported by these cloud services, but provided alongside new attack vectors, like vulnerable APIs, cloud configurations, or data-in-transit interception.

Besides, the fact that its functionality has to be based on wireless connecting protocols, e.g., Wi-Fi, Bluetooth, 5G, etc., adds an extra layer of vulnerabilities at the network tier. Man-in-the-middle attacks, spoofing, or packet sniffing are possible with man-in-the-middle targets when shared networks or insecure networks are used (Fereidouni et al., 2025; Muzammil et al., 2024). Also, a lot of XR apps involve the use of third-party SDKs and plug-in functionalities, which may add to the attack surface, especially when they are not thoroughly vetted securely (Abraham et al., 2022).

Table 1. Immersive system threat vector matrix

Attack Vector	Target Layer	Example Tactics	Potential Impact	Detection/Prevention Methods
Spoofing	Application Layer	Synthetic biometric input, replay attacks	Unauthorized access, impersonation	Multi-factor behavioral biometrics, liveness detection
Session Hijacking	Network/Transport Layer	Token theft via insecure Wi-Fi or Bluetooth	Real-time control of avatars, eavesdropping	Encrypted session tokens, short-lived credentials
Man-in-the-Middle	Network Layer	Interception of data between the device and the server	Data leakage, content injection, and control manipulation	End-to-end encryption (e.g., SRTP, TLS), mutual authentication
Hardware Tampering	Device/Physical Layer	Firmware manipulation, rogue sensors, unauthorized implants	Silent data exfiltration, persistent compromise	Secure boot, firmware attestation, tamper-evident casing
Sensor Spoofing	Sensor Input Layer	Fake inputs to depth cameras, motion sensors	Misleading system behaviors, disorientation, and false alerts	Sensor fusion validation, anomaly detection, and trusted hardware
Avatar Hijacking	Social/UX Layer	Taking control of user identity in collaborative VR spaces	Social engineering, trust violation, reputation damage	Behavioral signature matching, continuous re-authentication
Attack Vector	Target Layer	Example Tactics	Potential Impact	Detection/Prevention Methods

Continuous and Passive Nature of Data

The imminent problem in securing immersive systems is due to the ongoing, passive, and high-fidelity data collection of leaking information that is inherent in VR and AR environments (Gomes et al., 2021; Hutson & Hutson, 2024). Compared to conventional applications, where user activities are usually discrete (e.g., pressing a button or typing text) and happen only in clearly defined time intervals, immersive technologies are optimized to continuously sense users as they are always on. These platforms monitor user movement, facial proportions, speech, location, and environmental variations in real-time to provide synchronic responsiveness in the interaction of both parties (Krome & Kopp, 2023; Lee et al., 2021; Rubin, 2024). When this happens, users are left in the dark about just how much data is being tracked and how much developers are not aware of what uninterrupted surveillance means. This paradigm exponentially increases the attack surface, as every sensor, communication network, software dependency, or connection point may invite an attacker's exploitation. The scale of the information, including physical biometrics, spatial scans, and inferred behavioral patterns, provides more possibilities to burglars not just to take the information, but also to alter or masquerade as the user.

In the spoofing attacks, an attacker steals a biometric system by replicating or playing back communications, like the replication of hand gestures, using artificial voice commands, or the playback of eye movement patterns, to fool the system into allowing admission (Valluripally et al., 2023). As an example, say a system requires gaze-tracking or hand geometry in order to be granted permission to take an action; a good hacker can input synthetic or stored responses into the system so that it can pretend to be a bona fide user. In XR, spoofing is even more threatening since a number of platforms make use of implicit authentication, where the system identifies itself by behavior as opposed to passwords or tokens.

Another dreadful area of threat is session hijacking, which is a great concern, especially under multi-user virtual reality environments where avatars engage in real time. In situations where the headset of a user is linked via an unsafely Wi-Fi or Bluetooth connection, a hacker might capture session tokens, or even send forged packets containing them (Asif et al., 2024; Baldoni & Kavari, 2025; Frankl, 2024). This enables the adversary to hijack it and control the user session, modify their operational environment, or even pose as the user to them in group virtual meetings or collaborative design environments. These cyberattacks are very dangerous as they not only violate the privacy of information but also reduce social collaboration and trust in immersive media.

Almost concomitant with the aforementioned risk is the possibility of man-in-the-middle (MTI) attacks, in which the attacker inserts themselves between the XR device and backend servers, including cloud-based rendering engines and other real-time analytics platforms (Fereidouni et al., 2025; Mohamed & Ahmed, 2024; Salem et al., 2022). Here, the hacker can monitor data streams, steal sensitive data (such as spatial maps of someone's home), or even inject objectionable content (altered 3D objects, misleading audio cues, or controlled avatar actions). When perception determines cognition, as in immersive environments, as little as a small distortion creates disorienting and potentially hazardous effects, such as in training simulations or medical AR.

The most difficult to detect and most dangerous is the hardware-level tempering (Yekollu et al., 2024; Zhang et al., 2023). VR/AR devices develop frequently without the physical security that might have been on an enterprise-grade server or mobile phone. With physical access, an attacker may be able to alter firmware on sensors, put rogue tracking chips on them, or install rootkits that log or inject information into sensor data in a stealthy fashion. To give an example: a depth camera hacked into can leak environmental scans to the outside world, or haptic feedback can provide false information or coerce a user through its manipulation of firmware. This level of compromise may be below the operating system and may bypass the detection altogether, hence making it very difficult to detect and rectify.

Collectively, these sets of attack vectors point out the unprecedented combination of digital, physical, and behavioral vulnerabilities in XR systems. Since immersive environments involve real-world motion and space as part of the computing loop, a compromise is not only technical in nature; it is embodied, possibly impacting the perceptions, emotions, and even the physical safety of the users. Combining classic cybersecurity with cutting-edge biometric integrity verification, anomaly-based detection, tamper-resistant hardware design, and contextual user authentication processes, in a way that does not compromise the UN-surpassed immersive fidelity that the XR experiences are characterized by, requires a new generation of security measures to address this sort of threat.

In an adversarial VR game study by Nair et al., (2023), researchers showed that within minutes of gameplay, an adversarial program accurately inferred dozens of personal attributes (e.g., height, age, wingspan), revealing how motion-based inputs can expose sensitive data through behavioral inference. Additionally, Yang et al., (2024) demonstrated that an attacker observing avatar movements in a shared VR environment could recover sensitive inputs, such as keystrokes, which implies that even hand motion data can be reverse-engineered for identity or credential theft.. Examples like this point to the fact that security in immersive systems needs to be more than just the standard firewalls and anti-virus measures. Due to the more radically interconnected and sensor-manufactured nature of VR/AR devices, there are more ways they can be compromised; not only at the local data capturing level, but the cloud-based inference models. The response to these threats, therefore, needs thorough knowledge of the entire system stack with a view to finding the technical and human-oriented vulnerabilities and identifying the threats before they are transferred into real-life deployments. These vulnerabilities are not only raising ethical and policy issues, but also creating the feasibility of providing some technological protection to the immersive ecosystems with current and emerging technologies. Figure 1 illustrates the layered structure of immersive system vulnerabilities, organizing threats according to their point of origin, ranging from physical hardware to high-level user interaction.

Figure 1. Multi-layer threat taxonomy for immersive systems

ETHICAL AND REGULATORY CHALLENGES IN IMMERSIVE DATA PRIVACY

Both VR and AR technologies are no longer in their infancy stage, and the matter of data security is no longer seen as a completely technical issue, as it overlaps significantly with the perspectives of ethics, upon user rights, and regulation. Immersive environments exist within an area where behavioral, personal, and environmental information are integrated in real time. This convergence is creating a different breed of sensitive information. This type of information is highly intimate, constant, and context-aware, information that breaks the existing paradigm of privacy, consent, and data control. The data being shared inside VR/AR systems is the real world, biometric data, and even subconscious actions, which can make the systems an unprecedented source of highly personal data, unlike traditional digital platforms, where transactions are usually abstract (e.g., usernames, search queries, etc) (El-Hajj, 2024).

One of the greatest immediate questions of ethical concern in immersive technologies is who owns biometric and environmental information. Who is the owner of the real-time streams of data that can be gathered by body movements, facial expressions, tones, and vocal pitch, and direction of the gaze? What of environmental scans that take the images of the interiors of personal homes or offices? (Liyanaarachchi et al., 2024; Magee et al., 2024; Murala & Panda, 2023; Partarakis & Zabulis, 2024)This information is automatically gathered in most of the existing implementations by device manufacturers or other application developers, frequently in proprietary cloud infrastructures. Such control imbalance, in which users possess little knowledge or control about how their signals in closest areas are collected and their potential applications, evokes apprehensions of autonomy, online exploitation, spatial and bodily commodification. What is even worse, biometric information cannot be renewed: once it is hacked, you cannot be able to update your heartbeat rhythm or camera photo in your eye.

Consent in the context of immersive environments is also more complex, essential to the core, than in the context of web-based systems (Magee et al., 2024). Interactions in the VR/AR are usually liquid and ambient, and no active user-initiation of data collection is necessary, i.e., the user does not have to opt in. One might join a virtual meeting room or a communal AR workspace without knowing that his or her movement, accent, or eye movements are being recorded, illuminated, or saved. More conventional models of consent (pop-up agreements, check boxes, etc) are ineffective in immersive experiences where they are all paid and engaged. In addition, transparency is even more difficult to achieve: how are the developers going to keep the user informed at all times of what information is being collected and used, without it affecting the immersion? This gives rise to a situation where informed consent is performative or completely passed over, thus resulting in a high ethical blind spot. Table 2 highlights key categories of data collected in VR/AR environments.

Table 2. Regulatory coverage gaps for immersive data types

Data Type in VR/AR	Collected Via	Current Regulatory Coverage	Limitations/Gaps
Biometric Data (e.g., eye movement, gait, heart rate)	Sensors in HMDs, wearable devices	Partially under GDPR, HIPAA (if health-related)	Unclear coverage if collected for non-medical use (e.g., gaming, interaction)
Gaze Tracking & Facial Expression	Eye-tracking cameras, facial sensors	Not explicitly addressed	Can infer attention, emotions, and psychological state; no clear protections.
Spatial Mapping & Environmental Scans	Depth sensors, SLAM, LiDAR	Unregulated or weakly regulated	May capture private home interiors, third parties, or sensitive surroundings
Voice & Gesture Recognition Data	Microphones, motion sensors	GDPR (General Data)	Limited user control or awareness of persistent passive collection
Emotional & Behavioral Inference	ML models analyzing interaction patterns	Not covered by most frameworks	Intention prediction or emotional profiling lacks transparency or user oversight.
Location and Movement Trails	IMUs, GPS, and indoor localization systems	GDPR (location data), sectoral laws	Aggregated patterns reveal routines and identity; opt-out mechanisms are weak.

Regulatory and legal environments are finding it challenging to keep abreast with the peculiarities of immersive technologies based on the data protection systems that have been in place. Events such as the General Data Protection Regulation (GDPR) and the Health Insurance Portability and Accountability Act (HIPAA) were not formulated to capture spatial, biometric, and emotional data (Francesca, 2019; Li et al., 2019; Lutkevich, 2019). The existing regulation, e.g., GDPR, requires explicit consent and even a so-called right to be forgotten, yet it does not specify the application of these concepts to persistent biometric sensing in the XR environments. Regarding data related to health, HIPAA can take care of such data, whereas the physiological data, which is obtained by using a fitness-based VR app that works on the basis of heart rates, or body temperatures, and is used to gamify the interactions, may not fall under the protection of HIPAA. Moreover, immersive systems can be particularly characterized by cross-border data that can act as another jurisdictional issue in protecting the rights of the individual to control the privacy of their data when, through storage or analysis, that data is held by another country.

Adding to this are the new power asymmetries that have emerged. The companies that control VR/AR ecosystems are large tech companies that dictate the terms when it comes to the collection and processing of data and subsequent monetization. This establishes monopolistic pressures that can make users and minor developers extremely weak in terms of negotiation. Without specifically designed regulation, the immersive technology environment risks turning into a realm where the surveillance capitalism phenomenon not only would not be curbed but would be enhanced. To fill these ethical and regulatory gaps is necessary to reconsider privacy and consent concepts in spatial computing. And this should involve bringing dynamic consent to immersive spaces and integrating transparency into user interfaces that do not interfere with the flow-designing mechanisms, so that users can control and audit their immersive data, and advocating regulatory changes that directly reflect the behavioral and biometric characteristics of XR data. Figure 2 illustrates how data flows through a typical XR ecosystem, pinpointing where control is lost and consent mechanisms are often absent or insufficient.

Figure 2. Data control and consent breakdown in XR ecosystems

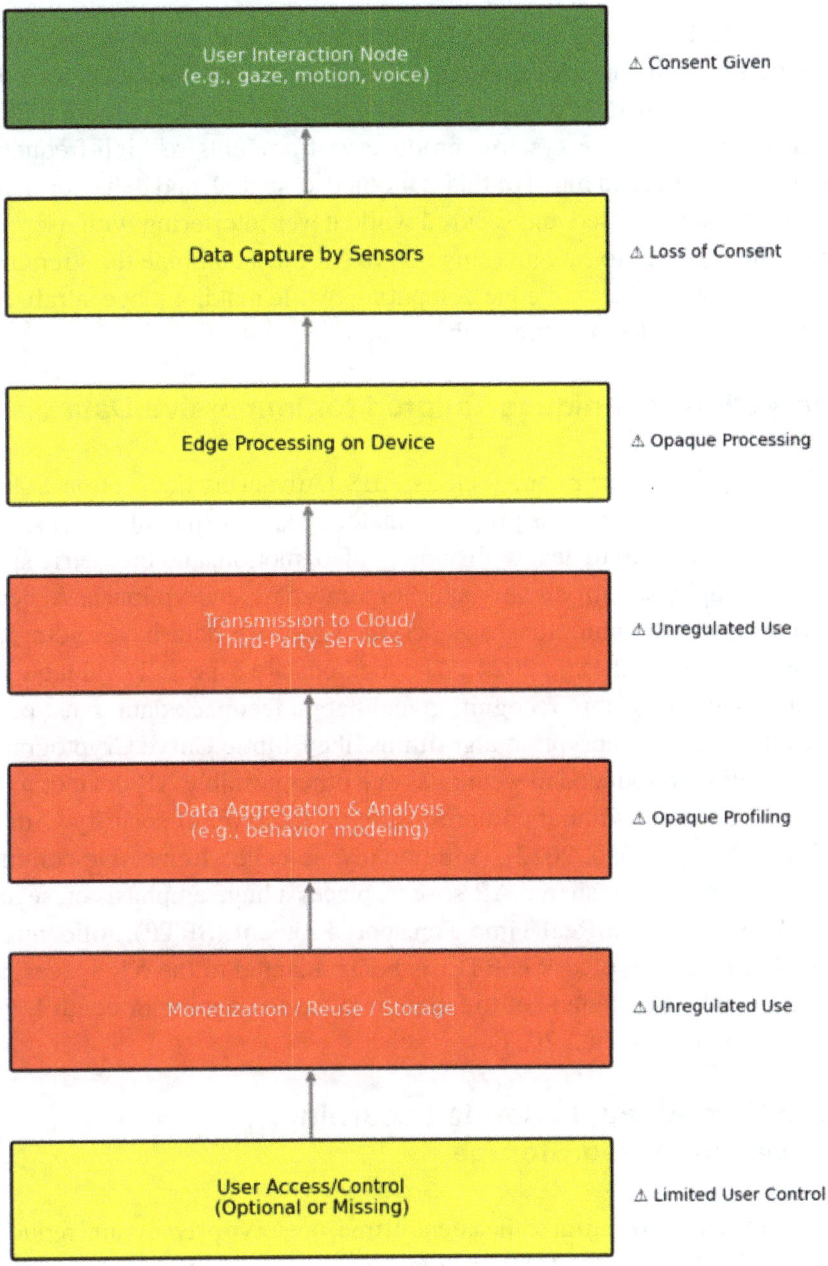

CURRENT AND EMERGING SECURITY SOLUTIONS

To meet the increasing risk of attacks on VR and AR systems, scientists and engineers have already developed a series of security solutions that respond to the specificity of immersive data and actuality. In comparison to a more traditional web application, immersive systems produce vast amounts of high-frequency, multi-dimensional data, and much of this is biometric, spatial, and behavioral information that has to be processed and secured while never interfering with user experience. The right approach to safeguarding in VR/AR must combine the strength of crypto and the resourcefulness of edge computing, while making it decentralized and able to learn how to adapt to unfavorable conditions.

Encryption Techniques Tailored for Immersive Data

More typical encryption, such as AES (Advanced Encryption Standard) and RSA, is being used, but it is proposed that low latency in context-sensitive encryptions may be needed to deal with audio, video, motion, and biometric applications. As an example, stream ciphers and homomorphic encryption have been used to provide secure computations on encrypted sensory data by avoiding sensitivity to the raw inputs (El-Hajj, 2024). The methods are especially valuable when gaze tracking data, or gesture recognition and haptic feedback data, must be processed in real time. Light encryption algorithms like Elliptic Curve Cryptography (ECC) are also being introduced in wearables and other portable XR devices to reduce the processing burden without compromising on the level of security (Adeniyi et al., 2024; X. Yang & Gao, 2022). Additionally, so-called immersive communication, i.e., multi-user VR or shared AR spaces, places a huge emphasis on secure session management. Secure Real-Time Transport Protocol (SRTP), following the work on end-to-end encrypted WebRTC, is being adapted to the XR spaces, so that the streams can be fine-tuned not to fall prey to eavesdropping or control (Gortázar et al., 2022; Rasanen et al., 2021).

Edge Computing, Federated Learning, and Decentralized Storage

In an attempt to minimize the latency time, preserve privacy, and reduce exposure to centralized attacks, VR/AR systems are migrating toward edge computing and federated learning. In such systems, sensitive information (gestures by the user or scans of the immediate environmental surroundings) can be processed at the IoT device or proxy nodes, and very limited raw data needs to be sent to the cloud. As an example, algorithms of pose estimation may be performed on the headset itself, and only aggregate or anonymized metrics may be transferred outside.

Federated learning provides a highly promising paradigm for immersive applications (Bashir et al., 2023; T. Zhang et al., 2022). It allows VR/AR devices to collaboratively learn AI and not centralize raw data. This technically translates to biometrics and behavioral data of millions of users being able to make systems smarter without breaking down the privacy of any individual user--which is vital to the healthcare or defense-related areas of XR applications. Work is already underway on projects such as Google TensorFlow Federated and Syft, which are attempting to adapt the models to edge-based XR.

In the meantime, blockchain and peer-to-peer protocols of decentralized storage (e.g., IPFS – Inter Planetary File System) provide an alternative to the centralized data stores, which are more susceptible to attacks (Huynh-The et al., 2023; Uddin et al., 2024). Such architectures not only increase data integrity and transparency but also grant power to the users to control access permissions. Immersive data would enable users to keep control of their spatial and biometric data by coupling self-sovereign identity (SSI) frameworks and decentralized identifiers (DIDs).

Real-Time Anomaly Detection in Immersive Behavior

In addition to the protection of data at rest and during transmission, immersive systems need to intercept malicious activities and anomalous patterns happening in real-time. Sophisticated behavioral anomaly-detecting algorithms have been in development, typically driven by AI, to keep track of user interaction, avatar movements, and session dynamics, being used to spot inconsistencies. Such systems are capable of picking up anomalies like avatar hijacking, anomalous motion patterns, gaze interference, or unauthorized access patterns in collaborative VR environments.

In the above, we could see a real-time threat detection engine used to monitor the movement normal signature of a user in VR and raise alerts when that signature is changed abruptly, indicating a spoofing or unauthorized control. In the same manner, authorship behavioral biometrics in the form of continuous authentication (e.g., typing cadence, gaze flow, and speech rhythm) can be used to keep sessions secure beyond initial login. This type of constantly changing security stance is essential in circumstances where conventional credentials have not been implemented, and the environment handled in terms of the user presence only exists virtually.

To put it into practice, companies are integrating AI-powered security measures into XR SDKs and engines (e.g., Unity, Unreal Engine) (Berrezueta-Guzman & Wagner, 2025). These modules work smoothly in combination with immersive content, giving the user a chance of having background monitoring without tampering with the content. Concurrently, immersive cybersecurity research considers visual or tactile feedback that can warn users of the threat wherever they are in the real sense -it makes threat awareness even when the virtual environment is very engaging. Collectively, these security innovations represent a paradigm shift based on reactive protection to the use of proactively and adaptive defense in XR ecosystems. This combination of encryption, edge intelligence, decentralized architecture, and AI-driven anomaly detection forms a stronger base on par with the special requirements of immersive technologies. Table 3 shows how technical innovations enhance trust and integrity in VR/AR ecosystems, whereas Figure 3 visualizes a multi-layered security architecture for VR/AR platforms.

Table 3. Security solutions mapped to immersive risk domains

Security Solution	Targeted Risk/ Vulnerability	Immersive Context	Key Advantage
Stream/Lightweight Encryption (e.g., ECC, SRTP)	Data interception, MITM attacks	Real-time audio, video, and biometric streaming	Maintains performance while securing dynamic data
Homomorphic Encryption	Data misuse during cloud-based computation	Biometric or gaze-based analytics	Enables secure processing without exposing raw data
Edge Computing	Latency, excessive cloud exposure	On-device gesture tracking, room scanning	Limits data transmission; preserves local privacy
Federated Learning	Centralized model training on sensitive data	Cross-user behavior modeling, personalization	Enhances AI utility while protecting user-level data
Decentralized Storage (e.g., IPFS, Blockchain)	Centralized data breaches, unauthorized access	Cross-platform identity/data sync	Offers transparency, tamper resistance, and user control
Real-Time Anomaly Detection	Avatar hijacking, spoofing, and abnormal interaction patterns	Collaborative VR sessions, virtual workspaces	Enables immediate threat identification
Continuous Behavioral Authentication	Session hijacking, identity spoofing	Identity verification in immersive interactions	Authenticates passively, preserving immersion

Figure 3. Layered security architecture for immersive systems

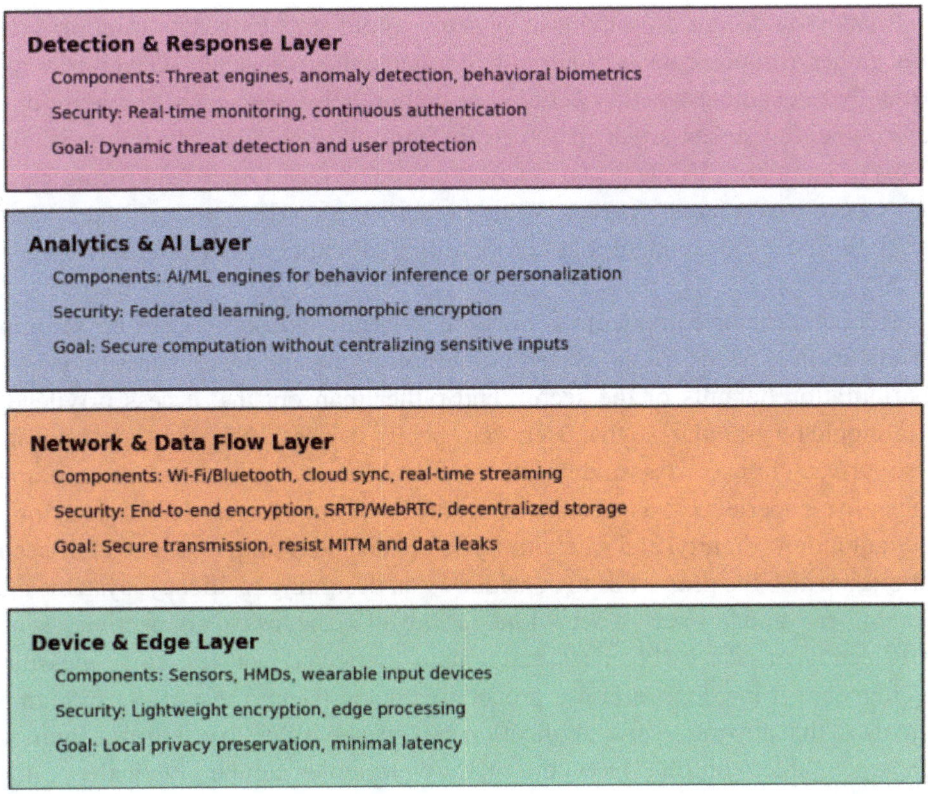

DESIGNING RESILIENT AND PRIVACY-FIRST IMMERSIVE SYSTEMS

This is the case, given that as immersive technologies enter the mainstream channels, ensuring security and privacy during the design phase could prove to be very important now more than ever before in the history of the technologies. This very ubiquitous and sensor-heavy aspect of VR/AR requires an active transition of defenses, which are historically more reactive and after-the-fact, to privacy-by-design, a process of proactively hiding problems before they get to the consumer. This not only entails using security tools but also takes a broader approach in which ethical standards, user rights, and the ability to withstand attacks are considered as an indispensable part of the construction process.

Immersive Development Privacy by Design Principles

Privacy-by-design in immersive systems would start with data minimization - only gather as much data as required to complete the experience. Developers must critically re-examine whether detailed or comprehensive scans of the body or the environment are necessary at all for certain features, or whether fuzzier or disguised forms of input are sufficient. An example would be that, rather than recording raw data of eye movements, systems would be able to record generalized measures of attention that indicate intent, but not identity (Qayyum et al., 2024; Sharma et al., 2025).

The other major component is the default security posture. Uses of XR applications include needs for encrypted communications and local data storage, with configuration defaults of the secure end rather than opt-ins; access privilege to data should be granular, so that users can specify its uses, recipients, and purposes. Also, privacy impact assessments (PIAs) must become the norm when developing immersive experiences, as an evaluation of the effect of each design decision on user autonomy, dignity, and safety must be conducted. Failure-safe and fail-secure actions are also the properties to consider when designing resiliency: systems must have fail-safe and fail-secure behaviors, react well to the loss of connectivity, sensor malfunction, or security breaches, and remain unaffected by them. This necessitates interdependent incident response procedures, local backup instances, and tamper signals so that any immersive application can resist both inadvertent and attempted sabotage. Table 4 outlines how core privacy principles can be practically realized in XR platforms through development tools, security mechanisms, and design strategies, whereas Figure 4 illustrates a privacy-by-design lifecycle tailored to immersive system development.

Table 4. Privacy-by-design principles and implementation in immersive systems

Privacy Principle	Immersive Application Context	Implementation Tools/Mechanisms
Data Minimization	Avoid unnecessary biometric/ spatial tracking	Adjustable sensor sensitivity, abstracted gaze data, and local filtering
Security by Default	Encrypt data from sensors by default	ECC, SRTP, on-device encryption modules
User Consent and Control	Allow granular permissions for data sharing	Voice/gaze-controlled privacy settings, contextual permission prompts
Transparency and Awareness	Communicate data usage without breaking immersion	AR overlays, ambient cues, just-in-time consent notifications
Privacy Embedded in Design	Integrate privacy checks into development workflows	Privacy SDKs, embedded PIAs, privacy champions in dev teams

continued on following page

Table 4. Continued

Privacy Principle	Immersive Application Context	Implementation Tools/Mechanisms
Resilience to Breach	Secure fallback during system failure	Offline local modes, tamper detection, secure error handling
Accountability and Governance	Enable auditability and compliance across systems	Activity logs, self-sovereign identity systems, and decentralized ID

Figure 4. Privacy-by-design lifecycle in immersive system development

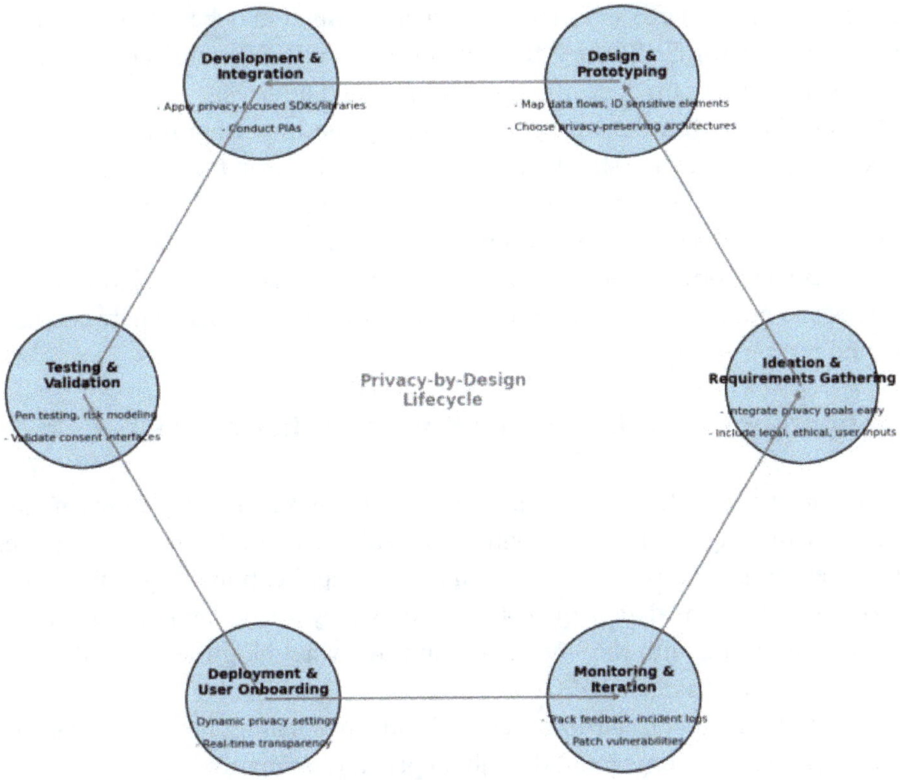

Promotion of cross-disciplinary cooperation

To make immersive systems truly privacy-first, it does not suffice to connect technical and non-technical proponents. The same issue should be co-designed by developers, UI/UX designers, hardware experts, lawyers, ethicists, and cybersecurity experts, aiming at developing solutions prepared based on both technical and ethical considerations. Take the example of the consents: designers can assist in making them more visually appealing and understandable by trying different ways, color-coded overlays or haptic feedback; all the legal advisors would have to ensure that the interfaces do not violate the data protection laws, both in the geographic region and internationally (Bhaskaran & Mahbub, 2024).

Security must also be incorporated in the design activities and prevailing tooling frameworks. Such platforms as Unity and Unreal Engine must integrate privacy-friendly SDKs or plug-ins to enable these developers to apply encryption, permission gating, or identity verification without having to possess advanced knowledge. Also, common standards in immersive privacy, which may be established by such organizations as IEEE, ISO, or XR Safety Initiative (XRSI), could facilitate interoperability and similar practices across platforms and devices.

Collegiality within the workplace also plays an important role. A member of immersive product teams should take upon themselves the title of a privacy champion, who can be trained in privacy engineering and ethical impact, and can help make decisions about the product throughout its life cycle. Such champions serve as in-house supporters who provide reviews, trade-offs, and mediation to enable services and goods to encounter problems that result in a balance between innovation and responsibility.

Transparency and User Education in XR Interfaces

An immersive system can be the most technically secure, but fail when the user is unaware of dangers or fails to control themselves. Thus, transparency and teaching to the user should be a part of the immersive application design. This includes information about the data being gathered, how they are being processed, and kept without interfering with the immersion and overwhelming the user (Maathuis & Datcu, 2025; Taninaka et al., 2025).

In place of the frozen "terms of service" hidden in menus, developers can powerfully bring up just-in-time reminders about privacy, interactive privacy dashboards, or even informative walkthroughs that can show their users how their data flows in an obvious and understandable way. The user in a given virtual meeting room may get an ambient visual notification of what participants are recording, which sensors are operational, and how long their interaction logs are to be kept. It is also key to make users able to act instead of making decisions. Users must be capable of adjusting the privacy levels in a convenient way during the onboarding and changing the settings throughout the interaction. Access to spatial space, audio recordings, or biometric data should be configurable by gestures, speech, or eye gaze, which are already built into XR systems.

Last, immersive developers could consider doing away with a culture of secrecy by being open about shortcomings. In a situation where full anonymity or security is not possible (such as in multi-user systems), strong notification about this and compensatory measures (such as pseudonymization or activity minimization) should be provided. The development of VR/AR resilient and privacy-conscious systems is an inter-dimensional problem that combines architecture, culture, and accountability. Incorporating privacy as a value proposition, scientific interdisciplinary design procedures, and providing the user with clarity and control, stakeholders can develop immersive ecosystems, which are not only captivating but also reliable in terms of being ethically and technically trustworthy. As immersive technologies achieve scale, these principles can be critical to ensuring long-term viability and adequate trust of the technologies in the eyes of the population.

CONCLUSION

Since virtual and augmented reality technologies have grown to be an innovative thing in healthcare, education, defense, enterprise environments, and other fields, the issue of securing immersive environments becomes very urgent and hard to manage. This chapter has examined how these VR/AR platforms have data ecosystems that are far more prone to potential security vulnerability points and ethical exploitation because, compared to traditional data-driven models, their ecosystems are covered in biometric, spatial, and behavioral information. Weaknesses seen in immersive systems range all the way back to spoofing attacks and session hijacking to the use of unauthorized biometric profiling, and impact both digital integrity and the individual autonomy and dignity of the users.

The security solutions discussed consist of an advanced encryption protocol, edge computing, federated learning, and real-time behavioral anomaly detection, and provide a powerful set of tools to alleviate these risks. Nevertheless, technical solutions are not enough. A safe, immersive experience has to be ethically built in, having transparency, control of users, and regulatory compliance. This requires a proactive, user-oriented, and reactive privacy-by-design philosophy to change threat models privacy-by-design philosophy. Cross-disciplinary collaboration is equally necessary, in which engineers, ethicists, legal minds, designers, and users collaborate to develop schemas that defend immersive spaces without eroding their functionality and level of realism.

One of the major aspects in this chapter is the balance between the immersion of the user and data security. Excessive security of an XR system might interfere with the interaction with fluids, its functionality, or even annoy the audience, whereas failure to sufficiently secure an XR system can result in its abuse, spying, and a lack of confidence in institutions. Immersive computing can exist or not depending on the attainment of this balance - to build systems that are both effortless to work with and feel, and, at the same time, are safe, transparent, and answerable.

The Key Stakeholders' Recommendations

- To Developers: Build in privacy and security at the low level. Apply SDKs and continuous threat modeling procedures, and have the users collaboratively design the control interfaces, which should be user-friendly and robust.
- To Regulators: Design immersive-specific data protection frameworks, which consider novel forms of data that exist: a pattern of gaze, a scan of space, and emotional inference. XR applications are mandated to have explainability of the mandate and transparency of consent.
- Researchers: Examine how paradigms of adaptive security may change in a real-time context, test the ethics of extended data capture in immersive technologies, and measure the levels of user perception and belief in XR security interfaces.

In the medium term, when XR technologies become full-body immersive, brain computer interfaces, and AI personalized, this aspect of going deeper can only increase. Therefore, the challenge of immersive ecosystems security is dynamic rather than fixed. Stakeholders can make the immersive future more than technically brilliant by balancing both innovation and ethics and regulation in ensuring that the city of the future is as safe and natural as it should be.

REFERENCES

Abraham, M., Saeghe, P., McGill, M., & Khamis, M. (2022). Implications of XR on Privacy, Security and Behaviour: Insights from Experts. *ACM International Conference Proceeding Series*. https://doi.org/DOI: 10.1145/3546155.3546691

Adeniyi, A. E., Jimoh, R. G., & Awotunde, J. B. (2024). A systematic review on elliptic curve cryptography algorithm for internet of things: Categorization, application areas, and security. *Computers & Electrical Engineering*, *118*, 109330. DOI: 10.1016/J.COMPELECENG.2024.109330

Adhanom, I. B., MacNeilage, P., & Folmer, E. (2023). Eye Tracking in Virtual Reality: A Broad Review of Applications and Challenges. *Virtual Reality (Waltham Cross)*, *27*(2). Advance online publication. DOI: 10.1007/s10055-022-00738-z PMID: 37621305

Al-Ansi, A. M., Jaboob, M., Garad, A., & Al-Ansi, A. (2023). Analyzing augmented reality (AR) and virtual reality (VR) recent development in education. *Social Sciences & Humanities Open*, *8*(1), 100532. DOI: 10.1016/J.SSAHO.2023.100532

Arena, F., Collotta, M., Pau, G., & Termine, F. (2022). An Overview of Augmented Reality. In *Computers* (Vol. 11, Issue 2). https://doi.org/DOI: 10.3390/computers11020028

Asif, A. U. Z., Sridhar, M., Ray, I., & Ortega, F. R. (2024). Breaking the Virtual Barrier of Exploit Chain Attacks in XR Systems. *Proceedings - 2024 IEEE International Symposium on Mixed and Augmented Reality Adjunct, ISMAR-Adjunct 2024*, 32–34. https://doi.org/DOI: 10.1109/ISMAR-ADJUNCT64951.2024.00017

Baldoni, S., & Kavari, A. (2025). *Security challenges for immersive media: threats and possible mitigations*. https://thesis.unipd.it/handle/20.500.12608/89886

Bashir, A. K., Victor, N., Bhattacharya, S., Huynh-The, T., Chengoden, R., Yenduri, G., Maddikunta, P. K. R., Pham, Q. V., Gadekallu, T. R., & Liyanage, M. (2023). Federated Learning for the Healthcare Metaverse: Concepts, Applications, Challenges, and Future Directions. *IEEE Internet of Things Journal*, *10*(24), 21873–21891. DOI: 10.1109/JIOT.2023.3304790

Berrezueta-Guzman, S., & Wagner, S. (2025). Immersive Multiplayer VR: Unreal Engine's Strengths, Limitations, and Future Prospects. *IEEE Access : Practical Innovations, Open Solutions*, *13*, 85597–85612. DOI: 10.1109/ACCESS.2025.3570166

Bhaskaran, V., & Mahbub, U. (2024). Immersive User Experiences: Trends and Challenges of Using XR Technologies. *Computer Vision: Challenges, Trends, and Opportunities*, 260–278. https://doi.org//DOI: 10.1201/9781003328957-12

El-Hajj, M. (2024). Cybersecurity and Privacy Challenges in Extended Reality: Threats, Solutions, and Risk Mitigation Strategies. *Virtual Worlds 2025, Vol. 4, Page 1, 4*(1), 1. https://doi.org/DOI: 10.3390/VIRTUALWORLDS4010001

Fang, K., & Wang, J. (2024). Interactive Design With Gesture and Voice Recognition in Virtual Teaching Environments. *IEEE Access : Practical Innovations, Open Solutions, 12*. Advance online publication. DOI: 10.1109/ACCESS.2023.3348846

Feng, Z., González, V. A., Amor, R., Spearpoint, M., Thomas, J., Sacks, R., Lovreglio, R., & Cabrera-Guerrero, G. (2020). An immersive virtual reality serious game to enhance earthquake behavioral responses and post-earthquake evacuation preparedness in buildings. *Advanced Engineering Informatics, 45*. Advance online publication. DOI: 10.1016/j.aei.2020.101118

Fereidouni, H., Fadeitcheva, O., & Zalai, M. (2025). IoT and Man-in-the-Middle Attacks. *Security and Privacy, 8*(2), e70016. DOI: 10.1002/SPY2.70016

Francesca, T. (2019). *Comparing privacy laws: GDPR v. CCPA*. https://futurium.ec.europa.eu/en/european-ai-alliance/open-library/comparing-privacy-laws-gdpr-v-ccpa

Frankl, D. (2024). *Exploring Security Weaknesses in VR Systems*. https://oda.uni-obuda.hu/handle/20.500.14044/25947

Gomes, P. V., Marques, A., Donga, J., Sá, C., Correia, A., & Pereira, J. (2021). Adaptive Model for Biofeedback Data Flows Management in the Design of Interactive Immersive Environments. *Applied Sciences 2021, Vol. 11, Page 5067, 11*(11), 5067. https://doi.org/DOI: 10.3390/APP11115067

Gortázar, F., Gallego, M., Maes-Bermejo, M., Chicano-Capelo, I., & Santos, C. (2022). Cost-effective load testing of WebRTC applications. *Journal of Systems and Software, 193*. Advance online publication. DOI: 10.1016/j.jss.2022.111439

Hamad, A., & Jia, B. (2022). How Virtual Reality Technology Has Changed Our Lives: An Overview of the Current and Potential Applications and Limitations. In *International Journal of Environmental Research and Public Health* (Vol. 19, Issue 18). https://doi.org/DOI: 10.3390/ijerph191811278

Hutson, J., & Hutson, P. (2024). Immersive Technologies. *Inclusive Smart Museums*, 153–228. https://doi.org/DOI: 10.1007/978-3-031-43615-4_5

Huynh-The, T., Gadekallu, T. R., Wang, W., Yenduri, G., Ranaweera, P., Pham, Q. V., da Costa, D. B., & Liyanage, M. (2023). Blockchain for the metaverse: A Review. *Future Generation Computer Systems, 143*. Advance online publication. DOI: 10.1016/j.future.2023.02.008

Krauß, V., Boden, A., Oppermann, L., & Reiners, R. (2021). Current practices, challenges, and design implications for collaborative ar/vr application development. *Conference on Human Factors in Computing Systems - Proceedings*. https://doi.org/DOI: 10.1145/3411764.3445335

Krome, N., & Kopp, S. (2023). Towards Real-time Co-speech Gesture Generation in Online Interaction in Social XR. *Proceedings of the 23rd ACM International Conference on Intelligent Virtual Agents, IVA 2023*. https://doi.org/DOI: 10.1145/3570945.3607315

Lee, J. H., Ostwald, M. J., & Kim, A. M. J. (2021). Characterizing Smart Environments as Interactive and Collective Platforms: A Review of the Key Behaviors of Responsive Architecture. *Sensors 2021, Vol. 21, Page 3417, 21*(10), 3417. https://doi.org/DOI: 10.3390/S21103417

Li, H., Yu, L., & He, W. (2019). The Impact of GDPR on Global Technology Development. In *Journal of Global Information Technology Management* (Vol. 22, Issue 1). https://doi.org/DOI: 10.1080/1097198X.2019.1569186

Liyanaarachchi, G., Viglia, G., & Kurtaliqi, F. (2024). Privacy in hospitality: Managing biometric and biographic data with immersive technology. *International Journal of Contemporary Hospitality Management, 36*(11), 3823–3840. DOI: 10.1108/IJCHM-06-2023-0861

Lutkevich, B. (2019). What is HIPAA (Health Insurance Portability and Accountability Act)? In *WhatIs.com*.

Maathuis, C., & Datcu, D. (2025). Transparency of AI-XR Systems: Insights from Experts. *Proceedings - 2025 IEEE International Conference on Artificial Intelligence and EXtended and Virtual Reality, AIxVR 2025*, 301–306. https://doi.org/DOI: 10.1109/AIXVR63409.2025.00058

Machala, S., Chamier-Gliszczynski, N., & Królikowski, T. (2022). Application of AR/VR Technology in Industry 4.0. *Procedia Computer Science, 207*, 2990–2998. DOI: 10.1016/J.PROCS.2022.09.357

Magee, P., Ienca, M., & Farahany, N. (2024). Beyond neural data: Cognitive biometrics and mental privacy. *Neuron, 112*(18), 3017–3028. DOI: 10.1016/J.NEURON.2024.09.004 PMID: 39326392

Mohamed, N., & Ahmed, A. A. (2024). AI in Combatting Man-in-the-Middle Attacks: A Comprehensive Review. *2024 15th International Conference on Computing Communication and Networking Technologies, ICCCNT 2024*. https://doi.org/DOI: 10.1109/ICCCNT61001.2024.10725789

Murala, D. K., & Panda, S. K. (2023). Metaverse: A study on immersive technologies. *Metaverse and Immersive Technologies: An Introduction to Industrial, Business and Social Applications*, 1–41. https://doi.org/DOI: 10.1002/9781394177165.CH1

Muzammil, M. Bin, Bilal, M., Ajmal, S., Shongwe, S. C., & Ghadi, Y. Y. (2024). Unveiling Vulnerabilities of Web Attacks Considering Man in the Middle Attack and Session Hijacking. *IEEE Access : Practical Innovations, Open Solutions*, *12*, 6365–6375. DOI: 10.1109/ACCESS.2024.3350444

Nair, V., Garrido, G. M., Song, D., & O'Brien, J. F. (2023). Exploring the Privacy Risks of Adversarial VR Game Design. *Proceedings on Privacy Enhancing Technologies. Privacy Enhancing Technologies Symposium*, *2023*(4), 238–256. DOI: 10.56553/popets-2023-0108

Neo, J. R. J., Won, A. S., & Shepley, M. M. C. (2021). Designing Immersive Virtual Environments for Human Behavior Research. In *Frontiers in Virtual Reality* (Vol. 2). https://doi.org/DOI: 10.3389/frvir.2021.603750

Parnandi, A., & Gutierrez-Osuna, R. (2013). Contactless measurement of heart rate variability from pupillary fluctuations. *Proceedings - 2013 Humaine Association Conference on Affective Computing and Intelligent Interaction, ACII 2013*. https://doi.org/DOI: 10.1109/ACII.2013.38

Partarakis, N., & Zabulis, X. (2024). A Review of Immersive Technologies, Knowledge Representation, and AI for Human-Centered Digital Experiences. *Electronics 2024, Vol. 13, Page 269*, *13*(2), 269. https://doi.org/DOI: 10.3390/ELECTRONICS13020269

Qayyum, A., Butt, M. A., Ali, H., Usman, M., Halabi, O., Al-Fuqaha, A., Abbasi, Q. H., Imran, M. A., & Qadir, J. (2024). Secure and Trustworthy Artificial Intelligence-extended Reality (AI-XR) for Metaverses. *ACM Computing Surveys*, *56*(7). Advance online publication. DOI: 10.1145/3614426

Rasanen, J., Altonen, A., Mercat, A., & Vanne, J. (2021). Open-source RTP Library for End-To-End Encrypted Real-Time Video Streaming Applications. *Proceedings - 23rd IEEE International Symposium on Multimedia, ISM 2021*, 92–96. https://doi.org/DOI: 10.1109/ISM52913.2021.00023

Rauschnabel, P. A., Babin, B. J., tom Dieck, M. C., Krey, N., & Jung, T. (2022). What is augmented reality marketing? Its definition, complexity, and future. In *Journal of Business Research* (Vol. 142). https://doi.org/DOI: 10.1016/j.jbusres.2021.12.084

Ross, A., Banerjee, S., & Chowdhury, A. (2022). Deducing health cues from biometric data. *Computer Vision and Image Understanding*, *221*. Advance online publication. DOI: 10.1016/j.cviu.2022.103438

Rubin, D. (2024). *Harnessing Eye and Face Movements: Bridging Technology and Human Interaction.*

Salem, O., Alsubhi, K., Shaafi, A., Gheryani, M., Mehaoua, A., & Boutaba, R. (2022). Man-in-the-Middle Attack Mitigation in Internet of Medical Things. *IEEE Transactions on Industrial Informatics*, *18*(3). Advance online publication. DOI: 10.1109/TII.2021.3089462

Sharma, S., Das, D., & Chaudhury, S. (2025). A decentralized privacy-preserving XR system for 3D medical data visualization using hybrid biometric cryptosystem. *Scientific Reports*, *15*(1), 1–22. DOI: 10.1038/S41598-025-08784-8 PMID: 40764519

Taninaka, K., Jain, R., Shi, J., Takashio, K., & Ramani, K. (2025). Transparent Barriers: Natural Language Access Control Policies for XR-Enhanced Everyday Objects. *Conference on Human Factors in Computing Systems - Proceedings*. https://doi.org//DOI: 10.1145/3706598.3713656

threekit. (2020). *What Is Augmented Reality (AR)? A Practical Overview*. Threekit.

Uddin, M., Obaidat, M., Manickam, S., Laghari, S. U. A., Dandoush, A., Ullah, H., & Ullah, S. S. (2024). Exploring the convergence of Metaverse, Blockchain, and AI: A comprehensive survey of enabling technologies, applications, challenges, and future directions. *Wiley Interdisciplinary Reviews. Data Mining and Knowledge Discovery*, *14*(6), e1556. DOI: 10.1002/WIDM.1556

Valluripally, S., Frailey, B., Kruse, B., Palipatana, B., Oruche, R., Gulhane, A., Hoque, K. A., & Calyam, P. (2023). Detection of Security and Privacy Attacks Disrupting User Immersive Experience in Virtual Reality Learning Environments. *IEEE Transactions on Services Computing*, *16*(4). Advance online publication. DOI: 10.1109/TSC.2022.3216539

Wang, P., Bai, X., Billinghurst, M., Zhang, S., Zhang, X., Wang, S., He, W., Yan, Y., & Ji, H. (2021). AR/MR Remote Collaboration on Physical Tasks: A Review. *Robotics and Computer-integrated Manufacturing*, *72*, 102071. DOI: 10.1016/J.RCIM.2020.102071

Wu, D., Yang, Z., Zhang, P., Wang, R., Yang, B., & Ma, X. (2023). Virtual-Reality Interpromotion Technology for Metaverse: A Survey. *IEEE Internet of Things Journal, 10*(18), 15788–15809. DOI: 10.1109/JIOT.2023.3265848

Yang, X., & Gao, F. (2022). The Overview of Elliptic Curve Cryptography (ECC). *Journal of Physics: Conference Series, 2386*(1), 012019. DOI: 10.1088/1742-6596/2386/1/012019

Yang, Z., Li, C. Y., Bhalla, A., Zhao, B. Y., & Zheng, H. (2024). *Inception Attacks: Immersive Hijacking in Virtual Reality Systems*. https://arxiv.org/abs/2403.05721

Yano, V., Zimmer, A., & Ling, L. L. (2015). Extraction and application of dynamic pupillometry features for biometric authentication. *Measurement: Journal of the International Measurement Confederation, 63*. Advance online publication. DOI: 10.1016/j.measurement.2014.12.001

Yekollu, R. K., Ghuge, T. B., Biradar, S. S., Haldikar, S. V., & Abdul Kader, O. F. M. (2024). Securing the Virtual Realm: Strategies for Cybersecurity in Augmented Reality (AR) and Virtual Reality (VR) Applications. *8th International Conference on I-SMAC (IoT in Social, Mobile, Analytics and Cloud), I-SMAC 2024 - Proceedings*, 520–526. https://doi.org/DOI: 10.1109/I-SMAC61858.2024.10714591

Zhang, T., Gao, L., He, C., Zhang, M., Krishnamachari, B., & Avestimehr, A. S. (2022). Federated Learning for the Internet of Things: Applications, Challenges, and Opportunities. *IEEE Internet of Things Magazine, 5*(1), 24–29. DOI: 10.1109/IOTM.004.2100182

Zhang, Y., Li, Y., & Li, Z. (2023). Aye: A Trusted Forensic Method for Firmware Tampering Attacks. *Symmetry, 15*(1). Advance online publication. DOI: 10.3390/sym15010145

Compilation of References

Aal-Asheakh, H. and Saud, W. (2024). The impact of gamification on developing foreign language within elementary students' speaking skills: an experimental study. Journal of Learning and Development Studies, 4(3), 01-16. DOI: 10.32996/jlds.2024.4.3.1

Abbas, N., Imran, A., Manzoor, R., Hussain, T., & Hussain, M. (2023). Role of artificial intelligence tools in enhancing students' educational performance at higher levels. *Journal of Artificial Intelligence Machine Learning and Neural Network*, (35), 36–49. DOI: 10.55529/jaimlnn.35.36.49

Abdul Talib, C., Romainor, N., & Aliyu, F. (2022). Augmented Reality in Chemistry Education: A Literature Review of Advantages on Learners. *Journal of Natural Science and Integration*, *5*(1), 126. DOI: 10.24014/jnsi.v5i1.16805

Abraham, M., Saeghe, P., McGill, M., & Khamis, M. (2022). Implications of XR on Privacy, Security and Behaviour: Insights from Experts. *ACM International Conference Proceeding Series*. https://doi.org/DOI: 10.1145/3546155.3546691

Abrahams, D. (2018). Engaging music students through Minecraft. In *ICERI 2018 proceedings* (pp. 1916–1921). IATED., DOI: 10.21125/iceri.2018.0142

Abrams, S. S. (2017). Emotionally crafted experiences: Layering literacies in Minecraft. *The Reading Teacher*, *70*(4), 501–506. DOI: 10.1002/trtr.1515

Adarkwah, M. (2021). The power of assessment feedback in teaching and learning: A narrative review and synthesis of the literature. *SN Social Sciences*, *1*(3), 75. DOI: 10.1007/s43545-021-00086-w

Adeniyi, A. E., Jimoh, R. G., & Awotunde, J. B. (2024). A systematic review on elliptic curve cryptography algorithm for internet of things: Categorization, application areas, and security. *Computers & Electrical Engineering*, *118*, 109330. DOI: 10.1016/J.COMPELECENG.2024.109330

Adeoye, M. A., & Otemuyiwa, B. I. (2024). Navigating the Future: Strategies of EdTech Companies in Driving Educational Transformation. JERIT. *Journal of Educational Research and Innovation Technology*, *1*(1), 43–50.

Adhanom, I. B., MacNeilage, P., & Folmer, E. (2023). Eye Tracking in Virtual Reality: A Broad Review of Applications and Challenges. *Virtual Reality (Waltham Cross)*, *27*(2). Advance online publication. DOI: 10.1007/s10055-022-00738-z PMID: 37621305

Agostinelli, S. (2021). *Actionable framework for city digital twin-enabled predictive maintenance and security management systems.*. https://doi.org/DOI: 10.2495/bim210191

Aguhayon, H., Tingson, R., & Pentang, J. T. (2023). Addressing students' learning gaps in mathematics through differentiated instruction. *International Journal of Educational Management and Development Studies*, *4*(1), 69–87. DOI: 10.53378/352967

Ahmad, F., Klaib, N. O., Alsrehin, W. Y., Melhem, H. O. B., & Magableh, A. A. (2021). Eye tracking algorithms, techniques, tools, and applications with an emphasis on machine learning and Internet of Things technologies. *Expert Systems with Applications*, *166*, 114037. DOI: 10.1016/j.eswa.2020.114037

Ahmed, A., & Sutton, M. J. (2017). Gamification, serious games, simulations, and immersive learning environments in knowledge management initiatives. *World Journal of Science. Technology and Sustainable Development*, *14*(2/3), 78–83.

Ajani, O. A., & Govender, S. (2023). Impact of ICT-driven teacher professional development for the enhancement of classroom practices in South Africa: A systematic review of literature. *Journal of Educational and Social Research*, *13*(5), 116. DOI: 10.36941/jesr-2023-0125

Ajit, G., Lucas, T., & Kanyan, R. (2021). A systematic review of augmented reality in stem education. In *Estudios de Economia Aplicada* (Vol. 39, Issue 1, pp. 1–22). https://doi.org/DOI: 10.25115/eea.v39i1.4280

Akavova, A., Temirkhanova, Z., & Lorsanova, Z. (2023). Adaptive learning and artificial intelligence in the educational space. *E3s Web of Conferences*, 451, 06011. https://doi.org/DOI: 10.1051/e3sconf/202345106011

Akgün, S., & Greenhow, C. (2021). Artificial intelligence in education: Addressing ethical challenges in k-12 settings. *AI and Ethics*, *2*(3), 431–440. DOI: 10.1007/s43681-021-00096-7

Akinrinola, O. (2024). Navigating and reviewing ethical dilemmas in ai development: strategies for transparency, fairness, and accountability. *GSC Advanced Research and Reviews,* 18(3), 050-058. https://doi.org/DOI: 10.30574/gscarr.2024.18.3.0088

Akintayo, O. T., Eden, C. A., Ayeni, O. O., & Onyebuchi, N. C. (2024). Evaluating the impact of educational technology on learning outcomes in the higher education sector: A systematic review. *International Journal of Management & Entrepreneurship Research*, *6*(5), 1395–1422.

Alali, R. (2024). Opportunities and challenges of integrating generative artificial intelligence in education. *International Journal of Religion*, *5*(7), 784–793. DOI: 10.61707/8y29gv34

Al-Ansi, A. M., Jaboob, M., Garad, A., & Al-Ansi, A. (2023). Analyzing augmented reality (AR) and virtual reality (VR) recent development in education. *Social Sciences & Humanities Open*, *8*(1), 100532. DOI: 10.1016/j.ssaho.2023.100532

Alaswad, Z., & Nadolny, L. (2015). Designing for game-based learning: The effective integration of technology to support learning. *Journal of Educational Technology Systems*, *43*(4), 389–402.

Alenezi, A. (2024). Obstacles to the use of ai applications in blackboard for faculty members at northern border university, saudi arabia. *Mier Journal of Educational Studies Trends & Practices,* 248-268. https://doi.org/DOI: 10.52634/mier/2024/v14/i2/2581

Alenezi, A. (2023). Teacher perspectives on ai-driven gamification: Impact on student motivation, engagement, and learning outcomes. *Information Technologies and Learning Tools*, *97*(5), 138–148. DOI: 10.33407/itlt.v97i5.5437

Aliabadi, R. (2023). *Transdisciplinary ai education: the confluence of curricular and community needs in the instruction of artificial intelligence.*, 137-151. https://doi.org/DOI: 10.1007/978-981-99-7947-9_11

Ali, D. F., Omar, M., Abdullah, A. H., Ibrahim, N. H., Mokhtar, M., Zaid, N. M., & Johari, N. (2021). 5 years into augmented reality technology in education: Research trends, bibliometric study and its application to enhance visualization skills. *WSEAS Transactions on Systems and Control*, *16*, 253–260. DOI: 10.37394/23203.2021.16.21

Ali, S. (2022). The effectiveness of immersive technologies for future professional education. *Futurity Education*, *2*(2), 14–22. DOI: 10.57125/FED/2022.10.11.25

Ali, S., Abdullah, Armand, T. P. T., Athar, A., Hussain, A., Ali, M., ... & Kim, H. C. (2023). Metaverse in healthcare integrated with explainable AI and blockchain: Enabling immersiveness, ensuring trust, and providing patient data security. *Sensors (Basel)*, *23*(2), 565. PMID: 36679361

Aliyeva, T. (2024). Innovative approaches to foreign language learning: A study of methods including Duolingo and beyond. *Global Spectrum of Research and Humanities*, *1*(2), 73–80. DOI: 10.69760/3twd9f85

Alkan, A. (2024). Artificial intelligence: its role and potential in education. *İnsan Ve Toplum Bilimleri Araştırmaları Dergisi,* 13(1), 483-497. https://doi.org/DOI: 10.15869/itobiad.1331201

Al-Kfairy, M., Alrabaee, S., & Alfandi, O. (2024, November). Ethical pathways in VR and the Metaverse: Frameworks for responsible innovation. In *2024 2nd International Conference on Intelligent Metaverse Technologies & Applications (iMETA)* (pp. 009-017). IEEE.

Alkire, S. (2015). Capability Approach and Well-being Measurement for Public Policy. OPHI Working Paper 94, Oxford University.

Alkire, S. (2005, March). Why the Capability Approach? *Journal of Human Development and Capabilities*, *6*(1), •••.

Alladi, T., Chamola, V., Parizi, R., & Choo, K. (2019). Blockchain applications for industry 4.0 and industrial iot: A review. *IEEE Access : Practical Innovations, Open Solutions*, *7*, 176935–176951. DOI: 10.1109/access.2019.2956748

Allahverdi, A. (2021). Sample senior design projects of industrial engineering program at kuwait university. *Asean Journal of Engineering Education*, *4*(1). Advance online publication. DOI: 10.11113/ajee2020.4n1.14

Almeman, K. E. L., Ayeb, F., Berrima, M., Issaoui, B., & Morsy, H. (2025). The integration of AI and metaverse in education: *A systematic literature review. Applied Sciences (Basel, Switzerland)*, *15*(2), 863.

Almusaed, A. (2023). Enhancing student engagement: Harnessing "aied"'s power in hybrid education—a review analysis. *Education Sciences*, *13*(7), 632. DOI: 10.3390/educsci13070632

Alrayes, A. (2024). Chatgpt in education – understanding the bahraini academics perspective. *Electronic Journal of e-Learning*, *22*(2), 112–134. DOI: 10.34190/ejel.22.2.3250

Alsadoon, H. (2023). The impact of gamification on student motivation and engagement: An empirical study. *Dirasat: Educational Sciences*, *50*(2), 386–396. DOI: 10.35516/edu.v50i2.255

Alshehri, B. (2023). Pedagogical paradigms in the ai era: Insights from saudi educators on the long-term implications of ai integration in classroom teaching. *IJESA*, *2*(8), 159–180. DOI: 10.59992/ijesa.2023.v2n8p7

Al-Sobhi, B. M. S., Rashid, S. M., Abdullah, A. N., & Darmi, R. (2017). Arab ESL secondary school students' spelling errors. *International Journal of Education and Literacy Studies*, *5*(3), 16–23.

Altmeyer, K., Kapp, S., Thees, M., Malone, S., Kuhn, J., & Brünken, R. (2020). The use of augmented reality to foster conceptual knowledge acquisition in STEM laboratory courses—Theoretical background and empirical results. *British Journal of Educational Technology*, *51*(3), 611–628. DOI: 10.1111/bjet.12900

Analyti, E., Χαρίτου, P., Pesmatzoglou, E., Stavrogiannopoulou, M., Schoina, I., Travlou, C., & Mitroyanni, E. (2024). Virtual reality in education: Transforming learning through immersive technology. *Technium Education and Humanities*, *10*, 1–11. DOI: 10.47577/teh.v10i.11766

Anisa, K. D., Marmanto, S., & Supriyadi, S. (2020). The effect of gamification on students' motivation in learning English. *Leksika: Jurnal Bahasa, Sastra dan Pengajarannya, 14*(1), 22–28.

Antonaci, A., Klemke, R., & Specht, M. (2019). The effects of gamification in online learning environments: A systematic literature review. *Informatics (MDPI)*, *6*(3), 32. DOI: 10.3390/informatics6030032

Anwar, M. S., Ullah, I., Ahmad, S., Choi, A., Ahmad, S., Wang, J., & Aurangzeb, K. (2023). Immersive learning and AR/VR-based education: cybersecurity measures and risk management. In *Cybersecurity management in education technologies* (pp. 1–22). CRC Press.

Aparicio-Gómez, O. (2024). Tejiendo conexiones: la simbiosis transformadora entre aprendizaje e inteligencia artificial. *Hachetetepé Revista Científica De Educación Y Comunicación,* (28). https://doi.org/DOI: 10.25267/hachetetepe.2024.i28.1103

Arena, F., Collotta, M., Pau, G., & Termine, F. (2022). An Overview of Augmented Reality. In *Computers* (Vol. 11, Issue 2). https://doi.org/DOI: 10.3390/computers11020028

Arieli-Attali, M., Ward, S., Thomas, J., Deonovic, B., & von Davier, A. A. (2019). The expanded evidence-centered design (e-ECD) for learning and assessment systems: A framework for incorporating learning goals and processes within assessment design. *Frontiers in Psychology, 10*, 853. DOI: 10.3389/fpsyg.2019.00853 PMID: 31105616

Armstrong, M. B., & Landers, R. N. (2017). An evaluation of gamified training: Using narrative to improve reactions and learning. *Simulation & Gaming, 48*(4), 513–538. DOI: 10.1177/1046878117703749

Asif, A. U. Z., Sridhar, M., Ray, I., & Ortega, F. R. (2024). Breaking the Virtual Barrier of Exploit Chain Attacks in XR Systems. *Proceedings - 2024 IEEE International Symposium on Mixed and Augmented Reality Adjunct, ISMAR-Adjunct 2024*, 32–34. https://doi.org/DOI: 10.1109/ISMAR-ADJUNCT64951.2024.00017

Auko, J. (2023). Current security and privacy posture in wireless body area networks. *World Journal of Advanced Research and Reviews, 18*(3), 1185–1206. DOI: 10.30574/wjarr.2023.18.3.1240

Aziz, F., Li, C., & Khan, A. U. (2025). Immersive learning in virtual worlds: A two-step analysis SEM and NCA for assessing the impact of Metaverse education on knowledge retention and student collaboration. *Technology in Society, 81*, 102871. DOI: 10.1016/j.techsoc.2025.102871

Azuma, R. T. (1997). A survey of augmented reality. *Presence (Cambridge, Mass.), 6*(4), 355–385. DOI: 10.1162/pres.1997.6.4.355

Babalola, A., Manu, P., Cheung, C., Yunusa-Kaltungo, A., & Bartolo, P. (2023). A systematic review of the application of immersive technologies for safety and health management in the construction sector. *Journal of Safety Research, 85*, 66–85. PMID: 37330902

Bacca-Acosta, J., Baldiris, S., Fabregat, R., & Graf, S. (2014). Augmented reality trends in education: A systematic review of research and applications. *Journal of Educational Technology & Society, 17*(4), 133–149.

Baiden, P., Essel, H. B., Vlachopoulos, D., Tachie-Menson, A., & Essuman, M. A. (2022). The effect of gamification on home economics students' motivation and engagement in drawing activities. *Technology. Knowledge and Learning, 27*(1), 161–182.

Bai, S., Hew, K. F., & Huang, B. (2020). Does gamification improve student learning outcome? Evidence from a meta-analysis and synthesis of qualitative data in educational contexts. *Educational Research Review, 30*, 100322. DOI: 10.1016/j.edurev.2020.100322

Balalle, H. (2024). Exploring student engagement in technology-based education in relation to gamification, online/distance learning, and other factors: A systematic literature review. *Social Sciences & Humanities Open*, *9*, 100870. DOI: 10.1016/j.ssaho.2024.100870

Balci, S., Secaur, J., & Morris, B. (2022). Comparing the effectiveness of badges and leaderboards on academic performance and motivation of students in fully versus partially gamified online physics classes. *Education and Information Technologies*, *27*(6), 8669–8704. DOI: 10.1007/s10639-022-10983-z

Baldoni, S., & Kavari, A. (2025). *Security challenges for immersive media: threats and possible mitigations*. https://thesis.unipd.it/handle/20.500.12608/89886

Balta, N. (2023). *Ethical considerations in using ai in educational research.,* 2(1), 14205. https://doi.org/DOI: 10.51853/jorids/14205

Bandura, A. (1997). *Self-efficacy: The exercise of control*. W. H. Freeman.

Bardach, L., & Murayama, K. (2025). The role of rewards in motivation—Beyond dichotomies. *Learning and Instruction*, *96*, 102056. DOI: 10.1016/j.learninstruc.2024.102056

Bartolomei, L., Blundo-Canto, G., & De Muro, P. (2024). How is the Capability Approach Applied to Assess Well-being Impacts? A Systematic Review. *Journal of Human Development and Capabilities*, *25*(3), 367–399. DOI: 10.1080/19452829.2024.2369502

Barua, P., Vicnesh, J., Gururajan, R., Oh, S., Palmer, E., Azizan, M., & Acharya, U. (2022). Artificial intelligence enabled personalised assistive tools to enhance education of children with neurodevelopmental disorders a review. *International Journal of Environmental Research and Public Health*, *19*(3), 1192. DOI: 10.3390/ijerph19031192

Bashir, A. K., Victor, N., Bhattacharya, S., Huynh-The, T., Chengoden, R., Yenduri, G., Maddikunta, P. K. R., Pham, Q. V., Gadekallu, T. R., & Liyanage, M. (2023). Federated Learning for the Healthcare Metaverse: Concepts, Applications, Challenges, and Future Directions. *IEEE Internet of Things Journal*, *10*(24), 21873–21891. DOI: 10.1109/JIOT.2023.3304790

Bastani, P., Kavosi, Z., Alipoori, S., & Imani-Nasab, M. (2023). Evidence- based policy and decision-making among health managers: A case of shiraz university of medical sciences. *Galen Medical Journal*, *6*(1). Advance online publication. DOI: 10.31661/gmj.v6i1.729

Basudan, S. (2023). A Scalable Blockchain Framework For Secure Transactions In Iot Based Dynamic Applications. *IEEE Open Journal of the Communications Society*, *4*, 1931–1945. DOI: 10.1109/ojcoms.2023.3307337

Baxter, G., & Hainey, T. (2024). Using immersive technologies to enhance the student learning experience. *Interactive Technology and Smart Education*, *21*(3), 403–425.

Bear, D. R., von Gillern, S., & Xu, W. (2018). Learning to spell in English by Chinese students: A cross-sectional study. *TESOL International Journal*, *13*(1), 47–66.

Beck, D., Morgado, L., & O'Shea, P. (2023). Educational practices and strategies with immersive learning environments: Mapping of reviews for using the metaverse. *IEEE Transactions on Learning Technologies*, *17*, 319–341.

Beetham, H., & Sharpe, R. (2013). *Rethinking Pedagogy for a Digital Age: Designing for 21st Century Learning* (2nd ed.). Routledge.

Belhaj, R. (2025). Gamified hybrid learning for neurodiverse students: Designing universally accessible instructional models. *J. Neosantara Hybrid Learning*, *3*(1), 38–46. DOI: 10.70177/jnhl.v3i1.2229

Benites, D. A. M., Villate, R. C., & Gouyon, F. (2023). Ear training applications in music education: A case study of music students in France. In *Proceedings of the 15th International Conference on Computer Supported Education (CSEDU 2023)* (pp. 381–388). SCITEPRESS. https://doi.org/DOI: 10.5220/0012054200003492

Bennani, S., Maalel, A., & Ghezala, H. (2021). Adaptive gamification in e-learning: A literature review and future challenges. *Computer Applications in Engineering Education*, *30*(2), 628–642. DOI: 10.1002/cae.22477

Benton, C. (2013). Promoting metacognition in music classes. *Music Educators Journal*, *100*(2), 52–59. DOI: 10.1177/0027432113495625

Berrezueta-Guzman, S., & Wagner, S. (2025). Immersive Multiplayer VR: Unreal Engine's Strengths, Limitations, and Future Prospects. *IEEE Access : Practical Innovations, Open Solutions*, *13*, 85597–85612. DOI: 10.1109/ACCESS.2025.3570166

Bhaskaran, V., & Mahbub, U. (2024). Immersive User Experiences: Trends and Challenges of Using XR Technologies. *Computer Vision: Challenges, Trends, and Opportunities*, 260–278. https://doi.org//DOI: 10.1201/9781003328957-12

Binytska, K. M., Bilyakovska, O. O., Yankovych, O. I., Buchkivska, G. V., Binytska, O. P., Greskova, V. V., & Ocheretna, I. P. (2023). Exploring the potential of immersive technologies in university education worldwide. *CEUR Workshop Proceedings*, *3436*, 203–217. https://ceur-ws.org/Vol-3482/paper292.pdf

Biryukov, A., Brikoshina, I., Mikhalevich, N., Sycheva, S., & Khalimon, E. (2021). Gamification in education: threats or new opportunities. SHS Web of Conferences, 103, 02001. DOI: 10.1051/shsconf/202110302001

Bissonette, J., Dubé, F., Provencher, M., & Morena Sala, M. (2015). Virtual reality exposure training for musicians: Its effect on performance anxiety and quality. *Medical Problems of Performing Artists*, *30*(3), 169–177. DOI: 10.21091/mppa.2015.3035 PMID: 26395619

Bitrián, P., Buil, I., & Catalán, S. (2021). Enhancing user engagement: The role of gamification in mobile apps. *Journal of Business Research*, *132*, 170–185. DOI: 10.1016/j.jbusres.2021.04.028

Bizami, N. A., Tasir, Z., & Kew, S. N. (2023). Innovative pedagogical principles and technological tools capabilities for immersive blended learning: A systematic literature review. *Education and Information Technologies*, *28*, 1373–1425. DOI: 10.1007/s10639-022-11243-w PMID: 35919874

Bloom, B. (1956). *Taxonomy of educational objectives: The classification of educational goals*. McKay.

Bloom, B. S. (1956). *Taxonomy of educational objectives: The classification of educational goals. Handbook 1: Cognitive Domain*. Longmans.

Bloom, B., Englehart, M., Furst, E., Hill, W., & Krathwohl, D. (1956). *Taxonomy of educational objectives: The classification of educational goals. Handbook I: Cognitive domain*. Longmans, Green.

Bos, B., Wilder, L., Cook, M., & O'Donnell, R. (2014). Learning mathematics through Minecraft. *Teaching Children Mathematics*, *21*(1), 56–59. DOI: 10.5951/teacchilmath.21.1.0056

Bosman, I. D. V., Ka, K. S. D., & Alemneh, D. G. (2024). *Immersive Technology in Education. Proceedings of the Association for Information Science and Technology*. https://doi.org/DOI: 10.1002/pra2.1086

Boudadi, N., & Gutiérrez-Colón, M. (2020). Effect of gamification on students' motivation and learning achievement in second language acquisition within higher education: A literature review 2011-2019. *The Eurocall Review*, *28*(1), 40. DOI: 10.4995/eurocall.2020.12974

Bowman, J. (1982). Please teach music theory in high school: A rebuttal of Earl Henry's "Please stop teaching college theory in high school." *American Music Teacher, 32*(1), 34–35. https://www.jstor.org/stable/43543846

Bowman, J. (1987). Bridging the gap: Preparing students for college music theory. *Music Educators Journal*, *73*(8), 49–53. https://www.jstor.org/stable/3400244

Buchner, J., Buntins, K., & Kerres, M. (2022). The impact of augmented reality on cognitive load and performance: A systematic review. *Journal of Computer Assisted Learning*, *38*(1), 285–303. DOI: 10.1111/jcal.12610

Buckley, P., & Doyle, E. (2014). Gamification and student motivation. *Interactive Learning Environments*, *24*(6), 1162–1175. DOI: 10.1080/10494820.2014.964263

Bullock, B. B., Nascimento, F. L., & Doore, S. A. (2021, March). Computing ethics narratives: Teaching computing ethics and the impact of predictive algorithms. In *Proceedings of the 52nd ACM Technical Symposium on Computer Science Education* (pp. 1020-1026).

Buonviri, N. O., & Paney, A. S. (2020). Technology use in high school aural skills instruction. *International Journal of Music Education*, *38*(3), 431–440.

Buragohain, D., Deng, C., Sharma, A., & Chaudhary, S. (2024). The impact of immersive learning on teacher effectiveness: A systematic study. *IEEE Access : Practical Innovations, Open Solutions*, *12*, 35924–35933.

Burton, L. (1990). Comprehensive musicianship: The Hawaii music curriculum project. *The Quarterly Journal of Music Teaching and Learning*, *1*(3), 67–76. DOI: 10.1177/875512339801700106

Burunat, I., Brattico, E., Hartmann, M., Vuust, P., Särkämö, T., & Toiviainen, P. (2018). Musical training predicts cerebello-hippocampal coupling during music listening. *Psychomusicology: Music, Mind, and Brain*, *28*(3), 152–163. DOI: 10.1037/pmu0000215

Cabrera-Duffaut, A., Pinto-Llorente, A. M., & Iglesias-Rodríguez, A. (2024, July). Immersive learning platforms: Analyzing virtual reality contribution to competence development in higher education—a systematic literature review. [). Frontiers Media SA.]. *Frontiers in Education*, *9*, 1391560.

Cacicio, S., Tinsley, B., Miller, A., & Luke Luna, C. (2022). *Inclusive Design Principles for Learning and Employment Records: Co-Designing for Equity*. Digital Promise.

Cai, S., Chiang, F.-K., Sun, Y., Lin, C., & Lee, J. J. (2017). Applications of augmented reality-based natural interactive learning in magnetic field instruction. *Interactive Learning Environments*, *25*(6), 778–791. DOI: 10.1080/10494820.2016.1181092

Callaghan, N. (2016). Investigating the role of Minecraft in educational learning environments. *Educational Media International*, *53*(4), 244–260. DOI: 10.1080/09523987.2016.1254877

Capatina, A., Patel, N. J., Mitrov, K., Cristea, D. S., Micu, A., & Micu, A. E. (2024). Elevating students' lives through immersive learning experiences in a safe metaverse. *International Journal of Information Management*, *75*, 102723.

Carter, M., & Egliston, B. (2023). What are the risks of virtual reality data? Learning analytics, algorithmic bias and a fantasy of perfect data. *New Media & Society*, *25*(3), 485–504.

Chai, F. (2024). Grading by ai makes me feel fairer? how different evaluators affect college students' perception of fairness. *Frontiers in Psychology*, *15*. Advance online publication. DOI: 10.3389/fpsyg.2024.1221177

Chang, C., Hwang, G., & Gau, M. (2021). Promoting students' learning achievement and self-efficacy: A mobile chatbot approach for nursing training. *British Journal of Educational Technology*, *53*(1), 171–188. DOI: 10.1111/bjet.13158

Chan, K., Wan, K., & King, V. (2021). Performance over enjoyment? effect of game-based learning on learning outcome and flow experience. *Frontiers in Education*, *6*. Advance online publication. DOI: 10.3389/feduc.2021.660376

Chapman, J. R., Kohler, T. B., Rich, P. J., & Trego, A. (2023). Maybe we've got it wrong: An experimental evaluation of self-determination and flow theory in gamification. *Journal of Research on Technology in Education*, •••, 1–20.

Chen, C. Y. (2025). Effects of worked examples with explanation types and learner motivation on cognitive load and programming problem-solving performance. *ACM Transactions on Computing Education*. Advance online publication.

Chen, C.-H. (2020). Impacts of augmented reality and a digital game on students' science learning with reflection prompts in multimedia learning. *Educational Technology Research and Development*, *68*(6), 3057–3076. DOI: 10.1007/s11423-020-09833-4

Chen, L., Chen, P., & Lin, Z. (2020). Artificial intelligence in education: A review. *IEEE Access : Practical Innovations, Open Solutions*, *8*, 75264–75278. DOI: 10.1109/access.2020.2988510

Chen, M., Chen, Y., Zuo, P., & Hou, H. (2023). Design and evaluation of a remote synchronous gamified mathematics teaching activity that integrates multi-representational scaffolding and a mind tool for gamified learning. *Education and Information Technologies*, *28*(10), 13207–13233. DOI: 10.1007/s10639-023-11708-6 PMID: 37361748

Chen, X., Gao, W., Chu, Y., & Song, Y. (2024). Enhancing interaction in virtual-real architectural environments: A comparative analysis of generative AI-driven reality approaches. *Building and Environment*, *266*, 112113. DOI: 10.1016/j.buildenv.2024.112113

Chen, Y. C., & Hou, H. T. (2025). Design of a digital gamified learning activity for relationship education with conceptual scaffolding and reflective scaffolding. *The Asia-Pacific Education Researcher*, *34*(1), 237–251.

Chomunorwa, S., & Mugobo, V. V. (2023). Challenges of e-learning adoption in South African public schools: Learners' perspectives. *Journal of Education and e-learning Research*, *10*(1), 80–85.

Chon, V., Sharif, S. b., & Saleh, N. M. (2024). Gamification for enhancing students' learning motivation: A systematic review. *Journal of Cognitive Sciences and Human Development*, *10*(2), 19–41. DOI: 10.33736/jcshd.7231.2024

Cho, Y., Coward, C., Lackner, J., Windleharth, T. W., & Lee, J. H. (2025). The use of an escape room as an immersive learning environment for building resilience to misinformation. *Journal of Librarianship and Information Science*, *57*(2), 524–538.

Christopher, L., & Waworuntu, A. (2021). Java programming language learning application based on octalysis gamification framework. [International Journal of New Media Technology]. *Ijnmt*, *8*(1), 65–69. DOI: 10.31937/ijnmt.v8i1.2049

Clark, D. A. (2005). *The Capability Approach: Its Development, Critiques and Recent Advances*. Global Poverty Research Group. https://base.socioeco.org/docs/developments_critiques_advances.pdf

Cleland, K. D., & Dobrea-Grindahl, M. (2014). *Developing musicianship through aural skills: A holistic approach to sight singing and ear training* (2nd ed.). Routledge.

Coppenbarger, B. (2014). *Music theory secrets: 94 strategies for the starting musician*. Rowman & Littlefield.

Corriveau, L. (2021). Technologies, institutions, development and growth. *Structural Change and Economic Dynamics*, *57*, 159–164. DOI: 10.1016/j.strueco.2021.03.005

Cranley, L., Doran, D., Tourangeau, A., Kushniruk, A., & Nagle, L. (2012). Recognizing and responding to uncertainty: A grounded theory of nurses' uncertainty. *Worldviews on Evidence-Based Nursing*, *9*(3), 149–158. DOI: 10.1111/j.1741-6787.2011.00237.x

Crofton, E. C., Botinestean, C., Fenelon, M., & Gallagher, E. (2019). Potential applications for virtual and augmented reality technologies in sensory science. *Innovative Food Science & Emerging Technologies*, *56*, 102178. DOI: 10.1016/j.ifset.2019.102178

Cruz, K., Noa, S., Turpo-Gebera, O., Montesinos-Valencia, C., Bazán-Velásquez, S., & Postigo, G. (2023). Use of gamification in english learning in higher education: A systematic review. *Journal of Technology and Science Education*, *13*(2), 480. DOI: 10.3926/jotse.1740

Csikszentmihalyi, M., Montijo, M. N., & Mouton, A. R. (2018). Flow theory: Optimizing elite performance in the creative realm. In Pfeiffer, S. I., Shaunessy-Dedrick, E., & Foley-Nicpon, M. (Eds.), *APA handbook of giftedness and talent* (pp. 215–229). American Psychological Association., DOI: 10.1037/0000038-014

Cui, Y., van Esch, P., & Spence, C. (2024). Multisensory technology in the wine industry: Where the senses meet technology. *Journal of Wine Research*, *35*(2), 75–84.

Czerniewicz, L., & Brown, C. (2013). The habitus and technological practices of rural students: A case study. *South African Journal of Education*, *33*(1).

D'Souza, R. (2024). Twelve tips for addressing ethical concerns in the implementation of artificial intelligence in medical education. *Medical Education Online*, *29*(1). Advance online publication. DOI: 10.1080/10872981.2024.2330250

Dahiya, M., Özen, E., & Yadav, K. (2023). The financial literacy of college students: Evidence from India. *ASR: Chiang Mai University Journal of Social Sciences and Humanities, 10*(1).

Dalgarno, B., & Lee, M. J. W. (2010). What are the learning affordances of 3D virtual environments? *British Journal of Educational Technology*, *41*(1), 10–32.

Dalim, C. S. C., Kolivand, H., Kadhim, H., Sunar, M. S., & Billinghurst, M. (2017). Factors influencing the acceptance of augmented reality in education: A review of the literature. In *Journal of Computer Science* (Vol. 13, Issue 11, pp. 581–589). https://doi.org/DOI: 10.3844/jcssp.2017.581.589

Dasgupta, D., & Sarkar, S. (2022). Privacy: A myth in online gaming? *International Journal of Advanced Mass Communication and Journalism*, *3*(2), 38–47. DOI: 10.22271/27084450.2022.v3.i2a.49

Davis, C. A., & Mobarak, A. M. (2020). The challenges of scaling effective interventions: A path forward for research and policy. *World Development*, *127*, 104817. DOI: 10.1016/j.worlddev.2019.104817

Davis, R. (2024). Korean in-service teachers' perceptions of implementing artificial intelligence (ai) education for teaching in schools and their ai teacher training programs. *International Journal of Information and Education Technology (IJIET)*, *14*(2), 214–219. DOI: 10.18178/ijiet.2024.14.2.2042

De Back, T. T., Tinga, A. M., & Louwerse, M. M. (2021). Learning in immersed collaborative virtual environments: Design and implementation. *Interactive Learning Environments*, *31*(8), 5364–5382. DOI: 10.1080/10494820.2021.2006238

Deci, E. L., & Ryan, R. M. (1993). Die Selbstbestimmungstheorie der Motivation und ihre Bedeutung für die Pädagogik [The self-determination theory of motivation and its importance for pedagogy]. *Zeitschrift für Pädagogik*, *39*(2), 223–238.

Deci, E. L., & Ryan, R. M. (Eds.). (2004). *Handbook of self-determination research.* University of Rochester Press.

DeCuir-Gunby, J. T., & Bindra, V. G. (2022). How does teacher bias influence students?: An introduction to the special issue on teachers' implicit attitudes, instructional practices, and student outcomes. *Learning and Instruction*, *78*, 101523. DOI: 10.1016/j.learninstruc.2021.101523

Dengel, A., Buchner, J., Mulders, M., & Pirker, J. (2024). *Levels of Immersive Teaching and Learning: Influences of Challenges in the Everyday Classroom.*

Department of Communications and Digital Technologies. (2020). *National Digital and Future Skills Strategy South Africa.* Government Gazette No. 43730.

Deri, M. N., Zaazie, P., & Singh, A. (2024). Digital Future of the Hospitality Industry and Hospitality Education Globally. In Sharma, A. (Ed.), *International Handbook of Skill, Education, Learning, and Research Development in Tourism and Hospitality. Springer International Handbooks of Education.* Springer., DOI: 10.1007/978-981-97-4318-6_14

Deterding, S., & Cutting, J. (2023). Objective difficulty-skill balance impacts perceived balance but not behaviour: A test of flow and self-determination theory predictions. *Proceedings of the ACM on Human-Computer Interaction, 7*(CHI PLAY), 1179-1205.

Deterding, S., Dixon, D., Khaled, R., & Nacke, L. (2011). From game design elements to "gamefulness": Defining gamification. In *Proceedings of the 15th International Academic MindTrek Conference* (pp. 9–15). ACM. https://doi.org/ DOI: 10.1145/2181037.2181040

Devakirubai, T. S. (2025). Digital Twins Supercharges Efficiency-Unlocking the Power of Industry 5.0. 6G Urban Innovation: AI and Digital Twin for Next-Gen Sustainable Cities, 163-178.

Devi, V., Vashe, A., Rao, R., Abraham, R., Pallath, V., & Torke, S. (2016). Curricular impact on learning approaches and critical thinking skills of medical students. *Education in Medicine Journal*, *8*(4). Advance online publication. DOI: 10.5959/eimj.v8i4.468

Dezuanni, M., O'Mara, J., & Beavis, C. (2015). "Redstone is like electricity": Children's performative representations in and around Minecraft. *E-Learning and Digital Media*, *12*(2), 147–163. DOI: 10.1177/2042753014568176

Dhakal, B. R. (2024). Differentiated Instruction: Tailoring learning for diverse learners. *Sikshya*, *40*(54), 167–176.

Dhar, P., Rocks, T., Samarasinghe, R. M., Stephenson, G., & Smith, C. (2021). Augmented reality in medical education: Students' experiences and learning outcomes. *Medical Education Online*, *26*(1). Advance online publication. DOI: 10.1080/10872981.2021.1953953 PMID: 34259122

Dichev, C., & Dicheva, D. (2017). Gamifying education: what is known, what is believed and what remains uncertain: a critical review. *International Journal of Educational Technology in Higher Education*, *14*(1). Advance online publication. DOI: 10.1186/s41239-017-0042-5

Dick, E. (2021). *The promise of immersive learning*. Information Technology & Innovation Foundation.

Dindar, M., Ren, L., & Järvenoja, H. (2020). An experimental study on the effects of gamified cooperation and competition on english vocabulary learning. *British Journal of Educational Technology*, *52*(1), 142–159. DOI: 10.1111/bjet.12977

Ding, A. C. E., Huang, K. T. T., DuBois, J., & Fu, H. (2024). Integrating immersive virtual reality technology in scaffolded game-based learning to enhance low motivation students' multimodal science learning. *Educational Technology Research and Development*, *72*(4), 2083–2102.

Dirgantoro, K., Bermuli, J., & Soesanto, R. (2022). Is moodle gamification effective in reviewing student's motivation related to interest in learning online? *Educational Journal Journal of Research Results and Literature Review in the Field of Education, Teaching, and Learning*, *8*(1), 114. DOI: 10.33394/jk.v8i1.4790

Domínguez Alfaro, J. L., Gantois, S., Blattgerste, J., de Croon, R., Verbert, K., Pfeiffer, T., & van Puyvelde, P. (2022). Mobile augmented reality laboratory for learning acid–base titration. *Journal of Chemical Education*, *99*(2), 531–537. DOI: 10.1021/acs.jchemed.1c00892

Dovleac, L., Chi u, I., Nichifor, E., & Brătucu, G. (2023). Shaping the inclusivity in the new society by enhancing the digitainability of sustainable development goals with education. *Sustainability*, *15*(4), 3782. DOI: 10.3390/su15043782

Du Plessis, A. E. (2019). Barriers to effective management of diversity in classroom contexts: The out-of-field teaching phenomenon. *International Journal of Educational Research*, *93*, 136–152. DOI: 10.1016/j.ijer.2018.11.002

Dubovi, I. (2022). Cognitive and emotional engagement while learning with VR: The perspective of multimodal methodology. *Computers & Education*, *183*, 104495. DOI: 10.1016/j.compedu.2022.104495

Duma, N. M., Mlambo, S., Mbambo-Mkwanazi, S., & Morgan, W. (2021). Digital Inequalities in Rural Schools in South Africa. *Ocean Science Journal*, *6*(3). Advance online publication. DOI: 10.23954/osj.v6i3.2984

Duncan, K. J. (2020). Examining the effects of immersive game-based learning on student engagement and the development of collaboration, communication, creativity and critical thinking. *TechTrends*, *64*(3), 514–524.

Edwards, J. (2022). Gamification, anxiety, & motivation in second language learners: A qualitative systematic review. Language, Education, & [LET Journal]. *Technology*, *2*(2), 98–127.

Egbert, J., & Borysenko, N. (2019). Standards, engagement, and Minecraft: Optimizing experiences in language teacher education. *Teaching and Teacher Education*, *85*, 115–124. DOI: 10.1016/j.tate.2019.06.015

Ejaz, H., McGrath, H., Wong, B., Guise, A., Vercauteren, T., & Shapey, J. (2022). Artificial intelligence and medical education: A global mixed-methods study of medical students' perspectives. *Digital Health*, *8*, 205520762210890. DOI: 10.1177/20552076221089099

El Mawas, N., Tal, I., Moldovan, A. N., Bogusevschi, D., Andrews, J., Muntean, G. M., & Muntean, C. H. (2018, March). Final frontier game: A case study on learner experience. In CSEDU-10th International Conference on Computer Supported Education.

El-Hajj, M. (2024). Cybersecurity and Privacy Challenges in Extended Reality: Threats, Solutions, and Risk Mitigation Strategies. *Virtual Worlds 2025, Vol. 4, Page 1, 4*(1), 1. https://doi.org/DOI: 10.3390/VIRTUALWORLDS4010001

Elmqaddem, N. (2019). Augmented Reality and Virtual Reality in education. Myth or reality? *International Journal of Emerging Technologies in Learning, 14*(3), 234–242. DOI: 10.3991/ijet.v14i03.9289

Englund, C. (2017). Exploring approaches to teaching in three-dimensional virtual worlds. *The International Journal of Information and Learning Technology, 34*(2), 140–151. DOI: 10.1108/IJILT-09-2016-0045

Erbaşı, Z. (2023). The role and potential of artificial intelligence and gamification in education: The example of vakıf participation bank. *Orclever Proceedings of Research and Development, 3*(1), 243–254. DOI: 10.56038/oprd.v3i1.329

Eslit, E. (2023). Blending boundaries in the new normal: Leveraging technology, ai and global perspectives in modern education. *Journal of Learning and Educational Policy*, (41), 8–18. DOI: 10.55529/jlep.41.8.18

Evayani, D., Jampel, I., & Widiana, I. (2021). Mission book game: Enhancing fifth-grade students' learning motivation on thematic learning. *Indonesian Journal of Educational Research and Review, 4*(3), 459. DOI: 10.23887/ijerr.v4i2.38492

Fajri, F. A., Haribowo, P. R. K., Amalia, N., & Natasari, D. (2021). Gamification in e-learning: The mitigation role in technostress. *International Journal of Evaluation and Research in Education, 10*(2), 606–614. DOI: 10.11591/ijere.v10i2.21365

Fälth, L., Brkovic, I., Kerestes, G., Svensson, I., Hjelmquist, E., & Tjus, T. (2023). The effects of a multimodal intervention on the reading skills of struggling students: An exploration across countries. *Reading Psychology, 44*(3), 225–241.

Familoni, B. (2024). Advancements and challenges in ai integration for technical literacy: A systematic review. *Engineering Science & Technology Journal, 5*(4), 1415–1430. DOI: 10.51594/estj.v5i4.1042

Fang, K., & Wang, J. (2024). Interactive Design With Gesture and Voice Recognition in Virtual Teaching Environments. *IEEE Access : Practical Innovations, Open Solutions, 12*. Advance online publication. DOI: 10.1109/ACCESS.2023.3348846

Fazil, A. (2024). Exploring the broad impact of ai technologies on student engagement and academic performance in university settings in afghanistan. *Riggs Journal of Artificial Intelligence and Digital Business*, *2*(2), 56–63. DOI: 10.31004/riggs.v2i2.268

Felzmann, H., Fosch-Villaronga, E., Lutz, C., & Tamò-Larrieux, A. (2020). Towards transparency by design for artificial intelligence. *Science and Engineering Ethics*, *26*(6), 3333–3361. DOI: 10.1007/s11948-020-00276-4

Feng, Z., González, V. A., Amor, R., Spearpoint, M., Thomas, J., Sacks, R., Lovreglio, R., & Cabrera-Guerrero, G. (2020). An immersive virtual reality serious game to enhance earthquake behavioral responses and post-earthquake evacuation preparedness in buildings. *Advanced Engineering Informatics*, *45*. Advance online publication. DOI: 10.1016/j.aei.2020.101118

Fereidouni, H., Fadeitcheva, O., & Zalai, M. (2025). IoT and Man-in-the-Middle Attacks. *Security and Privacy*, *8*(2), e70016. DOI: 10.1002/SPY2.70016

Fernandes, F. A., Rodrigues, C. S. C., Teixeira, E. N., & Werner, C. M. (2023). Immersive learning frameworks: A systematic literature review. *IEEE Transactions on Learning Technologies*, *16*(5), 736–747.

Ferrer-Torregrosa, J., Torralba, J., Jimenez, M. A., García, S., & Barcia, J. M. (2015). ARBOOK: Development and assessment of a tool based on augmented reality for anatomy. *Journal of Science Education and Technology*, *24*(2–3), 119–124. DOI: 10.1007/s10956-014-9526-4

Fırat, M. (2023). Integrating ai applications into learning management systems to enhance e-learning. *Öğretim Teknolojisi Ve Hayat Boyu Öğrenme Dergisi - Instructional Technology and Lifelong Learning*, 1-14. https://doi.org/DOI: 10.52911/itall.1244453

Foster, A. N., & Shah, M. (2020). Principles for advancing game-based learning in teacher education. *Journal of Digital Learning in Teacher Education*, *36*(2), 1–12. DOI: 10.1080/21532974.2019.1695553

Fowler, C. (2015). Virtual reality and learning: Where is the pedagogy? *British Journal of Educational Technology*, *46*(2), 412–422.

Francesca, T. (2019). *Comparing privacy laws: GDPR v. CCPA*. https://futurium.ec.europa.eu/en/european-ai-alliance/open-library/comparing-privacy-laws-gdpr-v-ccpa

Francis, R. S., Anantharajah, S., Sengupta, S., & Singh, A. (2024). Leveraging ChatGPT and Digital Marketing for Enhanced Customer Engagement in the Hotel Industry. In Bansal, R., Ngah, A., Chakir, A., & Pruthi, N. (Eds.), *Leveraging ChatGPT and Artificial Intelligence for Effective Customer Engagement* (pp. 55–68). IGI Global., DOI: 10.4018/979-8-3693-0815-8.ch004

Franco, C. (2022). Gamification in a textbook for brazilian learners of english. Belt – Brazilian English Language Teaching Journal, 13(1), e41062. DOI: 10.15448/2178-3640.2022.1.41062

Frankl, D. (2024). *Exploring Security Weaknesses in VR Systems*. https://oda.uni-obuda.hu/handle/20.500.14044/25947

Frolli, A., Cerciello, F., Esposito, C., Russo, M., & Bisogni, F. (2023). Learning italian as a second language in a sample of ukrainian children: A game-based learning approach. *Pediatric Reports*, *15*(3), 502–511. DOI: 10.3390/pediatric15030046 PMID: 37606450

Fromm, J., Radianti, J., Wehking, C., Stieglitz, S., Majchrzak, T. A., & vom Brocke, J. (2021). More than experience? On the unique opportunities of virtual reality to afford a holistic experiential learning cycle. *The Internet and Higher Education*, *50*, 100804. DOI: 10.1016/j.iheduc.2021.100804

Fuster-Guilló, A., Pertegal-Felices, M., Jimeno-Morenilla, A., Azorín-López, J., Soliveres, M., & Restrepo-Calle, F. (2019). Evaluating impact on motivation and academic performance of a game-based learning experience using kahoot. *Frontiers in Psychology*, *10*. Advance online publication. DOI: 10.3389/fpsyg.2019.02843

Galliher, A. (2024). Engaging aural skills students with model-eliciting activities. *Journal of Music Theory Pedagogy*, *38*(1), 67–94. https://digitalcollections.lipscomb.edu/cgi/viewcontent.cgi?article=1470&context=jmtp

Gamrat, C., Zimmerman, H., Dudek, J., & Peck, K. (2014). Personalized workplace learning: An exploratory study on digital badging within a teacher professional development program. *British Journal of Educational Technology*, *45*(6), 1136–1148. DOI: 10.1111/bjet.12200

Garcia-Bonete, M.-J., Jensen, M., & Katona, G. (2019). A practical guide to developing virtual and augmented reality exercises for teaching structural biology. *Biochemistry and Molecular Biology Education*, *47*(1), 16–24. DOI: 10.1002/bmb.21188

Garg, A., Singh, A., & Yanan, J. (2024). Exploring the Impact of Digital Detoxification on Higher Education Students' Learning. In Grima, S., Chaudhary, S., Sood, K., & Kumar, S. (Eds.), *Business Drivers in Promoting Digital Detoxification* (pp. 111–126). IGI Global Scientific Publishing., DOI: 10.4018/979-8-3693-1107-3.ch008

Garrison, D. R., Anderson, T., & Archer, W. (2000). Critical inquiry in a text-based environment: Computer conferencing in higher education. *The Internet and Higher Education*, *2*(2–3), 87–105.

Gautam, D. (2024). Revolutionizing Education through Innovative Technological Solutions. As the editors of Transforming Learning. *Power and Education*, •••, 60.

Ghory, S., & Ghafory, H. (2021). The impact of modern technology in the teaching and learning process. *International Journal of Innovative Research and Scientific Studies*, *4*(3), 219–227.

Gibson, D. C., Ostashewski, N., Flintoff, K., Grant, S., & Knight, E. B. (2013). Digital badges in education. *Education and Information Technologies*, *20*(2), 1–8. DOI: 10.1007/s10639-013-9291-7

Gladwell, M. (2008). *Outliers: The story of success*. Little, Brown and Company.

Gligorea, I., Yaseen, M., Cioca, M., Gorski, H., & Oancea, R. (2022). An interpretable framework for an efficient analysis of students' academic performance. *Sustainability*, *14*(14), 8885. DOI: 10.3390/su14148885

Gomes, P. V., Marques, A., Donga, J., Sá, C., Correia, A., & Pereira, J. (2021). Adaptive Model for Biofeedback Data Flows Management in the Design of Interactive Immersive Environments. *Applied Sciences 2021, Vol. 11, Page 5067*, *11*(11), 5067. https://doi.org/DOI: 10.3390/APP11115067

Gomes, J., Figueiredo, M., & Amante, L. (2014). Musical journey: A virtual world gamification experience for music learning. *International Journal on Advances in Education Research*, *1*(1), 1–21.

Gong, L., & Wang, J. (2023). Interactive Learning Environment for Effective Music Learning in Chinese Primary and Secondary Schools. *Sustainability*, *15*, 2143. DOI: 10.3390/su15032143

Gortázar, F., Gallego, M., Maes-Bermejo, M., Chicano-Capelo, I., & Santos, C. (2022). Cost-effective load testing of WebRTC applications. *Journal of Systems and Software*, *193*. Advance online publication. DOI: 10.1016/j.jss.2022.111439

Gotham, M., Micchi, G., López, N. N., & Sailor, M. (2023). When in Rome: A meta-corpus of functional harmony. *Transactions of the International Society for Music Information Retrieval, 6*(1).

Govender, T., & Arnedo-Moreno, J. (2021). An analysis of game design elements used in digital game-based language learning. *Sustainability, 13*(12), 6679. DOI: 10.3390/su13126679

Granić, A. (2022). Educational technology adoption: A systematic review. *Education and Information Technologies, 27*(7), 9725–9744. PMID: 35399780

Grashel, J. (1993). An integrated approach: Comprehensive musicianship. *Music Educators Journal, 79*(8), 38–41. DOI: 10.2307/3398596

Groff, J. S. (2018). The potentials of game-based environments for integrated, immersive learning data. *European Journal of Education, 53*(2), 188–201.

Grunhut, J., Wyatt, A., & Marques, O. (2021). Educating future physicians in artificial intelligence (ai): An integrative review and proposed changes. *Journal of Medical Education and Curricular Development, 8*. Advance online publication. DOI: 10.1177/23821205211036836

Güler, S., & Özkan, Y. (2018). Podcast applications in pre-service language teacher education from a constructivist perspective. *World Journal on Educational Technology Current Issues, 10*(3), 131–141. DOI: 10.18844/wjet.v10i3.3552

Gunder, A., & Buckner, M. (2023). Story as pedagogy: Leveraging narrative digital learning practices in the instructional design process. *Ubiquity Proceedings, 3*(1), 210–215. DOI: 10.5334/uproc.88

Gupta, M. S., & Warkhedkar, M. P. (2022). A Study of Impact of Edtech Companies on Education with Special Reference to Byjus and Vedantu. J. of Education: Rabindra Bharati University.

Haak, P. (1992). The acquisition of music listening skills. In Colwell, R. (Ed.), *Handbook of research on music teaching and learning* (pp. 451–465). Schirmer.

Hadi, R., & Park, E. S. (2024). Bridging the digital and physical: The psychology of augmented reality. *Current Opinion in Psychology, 58*, 101842. DOI: 10.1016/j.copsyc.2024.101842 PMID: 38986168

Halim, M., Hashim, H., & Yunus, M. (2020). Pupils' motivation and perceptions on esl lessons through online quiz-games. *Journal of Education and e-learning Research, 7*(3), 229–234. DOI: 10.20448/journal.509.2020.73.229.234

Hamad, A., & Jia, B. (2022). How Virtual Reality Technology Has Changed Our Lives: An Overview of the Current and Potential Applications and Limitations. In *International Journal of Environmental Research and Public Health* (Vol. 19, Issue 18). https://doi.org/DOI: 10.3390/ijerph191811278

Hamari, J., Koivisto, J., & Sarsa, H. (2014). Does gamification work? A literature review of empirical studies on gamification. In *2014 47th Hawaii International Conference on System Sciences* (pp. 3025–3034). IEEE. https://doi.org/DOI: 10.1109/HICSS.2014.377

Hanus, M. D., & Fox, J. (2015). Assessing the effects of gamification in the classroom: A longitudinal study on intrinsic motivation, social comparison, satisfaction, effort, and academic performance. *Computers & Education*, *80*, 152–161. DOI: 10.1016/j.compedu.2014.08.019

Harden, P., & Fanfarelli, J. R. (2023). Boundaries, Informed Consent, and Learning. In *Ethical Considerations of Virtual Reality in the College Classroom* (pp. 293–304). Routledge.

Haresamudram, K., Larsson, S., & Heintz, F. (2023). Three levels of ai transparency. *Computer*, *56*(2), 93–100. DOI: 10.1109/mc.2022.3213181

Harry, A. (2023). Role of ai in education. *Interdiciplinary Journal and Hummanity (Injurity)*, *2*(3), 260–268. DOI: 10.58631/injurity.v2i3.52

Henderson, M., Ryan, T., Boud, D., Dawson, P., Phillips, M., Molloy, E., & Mahoney, P. (2019). The usefulness of feedback. *Active Learning in Higher Education*, *22*(3), 229–243. DOI: 10.1177/1469787419872393

Henry, J., Li, F., & Arnab, S. (2024). On the pre-perception of gamification and game-based learning in higher education students: A systematic mapping study. *Simulation & Gaming*, *55*(6), 985–1010. DOI: 10.1177/10468781241271082

Hernández, C. (2023). Development of critical thinking in the university curriculum. International. *Journal of Human Sciences Research*, *3*(34), 2–9. DOI: 10.22533/at.ed.5583342313095

Hidayat, D. (2021). The implementation of gamification system in asian higher education teaching. *Journal of Games Game Art and Gamification*, *2*(1). Advance online publication. DOI: 10.21512/jggag.v2i1.7218

Hollands, F., Pan, Y., & Escueta, M. (2019). What is the potential for applying cost-utility analysis to facilitate evidence-based decision making in schools? *Educational Researcher*, *48*(5), 287–295. DOI: 10.3102/0013189x19852101

Hollow, D., & Jefferies, K. (2022). *How EdTech can be used to help address the global learning crisis: A challenge to the sector for an evidence-driven future.* EdTech Hub.

Honoris United Universities. (n.d). Regent Business School South Africa: MAHALABox, An Innovative Way to Address Unemployment. https://honoris.net/impactreport-refonte/regent-business-school-south-africa-mahalabox

Hoque, M. E. (2021). Tell me and I forget; teach me and I remember; involve me and I learn: Navigating the way of teaching. *The EDRC Journal of Learning and Teaching*, *7*(3), 30–42.

Hornbach, H. (2015). Singing and tonal audiation from early childhood to secondary. In Conway, C. (Ed.), *Musicianship-focused curriculum and assessment* (pp. 181–214). GIA Publications.

Horton, A. G., Gibson, K. B., & Curington, A. M. (2021). Exploring reflective journaling as a learning tool: An interdisciplinary approach. *Archives of Psychiatric Nursing*, *35*(2), 195–199. DOI: 10.1016/j.apnu.2020.09.009 PMID: 33781400

Höyng, M. (2022). Encouraging gameful experience in digital game-based learning: A double-mediation model of perceived instructional support, group engagement, and flow. *Computers & Education*, *179*, 104408.

Hsia, L., & Yamat, H. (2022). The use of kahoot and its role in improving irregular verbs learning among primary esl learners. *International Journal of Academic Research in Progressive Education and Development*, *11*(2). Advance online publication. DOI: 10.6007/ijarped/v11-i2/13358

Hsu, M. E., & Cheng, M. T. (2021). Immersion experiences and behavioural patterns in game-based learning. *British Journal of Educational Technology*, *52*(5), 1981–1999.

Huang, H. Y., Lin, Y. C. D., Li, J., Huang, K. Y., Shrestha, S., Hong, H. C., & Huang, H. D. (2020). miRTarBase 2020: Updates to the experimentally validated microRNA–target interaction database. *Nucleic Acids Research*, *48*(D1), D148–D154. PMID: 31647101

Huesca, G., Campos, G., Larre, M., & Pérez-Lezama, C. (2023). Implementation of a mixed strategy of gamification and flipped learning in undergraduate basic programming courses. *Education Sciences*, *13*(5), 474. DOI: 10.3390/educsci13050474

Huseinović, L. (2024). The effects of gamification on student motivation and achievement in learning English as a foreign language in higher education. *MAP Education and Humanities*, *4*, 10–36.

Hussain, M., Anuar, N., Jalil, N., & Sulaiman, N. (2023). Language attitudes and motivation of esl secondary school students. *International Journal of Academic Research in Business & Social Sciences*, *13*(12). Advance online publication. DOI: 10.6007/ijarbss/v13-i12/20246

Hutson, J., & Hutson, P. (2024). Immersive Technologies. *Inclusive Smart Museums*, 153–228. https://doi.org/DOI: 10.1007/978-3-031-43615-4_5

Hutson, J., & Hutson, P. (2024). Immersive technologies. In *Inclusive smart museums: Engaging neurodiverse audiences and enhancing cultural heritage* (pp. 153–228). Springer Nature Switzerland.

Huynh-The, T., Gadekallu, T. R., Wang, W., Yenduri, G., Ranaweera, P., Pham, Q. V., da Costa, D. B., & Liyanage, M. (2023). Blockchain for the metaverse: A Review. *Future Generation Computer Systems*, *143*. Advance online publication. DOI: 10.1016/j.future.2023.02.008

Ibáñez, M. B., Di Serio, Á., Villarán, D., & Delgado Kloos, C. (2014). Experimenting with electromagnetism using augmented reality: Impact on flow student experience and educational effectiveness. *Computers & Education*, *71*, 1–13. DOI: 10.1016/j.compedu.2013.09.013

Idris, M., Said, N., & Tan, K. (2020). Game-based learning platform and its effects on present tense mastery: Evidence from an esl classroom. *International Journal of Learning Teaching and Educational Research*, *19*(5), 13–26. DOI: 10.26803/ijlter.19.5.2

İlkay, A., Dalmış, İ., Şen, A., & Sarıkaya, Ö. (2025). Transformative 21st-century approaches in musical ear training. *SAGE Open*, *15*(1), 215824402513264. DOI: 10.1177/21582440251326438

Iqbal, M. Z., Mangina, E., & Campbell, A. G. (2022). Current Challenges and Future Research Directions in Augmented Reality for Education. *Multimodal Technologies and Interaction*, *6*(9), 1–29. DOI: 10.3390/mti6090075

Islam, M., & Moon, A. (2022). Motivation and attitudes towards learning a foreign language: A psycho-sociolinguistic study on the undergraduate students. *Shanlax International Journal of English*, *10*(4), 37–45. DOI: 10.34293/english.v10i4.5145

Isseks, M. (2022). *Engagement with EdTech: A Case Study on Student and Teacher Perceptions of Instructional Technology on Student Engagement in Middle School English Language Arts Classrooms* (Doctoral dissertation, State University of New York at Buffalo).

Jasrotia, S. S., Kamila, M. K., Chib, S., & Raj, V. A. (2025). BYJU'S–The Indian edtech giant under dark skies: Can they survive? *Journal of Information Technology Teaching Cases*, 20438869251347635.

Jayaraman, J. D., & Jambunathan, S. (2018). Financial literacy among high school students: Evidence from India. *Citizenship. Social and Economics Education*, *17*(3), 168–186. DOI: 10.1177/2047173418809712

Jayavardhini, P. (2024). Ai study partner: Development of an llm and gen ai-enhanced study assistant tool. *Interantional Journal of Scientific Research in Engineering and Management*, *08*(03), 1–5. DOI: 10.55041/ijsrem29626

Jiang, M. (2023). The impact and potential of educational technology: A comprehensive review. *Research and Advances in Education*, *2*(7), 32–49. DOI: 10.56397/rae.2023.07.05

Ji, H., Suo, L., & Hua, C. (2024). Ai performance assessment in blended learning: Mechanisms and effects on students' continuous learning motivation. *Frontiers in Psychology*, *15*. Advance online publication. DOI: 10.3389/fpsyg.2024.1447680

Jin, S., Huang, J., & Zhong, Z. (2024). Application of Immersive Technologies in Primary and Secondary Education. *Frontiers in Digital Education*, *1*(2), 142–152. DOI: 10.1007/s44366-024-0001-3

Jobin, A., & Ienca, M. (2019). The global landscape of ai ethics guidelines. *Nature Machine Intelligence*, *1*(9), 389–399. DOI: 10.1038/s42256-019-0088-2

Johnson, D., Deterding, S., Kuhn, K., Staneva, A., Stoyanov, S., & Hides, L. (2016). Gamification for health and wellbeing: A systematic review of the literature. *Internet Interventions : the Application of Information Technology in Mental and Behavioural Health*, *6*, 89–106. DOI: 10.1016/j.invent.2016.10.002

Joo, Y. J., Park, S., & Lim, E. (2018). Factors influencing preservice teachers' intention to use technology: TPACK, teacher self-efficacy, and technology acceptance model. *Journal of Educational Technology & Society*, *21*(3), 48–59.

Jose, D. (2024). Data privacy and security concerns in ai-integrated educational platforms. rmc, 5(2), 87-91. DOI: 10.46632/rmc/5/2/19

Juchniewicz, J., Kelly, S. N., & Acklin, A. I. (2014). Rehearsal characteristics of "superior" band directors. *Update: Applications of Research in Music Education*, *32*(2), 35–43. DOI: 10.1177/8755123314521030

Julita, R. (2024). The impact of gamification on efl students' reading comprehension. *JEFLE*, *4*(2), 136. DOI: 10.26418/jefle.v4i2.74901

Kabilan, M., Annamalai, N., & Chuah, K. (2023). Practices, purposes and challenges in integrating gamification using technology: A mixed methods study on university academics. *Education and Information Technologies*, *28*(11), 14249–14281. DOI: 10.1007/s10639-023-11723-7 PMID: 37361777

Kadriu, A., & Abazi Bexheti, L. (2022). The Who in VR/AR for Education: A Scoping Review from IEEE Publications. *ENTRENOVA - ENTerprise REsearch InNOVAtion, 8*(1), 1–8. https://doi.org/DOI: 10.54820/entrenova-2022-0001

Kahneman, D., & Tversky, A. (1979). Prospect theory: An analysis of decision under risk. *Econometrica*, *47*(2), 263–292. DOI: 10.2307/1914185

Kamarudin, N., Ikram, R., Azman, F., Ahmad, S., & Zainuddin, D. (2022). A study of the effects of short-term ai coding course with gamification elements on students' cognitive mental health. Tem Journal, 1854-1862. DOI: 10.18421/tem114-53

Kamruzzaman, M. (2023). Ai- and iot-assisted sustainable education systems during pandemics, such as covid-19, for smart cities. *Sustainability*, *15*(10), 8354. DOI: 10.3390/su15108354

Kang, H., & Kusuma, G. (2020). The effectiveness of personality-based gamification model for foreign vocabulary online learning. *Advances in Science, Technology and Engineering Systems Journal*, *5*(2), 261–271. DOI: 10.25046/aj050234

Kang, J., Kang, C., Yoon, J., Ji, H., Li, T., Hyunmi, M., & Han, J. (2023). Dancing on the inside: A qualitative study on online dance learning with teacher-ai cooperation. *Education and Information Technologies*, *28*(9), 12111–12141. DOI: 10.1007/s10639-023-11649-0

Kapp, K. (2015). *The gamification of learning and instruction: Game-based methods and strategies for training and education*. Wiley.

Karabıyık, Ü. (2024). Investigation of the effect of gamified learning on motivation and success in math class. *Journal of Education and Practice*, *8*(1), 32–52. DOI: 10.47941/jep.1645

Katiyar, P. (2024). Ai-driven personalized learning systems: enhancing educational effectiveness. *eatp*. https://doi.org/DOI: 10.53555/kuey.v30i5.4961

Kaur, N., Singh, V., Mahajan, N., & Garg, N. (2023, February). Game based learning-immersive teaching and learning platform through metaverse. In *2023 3rd International Conference on Innovative Practices in Technology and Management (ICIPTM)* (pp. 1-6). IEEE.

Kazu, İ., & Kuvvetli, M. (2024). Improve speaking skills with duolingo's mobile game-based language learning. *Asian Journal of Education and Training, 10*(1), 62–75. DOI: 10.20448/edu.v10i1.5488

Khakpour, A., & Colomo-Palacios, R. (2020). Convergence of gamification and machine learning: A systematic literature review. *Technology Knowledge and Learning, 26*(3), 597–636. DOI: 10.1007/s10758-020-09456-4

Khan, M. A. M., & Mishra, D. C. Digital Sales and Marketing: A Study of Private Coaching Industry.

Khasanova, O., Karimova, A., & Mubarakshina, A. (2020). Web quest technologies for learning english at university: opportunities and prospects.. DOI: 10.3897/ap.2.e1055

Khlaif, Z., Salama, N., Hamamra, B., & Mousa, A. (2025). Factors influencing educators' perspectives on accepting extended reality in health care education: Qualitative study. *JMIR Medical Education, 11*. Advance online publication. DOI: 10.2196/65042 PMID: 40310667

Khoza, R. T. (2023). *Digital Transformation Inequality in South African Secondary Schools Affecting the Implementation of 4IR Era Relevant Curriculum*. University of Johannesburg.

Kibici, V. B. (2022). Effects of online constructivist 5E instructional model on secondary school music lessons. *International Journal of Technology in Education, 5*(1), 117–131. DOI: 10.46328/ijte.241

Kien, L. and Nguyen, N. (2021). Gamification elements and their potential influence on employee motivation - a literature review of models.. DOI: 10.2991/aebmr.k.211119.016

Kilfoil, W. R. (Ed.). (2015). *Moving beyond the hype: A contextualised view of learning with technology in higher education*. Universities South Africa.

Kim, C., Kim, M. K., Lee, C., Spector, J. M., & DeMeester, K. (2013). Teacher beliefs and technology integration. *Teaching and Teacher Education, 29*, 76–85. DOI: 10.1016/j.tate.2012.08.005

Kim, J., & Castelli, D. (2021). Effects of gamification on behavioral change in education: A meta-analysis. *International Journal of Environmental Research and Public Health, 18*(7), 3550. DOI: 10.3390/ijerph18073550

Kim, S., Raza, M., & Seidman, E. (2019). Improving 21st-century teaching skills: The key to effective 21st-century learners. *Research in Comparative and International Education, 14*(1), 99–117. DOI: 10.1177/1745499919829214

Kirby, A., Lawrence, H., & Rowe, V. (2022). Musical play and young children's wellbeing. *Early Childhood Education Journal, 51*(2), 267–278. DOI: 10.1007/s10643-022-01309-2

Kolb, D. A. (1984). *Experiential learning: Experience as the source of learning and development*. Prentice Hall.

Krashen, S. D. (1982). *Principles and practice in second language acquisition.* Pergamon Press.

Krauß, V., Boden, A., Oppermann, L., & Reiners, R. (2021). Current practices, challenges, and design implications for collaborative ar/vr application development. *Conference on Human Factors in Computing Systems - Proceedings*. https://doi.org/DOI: 10.1145/3411764.3445335

Krishnan, S., Norman, H., & Yunus, M. (2021). Online gamified learning to enhance teachers' competencies using classcraft. *Sustainability, 13*(19), 10817. DOI: 10.3390/su131910817

Krome, N., & Kopp, S. (2023). Towards Real-time Co-speech Gesture Generation in Online Interaction in Social XR. *Proceedings of the 23rd ACM International Conference on Intelligent Virtual Agents, IVA 2023*. https://doi.org/DOI: 10.1145/3570945.3607315

Krug, M., Czok, V., Huwer, J., Weitzel, H., & Müller, W. (2021). Challenges for the design of augmented reality applications for science teacher education. In L. Gómez Chova, A. López Martínez, & I. Candel Torres (Eds.), *INTED2021 proceedings* (pp. 2484–2491). IATED.

Krug, M., Czok, V., Müller, S., Weitzel, H., Huwer, J., Kruse, S., & Müller, W. (2022). AR in science education—An AR based teaching-learning scenario in the field of teacher education. *CHEMKON, 29*(7), 312–318. DOI: 10.1002/ckon.202200017

Kuhail, M. A., Elsayary, A., Farooq, S., & Alghamdi, A. (2022). Exploring immersive learning experiences: A survey. *Informatics (MDPI), 9*(4), 75. DOI: 10.3390/informatics9040075

Kulkarni, M. (2019). Digital accessibility: Challenges and opportunities. *IIMB Management Review, 31*(1), 91–98. DOI: 10.1016/j.iimb.2018.05.009

Kumari, S., Pothu, L., Padmambika, P., & Bobbili, S. (2024). Bridging the digital divide: Addressing inequality and access disparities. *International Journal of Indiān Psychology, 12*(3), 1151–1156. DOI: 10.25215/1203.111

Kumar, R., Gupta, S. K., Wang, H. C., Kumari, C. S., & Korlam, S. S. V. P. (2023). From efficiency to sustainability: Exploring the potential of 6G for a greener future. *Sustainability, 15*(23), 16387.

Kurniawati, N., Maolida, E., & Anjaniputra, A. (2018). The praxis of digital literacy in the efl classroom: Digital-immigrant vs digital-native teacher. *Indonesian Journal of Applied Linguistics, 8*(1). Advance online publication. DOI: 10.17509/ijal.v8i1.11459

Kuzmich, J. (2015). Seamless classroom integration of national standards & cutting-edge music technology. *School Band & Orchestra, 18*(6), 38–40.

Laine, J., Korhonen, T., & Hakkarainen, K. (2023). Primary school students' experiences of immersive virtual reality use in the classroom. *Cogent Education, 10*(1), 2196896. Advance online publication. DOI: 10.1080/2331186X.2023.2196896

Laine, T., & Lindberg, R. (2020). Designing engaging games for education: A systematic literature review on game motivators and design principles. *IEEE Transactions on Learning Technologies, 13*(4), 804–821. DOI: 10.1109/tlt.2020.3018503

Lampropoulos, G., Keramopoulos, E., Diamantaras, K., & Evangelidis, G. (2022). Augmented reality and gamification in education: A systematic literature review of research, applications, and empirical studies. *Applied Sciences (Basel, Switzerland), 12*(13), 6809. Advance online publication. DOI: 10.3390/app12136809

Lampropoulos, G., Keramopoulos, E., Diamantaras, K., & Evangelidis, G. (2023). Integrating Augmented Reality, Gamification, and Serious Games in Computer Science Education. *Education Sciences, 13*(6). Advance online publication. DOI: 10.3390/educsci13060618

Langfeldt, V. (2023). Holistic and ecologically valid aural training within culturally diverse music education contexts. *Nordic Research in Music Education, 4*, 23–34. DOI: 10.23865/nrme.v4.5574

Lăpădat, L., & Lăpădat, M. (2024). The importance of motivation in foreign language learning. *Scientific Bulletin of the Politehnica University of Timişoara Transactions on Modern Languages, 22*(1), 142–152. DOI: 10.59168/vgle2734

Larsen, M., Gulis, G., & Pedersen, K. (2011). Use of evidence in local public health work in denmark. *International Journal of Public Health, 57*(3), 477–483. DOI: 10.1007/s00038-011-0324-y

Larsson, S., & Heintz, F. (2020). Transparency in artificial intelligence. *Internet Policy Review*, *9*(2). Advance online publication. DOI: 10.14763/2020.2.1469

Lascano Ortiz, A. A., Mejía Sánchez, E. J., Proaño López, G. L., & Silva Chávez, J. A. (2025). Spelling activities to reinforce vocabulary learning. *DATEH*, *7*(1), 1–5.

Lee, J. H., Ostwald, M. J., & Kim, A. M. J. (2021). Characterizing Smart Environments as Interactive and Collective Platforms: A Review of the Key Behaviors of Responsive Architecture. *Sensors 2021, Vol. 21, Page 3417, 21*(10), 3417. https://doi.org/DOI: 10.3390/S21103417

Lee, H. M., & Li, B. J. (2023). So far yet so near: Exploring the effects of immersion, presence, and psychological distance on empathy and prosocial behavior. *International Journal of Human-Computer Studies*, *176*, 103042. DOI: 10.1016/j.ijhcs.2023.103042

Legaki, N., Xi, N., Hamari, J., Karpouzis, K., & Assimakopoulos, V. (2020). The effect of challenge-based gamification on learning: An experiment in the context of statistics education. *International Journal of Human-Computer Studies*, *144*, 102496. DOI: 10.1016/j.ijhcs.2020.102496

Lehikko, A., Nykänen, M., Lukander, K., Uusitalo, J., & Ruokamo, H. (2024). Exploring interactivity effects on learners' sense of agency, cognitive load, and learning outcomes in immersive virtual reality: A mixed methods study. Computers & Education: X Reality, 4, 100066. https://doi.org/DOI: 10.1016/j.cexr.2024.100066

Levina, N., Petrenko, T., Airapetov, G., & Ryashchenko, M. (2021). Game-based language learning in the context of distance education. SHS Web of Conferences, 127, 01012. DOI: 10.1051/shsconf/202112701012

Li, H., Yu, L., & He, W. (2019). The Impact of GDPR on Global Technology Development. In *Journal of Global Information Technology Management* (Vol. 22, Issue 1). https://doi.org/DOI: 10.1080/1097198X.2019.1569186

Li, R. and Liu, J. (2022). *Applying gamification in english learning*. https://doi.org/DOI: 10.2991/assehr.k.220504.490

Li, D., & Jianxing, W. (2025). The effect of gamified learning monitoring systems on students' learning behavior and achievement: An empirical study. *Entertainment Computing*, *52*, 100907. DOI: 10.1016/j.entcom.2024.100907

Lim, L., Dawson, S., Gašević, D., Joksimovíc, S., Fudge, A., Pardo, A., & Gentili, S. (2020). Students' sense-making of personalised feedback based on learning analytics. *Australasian Journal of Educational Technology*, *36*(6), 15–33. DOI: 10.14742/ajet.6370

Limongi, R. (2024). The use of artificial intelligence in scientific research with integrity and ethics. *Rev. Artif. Intell. Educ*, *5*(00), e0022. DOI: 10.37497/rev.artif.intell.educ.v5i00.22

Lim, W. M. (2024). What is qualitative research? An overview and guidelines. *Australasian Marketing Journal*, *33*(2), 199–229. DOI: 10.1177/14413582241264619

Lin, J. (2017). The design process in VR, AR, and MR. *Hackernoon.* https://hackernoon.com/the-design-process-in-vr-ar-and-mr-b34b2247520f

Liu, G., Fathi, J., & Rahimi, M. (2024). Using digital gamification to improve language achievement, foreign language enjoyment, and ideal l2 self: A case of english as a foreign language learners. *Journal of Computer Assisted Learning*, *40*(4), 1347–1364. DOI: 10.1111/jcal.12954

Liu, L. (2024). Survey and analysis of primary school teachers' use of generative artificial intelligence. *Lecture Notes in Education Psychology and Public Media*, *74*(1), 43–52. DOI: 10.54254/2753-7048/2024.bo17693

Livingston, C. (1982). The role of the private instrumental teacher in preparing music students for college theory. *American Music Teacher, 31*(6), 14, 16. https://www.jstor.org/stable/43541444

Li, Y., & Chen, T. (2022). Blockchain Empowers Supply Chains: Challenges, Opportunities And Prospects. *Nankai Business Review International*, *14*(2), 230–248. DOI: 10.1108/nbri-06-2022-0066

Liyanaarachchi, G., Viglia, G., & Kurtaliqi, F. (2024). Privacy in hospitality: Managing biometric and biographic data with immersive technology. *International Journal of Contemporary Hospitality Management*, *36*(11), 3823–3840. DOI: 10.1108/IJCHM-06-2023-0861

Lopes, D. S., & Jorge, J. A. (2024). Extending medical interfaces towards virtual reality and augmented reality. *Annals of Medicine, 51*(sup1). https://doi.org/DOI: 10.1080/07853890.2018.1560068

López, C., & Tucker, C. (2020). Toward personalized adaptive gamification: A machine learning model for predicting performance. *IEEE Transactions on Games*, *12*(2), 155–168. DOI: 10.1109/tg.2018.2883661

Luan, H., Géczy, P., Lai, H., Gobert, J., Yang, S., Ogata, H., & Tsai, C. (2020). Challenges and future directions of big data and artificial intelligence in education. *Frontiers in Psychology*, *11*. Advance online publication. DOI: 10.3389/fpsyg.2020.580820

Luarn, P., Chen, C. C., & Chiu, Y. P. (2023). Enhancing intrinsic learning motivation through gamification: A self-determination theory perspective. *The International Journal of Information and Learning Technology*, *40*(5), 413–424.

Luarn, P., Chen, C., & Chiu, Y. (2023). Enhancing intrinsic learning motivation through gamification: A self-determination theory perspective. *International Journal of Information and Learning Technology*, *40*(5), 413–424. DOI: 10.1108/ijilt-07-2022-0145

Lumadi, R. I. (2024). The influence and effects of digital revolution on Africa's higher education systems. *South African Journal of Higher Education*, *38*(3), 114–130.

Luo, Y. (2024). Innovative research on ai-assisted teaching models for college english listening and speaking courses. *Applied and Computational Engineering*, *69*(1), 155–160. DOI: 10.54254/2755-2721/69/20241493

Luo, Z. (2023). The effectiveness of gamified tools for foreign language learning (fll): A systematic review. *Behavioral Sciences (Basel, Switzerland)*, *13*(4), 331. DOI: 10.3390/bs13040331 PMID: 37102845

Lusardi, A., & Mitchell, O. S. (2014). The economic importance of financial literacy: Theory and evidence. *Journal of Economic Literature*, *52*(1), 5–44. DOI: 10.1257/jel.52.1.5 PMID: 28579637

Lutkevich, B. (2019). What is HIPAA (Health Insurance Portability and Accountability Act)? In *WhatIs.com*.

Maathuis, C., & Datcu, D. (2025). Transparency of AI-XR Systems: Insights from Experts. *Proceedings - 2025 IEEE International Conference on Artificial Intelligence and EXtended and Virtual Reality, AIxVR 2025*, 301–306. https://doi.org/DOI: 10.1109/AIXVR63409.2025.00058

Machala, S., Chamier-Gliszczynski, N., & Królikowski, T. (2022). Application of AR/VR Technology in Industry 4.0. *Procedia Computer Science*, *207*, 2990–2998. DOI: 10.1016/J.PROCS.2022.09.357

Magee, P., Ienca, M., & Farahany, N. (2024). Beyond neural data: Cognitive biometrics and mental privacy. *Neuron*, *112*(18), 3017–3028. DOI: 10.1016/J.NEURON.2024.09.004 PMID: 39326392

Maggio, I., Ginevra, M., Santilli, S., Nota, L., & Soresi, S. (2021). *Life design for an inclusive and sustainable future.*, 251-270. https://doi.org/DOI: 10.1007/978-3-030-64537-3_10

Magi, C. E., Bambi, S., Iovino, P., El Aoufy, K., Amato, C., Balestri, C., Rasero, L., & Longobucco, Y. (2023). Virtual Reality and Augmented Reality Training in Disaster Medicine Courses for Students in Nursing: A Scoping Review of Adoptable Tools. In *Behavioral Sciences* (Vol. 13, Issue 7, pp. 1–13). https://doi.org/DOI: 10.3390/bs13070616

Magne, C., Schön, D., & Besson, M. (2006). Musician children detect pitch violations in both music and language better than nonmusician children: Behavioral and electrophysiological approaches. *Journal of Cognitive Neuroscience*, *18*(2), 199–211. DOI: 10.1162/jocn.2006.18.2.199 PMID: 16494681

Mahardika, I. (2023). Science textbook based on merdeka belajar curriculum: Integration of learning implementation for critical thinking skills. *Journal of Education Society and Behavioural Science*, *36*(10), 109–115. DOI: 10.9734/jesbs/2023/v36i101273

Majdzadeh, R., Yazdizadeh, B., Nedjat, S., Gholami, J., & Ahghari, S. (2011). Strengthening evidence-based decision-making: Is it possible without improving health system stewardship? *Health Policy and Planning*, *27*(6), 499–504. DOI: 10.1093/heapol/czr072

Makransky, G., & Petersen, G. B. (2021). The cognitive affective model of immersive learning (CAMIL): A theoretical research-based model of learning in immersive virtual reality. *Educational Psychology Review*, *33*(3), 937–958.

Makri, A., Vlachopoulos, D., & Martina, R. A. (2022). *Digital escape rooms as innovative pedagogical tools in education: a systematic literature review. Sustainability 13, 4587 (2021).*

Marone, V. (2016). Playful constructivism: Making sense of digital games for learning and creativity through play, design, and participation. *Journal of Virtual Worlds Research*, *9*(3), 1–18. DOI: 10.4101/jvwr.v9i3.7244

Marquardt, J., Fünfgeld, A., & Elsässer, J. P. (2023). Institutionalizing climate change mitigation in the Global South: Current trends and future research. *Earth System Governance*, *15*, 100163. DOI: 10.1016/j.esg.2022.100163

Martinez, L., Gimenes, M., & Lambert, É. (2022). Entertainment video games for academic learning: A systematic review. *Journal of Educational Computing Research*, *60*(5), 1083–1109. DOI: 10.1177/07356331211053848

Martín-Gutiérrez, J., Roca González, C., & García Domínguez, M. (2012). Training of spatial ability on engineering students through a remedial course based on augmented reality. In *Volume 7: 9th international conference on design education; 24th international conference on design theory and methodology*. American Society of Mechanical Engineers. https://doi.org/DOI: 10.1115/DETC2012-70928

Mayer, R. E. (2021). Evidence-based principles for how to design effective instructional videos. *Journal of Applied Research in Memory and Cognition, 10*(2), 229–240.

Mayer, R. E. (Ed.). (2014). *The Cambridge handbook of multimedia learning* (2nd ed.). Cambridge University Press., DOI: 10.1017/CBO9780511816819

McCarrick, C. A., Moynihan, A., McEntee, P. D., Boland, P. A., Donnelly, S., Heneghan, H., & Cahill, R. A. (2025). Impact of simulation training on communication skills and informed consent practices in medical students-a randomised controlled trial. *BMC Medical Education, 25*(1), 1078. PMID: 40682099

McKeever, M. (2023). Social stratification and inequality in South Africa. *Sociology Compass, 13173*. Advance online publication. DOI: 10.1111/soc4.13173

McKenzie, J. A., & Dalton, E. M. (2020). Universal design for learning in inclusive education policy in South Africa'. *African Journal of Disability, 9*(0), a776. DOI: 10.4102/ajod.v9i0.776 PMID: 33392062

Meekaew, N., & Ketpichainarong, W. (2018). An augmented reality to support mobile game-based learning in science museum on biodiversity. In *Proceedings of the 2018 7th international congress on advanced applied informatics (IIAI-AAI)* (pp. 250–255). IEEE. https://doi.org/DOI: 10.1109/IIAI-AAI.2018.00054

Mehrpour, S., Shavoun, A., Kheiltash, A., Masoomi, R., & Seraji, R. (2023). Evaluating and comparing critical thinking skills of residents of tehran university of medical sciences. *BMC Medical Education, 23*(1). Advance online publication. DOI: 10.1186/s12909-023-04094-7

Mendoza-Ramírez, C. E., Tudon-Martinez, J. C., Félix-Herrán, L. C., Lozoya-Santos, J. J., & Vargas-Martínez, A. (2023). Augmented reality: Survey. *Applied Sciences (Basel, Switzerland), 13*(18), 10491. DOI: 10.3390/app131810491

Meyer, A., Rose, D. H., & Gordon, D. (2014). *Universal design for learning: Theory and practice*. CAST Professional Publishing.

Mhlongo, S., Mbatha, K., Ramatsetse, B., & Dlamini, R. (2023). Challenges, opportunities, and prospects of adopting and using smart digital technologies in learning environments: An iterative review. *Heliyon, 9*(6), e16348. DOI: 10.1016/j.heliyon.2023.e16348 PMID: 37274691

Milgram, P., Takemura, H., Utsumi, A., & Kishino, F. (1995). Augmented reality: A class of displays on the reality-virtuality continuum. In Das, H. (Ed.), *Telemanipulator and telepresence technologies* (Vol. 2351, pp. 282–292). SPIE., DOI: 10.1117/12.197321

Mimeau, C., Ricketts, J., & Deacon, S. H. (2025). Learning spellings and meanings: Longitudinal relations to reading. *Journal of Research in Reading*. Advance online publication.

Mishra, P., & Koehler, M. J. (2006). Technological pedagogical content knowledge: A framework for integrating technology in teachers' knowledge. *Teachers College Record, 108*(6), 1017–1054. DOI: 10.1177/016146810610800610

Mkhonto, B. S., & Mubangizi, B. C. (2024). Digital Divide or Digital Bridge? Evaluating the Impact of ICT Integration in South Africa's Rural Schools. *International Journal of Social Science Research and Review, 7*(7), 132–145. DOI: 10.47814/ijssrr.v7i7.2142

Mohamed, N., & Ahmed, A. A. (2024). AI in Combatting Man-in-the-Middle Attacks: A Comprehensive Review. *2024 15th International Conference on Computing Communication and Networking Technologies, ICCCNT 2024*. https://doi.org/DOI: 10.1109/ICCCNT61001.2024.10725789

Mohsen, M. A., & Alangari, T. S. (2024). Analyzing two decades of immersive technology research in education: Trends, clusters, and future directions. *Education and Information Technologies, 29*(3), 3571–3587.

Moldt, J. (2024). Assessing ai awareness and identifying essential competencies: Insights from key stakeholders in integrating ai into medical education. *JMIR Medical Education, 10*, e58355–e58355. DOI: 10.2196/58355

Molloy, C., & Farrell, R. (2024). Cultivating positive classroom environments: Exploring the efficacy of immersive technologies in removing barriers to learning among primary school students. *Computers in the Schools, 41*(2), 164–192. DOI: 10.1080/07380569.2024.2325441

Morales, M., Amado-Salvatierra, H., Medina, J., Barchino, R., Hernández-Rizzardini, R., & Teixeira, A. (2024). Personalized feedback in massive open online courses: Harnessing the power of langchain and openai api. *Electronics (Basel), 13*(10), 1960. DOI: 10.3390/electronics13101960

Moreira, F. T., & Teles, R. O. (Eds.). (2024). *Improving student assessment with emerging AI tools*. IGI Global.

Moreno, S., Marques, C., Santos, A., Santos, M., Castro, S. L., & Besson, M. (2009). Musical training influences linguistic abilities in 8-year-old children: More evidence for brain plasticity. *Cerebral Cortex (New York, N.Y.), 19*(3), 712–723. DOI: 10.1093/cercor/bhn120 PMID: 18832336

Mueller-Csernetzky, P., Malakhatka, E., Thuvander, L., Kragic, D., & Kabo, J. (2025). Technological Frontiers in Education: Exploring the Impact of AI and Immersive Learning. In *Human-Technology Interaction: Interdisciplinary Approaches and Perspectives* (pp. 291–328). Springer Nature Switzerland.

Mugisha, M., Uwitonze, A., Chesire, F., Senyonga, R., Oxman, M., Nsangi, A., & Rosenbaum, S. (2021). Teaching critical thinking about health using digital technology in lower secondary schools in rwanda: A qualitative context analysis. *PLoS One, 16*(3), e0248773. DOI: 10.1371/journal.pone.0248773

Mulaudzi, L. (2024). Evaluating impact: South Africa's e-education white paper on digital equity and post-COVID education leadership. *Cogent Education, 11*(1), 2415749.

Mulcahy, R., Zainuddin, N., & Russell-Bennett, R. (2020). Transformative value and the role of involvement in gamification and serious games for well-being. *Journal of Service Management, 32*(2), 218–245. DOI: 10.1108/josm-05-2019-0137

Munirah, M., & Sahriani, S. (2024). Transformation of student motivation through the use of quizizz in language learning: A longitudinal approach in secondary education. *International Journal for Multidisciplinary Research, 6*(6). Advance online publication. DOI: 10.36948/ijfmr.2024.v06i06.30354

Munje, P., & Jita, T. (2020). The impact of the lack of ICT resources on teaching and learning in selected South African primary schools. *International Journal of Learning Teaching and Educational Research, 19*(7), 263–279. DOI: 10.26803/ijlter.19.7.15

Murala, D. K., & Panda, S. K. (2023). Metaverse: A study on immersive technologies. *Metaverse and Immersive Technologies: An Introduction to Industrial, Business and Social Applications*, 1–41. https://doi.org/DOI: 10.1002/9781394177165.CH1

Muralidharan, V., Tran, M. M., Barrios, L., Beams, B., Ko, J. M., Siegel, D. H., & Bailenson, J. (2024). Best Practices for Research in Virtual and Augmented Reality in Dermatology. *The Journal of Investigative Dermatology, 144*(1), 17–23. DOI: 10.1016/j.jid.2023.10.014 PMID: 38105083

Murtaza, M., Ahmed, Y., Shamsi, J., Sherwani, F., & Usman, M. (2022). Ai-based personalized e-learning systems: Issues, challenges, and solutions. *IEEE Access : Practical Innovations, Open Solutions, 10*, 81323–81342. DOI: 10.1109/access.2022.3193938

Musumeci, O. (2000). The cognitive pedagogy of aural training. In Proceedings of the *2000 ISME seminar on the education of the professional musician*. ISME.

Muzammil, M. Bin, Bilal, M., Ajmal, S., Shongwe, S. C., & Ghadi, Y. Y. (2024). Unveiling Vulnerabilities of Web Attacks Considering Man in the Middle Attack and Session Hijacking. *IEEE Access : Practical Innovations, Open Solutions, 12*, 6365–6375. DOI: 10.1109/ACCESS.2024.3350444

Muzata, A. R., Singh, G., Stepanov, M. S., & Musonda, I. (2024, November). Immersive learning: A systematic literature review on transforming engineering education through virtual reality. In *Virtual Worlds* (Vol. 3, No. 4, pp. 480-505). MDPI.

Mystakidis, S., & Lympouridis, V. (2024). Immersive Learning Design in the Metaverse: A Theoretical Literature Review Synthesis. *Application of the Metaverse in Education*, 55-71.

Nacional, R. (2024). Gamifying education: Enhancing student engagement and motivation. *Puissant, 5*, 716–729.

Nah, F. F.-H., Zeng, Q., Telaprolu, V. R., Ayyappa, A. P., & Eschenbrenner, B. (2014). Gamification of education: A review of literature. In Hutchison, D., Kanade, T., Kittler, J., Kleinberg, J. M., Kobsa, A., Mattern, F., Mitchell, J. C., Naor, M., Nierstrasz, O., & Pandu Rangan, C. (Eds.), *HCI in business* (pp. 401–409). Springer International Publishing., DOI: 10.1007/978-3-319-07293-7_39

Nair, V., Garrido, G. M., Song, D., & O'Brien, J. F. (2023). Exploring the Privacy Risks of Adversarial VR Game Design. *Proceedings on Privacy Enhancing Technologies. Privacy Enhancing Technologies Symposium, 2023*(4), 238–256. DOI: 10.56553/popets-2023-0108

Namaziandost, E., Shobeiry, M., & Heydarnejad, T. (2024). Enhancing the SHAD platform: Exploring the emotional influence of telegram-supported supplementary tasks on learners' happiness, technostress, autonomy, growth mindfulness, and resilience. *Journal of Studies in Language Learning and Teaching, 1*(2), 251–267. DOI: 10.22034/jsllt.2024.21648.1043

Narayanan, K. (2024). Hybrid gamification and ai tutoring framework using machine learning and adaptive neuro-fuzzy inference system. *Journal of Advanced Research in Applied Sciences and Engineering Technology*, *42*(2), 221–233. DOI: 10.37934/araset.42.2.221233

Nasereddin, M., & Price, A. (2021). Addressing the capital cost barrier to sustainable construction. *Developments in the Built Environment*, *7*, 100049. DOI: 10.1016/j.dibe.2021.100049

National Association for Music Education. (2014). *2014 music standards: PK–8 strand.* https://nafme.org/wp-content/files/2014/11/2014-Music-Standards-PK-8-Strand.pdf

National Centre for Financial Education (NCFE). (2019). *Financial Literacy and Inclusion Survey (NFLIS).* NCFE.

National Financial Inclusion Benchmarks. (2021).

NCR Youth Survey. (2025). *[Unpublished survey – cited in text as "Delhi–NCR Youth Survey (2025)"].*

Nebel, S., Schneider, S., & Rey, G. D. (2016). Mining learning and crafting scientific experiments: A literature review on the use of Minecraft in education and research. *Journal of Educational Technology & Society*, *19*(2), 355–366.

Neo, J. R. J., Won, A. S., & Shepley, M. M. C. (2021). Designing Immersive Virtual Environments for Human Behavior Research. In *Frontiers in Virtual Reality* (Vol. 2). https://doi.org/DOI: 10.3389/frvir.2021.603750

Netta, A. (2023). Motivation in second language acquisition: A review. *ACCENTIA*, *3*(1), 1–8. DOI: 10.37598/accentia.v3i1.1713

Ng'ambi, D., Gachago, D., Backhouse, J., Bozalek, V., Ivala, E., & Bosman, J. P. (2013). Towards a Shared Understanding of emerging technologies: experiences in a collaborative research project in South Africa. *The African Journal of Information Systems*, http://hdl.handle.net/11427/8863

Nguyen, D., & Meixner, G. (2019). Gamified augmented reality training for an assembly task: A study about user engagement. In *Proceedings of the 2019 federated conference on computer science and information systems* (pp. 901–904). IEEE. https://doi.org/DOI: 10.15439/2019F135

Nguyen, T. (2023). Artificial intelligent based teaching and learning approaches: A comprehensive review. *International Journal of Evaluation and Research in Education (Ijere)*, *12*(4), 2387. DOI: 10.11591/ijere.v12i4.26623

Nhlapo, L., Mosethle, T., Monchusi, B. B., & Yusuff, A. (2024, November). Design of a Microgrid for a Rural Area: A Systematic Approach. In 2024 4th International Conference on Electrical, Computer, Communications and Mechatronics Engineering (ICECCME) (pp. 1-4). IEEE.

Ningrum, N., Harisa, A., & Umaroh, L. (2024). Learning through play: Utilizing board games to enhance english vocabulary for early students. *TCV, 1*(2), 117. DOI: 10.62411/tcv.v1i2.1784

Nocilla, S., & Nocilla, M. (2024). Empowering Learning Through Game Creation: Investigating the Impact of Educational Technology on Learners' Engagement and Attainment Level in Subject-Based Game Design (Phase I). MCAST Journal of Applied Research & Practice, 8(1), 203-22

Nottingham, E., Stockman, C., & Burke, M. (2022). Education in a datafied world: Balancing children's rights and school's responsibilities in the age of Covid 19. *Computer Law & Security Review, 45*, 105664. DOI: 10.1016/j.clsr.2022.105664

Nunnally, J. C. (1978). *Psychometric theory* (2nd ed.). McGraw-Hill.

Nuong Deri, M., Singh, A., Zaazie, P., & Anandene, D. (2024). Leveraging Artificial Intelligence in Higher Educational Institutions: A Comprehensive Overview. *Education and Law Review*, (30). Advance online publication. DOI: 10.1344/REYD2024.30.45777

Nussbaum, M. C. (2011). *Creating capabilities: The human development approach.* Harvard University Press.

Nyathi, T., & Joseph, R.M. (2024). Empowering South African educators: Navigating the challenges of digital teaching and learning competencies. *SA Journal of Human Resource Management/SA Tydskrif vir Menslikehulpbronbestuur, 22*(0), a2591. https://doi.org/DOI: 10.4102/sajhrm.v22i0.2591

Obourdin, G., De Maeyer, S., & Van den Bossche, P. (2024). Unlocking the power of immersive learning: The FAIRI instructional design proposition for adaptive immersive virtual reality. *Computers & Education: X Reality, 5*, 100084.

OECD. (2013). *OECD/INFE toolkit for measuring financial literacy and financial inclusion.* OECD Publishing.

OECD. (2020). *OECD/INFE 2020 international survey of adult financial literacy.* OECD Publishing.

Ogino, H., & Matsuguma, H. (2024). Effective implementation of feedback in gamification. *International Journal of Asia Digital Art and Design, 28*(2), 9–17.

Okoye, K., Hussein, H., Arrona-Palacios, A., Quintero, H. N., Ortega, L. O. P., Sanchez, A. L., & Hosseini, S. (2023). Impact of digital technologies upon teaching and learning in higher education in Latin America: An outlook on the reach, barriers, and bottlenecks. *Education and Information Technologies*, *28*(2), 2291–2360. PMID: 35992366

Onesi-Ozigagun, O. (2024). Revolutionizing education through ai: A comprehensive review of enhancing learning experiences. *International Journal of Applied Research in Social Sciences*, *6*(4), 589–607. DOI: 10.51594/ijarss.v6i4.1011

Orak, S. D. (2025). EFL students' perception of gamification-integrated English language education. *Pegem Journal of Education and Instruction*, *15*(1), 143–158.

Oroszi, T. (2020). Competency-based education. *Creative Education*, *11*(11), 2467–2476. DOI: 10.4236/ce.2020.1111181

Orton, L., Lloyd-Williams, F., Taylor-Robinson, D., O'Flaherty, M., & Capewell, S. (2011). The use of research evidence in public health decision making processes: Systematic review. *PLoS One*, *6*(7), e21704. DOI: 10.1371/journal.pone.0021704

Osadchyi, V. V., Valko, N. V., & Kuzmich, L. V. (2021). Using augmented reality technologies for STEM education organization. *Journal of Physics: Conference Series*, *1840*(1), 1–10. DOI: 10.1088/1742-6596/1840/1/012027

Osmani, S. (2016). *The Capability Approach and Human Development: Some Reflections*. UNDP Human Development Report. https://hdr.undp.org/system/files/documents/osmanitemplate.pdf

Otero, L., Catalá, A., Morante, M., Taboada, M., López, B., & Barro, S. (2023). Ai literacy in k-12: A systematic literature review. *International Journal of STEM Education*, *10*(1). Advance online publication. DOI: 10.1186/s40594-023-00418-7

Ouanes, K. (2024). Transforming medical and health sciences education with gamification.. DOI: 10.5772/intechopen.1005500

Overby, A., & Jones, B. L. (2015). Virtual Legos: Incorporating Minecraft into the art education curriculum. *Art Education*, *68*(1), 21–27. DOI: 10.1080/00043125.2015.11519302

Owusu-Cole, C., Entsie, N. Y., Bosu, L., Akore Sarpong, E., & Kwadwo Mensah, E. (2025). Exploring educational technology dynamics: A dive into student engagement and educator empowerment. *Cogent Education*, *12*(1), 2477366.

Özhan, Ş., & Kocadere, S. (2019). The effects of flow, emotional engagement, and motivation on success in a gamified online learning environment. *Journal of Educational Computing Research, 57*(8), 2006–2031. DOI: 10.1177/0735633118823159

Panchal, N. (2024). The Indian Edtech Evolution: From Boom to Struggle and the Path Forward. *Open Access Cases, 1*(2).

Paramita, A., Yulia, C., & Nikmawati, E. E. (2021). Augmented reality in nutrition education. *IOP Conference Series. Materials Science and Engineering, 1098*(2), 1–8. DOI: 10.1088/1757-899x/1098/2/022108

Pardosi, V., Xu, S., Umurohmi, U., Nurdiana, N., & Sabur, F. (2024). Implementation of an artificial intelligence based learning management system for adaptive learning. *Al-Fikrah Jurnal Manajemen Pendidikan, 12*(1), 149. DOI: 10.31958/jaf.v12i1.12548

Parizad, A., Baghaee, H. R., Alizadeh, V., & Rahman, S. (2025). Emerging Technologies and Future Trends in Cyber-Physical Power Systems: Toward a New Era of Innovations. *Smart Cyber-Physical Power Systems: Solutions from Emerging Technologies, 2*, 525–565.

Park, S., & Kim, S. (2021). Is sustainable online learning possible with gamification?—The effect of gamified online learning on student learning. *Sustainability, 13*(8), 4267. DOI: 10.3390/su13084267

Parnandi, A., & Gutierrez-Osuna, R. (2013). Contactless measurement of heart rate variability from pupillary fluctuations. *Proceedings - 2013 Humaine Association Conference on Affective Computing and Intelligent Interaction, ACII 2013*. https://doi.org/DOI: 10.1109/ACII.2013.38

Partarakis, N., & Zabulis, X. (2024). A Review of Immersive Technologies, Knowledge Representation, and AI for Human-Centered Digital Experiences. *Electronics 2024, Vol. 13, Page 269, 13*(2), 269. https://doi.org/DOI: 10.3390/ELECTRONICS13020269

Paskevicius, M. (2023). Empowering future educators: Leveraging openness by design when integrating technology in teacher education programs. Edutec. *Revista Electrónica de Tecnología Educativa*, (85), 103–119.

Patel, S. (2023). Addressing racial injustice: Examining systems of oppression and promoting equity in contemporary society. *Joura, 1*(2), 13–17. DOI: 10.61963/jkt.v1i2.33

Patel, S., & Ragolane, M. (2024). The Implementation of Artificial Intelligence in South African Higher Education Institutions: Opportunities and Challenges. *Technium Education and Humanities*, *9*, 51–65. DOI: 10.47577/teh.v9i.11452

Pather, B., & Ragolane, M. (2025). Innovative Teaching through Technology: Preparing Educators for ICT-Based Modelling and Simulation Integration. *American Research Journal of Humanities & Social Science. 08(03), 66 – 75.* https://www.arjhss.com/wp-content/uploads/2025/03/H836675.pdf

Pellas, N., & Mystakidis, S. (2020). A systematic review of research about game-based learning in virtual worlds. *Journal of Universal Computer Science*, *26*(8), 1017–1042. DOI: 10.3897/jucs.2020.054

Pendy, B. (2023). Artificial intelligence: The future of education. *Jurnal Indonesia Sosial Sains*, *2*(11). Advance online publication. DOI: 10.59141/jiss.v2i11.801

Pereira, D., Aguiar Vieira, D., Flores, M. A., Machado, E. A., & Fernandes, E. (2025). Teachers' concerns and teaching experience during the pandemic and beyond: Implications for research, policy and practice. *Cogent Education*, *12*(1), 2461395. Advance online publication. DOI: 10.1080/2331186X.2025.2461395

Perin, A., Galbiati, T. F., Ayadi, R., Gambatesa, E., Orena, E. F., Riker, N. I., & DiMeco, F. (2021). Informed consent through 3D virtual reality: A randomized clinical trial. *Acta Neurochirurgica*, *163*(2), 301–308. PMID: 32242272

Petrusly, P. (2024). *The effect of gamification using kahoot on students' critical thinking abilities: the role of mediating learning engagement and motivation*. Kuey., DOI: 10.53555/kuey.v30i5.1524

Pettersen, K., Arnseth, H. C., & Silseth, K. (2025). Playing Minecraft: Young children's postdigital play. *Journal of Early Childhood Literacy*, *25*(1), 133–157. DOI: 10.1177/14687984221118977

Philippe, S., Souchet, A. D., Lameras, P., Petridis, P., Caporal, J., Coldeboeuf, G., & Duzan, H. (2020). Multimodal teaching, learning and training in virtual reality: A review and case study. *Virtual Reality & Intelligent Hardware*, *2*(5), 421–442. DOI: 10.1016/j.vrih.2020.07.008

Phuong, T. (2020). Gamified learning: Are vietnamese efl learners ready yet? *International Journal of Emerging Technologies in Learning (Ijet)*, *15*(24), 242. DOI: 10.3991/ijet.v15i24.16667

Piaget, J. (1971). *Biology and knowledge*. Edinburgh University Press.

Pierson, J. (2025). Indexed piano repertoire in support of music theory and aural skills reinforcement. *MTNA e-Journal, 16*(3), 14–29.

Pimentel, J., López, P., Correal, C., Cockcroft, A., & Andersson, N. (2022). Educational games created by medical students in a cultural safety training game jam: A qualitative descriptive study. *BMC Medical Education, 22*(1). Advance online publication. DOI: 10.1186/s12909-022-03875-w PMID: 36419048

Pitsikalis, S., Lasica, I. E., Kostas, A., & Vitsilaki, C. (2024). Educational Design Guidelines for Teaching with Immersive Technologies—Updating Learning Outcomes of the European Qualification Framework. *Trends in Higher Education, 3*(4), 1091–1108.

Pitsikalis, S., Lasica, I. E., Kostas, A., & Vitsilaki, C. (2024). Educational design guidelines for teaching with immersive technologies—Updating learning outcomes of the European Qualification Framework. *Trends in Higher Education, 3*(4), 1091–1108. DOI: 10.3390/higheredu3040064

Piyathanavong, V., Huynh, V. N., Karnjana, J., & Olapiriyakul, S. (2024). Role of project management on Sustainable Supply Chain development through Industry 4.0 technologies and Circular Economy during the COVID-19 pandemic: A multiple case study of Thai metals industry. *Operations Management Research, 17*(1), 13–37. DOI: 10.1007/s12063-022-00283-7

Polat, E. (2023). Gamification implementation for educational purposes: A scoping review (2013-2018). *Educational Technology Quarterly, 2023*(3), 367–400. DOI: 10.55056/etq.589

Popenici, S., & Kerr, S. (2017). Exploring the impact of artificial intelligence on teaching and learning in higher education. *Research and Practice in Technology Enhanced Learning, 12*(1). Advance online publication. DOI: 10.1186/s41039-017-0062-8

Poupard, M., Gallo, A., Boulord, R., Guillem, P., Rolland, G., Simonneau, T., & Pallas, B. (2025). Source–sink manipulations through shading, crop load and water deficit affect plant morphogenesis and carbon sink priorities leading to contrasted plant carbon status in grapevine. *Annals of Botany, 136*(1), 49–66. PMID: 39656901

Pratama, M. (2023). Revolutionizing education: Harnessing the power of artificial intelligence for personalized learning. *Klasikal Journal of Education Language Teaching and Science, 5*(2), 350–357. DOI: 10.52208/klasikal.v5i2.877

Pratisto, E. H., Thompson, N., & Potdar, V. (2022). Immersive technologies for tourism: A systematic review. *Information Technology & Tourism, 24*(2), 181–219.

Priyadharsini, V., & Sahaya Mary, R. (2024). Universal Design for Learning (UDL) in Inclusive Education: Accelerating Learning for All. Shanlax International Journal of Arts. *Science and Humanities*, *11*(4), 145–150.

Pu, D., Ni, J., Song, D., Zhang, W., Wang, Y., Wu, L., & Wang, Y. (2019). Influence of critical thinking disposition on the learning efficiency of problem-based learning in undergraduate medical students. *BMC Medical Education*, *19*(1). Advance online publication. DOI: 10.1186/s12909-018-1418-5

Qasserras, L. (2024). The role of visual learning aids across diverse learning styles in high school education. *European Journal of Applied Linguistics Studies*, *7*(2), 68. DOI: 10.46827/ejals.v7i2.550

Qayyum, A., Butt, M. A., Ali, H., Usman, M., Halabi, O., Al-Fuqaha, A., Abbasi, Q. H., Imran, M. A., & Qadir, J. (2024). Secure and Trustworthy Artificial Intelligence-extended Reality (AI-XR) for Metaverses. *ACM Computing Surveys*, *56*(7). Advance online publication. DOI: 10.1145/3614426

Qudsi, H. (2024). Gamification in education: Boosting student engagement and learning outcomes. ShodhKosh. *Journal of Visual and Performing Arts*, *5*(4), 686–693. DOI: 10.29121/shodhkosh.v5.i4.2024.2542

Rafiq, K., Hashim, H., & Yunus, M. (2021). Sustaining education with mobile learning for english for specific purposes (esp): A systematic review (2012–2021). *Sustainability*, *13*(17), 9768. DOI: 10.3390/su13179768

Ragolane, M., & Patel, S. (2024). Artificial Intelligence, Digital Grades and Human Voices: Students' Perceptions on AI Grading in Higher Education. *International J. Soc. Sci. & Education*. 2024(14), 32-64. http://ijsse.com/Paper-04.pdf

Ragolane, M., & Patel, S. (2025). AI Grading Systems in Education: A Panacea or Drawback for South African Higher Education. In Moreira, F., & Teles, R. (Eds.), *Improving Student Assessment With Emerging AI Tools* (pp. 245–272). IGI Global Scientific Publishing., DOI: 10.4018/979-8-3693-6170-2.ch009

Rahimi, S., Walker, J. T., Lin-Lipsmeyer, L., & Shin, J. (2024). Toward defining and assessing creativity in sandbox games. *Creativity Research Journal*, *36*(2), 194–212. DOI: 10.1080/10400419.2022.2156477

Raizada, A., & Sinha, S. (2024). The falling star: What went wrong with BYJU'S? *Journal of Information Technology Teaching Cases*, 20438869251329034.

Ramírez-Cedillo, E., Armendáriz-Rodríguez, M., García-Ávila, J., Quintero-Sánchez, D., Ortiz-Espinoza, A. A., & Vargas-Martínez, A. (2025, April). Student 5.0: Immersive learning in next-gen Automation of Manufacturing Systems courses for the Industry 5.0 era. []). Frontiers Media SA.]. *Frontiers in Education, 10*, 1416761.

Ramtohul, A., & Khedo, K. K. (2021). Location-based mobile augmented reality systems: a systematic review. *Immersive Technology in Smart Cities: Augmented and Virtual Reality in IoT*, 41-65.

Rapp, A., Hopfgartner, F., Hamari, J., Linehan, C., & Cena, F. (2019). Strengthening gamification studies: Current trends and future opportunities of gamification research. *International Journal of Human-Computer Studies, 127*, 1–6. DOI: 10.1016/j.ijhcs.2018.11.007

Rasanen, J., Altonen, A., Mercat, A., & Vanne, J. (2021). Open-source RTP Library for End-To-End Encrypted Real-Time Video Streaming Applications. *Proceedings - 23rd IEEE International Symposium on Multimedia, ISM 2021*, 92–96. https://doi.org/DOI: 10.1109/ISM52913.2021.00023

Rathore, A. (2023). Artificial intelligence and curriculum prospects for elementary school. *Pakistan Journal of Humanities and Social Sciences, 11*(4). Advance online publication. DOI: 10.52131/pjhss.2023.v11i4.1909

Rauschnabel, P. A., Babin, B. J., tom Dieck, M. C., Krey, N., & Jung, T. (2022). What is augmented reality marketing? Its definition, complexity, and future. In *Journal of Business Research* (Vol. 142). https://doi.org/DOI: 10.1016/j.jbusres.2021.12.084

Ravichandran, R., & Mahapatra, J. (2023). Virtual reality in vocational education and training: Challenges and possibilities. *Journal of Digital Learning and Education, 3*(1), 25–31. DOI: 10.52562/jdle.v3i1.602

Reisenweaver, A. (2012). Guido of Arezzo and his influence on music learning. *Musical Offerings, 3*(1), 37–59. DOI: 10.15385/jmo.2012.3.1.3

Reserve Bank of India. (2021). *Report on trends and progress of banking in India 2020–21*. Reserve Bank of India.

Rivera, E., & Garden, C. (2021). Gamification for student engagement: A framework. *Journal of Further and Higher Education, 45*(7), 999–1012. DOI: 10.1080/0309877x.2021.1875201

Robb, C. A., & Sharpe, D. L. (2009). Effect of personal financial knowledge on college students' credit card behavior. *Financial Counseling and Planning, 20*(1), 25–43.

Rohmah, N. (2022). A vocational school cutting-edge learning strategy: Examining gamification towards student engagement and achievement. *Jurnal Kependidikan Jurnal Hasil Penelitian Dan Kajian Kepustakaan Di Bidang Pendidikan Pengajaran Dan Pembelajaran*, *8*(3), 655. DOI: 10.33394/jk.v8i3.5779

Rohmana, W. (2022). The use of livemocha: A platform for independent language learning. *Abjadia International Journal of Education*, *7*(1), 103–113. DOI: 10.18860/abj.v7i1.15234

Ross, A., Banerjee, S., & Chowdhury, A. (2022). Deducing health cues from biometric data. *Computer Vision and Image Understanding*, *221*. Advance online publication. DOI: 10.1016/j.cviu.2022.103438

Rowe, L. W., & Pennington, V. (2025). Multilingual learners' digital book composing: Examining circulation of translingual, multimodal resources in an elementary classroom. *Journal of Second Language Writing*, *67*, 101180.

Rubin, D. (2024). *Harnessing Eye and Face Movements: Bridging Technology and Human Interaction*.

Rueckert, D., Pico, K., Kim, D., & Sánchez, X. (2020). Gamifying the foreign language classroom for brain-friendly learning. *Foreign Language Annals*, *53*(4), 686–703. DOI: 10.1111/flan.12490

Rugaiyah, R. (2023). The potential of artificial intelligence in improving linguistic competence: A systematic literature review. *Arkus*, *9*(2), 319–324. DOI: 10.37275/arkus.v9i2.313

Rybchynska, A. (2023). Development of communication skills through the introduction of interactive teaching methods in english lessons. Scientific Bulletin of Mukachevo State University Series. *Pedagogy and Psychology*, *9*(2). Advance online publication. DOI: 10.52534/msu-pp2.2023.09

Rye, S., Sousa, M., & Sousa, C. (2025a). Beyond Scholastic Disciplines: The Need for Complex Game-Based Learning in a Complex World. In *Transformative Learning Through Play: Analogue Games as Vehicles for Educational Innovation* (pp. 1–27). Springer Nature Switzerland.

Sabornido, E., Garma, V., Niepes, G. L., & Cabria, F. M. N. (2022). Key challenges and barriers in gamification: A systematic review. APJAET - Journal of Asia Pacific Journal of Advanced Education and Technology, 1(1), 13–19. https://doi.org/DOI: 10.54476/apjaetv1i1mar20221054

Saca, P. (2023). Designing accessible immersive learning experiences. *Journal of Technology-Integrated Lessons and Teaching*, *2*(1), 78–87. DOI: 10.13001/jtilt.v2i1.7669

Saidin, N. F., Halim, N. D. A., & Yahaya, N. (2015). A review of research on augmented reality in education: Advantages and applications. *International Education Studies*, *13*, 1–8. DOI: 10.5539/ies.v8n13p1

Sailer, M., & Homner, L. (2020). The gamification of learning: A meta-analysis. *Educational Psychology Review*, *32*(1), 77–112. DOI: 10.1007/s10648-019-09498-w

Salem, O., Alsubhi, K., Shaafi, A., Gheryani, M., Mehaoua, A., & Boutaba, R. (2022). Man-in-the-Middle Attack Mitigation in Internet of Medical Things. *IEEE Transactions on Industrial Informatics*, *18*(3). Advance online publication. DOI: 10.1109/TII.2021.3089462

Šarić, M., Russo, M., Kraljević, L., & Meter, D. (2024). Extended Reality Telemedicine Collaboration System Using Patient Avatar Based on 3D Body Pose Estimation. *Sensors (Basel)*, *24*(1), 1–12. DOI: 10.3390/s24010027 PMID: 38202889

Sari, R. C., Pranesti, A., & Solikhatun, I. (2024). Cognitive overload in immersive virtual reality in education: More presence but less learnt? *Education and Information Technologies*, *29*, 12887–12909. DOI: 10.1007/s10639-023-12379-z

Schiff, R., Levy-Shimon, S., Oanunu Shashoua, L., & Sasson, A. (2025). Same spelling, different meaning: An EF-based homograph reading intervention for struggling readers. *Reading & Writing Quarterly*, *41*(1), 28–49.

Schneider, P., Scherg, M., Dosch, H. G., Specht, H. J., Gutschalk, A., & Rupp, A. (2002). Morphology of Heschl's gyrus reflects enhanced activation in the auditory cortex of musicians. *Nature Neuroscience*, *5*(7), 688–694. DOI: 10.1038/nn871 PMID: 12068300

Schoenfeld, A., & Zhang, D. (2019). *Gamified simulations in financial education: A review of outcomes*.

Schrader, C., Kalyuga, S., & Plass, J. L. (2021). *Motivation and affect in multimedia learning*. Cambridge University Press.

Scopes, L. (2009). Learning archetypes as tools of cybergogy for a 3D educational landscape: A structure for eTeaching in Second Life (Master's thesis, University of Southampton). University of Southampton Repository.

Sen, A. (1999). *Development as freedom*. Oxford University Press.

Serrano-Ausejo, E., & Mårell-Olsson, E. (2024). Opportunities and challenges of using immersive technologies to support students' spatial ability and 21st-century skills in K-12 education. *Education and Information Technologies*, *29*, 5571–5597. DOI: 10.1007/s10639-023-11981-5

Setyoadi, E., & Patmanthara, S. (2024). Students' goal orientation and gamification in learning for academic performance: A systematic literature review. *Research and Development in Education (Raden)*, *4*(1), 390–403. DOI: 10.22219/raden.v4i1.32630

Sewell, A., Kennett, A., & Pugh, V. (2022). Universal Design for Learning as a theory of inclusive practice for use by educational psychologists. *Educational Psychology in Practice*, *38*(4), 364–378. DOI: 10.1080/02667363.2022.2111677

Shah, J. (2024). *Rethinking higher education through multidisciplinary studies.* jes, 20(4s), 2060-2063. https://doi.org/DOI: 10.52783/jes.2309

Shala, D. (2024). Learning styles and motivation: Their role in academic performance. *Journal of Educational and Social Research*, *14*(3), 258. DOI: 10.36941/jesr-2024-0071

Sharma, D., Sharma, J., & Mehta, N. (2024). The art of gamification for societal mind shifts: Refining human behaviour through strategic engagement. *Shodhkosh Journal of Visual and Performing Arts*, *5*(1). Advance online publication. DOI: 10.29121/shodhkosh.v5.i1.2024.855

Sharma, M., & Singh, A. (2024a). Embracing Technological Innovation: A Review of Hi-Tech Services in Hospitality Industry. *Evergreen*, *11*(4), 2818–2830. DOI: 10.5109/7326926

Sharma, R., & Singh, A. (2024b). Use of Digital Technology in Improving Quality Education: A Global Perspectives and Trends. In Nadda, V., Tyagi, P., Moniz Vieira, R., & Tyagi, P. (Eds.), *Implementing Sustainable Development Goals in the Service Sector* (pp. 14–26). IGI Global., DOI: 10.4018/979-8-3693-2065-5.ch002

Sharma, S., Das, D., & Chaudhury, S. (2025). A decentralized privacy-preserving XR system for 3D medical data visualization using hybrid biometric cryptosystem. *Scientific Reports*, *15*(1), 1–22. DOI: 10.1038/S41598-025-08784-8 PMID: 40764519

Shen, Z., Lai, M., & Wang, F. (2024). Investigating the influence of gamification on motivation and learning outcomes in online language learning. *Frontiers in Psychology*, *15*, 1295709. DOI: 10.3389/fpsyg.2024.1295709 PMID: 38860036

Shobeiry, M. (2021a). Personalized learning reliability of Tell Me More: A dynamic approach. *Revista EntreLinguas*, e021068.

Shobeiry, M. (2021b). A survey study on the potential educational value of WhatsApp in the Iranian EFL settings. *Journal of Applied Linguistics and Language Research, 8*(1), 126–148.

Shortt, M., Tilak, S., Kuznetcova, I., Martens, B., & Akinkuolie, B. (2021). Gamification in mobile-assisted language learning: A systematic review of duolingo literature from public release of 2012 to early 2020. *Computer Assisted Language Learning, 36*(3), 517–554. DOI: 10.1080/09588221.2021.1933540

Siko, J., Barbour, M., & Toker, S. (2011). Beyond jeopardy and lectures: Using Microsoft PowerPoint as a game design tool to teach science. *Journal of Computers in Mathematics and Science Teaching, 30*(3), 303–320.

Sikora, Y., Chernykh, V., Shaforost, Y., Danylyuk, S., & Chemerys, I. (2024). Leveraging gamification and game-based technologies for educational purposes. Multidisciplinary Reviews, 7.

Silić, M., Marzi, G., Caputo, A., & Bal, P. (2020). The effects of a gamified human resource management system on job satisfaction and engagement. *Human Resource Management Journal, 30*(2), 260–277. DOI: 10.1111/1748-8583.12272

Sims, S., Fletcher-Wood, H., O'Mara-Eves, A., Cottingham, S., Stansfield, C., Goodrich, J., Van Herwegen, J., & Anders, J. (2023). Effective teacher professional development: New theory and a meta-analytic test. *Review of Educational Research, 95*(2), 213–254. DOI: 10.3102/00346543231217480

Sindberg, L. (2009). The evolution of comprehensive musicianship through performance (CMP): A model for teaching performing with understanding in the ensemble setting. *Contributions to Music Education, 36*(1), 25–39. https://www.jstor.org/stable/24127216

Singh, A. (2022). Conceptual framework on Smart Learning Environment- An Indian perspective. *Journal of Education and Law*, (25). Advance online publication. DOI: 10.1344/REYD2022.25.36706

Singh, A. (2024a). Endorsing Gamification Pedagogy for Nurturing Employability Skills in Higher Education Institutions (HEI). In Membrive, V. (Ed.), *Practices and Implementation of Gamification in Higher Education* (pp. 172–183). IGI Global Scientific Publishing., DOI: 10.4018/979-8-3693-0716-8.ch008

Singh, A. (2024b). Impact of E-learning on Student Motivation in Higher Education Institutions: An Indian Perspective. *Journal of Education and Law*, (29). Advance online publication. DOI: 10.1344/REYD2024.29.43214

Singh, A., & Kumar, P. (2024). E-Learning Ecosystem in Higher Education Institutions: Trends and Practices. In Al Husseiny, F., & Munna, A. (Eds.), *Preparing Students for the Future Educational Paradigm* (pp. 1–18). IGI Global Scientific Publishing., DOI: 10.4018/979-8-3693-1536-1.ch001

Singh, B., & Goyal, S. (2024). "Unacademy": Journey from online disruptor to omnichannel EdTech. *Emerald Emerging Markets Case Studies*, *14*(4), 1–35.

Singh, G., Mantri, A., Sharma, O., Dutta, R., & Kaur, R. (2019). Evaluating the impact of the augmented reality learning environment on electronics laboratory skills of engineering students. *Computer Applications in Engineering Education*, *27*(6), 1361–1375. DOI: 10.1002/cae.22156

Skoe, E., & Kraus, M. (2012). A little goes a long way: How the adult brain is shaped by musical training in childhood. *The Journal of Neuroscience : The Official Journal of the Society for Neuroscience*, *32*(34), 11507–11510. DOI: 10.1523/JNEUROSCI.1949-12.2012 PMID: 22915097

Slater, M., & Wilbur, S. (1997). A framework for immersive virtual environments (FIVE): Speculations on the role of presence in virtual environments. *Presence (Cambridge, Mass.)*, *6*(6), 603–616.

Slattery, E. J., Butler, D., O'Leary, M., & Marshall, K. (2024). Teachers' experiences of using Minecraft Education in primary school: An Irish perspective. *Irish Educational Studies*, *43*(4), 965–984. DOI: 10.1080/03323315.2023.2185276

Slattery, E. J., Lehane, P., Butler, D., O'Leary, M., & Marshall, K. (2025). Assessing the benefits of digital game-based learning with Minecraft in children, adolescents and young adults: A broad systematic review. *Review of Education*, *13*(1), e70035. DOI: 10.1002/rev3.70035

Smail, L., Mahmoud, G., & Adel, D. (2025). The role of morphological awareness and orthographic awareness in reading comprehension in Arabic: Do reading fluency and working memory count? *Reading Psychology*, *46*(1), 1–42.

Spanellis, A., Pyrko, I., & Dörfler, V. (2021). Gamifying situated learning in organisations. *Management Learning*, *53*(3), 525–546. DOI: 10.1177/13505076211038812

Statistics South Africa. (2019). *Inequality Trends in South Africa: A Multidimensional Diagnostic*. Report No. 03-10-19

Statistics South Africa. (2024). *Poverty and Inequality Statistics in South Africa*. Presentation to the NCOP by Patricia Koka.

Stephenson, M., & McKee, S. (2022). Interventions for Change: An Inclusive Curriculum Design for Social Justice. *Investigations in University Teaching and Learning*, 13. https://repository.londonmet.ac.uk/7748/1/MARIE_Investigations22_FINAL-Accessible.pdf

Stiver, M., Naveed, A., Chilton, J., & Moyes, S. (2025). Gamifying anatomy outreach: An underexplored opportunity. *Anatomical Sciences Education*. Advance online publication. DOI: 10.1002/ase.70019 PMID: 40099809

Story, K. M. (2014). Music therapy and avatars: Reflections on virtual learning environments for music therapy students. *Voices: A World Forum for Music Therapy, 14*(1). https://doi.org/DOI: 10.15845/voices.v14i1.722

Struwig, M., & Watson, S. (2023). *Re-Imagining Teaching and Learning at South African Higher Education Institutions in the Digital Landscape. International Conference on Education Research*, Nelson Mandela University. https://doi.org/DOI: 10.34190/icer.1.1.3145

Strydom, W., Funke, N., Nienaber, S., Nortje, K., & Steyn, M. (2010). Evidence-based policymaking: A review. *South African Journal of Science*, *106*(5/6). Advance online publication. DOI: 10.4102/sajs.v106i5/6.249

Suárez-Coalla, P., Hevia-Tuero, C., Martínez-García, C., & Afonso, O. (2024). Spanish children spelling in English as a foreign language: Central and peripheral processes. *Journal of Research in Reading*, *47*(4), 475–496.

Suero Montero, C., & Oliveira Leite, L. (2022). Towards local community involvement in students' science learning: Perspectives of students and teachers. *Journal of Teaching and Learning*, *16*(3), 21–43.

Sughra, U., & Usmani, A. (2022). Comparison of critical thinking among undergraduate medical students of conventional and integrated curricula in twin cities. *Pakistan Journal of Medical Sciences*, *38*(6). Advance online publication. DOI: 10.12669/pjms.38.6.5409

Sujana, D. S., Kureethara, J. V., Augustine, D. P., & Augustine, L. (2025). Meta-Teaching on Leveraging the Metaverse for Definitive Efficiency in Learning in Higher Education. In *Transformations and Changing Perspectives in Higher Education* (pp. 207–226). Routledge India.

Sun, X., & Sailer, M. (2025). Students' behavioural, cognitive and affective outcomes in gamified flipped classrooms: A meta-analysis. *Review of Education*, *13*(1), e70039.

Sweller, J. (2011). Cognitive load theory. In Ross, B. H. (Ed.), *Psychology of learning and motivation* (Vol. 55, pp. 37–76). Academic Press.

Tablatin, C. L. S., Casano, J. D. L., & Rodrigo, M. M. T. (2023). Using Minecraft to cultivate student interest in STEM. *Frontiers in Education*, *8*, 1127984. DOI: 10.3389/feduc.2023.1127984

Takbiri, Y., Bastanfard, A., & Amini, A. (2023). A gamified approach for improving the learning performance of k-6 students using easter eggs. *Multimedia Tools and Applications*, *82*(13), 20683–20701. DOI: 10.1007/s11042-023-14356-7 PMID: 36685015

Taninaka, K., Jain, R., Shi, J., Takashio, K., & Ramani, K. (2025). Transparent Barriers: Natural Language Access Control Policies for XR-Enhanced Everyday Objects. *Conference on Human Factors in Computing Systems - Proceedings*. https://doi.org//DOI: 10.1145/3706598.3713656

Tan, L. Y., Hu, S., Yeo, D. J., & Cheong, K. H. (2025). Artificial intelligence-enabled adaptive learning platforms: A review. *Computers and Education: Artificial Intelligence*, *9*, 100429. DOI: 10.1016/j.caeai.2025.100429

Tariq, M. U. (2025). Gamification and virtual reality: Transforming early childhood language learning. In *Digital pedagogy in early childhood language development* (pp. 25–52). IGI Global Scientific Publishing.

Taylor, J. A., & Urquhart, D. M. (1974). Florida State University: An experimental approach to comprehensive musicianship for freshman music majors. *College Music Symposium, 14*, 76–88. https://www.jstor.org/stable/40373355

TEAL Center. (2010). *Universal Design for Learning Fact Sheet*. https://lincs.ed.gov/sites/default/files/2_TEAL_UDL.pdf

Tene, T., Marcatoma Tixi, J. A., Palacios Robalino Md, L., Mendoza Salazar, M. J., Vacacela Gomez, C., & Bellucci, S. (2024). Integrating immersive technologies with STEM education: A systematic review. *Frontiers in Education*, *9*, 1410163. DOI: 10.3389/feduc.2024.1410163

Thees, M., Kapp, S., Strzys, M. P., Beil, F., Lukowicz, P., & Kuhn, J. (2020). Effects of augmented reality on learning and cognitive load in university physics laboratory courses. *Computers in Human Behavior*, *108*, 106316. Advance online publication. DOI: 10.1016/j.chb.2020.106316

Thimmanna., Sharma, A.V.N.S., Naik, M. S., Radhakrishnan, S., Sharma, A., (2024). Personalized Learning Paths: Adapting Education with AI-Driven Curriculum. *European Economic Letters (EEL), 14*(1), 31–40. https://doi.org/DOI: 10.52783/eel.v14i1.993

Thomas, S. (2016). *Future Ready Learning: Reimagining the Role of Technology in Education. 2016 National Education Technology Plan*. Office of Educational Technology, US Department of Education.

threekit. (2020). *What Is Augmented Reality (AR)? A Practical Overview*. Threekit.

Thurlings, M., Vermeulen, M., Bastiaens, T., & Stijnen, S. (2013). Understanding feedback: A learning theory perspective. *Educational Research Review*, *9*, 1–15. DOI: 10.1016/j.edurev.2012.11.004

Th y, N. and Hung, L. (2021). Teachers' perceptions of using gamification apps in teaching speaking skill to efl young learners. International Journal of Science and Management Studies (Ijsms), 81-97. DOI: 10.51386/25815946/ijsms-v4i5p108

Tiede, J., Grafe, S., & Mangina, E. (2022). Teachers' attitudes and technology acceptance towards AR apps for teaching and learning. In *Proceedings of the 2022 8th international conference of the immersive learning research network (iLRN)* (pp. 1–8). IEEE. https://doi.org/DOI: 10.23919/iLRN55037.2022.9815965

Tolentino, R. (2024). Curriculum frameworks and educational programs in ai for medical students, residents, and practicing physicians: Scoping review. *JMIR Medical Education*, *10*, e54793. DOI: 10.2196/54793

Tonbuloğlu, B. (2023). An evaluation of the use of artificial intelligence applications in online education. *Journal of Educational Technology and Online Learning*, *6*(4), 866–884. DOI: 10.31681/jetol.1335906

Trang, N., & Thư, P. (2024). The role of ai in improving student learning outcomes: Evidence in vietnam. *International Journal of Multidisciplinary Research and Analysis*, *07*(06). Advance online publication. DOI: 10.47191/ijmra/v7-i06-48

Trilling, B., & Hood, P. (1999). Learning, technology, and education reform in the knowledge age or" we're wired, webbed, and windowed, now what? *Educational Technology*, •••, 5–18.

Tromba, P. (2013). Build engagement and knowledge one block at a time with Minecraft. *Learning and Leading with Technology*, *40*(8), 20–23.

Trust, T., Krutka, D. G., & Carpenter, J. P. (2016). "Together we are better": Professional learning networks for teachers. *Computers & Education*, *102*, 15–34. DOI: 10.1016/j.compedu.2016.06.007

Tubino, L. & Adachi, C. (2022). Developing feedback literacy capabilities through an ai automated feedback tool. *Ascilite Publications*, e22039. https://doi.org/DOI: 10.14742/apubs.2022.39

Turhan, M. E., Metin, M., & Çevik, E. E. (2022). A content analysis of studies published in the field of augmented reality in education. *Journal of Educational Technology and Online Learning*, *5*(1), 243–262. DOI: 10.31681/jetol.925340

Turkle, S. (2011). *Alone together: Why we expect more from technology and less from each other. Basic Books World Bank. (2022). Inequality in Southern Africa.* An Assessment of the Southern African Customs Union.

Tyni, J., Tarkiainen, A., López-Pernas, S., Saqr, M., Kahila, J., Bednarik, R., & Tedre, M. (2022). Games and rewards: A scientometric study of rewards in educational and serious games. *IEEE Access : Practical Innovations, Open Solutions*, *10*, 31578–31585. DOI: 10.1109/access.2022.3160230

Tzafilkou, K., Perifanou, M., & Economides, A. (2023). Assessing teachers' digital competence in primary and secondary education: Applying a new instrument to integrate pedagogical and professional elements for digital education. *Education and Information Technologies*, *28*(12), 16017–16040. DOI: 10.1007/s10639-023-11848-9

Uddin, M., Obaidat, M., Manickam, S., Laghari, S. U. A., Dandoush, A., Ullah, H., & Ullah, S. S. (2024). Exploring the convergence of Metaverse, Blockchain, and AI: A comprehensive survey of enabling technologies, applications, challenges, and future directions. *Wiley Interdisciplinary Reviews. Data Mining and Knowledge Discovery*, *14*(6), e1556. DOI: 10.1002/WIDM.1556

Udeozor, C., Chan, P., Russo Abegão, F., & Glassey, J. (2023). Game-based assessment framework for virtual reality, augmented reality and digital game-based learning. *International Journal of Educational Technology in Higher Education*, *20*(1), 36. PMID: 36644670

Ulagammal, S., & Chaluvarayaswamy, R. (2023). Expanding access to mindfulness education in adaptive learning: Enhancing student well-being and academic success. *Thiagarajar College of Preceptors Edu Spectra*, *5*(S1), 81–84. DOI: 10.34293/eduspectra.v5is1-may23.014

Uygun, D. (2024). Teachers' perspectives on artificial intelligence in education. *Advances in Mobile Learning Educational Research*, *4*(1), 931–939. DOI: 10.25082/amler.2024.01.005

Uymaz, P., & Uymaz, A. O. (2022). Assessing acceptance of augmented reality in nursing education. *PLoS ONE, 17*(2 February). https://doi.org/DOI: 10.1371/journal.pone.0263937

Valluripally, S., Frailey, B., Kruse, B., Palipatana, B., Oruche, R., Gulhane, A., & Calyam, P. (2022). Detection of security and privacy attacks disrupting user immersive experience in virtual reality learning environments. *IEEE Transactions on Services Computing, 16*(4), 2559–2574.

Valluripally, S., Frailey, B., Kruse, B., Palipatana, B., Oruche, R., Gulhane, A., Hoque, K. A., & Calyam, P. (2023). Detection of Security and Privacy Attacks Disrupting User Immersive Experience in Virtual Reality Learning Environments. *IEEE Transactions on Services Computing, 16*(4). Advance online publication. DOI: 10.1109/TSC.2022.3216539

Varas, J., Coronel, B., Villagrán, I., Escalona, G., Hernández, R., Schuit, G., & Achurra, P. (2023). Innovations in surgical training: exploring the role of artificial intelligence and large language models (llm). *Revista Do Colégio Brasileiro De Cirurgiões,* 50. https://doi.org/DOI: 10.1590/0100-6991e-20233605-en

Värtinen, S., Hämäläinen, P., & Guckelsberger, C. (2024). Generating role-playing game quests with gpt language models. *IEEE Transactions on Games, 16*(1), 127–139. DOI: 10.1109/tg.2022.3228480

Vega, K., Pereira Soares, A., Robichez, G., & Fuks, H. (2010). TREG usability tests: Evaluating a training game in Second Life. In *2010 VII Brazilian symposium on collaborative systems (SBSC 2010)* (pp. 63–70). IEEE. https://doi.org/DOI: 10.1109/SBSC.2010.17

Vygotsky, L. (1978). Interaction between learning and development. In Gauvain& Cole (Eds.), Readings on the Development of Children (pp. 34–40). Scientific American Books.

Vygotsky, L. S. (1978). *Mind in society: The development of higher psychological processes*. Harvard University Press.

Wagner, P., & Alharthi, D. (2023). Leveraging VR/AR/MR/XR Technologies to Improve Cybersecurity Education, Training, and Operations. *Journal of Cybersecurity Education Research and Practice, 2024*(1), 1–26. DOI: 10.32727/8.2023.32

Walter, Y. (2024). Embracing the future of artificial intelligence in the classroom: The relevance of ai literacy, prompt engineering, and critical thinking in modern education. *International Journal of Educational Technology in Higher Education, 21*(1). Advance online publication. DOI: 10.1186/s41239-024-00448-3

Wang, F., & Burton, J. K. (2013). Second Life in education: A review of publications from its launch to 2011. *British Journal of Educational Technology, 44*(3), 357–371. DOI: 10.1111/bjet.12034

Wang, H., Gao, Z., Zhang, X., Du, J., Xu, Y., & Wang, Z. (2024). Gamifying cultural heritage: Exploring the potential of immersive virtual exhibitions. *Telematics and Informatics Reports*, *15*, 100150. DOI: 10.1016/j.teler.2024.100150

Wang, M., Callaghan, V., Bernhardt, J., White, K., & Peña-Rios, A. (2018). Augmented reality in education and training: Pedagogical approaches and illustrative case studies. *Journal of Ambient Intelligence and Humanized Computing*, *9*(5), 1391–1402. DOI: 10.1007/s12652-017-0547-8

Wang, P., Bai, X., Billinghurst, M., Zhang, S., Zhang, X., Wang, S., He, W., Yan, Y., & Ji, H. (2021). AR/MR Remote Collaboration on Physical Tasks: A Review. *Robotics and Computer-integrated Manufacturing*, *72*, 102071. DOI: 10.1016/J.RCIM.2020.102071

Welbers, K., Konijn, E. A., Burgers, C., de Vaate, A. B., Eden, A., & Brugman, B. C. (2019). Gamification as a tool for engaging student learning: A field experiment with a gamified app. *E-Learning and Digital Media*, *16*(2), 92–109. DOI: 10.1177/2042753018818342

Weng, Y., Schmidt, M., Huang, W., & Hao, Y. (2024). The effectiveness of immersive learning technologies in K–12 English as second language learning: A systematic review. *ReCALL*, *36*(2), 210–229.

West, D. M., & Bleiberg, J. (2013). *Education technology success stories*. Brookings Institution.

Witzel, B., Görgen-Rein, R., Galuschka, K., Huemer, S., Del Toro, I. C., Schulte-Körne, G., & Moll, K. (2024). Digital game-based spelling intervention for children with spelling deficits: A randomized controlled trial. *Learning and Instruction*, *89*, 101842.

Wood, E., Ange, B., & Miller, D. (2021). Are we ready to integrate artificial intelligence literacy into medical school curriculum: Students and faculty survey. *Journal of Medical Education and Curricular Development*, *8*. Advance online publication. DOI: 10.1177/23821205211024078

World Bank. (2022). *The Global Findex Database 2021: Financial inclusion, digital payments, and resilience in the age of COVID-19*. World Bank. https://doi.org/DOI: 10.1596/978-1-4648-1897-4

Wu, D., Yang, Z., Zhang, P., Wang, R., Yang, B., & Ma, X. (2023). Virtual-Reality Interpromotion Technology for Metaverse: A Survey. *IEEE Internet of Things Journal*, *10*(18), 15788–15809. DOI: 10.1109/JIOT.2023.3265848

Wulan, D. R., Nainggolan, D. M., Hidayat, Y., Rohman, T., & Fiyul, A. Y. (2024). Exploring the benefits and challenges of gamification in enhancing student learning outcomes. *Global International Journal of Innovative Research*, *2*(7), 1657–1674. DOI: 10.59613/global.v2i7.238

Wulantari, N. P., Rachman, A., Sari, M. N., Uktolseja, L. J., & Rofi'i, A. (2023). The role of gamification in English language teaching: A literature review. *Journal of Education*, *6*(01), 2847–2856.

Xiong, J., Hsiang, E. L., & He, Z. (2021). Augmented reality and virtual reality displays: Emerging technologies and future perspectives. *Light, Science & Applications*, *10*, 216. Advance online publication. DOI: 10.1038/s41377-021-00658-8 PMID: 34697292

Xu, E., Wang, W., & Wang, Q. (2023). The effectiveness of collaborative problem solving in promoting students' critical thinking: A meta-analysis based on empirical literature. *Humanities & Social Sciences Communications*, *10*, 16. DOI: 10.1057/s41599-023-01508-1

Xu, W.-W., Su, C.-Y., Hu, Y., & Chen, C.-H. (2022). Exploring the effectiveness and moderators of augmented reality on science learning: A meta-analysis. *Journal of Science Education and Technology*, *31*(5), 621–637. DOI: 10.1007/s10956-022-09979-2

Yadav, A., & Reddy, K. N. (2024). Virtual Dilemmas: Legal and Ethical Rollercoasters in Immersive Tech Land. In *Multidisciplinary Applications of Extended Reality for Human Experience* (pp. 64-80). IGI Global.

Yadav, N., Gupta, K., & Khetrapal, V. (2018). Next education: Technology transforming education. *South Asian Journal of Business and Management Cases*, *7*(1), 68–77.

Yan, T. and Zhao, Y. (2023). Gamification teaching design and application based on self-determination theory., 846-857. DOI: 10.2991/978-94-6463-172-2_89

Yang, C., Yang, P., & Feng, Y. (2021). Effect of achievement-related gamification on brand attachment. *Industrial Management & Data Systems*, *122*(1), 251–271. DOI: 10.1108/imds-02-2021-0088

Yang, X., & Gao, F. (2022). The Overview of Elliptic Curve Cryptography (ECC). *Journal of Physics: Conference Series*, *2386*(1), 012019. DOI: 10.1088/1742-6596/2386/1/012019

Yang, Z., Li, C. Y., Bhalla, A., Zhao, B. Y., & Zheng, H. (2024). *Inception Attacks: Immersive Hijacking in Virtual Reality Systems*. https://arxiv.org/abs/2403.05721

Yano, V., Zimmer, A., & Ling, L. L. (2015). Extraction and application of dynamic pupillometry features for biometric authentication. *Measurement: Journal of the International Measurement Confederation, 63*. Advance online publication. DOI: 10.1016/j.measurement.2014.12.001

Yasir, G., Shaheen, A., & Hafeez, M. (2021). A systematic review on digital game-based versus traditional learning approaches. *Global Social Sciences Review, VI*(IV), 124–135. DOI: 10.31703/gssr.2021(vi-iv).12

Yazdanpanah, V., Gerding, E., Stein, S., Dastani, M., Jonker, C., Norman, T., & Ramchurn, S. (2022). Reasoning about responsibility in autonomous systems: Challenges and opportunities. *AI & Society, 38*(4), 1453–1464. DOI: 10.1007/s00146-022-01607-8

Yekollu, R. K., Ghuge, T. B., Biradar, S. S., Haldikar, S. V., & Abdul Kader, O. F. M. (2024). Securing the Virtual Realm: Strategies for Cybersecurity in Augmented Reality (AR) and Virtual Reality (VR) Applications. *8th International Conference on I-SMAC (IoT in Social, Mobile, Analytics and Cloud), I-SMAC 2024 - Proceedings*, 520–526. https://doi.org/DOI: 10.1109/I-SMAC61858.2024.10714591

Young, S. (2024). *Music, children and other languages*. Routledge., DOI: 10.4324/9781003331193

Yunus, C., & Tan, K. (2021). Exploring a gamified learning tool in the esl classroom: The case of quizizz. *Journal of Education and e-learning Research, 8*(1), 103–108. DOI: 10.20448/journal.509.2021.81.103.108

Yusufjanovna, R. N. (2022). Prospects for the use of Augmented Reality in Education. *Embedded Selforganising Systems, 9*(4), 26–29. https://doi.org/DOI: 10.14464/ess.v9i4.552

Zainal, N. (2023). University students' perspectives on gamification in vocabulary learning: A literature review. *Malaysian Journal of Social Sciences and Humanities (Mjssh), 8*(5), e002314. DOI: 10.47405/mjssh.v8i5.2314

Zainuddin, Z., Chu, S. K. W., Shujahat, M., & Perera, C. J. (2020). The impact of gamification on learning and instruction: A systematic review of empirical evidence. *Educational Research Review, 30*, 100326. DOI: 10.1016/j.edurev.2020.100326

Zhang, Y., Dewitt, D., & Cheah, K. S. (2025). Virtual Reality for Sustainable and Responsible Pedagogy in Art and Design Education: A Systematic Review of Motivation and Digital Leadership. *Cleaner and Responsible Consumption*, 100311.

Zhang, J. (2024). AI in teacher education: Unlocking new dimensions in teaching support, inclusive learning, and digital literacy. *Journal of Computer Assisted Learning*, *40*(4), 1871–1885. DOI: 10.1111/jcal.12988

Zhang, S., Gao, Q., Sun, M., Cai, Z., Li, H., Tang, Y., & Liu, Q. (2022). Understanding student teachers' collaborative problem solving: Insights from an epistemic network analysis (ENA). *Computers & Education*, *183*, 104485. DOI: 10.1016/j.compedu.2022.104485

Zhang, S., & Hasim, Z. (2023). Gamification in efl/esl instruction: A systematic review of empirical research. *Frontiers in Psychology*, *13*. Advance online publication. DOI: 10.3389/fpsyg.2022.1030790 PMID: 36687912

Zhang, T., Gao, L., He, C., Zhang, M., Krishnamachari, B., & Avestimehr, A. S. (2022). Federated Learning for the Internet of Things: Applications, Challenges, and Opportunities. *IEEE Internet of Things Magazine*, *5*(1), 24–29. DOI: 10.1109/IOTM.004.2100182

Zhang, Y., Li, Y., & Li, Z. (2023). Aye: A Trusted Forensic Method for Firmware Tampering Attacks. *Symmetry*, *15*(1). Advance online publication. DOI: 10.3390/sym15010145

Zhao, J., Juithong, S., & Nilnopkoon, P. (2024). Effecting an adaptive learning system on academic achievement as regulations for measuring pharmacist qualifications to licensure of pharmaceutical management students. *IJSASR*, *4*(3), 573–582. DOI: 10.60027/ijsasr.2024.4357

Zhao, X., & McClure, C. D. (2024). Gather.Town: A gamification tool to promote engagement and establish online learning communities for language learners. *RELC Journal*, *55*(1), 240–245.

Zhou, G. (2024). Navigating the future landscape of gamified education. SHS Web of Conferences, 187, 02005. DOI: 10.1051/shsconf/202418702005

Zhou, J., & Gu, Y. (2024). Unraveling students' liking of teachers: The impact of multimodal cues during L2 English vocabulary teaching. [ISCA.]. *Speech Prosody (Urbana, Ill.)*, *2024*, 881–885.

Zhuang, Z. (2021). Interactive media information security immersive experience system based on virtual reality technology. *Journal of the Institution of Electronics and Telecommunication Engineers*, •••, 1–8.

Zhyhadlo, O. (2022). Application of digital game-based tools for formative assessment at foreign language lessons. *Information Technologies and Learning Tools*, *87*(1), 139–150. DOI: 10.33407/itlt.v87i1.4703

Zourmpakis, A., Kalogiannakis, M., & Papadakis, S. (2023). Adaptive gamification in science education: An analysis of the impact of implementation and adapted game elements on students' motivation. *Computers*, *12*(7), 143. DOI: 10.3390/computers12070143

About the Contributors

Filipe T. Moreira holds a PhD in Multimedia in Education and has a large experience in developing national and international ICT projects in Education. His interests lie in understanding how technology can influence children's learning processes and general development, and the philosophy of technology. At the moment he is Assistant Professor at Polytechnic University of Porto and researcher at TECHN&ART and at DigiMedia Research Centre of the University of Aveiro.

Rui Oliva Teles holds a PhD in the field of Educational Technologies by University of Minho (Portugal), currently he is Adjunct professor at ESE do Porto and teaches on various undergraduate, master's and CTeSp courses. He is the coordinator of ESE/IPP's Digital Inclusion Support Centre (2005/ -), a resource centre specialising in assistive technologies for people with special needs (). He has participated in national programmes (PORTIC_2002, CEFPI_2006, PNEP_2006, MAT_2006 DIVERTIR_2007) and represented ESE in Língua (1999), EDIN (1999) Comenius (2000), Grundtvig (2009) and Erasmus (2011) projects in the area of Educational Technologies and Support Technologies. He was coordinator of the ESE/IPP Knowledge Resource Centre (2003/2009) and collaborated in the creation and development of the IPP eLearning Unit, of which he is a representative. He is also the manager of the ESE Content Platform (2004/ -). He is a certified trainer (CAP and CCPFCO) with training activities in the area of ICT and Support Technologies for groups 910, 920 and 930. He supervises internships and master's projects (2008/ -). He is a founding member of SUPERA - Society for Rehabilitation Engineering and Accessibility (2006/-), of which he was vice-president. His areas of research are centred on learning technologies and support technologies, as a non-integrated researcher at INED.

***

Munir Ahmad is a seasoned professional in the realm of Spatial Data Infrastructure (SDI), Geo-Information Productions, Information Systems, and Information Governance, boasting over 25 years of dedicated experience in the field. With a PhD in Computer Science, Dr. Ahmad's expertise spans Spatial Data Production, Management, Processing, Analysis, Visualization, and Quality Control. Throughout his career, Dr. Ahmad has been deeply involved in the development and deployment of SDI systems specially in the context of Pakistan, leveraging his proficiency in Spatial Database Design, Web, Mobile & Desktop GIS, and Geo Web Services Architecture. His contributions to Volunteered Geographic Information (VGI) and Open Source Geoportal & Metadata Portal have significantly enriched the geospatial community. As a trainer and researcher, Dr. Ahmad has authored over 50 publications, advancing the industry's knowledge base and fostering innovation in Geo-Tech, Data Governance, and Information Infrastructure, and Emerging Technologies. His commitment to Research and Development (R&D) is evident in his role as a dedicated educator and mentor in the field.

Oindrilla Ghosh is a Research Scholar hailing from the School of Law at Christ (Deemed to be University) Bangalore, India, focuses her research on health of tribal communities. Her work includes total 32 publications on Neuroscience on Organizational Behavior at IGI Global and also Environmental Disasters that are indexed in SCOPUS and Web of Sciences conference proceedings. She completed her early education at Loreto Day School, Bowbazar and went on to achieve distinction in her undergraduate (B.A/LL.B) and postgraduate (LL.M) studies at Calcutta University. Having served as an Assistant Professor of Law at Kingston Law College,Barasat, Kolkata, Ghosh has actively participated in numerous National Conferences, International Conferences, UN Global Summits, webinars, and seminars organized by prestigious academic institutions. Her expertise lies in health perspectives, environmental studies, human behavior, and related areas. Additionally, she has conducted various workshops, lectures in educational institutions, and is engaged with NGO's to help the needy.

S. Ida Evangeline, presently working as an Assistant Professor in the Department of Electrical and Electronics Engineering at the Government College of Engineering, Tirunelveli, Tamilnadu, India. She obtained her Bachelor's in Electrical and Electronics Engineering from Manonmaniam Sundaranar University in 2003, and Master's in Power Systems Engineering from Anna University, Chennai, Tamilnadu, India in 2005. She completed her PhD degree in 2023 at Anna University, Chennai, Tamilnadu, India. She has published six research papers in international journals. Her current research interests include optimal power flow, renewable energy, soft computing, machine learning, and deep learning.

Binod Kumar is a graduate student known for his academic excellence, with his total 22 scholarly works indexed in Scopus database on Neuroscience in Organizational Behavior, Neuromarketing and AI Applications on Wildlife Conservation. Hailing from Ranchi, Jharkhand in India, Binod is currently pursuing a Master of Laws (LL.M) at the prestigious Radha Govind University. His passion for technology and innovation along with climate changes is evident through his high academic performance and numerous projects. Binod has a keen interest in artificial intelligence, machine learning, neuropsychology, climate changes and disaster management, fields in which he has undertaken several research projects. He is particularly fascinated by the potential of AI to solve real-world problems and is dedicated to learning and applying new techniques in these areas. He volunteers at local NGOs, teaching underprivileged children basic computer skills. With a strong foundation in law and a commitment to making a positive impact, Binod Kumar is poised to become a future leader in the legal industry.

Peter Leong is a Professor with the Department of Learning Design & Technology, University of Hawaii-Manoa. He has extensive experience in the development and delivery of online courses and distance education. Dr. Leong was honored as one of Hawaii's 2007 top high-technology leaders and was recognized with the University of Hawaii Board of Regents' Medal for Teaching Excellence award in 2012. He was a co-investigator on a National Science Foundation (NSF) grant to evaluate new approaches to improving engagement, diversity, and retention in undergraduate computer science and currently serves as a co-investigator of a Computer Science for All NSF grant focused on culturally-relevant computing . His research interests include culturally-relevant computing, student satisfaction with online learning, faculty support for technology integration, technologies for distance education and teaching & learning in virtual worlds.

Zokir Mamadiyarov is working in the Department of Finance and Tourism at Termez University of Economics and Service, Termez, Uzbekistan.

Barno Matchanova is working at Department of National Idea and Philosophy, Urgench State Pedagogical Institute, Uzbekistan

Gaman Palem is a visual artist, comic creator, and graphic novelist whose practice bridges fine art and sequential storytelling. With a PhD in visual arts and over 200 published comics and storybooks, he integrates traditional media and digital practices with the narrative dynamism of comic panels to craft a distinctive visual language. Gaman's work explores the interplay of human and natural forms, weaving philosophical concepts into figurative and nature-driven compositions. His projects range from intimate, hand-painted pieces to large-scale narrative works that challenge the boundaries between comics and fine art. Alongside his studio practice, Dr. Palem is an educator and researcher in media and design, developing innovative courses on comic design, storytelling, and digital-traditional narrative integration. His academic writings examine multimodal storytelling and the use of comics as tools for social change and education, reflecting a commitment to scholarship that informs practice. Whether through gallery exhibitions, published graphic novels, or collaborative educational initiatives, Gaman Palem continues to push the possibilities of visual storytelling, inspiring emerging artists and engaging diverse audiences in the evolving dialogue between art, narrative, and culture.

Shahiem Patel holds a Bachelor of Commerce degree from the University of the Witwatersrand and a Bachelor of Commerce Honours degree in Business Management from the University of South Africa (UNISA). He earned his Master of Commerce in Leadership Studies from the University of KwaZulu-Natal on a full scholarship and later completed his PhD in Leadership Studies in 2018, also on a full scholarship. Dr. Patel brings extensive experience across academia and the corporate sector. He has held roles in the banking sector with Standard Bank, served as a management consultant with McKinsey, worked as a business analyst, and lectured at various institutions. Additionally, he is a sought-after speaker and radio personality. Dr. Patel frequently delivers lectures and keynote addresses at leading organisations and business schools, focusing on topics such as leadership, management and organisational change. As a scholar, Dr. Patel co-authored a book chapter titled AI Grading Systems in Education: A Panacea or Drawback for South African Higher Education (Chapter 9, published by IGI Global and Scopus-indexed). He has also published peer-reviewed articles in both accredited and non-accredited journals. His multidisciplinary expertise and thought leadership make him a valuable contributor to discussions at the intersection of academia and industry.

Mahlatse Ragolane is an academic and Head of Department for the Centre of Excellence at Regent Business School. He also serves as Programme Coordinator for the MBA, supervises postgraduate research projects, and lectures in the School of Commerce and Management. He holds a Master of Arts in Public Management and Governance from the University of Johannesburg (UJ), as well as a Bachelor of Administration and BA Honours in Public Administration from the University of Limpopo (UL). He is currently a Doctor of Business Administration (DBA) candidate. As a Research Fellow at the International Council of Human Rights, Peace and Politics (ICHRPP) and a Researcher at the Institute for Community Safety and Criminal Justice (ICSCJ), Mahlatse engages in interdisciplinary projects addressing governance, social justice, and conflict resolution. His growing body of work includes peer-reviewed publications on artificial intelligence in education, hybrid governance and political stability. Mahlatse is also the co-author of the forthcoming book Local Government Administration in Eastern and Southern Africa, 1st Ed), Van Schaik, 2026. Through scholarship and practice, he continues to shape public policy discourse and higher education innovation across Africa

Jitendra Singh Rathore is an Assistant Professor at Department of Commerce and Management – WISDOM, Banasthali Vidyapith, India. He has over 18 years of experience in both industry and academics and teaches Marketing Management, Sales and Distribution Management, and International marketing to undergraduate and postgraduate students. Prior to joining academics, he worked in the Banking, Financial Services and Insurance (BFSI) sector with organizations such as Bajaj Allianz, Kotak Securities and SBI cards in various capacities for around 5 years. His areas of research interest include e-commerce, sharing economy, channel and distribution management, the shopping behaviour of consumers in the digital age etc.

Vivit Rosmayanti, S.Pd.I., M.Pd was born in Botta on June 26, 1987. She has over 10 years of experience teaching at the University. She obtained a bachelor's degree in English Education from Alauddin State Islamic University. She completed her master's and doctoral degrees in English Education from Makassar State University. She is currently a lecturer in the Post Graduate Program, Department of English Education at Makassar State University, South Sulawesi, Indonesia. She is also actively writing research articles to be published in nationally and internationally accredited journals. She has written in some chapter books, monographs, and reference books. She is interested in teaching methods for teaching English. Her research interests include language teaching methodology, ICT instruction, and ESP teaching. She can be contacted at email: rosmayantivivit@gmail.com

S Md Azash serves as Assistant Professor (Senior Scale) at the Presidency School of Law, where he blends strong academic training with a multidisciplinary approach to legal education. He holds a PhD, Master's in Human Resource Management (M.H.R.H.), and LL.M., and has cleared both APSET and UGC-NET, reflecting a solid foundation in research and teaching excellence. Dr. Azash's scholarship spans a wide spectrum of law and management, with research interests in Human Resource Management, Organisational Behaviour, Labour and Industrial Laws, Industrial Relations, Intellectual Property Rights, Taxation, Corporate Laws, and the evolving field of Capital Market and Securities Laws. His work emphasises the dynamic interface between business practices and legal frameworks, aiming to create practical insights for industry and policy. At Presidency School of Law, he mentors students in critical legal reasoning, fosters participatory classroom learning, and encourages interdisciplinary dialogue between management and law.

Through publications, seminars, and continuous professional engagement, Dr. Azash contributes to both academic discourse and practical legal development, positioning himself as a committed educator and researcher dedicated to advancing contemporary legal studies and nurturing the next generation of legal professionals.

Maria Shobeiry is a postdoctoral researcher at the University of Tehran and the University of Tennessee, Knoxville, United States. She holds a PhD in Applied Linguistics and currently serves as a lecturer at the University of Tehran. Maria's research focuses on innovative language learning methodologies, with a particular emphasis on gamification and technology-enhanced language education. Her work aims to improve learner motivation and engagement through the integration of digital tools in language acquisition. Maria has published extensively in peer-reviewed journals and presented her research at international conferences, contributing valuable insights to the field of Applied Linguistics. Committed to bridging theory and practice, she collaborates with educators to implement effective, technology-driven teaching strategies. Maria's dedication to advancing language education is reflected in her dynamic approach to research and teaching, inspiring both students and colleagues alike.

Amrik Singh is working as Professor in the School of Hotel Management and Tourism at Lovely Professional University, Punjab, India. He obtained his Ph.D. degree in Hotel Management from Kurukshetra University, Kurukshetra. He started his academic career at Lovely Professional University, Punjab, India in the year 2007. He has published more than 40 research papers in UGC and peer-reviewed and Scopus/Web of Science) journals. He has published 12 patents and 01 patent has been granted in the inter-disciplinary domain. Dr. Amrik Singh participated and acted as a resource person in various national and international conferences, seminars, research workshops, and industry talks. His area of research interest is accommodation management, ergonomics, green practices, human resource management in hospitality, waste management, AR VR in hospitality, etc. He is currently guiding 8Ph.D. scholars and 2 Ph.D. scholars have been awarded Ph.D.

Sonam Tripathi is a dedicated research scholar pursuing her Ph.D. at Banasthali Vidyapith, Rajasthan, India. Her research expertise lies in the area of education-based earning outcomes, with a focus on understanding the link between academic pathways and economic advancement

Samiksha Vyas is an Assistant Professor at Vivekananda Global University, Jaipur. She earned her Ph.D. from Banasthali Vidyapith, with a research focus on the sharing economy. Her academic interests lie in developing innovative models to enhance collaboration and resource utilization within this emerging field. Prior to her academic role, she gained valuable industry experience in the forensic department at KPMG, Gurgaon. She has multiple publications in reputed ABDC and Scopus-indexed journals, reflecting her commitment to impactful and sustainable research.

Seema Yadav has academic qualifications of M. Sc. (Chemistry), M Ed (RIE), UGC-NET, and PhD in Education. Presently she is working as an Assistant Professor, in the Department of Education at The Bhopal School of Education, Bhopal. She has almost 18 years of teaching experience. Her areas of specialization are educational psychology, environmental education, digital learning, and curriculum development.

Index

F

G

H

I

L

M

N

P

R

S

U

V

X